OPTION	EFFECT
FRAME	
Margins & Columns	Controls the margins and columns for underlying-page and standard frames.
Sizing & Scaling	Controls frame position, dimensions, padding, flow-around, picture scale, crop, and column balance.
Repeating Frame	Allows a frame to be repeated on every page. Controls the repeating page on the current page.
Anchors & Captions	Assigns an anchor name to a frame. Allows you to specify a caption for a frame.
Table Counter	Sets the style and beginning number for numbering table captions.
Figure Counter	Sets the style and beginning number for numbering figure captions.
Vertical Rules	Places rules between columns of a frame and vertical page rules.
Ruling Line Above	Places rules at the top of a frame.
Ruling Line Below	Places rules at the bottom of a frame.
Ruling Box Around	Places boxes at and within the edges of a frame.
Frame Background	Sets the color and pattern of a frame's background.
PARAGRAPH	
Font	Controls the font face, size, style and color for a paragraph tag.
Alignment	Sets the alignment, hyphenation, width, and first-line indent for a paragraph tag.
Spacing	Sets the spacing between paragraph lines and the in-from-left/right values.
Breaks	Sets the positioning of text when one paragraph ends and another begins.
Tab Settings	Assigns the tab type, location, and leaders to a paragraph's tab settings.
Special Effects	Sets dropped capitals (big first characters) and bullets for a paragraph tag.
Typographical Controls	Sets horizontal spacing between characters and the position of text-attribute lines.
Ruling Line Above	Places rules above paragraphs so tagged.
Ruling Line Below	Places rules below paragraphs so tagged.
Ruling Box Around	Places boxes around paragraphs so tagged.
Remove Tag	Removes a tag from the assignment list and reassigns its paragraphs.
Rename Tag	Changes the name of a paragraph tag.
Assign Function Keys (^ K)	Allows you to assign paragraph tags to the function keys or view the assignments.
GRAPHIC	
Send to Back (^ Z)	Sends a graphic to the back of a graphics pile.
Bring to Front (^ A)	Brings a graphic to the front of a graphics pile.
Line Attributes (^ L)	Sets the thickness, color, and end style of graphics.
Fill Attributes (^ F)	Sets the fill color and fill pattern of graphics.
Select All (^ Q)	Selects all the graphics associated with the selected frame.
Grid Settings	Defines a grid that positions graphics.
OPTIONS	
Set Preferences	Sets generated tag display, greeking, backup files, double-click speed, decimal-tab character, on-screen kerning, and automatic adjusting of inter-line spacing.
Set Ruler	Sets the measurement system and zero point for the screen rulers.
Set Printer Info	Sets printer name, screen fonts, output port, and width table.
Add/Remove Fonts	Allows you to add fonts and indicate their download status.
Show/Hide Side-Bar (^ W)	Displays or hides the Side-bar.
Show/Hide Rulers	Displays or hides the rulers along the edges of the working area.
Show/Hide Column Guides	Displays or hides the edges of columns in the underlying-page frame.
Show/Hide Pictures	Displays or hides pictures on the screen.
Show/Hide Tabs & Returns (^ T)	Displays or hides tabs, returns, solid spaces, and line breaks, end of file, and other codes.
Show/Hide Loose Lines	Displays or hides darkening of lines that exceed the maximum space width as specified.
Turn Column Snap On/Off	Turns on or off alignment of frames with columns in the underlying-page frame.
Turn Line Snap On/Off	Turns on or off alignment of frames with lines of text in the underlying-page frame.
Multi Chapter	Allows you to perform operations associated with publications and to copy chapters.

MASTERING VENTURA

MASTERING VENTURA™

Matthew Holtz

SAN FRANCISCO • PARIS • DÜSSELDORF • LONDON

Cover design by Thomas Ingalls + Associates
Cover photograph by Casey Cartwright
Series design by Julie Bilski
Technical illustrations by Lucie Zivny

Library of Congress Card Number: **87-62723**
ISBN **0-89588-427-5**
Manufactured in the United States of America
10 9 8 7 6 5 4 3 2 1

To Barbara Gordon, *with thanks for the professionalism and patience.*

It is one thing to write, and another to publish.

—Edward George Earle Bulwer-Lytton

ACKNOWLEDGMENTS

Thanks to all those at SYBEX who assisted in the production of this book, especially Jon Strickland, Geta Carlson, and Michael Wolk for editorial assistance. Thanks also to Hannah Robinson for the helpful input. Thanks to Joel Kroman for work on the full-page screens, and to the following people for their efforts at all stages of the book: John Kadyk, word processing; Charlie Cowens, typesetting; Winnie Kelly, proofreading; Ingrid Owen, paste-up and layout; Julie Bilski, book design; Lucie Zivny, technical illustrations; and Michelle Hoffman, screen reproduction.

Thanks to Gene Brott for the special help, and to those at the Berkeley Adult School for their support. Thanks to Gerald Harland and Chas Smith for word processing assistance.

Thanks especially to the following companies for providing hardware that assisted in the production of this book: Hewlett-Packard for the LaserJet Series II; Micro Display Systems, Inc. for the Genius Full-Page Display; and Princeton Graphics Systems for the LS-300 Image Scanner.

TABLE OF CONTENTS

INTRODUCTION

At last the full power of desktop publishing, formerly the sole province of the Apple Macintosh, has come to the IBM PC and compatibles, in the form of Ventura Publisher, or simply Ventura.

Despite this innovative program's sophistication and capability, it lacks two "user-friendly" features. There is no online help for you to reference while at the computer. In addition, there is no undo feature to allow you to recover from some mishaps. This means that access to a well-written, understandable tutorial, usable in combination with any software, is all the more important with Ventura. This book is here to fill this role.

To make the program comprehensible, this book describes all of Ventura's major procedures step by step, with illustrations and examples. The methods used allow you to practice these procedures in order to get to know them, or to reference and use them as your practical needs demand.

This book makes liberal use of the extensive samples that Ventura provides with its software. By examining and dissecting these samples, you'll come to understand the innermost workings of the program. This means that in order to learn, you don't need to type in a lot of text in order to see the program in action. By using the material at hand, you'll quickly become acquainted with Ventura's features.

Once you understand Ventura's fundamentals, you can use various chapters of this book as necessary. For example, if you are especially interested in incorporating 1-2-3 graphs into Ventura, you can simply consult Chapter 7. Each chapter contains cross references to other chapters that contain related information.

In order to use Ventura effectively, you will probably find it necessary to have other software in place, especially a word processor. With Ventura, you can use text from a variety of word processors, and even combine text created from different word processors in the same document. You will also need graphics software if you wish to include sophisticated graphs or other pictures. This book discusses your additional software needs in the context of their use with Ventura.

IMPORTANT

Ventura has some potential pitfalls that you need to watch out for. Throughout the text, we've flagged these pitfalls with the word *Important*, as we have done with this paragraph.

Let's begin by taking a look at this book's contents, chapter by chapter:

Chapter 1, "Introducing Ventura," provides an overview of what Ventura can do, how it does it, and what you'll need to do to make Ventura operational. It also looks at the unique ways in which Ventura uses the mouse and the keyboard.

Chapter 2, "How Ventura Operates," examines the Ventura screen and the conventions Ventura uses to communicate to the user. It also examines Ventura's four operating modes, and provides an overview of how to use them.

Chapter 3, "Setting Up a Newsletter," is the first to work with one of the samples, showing you how you can adapt it to your needs. We examine using and saving files, and specifying the size of pages, margins, and columns. We'll also see how to use *frames*, Ventura's primary means of organizing the page.

Chapter 4, "Using Electronic Scissors and Glue," shows you how to use Ventura's editing abilities to rework text. We'll see how to manipulate frames as well.

Chapter 5, "Paragraph Tags and Text Attributes: Building Blocks for Formatting," examines a fundamental formatting tool in Ventura: the *paragraph tag*. You'll see how to set fonts and create italics, boldface, underlining, and other attributes. In this chapter, we'll also examine centering of text and justification, as well as hyphenation, indenting, spacing between lines, and various other formats you can apply to paragraphs.

Chapter 6, "Start the Presses: Printing and Other Output," explains how you can use Ventura to print your work. Although printing with Ventura is generally a simple and straightforward process, the program nevertheless provides many sophisticated printing abilities, allowing for a high degree of flexibility. The chapter contains a discussion of various printers, with sections on setting up printers, printing multiple copies, and so on. There is also a section on how to add fonts to your printer, as well as how to use Ventura for printing with a typesetter.

Chapter 7, "Adding Pictures from Lotus 1-2-3 and Other Sources," shows how you use Ventura's uncanny ability to integrate pictures from a variety of sources with word processed text. We'll discuss the characteristics of the two kinds of pictures that Ventura uses and see how to adjust pictures to fit your needs. We'll also look at how text interacts with pictures, how to create captions, and how to keep a picture with its associated text as you edit.

Chapter 8, "Lines, Circles, and Boxes," is an examination of the graphics capabilities that are built into Ventura. You'll see how such graphics can be assigned to frames or paragraph tags. You'll see how to use Ventura's Graphics mode to create arrows, ovals, and custom shapes as well. You'll also see how text works with these graphics in special ways.

Chapter 9, "Creating Tables," is a discussion of how to make tables of text in Ventura. To accommodate a variety of needs, Ventura provides you with four different ways to create tables. By using this chapter, you'll see how these methods differ and so be able to choose the one that suits you best.

Chapter 10, "Working with Pages: Formats and Page Headings," provides a look at how to format the page and create headings that are automatically repeated on each page. We'll see how automatically generated pages differ from pages that you insert individually. We'll also see how to make material repeat on every page and look at some methods for speeding up the page layout process.

Chapter 11, "Multichapter Features: Tables of Contents, Indexes, Footnotes, and Numbering," discusses the features you would usually press into service for long documents. We'll see how to make copies of chapters and publications, rearrange chapters, and create a table of contents and an index. We'll also see how to number and renumber section headings, as well as pages and chapters, automatically.

Chapter 12, "Using Other Programs with Ventura," provides a discussion of how to use word processors and other programs with Ventura. We'll see how you can use your favorite word processor to create text and assign formatting to Ventura documents. We'll specifically examine the use of Microsoft Word, WordStar, and WordPerfect with Ventura. We'll also look at using macro generators with Ventura and see how to use word processors that Ventura does not fully support. The chapter also contains a discussion of the use of dBASE III PLUS and other database systems for providing data for Ventura documents.

Chapter 13, "Typographical Elements and Effects," is an examination of Ventura's sophisticated typographical capabilities, many of which are new with Version 1.1. We'll see how to begin paragraphs with special effects and how to create reverse text and other unusual effects. We'll also show how to make adjustments to the spacing between letters and words, as well as between paragraphs. We'll see how fine-tuning like this can put the finishing touches on your Ventura documents.

The appendices provide some supplemental information that you will find a useful reference as you work with Ventura. Appendix A is a listing of the sample documents provided with Ventura, along with a display of each and a discussion of their features. Appendix B discusses some alternative setups that you can use to run Ventura, including operating without a mouse, with a RAM drive, and with a full-page display. Appendix C contains a discussion of the DOS conventions that Ventura uses; you may wish to consult this appendix if you are unfamiliar with DOS. Appendix D is a listing of companies that provide fonts for use with Ventura. Appendix E contains a listing of unusual characters and special codes that Ventura makes available for additional typographical flexibility.

This edition of this book covers the features available with Versions 1.0 and 1.1. Where a feature became available only in Version

1.1, this has been indicated in the text. If you are not sure which version you have, you will be able to tell once you have Ventura up and running. (To see the version number once you've installed the product, as discussed in Chapter 1, check the title line as you start the program. There is also another way to check, which you can use once the program is loaded. Point the mouse cursor to Desk on the menu line and then click Publisher Info.)

Congratulations. You are about to participate in a technological adventure. Now the adventure begins.

CHAPTER ONE

Introducing Ventura

VENTURA OVERCOMES A FUNDAMENTAL LIMITATION initially imposed upon the PC when IBM designed it in 1981. Because of that design, all IBM personal computers (and compatibles) possess something of a dual personality. They operate in either of two modes: *text mode* or *graphics mode*. Until recently the mode used had far-reaching effects in numerous areas, including choice of monitor and program design. The impact also extended to printer selection and, perhaps most importantly, to the appearance of the printed page.

In text mode, the computer can manipulate the letters, numbers, and symbols that appear on the keyboard. Word processing software governs the realm of text-related printing that is done through the IBM personal computer. As such, the computer is more or less an extension of the typewriter.

The main attraction of the word processor (as opposed to the typewriter) is its ability to make revisions easily. Once printed, however, word-processed text closely resembles standard typewritten text.

On the other hand, there are a variety of charting, graphing, drawing, and painting programs that have coexisted with text programs in the IBM world. Because they operate in *graphics mode*, these programs are not restricted to character choices, as text programs are; they afford material a visual dimension that text programs cannot. But their text capabilities are quite restricted; traditionally, characters printed in graphics mode have looked "dotty," like computer printout characters.

Until now, graphics mode was quite different from text mode and demanded different programs and hardware. Electronically incorporating graphics on the same page as word processed text was out of the question.

Now, though, with the laser printer and a whole breed of new programs, desktop publishing has come to the IBM. Among these programs, Xerox's Ventura Publisher has probably captured the computer world's attention most strongly. Considering its capabilities, it's no wonder.

Strictly speaking, Ventura operates in the graphics mode. As such, it has the capability of printing graphics remarkably well, as might be expected. In addition, Ventura's text, with the right printer, surpasses typewriter quality and appears almost typeset. Columns of varying widths, text of varying sizes, and complete integration of text and graphics on the same page is now possible. With

Ventura, the IBM PC or compatible moves closer to becoming a complete typographer's shop rather than being simply an extension of the office typewriter. In conjunction with a wide variety of software, Ventura provides you with a tool kit of electronic typesetting and pasteup equipment.

With Ventura, you can create newsletters, brochures, letterhead, books, catalogs, and all sorts of other professional-looking documents with ease and speed. Now, in your own office or at home, you can lay out the finest quarterly reports or a simple interoffice memo on a company letterhead. The same computer that yesterday created only typewriter-quality work can now provide typeset-quality work as well. Figure 1.1 shows some examples of work created using Ventura.

WHAT MAKES VENTURA SPECIAL?

Xerox's Ventura Publisher was the first full-featured desktop publisher available for the IBM personal computer and compatibles. It has been so successful in its features and design that it is now the standard with which other desktop publishers are compared.

Several covers of the most popular computer magazines have showcased Ventura. Periodicals have given it one rave review after another. Some have called it the best piece of software since Lotus 1-2-3. Perhaps that's because Ventura has accomplished what many thought was impossible with an IBM.

To get a sense of why Ventura has garnered such high praises, let's take a quick look at its capabilities in the categories that are generally most important to users.

PRICING

Ventura is the first program to make IBM desktop publishing affordable. For under $1000, it offers capabilities previously available only on machines costing upward of $200,000.

In addition, it has kept hardware requirements to a minimum. While other desktop publishers require an IBM AT or its equivalent, Ventura performs just fine on an XT. It will even work on a standard PC that's been upgraded.

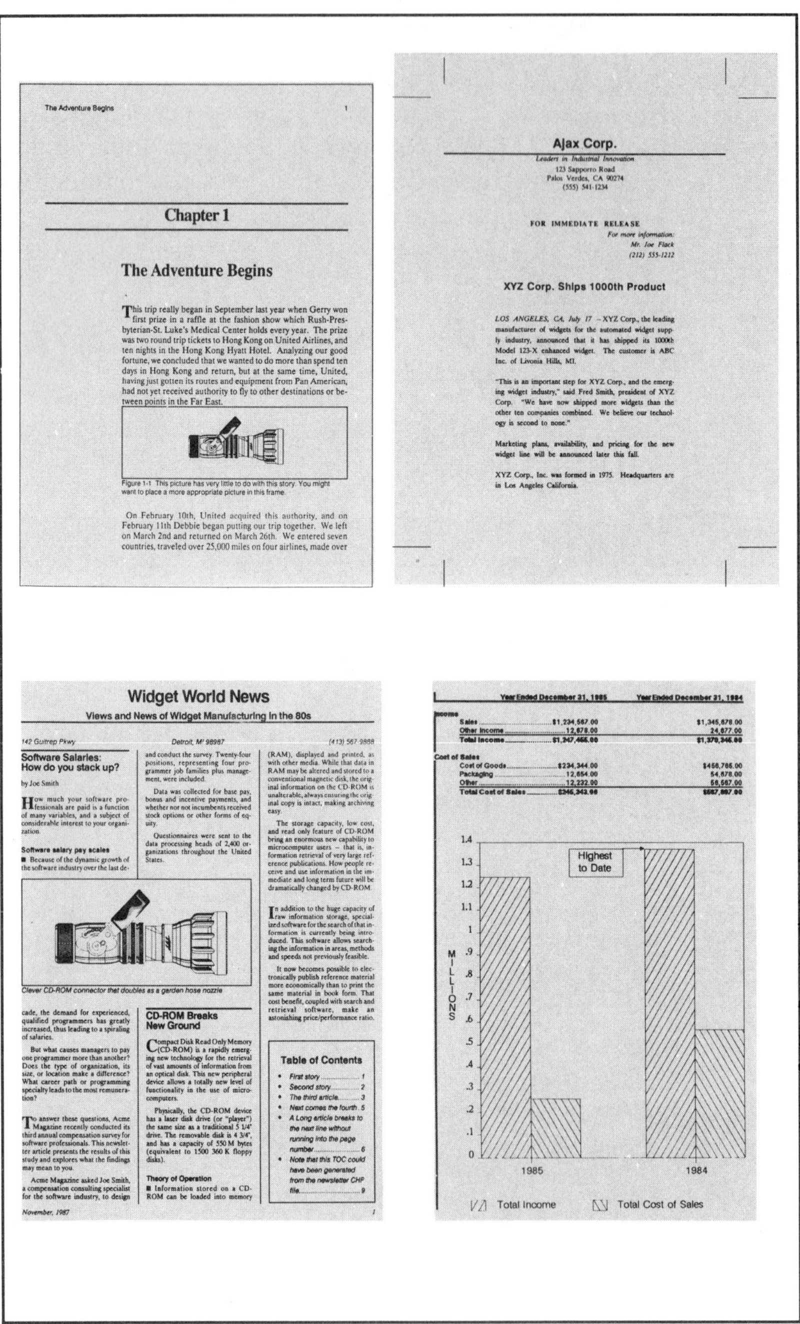

The Adventure Begins 1

Chapter 1

The Adventure Begins

This trip really began in September last year when Gerry won first prize in a raffle at the fashion show which Rush-Presbyterian-St. Luke's Medical Center holds every year. The prize was two round trip tickets to Hong Kong on United Airlines, and ten nights in the Hong Kong Hyatt Hotel. Analyzing our good fortune, we concluded that we wanted to do more than spend ten days in Hong Kong and return, but at the same time, United, having just gotten its routes and equipment from Pan American, had not yet received authority to fly to other destinations or between points in the Far East.

Figure 1-1 This picture has very little to do with this story. You might want to place a more appropriate picture in this frame.

On February 10th, United acquired this authority, and on February 11th Debbie began putting our trip together. We left on March 2nd and returned on March 26th. We entered seven countries, traveled over 25,000 miles on four airlines, made over

Ajax Corp.

Leaders in Industrial Innovation
123 Sapporro Road
Palos Verdes, CA 90274
(555) 541-1234

FOR IMMEDIATE RELEASE

For more information:
Mr. Joe Flack
(212) 555-1212

XYZ Corp. Ships 1000th Product

LOS ANGELES, CA, July 17 – XYZ Corp., the leading manufacturer of widgets for the automated widget supply industry, announced that it has shipped its 1000th Model 123-X enhanced widget. The customer is ABC Inc. of Livonia Hills, MI.

"This is an important step for XYZ Corp., and the emerging widget industry," said Fred Smith, president of XYZ Corp. "We have now shipped more widgets than the other ten companies combined. We believe our technology is second to none."

Marketing plans, availability, and pricing for the new widget line will be announced later this fall.

XYZ Corp., Inc. was formed in 1975. Headquarters are in Los Angeles California.

Widget World News

Views and News of Widget Manufacturing in the 80s

142 Guitrep Pkwy *Detroit, MI 98987* *(413) 567-9888*

Software Salaries: How do you stack up?

by Joe Smith

How much your software professionals are paid is a function of many variables, and a subject of considerable interest to your organization.

Software salary pay scales

■ Because of the dynamic growth of the software industry over the last decade, the demand for experienced, qualified programmers has greatly increased, thus leading to a spiraling of salaries.

But what causes managers to pay one programmer more than another? Does the type of organization, its size, or location make a difference? What career path or programming specialty leads to the most remuneration?

To answer these questions, Acme Magazine recently conducted its third annual compensation survey for software professionals. This newsletter article presents the results of this study and explores what the findings may mean to you.

Acme Magazine asked Joe Smith, a compensation consulting specialist for the software industry, to design and conduct the survey. Twenty-four positions, representing four programmer job families plus management, were included.

Data was collected for base pay, bonus and incentive payments, and whether nor not incumbents received stock options or other forms of equity.

Questionnaires were sent to the data processing heads of 2,400 organizations throughout the United States.

Clever CD-ROM connector that doubles as a garden hose nozzle

CD-ROM Breaks New Ground

Compact Disk Read Only Memory (CD-ROM) is a rapidly emerging new technology for the retrieval of vast amounts of information from an optical disk. This new peripheral device allows a totally new level of functionality in the use of microcomputers.

Physically, the CD-ROM device has a laser disk drive (or "player") the same size as a traditional 5 1/4" drive. The removable disk is 4 3/4", and has a capacity of 550 M bytes (equivalent to 1500 360 K floppy disks).

Theory of Operation

■ Information stored on a CD-ROM can be loaded into memory (RAM), displayed and printed, as with other media. While that data in RAM may be altered and stored to a conventional magnetic disk, the original information on the CD-ROM is unalterable, always ensuring the original copy is intact, making archiving easy.

The storage capacity, low cost, and read only feature of CD-ROM bring an enormous new capability to microcomputer users – that is, information retrieval of very large reference publications. How people receive and use information in the immediate and long term future will be dramatically changed by CD-ROM.

In addition to the huge capacity of raw information storage, specialized software for the search of that information is currently being introduced. This software allows searching the information in areas, methods and speeds not previously feasible.

It now becomes possible to electronically publish reference material more economically than to print the same material in book form. That cost benefit, coupled with search and retrieval software, make an astonishing price/performance ratio.

Table of Contents

November, 1987 1

	Year Ended December 31, 1985	Year Ended December 31, 1984
Income		
Sales	$1,234,567.00	$1,345,678.00
Other Income	12,678.00	24,677.00
Total Income	**$1,247,465.00**	**$1,370,345.00**
Cost of Sales		
Cost of Goods	$234,344.00	$456,765.00
Packaging	12,654.00	54,678.00
Other	12,232.00	56,567.00
Total Cost of Sales	**$246,342.99**	**$567,997.00**

Figure 1.1: Ventura Creations

PERFORMANCE

Despite its low price and minimal investment requirement, there is no sacrifice in performance. The speed with which the product operates is immediately apparent and impressive. Ventura has completely belied the prediction that desktop publishing with an IBM would be sluggish and severely limited.

In addition, Ventura offers all the features users need in a desktop publisher. For example, as you make changes in one place, Ventura updates any material affected by those changes; generally, you don't need to execute separate processing operations. This means that whenever you look at any part of the document, what you see on the screen is what you'll get when you print on the printer (except the printed version may be sharper). So, if adding a paragraph or graphic on page 1 means that a 20-page manuscript is now 21 pages long, you'll know that just by checking the page number on the last page.

COMPATIBILITY

In a shrewd and unprecedented move, the makers of Ventura have designed it so you can use your favorite piece of word processing software to edit Ventura documents. Thus, you work with text in the manner that's most familiar to you.

Ventura also operates with a variety of graphics packages. So, you can create the finest graphics using the most appropriate means. Ventura provides the common ground that ties all these elements together, allowing your various software packages as well as your hardware to perform in "symphony" in a way no other piece of software has been able to orchestrate (see Table 1.1).

EASE OF USE

Despite its capabilities, Ventura doesn't require the typically steep computer learning curve. As encompassing as the program is, its structure is logical, intuitive, and easy to grasp. With this book and a minimal investment of your time, you'll go far quickly.

Using the built-in *GEM user interface* (GEM stands for Graphics Environment Manager), the program presents itself to you with

LINE ART	IMAGES	WORD PROCESSING
AutoCAD CGM Encapsulated PostScript GEM HPGL Lotus 1-2-3 Macintosh PICT Mentor Graphics VideoShow	DFX format GEM PC Paintbrush Publishers Paintbrush VideoShow format	ASCII format IBM DCA (DisplayWrite) Microsoft Word MultiMate WordPerfect WordStar Xerox Writer XyWrite

Table 1.1: Software Packages Supported by Ventura

icons, pull-down menus, dialog boxes, and other graphics displays that are the hallmarks of that interface system. This format, originated on the Apple Macintosh computer, has a well-deserved reputation for ease of use, because its components are visually-oriented. The GEM machinery is fully integrated into the program. You need know no more about GEM than what you'll learn by studying Ventura Publisher with this book.

WHAT VENTURA CAN DO

Not only can Ventura integrate the creations of state-of-the-art programs into its documents, it also possesses its own exceptional features. Let's take a look at the kinds of operations you can perform with it.

CUT AND PASTE

With Ventura, you can easily delete or duplicate text, graphics, or formatting elements, or move them from one area or page to another.

You can cut text from files created with one word processor and paste that text into files created by a different word processor. You can then edit the transplanted text fully, using the receiving word processor. We'll examine cut and paste operations in Chapter 4.

You can also add graphics elements to existing graphics files. Ventura's own arrows, lines, circles, and boxes can either augment existing graphics files or be used on their own. We will discuss this capability in Chapter 8.

HEADERS AND FOOTERS

In Ventura, a *header* or *footer* is one or two lines of text that appear at the top or bottom, respectively, of each page. Rather than retype text at the top or bottom of each page, you need type it only once and designate it as a header or footer. Ventura will reprint it on each page in the manner you stipulate.

You can have each header appear at the left, right, or center of the page. The same holds true for footers. In addition, Ventura allows you to specify an entirely different set of headers and footers for odd- and even-numbered pages. You can also have the page number and the chapter number appear as part of the header or footer. Finally, you can insert a catch phrase from the text into the header or footer, just as a phone directory shows the first and last names on each page. Chapter 10 examines headers and footers.

FOOTNOTES

You can insert footnotes using either Ventura or your word processor. By typing special codes into the text, you can even create footnotes with a word processor that doesn't normally support footnotes. As you add or delete footnotes, Ventura renumbers the ones that follow automatically .

Ventura allows you to use a variety of footnote formats, including automatic numbers or your own defined characters, such as the asterisk or double dagger. You can also decide how to display the number, for instance, in superscript or with parentheses around it (see Figure 1.2). We'll cover footnotes in Chapter 11.

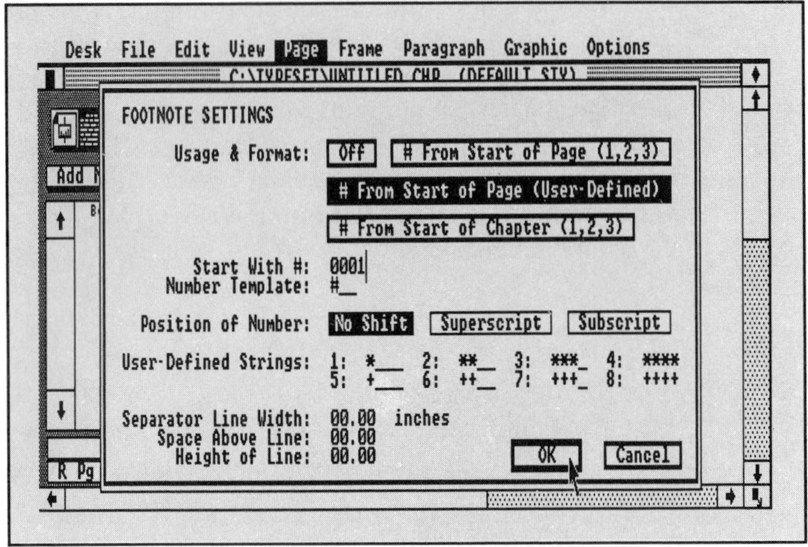

Figure 1.2: Footnote Creation with Ventura

PAGE NUMBERS

Ventura numbers pages for you automatically, and it does so in a variety of formats. It supports standard Arabic numbers, Roman numerals in both uppercase (I,II,III) and lowercase (i,ii,iii), or letters of the alphabet in upper- and lowercase. All numbering is automatic: once you place a page number, it remains in position on the page, regardless of how you edit the text around it. Inserting or removing a page will automatically renumber the subsequent pages. In Chapter 11 we'll examine page numbering.

HOW CHAPTERS AND PUBLICATIONS COORDINATE MATERIAL

A *chapter* is the fundamental unit that Ventura uses to coordinate files and other elements that go into creating a document. Multiple chapters combine together to make a *publication*. Version 1.1 allows you to assign up to 128 files to a chapter or publication. Each chapter can contain up to 500K bytes of text.

To coordinate the composition of text and graphics, a *chapter file* locates the appropriate word processed and picture files as well as other files, such as one it uses to create and hold captions, on the disk. Then the chapter file positions their contents properly on the page. Figure 1.3 shows the relationship among these elements. (We'll discuss style sheets later in this chapter.) To hold and position these elements, Ventura uses containers that it calls *frames*. The chapter file presents the resulting page, consisting of frames that hold files, on the screen.

In turn, you (and Ventura) can combine multiple chapters together. Ventura calls the resulting conglomeration a *publication*. In a publication, Ventura automatically coordinates printing of the publication's various chapters.

AN INDEX AND A TABLE OF CONTENTS

Based on entries that you make into chapters, Ventura will create an index and a table of contents for your publication automatically. Then, if you add or remove material, you can simply recompile to generate a new index and table of contents. Sorting is automatic, and the program updates the page numbers for you. Figure 1.4 shows the relationship between the publication and the chapters, table of contents, and index. Chapter 11 examines the way that these elements are coordinated.

CAPTIONS

You can *tie* a caption to the particular frame of text or graphic (see Figure 1.5). You can even specify its position in one of a variety of locations with respect to that frame. Ventura will automatically number figure and table captions throughout the chapter and the publication. Adding, removing, or rearranging illustrations will result in automatic renumbering, as you may have guessed.

There are two separate automatic counters: one keeps track of numbers for figures and the other numbers your tables. If you desire, Ventura will also include the chapter number in captions automatically. This makes possible a numbering system such as *Figure 2-1*, where *2* is the chapter number. In Chapter 7 we'll see how to tie captions to frames.

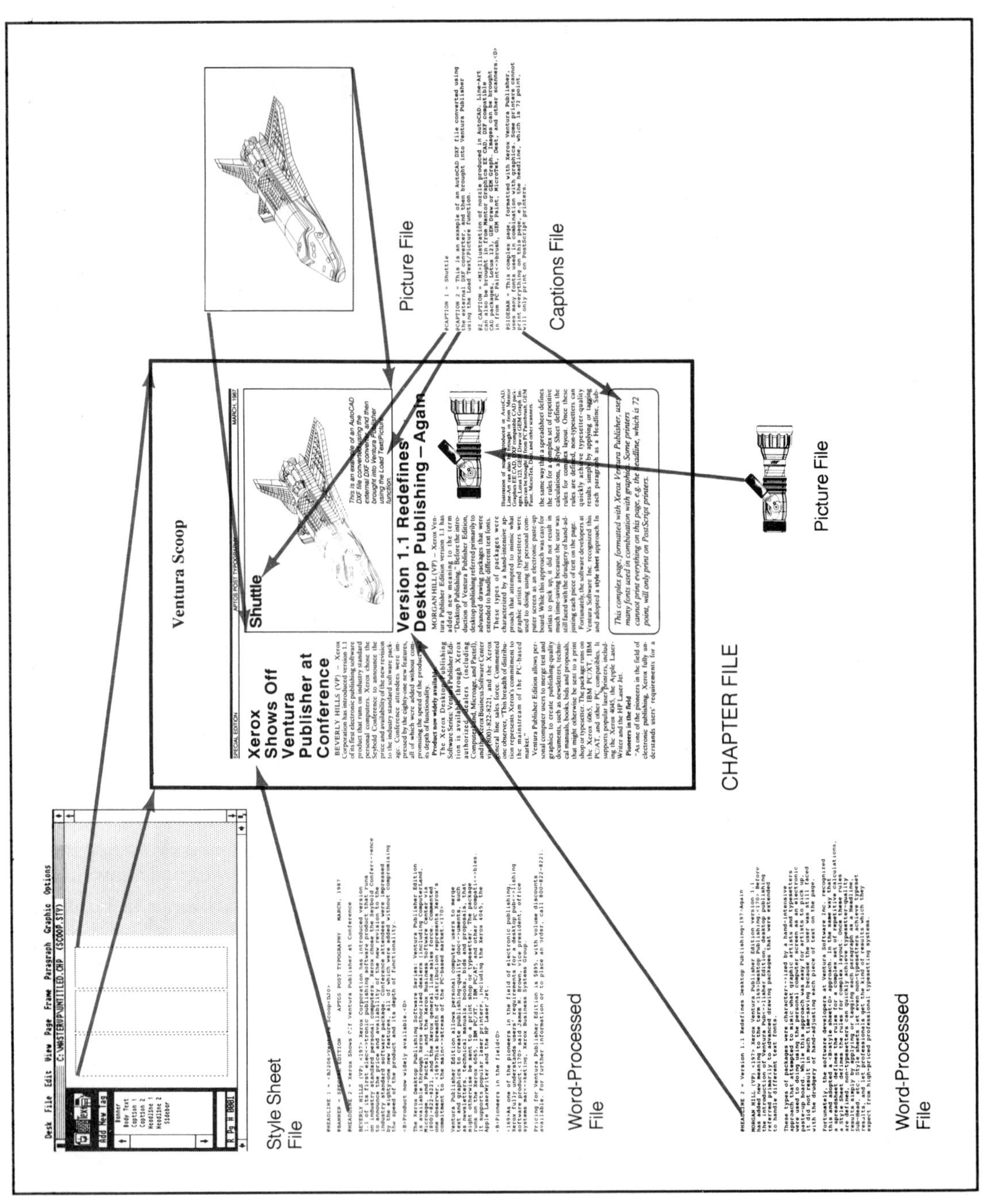

Figure 1.3: Chapters in Ventura

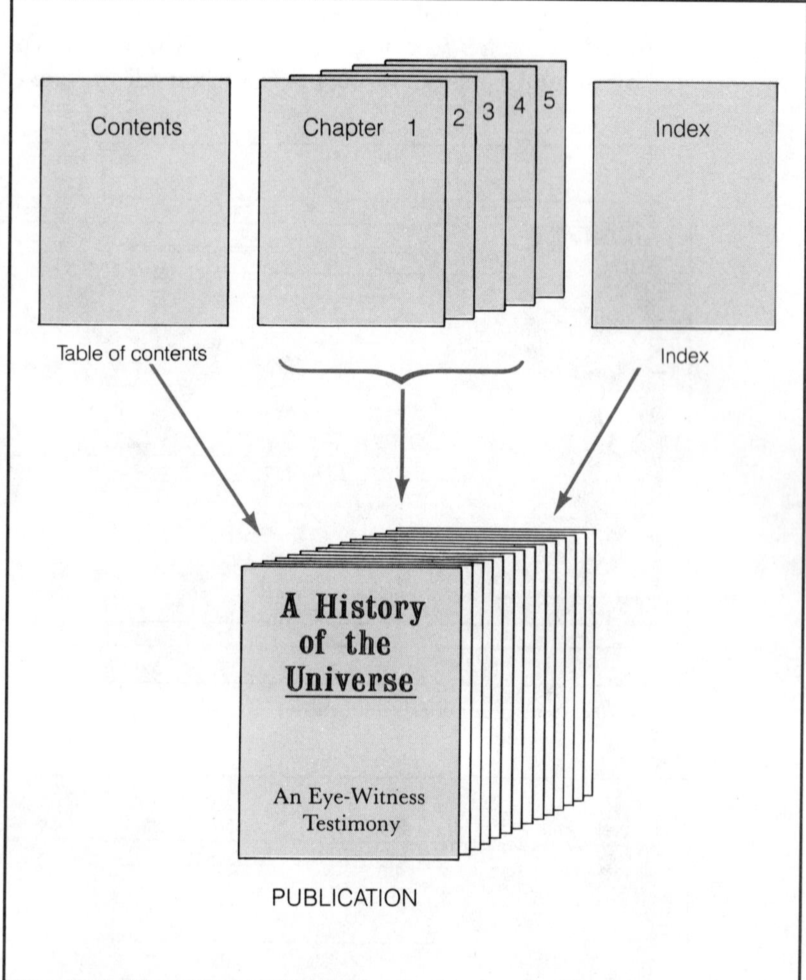

Figure 1.4: Publications in Ventura

TABLES

Ventura allows you to create tables in your chapters in several ways. One way is to use tabs, just as you would on a conventional typewriter. Each tab setting can have any one of a variety of alignment assignments. Thus, you can make decimals line up easily, center a heading over a column, and so forth.

The second way that you can make a table is with a graphic element called *box text* (see Figure 1.6). With box text, you create a *grid* by lining up blocks of boxes. You then fill the boxes with the

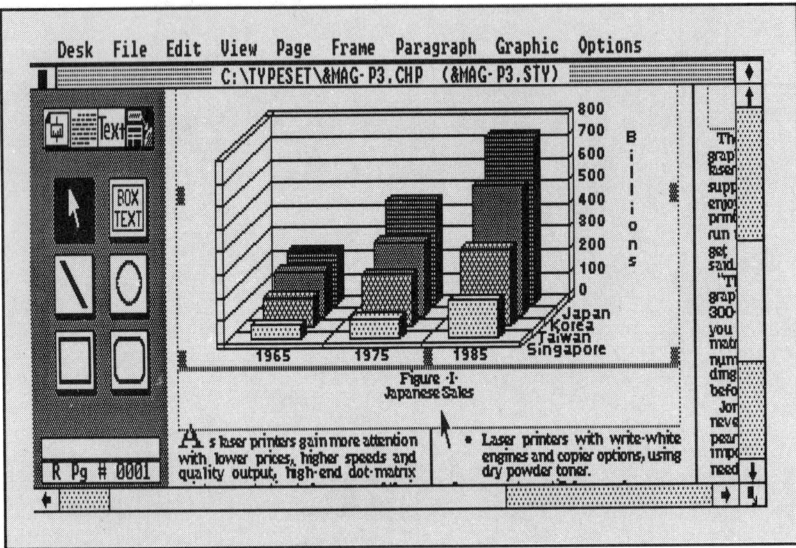

Figure 1.5: A Caption Tied to a Frame

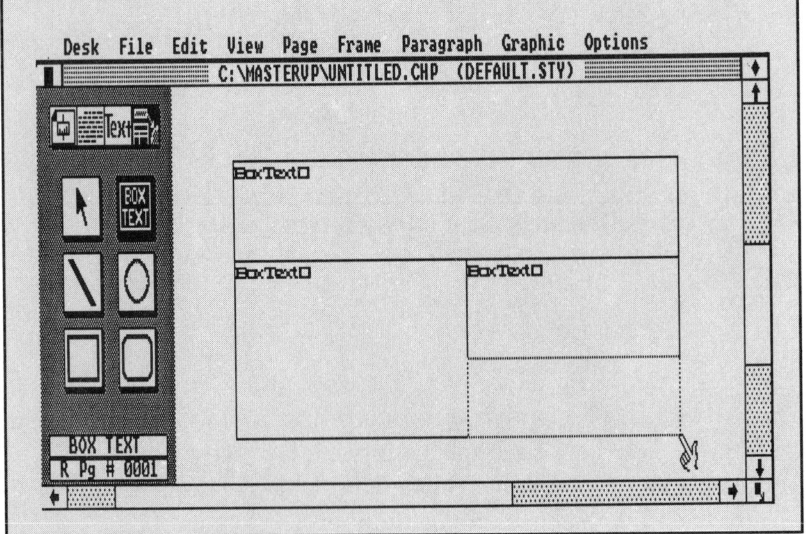

Figure 1.6: Box Text in Ventura

appropriate material. Along with another method of creating tables, these methods are discussed fully in Chapter 9.

We've looked at some of Ventura's chief features. Now let's examine one of its handiest abilities.

VENTURA AND YOUR WORD PROCESSING SYSTEM

As we mentioned, Ventura has the capacity to work with a variety of word processing systems (see Table 1.1). It also has some word processing capabilities itself.

With the most popular word processors (such as Microsoft Word, WordStar, WordPerfect and MultiMate), Ventura Publisher is capable of a kind of two-way communication. That is, changing text in Ventura changes the text in the original word processed file as well. Likewise, if you change the file with your word processor, the text changes in your Ventura chapter, too.

What's more, Ventura can also understand some of your word processor's formatting codes, such as those used for underlining and boldface. Changing these formats with Ventura changes them in the word processed file as well. You can also use the word processing capabilities of Ventura to enter your text initially.

Be aware, though, that the program does not feature a full word processing system. You can use it to cut and paste, but it's missing other features that are standard with most word processors, such as a search capability and a spelling checker. For these operations, you have to use your word processor. This limitation of Ventura, however, is an advantage rather than a drawback. It means that you needn't learn an entirely new word processing system to do desktop publishing.

As mentioned, Ventura fully supports several word processors. Within the same document, you can use files created by any or all of these. You can also use word processors that Ventura does not support fully. To do that, you simply save the text in standard, plain vanilla ASCII format. Ventura understands ASCII and can save in that format, too. In addition, you can use data from other programs that have the ability to output in ASCII format. This includes Lotus

1-2-3 and dBASE III PLUS. Chapter 12 discusses Ventura's performance with word processors and other kinds of software packages.

Finally, different word processor programs use different methods for storing text. With Ventura you can *convert* files from one word processing format to another. Thus, you could create a file using Microsoft Word and place it in your chapter. Then, if you have a copy editor who prefers to use WordStar, for instance, you can convert the file to WordStar format. The editor can then use WordStar to edit that file.

GRAPHICS AND VENTURA

Ventura's graphics capabilities are similar to its word processing capabilities. It can import graphics from a variety of sources. As with word processing, it can also create modest graphics, or fine tune those that it imports. Ventura supports graphics created by Lotus, GEM, AutoCAD, and ZSoft, among others.

By means of a *scanner*, you can even use paper graphics or photos within documents. A scanner is a peripheral input device for the computer. To use a scanner, you just feed it camera-ready art. The scanner "looks" at the art and digitizes it, creating an electronic equivalent of the picture. You can then use Ventura to manipulate the electronic image in a variety of ways. For instance, you can stretch it in one direction or another, magnify or reduce it, or you can *crop* it (that is, cut parts of the image away). Princeton Graphics Systems manufactures one such scanner.

Even if you make changes to pictures that appear in your Ventura document, you can always restore the originals later. That's because Ventura always leaves the file containing the original art intact. Thus, if your boss points out that you cut off her left ear in the company newsletter, it's simplicity itself to crop the picture differently so that she's whole again.

Ventura can also create lines, boxes, and circles. You can use its graphics and fonts, for instance, to add legends or text to an existing graphics file, or to expand upon text that is already there.

STYLE SHEETS

Style sheets are a special kind of file that control the formatting characteristics of documents that you prepare with Ventura. Unlike text and graphics files, style sheets are always created with Ventura, not some outside program. Every chapter must have a style sheet associated with it. You can either use sample style sheets that Ventura provides or you can create your own. You can also customize the sample style sheets to suit your own needs. (See Appendix A to get a sense of what these style sheets are like.)

Style sheets contain specifications for such style elements as fonts, alignment, spacing, and tabs. You group these elements into modular components that Ventura calls *tags*. A group of tags, in turn, composes a style sheet. In Version 1.1 you can have up to 128 such tags to a style sheet.

Within your chapter, you assign tags by the paragraph. The names of your tags should signal the purpose of the paragraph. For instance, you may have tags for a headline, sub-heading, body text, caption, and footnote.

By associating formats with tags, you guarantee a consistent formatting appearance throughout your chapter. Each time the tag appears, the proper font size and style, paragraph alignment, spacing, and so on are set in place automatically.

Note that style sheet file names have the extension STY unless you specify otherwise.

AUTOMATIC SCREENING OF FILES

Ventura uses file-name extensions to filter file names automatically according to type. In doing so, it assumes that the file names have the standard extensions listed in Table 1.2. (It automatically assigns extensions to the files it creates.) Many of the extensions listed for "Other Software" come from the various programs that originally generate the file. Some, however, you must assign yourself, such as the WS extension used for WordStar, if you wish to take advantage of the way Ventura filters filenames.

EXTENSION	VENTURA PUBLISHER
.C00	Print to disk output
.CAP	Captions
.CHP	Chapters
.CIF	Chapter information
.CNF	Printer information
.DIC	Hyphenation dictionaries
.FNT	Fonts
.GEN	Generated text
.HY1, .HY2	Hyphenation algorithms
.PUB	Publications
.STY	Style sheets
.VGR	Graphics
.WID	Width tables
EXTENSION	**OTHER SOFTWARE**
.CGM	Computer Graphics Metafile
.DCA	IBM Document Content Architecture
.DOC	Microsoft Word
.DOC	Multimate
.EPS	Encapsulated PostScript
.GEM	GEM line art
.HPG	Hewlett-Packard Graphics Language
.IMG	GEM image
.P*	Mentor Graphics
.PCT	Macintosh PICT
.PCX	PC Paintbrush

Table 1.2: File-Name Extensions and Ventura

EXTENSION	OTHER SOFTWARE
.PIC	Lotus 1-2-3 graph
.PIC	VideoShow
.PNT	Macintosh Paint
.SLD	AutoCAD Slides
.TXT	ASCII
.TXT	WordStarUK
.TXT	XyWrite
.WP	WordPerfect
.WS	WordStar US
.XWP	Xerox Writer

Table 1.2: File-Name Extensions and Ventura (continued)

SYSTEM REQUIREMENTS FOR VENTURA

Now that we've looked at the various files that are used to create a Ventura document, let's see what you will need to take the first step in the construction of a Ventura publication.

Of course, you'll need the Ventura software, distributed by Xerox Corporation, as well as a minimum of 512K of RAM on your computer. If you plan to create chapters longer than 20 pages, it's recommended that you have at least 640K.

You'll also need to have a graphics card, such as the one manufactured by Hercules for monochrome display. Ventura supports a variety of graphics cards, including CGA and EGA cards for color display. Just be certain that the graphics card you get will work with your monitor, and the resulting resolution is acceptable to you. You can have a computer dealer install it in your computer, or you can install the board yourself.

In addition to at least one floppy drive, a hard disk is necessary as well. You cannot use Ventura if you have only floppy drives. (If you choose, however, you can use floppy disks to store your documents.) Before you install Ventura, be sure that the hard disk has from one to three megabytes of storage available. The exact amount depends on the printer you will be using.

Xerox says that you will need a mouse. Because the program is designed to be used with a mouse, we will assume that you have one and will be using it with Ventura. While it is possible to use the program without a mouse, doing so is quite difficult, especially if you are new to the program. However, you can improve mouseless performance if you use a keyboard enhancer, such as SmartKey. Appendix B provides information on the use of Ventura without a mouse.

To print your documents, you need a printer that Ventura supports. The list currently includes the Epson MX-80, RX-80, the Hewlett-Packard LaserJet Plus, the LaserJet with F cartridge or LaserJet Series II, the IBM ProPrinter, the Xerox 4020 Color or 4045 Laser printers, and any printer that uses the PostScript command language, such as the Apple LaserWriter. You can also use a JLaser card with a printer that's compatible with it.

As your system and your skills in using Ventura become increasingly sophisticated, you may find that your normal screen is simply too small. That's because standard screens cannot display a full $8^1/_2 \times 11$-inch page. To alleviate this problem, it's a pleasure to use a full-page display, such as the Genius from Micro Display Systems. With this ingenious piece of hardware, you can finally have a screen that displays a full $8^1/_2 \times 11$ inches (see Figure 1.7). If you've yet to purchase your hardware, you may wish to consider a full-page display. Some experts estimate that using such a display can double the efficiency of your desktop publishing work. (If you purchase a full-page display, you'll also need to use a special graphics card.) As we proceed in this book, we'll occasionally use the Genius to display some of the examples.

There are even displays that are large enough to show a full size two-page spread, such as one manufactured by Wyse. We'll use the term *large display* to indicate either a full-page or a two-page display.

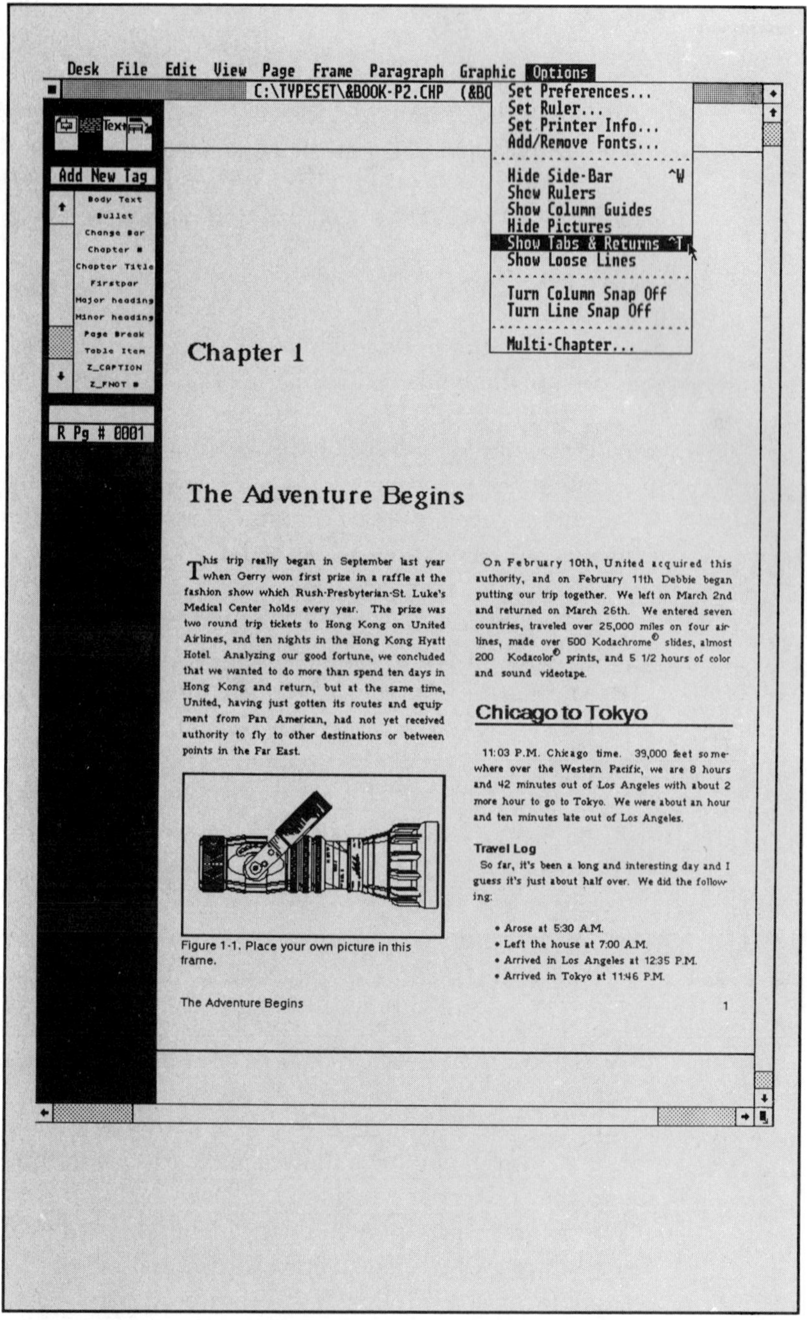

Figure 1.7: Ventura on a Genius Full-Page Display

HOW VENTURA WORKS WITH THE OPERATING SYSTEM

Since Ventura is designed for IBM systems, it naturally requires you to use the IBM DOS or the Microsoft MS-DOS operating system. You must use Version 2.10 or higher. If you are uncertain of the version of DOS you have, you can find out by typing

```
ver
```

at your system prompt and hitting the Return key.

If you are unfamiliar with the use of DOS conventions, especially the use of directories, you may wish to consult Appendix C, which provides an overview of the DOS operations necessary to use Ventura Publisher.

Various elements of the program, such as chapter text, graphics elements, and so on, are each stored in a file. You may wish to organize your work so that each publication has all its associated material in one directory. As you learn to use Ventura's various file commands, you'll be able to specify the appropriate directories. Ventura can also create directories and remove them from the disk.

Alternatively, you may wish to store material according to the type of file. Using this method, you could store word processed material with its asscociated word processor software, graphics images with their appropriate graphics package, and so on. In either case, keep close tabs on where you are storing your files.

THE VENTURA PACKAGE

When you acquire Ventura, you'll know right away that it is a formidable piece of software. The program consists of 11 disks, and the documentation is divided into three volumes. This book does not assume that you have used the documentation or any other means to study Ventura. If you have, however, working with this book should add to your understanding of the program.

The program's disks have labels with various names and are numbered 1 through 11. They contain the program itself as well as specifications for various printers that Ventura supports. When you install

Ventura, a process we'll look at in a moment, the specifications for your printer or printers are automatically copied onto your hard disk. When you install the program, fan the disks out as they appear in Figure 1.8. In this way, you'll be able to see the numbers that appear along the left edge of each disk easily. The installation program will prompt you for which disks you need to insert according to number.

The disks also contain examples of various documents. In conjunction with these examples, there are also 25 style sheets.

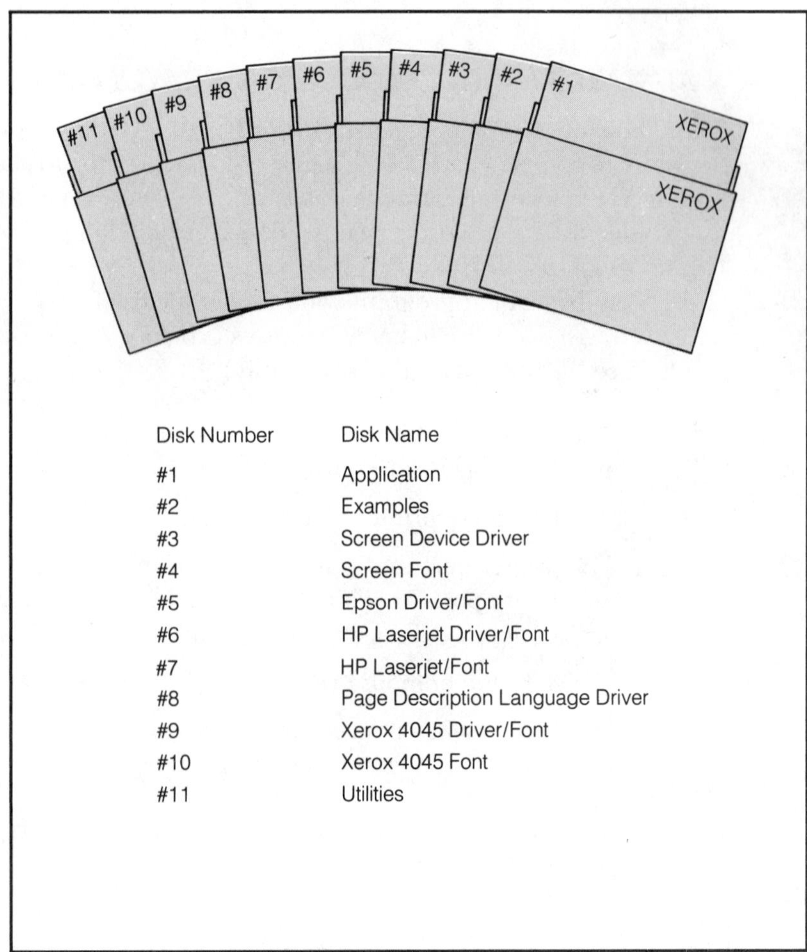

Disk Number	Disk Name
#1	Application
#2	Examples
#3	Screen Device Driver
#4	Screen Font
#5	Epson Driver/Font
#6	HP Laserjet Driver/Font
#7	HP Laserjet/Font
#8	Page Description Language Driver
#9	Xerox 4045 Driver/Font
#10	Xerox 4045 Font
#11	Utilities

Figure 1.8: The Ventura Package

GETTING VENTURA READY TO USE

As with most software, you must *install* Ventura before you can use it on your computer. When you install the program, you provide it with the specifications for your computer system, telling it what your monitor is like, what printer you will be using, and so forth. Ventura transfers the appropriate information from its disks onto your hard disk.

USING THE INSTALLATION PROGRAM

The installation program (VPPREP) can take up to a half hour or more to complete its work. If you should later decide to change some aspect of the installation, you can easily do so with Version 1.1. (With Version 1.0, you must repeat the entire installation process to make any changes.)

The installation program will ask you for the following information (it is a good idea to know the answers before you run the installation, so the process proceeds smoothly):

- The type of graphics board that's installed in your computer and the display you're using.
- What brand of printer you are using.
- The printer port that connects your printer. If you're unfamiliar with ports or printers, you may wish to consult Chapter 6, where we discuss them in detail.
- Which brand of mouse you are using.
- How that mouse connects to your computer. It may connect via a serial port or it may be using a board.

To install Ventura, insert disk #1, the Application disk, into drive A. Then type

```
a:vpprep
```

and hit the Return key.

The installation program will proceed to ask you about your equipment (see Figure 1.9) and then prompt you to insert the appropriate disks. As you install, you will probably find that there are some disks you use more than once and some you don't use at all; this is normal. Just follow the instructions on the screen. If you decide that it's necessary to abort the installation at any time, you can do so by pressing the Ctrl key and holding it down while you push the key labeled Scroll Lock Break.

If you are going to install more than one printer, decide which one you will install first. The one that you specify first will be the *default* printer: the first one that Ventura displays when you print your documents.

Though lengthy, the installation process is simple because its questions are straightforward; Ventura creates its own directories (VENTURA, which contains the program, and TYPESET, which contains the examples) for you and copies the appropriate information into the directories automatically.

COMPLETING THE INSTALLATION PROCESS

When VPPREP is finished, there are a couple of other steps you should perform to complete the installation process. You'll need to use your word processor to create or modify certain files on disk, including VP.BAT, which is created with the installation process and loads Ventura, and AUTOEXEC.BAT (you create this file if you like), which runs programs when you turn the computer on. You'll also work with the CONFIG.SYS file, which configures the operating system to your specifications.

Use your word processor in the ASCII mode to modify these files. If you're unsure how to do this, check Chapter 12. It describes the methods of creating ASCII text with some of the more popular word processing systems. If your word processor is not listed, check the documentation that came with it or with another reference.

When you create these files, be certain that you spell their names correctly. Also be sure to type the commands exactly as shown, with no extra spaces. Each line must end with a Return.

First, you'll need to add the following line to the CONFIG.SYS file on your hard disk or another disk from which you boot your

```
Which graphics card and display do you have?

A    IBM Color Card / Color Display (640x200)
B    IBM Enhanced Card / Color Display (640x200)
C    IBM Enhanced Card / Enhanced Display (640x350)
D    IBM Enhanced Card / Monochrome PC Display (640x350)
E    IBM Personal System/2 (640x480) two colors.
F    IBM 3270 Pc / Monochrome PC Display (640x350)
G    Hercules Card / Monochrome PC Display (720x348)
H    Xerox 6065 / AT&T 6300 (640x400)
I    MDS Genius Full Page Display (720 x 1000)
J    Xerox Full Page Display (720 x 992)
K    Wyse WY-700 Display (1280 x 800)
L    ---THE FOLLOWING DRIVERS SHOULD ONLY BE USED WITH COLOR PRINTERS---
M    IBM Enhanced Card / Color Display 16 Colors 640x200
N    IBM Enhanced Card / Enhanced Display 16 Colors 640x350
O    AT&T Display Enhancement Board (640 x 400) 16 colors

Type the letter of the graphics card you have: _
```

Figure 1.9: Installing Ventura

computer:

```
BUFFERS = 15
FILE = 15
```

These numbers control the amount of data (number of buffers) read from the disk at one time and the number of files that can be opened at one time. You can use numbers greater than 15 if another program you're using demands that you do. If you see these lines already in the file, and if they're set for 15 or greater, leave them. If not, change them to 15.

If you have a *bus* mouse (one that uses its own board instead of plugging into a serial port), the software that runs the mouse must be installed before each work session. You'll probably want to automate this installation of your mouse. That way, you won't have to reload it each time you use Ventura Publisher. To do this, add the line

```
c:\mouse
```

to the VP.BAT file or the AUTOEXEC.BAT file. Be sure to specify the path, if any, where you have the mouse software located. Thus, if your Microsoft Mouse software is stored in the MSMOUSE directory on drive C, you'd enter

```
c:\msmouse\mouse
```

VENTURA AND THE MOUSE

As mentioned earlier, Ventura makes liberal use of the mouse. As you move the mouse around, an indicator on the screen moves in a corresponding fashion. This indicator, which Ventura calls a *mouse cursor*, changes shape depending on the operation of the program. We'll look at mouse shapes as we study Ventura's screen in the next chapter.

Although the mouse can be used in Ventura in several different ways, you'll use only one of the mouse buttons: the one on the left.

You can use the mouse to select a designated item or feature by pointing to a choice on the screen and pushing the mouse button. Pushing and releasing the mouse button is often referred to as *clicking* the mouse. Pointing the mouse cursor at a choice and pushing the mouse button to select it is called *clicking the choice*.

You can also use the mouse cursor to move to the spot where you next wish to type. By pointing to a certain spot, you can cause another indicator, called the *text cursor* or *keyboard cursor*, to appear. As you then start to type, your typing appears in that spot.

For other effects, you'll use a technique called *dragging* the mouse. To drag the mouse, you point to one spot and press the mouse button down. Then, with your finger still holding the mouse button down, you move the mouse to another location. When you reach the appropriate location, you release the mouse button. This action affects the area between the two points in some manner. For instance, should you wish to underline some text previously typed in, you would drag the mouse to indicate the text that you want underlined.

THE VENTURA KEYBOARD

Despite Ventura's sophisticated capabilities, its use of the keyboard is rather simple and straightforward. Let's look at some of the keys that operate in a special way in Ventura. Table 1.3 summarizes the operation of these keys.

Some Things to Know About Buying and Using the Mouse

- If you get a bus mouse, you'll use one of the slots inside the computer for its board. If you get a serial mouse, you'll use an RS-232 port. Consider which type is most advantageous to you before you purchase one.
- The mouse comes in a variety of styles. Some roll on the desk, some slide on a card. Some, like the Keytronic Keyboard Touchpad, don't even use a mouse: you use your finger on a pad instead.
- If some part of your computer stops operating once you install a bus mouse, you may need to change the *jumper clip*. It's a small plastic block that fits over a pair of prongs on the card and can be changed to various settings.
- If you run out of room on your desktop as you move the mouse in one direction or another, just lift the mouse and position it elsewhere on the surface. The pointer won't move as you relocate the mouse.
- Single clicking with the mouse seems to work best when you keep the click short (just hold down the mouse button briefly). Double clicking seems to work best when you make the first click short and the second click long.
- Keep your desktop or slide card clean so that the mouse can roll or slide smoothly.
- By sliding a cover off the bottom, you may be able to dissect the mouse for cleaning. Be sure to turn off the computer and disconnect the mouse before you do. Check your mouse documentation for full details on cleaning.
- You may find it interesting to know that programmers measure mouse movement in tiny increments called *mickeys*—about 1/100th of an inch.

KEY	ACTION
Alt with the keypad	Creates special characters
Alt with the mouse	Crops pictures
Arrow keys on the keypad	Moves the keyboard cursor
Backspace	Erases text as it backs up
Ctrl with the mouse	Selects hidden graphics
Ctrl with various keys	Activates commands or creates special characters
Ctrl-Hyphen	Inserts a discretionary hyphen
Ctrl-Return	Starts a new line but not a new paragraph
Ctrl-Right Shift	Allows directional arrows to move the mouse cursor
Ctrl-Space	Creates a NoBreak Space (a space that prevents text on either side from breaking across lines)
Del	Deletes (cuts) text to the right or selected material
End	Displays the end of the chapter
Esc	Re-inks the screen in the working area
	Erases a displayed entry field
	Interrupts printing or a GoTo operation
Home	Displays the beginning of the chapter
Ins	Inserts (pastes) text or other selected material
PgUp, PgDn	Displays the previous and next page, respectively
Return	Starts a new paragraph

Table 1.3: Important Keys in Ventura

KEY	ACTION
Shift-Del	Copies text or other selected material
Shift with the mouse	Selects multiple elements Adds multiple frames or graphics
Tab	Moves to the next tab setting in the paragraph

Table 1.3: Important Keys in Ventura (continued)

Return As with word processing, you use the Return key to end a paragraph. However, there may be times when it is necessary to begin a new line without beginning a new paragraph. By pressing Ctrl-Return, you can create a *line break*, which does this. Paragraph formatting (the tagging we discussed earlier) remains unbroken between the two lines separated by a line break.

Tab As mentioned above, you can use the Tab key to separate items that appear in a table. You can also use the Tab key (or an arrow key or the mouse) to move among fields on the screen and set their respective values. Note that you don't usually use tabs to indent the first line of a paragraph. Ventura provides that format with a paragraph tag. Thus, when creating text with your word processor, always press only the Return key to start a new paragraph; do not press Return and then Tab.

Del and Ins You can use the Del key to delete (or cut) material that you've selected, such as text. Use the Ins key to insert (or paste) that material into a new location.

Esc The Esc (Escape) key has a variety of uses depending upon Ventura's display when the key is pressed. First, as you work with the program, parts of the screen may become sloppy. Material that you've removed or changed may remain on the screen along with the revised version. These odd occurrences result from the complex interaction that various parts of the program have on each other. Such screen surprises can be quite disconcerting. You can remedy the problem by hitting the Esc key. Doing so when the page is displayed causes Ventura to *re-ink* the screen, that is, make it appear as it should.

The Esc key has two other major functions. First, you can use it to erase values that have been previously entered into a field. Second, when you're printing a document or moving the screen display to a certain page in the chapter, pressing Esc will interrupt that operation. You can then either continue the procedure or go on to something else instead.

Home and End These keys are used to reposition the display of the document quickly. The Home key moves to the very beginning of the chapter. The End key moves to the end of the chapter.

PgUp and PgDn These keys move the display through the document one page at a time. Pressing PgUp causes Ventura to display the previous page of the document. PgDn displays the next page.

Note that these keys actually move one *page* at a time. They do not move one screen at a time, as they do in some word processing systems.

Alt The Alt key serves two purposes in Ventura Publisher. When used with the mouse, it moves cropped images behind frames. We'll study this application in Chapter 7.

You can also use the Alt key to create a variety of special characters, such as the copyright symbol, that do not appear on the keyboard. Appendix E lists these characters along with their respective Alt codes. To create one of these characters, press the Alt key and hold it down while you type the code number on the numeric keypad at the right of the keyboard. To display a copyright symbol, for instance, you'd type Alt-**189**. Be sure to use the numeric keypad to enter the code. Do not use the number keys at the top of the keyboard.

Ctrl Used with other keys, the Ctrl (Control) key works in the same press-and-hold fashion as the Alt key. Pressing Ctrl and the Space bar, for example, creates a NoBreak Space, which keeps the words on either side of it together on the same line.

With Version 1.1, you can use the Ctrl key in conjunction with the Shift key to create some of the more popular special characters. For instance, you can display a copyright symbol by typing Ctrl- Shift-C. The special characters you can create with Ctrl-Shift are listed in Appendix E.

Pressing Ctrl and the right Shift key allows you to use the directional arrows to move the mouse cursor without a mouse. Appendix B discusses use of Ventura without a mouse.

F1–F10 Ventura does not assign mandatory duties to the function keys, as many programs do. Instead, it allows you to assign paragraph tags to them if you choose. This makes it possible to tag paragraphs without using the mouse. It also allows you to use the function keys in conjunction with a keyboard enhancer, such as SmartKey (see Chapter 12).

You should now have an idea *what* kinds of things Ventura can do for your publication. In the next chapter, you'll get an idea of *how* it accomplishes these marvels.

CHAPTER TWO

How Ventura Operates

AS YOU CAN PROBABLY TELL BY NOW, VENTURA IS quite a sophisticated program. To be able to perform its many multi-faceted operations, it has, in one sense, a very complex structure. Fortunately for us, though, this structure is exquisitely designed to give users *intuitive* access to the program's features; that is, the program operates in a fashion that seems natural and flows logically. Ventura's commands, for example, are categorized in menus whose names are easy to remember and locate. The menus have straightforward, descriptive names, such as Page and Paragraph. As you continue to work with Ventura, you may find yourself second-guessing the way in which an operation will perform, even before you learn it.

The first step in developing an understanding of the program's operations is to learn how they are compartmentalized. Ventura is divided into four functions or *operating modes*, only one of which is active at any given time. The active mode controls the manner in which Ventura behaves and the way it looks to the user.

The purpose of this chapter is to give you an overview of the workings of Ventura. That way, you'll have a chance to see how the program's features operate before you actually try them out. As part of this overview, we'll provide you with a short tour of Ventura's four modes of operation.

VENTURA'S TWO CURSORS

Ventura's two cursors, the mouse cursor and the keyboard cursor, act as your servants throughout the program. These cursors open doors to Ventura's commands, so you can see what's available and instruct the program to do your bidding.

As described in Chapter 1, the *mouse cursor* moves all around the screen. Like a shadow, its motion corresponds to movements that you make on your desk with the mouse. With a somewhat jerky action, it causes a variety of activities to occur. For example, as it passes over menu names, it causes their corresponding menus to drop down from those names like a window shade. As it passes over available menu items, it causes them to darken, indicating that they're available for you to select. Also, its own shape changes as it goes from one task to another. The various shapes the mouse cursor can take are shown in Table 2.1, along with a summary of their meanings.

Mouse Cursor Shapes	**Mode**	**Operation**
	Frame	
		Add new frame
		Resize frame
		Crop image
		Move frame
	Paragraph	
	Text	
	Graphic	
		Box text
		Line drawing
		Circle drawing
		Rectangle drawing
		Rounded rectangle drawing

Note: The mouse cursor changes to when you make selections from pull-down menus, dialog boxes, and the Side-bar.

Table 2.1: Mouse Cursor Shapes

The other cursor in Ventura is the *keyboard cursor* or *text cursor*. This cursor operates in a more staid manner than the mouse cursor. Its shape is always that of a slender vertical bar (see Figure 2.1), which blinks at certain times and at other times stays constant. The purpose of this cursor is straightforward. As you type at the keyboard, it simply marks the point at which the letters, numbers, and other characters that you type appear. To move the keyboard cursor without entering characters, you use the arrow keys on the right of the keyboard.

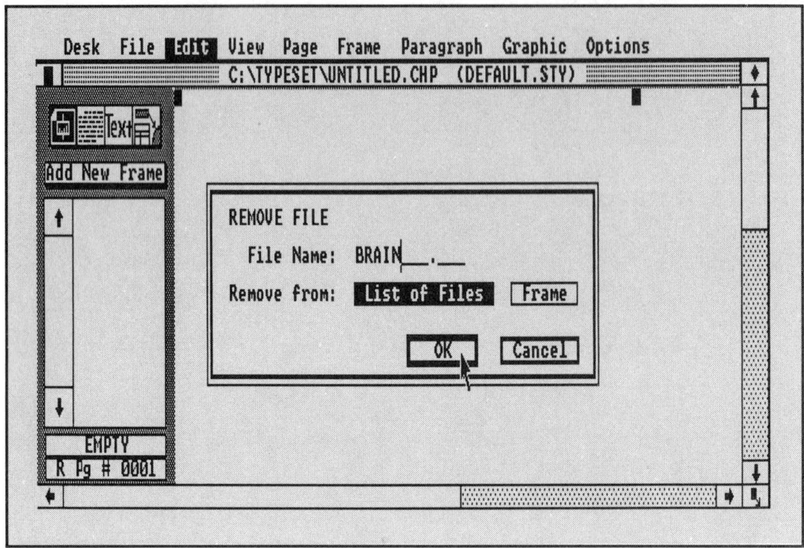

Figure 2.1: Using the Keyboard Cursor to Type a File Name

Although the mouse and keyboard cursors differ completely in the way they perform, they cooperate fully and complement each other's activities. In fact, when you are working with one, the other often disappears. Like perfect servants, though, they return to the screen the moment you need them.

EXPLORING THE MAIN SCREEN

The main screen in Ventura is shown in Figure 2.2. When you start Ventura, this is the sight that will greet you. It's like a main gate that opens into the program. Let's take a moment to look at this screen and see how it is used to gain access to Ventura's many features. Refer to Figure 2.2 as we discuss the different elements of the main screen.

As you read this discussion, you may also wish to look at the main screen on your monitor. If so, start up Ventura by typing

```
VP
```

at the system prompt. (Of course, you must first install the program as described in Chapter 1.)

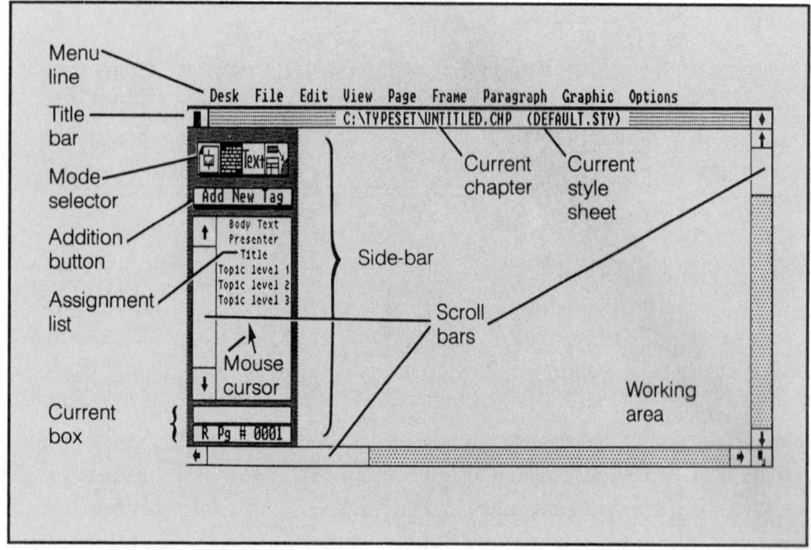

Figure 2.2: The Main Screen

THE WORKING AREA

The screen's main blank space is the *working area*. This is the area in which you'll lay out your document and see it take shape. It's here that you'll indicate your columns, insert your headlines and titles, position your illustrations, and view the results as you compose your document.

Besides the keyboard cursor, there are six unusual symbols that you may encounter as you work in the working area. They are shown in Table 2.2. The Paragraph End symbol (¶) indicates the spot where you hit the Return key in text in order to start a new paragraph. The Line Break symbol (↵) indicates the spot where you hit Ctrl-Return to start a new line. You create a Horizontal Tab symbol (→) by hitting the Tab key. Ventura automatically displays the End of File symbol (□) so that you know when the file text ends. You create a NoBreak Space symbol (␣) by typing Ctrl-Space in order to keep the text on either side of the symbol together on the same line. In Version 1.1, Ventura also uses this symbol to indicate an Em Space, an En Space, a Figure Space, and a Thin Space. Respectively, these are spaces about the width of the letter M, the letter N, a numeric digit, and a period. We'll discuss their use in Chapter 13. Finally,

NAME IN THE CURRENT BOX	SYMBOL ON THE SCREEN	HOW CREATED
Paragraph End	¶	Return key
Line Break	↵	Ctrl-Return
Horizontal Tab	→	Tab key
End of File	□	(Automatically)
NoBreak Space Em Space En Space Thin Space Figure Space	␣	Ctrl-Space Ctrl-Shift-M Ctrl-Shift-N Ctrl-Shift-T Ctrl-Shift-F
Frame Anchor	°	Edit Menu's Insert/Edit Anchor command
Index Entry	°	Edit Menu's Insert/Edit Index command
Footnote	°	Edit Menu's Insert/Footnote Index command

Table 2.2: Keyboard Symbols

Version 1.1 displays a very small circle (°), like a temperature degree symbol, to indicate the position of a Frame Anchor, Footnote, or Index Entry. We'll study the special commands you use to create this symbol in Chapter 11.

Normally, these symbols will appear on the screen where you type them. If they're distracting, however, you can use the Options pull-down menu to make them invisible by clicking the Hide Tabs and Returns option. You can achieve the same result by typing Ctrl-T. We'll see how to use pull-down menus in a moment.

THE SIDE-BAR

To the left of the working area is a panel with several boxes within it. This area is the *Side-bar*.

A Note About the NoBreak Space

Proper typesetting requires that certain words that belong together always stay on the same line. For instance, titles should not be separated from names, as in Dr. Jones or Jane Jones, M.D. The rule also applies to numbers that follow categories, as in January 1 or Chapter 10. You use a NoBreak Space (Ctrl-Space) instead of a regular space to keep words together on the same line.

Ventura creates a NoBreak Space automatically under one condition. If you type two spaces after a period, the second space becomes a NoBreak Space when you save your material. In this case, however, it doesn't actually operate as a NoBreak Space; that is, it doesn't force text on either side of it to stay together. Apparently, its purpose is to draw your attention to the second space so you can delete it. In typesetting, as opposed to typing with a typewriter, it's standard procedure to insert only *one* space between one sentence and the next. Inserting two spaces, the typewriter standard, creates too much room between sentences.

The Mode Selector

The first area of the Side-bar is officially referred to as the *Function selector*. We'll call it the *Mode selector;* the term is more accurate and avoids confusion with the keyboard's function keys. The Mode selector consists of four boxes or *buttons*.

(We'll use the term *button* to describe any labeled box that you can use to change something. You ''push'' a button by pointing to it with the mouse and clicking. Generally, this causes the button to darken. Note that while most button labels are short, as suits a button, some are not; button labels can be up to a sentence in length.)

The buttons of the Mode selector indicate which mode of Ventura is operating at any moment. A darkened button indicates the mode that is currently in effect or *active*. By pointing to one of the buttons and clicking the mouse, you can change the operating mode, *activating* one mode or another. You'll see that there are other ways to change the operating mode as well.

The Addition Button

Below the mode selector is the *Addition button*. What appears inside it will vary depending upon which mode is active. It may say "Add New Frame," "Add New Tag," or "Set Font," or it may disappear altogether. You use it to add various attributes to the document you're formatting in the working area.

The Assignment List

Generally, when you use the Addition button, you do so in conjunction with the elements that appear in the area below it. This area is called the *Assignment list*. A listing of the items that are available for assigning appears in this box.

The kinds of choices that are available will depend upon the mode that's active. You may see the names of text files, paragraph tags that are available for formatting, or text attributes, such as italic, bold, and underline. We'll discuss the contents of the Assignment list further when we examine the various modes in detail.

Scroll Bars

To the left of the Assignment list is a *scroll bar*. Scroll bars are used to bring hidden material into view. When the total number of available choices exceeds that which the Assignment list can accommodate, you can use the scroll bar to move the list up and down in order to view and select additional items.

Scroll bars appear in various places within Ventura. For instance, there are scroll bars to the right of the working area as well as below it. If you can't see the entire page at once, you'll want to use the Vertical scroll bar (to the right of the working area). This bar moves the displayed page up and down. Vertical scrolling will probably be necessary unless you have a monitor with a large display, such as the Genius. You'll use the Horizontal scroll bar (at the bottom of the screen) to move the page left and right as necessary.

Scroll bars indicate when there is more available than meets the eye. The amount of white area (as opposed to shaded) shows the relative amount that the display occupies as opposed to the amount that is unseen in either direction.

The operation of scroll bars is similar throughout the program. We'll see how to use them in a moment.

The Current Box

The *Current box* appears below the Assignment list. It shows the current status of some elements in Ventura. Its contents, like those of the Assignment list, will vary depending upon the active mode.

Note that the Current box is not a button, but simply an *indicator;* its contents are for display purposes only. You can't change the Current box by clicking it, as you would a button.

The top half of the Current box provides information about the *current selection.* As dictated by the mode, it identifies the contents of the selected frame, paragraph, text, or graphic. To work on a given frame, paragraph, and so on, you must first select it. By using the mouse to click material in the working area, you indicate that you want the program to focus its attention on that element.

The bottom half of the Current box gives you information about the page that you have displayed in the working area. It indicates the page number and whether it is a left or right page.

THE TITLE BAR AND THE MENU LINE

The *Title bar* appears just above the Working area. The Title bar displays the name of the chapter that's on the screen along with the disk drive and directory that store it. Until you assign a name, Ventura calls the document UNTITLED.CHP.

The Title bar also shows the name of the style sheet you've assigned to the document. With a new chapter, Ventura initially assigns the style sheet for you. It assigns the same style sheet that you were last using.

At the right end of the Title bar is a small box called the Full box. This box and the box at the bottom right corner of the screen (called the Size box) serve no useful purpose, although they do operate.

They change the size of Ventura's display area (as does the Title bar itself). Perhaps future versions of Ventura will make productive use of these boxes, which are vestiges of GEM.

At the very top of the screen, the *Menu line* (Desk, File, Edit, View, and so on) displays the names of nine *pull-down menus* that you can expose with the mouse. This Menu line provides your main entree into the operations of Ventura.

PULL-DOWN MENUS AND ASSOCIATED FEATURES

As you move the mouse cursor up to the Menu line, it always takes on an arrow shape. As long as the screen isn't displaying a *dialog box* or the *Item Selector* box (both of which we'll discuss shortly), the mouse arrow will activate the pull-down menus associated with each of the names on the Menu line.

In this section we'll examine these menus and see how they operate. We'll also examine some commands, shortcuts, and other features that work hand-in-glove with these menus.

PULL-DOWN MENUS

Ventura's menus are called *pull-down menus* because they seem to be pulled down from the menu name that you point at with the mouse. Figure 2.3 shows how pointing at File on the Menu line reveals the File pull-down menu.

Once a pull-down menu appears, you can use the mouse cursor—an arrow—to select one of the offered choices, which we'll call *commands*. As you move the arrow up or down the pull-down menu, you will see each command darken as the arrow passes in front of it. To choose a darkened command, you click the mouse button. Figure 2.4 shows how the darkened Save command on the File pull-down menu is standing by, ready for selection.

Keyboard Shortcuts

Notice, too, that the Save choice has a ^S appearing at the right of the darkened bar. This ^S is an abbreviation for Ctrl-S, a *keyboard shortcut*. Several of Ventura's commands have shortcuts such as this that you may prefer to use.

Thus, in order to save, you can pull down the File menu and click Save with the mouse, or you can simply type Ctrl-S at the keyboard.

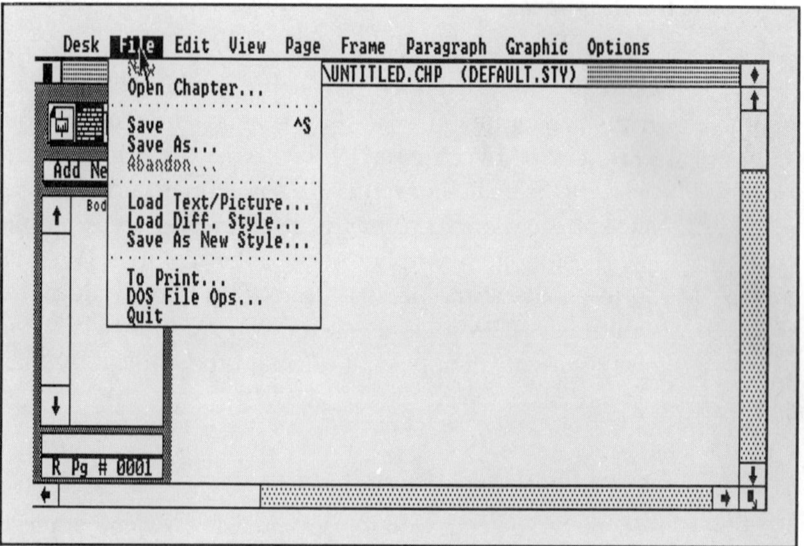

Figure 2.3: Activating a Pull-Down Menu

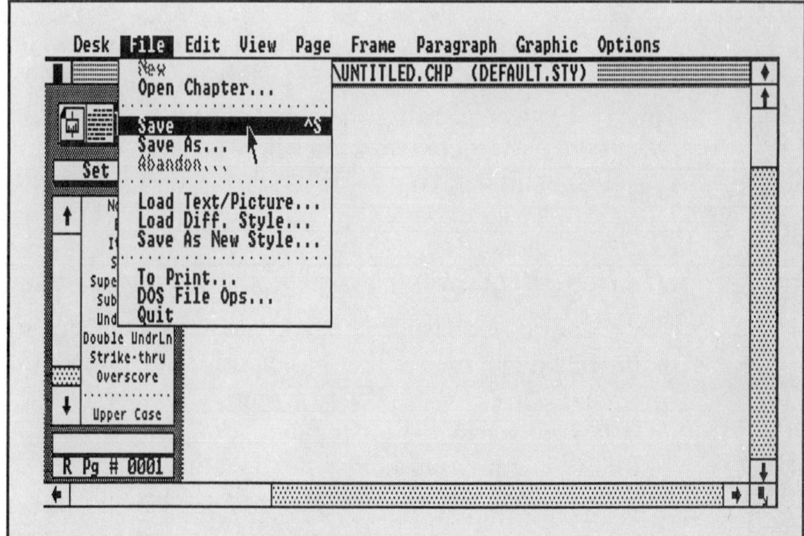

Figure 2.4: Selecting from a Pull-Down Menu

Both methods accomplish the same thing. Table 2.3 shows a listing of Ventura's keyboard shortcuts, along with their pull-down menu counterparts.

Ghosting Items

As you move the cursor arrow across the various items on the Menu line, you'll notice that some commands on the pull-down menus are lighter in type than others, and that as you move the mouse cursor over these lighter items, they do not darken as the others do. Such lighter items are sometimes said to be *ghosting*. (The New and Abandon commands in Figure 2.4 are examples of this.)

A ghosting item simply indicates that the item is not available for you to choose at the present time. This may be due to a variety of conditions. As you change these surrounding circumstances, the ghosting item will appear in normal type, indicating that it is available for you to select.

Closing Pull-Down Menus

If you decide you want to use a pull-down menu other than the one you've opened, just point the mouse cursor at the desired menu name (such as Edit) on the Menu line. The new menu will open and the old menu will close.

If you wish to close a menu without opening a new one, click the mouse when it's not pointing at a darkened (available) command. Thus, you can be pointing anywhere outside the pull-down menu, at any ghosting command, or somewhere between commands, in order to close a menu.

DIALOG BOXES

A dialog box is a display that is generated by one of the commands on the pull-down menus that has ellipsis points, three dots after the command (for example, Page Layout...). Dialog boxes use the settings you provide in them to regulate related items, as grouped by the pull-down menu commands. For instance, Figure 2.5 shows the Page Layout dialog box, one of the first you may have to use. You

KEYBOARD SHORTCUT	PULL-DOWN EQUIVALENT	
	MENU	COMMAND
^A	Graphic	Bring to Front
^B	Page	Renumber Chapter
^E	View	Enlarged View
^F	Graphic	Fill Attributes
^G	Page	Go to Page
^I	View	Paragraph Tagging
^K	Paragraph	Assign Function Keys
^L	Graphic	Line Attributes
^N	View	Normal View
^O	View	Text Editing
^P	View	Graphic Drawing
^Q	Graphic	Select All
^R	View	Reduced View
^S	File	Save
^T	Options	Show/Hide Tabs & Returns
^U	View	Frame Setting
^W	Options	Show Hide Side-Bar
^X		*Equivalent varies: recalls last dialog box*
^Z	Graphic	Sent To Back
Del	Edit	Cut
Ins	Edit	Paste
Shift-Del	Edit	Copy
^2	Side-bar	Addition Button (available in Version 1.1)
Note: ^ stands for the Ctrl key.		

Table 2.3: Keyboard Shortcuts

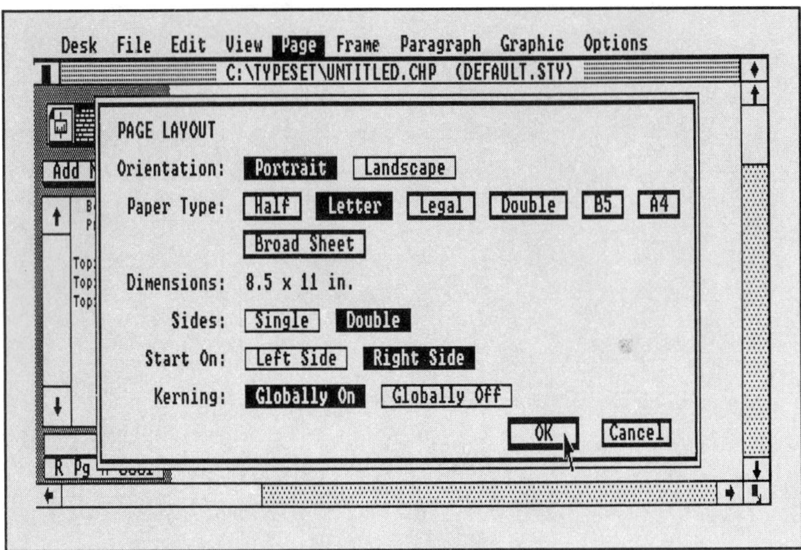

Figure 2.5: The Page Layout Dialog Box

find this box by pulling down the Page menu and clicking Page Layout. Within it, you can view, choose, or change the various settings that deal with the layout of the page.

Changing Settings in a Dialog Box

The darkened boxes (buttons) in the dialog box indicate the current settings of various features. To change one of the features, you point the mouse cursor to one of the outlined (not darkened) buttons. Then you click the mouse. The button you're pointing at will darken.

Changing a setting will undo a different setting within the same category. Any darkened button deactivated by your new choice will change to outline style (not darkened), indicating that this setting is no longer in effect. For example, in the dialog box shown in Figure 2.5, you could change the paper type from letter size to legal size by pointing to Legal and clicking the mouse. The Legal button would darken and the Letter button would change to outline. (The page measurements, shown after the word Dimension, would automatically change as well. The Dimension setting is merely an indicator; you can't change it directly.)

Giving the OK

Once you change the settings, they don't take effect until you *give the OK*. There are two ways to do that. You can point to the OK button and click the mouse, or you can hit the Return key on the keyboard. Both methods register the features as you've set them in the dialog box. The heavy outline of the OK button reminds you that the button does the same thing as pressing Return.

Canceling Your Changes

If you decide you don't want to make any changes after all, you can click the Cancel button instead of giving the OK. Ventura will then leave the settings in the dialog box as they were before you opened the box; that is, any resetting that you've done will not take place.

Ghosting in a Dialog Box

Consider another property of dialog boxes. Figure 2.6 shows the File menu's Load Text/Picture dialog box. Some of the buttons are ghosting, which indicates that they are not available for you to

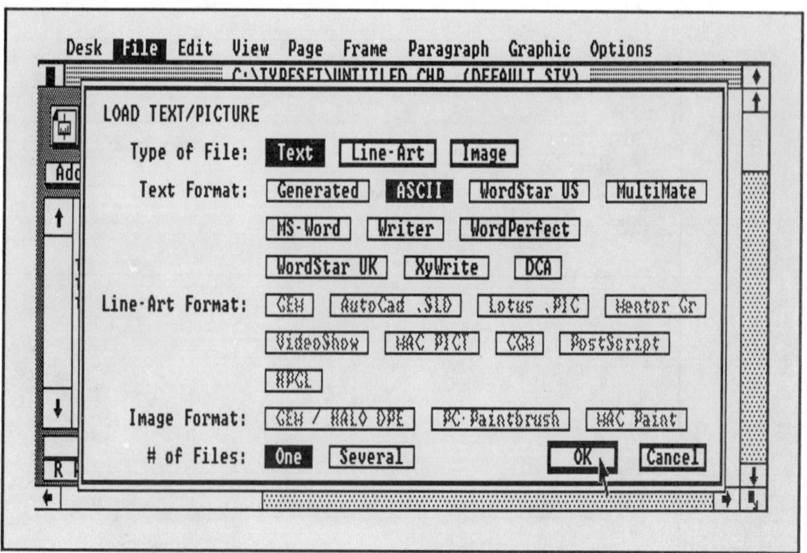

Figure 2.6: The File Menu's Load Text/Picture Dialog Box

choose. Generally, previous selections you've made in the same dialog box will have determined which items are available.

For instance, in the first group of choices, Type of File is set for Text. For that reason, the Text Format grouping (Generated, ASCII, WordStar US, and so on) appears in normal outline type. You can click any of these choices. The other groups, though, are ghosting.

If, however, you set the Type of File to Line-Art, the grouping for Line-Art Format (GEM, AutoCad .SLD, Lotus .PIC, and so on) will change to normal type, indicating that these choices are now available to you. Simultaneously, the Text Format grouping will ghost.

To experiment with this property of dialog boxes, check what happens when you click the Image button.

ITEM SELECTOR BOXES

Ventura also has a display that it calls the *Item Selector* box. The Item Selector box is very much like a dialog box. However, rather than showing settings for Ventura's features, the Item Selector box lists the names of files that are in a directory of your disk. For instance, after giving the OK to the Load Text/Picture dialog box shown in Figure 2.6, you see the Item Selector box shown in Figure 2.7. You use

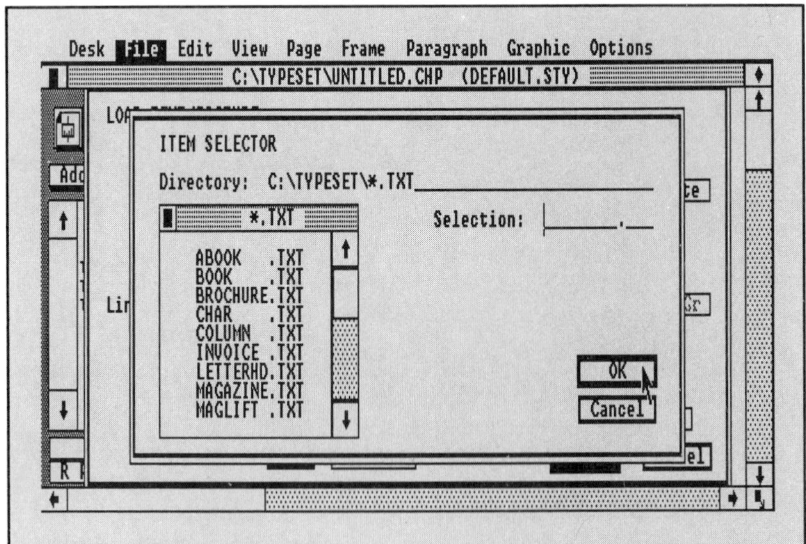

Figure 2.7: The Item Selector Box

this box to retrieve a file of the type you've specified with the Load Text/Picture dialog box. The Item Selector list will also display the names of available directories. A diamond-shaped character (◆) precedes directory names.

There are two ways to make a choice using the Item Selector box. You can use the "fill-in-the-blanks" method or the multiple-choice method. (These techniques also work with many dialog boxes.)

The Fill-in-the-Blanks Method

To fill in the blanks, you use the keyboard cursor, the thin vertical bar that appears on one of the horizontal lines (*fields*) in the Item Selector box. (In Figure 2.7, the keyboard cursor is to the right of the word Selection.) As you type at the keyboard, the characters you type appear at the keyboard cursor.

One at a time, you can erase characters that appear in the field by pressing the Backspace key. You can wipe out all characters that are in a field by pressing the Esc key. Without erasing, you can move the keyboard cursor back and forth over characters that appear by using the ← and → keys on the numeric keypad.

You move the keyboard cursor from one field to another in any of several ways. You can use the ↓ key on the numeric keypad at the right of your keyboard or the Tab key to move to the next field. To move back to the previous field, you can press the ↑ key or you can use Shift-Tab. Note that you cannot use the Return key to move to the next field, as you can with some programs. As in dialog boxes, pressing Return has the effect of giving the OK to the selections that you've made.

You can also relocate the keyboard cursor by using the arrow-shaped mouse cursor. Just move the mouse cursor to the field where you wish the keyboard cursor to appear and click the mouse button. The keyboard cursor will appear at the end of the field.

The Multiple-Choice Method

The other way to make an item selection is to use the mouse. Just point to the file you wish to choose and click. The item you've chosen darkens, as it does with dialog boxes. Simultaneously, your choice appears in the appropriate field. If you wish, you can then edit the field, as you would with the fill-in-the-blanks method.

Once your choices are made, you can give the OK in the same way that you do with dialog boxes; that is, you can either click the OK button or hit Return.

There is a third way to give the OK to the Item Selector box. When you point to an item you wish to select, you can choose the item *and* give the OK by clicking it *twice* in rapid succession. We'll work with this technique, which is called *double-clicking*, in Chapter 3.

SCROLL BARS IN THE ITEM SELECTOR BOX

As mentioned, the choices available in Item Selector boxes are files on the disk. However, you won't always be able to see the names of all the files that you can use. To see additional files, you may need to use the scroll bar that appears at the right of the directory list. This scroll bar operates in the same manner as the scroll bar used to manipulate the Side-bar's Assignment list.

To see the scroll bar in action, bring the mouse cursor to the *down button*, which is the box with the ↓ at the bottom of the scroll bar. You use the down button when you want to scroll down the list. With the mouse cursor on the down button, press the mouse button and hold it down. You'll see the list of directories and files move up the box. Notice that as the list of file names moves up, the white area of the scroll bar, like a counterweight, moves down. This action can be a little disconcerting at first, but you'll grow used to it quickly. At the top of the scroll bar there is an up button you can use to scroll up the list. With this button, the action is reversed.

You can also move the list by *grabbing* the scroll bar directly, rather than moving it with the up and down buttons. To do this, point to the white area of the scroll bar, press the mouse button, and hold it down. Move the mouse cursor up or down as desired. As you do, you'll see a ghost of the white area move along with you. There will be no change in the directory display until you release the mouse button (when the ghost is at the new, desired position). At that moment, both the scroll bar and the file display will jump to the new position.

There is a third way to move a scroll bar. You can click one of the shaded areas that may appear either before or after the white area of the scroll bar. Doing so causes the white area to jump in the direction you indicate. The display is then relocated in that direction. Each click of the shaded area moves the white area a distance equal to the size of the white area.

This completes our examination of the main screen and the kinds of operations that can be performed from it. Now let's take a look at Ventura's four operating modes, which we mentioned at the outset of this chapter.

THE FOUR OPERATING MODES

Ventura has four main modes of operation. At any time, the program will be operating in one of these four modes. Each mode affects most operations in many basic ways. (By the way, the mode that is active when you start a work session with Ventura will be the same mode that was active when you last quit.)

We'll study the techniques for changing the operating mode in Chapter 3 when we begin to work with the Frame mode. But for the present, you should know that you can change or choose a mode by clicking one of the buttons of the Mode selector that appears at the top of the Side-bar. We'll see later that you can also use a pull-down menu or the keyboard to change modes.

Each of the four buttons of the Mode selector corresponds to one of the modes we'll now examine in turn. The first is the Frame mode.

THE FRAME MODE

To lay out and set the various text and graphic elements of your documents, Ventura allows you to divide each page into box-shaped areas of varying dimensions. These areas are called *frames*. To create these frames, and to manipulate them, you use the *Frame setting mode*, or simply the *Frame mode*. Once you create a frame, you place text or a picture within it. Unless you outline it, the frame itself is invisible when you print the document. All you see are its contents. Thus the elements that make up a page appear to be seamlessly integrated.

On the other hand, if you wish to outline the frame in your final document, you can have up to three lines above, below, or within the periphery of the frame. You can set the thickness and spacing of these lines in any way you wish. There is a great deal of flexibility in creating lines; we'll work with them later in the book. You can also shade the background of a frame.

The Underlying-Page Frame

Initially, each page consists of a single frame. This main frame is the size of the page. Imagine pasting down on a page by conventional means: you would paste all other *standard* frames on top of this one. For this reason, this main frame is called the *underlying-page frame*. (By standard frame, we mean any frame that is not the underlying-page frame.)

As you view the screen, you can imagine the underlying-page frame as being at the bottom—that is, furthest away from you, the viewer. You can place standard frames on top of it (closer to you). There is no apparent limit to the number of frames you can stack in this manner.

In many respects, the underlying-page frame is just a frame like the standard frames that might be laid on top of it. Many of the settings for the Frame mode apply to both the underlying-page frame and to standard frames. In other ways, however, the underlying-page frame is special and different from standard frames. For instance, if you place a graphic in an underlying-page frame, that graphic will appear on all pages of the document. If, however, it is placed in a standard frame, it will appear only in that particular frame.

Margins and Columns

Each frame can contain up to eight columns. This holds true for the underlying-page frame as well as for any frame on top of it. Should it be necessary to create additional columns, you can simply add as many standard frames, side by side, as the paper allows.

You can also specify margins for either kind of frame. Text will not appear in these areas of the frame.

Moving Frames

There are two ways to relocate or change the size of a standard frame. One way is to grab the frame with the mouse and move the mouse. You can also pull down the Frame menu and change the various settings in its Sizing & Scaling dialog box. We'll see how to do this in Chapter 3.

When you move a frame with the mouse, you have the option of using *column snap*. Column snap allows the left and right edges of the frame to land only on the edges of columns specified for the underlying-page frame. This ensures that columns will line up where they should and won't end up too close together. It also aids in keeping the distance between frames similar, or in regular multiples. You turn column snap on by pulling down the Options menu and clicking the Turn Column Snap On command. If, when you pull down the menu, the command says "Turn Column Snap Off," column snap is already on. (You can then turn it off by clicking that command.)

You can see the column edges displayed as light dashes. To do that, you use the Options menu and select Show Column Guides. You can also use the Options menu to turn line snap on or off. *Line snap* operates like column snap, but it regulates the upper and lower edges of standard frames. It forces the edges to line up according to spacing set for standard text (*body text*) that makes up the underlying-page frame.

Text and Frames

When you assign word processed text files to a frame, Ventura handles the text slightly differently for the underlying-page frame than for other frames. If all the text in a text file does not fit in an underlying-page frame, Ventura will create additional pages as necessary to accommodate all the text in the file. If, however, you assign the text file to a standard frame, the frame will show only as much of the file as it has room for, and Ventura will not create additional standard frames for leftover text. If you wish the entire text to appear, you must create the additional frames yourself. Alternatively, you can increase the size of the initial frame.

You can assign text files to as many standard or underlying-page frames as you like. You can use both types of frame with the same text file. The order in which you create multiple frames determines the order in which the text appears in the frames. Ventura will first fill the first-assigned frame; then, if there is text left over, it will start to fill the second-assigned frame, picking up where it left off with the first frame. If there is text left over from the second, it will go on to fill the third frame, and so on (see Figure 2.8).

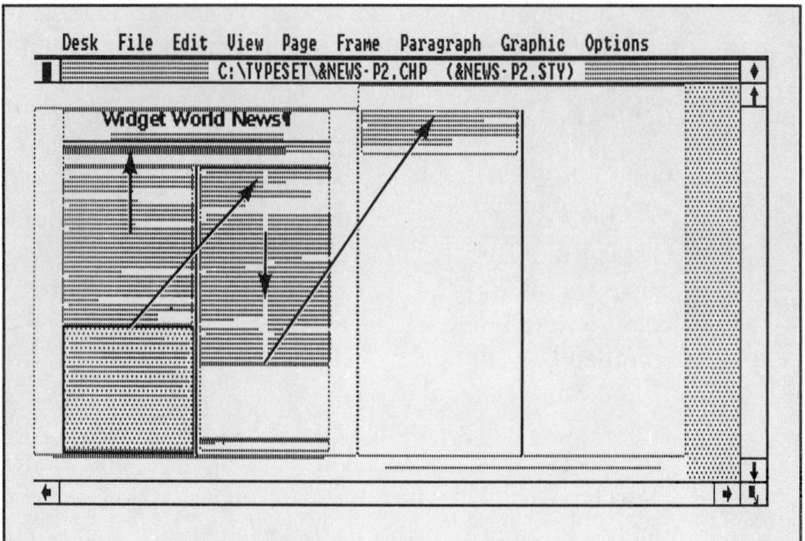

Figure 2.8: Text Filling Frames

THE PARAGRAPH MODE

The second of Ventura's operational modes is the *Paragraph tagging mode* or simply the *Paragraph mode*. We'll study tagging in Chapter 4. Paragraphs, along with text attributes, constitute the main building blocks for formatting with Ventura.

Paragraph formatting controls the alignment (justification, indent, and so on), tab settings, spacing, and other attributes of chunks of text. The size of these chunks is generally about the size of a paragraph. However, you do not have to use true paragraphs as these formatting components. A series of short lines—such as an address, for instance—qualifies as a paragraph for the purpose of formatting.

Alignment is one of the attributes handled with paragraph tags. This feature determines if a paragraph is ragged, justified, or centered. It can also indent (or outdent) the first line of each paragraph automatically. Spacing is another feature Ventura can set automatically; you set the distance between characters, lines, and paragraphs once, and Ventura adjusts all similar paragraphs simultaneously. Tab settings are also handled with paragraph tags, although there are other ways to create tables, as you'll see in Chapter 9.

In addition, Paragraph tagging governs whether a paragraph should be kept together (not split between the bottom of one column and the top of the next, for instance). You can also use tagging to create lines or boxes around paragraphs, as you can with frames.

Initially, Ventura assigns a tag with the name *body text* to all paragraphs in the text. All the attributes that you assign to the body-text tag will affect all the paragraphs so designated. You can tag paragraphs with other paragraph tags that you create or that Ventura Publisher has created for you already. All paragraphs tagged with the same tag will share the attributes that you have assigned. In Paragraph mode, tags appear in the Assignment list in the Side-bar. You assign them from the list with the mouse.

Ventura has two tools to assist in expediting the tagging procedure. First, you can assign the ten function keys to various paragraph tags. Second, you, or others who are writing articles for you, can assign the tag directly with your word processor as you create or edit the text. You do this by typing in a special code along with the tag's name. Paragraph tagging is discussed in Chapter 5.

THE TEXT MODE

As you work with Ventura, you're certain to find that you need to edit the text that appears on your pages. Of course, you can use your word processor to make the changes in the original text files. Alternatively, you can use Ventura's *Text mode* to edit. The technique is simple: once you activate the Text mode, you use the mouse cursor to place the keyboard cursor in the text. Then you simply edit from the keyboard.

One beautiful aspect of the Text mode is that as you type and eventually save the document, the changes you make are made in the original word processed files as well. Thus, for instance, if you need to search for a string (remember that Ventura has no search capabilities), you can simply switch to your word processor and use the search command to find the string. Using a word processor to work on Ventura files is dicussed in Chapter 12.

Ventura allows you to translate a text file from one word processing system to another. So if an author submits the document in WordPerfect format, but you use MultiMate, it's no problem. Ventura can convert the file from one to the other for you.

You can also use Text mode to change some text *attributes*, such as boldface, italics, underline, and so on, for text that you designate. Alternatively, you can use your word processor to insert such formatting. Ventura will then convert the word processor's formatting to its own system, and vice versa. You can also capitalize a whole block of text, such as the title of a table, automatically without retyping it. You can use Text mode to type in special characters, such as accents and em dashes. You can set fonts selectively and *kern* (change the distance between characters) as well.

You can even use the Text mode to enter the original text. The text for this book, for instance, was originally created using Ventura's Text mode (with help from SmartKey).

Finally, you can use the Text mode for cut-and-paste applications. You can move or copy text to any place in the chapter. Ventura does not confine cut-and-paste operations to Text mode, however. You can also move and copy frames along with all their attributes in Frame mode. (You can cut-and-paste in Graphics mode as well.)

THE GRAPHICS MODE

As if its impressive text capabilities aren't enough, Ventura has graphics capabilities, too. Most importantly, it can *import* graphics. You can create graphic designs with a variety of programs—AutoCAD or Publisher's Paintbrush, for instance. You can then use Ventura to display the file you created with the graphics program. As mentioned earlier, any changes you make will not affect the original artwork.

USE OF THE FOUR MODES

Throughout Ventura, there is a consistent approach in the use of the various modes. Only the Graphics mode differs slightly. To accomplish much of your work with the program, you'll find that you generally follow these steps:

1. Activate the appropriate mode (Frame, Paragraph, Text, Graphics.)

2. Select the particular item in the mode that you wish to change; that is, use the mouse to click the appropriate frame, paragraph, piece of text, or graphic as it appears in the working area.
3. Make the change you desire. You can do this in one of three ways, depending upon the nature of the change you wish to make:
   a) Click the correct item on the Assignment list in the Sidebar.
   b) Activate a pull-down menu and make a selection from it.
   c) Use the keyboard.

IMPORTANT

The Graphics mode differs in the following way. Graphics are always *tied* to a particular frame. You must first use the Frame mode and select the frame to which the graphic is tied before proceeding with step 1 above.

As we work with frames in the next chapter, you'll see this consistent approach in action. You'll see it in the work you perform with other modes as well.

CHAPTER THREE

Setting Up a Newsletter

EFFECTIVE DESKTOP PUBLISHING CAN ORGANIZE SO many different elements that creating a complex newsletter is now a manageable task, even for non-designers. With Ventura, you can align columns evenly, leapfrog stories over different pages, mix variably-sized graphic and text elements, and number pages automatically. These elements, done right, can combine to catch the interest of readers as well as provide them with comprehensible copy and create a coherent visual impression that stays with them long after they finish reading. Because of the variety of challenges a newsletter presents, its creation encapsulates many of the capabilities desktop publishing has to offer.

Designing a sophisticated newsletter has long been outside the realm of the conventional word processor. On the other hand, the prospect of doing it with scissors and glue is intimidating, to say the least. So up until recently, when it came to creating good-looking newsletters, the prospective do-it-yourselfer has done without or has had it done.

In this chapter we will use Ventura to create a newsletter without scissors and paste. Doing so will provide a good introduction to frames and how to use them. It will demonstrate how Ventura pours word processed text into columns on the page automatically. It will also show how to make changes to one of the standard style sheets provided with Ventura, in order to customize the design of your publication.

ADAPTING A SAMPLE

The first step in creating a good document with Ventura Publisher is to envision the final document in your mind's eye. Always have a good idea of where you are heading. It's especially important to consider how the pages will be laid out.

In this example, let's say that you want to create a newsletter on letter-size paper. This is because you want to copy the newsletter on your office copier, which has only letter and legal size, and you feel that letter size would be easier for your readers to grab and run with.

You want your newsletter to have a good-sized masthead at the top of the first page. You also plan to use headlines and subheads.

With Ventura you could create such a publication from scratch. You could select all the typefaces, column widths, margins, spacing, and so on, one by one.

However, as you work with Ventura, you'll probably find chapter creation easiest, at least initially, if you build on the samples that come with the program. To do that, you just pick out one of the sample style sheets and one of the sample chapters and adapt them to suit your needs.

The samples that come with the program are displayed in Appendix A. As you begin work on a new chapter, leaf through those samples. Find one that resembles the way you'd like your document to look. Then copy the sample and proceed to work on the duplicate.

As you consider the sample, compare its purpose with yours. Also consider the page layout, type size and style, paragraph formats, and margins. Don't forget to consider your gut reaction to the style.

For this exercise, we'll say that you decide on the sample that's called &NEWS-P2.CHP, shown in Figure 3.1. It has the masthead and headline style you want, and it uses letter-size paper. Perhaps the small table of contents appeals to you, too.

LOADING A SAMPLE

It's important to protect the original samples against alteration. That way, if you want to use them again, they're sure to look like the samples in the back of this book. To accomplish this first important step, we'll make a copy of the samples we'll use, stored under different names.

The first thing you'll want to do is to copy the sample chapter to a new file. Let's suppose that your publication is going to be called *The Brainstorm*. We'll call the new file BRAIN.CHP. Once copied, you can substitute your headlines and articles for those in the sample.

You'll also want to copy the style sheet associated with the sample chapter, &NEWS-P2.STY. We'll call the new style sheet BRAIN.STY. As you make formatting changes in the document, the new style sheet will store your specifications.

To make the copies of the sample chapter and style sheet, you first load Ventura. Then you load the original samples. Before you make any changes, save the chapter and the style sheet under new names.

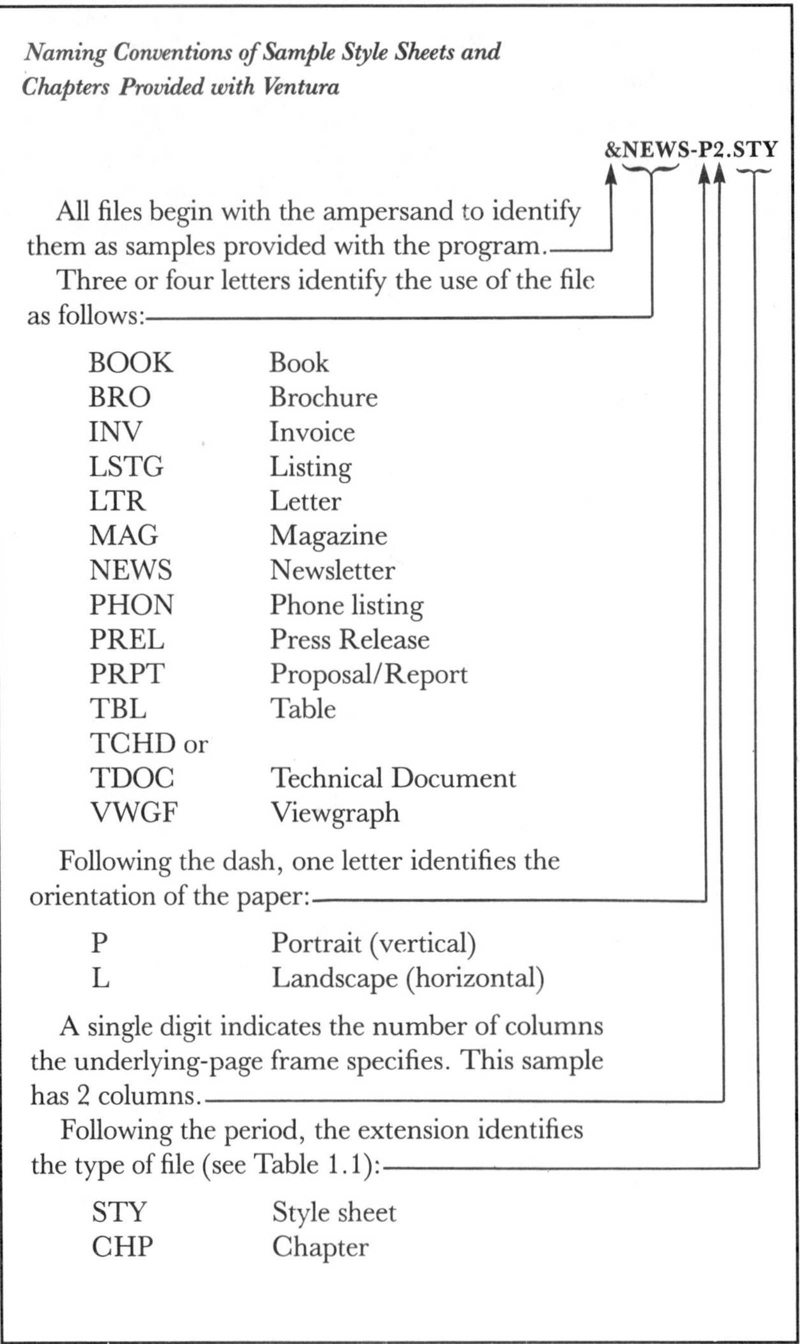

Naming Conventions of Sample Style Sheets and Chapters Provided with Ventura

&NEWS-P2.STY

All files begin with the ampersand to identify them as samples provided with the program.

Three or four letters identify the use of the file as follows:

BOOK	Book
BRO	Brochure
INV	Invoice
LSTG	Listing
LTR	Letter
MAG	Magazine
NEWS	Newsletter
PHON	Phone listing
PREL	Press Release
PRPT	Proposal/Report
TBL	Table
TCHD or	
TDOC	Technical Document
VWGF	Viewgraph

Following the dash, one letter identifies the orientation of the paper:

P	Portrait (vertical)
L	Landscape (horizontal)

A single digit indicates the number of columns the underlying-page frame specifies. This sample has 2 columns.

Following the period, the extension identifies the type of file (see Table 1.1):

STY	Style sheet
CHP	Chapter

Widget World News

Views and News of Widget Manufacturing in the 80s

Software Salaries: How do you stack up?

by Joe Smith

How much your software professionals are paid is a function of many variables, and a subject of considerable interest to your organization.

Software salary pay scales

Because of the dynamic growth of the software industry over the last decade, the demand for experienced, qualified programmers has greatly increased, thus leading to a spiraling of salaries.

But what causes managers to pay one programmer more than another? Does the type of organization, its size, or location make a difference? What career path or programming specialty leads to the most remuneration?

To answer these questions, Acme Magazine recently conducted its third annual compensation survey for software professionals. This newsletter article presents the results of this study and explores what the findings may mean to you.

Acme Magazine asked Joe Smith, a compensation consulting specialist for the software industry, to design and conduct the survey. Twenty-four positions, representing four programmer job families plus management, were included.

Data was collected for base pay, bonus and incentive payments, and whether nor not incumbents received stock options or other forms of equity.

Questionnaires were sent to the data processing heads of 2,400 organizations throughout the United States.

Table of Contents

First story 1
Second story 2
The third article 3
Next comes the fourth 5
A Long article breaks to the next line without running into the page number 6
Note that this TOC could have been generated from the newsletter CHP file. 9

CD-ROM Breaks New Ground

Compact Disk Read Only Memory (CD-ROM) is a rapidly emerging new technology for the retrieval of vast amounts of information from an optical disk. This new peripheral device allows a totally new level of functionality in the use of microcomputers.

Physically, the CD-ROM device has a laser disk drive (or "player") the same size as a traditional 5 1/4" drive. The removable disk is 4 3/4", and has a capacity of 550M bytes (equivalent to 1500 360K floppy disks).

Theory of Operation

Information stored on a CD-ROM can be loaded into memory (RAM), displayed and printed, as with other media. While that data in RAM may be altered and stored to a conventional magnetic disk, the original information on the CD-ROM is unalterable, always ensuring the original copy is intact, making archiving easy.

The storage capacity, low cost, and read only feature of CD-ROM bring an enormous new capability to microcomputer users – that is, information retrieval of very large reference publications. How people receive and use information in the immediate and long term future will be dramatically changed by CD-ROM.

In addition to the huge capacity of raw information storage, specialized software for the search of that information is currently being introduced. This software allows searching the information in areas, methods and speeds not previously feasible.

It now becomes possible to electronically publish reference material more

Caption

Figure 3.1: A Sample Newsletter

To perform both loading operations, proceed as follows:

1. Load Ventura by typing

   vp

   at the system prompt and hitting the Return key.

2. Once you have Ventura's main screen, point to File on the Menu line to pull down the File menu.

3. Move the mouse cursor (shaped like an arrow) down the menu to Open Chapter. The command name darkens, as shown in Figure 3.2.

4. Click the mouse button while the arrow is on that choice. When you do, the Item Selector box appears, as shown in Figure 3.3. Notice that the keyboard cursor (the thin vertical bar) initially appears in the Selection field.

5. If Ventura Publisher has been properly installed, your hard drive is C, and no one has used the program yet, the directory and disk drive (in the Directory field) will say

   C:/TYPESET/*.CHP

   If it doesn't, you'll need to make the some changes.

   To change the directory, you first move the keyboard cursor up to the Directory field. As discussed in Chapter 2, you can use the ↑ key, the Shift-Tab key combination, or the mouse. Once there, you can wipe out the entire field by hitting the Esc key, or you can delete one character at a time by using the Backspace or Del key. You can float the cursor over the characters by using the ← and → keys as well. Type in your corrections. (Instead of typing, you can use the mouse to change directories, as we'll see shortly.)

6. If you had to change the directory, the items in the list would not yet be the proper ones, because Ventura would still be showing the incorrect directory's display. However, the program will display the correct files when you give the OK by hitting Return or clicking the mouse on the OK button. With that, the samples stored in the TYPESET directory will appear on the screen, as shown in Figure 3.3. The keyboard cursor will move from the Directory field to the Selection field.

7. Next you'll want to indicate the file for Ventura Publisher to load. Depending on the version, and if others have been using the program, the sample file may not be in view. If necessary,

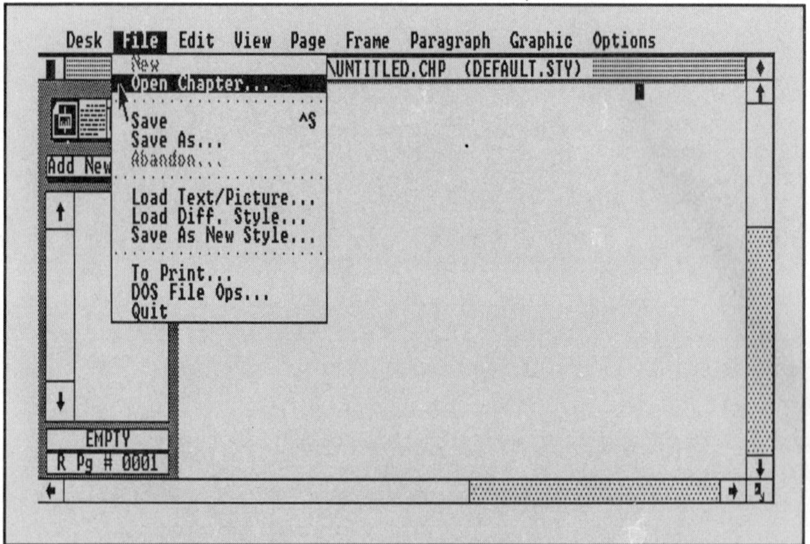

Figure 3.2: Pulling Down the File Menu and Clicking Open Chapter

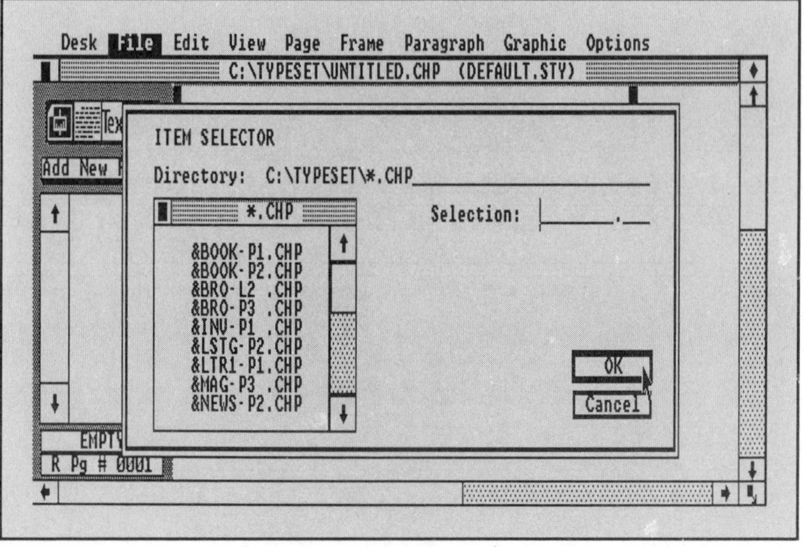

Figure 3.3: The Item Selector Box for the File Menu's Open Chapter Command

scroll down the list of file names. (Scrolling techniques are described in Chapter 2.) When you see the name

&NEWS-P2.CHP

darken it by pointing to it with the mouse cursor and clicking. You could also simply type in the file name, rather than picking it from the list.

8. Give the OK by clicking the OK button or by hitting Return.

You can combine steps 7 and 8 by pointing to the file name and clicking twice in rapid succession, which we'll discuss next. Doing so both selects the file and gives the OK.

Once you give the OK, Ventura flashes some loading and hyphenating messages on the screen. When they're done, you've successfully loaded the sample chapter into Ventura.

Changing the Mouse Double Click Speed

You can vary the amount of time that's required between successive clicks. Pull down the Options menu and click Set Preferences. You'll see the dialog box shown in Figure 3.4. You use the Options

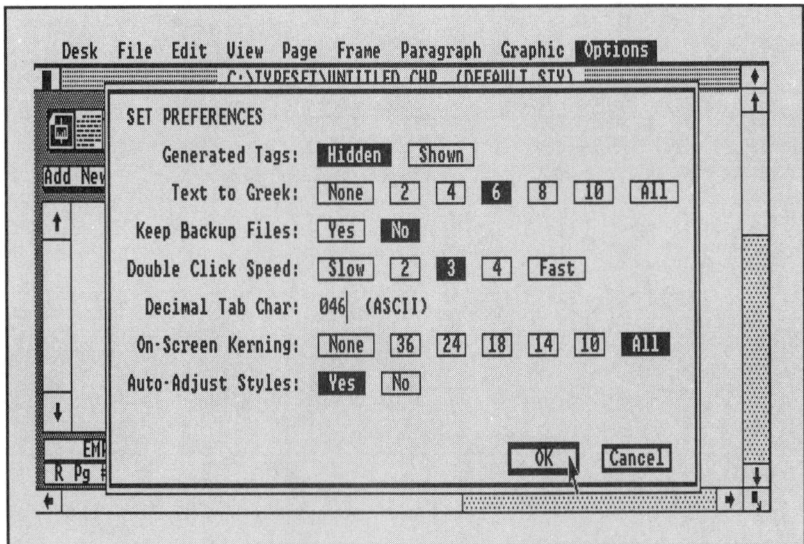

Figure 3.4: The Options Menu's Set Preferences Dialog Box

pull-down menu, and especially this dialog box, to customize the manner in which the program operates, so it best suits your needs. Throughout this book, we'll examine various options as they pertain to the subject matter at hand.

Notice that there are five settings, from slow to fast, in the Double Click Speed grouping. Choose one of the five settings and give the OK. Experiment to determine the setting that's most comfortable for you. When you quit Ventura, the setting is saved and is still in place the next time you use the program.

MAKING A NEW DIRECTORY

Before saving the files with new names, we'll create a special directory called MASTERVP. You'll use this directory to hold the exercises you work with in this book.

Judicious use of directories is an aid to categorizing the various files you use with Ventura. Some people like to create a new directory for each new document they compose. Others like to use directories to group similar elements, such as text, chapter, or graphics files, regardless of the document.

Whatever the strategy, it's wise to use your own directories. Don't just dump everything into the TYPESET directory, which Ventura uses to house its sample documents.

Here's how to make a directory with Ventura. (You can also use DOS's MD command to make directories.)

1. Pull down the File menu. (With Version 1.0, use the Options menu instead.)
2. Click DOS File Ops. Doing so displays the dialog box for DOS File Operations. The File Spec field reads

   C:/*.*

3. Use the Backspace key to erase the *.* that's showing. Type in a name for the new directory. The dialog box now looks like Figure 3.5.
4. Click the Make Directory button as shown in the figure.
5. To make the dialog box disappear, click the Done box or press Return.

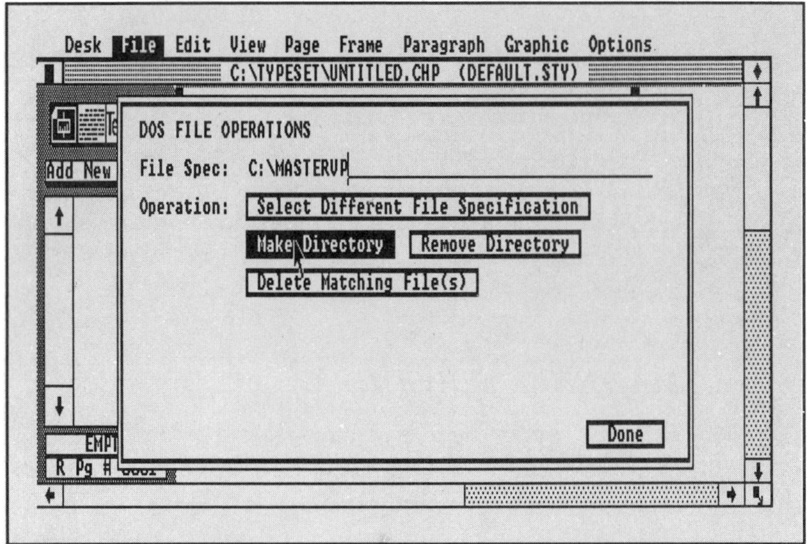

Figure 3.5: The Dialog Box for the File Menu's DOS File Operations

Note that you can also use this dialog box to delete files and remove directories from the disk. These capabilities are useful for cleaning up the disk once you're finished with a document. For more on DOS, see Appendix C.

SAVING A COPY OF THE CHAPTER FILE

Now that we've created our special directory, save the chapter with a new name in that directory. This action will make a copy of the chapter file on the disk. You can then make changes in the chapter specifications and save the changed version. The original is separate and will not reflect those changes. Note, however, that this does not copy text files that are loaded into the chapter. Doing that is a separate procedure we'll examine later.

To save the copy of the chapter file, follow these steps:

1. Pull down the File menu and click the Save As command. The Item Selector box appears.
2. Change the directory or disk drive, if desired, as specified earlier or by using the Backup button, which we'll describe in

a moment. You may wish, for instance, to place the new files on a floppy disk in drive A.

3. Type in the name we're assigning to the copy of the chapter file, **BRAIN**. Do not type the period or the CHP extension; Ventura will assign the CHP extension automatically.

To use the mouse to change directories and drives, you can click the Backup button which is located in the top-left corner of the box of listings. When backing out of a directory, the system will first change to the root directory (or the parent directory, which holds the directory the system is backing out of). Clicking the button again will cause the disk drives to be listed, as shown in Figure 3.6. At this point you can then click a different drive, and then choose one of its directories, if necessary.

COPYING THE STYLE SHEET

Now that the chapter is safe, to protect the original style sheet, you must save it with a new name as well. The procedure is basically the same as that used to save the chapter. Ventura Publisher has already

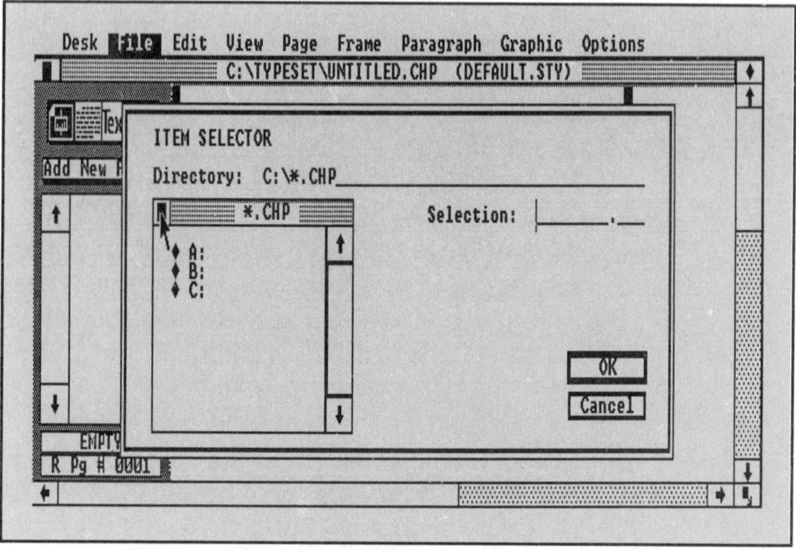

Figure 3.6: Backup Button Used to Display Disk Drives in the Item Selector Box

Backup Files

When you save your various Ventura Publisher files, consider whether you want the program to keep backup versions of the files. Normally, it does not. However, if you have the disk space, saving backups is a good precaution against accidental file losses.

If you want Ventura Publisher to retain the previous version of its files each time it saves, indicate that with the Options menu's Set Preferences dialog box (see Figure 3.4). Simply change the Keep Backup Files setting to Yes. Ventura Publisher will save previous versions by keeping the same file name for the backup but replacing the first character in the extension with a dollar sign. Thus, the backup file for the chapter BRAIN.CHP would be named BRAIN.$HP.

loaded the style sheet along with the document, so all you need do is save it under a new name. To do that, you again use the File pull-down menu. This time, though, click the Save As New Style command. The Item Selector box that appears (see Figure 3.7) is similar to the one you saw for the chapter save. This time, however, the system assumes an extension of STY.

Complete the Item Selector box. Use the name BRAIN; Ventura Publisher will add the STY extension.

Let's discuss why we've saved the material before making any changes. You could have made the changes first and then performed the saves. However, saving them before you start to make changes guards against accidentally saving those changes with the original files.

If, however, you should change the originals accidentally, you can simply recopy them from the original disk #2; this is the disk labeled "Examples."

IMPORTANT

As mentioned, the procedures we've just examined do not make copies of the text files that hold the newsletter articles. They only copy the style-sheet file, which dictates the format of the newsletter, and the chapter file, which coordinates the various elements of the document.

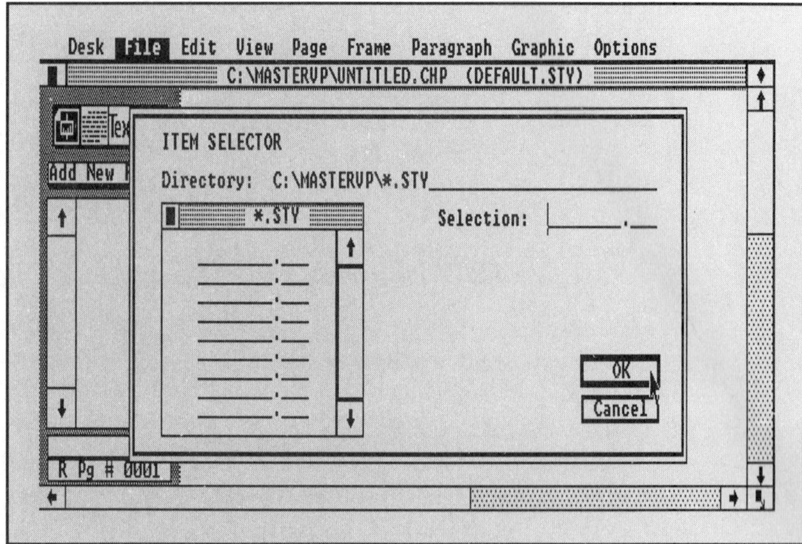

Figure 3.7: Saving a Style Sheet under a New Name

If you plan to make alterations in the content of these files you must also save the text files under a different name to protect the originals. Alternatively, you can pull in new text files that you create with a word processor (See Chapter 12). You can also use the Options menu's Multi-Chapter command, discussed in Chapter 11, to copy all the material associated with a chapter, including text files.

We'll look at how to change the text as well as the layout presently. As we do, though, it will prove useful to have the following viewing tools at our disposal.

A CHANGE OF VIEW: ENLARGING AND REDUCING

As you begin to make changes in the content and layout of your newsletter or other documents, you may find it necessary to have a magnified look at your work. Just as an artist does, you may wish to step in closer to perform some delicate detail work. Similarly, there will be times when you'd like to step back to take in a more removed view of the page. That way, you can check general layout and initial impact on the reader, as well as see how a headline, for instance, looks compared to the rest of the page.

To afford you alternative ways of scrutinizing your document, Ventura offers four different views: Normal, Enlarged, Reduced, and Facing Pages. You can see these views as the first four commands on the View pull-down menu (see Figure 3.8).

NORMAL VIEW (Ctrl-N)

Normal view is the view that most closely represents the true size and proportions of your document. The (1x) next to the command name indicates that Normal view is the same size as the printed version. Note that because of differences between the way a monitor and a printer operate, there may still be some difference in what is called the *aspect ratio*, the ratio of the height (of the screen or page) to the width.

Generally, you will use the Normal view to read text and make changes in it. You can activate Normal view either by clicking Normal View on the View menu or by typing Ctrl-N at the keyboard. The pull-down menu reminds you of this keyboard shortcut by displaying a ^N next to the words *Normal View.*

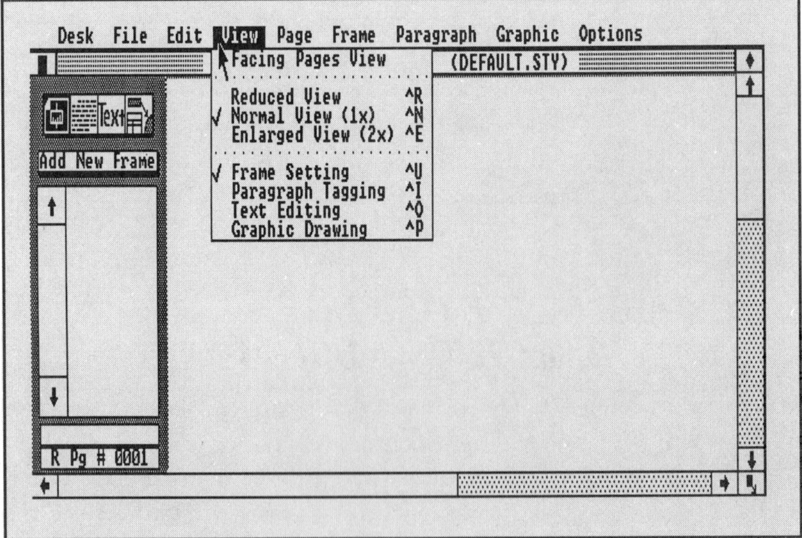

Figure 3.8: The View Pull-Down Menu

ENLARGED VIEW (Ctrl-E)

Like Normal view, Enlarged view can be triggered in either of two ways: by using the View pull-down menu and clicking Enlarged View or by typing Ctrl-E. As indicated by the (2x) next to the command name, Enlarged view is twice the normal size of the layout. You'll find Enlarged view helpful when you want to check the details of pictures, or when you are working with very small type.

In Version 1.1, when you use a keyboard shortcut (such as Ctrl-E) to change to a larger view, Ventura takes the approximate location of the mouse cursor as its cue for positioning the top-left corner of the larger view. This new feature makes the program operate more efficiently: it's no longer necessary to use the scroll bars after you enlarge the view because the screen will be properly positioned. If you don't wish to make use of this feature, use the pull-down menu method instead.

REDUCED VIEW (Ctrl-R)

If you have a standard monitor, you'll find it helpful to use Reduced view to check the entire page at once. Of course with a full-page monitor, such as the Genius, you can usually see the entire page with Normal view.

When you use Reduced view, Ventura may *greek* some of the text, that is, substitute plain straight lines for some lines of text. By greeking text, the program can operate more quickly as you make changes that affect the page. (Due to the reduction in size, these lines of text would probably be too small to read anyway.)

Figure 3.9 shows how the displayed document appears with greeked text. The height and width of the greek lines approximate the true dimensions of the actual text.

If you want Ventura to greek more or less of the text, pull down the Options menu and click Set Preferences. You'll see the Set Preferences dialog box, shown in Figure 3.4. Set the Text to Greek preference to None, All, or any one of the sizes shown. The sizes represent the number of screen dots (pixels). If you choose a size, Ventura will greek all text that size and smaller. Thus, the larger the size you choose, the more text will be greeked.

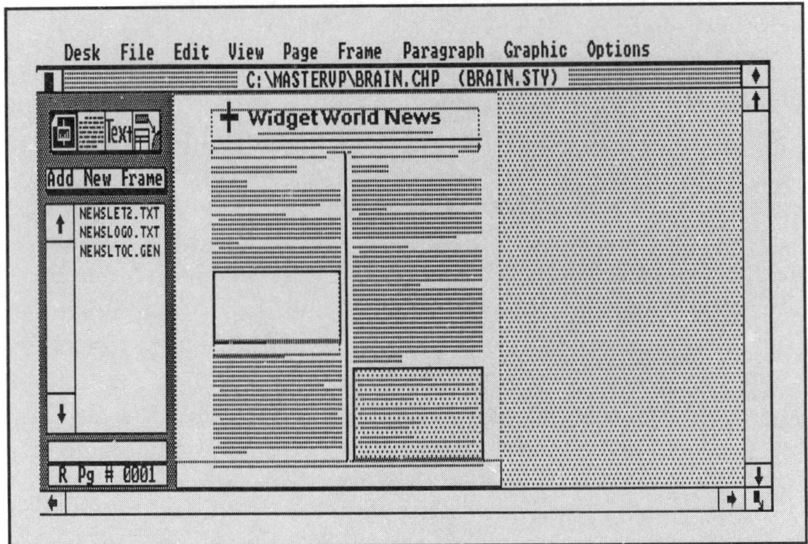

Figure 3.9: Greeked Text in the Reduced View

FACING PAGES VIEW

Facing Pages view displays left- and right-hand pages simultaneously for documents that are so designed. We'll see how you specify double sides shortly.

Using Facing Pages view allows you to assess the combined impact of the two pages that your reader will be viewing together. As with Reduced view, Ventura Publisher may greek some text. Note that there is no keyboard shortcut for triggering Facing Pages view.

As you construct your documents, use these four views freely to your advantage.

You probably noticed that besides these four views, there are four other commands available on the View pull-down menu. We'll examine these commands shortly, as we begin to adapt the newsletter.

SPECIFYING PAPER SIZE AND DOUBLE SIDES

Let's assume that, as mentioned, one reason you selected the &NEWS-P2 sample was that it is designed for letter-size paper.

There are seven standard sizes of paper that are available with Ventura. They are illustrated in Figure 3.10. (A4 and B4 are international paper sizes.) Your choice of paper size is stored as part of the style sheet. You're not, however, confined to these standard sizes. You can also create your own custom sizes. We'll see how that's done later in this chapter.

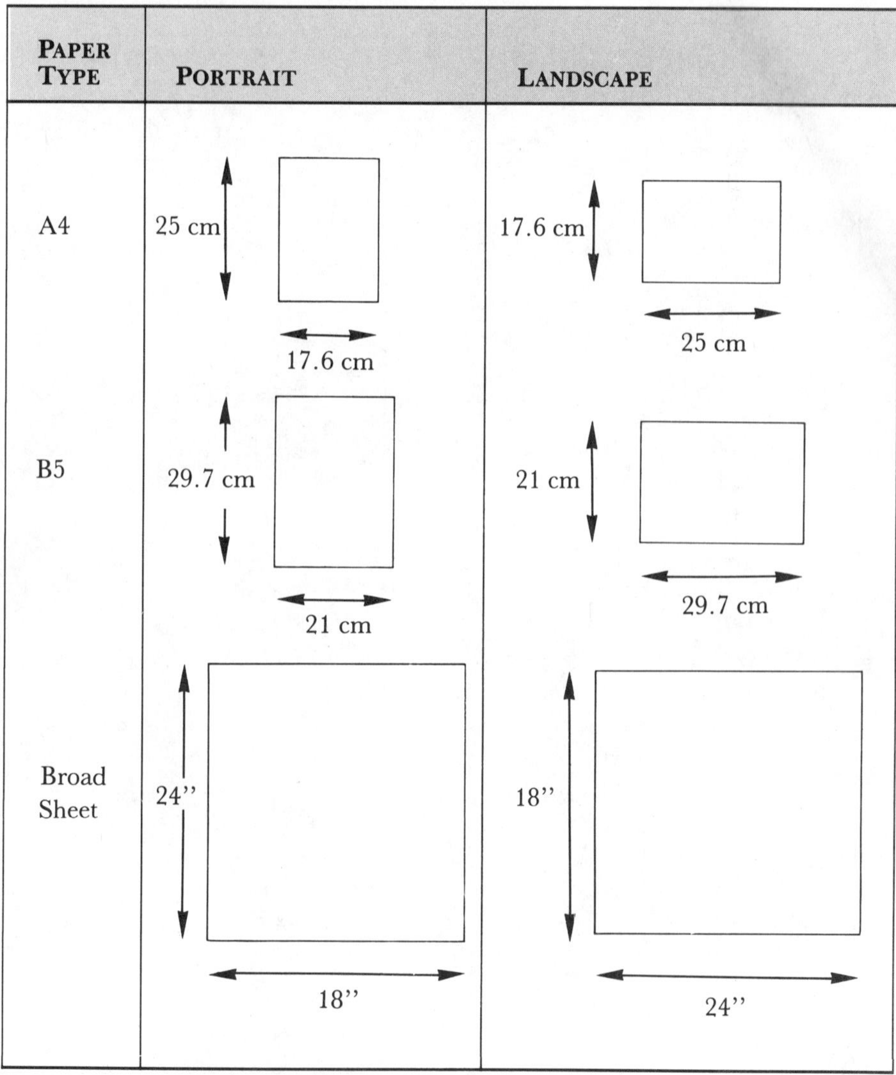

PAPER TYPE
PORTRAIT
LANDSCAPE
A4
25 cm
17.6 cm
17.6 cm
25 cm
B5
29.7 cm
21 cm
21 cm
29.7 cm
Broad Sheet
24''
18''
18''
24''

Figure 3.10: Standard Paper Sizes

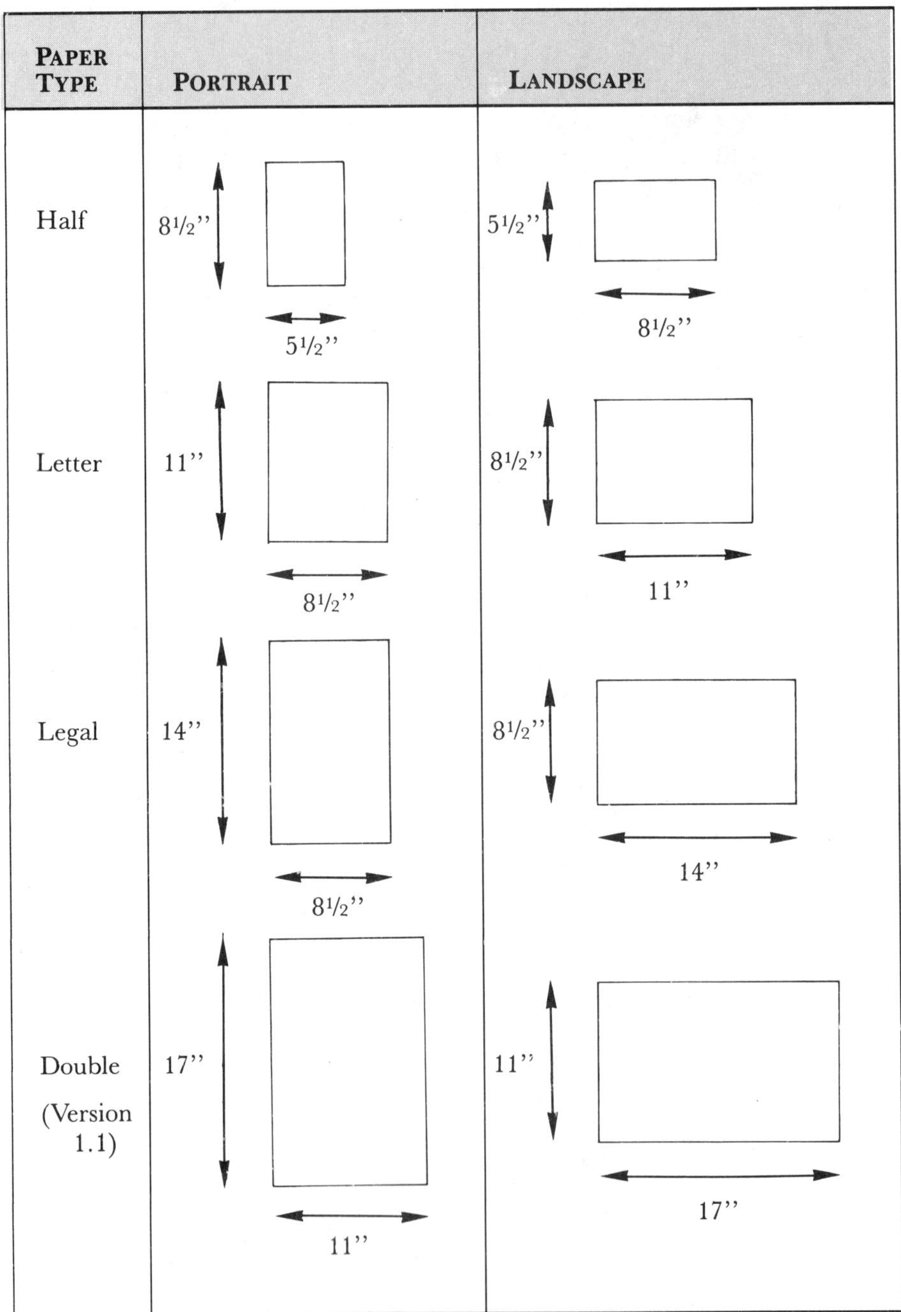

Figure 3.10: Standard Paper Sizes (continued)

To check the size and shape of your pages, and change them when necessary, pull down the Page menu and click the Page Layout command. The Page Layout dialog box, shown in Figure 3.11, will appear.

SPECIFYING THE PAPER SIZE

As you can see from Figure 3.11, you have two choices for Orientation: Portrait, for a vertical layout, and Landscape, for a horizontal one. Portrait orientation is considered to be easier to read and handle; hence, it's generally preferred. With some tables or pictures, however, you may find it necessary to use the landscape orientation. The sample should already be set to use portrait orientation.

Next look at the Paper Type setting. When you click any of the six types listed (Half, Letter, Legal, and so on), corresponding dimensions appear in the field below. You cannot change the dimensions by typing numbers in this field. You must chose one of the five boxes. Later, we'll see how you can use frames margins to specify sizes that aren't available here. In this example, the dialog box should indicate letter size.

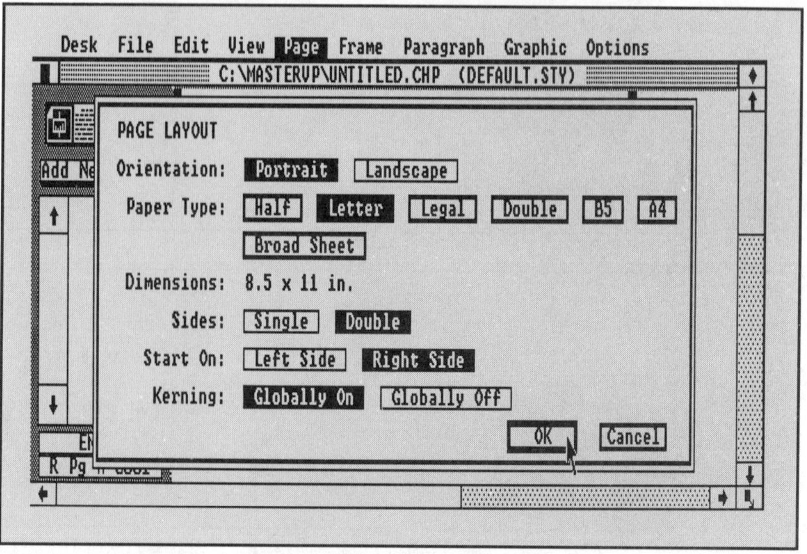

Figure 3.11: The Page Menu's Page Layout Dialog Box

INDICATING SINGLE OR DOUBLE SIDES

With the Sides setting, you indicate whether you will be printing single or double sided. We won't be using double sides with our example, so the setting should be set to Single.

Specifying double-sided allows you to treat special features, such as headers and footers, differently for left- and right-facing pages. That way, the features appear consistently on the inside or outside edges of the document. The features that you affect by specifying double sided are listed in Table 3.1. Shortly, we'll see how specifying double sides affects margins and columns.

With the Starts On setting, you indicate whether the chapter should have its first page on the left or the right as you look at the document. This setting will take effect only if you've set the Sides setting to Double. Generally, a simple document that starts with page one should begin on the right side. This is because, by convention, odd-numbered pages are on the right.

MENU	COMMAND	SETTING
File	To Print	Which Pages
View	Facing Pages View	(No Dialog Box)
Page	Page Layout	Sides Starts On
	Headers & Footers	Define
Frame	Margins & Columns	Settings For Inserts
	Repeating Frame	For All Pages
	Vertical Rules	Setting For Inserts
Paragraph	Spacing	Inserts
	Breaks	Page Break

Table 3.1: Settings Affected by Setting the Page Menu's Page Layout Command to Double Sides

Kerning, the last setting in this dialog box, is new with Version 1.1. *Kerning* is a typographic feature that can be applied to the entire document. It regulates the distance between characters and makes reading easier. We'll study kerning as well as other typographic controls in Chapter 13.

Once you set the settings to your satisfaction, give the OK with the mouse or the Return key. (Note that you cannot give the OK by double-clicking a choice, as you could earlier with the file names in the Item Selector box. Double-clicking operates only with the Item Selector box, not dialog boxes.)

SETTING UP MARGINS AND COLUMNS

The work we've performed so far has involved the File, View, and Page pull-down menus. You can choose from these three menus while any of Ventura's four modes (Frame, Paragraph, Text, or Graphic) is active.

However, you cannot utilize some of Ventura's menus unless the appropriate mode is active. To work with the Frame menu, for example, the Frame mode must be active, and the actual frame whose settings we wish to change must be selected in the working area. Only then can we choose commands from the Frame pull-down menu. Otherwise, the menu choices ghost in a light gray, and the mouse doesn't work on them.

You'll follow this sequence of events repeatedly throughout Ventura. That is, first you must have Ventura operating in the correct mode, then you must designate (*select*) the item you wish to change. Only then can you change it. To make such a change, you generally use one of the pull-down menus or the Assignment list on the Side-bar.

Let's examine the frames that comprise our newsletter sample. Then we'll consider which frame to alter and how to activate the Frame mode to do it. In Figure 3.12, the Frame mode is operational and you can see the frames. We used a Genius full-page display to create this figure, so you can study the page and its frames as a unit.

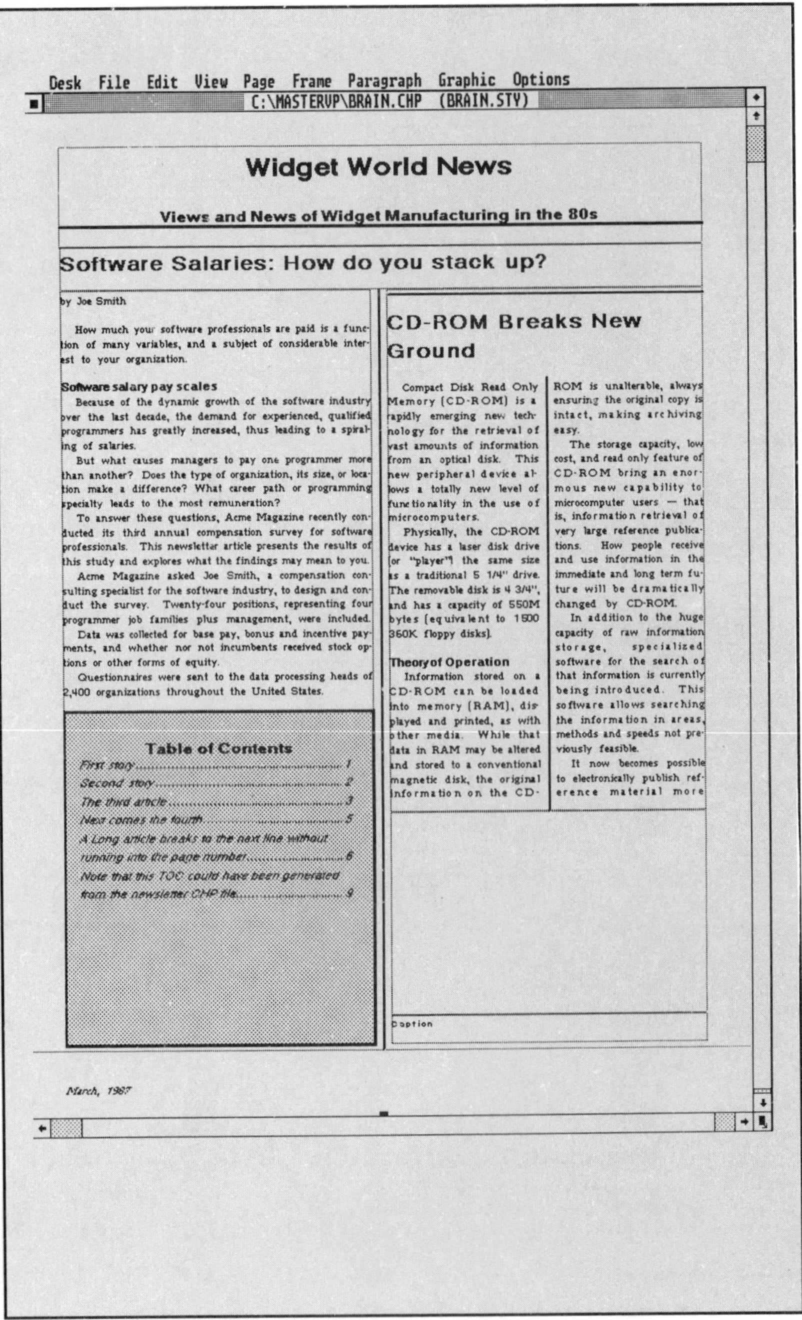

Desk File Edit View Page Frame Paragraph Graphic Options

C:\MASTERVP\BRAIN.CHP (BRAIN.STY)

Widget World News

Views and News of Widget Manufacturing in the 80s

Software Salaries: How do you stack up?

by Joe Smith

How much your software professionals are paid is a function of many variables, and a subject of considerable interest to your organization.

Software salary pay scales

Because of the dynamic growth of the software industry over the last decade, the demand for experienced, qualified programmers has greatly increased, thus leading to a spiraling of salaries.

But what causes managers to pay one programmer more than another? Does the type of organization, its size, or location make a difference? What career path or programming specialty leads to the most remuneration?

To answer these questions, Acme Magazine recently conducted its third annual compensation survey for software professionals. This newslettar article presents the results of this study and explores what the findings may mean to you.

Acme Magazine asked Joe Smith, a compensation consulting specialist for the software industry, to design and conduct the survey. Twenty-four positions, representing four programmer job families plus management, were included.

Data was collected for base pay, bonus and incentive payments, and whether nor not incumbents received stock options or other forms of equity.

Questionnaires were sent to the data processing heads of 2,400 organizations throughout the United States.

Table of Contents

CD-ROM Breaks New Ground

Compact Disk Read Only Memory (CD-ROM) is a rapidly emerging new technology for the retrieval of vast amounts of information from an optical disk. This new peripheral device allows a totally new level of functionality in the use of microcomputers.

Physically, the CD-ROM device has a laser disk drive (or "player") the same size as a traditional 5 1/4" drive. The removable disk is 4 3/4", and has a capacity of 550M bytes (equivalent to 1500 360K floppy disks).

Theory of Operation

Information stored on a CD-ROM can be loaded into memory (RAM), displayed and printed, as with other media. While that data in RAM may be altered and stored to a conventional magnetic disk, the original information on the CD-ROM is unalterable, always ensuring the original copy is intact, making archiving easy.

The storage capacity, low cost, and read only feature of CD-ROM bring an enormous new capability to microcomputer users — that is, information retrieval of very large reference publications. How people receive and use information in the immediate and long term future will be dramatically changed by CD-ROM.

In addition to the huge capacity of raw information storage, specialized software for the search of that information is currently being introduced. This software allows searching the information in areas, methods and speeds not previously feasible.

It now becomes possible to electronically publish reference material more

Caption

March, 1987

Figure 3.12: Frames in the Frame Mode on a Genius Monitor

The sample page has nine frames in it. There is one around the masthead (*Widget World News* . . .) and one surrounding the headline (*Software Salaries* . . .). There's a frame set aside for the figure in the bottom right and one for the caption below it. Another frame holds the Table of Contents. The left and right halves of the main text area are each framed, and there's also a footer frame at the bottom. The last frame is the main one, the *underlying-page frame.* This is the frame you reset to change settings for the entire page. The underlying page frame holds the other frames (standard frames) but, in this example, it does not contain any text itself.

Notice that in the printed version of this newsletter (Figure 3.1) the footer doesn't appear. That's because the LaserJet, with which it was printed, does not print to the edge of the page. In Chapter 6, you'll see how to determine the limitations of your printer.

CHANGING MODES

Let's say that you don't like the two narrow columns on the right side of the page. You'd like to change this frame to a single-column format. To work with a frame, you must first activate the Frame mode.

The mode that was active when you (or someone else) last used Ventura will be the one that's active when you start a work session. You can tell which of the four modes is active by consulting the Mode selector at the top of the Side-bar (see Figure 2.1). The first button is for the Frame mode. If it's darkened, the Frame mode is active. Buttons for Paragraph, Text, and Graphic mode follow the Frame mode button in turn. If one of them is darkened instead (only one can be active at a time), its corresponding mode is active. If this is the case, you must change to the Frame mode before proceeding.

There are three ways that you can change modes in Ventura. First, you can click the appropriate button in the Mode selector at the top of the Side-bar.

The second method is to use the View pull-down menu, shown in Figure 3.8. The lower four choices on this menu are the four modes, in the same order as they appear at the top of the Side-bar. A check mark to the left of a menu choice indicates which mode is active, in the same way that the darkened button in the Mode selector does.

The third method of changing modes is the keyboard method. The key you use is indicated on the View pull-down menu. Thus, you type Ctrl-U to activate the Frame mode. Notice that the four keys you use to change modes are positioned on the keyboard in the same order as the buttons in the Mode selector.

You can use any of these three methods to change modes. All three accomplish the same end. The methods are summarized in Figure 3.13.

Once you activate the Frame mode, you'll notice that the mouse cursor changes to a plus sign. This serves as a reminder that the Frame mode is active. As Figure 3.13 shows, each mode has a corresponding shape for the mouse cursor.

SELECTING A FRAME

Once you activate the Frame mode, you must select a frame in the working area before you can alter it. Here are the steps for selecting a frame (use them to select the frame that contains the two columns on the right of the page):

1. Change to Reduced view or scroll the screen, if necessary, so that the frame you want is visible on the screen.
2. Make sure Frame mode is active, as shown by the Mode selector at the top of the Side-bar.
3. Move the mouse cursor anywhere inside the frame.
4. Click the mouse button.

Ventura indicates that a frame is selected by displaying small black boxes along the edges of the frame, as shown in Figure 3.14. These boxes are called *handles*. Usually, there are eight handles to a frame, but there may be fewer if the box is too small to accommodate eight. Shortly, we'll see how you can grab these handles to manipulate a frame.

CHANGING THE SELECTED FRAME

To select a different frame, just position the plus-shaped mouse cursor within the new frame and click. The handles will appear on the new frame and disappear from the first one. This works well as long as the two frames are completely separate.

This method also works if the first frame lies within the second frame. In that case, just move the mouse cursor to a point that's within the

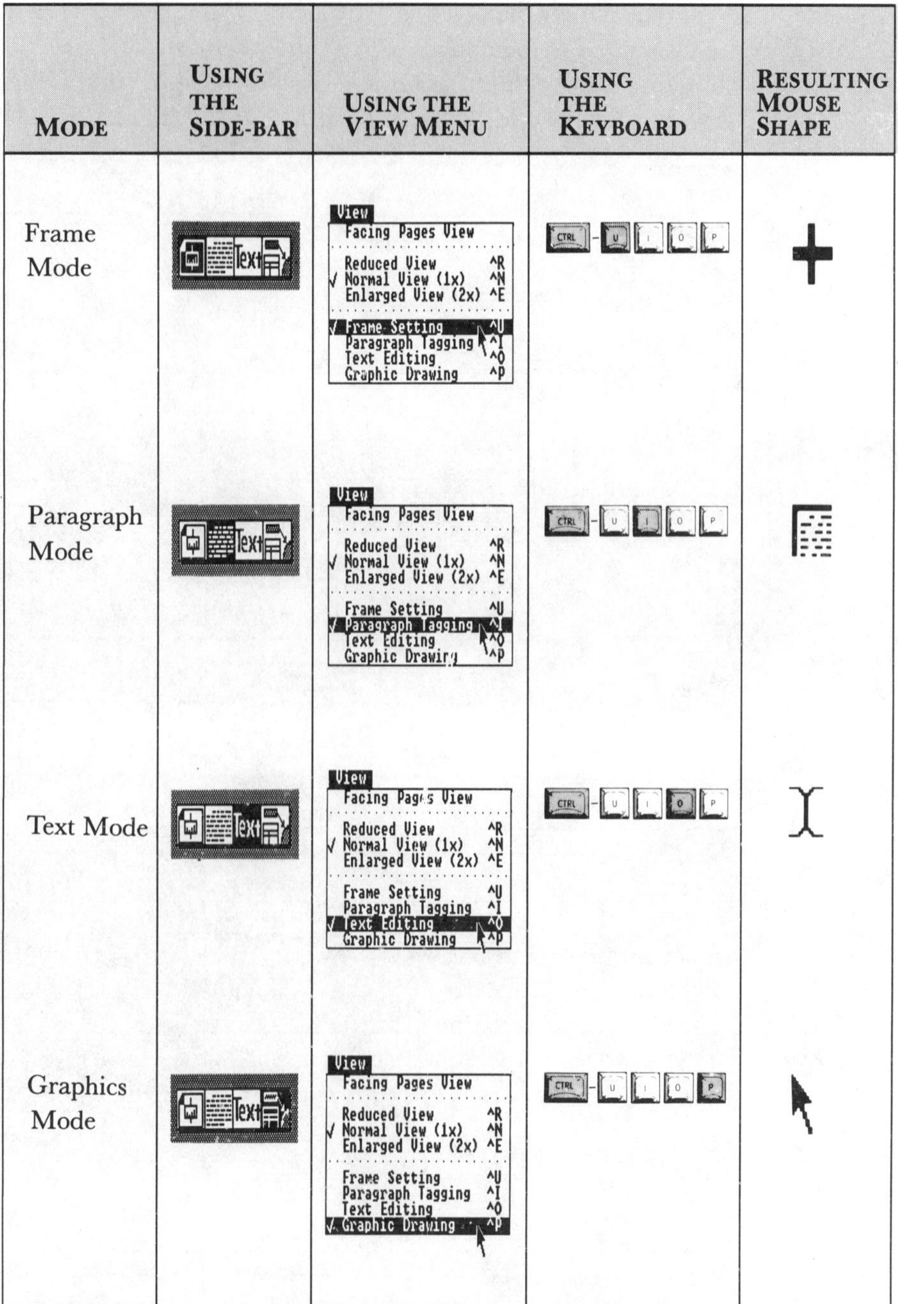

MODE	USING THE SIDE-BAR	USING THE VIEW MENU	USING THE KEYBOARD	RESULTING MOUSE SHAPE
Frame Mode				
Paragraph Mode				
Text Mode				
Graphics Mode				

Figure 3.13: Methods for Changing Modes and Resultant Mouse Shapes

second frame but not the first (see Figure 3.15). Then click. This is how you could change to the underlying-page frame, for instance.

Changing back to the first frame is trickier since the first frame is fully within the second. To select the first frame again, begin by

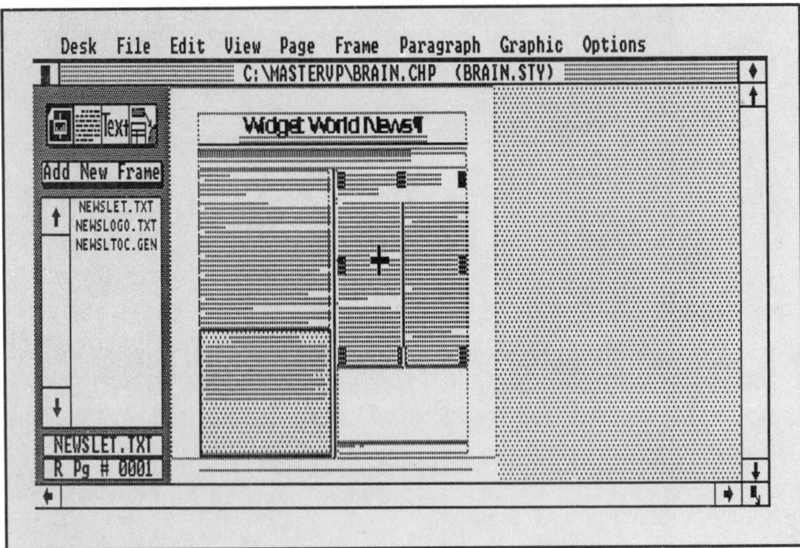

Figure 3.14: Handles on a Selected Frame

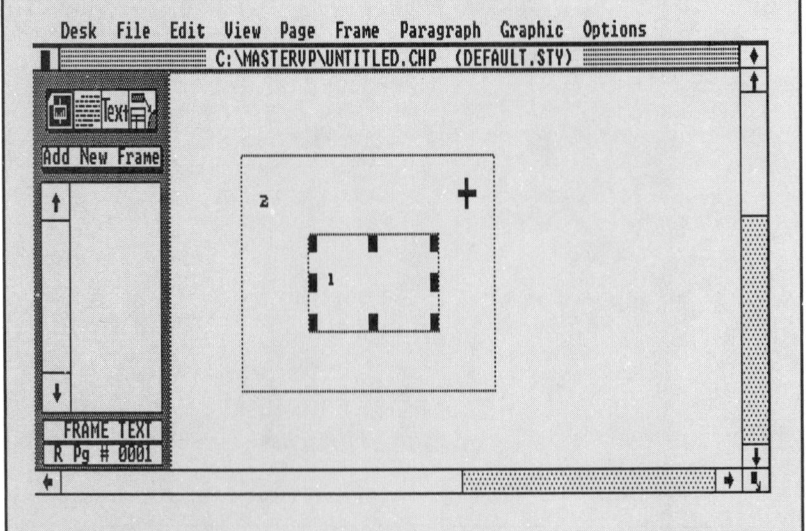

Figure 3.15: Selecting a Frame that Contains the Currently Selected Frame

selecting some *third* frame that doesn't contain these frames (see Figure 3.16). Then you can select the first frame. (You may add a third frame temporarily just for this purpose.)

Alternatively, you could move the second frame away temporarily, so that it doesn't surround the first frame. Once you've completed your work with the first frame you would move the second frame back in position. We'll see how to add and move frames shortly. Version 1.1 provides a third method for selecting a frame within a frame. By holding down the Ctrl key as you click, you can select frames piled on top of each other. Each Ctrl-click successively selects a different frame in the pile.

Once you select a frame, the name of the text file that's assigned to the selected frame appears in the Current box (at the bottom of the Side-bar). In Figure 3.14, for instance, the Current box shows that the sample chapter is using the NEWSLET.TXT file to fill the two-column frame on the right.

When you use a sample's format, you'll undoubtedly want to exchange the text files that appear in the frames of the sample newsletter for the files that have the stories that are to appear in your newsletter. We'll see how to do that in Chapter 4.

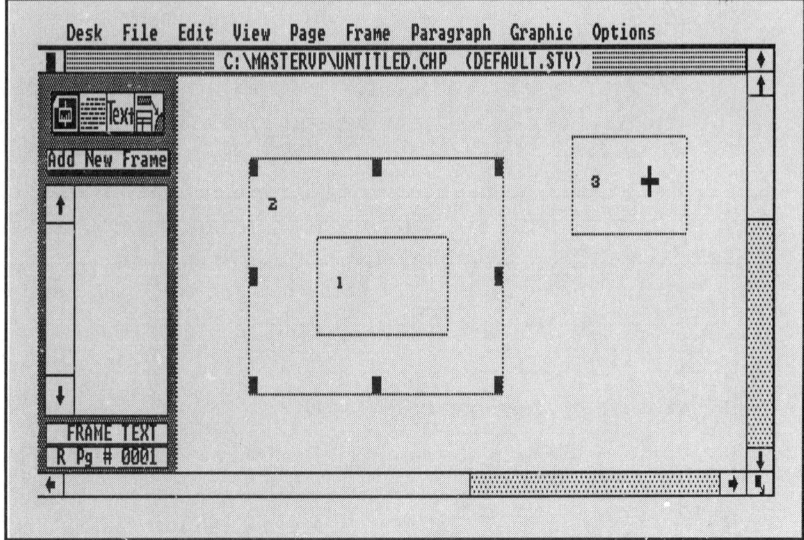

Figure 3.16: Using a Third Frame to Select a Frame Within the Currently Selected Frame

DIALOG BOX FOR MARGINS AND COLUMNS

Now let's see how to change the margins and columns for the right half of our example page. To do that, we'll use the Frame menu's Margins & Columns command. Follow these steps to display this command's dialog box:

1. Make sure that the Frame mode is active and you've selected the proper frame.
2. Display the Frame pull-down menu.
3. Click Margins & Columns.

The dialog box shown in Figure 3.17 should appear.

The parameters you set with this dialog box will affect the selected frame. When you select the underlying-page frame, the settings apply to the entire page. In that case, they generally affect every page in the chapter, because you usually have only one basic page format to a chapter (see Chapter 10).

Setting Margins

Now let's examine this dialog box. First look at the Margins settings on the right. When you work with margins and columns, you'll probably find it easiest to set the margins first and then allocate column widths according to what's left. (We won't change the margin settings for the frame in our example.)

The top, bottom, left and right margin settings are the widths of the margins from their respective edges of the frame. (In the case of the underlying-page frame, these measurements are from the edge of the page.) Contents of the frame, such as text, will not be allowed in the margins, thus creating a blank area between the contents and the edges of the frame.

Systems of Measurement

In its dialog boxes, Ventura can display measurements in four ways. You can change the system of measurement that a dialog box uses.

In the Frame menu's Margins & Columns dialog box (see Figure 3.17), notice that the word *inches* appears to the right of the

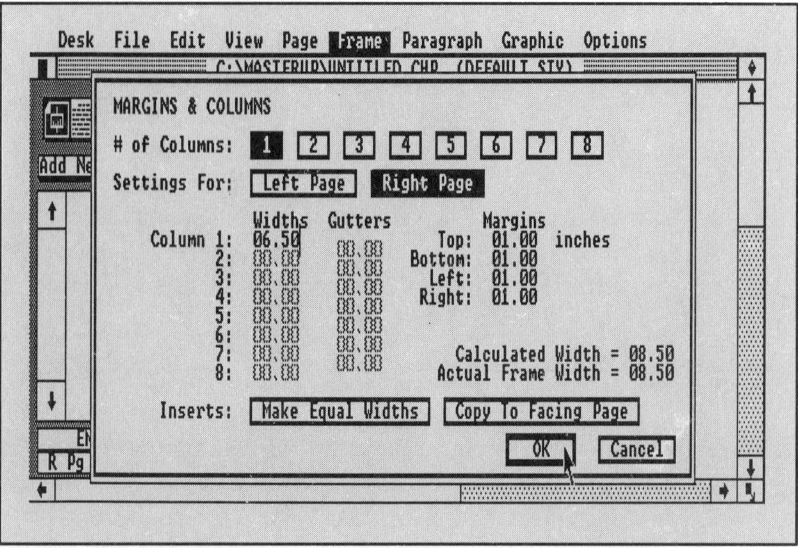

Figure 3.17: The Frame Menu's Margins & Columns Dialog Box

top-margin setting. This label indicates the system of measurement Ventura Publisher is using to display values in the dialog box.

To change to a different system of measurement, click the mouse cursor directly on the word *inches*. The word *centimeters* will replace the word *inches*, and all measurements will be converted to centimeters. Click several times. Ventura will display other systems of measurement (*picas & points* and *fractional points*) before it returns to inches. For example, typesetters can use picas and points for vertical and linear measurement of type. (There are about 6 picas in 1 inch, and there are 72 points in 1 inch.) With picas & points, Ventura displays the number of picas, followed by a comma and the number of points. Thus, 1.25 inches, which is equal to 7 picas plus 6 points, would be displayed as

07,06 picas & points

Fractional points appear as the number of points, a decimal, then fractions of points. Thus, the same value would convert to

90.00 fractional pts

Figure 3.18 shows the various systems of measurement that Ventura has available for you. The figure also shows how they correspond and, as the figure is actual size, you can use it for measuring.

Once you convert a value, if the field in a dialog box is too small to display the resulting large value, a tilde (˜) appears in the field instead. To see the true value, simply click the measurement name, as we've discussed, to convert the value to a different system of measurement.

Be aware, too, that slight rounding errors may occur when you convert. This is normal and usually inconsequential.

Odd Size Paper

As mentioned earlier, Ventura accommodates seven standard sizes of paper, each in two orientations (portrait and landscape). These choices are found in the Page menu's Page Layout dialog box, shown in Figure 3.11.

If none of these sizes suit you, choose one that is bigger than the size you need and adapt it. You do this by increasing the margins of the underlying-page frame. It may take some doing, so be prepared to experiment. When using this technique, avoid using double-sided pages if possible. With odd size paper, double-sized pages complicate the process considerably.

You can also use a repeating frame to reduce the printed area of a page. Repeating frames are discussed in Chapter 10.

Setting Columns

Continuing with our exploration of the Frame menu's Margins & Columns box (Figure 3.17), notice that you can have from one to eight columns of text in the frame. To change the number of columns, simply click the button of your choice. To change our example frame to single-column format, click the 1 button.

When you set columns, the appropriate number of Widths fields will darken automatically. You can then enter each width individually or make them equal automatically, as we'll see.

Gutters are the distances between the columns. As with column widths, you can set gutters individually or make them equal automatically.

Next look at the two fields labeled Calculated Width and Actual Frame Width. You cannot enter values for these fields, but it is important that you pay close attention to them as you set up your columns.

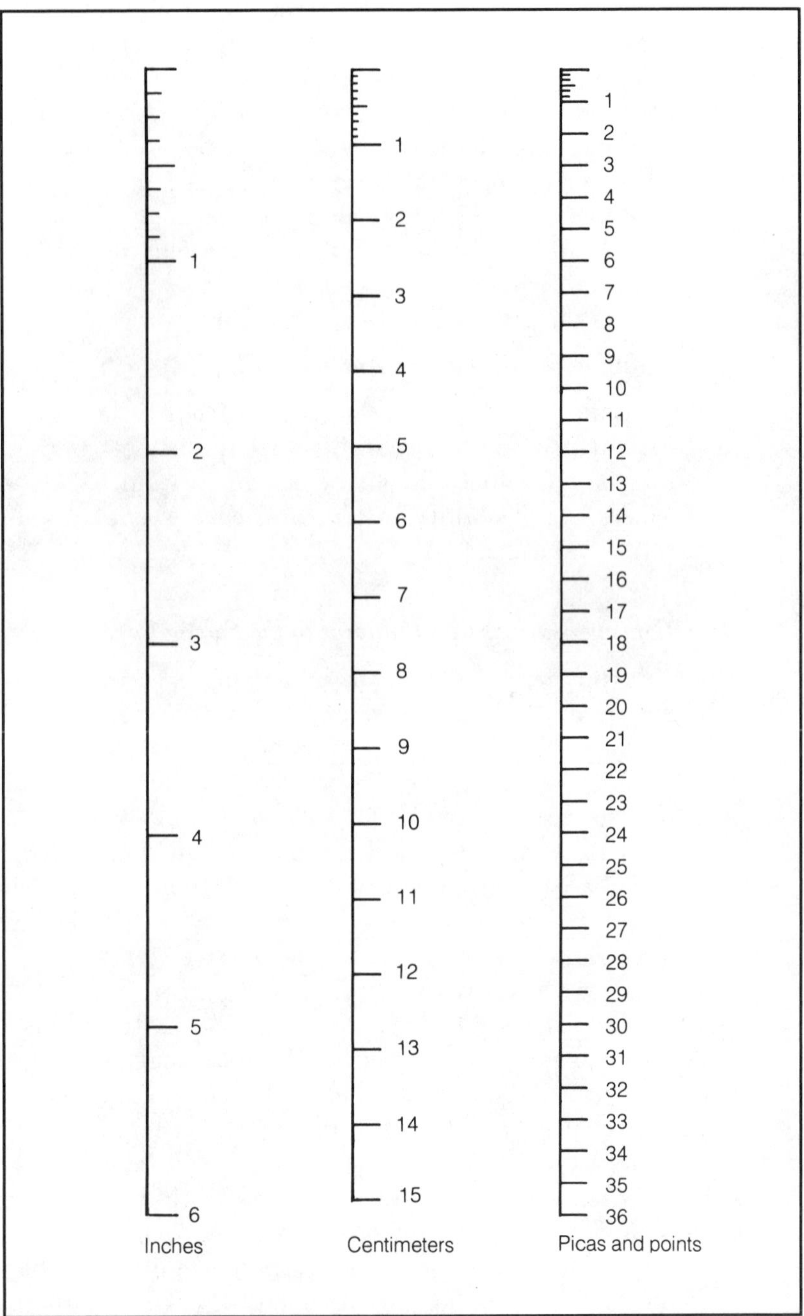

Figure 3.18: Ventura's Systems of Measurement

The values in these two fields must be equal. Otherwise, you could cause formatting irregularities to occur within your document.

Ventura computes the calculated width by adding values that you have specified in this dialog box. That is, it adds together the left and right margins, all the columns, and all the gutters. It gets the value for Actual Frame Width from the Sizing & Scaling dialog box, which also springs from the Frame pull-down menu. This box works in close connection with the Margins & Columns dialog box. We'll study the Sizing & Scaling dialog box next.

Creating Equal Columns Automatically

To make the columns and gutters for the frame equal in width (once you've set the margins and number of columns), all you need do is assign a value to the first gutter width. Then, point to the Make Equal Widths button, and click. Ventura will fill in the correct values.

Copying Margins and Columns to the Facing Page

If you are working on the underlying-page frame, you can copy the margin and column settings to the page facing the one you're working on. For this to work, you must first use the Page pull-down menu and click the Page Layout command. In the resulting dialog box, specify the Sides setting as Double.

Then, with the underlying-page frame active, use the Frame menu's Margins & Columns dialog box to set your margins and columns, as discussed above. Point to the Copy To Facing Page button and click. Ventura will change the settings for the facing page to match those you've specified.

When you use this technique, the left and right margins will be copied as mirror images on the opposite page. That is, the left will be right and the right will be left. Because of this, the pages' inside margins will match, as will their outside margins. This mirroring effect will only occur for the margins, not the columns or gutters. That is, column 1 on the facing page will be the same width as column 1 on the original page.

If you don't want to have the margins mirrored, change the settings for the opposite page *after* you copy them to that page. To do that, copy the settings and then simply click the opposite Settings For setting (Left Page or Right Page). Ventura will display the newly copied settings, and you can change them as you wish.

MANIPULATING FRAMES WITH THE MOUSE

So far, we've discussed how to adapt existing frames for new uses. Naturally, there are times when it's necessary to create an entirely new frame. Let's say that you want to add a picture or an accompanying article or information about the author at the beginning of the first article. Doing this would call for a new frame.

SHOWING RULERS

To assist in placing a new frame, you may wish to display rulers. Rulers are measuring sticks that can appear at the top and the left of the working area. With Version 1.1, these rulers each display a traveling marker that shows the position of the mouse cursor.

To display the rulers, pull down the Options menu and click Show Rulers. (If the option reads "Hide Rulers," the rulers are already showing, and clicking the command makes them disappear.)

You can change the system of measurement in which the rulers are calibrated, and in Version 1.1, you can use different measuring systems for the top and left rulers. Pull down the Options menu and click Set Ruler. You'll see the Set Ruler dialog box, as shown in Figure 3.19. This figure also shows the rulers.

Notice that you can also set the horizontal and vertical *zero point*. This is the distance that the beginning of the ruler is offset into the working area (that is, indented from the left or from the top). You might set the zero point to some value other than zero in order to measure from the center of the page rather than the left edge, for instance.

You can also use the mouse cursor to change the zero point. To do that, point to the 0,0 box in the top-left corner of the working area. Then drag (press and hold the left mouse button and move) the mouse to the desired location. When you release the mouse button, the zero point relocates to the position you've indicated. To make the ruler revert to normal, simply click the 0,0 box.

CREATING NEW FRAMES

To create a new frame, the Frame mode must be active. Click the Add New Frame button near the top of the Side-bar. Then move the mouse cursor out to the working area. As you do, the mouse cursor will change to a bracket shape that includes the letters FR (see Figure 3.20).

Move the mouse cursor to the spot where you want to place the top-left corner of the frame. Then press the mouse button and drag the mouse cursor to the spot you have in mind for the bottom-right corner of the frame. As you *stretch* the frame in this way, the cursor looks like a pointing finger (see Figure 3.21). Release the button and you establish the new frame.

You can add several frames in succession without clicking the Add New Frame button for each frame. To do that, hold down the Shift key as you create and stretch the new frames. Release the Shift key before you create the final frame.

RELOCATING FRAMES

To use the mouse to relocate a frame, first activate the Frame mode. Then bring the mouse cursor to a point somewhere within the

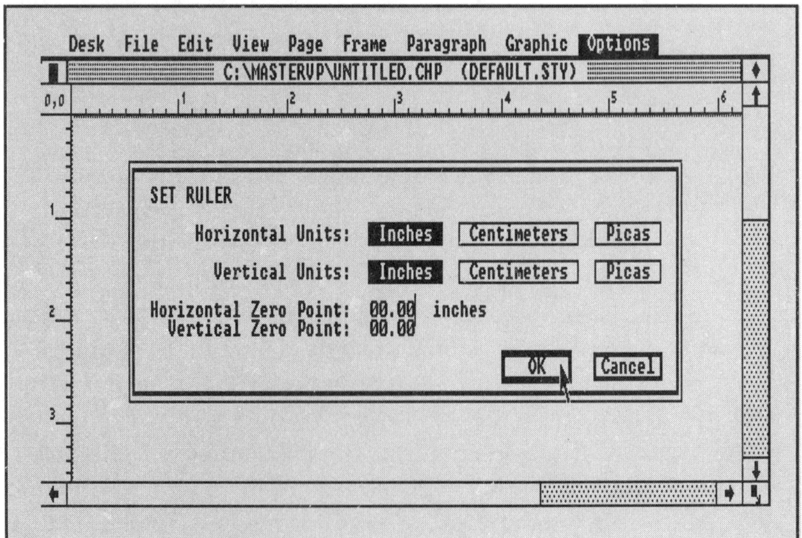

Figure 3.19: The Options Menu's Set Ruler Dialog Box and the Rulers It Controls

frame. Press the mouse button and hold it down. The mouse cursor will change to the shape of four arrows (see Figure 3.22).

Holding the mouse button, drag the frame to a new location. As you do, you'll see a ghost of the frame move along with you. Release

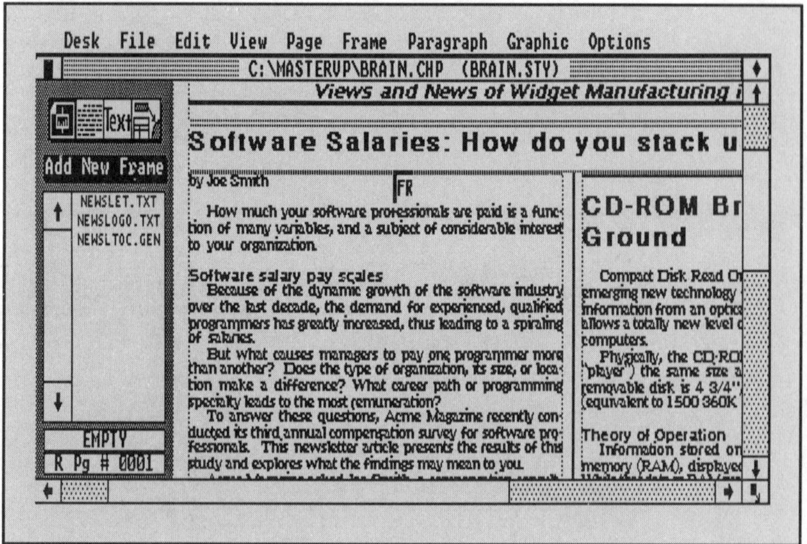

Figure 3.20: Starting to Create a New Frame

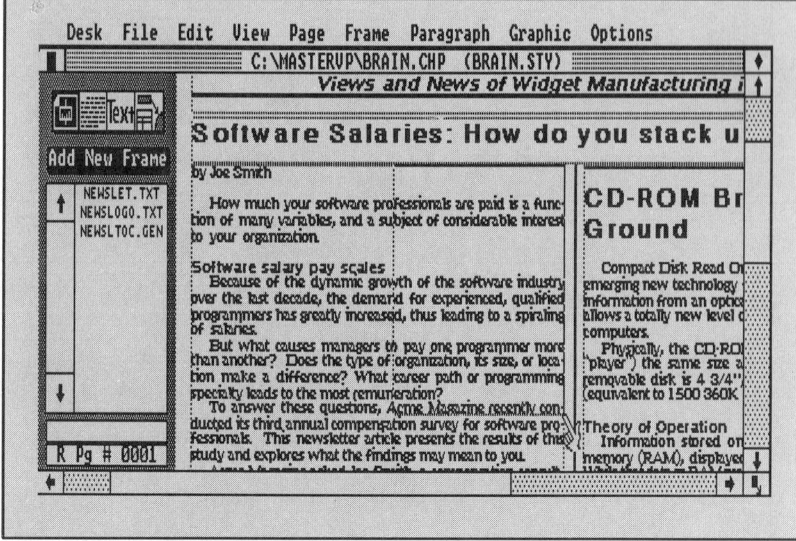

Figure 3.21: Finishing the Creation of a New Frame

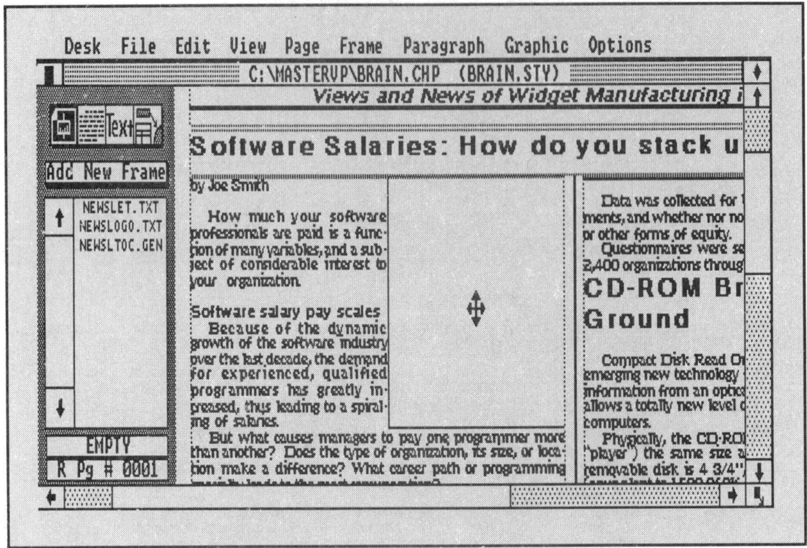

Figure 3.22: Relocating a Frame

the button, and the frame will jump to the new location.

As you move the frame, you may see it snap jerkily from one place to the next. This occurs when you have column snap or line snap turned on. In such a case, the underlying-page frame dictates the positions that the selected frame snaps into. To turn either column snap or line snap on and off, use the Options pull-down menu. Using these features allows you to make your frames line up exactly.

RESIZING FRAMES

You can also use the mouse to resize frames. To do so, grab the frame (once you've selected it) by one of its eight black handles. Press and hold the mouse button; the mouse cursor changes to the shape of a pointing finger, as it does when you are creating a frame. Drag the handle to a new location; the frame's ghost will stretch or shrink in the direction that you move the handle. When you reach the desired location, release the mouse button.

If you grab a corner handle, you stretch and contract both edges of the frame that meet at that corner. If you grab a handle in the middle of either the top or bottom of the frame, the top or bottom edge

Selecting Multiple Frames

If you need to move or resize several frames in a similar fashion, you don't have to do so for one frame at a time. Instead, you can select *multiple frames*.

To select multiple frames, begin by selecting the first frame as usual. Then, press the Shift key and, as you hold it down, click the additional frames, one by one. Each frame will display its handles and any moves you make with the mouse will affect all of the selected frames.

To unselect one of the multiple frames, Shift-click the frame you wish to unselect. The others will remain selected. To unselect all the frames, just select some other frame as usual or change the operating mode.

adjusts up and down. The action is rather like that of a window shade. If you use one of the handles centered along the left or right edge of the frame, the frame adjusts left and right, somewhat like a sliding door.

SIZING AND SCALING FRAMES

As you resize or relocate a frame with the mouse, Ventura Publisher keeps accurate track of the frame's edges. It stores the values for their location in the Frame menu's Sizing & Scaling dialog box (see Figure 3.23). You can change these values directly in the dialog box, rather than by using the mouse on a frame. You may find it handiest to do your major moves with the mouse and fine-tune with this dialog box. You need to use the Sizing & Scaling dialog box only when you are working with a frame other than the underlying-page frame.

As we mentioned earlier, the Frame menu's Sizing & Scaling (S&S) dialog box works closely with its Margins & Columns (M&C) dialog box. The manner in which these values influence each other is summarized in Figure 3.24.

TEXT AROUND A FRAME

There are two on/off settings in the Sizing & Scaling dialog box: Flow Text Around and Column Balance. The first, Flow Text Around, is usually set to On. When you add a frame on top of existing text, as we did earlier, this feature makes the text flow around the new frame automatically, preventing the new frame from obscuring text that previously occupied the frame's space. An example of this is shown in Figure 3.22.

You may wish to change this setting to Off for certain graphic effects, as you'll see in Chapter 7, where you'll also learn how to use other features in the S&S box that are shown ghosting in Figure 3.23.

FRAME POSITION AND SIZE

The X value indicates the distance of the left edge of the frame from the left edge of the paper. The Y value is the distance of the top edge of the frame from the top edge of the paper. (If you are working with the underlying-page frame, these two values, naturally, will be zero: the underlying-page frame is the same as the page.)

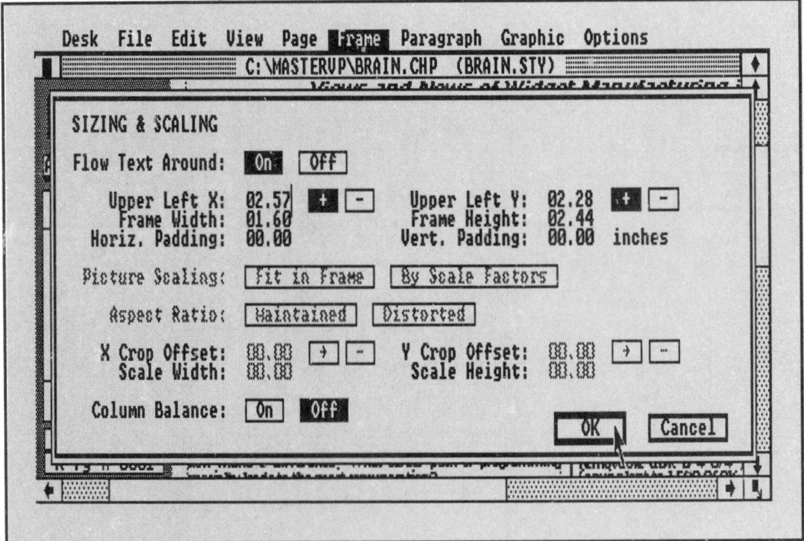

Figure 3.23: Frame Menu's Sizing & Scaling Dialog Box

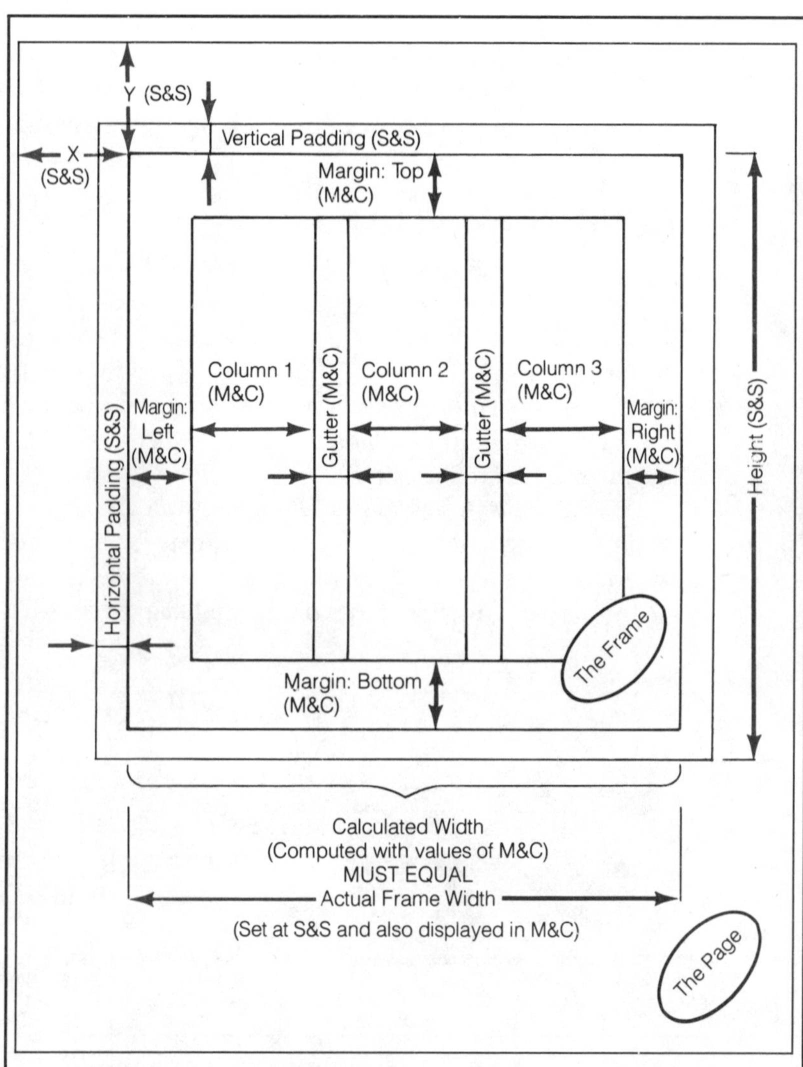

Note: Activate the appropriate frame to find its settings via the Frame pull-down menu.

M&C = Margins & Columns dialog box

S&S = Sizing & Scaling dialog box

If the frame is the same size as the page (i.e., you are working with the underlying-page frame), X and Y will be equal to 0, and Height and Width will match the page size.

Figure 3.24: Interaction of Frame Values

The Width and Height settings represent the dimensions of the frame. For the underlying-page frame, these values will match those set with the Page menu's Page Layout dialog box. Do not change them here when you are working with the underlying-page frame.

PADDING AND BALANCE

The Horiz. Padding and Vert. Padding settings, new with Version 1.1, control the border area just *outside* the frame. They won't allow text from adjacent frames into this area so that the text cannot touch the padded frame. Figure 3.25 shows how padding keeps text away from our new frame. Notice how these settings contrast with margins in the Frame menu's Margins & Columns dialog box. Margins regulate the border area within the frame.

You set Column Balance to On if you want all columns within the frame to be the same length, even when there is not enough text to fill the frame. Don't overdo the use of this feature, as it may slow down Ventura's performance (more on this in Chapter 5).

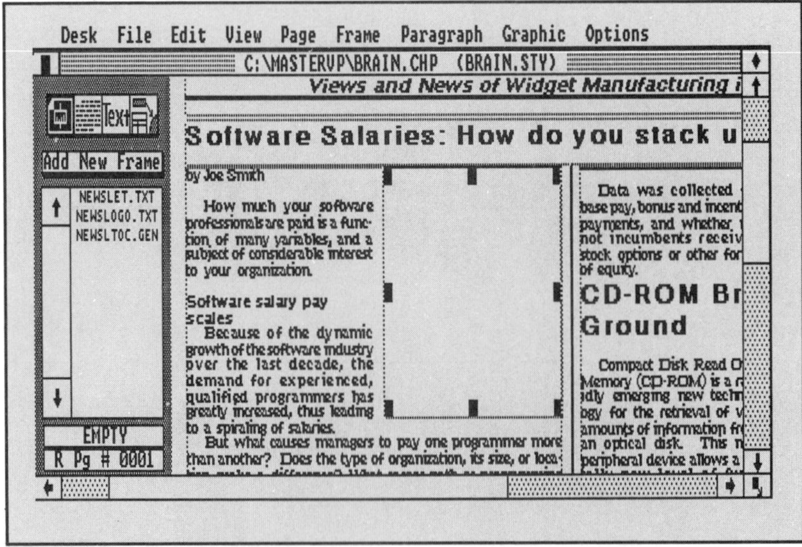

Figure 3.25: Frame Padding

SAVING YOUR WORK

Though there remains quite a bit of work to do on our newsletter, you have already learned how to do most of the initial setting up. To save the work that you've done, pull down the File menu and click Save.

As the menu indicates, there is a keyboard shortcut for saving: Ctrl-S. Either way, Ventura Publisher saves all elements of the displayed chapter that you've changed since you last saved. This includes the style sheet.

Remember that if you wish to save the chapter under a new name, use the Save As command instead.

NEW AND ABANDONED DOCUMENTS

There are two other commands on the File pull-down menu with which you should become familiar. Use the New command when you want to clear the document that's displayed in order to commence work on a brand new (currently nonexisting) chapter. Use the Abandon command if you've loaded a chapter and then made changes to it that you don't want to keep. After getting verification from you, Ventura will discard the revisions you've made and reload the previous version of the chapter from the disk.

QUITTING

When you are finished with a Ventura Publisher work session, use the File pull-down menu and click Quit. If you've made any changes in the chapter since you last saved, Ventura Publisher will display the message

> STOP
> Save or Abandon changes
> to this chapter?

If you haven't saved and you want to keep the changes that you've made, carefully click Save or Don't Quit. Use Abandon if you've made changes that you don't want to save.

IMPORTANT

Even though the Quit command allows you to save, don't rely on it. Sometimes, as in the case of a full disk, quitting will not allow you to save before quitting. Always use the File menu's Save command to save before quitting.

For now, quit or practice quitting, even if you want to go on. In the next chapter, we'll see how to make changes in the material that we've been setting up.

CHAPTER FOUR

Using Electronic Scissors and Glue

IN CHAPTER 3, YOU LEARNED HOW TO CREATE AND position frames on the page, using the sample frames and pages provided with Ventura. From this starting point, you can develop your own frames. Once you have your frames laid out, at least preliminarily, you'll need to assign material to them. Since you've used one of the sample chapters as a starting block, you must first remove the sample material from the frames and then replace it with your own.

As you assign material to frames, you'll probably find it necessary to make some changes in the material that appears; you'll need to play the role of editor as you create layouts. For example, you may see that you have to shorten an article or correct a misspelling. You might prepare a frame completely and then find that it would be better to locate it on a different page, perhaps next to a frame that contains material of a similar nature. You might even come up with a complex set of formats for your document and then decide to reformat completely.

Before desktop publishing, such changes, small or large, would call for scissors, glue, and a lot of effort. With Ventura, though, you use electronic equivalents of scissors and glue (and much less effort). For this reason, Ventura refers to editing work as *cut, copy,* and *paste operations*.

There are different ways to perform editing operations with Ventura. Roughly, they correspond to the operational modes of the program. In Frame mode, you can cut, copy, and paste frames. In Text mode, you cut, copy, and paste text. In Graphics mode, you use these procedures on graphics. Paragraph mode, however, has no cut, copy, and paste procedure. You can duplicate and remove paragraph tags. However, that procedure is quite different from cut, copy, and paste operations. We'll see how that's handled in Chapter 5.

In this chapter, you'll learn how to cut, copy, and paste frames and text. (You'll perform these operations on graphics when we study graphics features in Chapter 7.) We'll look at how you assign text files created with your word processor to frames in your document. You can use this procedure to replace the sample text files originally assigned by Ventura. Then we'll see how to make changes in your text, from minor line editing to moving whole blocks. Finally, we'll see how you can cut, copy, and paste frames themselves, along with the contents they hold.

WORKING WITH TEXT CREATED WITH A WORD PROCESSOR

Each frame can have only one text file assigned to it. When a frame is active, the name of that text file appears above the page number in the Current box.

You can, however, assign the same file to several frames. In this case, Ventura will first use the text to fill the first frame that you assign, and then go on to fill the next frame, picking up where it left off.

ADDING A FILE TO THE ASSIGNMENT LIST

The first step in assigning a text file to a frame is to add its name to the Assignment list on the Side-bar. Doing so makes it available for you to use. Once the name appears on the list, you can assign it to a frame. Let's say, for instance, that you have a file you created with WordPerfect called IDEAS.WP, which you want to take the place of the article entitled "CD-ROM Breaks New Ground" on the right side of the sample newsletter we've been working with. To add the file's name to the assignment list, follow these steps:

1. Pull down the File menu and click Load Text/Picture. Use the Load Text/Picture dialog box that appears (see Figure 2.7) to specify the format of the text file (that is, the word processor used to create the file). Then give the OK by pressing Return or clicking the OK box.
2. Use the Item Selector box that appears to specify the directory and the name of the file you wish to add (IDEAS.WP). Give the OK.

Note that when you create text for Ventura with a word processor, do not press Return except at the end of a paragraph. Don't indent paragraphs, center headings, or concern yourself with page layout: such features will be handled by Ventura. For more on entering text with a word processor, see Chapter 12.

ASSIGNING THE FILE TO A FRAME

When you've completed these steps, the file's name will appear on the Assignment list. To assign its contents to any frame, including the underlying-page frame, follow these steps:

1. With the Frame mode operational, select the frame you wish to fill with text.
2. In the Assignment list, click the file name whose contents you want assigned to that frame. The file's contents should then appear in the frame, and the file's name will appear in the Current box.

Ventura will fill the selected frame with as much of the text file as the frame can accommodate.

IMPORTANT

Before you attempt to click a file name on the assignment list, be sure that the Frame mode is active and you've selected the appropriate frame.

For instance, to change the frame with the CD-ROM article so that it holds the IDEAS.WP article, pull down the Frame menu and click Load Text/Picture. You'll see the Load Text/Picture dialog box that we examined in Chapter 2 (see Figure 2.6). For Type of File indicate Text, and for Text Format indicate WordPerfect.

Upon giving the OK for this dialog box, you'll see the Item Selector box. Use it to specify the directory and name of the file, IDEAS.WP. Once you give the OK, the name IDEAS.WP appears on the Assignment list when the Frame mode is active, indicating that this file is available for use with the displayed chapter. (Note that although Ventura is designed to assume that a WP extension denotes a WordPerfect file, this extension is not assigned automatically by WordPerfect. If you want to take advantage of the way Ventura uses this extension, you must assign it yourself when you create a file in WordPerfect.)

Next, in the Frame mode, select the right-hand frame of the newsletter. By clicking the IDEAS.WP file name in the Assignment list, you cause Ventura to replace the NEWSLET.TXT file with IDEAS.WP. Since the frame is still selected, the new file's name will appear in the Current box.

IMPORTANT

Be sure to look for the End of File marker so that you know all of the file is showing in your frame (unless you deliberately want to cut an article short). The End of File marker is a small square box, the size of other characters, that always appears at the very end of the file when tabs and returns are showing. If this code doesn't appear, there is additional text in the file. In this case, enlarge the frame or assign the file to an additional frame, to accommodate the rest of the file. (If the additional text is simply blank spaces or unnecessary Returns, you can delete them, so that the End of File mark comes after the last character of true text. We'll see how to edit text later in this chapter.)

To assign a file to an additional frame on the same page, simply select the second frame and click the file's name again on the Assignment list. Ventura will pick up the text where it left off when the first frame was full. The program will always display text in frames in the same order that you create the frames (not necessarily in the order that the frames appear on the page). You can change the assigned order by cutting frames and repasting them, as discussed later in this chapter. Repasting is the same as creating the frame anew, and the text will be assigned accordingly.

Note, however, that Ventura always assigns text to pages in order. You cannot have text continue on a previous page, even by assigning it after you assign text to a later page.

If another file occupies a frame when you assign a new file, the new assignment will take its place in the frame. However, the old file's name will still appear on the Assignment list. You can easily assign that file to another frame elsewhere in the chapter by just selecting a new frame and clicking the file's name on the Assignment list.

REMOVING A FILE FROM THE ASSIGNMENT LIST OR FROM A FRAME

If you don't plan to use the file that you've eliminated from a frame, you'll probably want to remove it from the Assignment list. Doing so may speed up operations and allow you to create larger chapters. Here's how to remove a file from the Assignment list:

1. Activate the Frame mode and select the appropriate frame.

2. Pull down the Edit menu and click Remove Text/File. This causes the dialog box shown in Figure 4.1 to appear. The name of the file contained in the selected frame appears in the File Name field.
3. Click the List of Files button and give the OK.

When you remove a file name from the Assignment list, it makes that file unavailable for use with the chapter. This action does not, however, erase the file from the disk. Thus, if you later wish to use the file, just add it to the Assignment list again, as described earlier. To remove a file from the disk, use the File menu's DOS File Operations command.

Notice that the Remove File dialog box has two choices for Remove from: namely, List of Files and Frame. There'll be times when you want to remove a text file from a frame, even though you don't have another file ready to replace the text immediately (as we did above). You might want to do this, for instance, if someone working on an article for your newsletter has not yet finished it. To remove a text file in this manner, activate the appropriate frame and click the Frame button in this dialog box. This action removes all text from the chosen frame. You can later assign a text file to this frame.

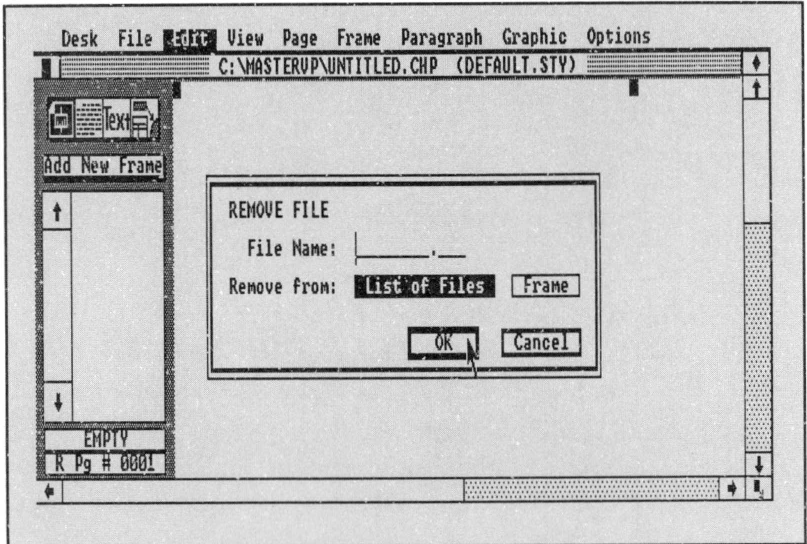

Figure 4.1: The Remove File Dialog Box

Once a frame is empty, you can also type text directly into it. We'll see how to do this shortly using the Edit mode.

RENAMING FILES AND CHANGING THE FORMAT TYPE

If you wish to make changes in the contents of a text file but you want to keep the original intact, simply change the file's name. Here are the steps you need to perform:

1. Activate the Frame mode.
2. Pull down the Edit menu.
3. Click File Type/Rename.

This action displays the File Type/Rename dialog box, shown in Figure 4.2. If you have selected a particular frame that holds a text file before you take these steps, that file's name will appear in both the Old Name and the New Name fields. Change the New Name field as desired.

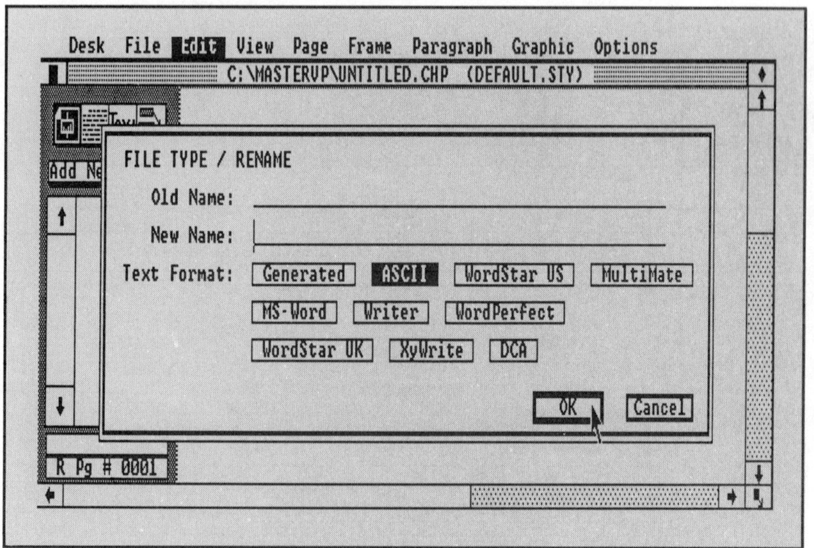

Figure 4.2: The File Type/Rename Dialog Box

Note that you can also use this dialog box to change the word processor format that any file uses. Just click the appropriate button. The next time you save the chapter (with the File menu's Save or Save As commands), the file will be converted to the new format.

MOVING WITHIN THE DOCUMENT

Shortly, we'll see how to perform various editing procedures on the files you've assigned to frames. To do so, however, you'll need to be able to display any page in your document that needs work.

With Ventura, you can easily move to any page. The two methods of doing this are the Go To Page dialog box, shown in Figure 4.3, and the shortcut keys associated with it.

The easiest way to display the Go To Page dialog box is to type Ctrl-G. You can also display it by pulling down the Page menu and clicking Go To Page.

Usually, the Document button is darkened, indicating that the settings you choose will operate relative to the document. Let's examine this setup first.

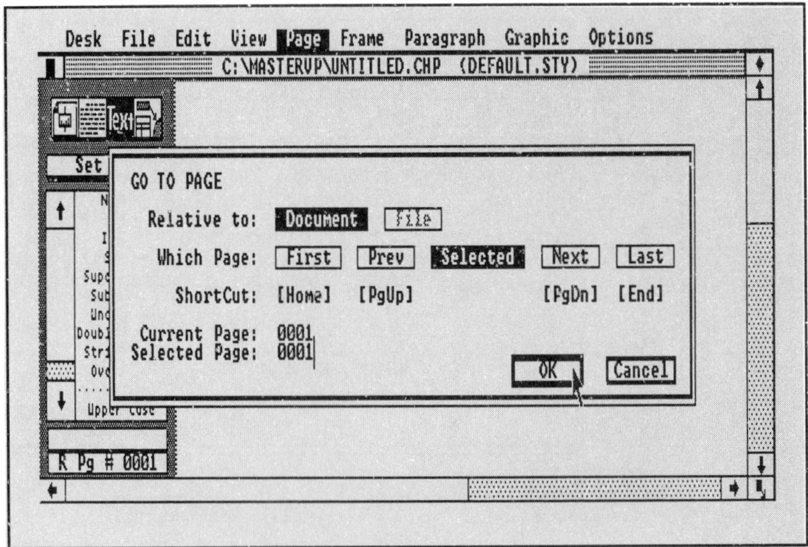

Figure 4.3: The Go To Page Dialog Box

MOVING RELATIVE TO THE DOCUMENT

The set of buttons in the Which Page grouping allows you to specify which page you want displayed on the screen. Choosing First displays the first page in the document (once you give the OK). Prev displays the previous page in the document; that is, the page before the one currently on the screen. The Next and Last buttons display the next page and the last page of the document, respectively.

For the Which Page grouping, the button labeled Selected is initially darkened. It operates in conjunction with the Selected Page field at the bottom of this dialog box. The Current Page field is an indicator that shows the page number of the page displayed on the screen. (You can also see the current page number at the bottom of the Side-bar.)

Initially, the Selected Page field displays the same number as the Current Page. Inserting a page number for Selected Page and giving the OK will display the page that you specify. Remember, you can wipe out the entire value that initially appears for Selected Page by pressing the Esc key.

Except for the button labeled Selected, each of the Which Page buttons has a shortcut key associated with its operation, as indicated immediately below these buttons. Instead of displaying this dialog box and clicking one of these buttons, you can use a corresponding shortcut key. Thus, to go to the first page in your document you can simply press the Home key (the equivalent of clicking First and giving the OK). As you can tell, these shortcut keys certainly warrant their name.

MOVING RELATIVE TO THE FILE

You can also use the settings in the Go To Page dialog box to move relative to the file. This ability of Ventura is designed for use with newsletters or magazine articles, for instance, that begin on one page and continue on another, many pages later.

As an example, assume that the Frame mode is active and you have selected a frame with an article that leaves off at the bottom of the frame. The Go To Page dialog box, when you display it, will have the File button darkened. By clicking the Next button and giving the OK, you will move to the page where the article picks up.

Note that you must use the Which Page buttons if you want to display a page relative to a file. The shortcut keys operate only with respect to the document.

If you go to a selected page, and the file you've specified does not appear on the page you've indicated, Ventura will display the next page that does contain the file. If your selected page is after the last page containing the file, Ventura will display the last page on which the file appears.

PREPARING TO EDIT TEXT

Once you begin to move through your document and examine its contents, you may find that you need to make some changes in the text. You may even want to make a rough draft of your text and let another person proofread it for you. For major edits, it's best to use a word processor because of Ventura's limitations. For example, with Ventura you can't edit text across pages, even when using the Facing Pages view. However, Ventura can handle minor and medium edits quite well. To make changes in text, you use the Text mode.

ACTIVATING THE TEXT MODE

There are three ways to activate the Text mode. You can pull down the View menu and click Text Editing. More directly, you can click the Text button of the Mode selector at the top of the Side-bar. Finally, you can press Ctrl-O on the keyboard. (Remember that the four shortcut keys, U, I, O, and P, are located on the keyboard in the same order as the four buttons of the Mode selector.)

THE MOUSE I-BEAM

Once you activate the Text mode, the mouse cursor turns into an *I-beam* shape, resembling an oversized capital I, as shown in Figure 4.4.

You use this mouse I-beam to accomplish two important tasks. First, you use it to position the keyboard cursor in the text. That is, clicking the mouse at a certain spot causes the keyboard cursor to appear in or move to that spot. If the keyboard cursor is not on the

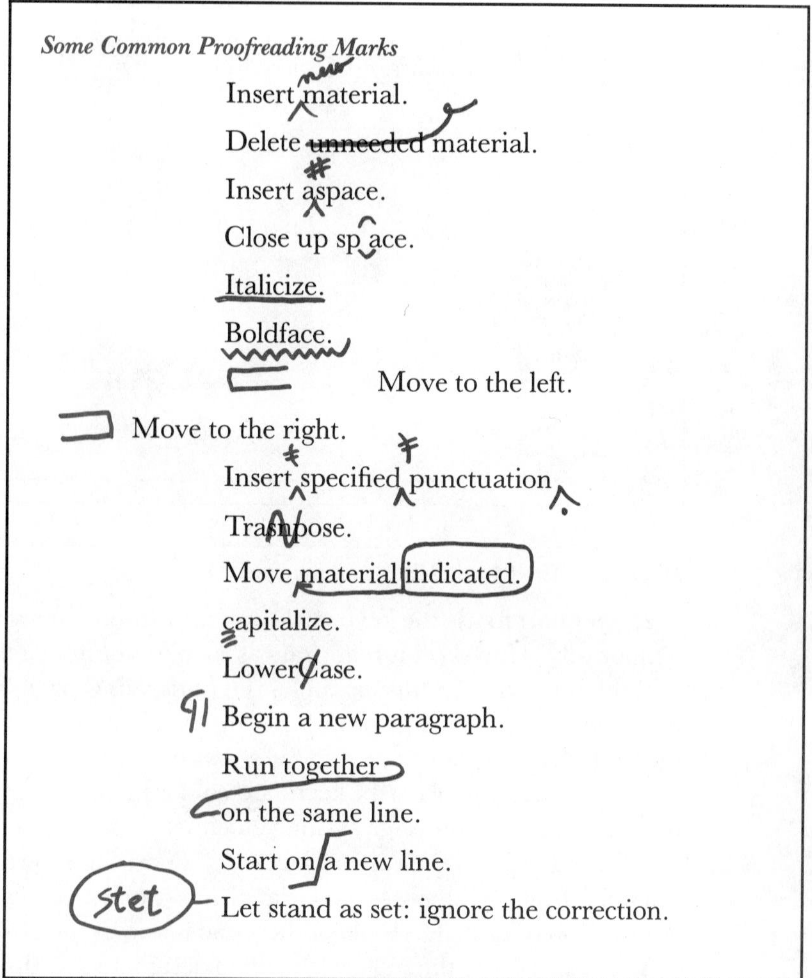

screen (as is the case when you initially activate the Text mode), this action causes it to appear where clicked. If the keyboard cursor is elsewhere on the page, this action relocates it to the new position. Either way, the two cursors then appear at the same location. With the keyboard cursor in position, you can then edit.

Some Common Proofreading Marks
Insert material.
new
Delete unneeded material.
Insert aspace.
#
Close up sp ace.
Italicize.
Boldface.
Move to the left.
Move to the right.
Insert specified punctuation
Trasnpose.
Move material indicated.
capitalize.
LowerCase.
Begin a new paragraph.
Run together
on the same line.
Start on a new line.
stet
Let stand as set: ignore the correction.

The arrow keys on the keypad also maneuver the keyboard cursor. Each arrow key moves the keyboard cursor in its respective direction on the screen. As it does, the cursor moves over any text that appears without disturbing it (for example, by erasing it).

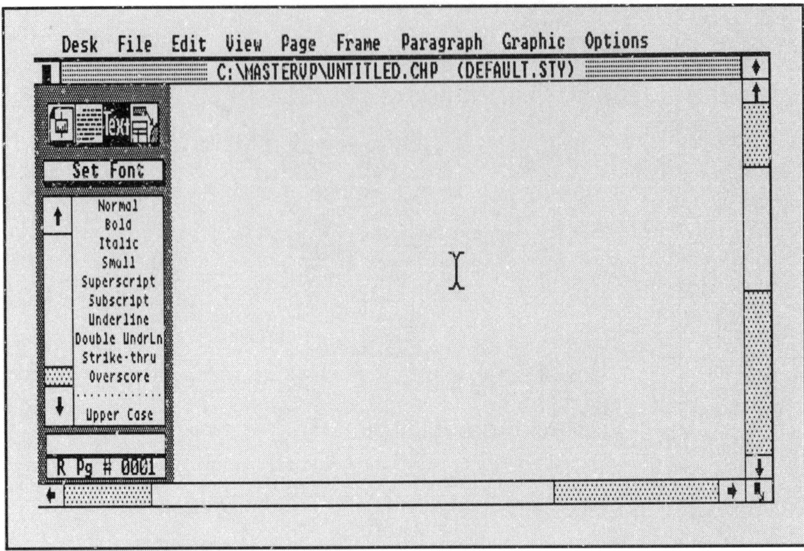

Figure 4.4: The Mouse I-Beam in the Text Mode

As you start to use the keyboard cursor, the mouse cursor vanishes temporarily. However, it reappears as soon as you move the mouse.

Remember that in this example, the underlying-page frame does not have a text file assigned to it. Because you cannot enter text into the underlying-page frame without a text file, if you attempt to use the mouse cursor to place the keyboard cursor in the underlying-page frame, you'll see a message asking you either to provide a name for a new file or to cancel the cursor placement. (You can insert text into a standard frame without an associated file. Such text, called *Frame Text,* is stored in the CAP file of the same name as the chapter file.)

You can also use the mouse I-beam to designate text that you wish to change. This process is called *selecting text.* Ventura darkens the text to indicate that you've selected it. Then you can cut or copy that text. We'll examine the process later in this chapter, under "Selecting and Cutting Text." (In Chapter 5, we'll also see how you can change the attributes of the selected text. You can use this technique to italicize, for instance.)

Whether you use the mouse to position the keyboard cursor or to select text, deactivating the Text mode will undo your efforts. For instance, if you switch to Frame mode, the keyboard cursor disappears. When you reactivate Text mode, you will have to use the mouse cursor to reposition the keyboard cursor. Likewise, switching out of the Text mode will cause any text you've darkened (by selecting) to return to normal. Switching the page will also cause the keyboard cursor to disappear and any selections you've made to return to normal.

KEEPING THE KEYBOARD CURSOR IN SIGHT

There is another circumstance under which you may find the keyboard cursor disappearing. If you move the cursor too far up, down, left, or right, it may go off the screen. This problem occurs especially when you use a standard-size screen.

Once off the screen, the keyboard cursor may continue to operate as you type and so affect unseen material in your document. So be careful. Make sure that you can always see the keyboard cursor as you type in text.

If you lose the keyboard cursor off the screen, use one of the following methods to get it back. (Using these techniques can also keep it from disappearing in the first place.)

- Use the mouse. Click and reposition the keyboard cursor on some text that's displayed.
- Reverse the direction in which you were moving when the keyboard cursor went off the screen. Often, such a turnabout will bring the cursor back on.
- Change the view (Reduced, Normal, Enlarged). With a more general view, you may be able to display the portion of the page with the keyboard cursor. Remember that with the keyboard shortcuts, Ventura will use the mouse cursor to position the top-left corner of a more reduced view.
- If the keyboard cursor has moved to the next or previous page, you can change the displayed page with the PgDn or PgUp key. When you do, however, you will still not see the keyboard cursor; as mentioned, switching pages causes the keyboard cursor to disappear. To redisplay it, you will have to click the mouse on the new page.
- If the Side-bar is visible (as it normally is), you can remove it to see more of the page and perhaps the keyboard cursor. To

do that, pull down the Options menu and click Hide Side-Bar. You can also use the keyboard shortcut, Ctrl-W, to show or hide the Side-bar.

- If the keyboard cursor is on the same page but it's not visible on the displayed portion, you can use the scroll bars to move the working area to another part of the page. The scroll bar on the right of the screen moves the working area up and down the page. The scroll bar at the bottom moves the working area to the left and right.

RE-INKING IN TEXT MODE

As you edit your chapter, you may find it necessary to re-ink the page as you work. Due to its size, the keyboard cursor often extends into text above and below the line that it's on. Thus, as you type, the keyboard cursor will sometimes erase parts of such text as it passes. To reset the text correctly, just press the Esc key when you have the working area displayed.

The kind of monitor you have may determine how often you need to re-ink. For instance, you'll find that a standard color/graphics monitor needs re-inking more often than a Genius monitor. This is apparently due to the low resolution provided by the color/graphics monitor.

WATCHING FOR PARAGRAPH END SYMBOLS

As you edit, you'll also need to keep an eye out for Paragraph End (¶) symbols. This mark shows where a paragraph ends—that is, where the Return key has been pressed. As we'll see in Chapter 5, this mark terminates the paragraph formatting. So be careful not to erase a Paragraph End symbol accidentally, or you may have to retag the following paragraph in order to regain its formatting.

So that you don't erase them accidentally, it's best to keep Paragraph End symbols showing as you edit. Hide them only temporarily to check the appearance of your page; then redisplay them right away. To hide or display Paragraph End symbols, pull down the

Options menu and click Hide (or Show) Tabs and Returns. (The wording that actually appears will vary depending on the current status of the tabs and returns.) Alternatively, you can type Ctrl-T to change the status of tabs and returns.

USING THE CURRENT BOX TO WATCH FOR SPECIAL SYMBOLS

Besides the Paragraph End symbol, there are several other special symbols that may appear on the screen, such as the Line Break and Horizontal Tab symbols (see Table 2.2). If tabs and returns are hidden, you won't be able to see them. However, Ventura does provide you with a way to make their presence known, with or without displaying them. The Current box serves this function.

The Current box is located below the Assignment list in the Side-bar (see Figure 4.5). The upper half of this box is often empty. However, when the working area has a special symbol to the *right* of the keyboard cursor, the name of that symbol appears in the Current box. When a standard character that is always visible (such as a letter or number) appears to the right of the keyboard cursor, the Current box is empty.

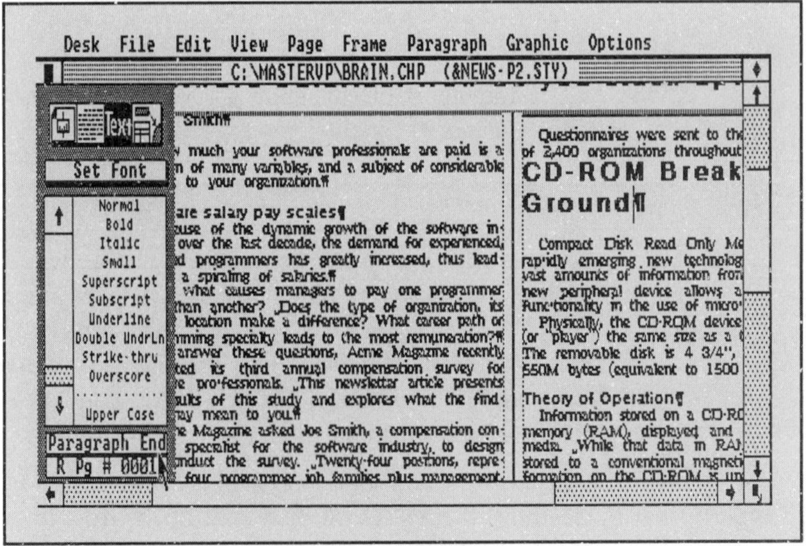

Figure 4.5: The Current Box in the Side-bar

Use this flagging mechanism to judge your editing maneuvers, especially when you delete using the Del key. With the keyboard cursor showing in the working area, pressing the Del key deletes the character to the right of the keyboard cursor. By checking the Current box you can be certain not to accidentally remove a special symbol that's invisible. You should also check the Current box as you select text. That way, you'll be certain to darken only those special symbols that you want to affect, without unintentionally selecting or missing any.

CHANGING A TITLE

Now that you're aware of some possible pitfalls, you can practice editing with Ventura. Our first editing task will be to change the title of the sample newsletter. We'll replace *Widget World News* with *The Brainstorm*. Be aware, though, that the original title is still in the NEWSLOGO.TXT file. To keep the original file intact, be sure to rename the text file, as described earlier in this chapter.

1. If Text mode is not operational, activate it as described earlier in the section "Activating the Text Mode."
2. To observe differences in the way the Backspace and Del keys erase, point the mouse I-beam to a spot somewhere in the middle of the title, say before the W in World.
3. Click the mouse on that spot. The keyboard cursor, a vertical bar, appears in the title (see Figure 4.6).
4. Move the mouse cursor, so that you can see what you're doing.
5. Remove all characters to the *right* of the keyboard cursor except the Paragraph End symbol. To do so, simply press the Del key; each repeated press removes one character. However, if you *hold* the Del key down, it removes characters one after another; be careful that you don't hold it down too long, or the keyboard cursor may eat up more characters than you want.
6. Remove the text to the *left* of the keyboard cursor. To do so, press the Backspace key. The same "hit-or-hold" rule just mentioned for the Del key also applies to the Backspace key.

7. Once you have removed all the characters except the Paragraph End symbol, as shown in Figure 4.7, type in the new title, **The Brainstorm**. As you do, you'll see that it appears in the same typeface as the previous title.

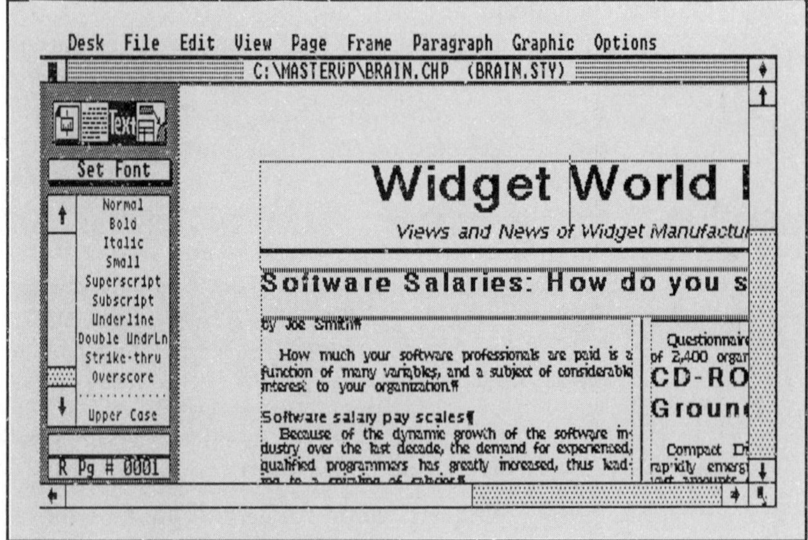

Figure 4.6: Keyboard Cursor in a Newsletter Title

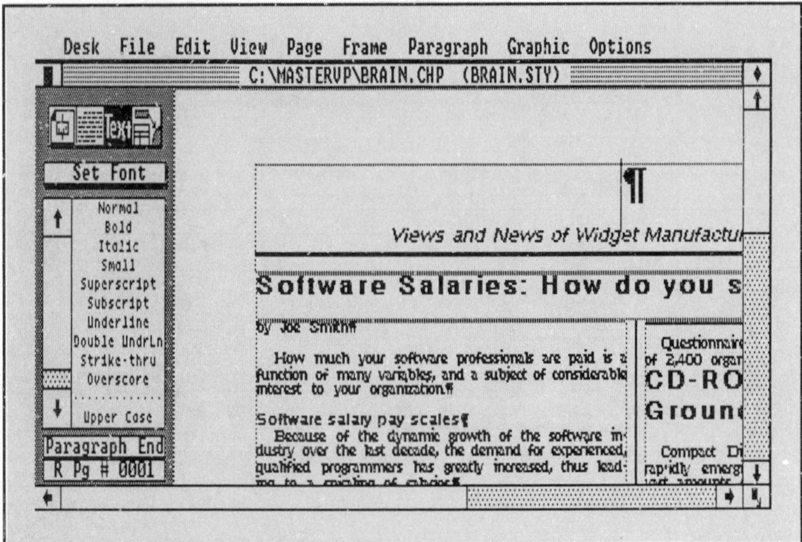

Figure 4.7: Paragraph End Symbol

SELECTING AND CUTTING TEXT

Using the Backspace key or the Del key in conjunction with the keyboard cursor works well for deletions of a single character or a few words. If you need to delete several words or more, however, it's best to use the mouse.

You can use the mouse in one of two ways to indicate the text that you want to delete. Once selected, the text appears darkened or in *reverse video* (see Figure 4.8). You can then perform a variety of operations on the selected text, such as copying or cutting it from its surroundings.

There are two ways to select text with the mouse: dragging the mouse and Shift-clicking. To select and cut text by dragging the mouse, follow these steps:

1. Bring the mouse cursor (in the shape of an I-beam) to either the beginning or the end of the text that you want to select.
2. With the mouse I-beam at one end of the passage, press the mouse button and hold it down.
3. While holding down the mouse button, drag the mouse to the other end of the passage you want to select. As you move

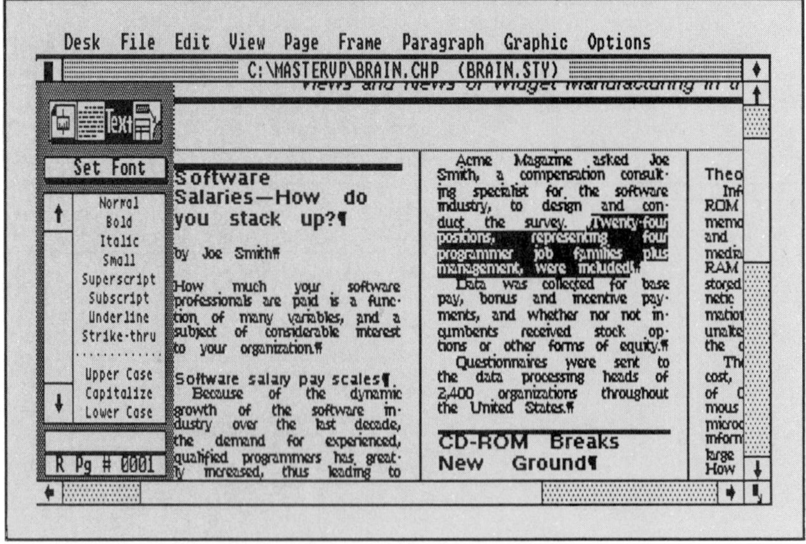

Figure 4.8: Selecting Text

the mouse, the text that it passes over will darken. Release the button. The text is now selected.

4. To cut the selected text, press the Del key or pull down the Edit menu and click Cut Text. The text is extracted from the screen and placed on an invisible clipboard (which we'll discuss shortly).

To select text by *Shift-clicking,* follow these steps:

1. With Text mode active, click the mouse at the beginning or end of the text you wish to select. The keyboard cursor will appear in that spot.
2. Move the mouse to the opposite end of the selected text. (Do not hold the mouse button and drag.)
3. Press the Shift key and hold it down while you click the mouse at that spot. This action will darken the text between the two spots. You can then cut the text as in step 4 above.

This second technique is especially handy when the keyboard cursor already happens to be positioned correctly at one end of the desired text. All you need to do is Shift-click the mouse at the other end.

We could use either of these techniques to remove the old title, *Widget World News,* from the newletter. Pressing the Del key will delete the darkened title.

CORRECTING ERRORS IN A SELECTION OPERATION

You may make a mistake in the selection operation using either of the above methods. You may find that you have selected too little or too much. If so, you can use the Shift-click method of selection to shorten *or* extend the darkened area. Simply hold down the Shift key and click at the correct spot. The darkened area will adjust accordingly.

If you shorten the darkened area by Shift-clicking, Ventura assumes that the beginning of the selected text (that is, the spot closest to the top of the page) is correct. The new darkened area covers text from that spot to the new spot you indicate.

However, if you make a cutting mistake and find that you have cut the wrong material, stop. Don't touch anything! See "Pasting Text in a New Location" below to learn how to restore the cut text.

THE CLIPBOARD

At any one time, you can cut any amount of text that's displayed on the page, as long as all the material you cut is initially on the same page. Once the material is on the clipboard, however, you can paste it on any page you desire.

The *clipboard* is an unseen area of Ventura. When you cut text, Ventura removes it from the page and places it on the clipboard. From the clipboard, you can paste it into the chapter at another location. You can even insert the contents of the clipboard into a different chapter. The contents of the clipboard remain intact when you load another chapter. Ventura clears the clipboard only when you quit the program or replace it with new cut or copied text. That is, when you cut new text to the clipboard, the old text that was on the clipboard disappears forever. So if you plan to use text that's on the clipboard, be certain that you insert it somewhere in your document before you cut other text.

Unlike text selected on the screen, the contents of the clipboard remain there when you switch modes. In fact, Ventura has a total of *three* clipboards. One is used to store frames, one stores text, and one stores graphics. The content of each clipboard is separate. What you do to any one does not affect the other two.

Thus, if we select the old title and then cut it with the Del key, the words *Widget World News* would be deleted from the document and sent to the Text clipboard. They will remain there even as we change modes or documents, until replaced by some other text.

COPYING TEXT

The procedure for copying text is similar to that for cutting text. Both procedures place the selected text on the clipboard. When you are cutting, you remove text from the page, and Ventura places it on the clipboard. Copying, however, places an exact *copy* of the selected text on the clipboard. The selected text remains on the page as well.

To copy text, perform these steps (notice how similar they are to the steps used to cut):

1. Activate the Text mode if it's not already active.
2. Select your text by darkening it with the mouse. Do so by dragging the mouse or Shift-clicking.
3. Copy the darkened text to the clipboard. Do this by pulling down the Edit menu and clicking Copy Text or by pressing Shift-Del.
4. To insert a copy of the text in a new location, follow the steps for pasting text outlined below.

PASTING TEXT IN A NEW LOCATION

Once you have cut or copied text to the clipboard, you can paste that text in a new location. By cutting and pasting you effect a move; that is, you remove the text from one location and place it in another. This kind of operation is routinely performed when documents are revised for readability.

By copying and pasting, however, you place an exact copy of the text that's in one location in another location. This is handy when you're working with forms, for instance, or other applications that involve repeating patterns.

To paste text, follow these steps:

1. You must, of course, have some text on the clipboard already. That is, you must have cut or copied text to it, as described above. Text mode must be active.
2. Position the keyboard cursor in the exact spot where you want the first character of the text to appear.
3. Press the Ins key. Alternatively, pull down the Edit menu and click Paste Text.

When you paste, the first character of text on the clipboard appears right after (to the right of) the flashing keyboard cursor. The remaining clipboard text follows. Text already on the page, originally following the keyboard cursor, is pushed down the page and follows the newly pasted (inserted) text.

You can easily make multiple copies of the text that's on the clipboard. When you paste, you are pasting a *copy* of the text that's on the clipboard; even after you paste, the same text remains on the clipboard. You can then relocate the keyboard cursor and simply paste the same text again as many times as you like.

Use Text mode and these cut, copy, and paste operations when you want to edit the text file that appears in a frame. If you are editing a great deal of a file, however, it is better to use your word processor. That way you won't have to worry about selecting text across pages, for instance. You can also use the word processor's search capability if you need to. Searching is necessary if the file is long and you have cross references that you must check. See Chapter 12 for a discussion of word processors.

CUTTING, COPYING, AND PASTING FRAMES

As we mentioned earlier, you can perform cut, copy, and paste operations on frames as well as text. Many of the techniques used to manipulate frames are similar to those used for text. By applying these techniques, you can move or remove frames, or create duplicate frames with similar specifications.

Just as you must activate the Text mode to manipulate text, so you must activate the Frame mode to manipulate frames. Also, just as you must indicate the text you want to change, so too you must indicate which frame is to change.

In Chapter 3, you saw how you can use the mouse to move a frame. Although moving frames with the mouse is easy to do, mouse moves will reposition a frame only on the same page. If you wish to move a frame to a new page, you must cut it from the first page and then paste it on the new page. You may also wish to cut a frame simply to delete it and its contents from the page.

CUTTING FRAMES

Cutting a frame that you either no longer need or that you want to move to another location is quite similar to cutting unwanted text. Doing so places the cut frame on a *Frame clipboard;* you can then paste it elsewhere from there. To cut a frame, follow these steps:

1. Activate the Frame mode.
2. Select the frame that you wish to remove. The frame's black handles should appear at its edges.
3. Press the Del key or pull down the Edit menu and click Cut Frame. The frame, and any file in it, will disappear from the page. (It is now on the Frame clipboard.)

If you inadvertently cut the wrong frame, reinsert it in the same spot before you do anything else (see "Pasting Frames" below).

COPYING FRAMES

Often, you may find that you wish to make several frames that are alike in some or all respects. In a newsletter, for instance, you may have an article that continues from page to page. To draw your readers to the continuing story, you may want to place it in sequential frames of the same size. To do that, you can create one version of the frame and then copy it.

When you copy a frame, you leave it where it is on the page as well as make a copy of it on the Frame clipboard. You can then insert that copy elsewhere within the chapter or in other chapters. (Remember, the clipboards are not cleared when you change chapters.)

The steps for copying frames are similar to those for cutting. Make sure the Frame mode is active and that you've selected the appropriate frame. As with text, you use Shift-Del or the Edit menu's Copy Frame command to copy a frame.

PASTING FRAMES

Once you cut or copy a frame to the Frame clipboard, you can paste it on the same page or a different one. (It's tricky to paste a frame on the same page that you copied it from, as we'll see shortly.)

To paste a frame on a page, follow these steps:

1. Activate the Frame mode.
2. Go to the page where you want to paste the frame.
3. Press the Ins key or pull down the Edit menu and click Paste Frame.

When you paste a frame on a new page, it initially appears *in the same position* that it occupied on the page you cut or copied it from. If you are inserting it on a different page, this arrangement is no problem. Once the frame is pasted, simply use the mouse (or the Frame menu's Sizing and Scaling command) to place the frame where you want it on the page.

IMPORTANT

If you copy a frame to the clipboard and then insert it on the same page, you'll end up with *two* frames of the same size, one on top of the other. You won't be able to see the one that's underneath. The situation could be quite disconcerting should you later try to resize. To see and use both frames under such circumstances, select the frame on top. Then use the mouse to move it off the one underneath. Alternatively, *before* you paste the copy of a frame from the clipboard, move the original frame to a different location.

As we mentioned, cut, copy, and paste operations also apply to graphics. We'll see how to use these operations in that mode when we study graphics in Chapter 8. Next, however, we will look at Ventura's Paragraph (tagging) mode, to see how to format text.

CHAPTER FIVE

Paragraph Tags and Text Attributes: Building Blocks for Formatting

FORMATTING IS THE PROCESS OF ASSIGNING FONTS and other typographical elements to text. The letter A is always the letter A, but a plain A, an italic one, a boldface one, and one set in boldface italic each have a quite different impact.

Similarly, a paragraph that is single spaced produces a different effect from one that is double spaced, and text that is flush only along the left edge produces a different effect from text that is flush along both edges.

By formatting with Ventura, you can make the form of your documents help convey your thoughts. For instance, by using a certain type style consistently under similar circumstances you make your ideas organized and clear. By using type sizes judiciously, you can create a sense of relative importance for each item. In addition, you are sometimes required to format according to certain conventions, such as italicizing the title of a book.

Ventura provides you with two means of formatting text. Because there is some overlap in the way they are used, we will present them together.

One method of formatting involves the use of *text attributes*, which are formatting characteristics that you apply by activating the Text mode. Text attributes affect individual characters in reading order (that is, left to right, line by line). You apply text attributes only to text you specifically indicate; it can be as little as one character but should usually be less than a paragraph.

The second method uses *paragraph tags*. A *tag* is a collection of formatting specifications that you assign to a unit of text, called a *paragraph*. You apply tags by activating the Paragraph mode. With paragraph tags, the features you set influence the selected paragraph and all other paragraphs in the document that are similarly tagged. The effect can even extend to other documents by way of the style sheet.

Before we begin to the examine the formatting features themselves, let's look in more detail at these two methods of formatting.

PARAGRAPH TAGS

Paragraph tagging is the tool that Ventura uses to apply features to a self-contained cluster of text called a paragraph. This component is not necessarily a conventional paragraph. In fact, the paragraph is defined in Ventura simply as a unit of text that is tagged. A Ventura paragraph always ends with a Return. Its size is not restricted by the program.

APPLYING TAGS

Paragraphs with similar formatting share the same tag. Unless otherwise indicated, Ventura tags paragraphs as *body text.* This tag dictates the default or standard format for paragraphs in the chapter. When you pull text into a chapter, such as the articles for your newsletter, all text—headlines, subheads, bylines, and so on, as well as the main body of the articles—has the tag of body text and therefore appears the same. You can change the characteristics of the body-text tag, but you cannot eliminate or rename this tag.

To change the formatting characteristics of a paragraph, you can either change the tag's format or apply a different tag to the paragraph. If you want to change the format of a paragraph, such as the text of a headline to an existing headline format, proceed as follows:

1. Activate the Paragraph mode. Do this by clicking the Paragraph button at the top of the Side-bar, pulling down the View menu and clicking Paragraph Tagging, or typing Ctrl-I.
2. Click the paragraph whose format you wish to change. The paragraph darkens, indicating that it is selected. The name of the tag (for example, Body Text) currently assigned to the paragraph appears in the Current box, towards the bottom of the Side-bar.
3. Move the mouse cursor to the tag on the Assignment list you wish to apply. The tag name darkens when you point to it, as shown in Figure 5.1.
4. Click the mouse to apply the indicated tag. The paragraph takes on the new format, and the selected tag's name appears in the Current box, as shown in Figure 5.2.

There's a tool you can use that will speed up your application of tags to text. Ventura allows you to assign paragraph tags to the ten

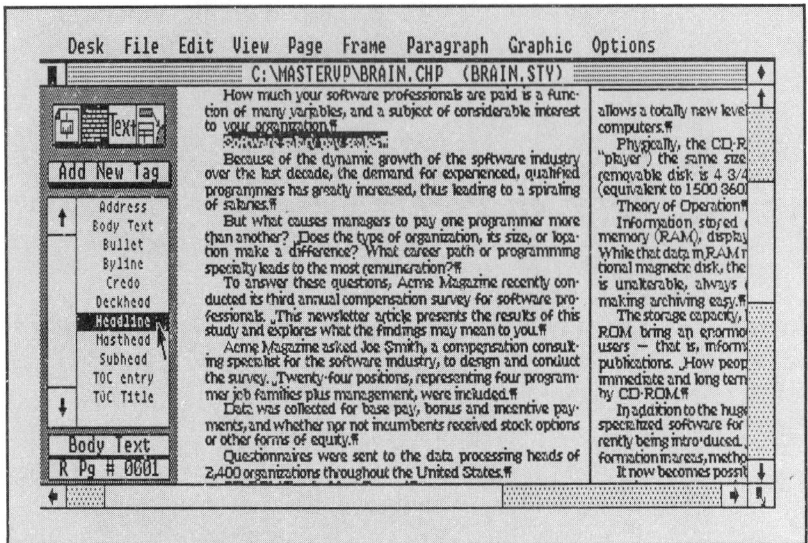

Figure 5.1: Selecting a Tag to Apply to a Paragraph

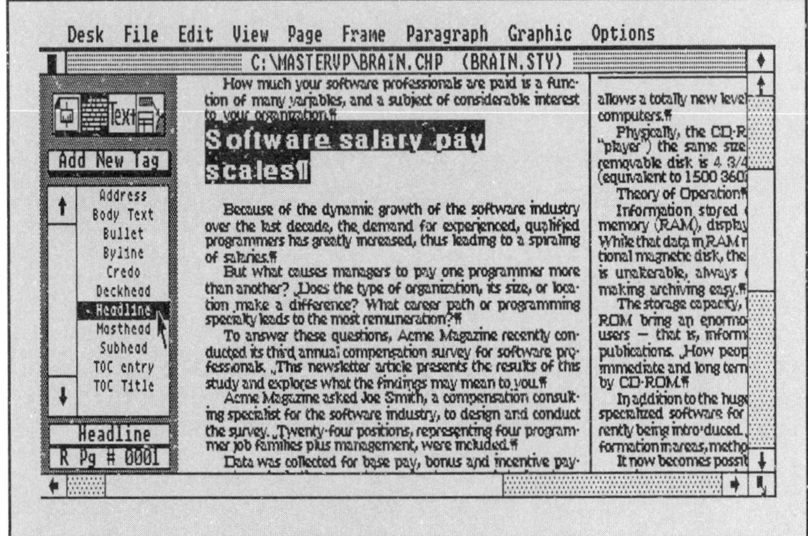

Figure 5.2: The Selected Tag Applied

Function keys on the left of your keyboard. To do this, just pull down the Paragraph menu and click Assign Func. Keys or type Ctrl-K. You'll see the dialog box shown in Figure 5.3. Enter the names of the tags you plan to use on the lines corresponding to the Function keys.

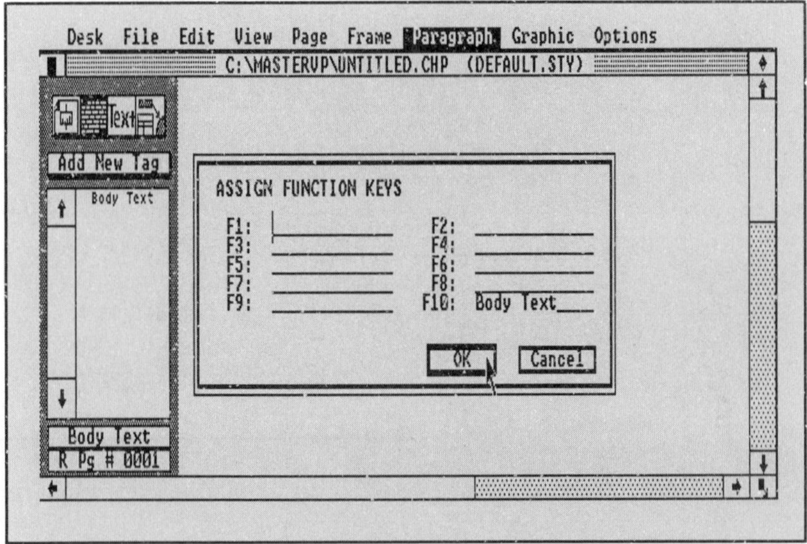

Figure 5.3: The Paragraph Menu's Assign Function Keys Dialog Box

F10 is automatically assigned to Body Text, but you can change it to another tag if you like. Once the tags are assigned, you can use the Function keys to apply the tags in either Paragraph mode or Text mode. Just select the paragraph you want to format and press the appropriate Function key.

In addition to applying tags to paragraphs, you can add, rename, and remove tags on the Assignment list. We'll study these procedures at the end of this chapter.

CHANGING A TAG'S FORMAT

When you change format specifications for a paragraph, all the paragraphs that are similarly tagged change to the new settings as well. It is therefore important to think of your chapter as a whole. You'll want to group paragraphs mentally according to their purpose and provide each group with a tag. For instance, you can use one tag for headings, another for subheadings, one for step-by-step instructions, another for callouts, and so on.

A *style sheet* is a collection of tags as well as other elements that are used with at least one chapter. Table 5.1 is a listing of the commands that control the elements of the style sheet. Every chapter has a style

PULL-DOWN MENU	COMMAND
File	Load Diff. Style Save as New Style
Page	Page Layout Auto-Numbering
Frame (Underlying-page frame only)	Margins & Columns Sizing & Scaling Vertical Rules Ruling Line/Box Frame Background
Paragraph	All Commands
Options	Set Printer Info (Width Table setting only)

Table 5.1: Commands that Affect Style Sheets

sheet associated with it. As you work with a chapter and its style sheet, however, you must keep in mind that other documents may reference the same style sheet. Changes you make in tags could affect paragraphs in the other document. For example, if you change a tag in a newsletter, all paragraphs in the newsletter that are similarly tagged will change. Moreover, any similarly tagged paragraphs in other documents that reference the same style sheet will change as well. So it's important to keep track of which documents reference a style sheet, or you will find yourself changing the format of documents without realizing it. The positive side of this feature is that you can use it to achieve a consistent look in a group of similar documents. Just have them reference the same style sheet.

Appendix A shows a listing of the sample style sheets that come with Ventura, along with their paragraph tags. Be sure to consult this appendix for the tags that you can use, as well as some ideas of how to use them.

GENERATED TAGS

Tags that Ventura manufactures automatically, such as those for captions, are called *generated tags*. Table 5.2 lists the names Ventura

GENERATED TAG	**FORMAT**
Z_BOXTEXT	Box text
Z_CAPTION	Free form captions (Text mode)
Z_FNOT #	Footnote numbers: reference numbers (or symbols such as *) in text
Z_FNOT ENTRY	Footnote entries: entries at the bottom of the page
Z_FOOTER	Footers
Z_HEADER	Headers
Z_LABEL CAP	Caption labels without an automatic number
Z_LABEL TBL	Caption labels with a table number
Z_LABEL FIG	Caption labels with a figure number
Beginning with Z_SEC	Automatic section numbers
Beginning with Z_INDEX	Entries in the index
Beginning with Z_TOC	Entries in the table of contents

***Table** 5.2:* Generated Tags

assigns its generated tags, along with the kinds of paragraphs they're created for.

Normally, the names of generated tags do not appear with those of normal tags on the Paragraph mode's Assignment list. However, you can have Ventura display generated tags. Use the Options menu's Set Preferences dialog box to change the Generated Tags setting to Shown. The names of tags that have been generated for the displayed document will then appear in the Assignment list.

All generated tags begin with the letter Z. This is so that if they appear on the Assignment list, where tags are listed in alphabetical order, generated tags will be placed at the bottom of the list. Besides keeping the generated tags together, this positioning gives them lowest priority in terms of scrolling the Assignment list. As generated tags are assigned automatically, you shouldn't need to reference them as often as regular tags; hence the low priority.

You can change formatting for these tags. In fact,you can do just about anything with them that you can do to a normal tag. Activate the Paragraph mode and use the mouse cursor to select a sample paragraph. Then pull down the Paragraph menu and make the changes you desire.

TEXT ATTRIBUTES

In Text mode, you format by choosing text and then applying *text attributes* to the selected text. Text attributes include characteristics—such as italics, boldface, underline, and fonts—that are more localized in nature than formatting that you set with the Paragraph mode. Usually, you'll use this technique for text units that are smaller than a paragraph.

As mentioned, formatting that you set by using text attributes affects only the text that you indicate; it has no effect on other documents by way of the style sheet. It doesn't even affect other parts of the same chapter.

When you make such local formatting changes, how does Ventura keep track which text differs from normal text? The system it uses is rather ingenious. Once you understand how it operates, you'll have a command of the program's formatting capabilities and will avoid a lot of undesirable surprises as you edit.

Begin by remembering that the settings in any paragraph tag are the standard or default values for all paragraphs formatted with that tag. At the place in text (in regular reading order) where nonstandard text begins, Ventura inserts an invisible *attribute-setting* code. This code is a flag that says that formatting changes take place at that spot. The code also contains a register that records the nature of the change.

Ventura also flags the spot where the text returns to the normal settings dictated by the paragraph tag. Again, it uses an invisible attribute-setting code to accomplish this neutralizing operation.

To examine how paragraph tags and text attribute settings operate, let's examine the various formatting elements that utilize these building blocks. Although you can't use all formatting features with both methods, you can set some in more than one way. Table 5.3 lists the formatting features that you can control in several ways. We'll begin by looking at fonts.

SETTING FONTS

One of the first formatting elements that you'll need to consider is the font. A *font* is a collection of letters of the alphabet, numbers, and other symbols with a particular design.

As with several other formatting features, there are two ways that you can set fonts. The method you choose depends upon the amount of text you want to affect. You can go for a universal effect, or you can choose text selectively. When you want your choice of font to extend

FEATURE	METHODS OF SETTING
Font face, size, and color	Paragraph menu's Font command Text mode's Set Font button Text Mode's Assignment list (Small size only)
Italic and Bold	Paragraph menu's Font command Text mode's Set Font button Text mode's Assignment list
Superscript and Subscript	Paragraph menu's Font command (Shift setting) Text mode's Set Font button (Shift setting) Text mode's Assignment list
Underline, Double Underline, Strike-thru, Overscore	Text mode's Assignment list Paragraph menu's Typographic Controls
Kerning	Text mode's Assignment list Paragraph menu's Typographic Controls Page menu's Page Layout Options menu's Set Preferences

Table 5.3: Text Formatting Features

throughout a document, set the font in the Paragraph mode. When your choice of font is local, use the Text mode.

SETTING FONTS IN THE PARAGRAPH MODE

To set fonts in the Paragraph mode, you change the paragraph tag for a sample paragraph. Once set, Ventura will apply the font to all characters in the selected paragraph as well as in all paragraphs with the same tag.

To set the font for a paragraph tag, follow these steps:

1. Activate the Paragraph mode.
2. Click a sample paragraph whose settings you wish to change. You may click anywhere within the paragraph. The paragraph will darken, as shown in Figure 5.1.
3. Pull down the Paragraph menu.
4. Click Font on that menu.

IMPORTANT

Before you can use a command on the Paragraph menu, you must activate the Paragraph mode and select a sample paragraph by clicking it. If you neglect to click a paragraph before pulling down the Paragraph menu, the commands on the menu will ghost, showing that you can't use them.

At this point, you'll see the Font dialog box appear, as shown in Figure 5.4. The fonts that you actually see may differ, depending on what's available for your printer. (Those shown in the figure are for the HP LaserJet.) You can also add fonts to those initially available. We'll study more about fonts and printers in Chapter 6.

Note that this dialog box allows you to set a number of font features, not just the typeface and size. Ventura provides a great deal of font flexibility.

Face refers to the actual design of the characters themselves. *Size* is the height of the font as measured in points. There are 72 points in one inch. The smaller the number that's listed for Size, the smaller the type. 10-point type is probably the most common type size and a good size for body text.

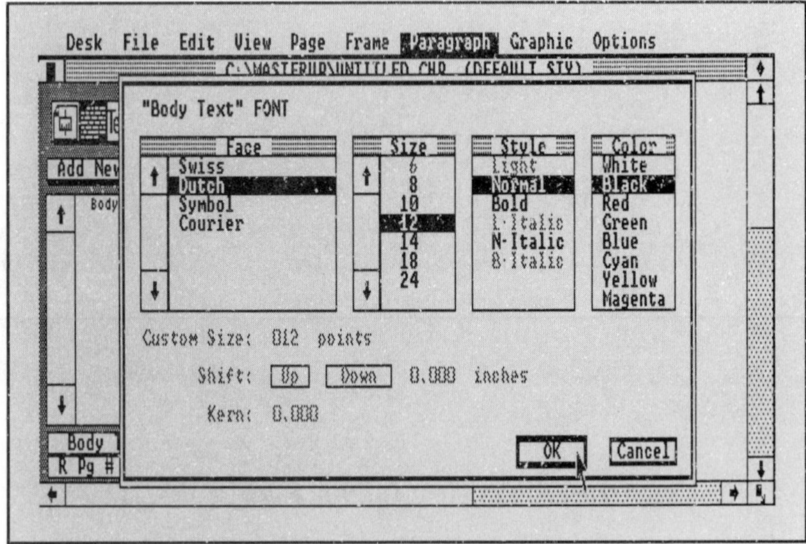

Figure 5.4: The Paragraph Menu's Font Dialog Box

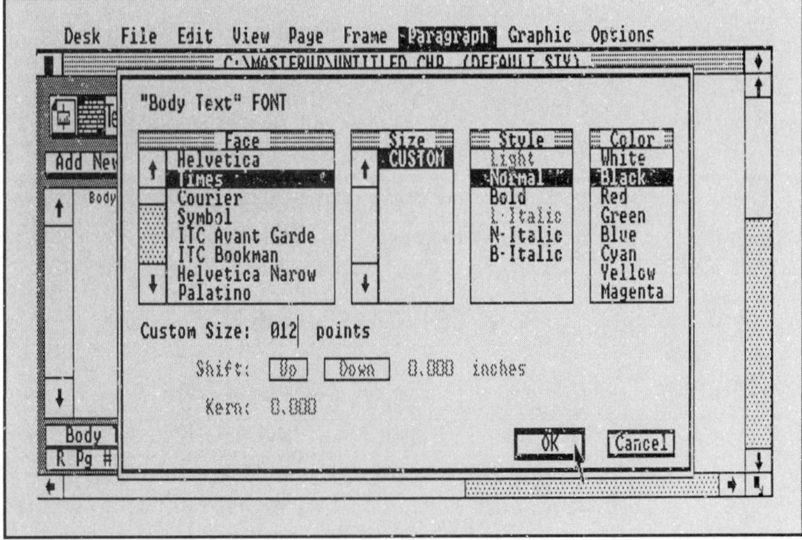

Figure 5.5: Custom Size Fonts with PostScript Printers

With PostScript printers, the word CUSTOM will appear in the Size column, as shown in Figure 5.5. For these printers, you simply enter a value between 1 and 254 points into the Custom Size field.

Figure 5.6 shows some sample typefaces that are available with Ventura on the HP LaserJet. Once you learn how to format, you may wish to create a sheet like this that lists the fonts you have and keep it near the computer as a handy reference.

As with other dialog boxes, the choices that you make in one category of the box may affect the choices that are available to you in other categories. For instance, the typeface that you choose will usually affect the sizes that are available. As usual, choices that are not available will ghost. In Figure 5.4, you can see that the Dutch typeface is not available in 6-point size.

Before we look at the other settings that appear in this dialog box, let's consider an alternative way to gain access to the box, using Ventura with the Text mode.

SETTING FONTS IN THE TEXT MODE

In Figure 5.7, in the headline from our newsletter, the word *you* is an example of a font change within a paragraph. Such a change calls for formatting in the Text mode.

To set a font in this manner, follow these steps:

1. Activate the Text mode. The Set Font button appears in the Side-bar.
2. Use the mouse to darken the text you want to change.
3. Click the Set Font button in the Side-bar, as shown in Figure 5.8. The Font dialog box appears. It looks as it does in Paragraph mode, except that its title appears as

   FONT SETTING FOR SELECTED TEXT

4. Change the settings as necessary. Then give the OK by pressing Return or clicking the mouse.

Ventura marks the spot where the new font takes effect (before the y in *you*) with an attribute setting that stores the name of the typeface and the size of the font. We'll call such an initializing mark a *beginning*

Face	Size	Style
Swiss	6	Normal
Swiss	8	Normal
Swiss	10	Normal, **Bold,** *Normal Italic*
Swiss	12	Normal, **Bold**, *Normal Italic*
Swiss	**14**	**Bold**
Swiss	**18**	**Bold**
Swiss	**24**	**Bold**
Dutch	8	Normal
Dutch	10	Normal, **Bold,** *Normal Italic*
Dutch	12	Normal, **Bold,** *Normal Italic*
Dutch	**14**	**Bold**
Dutch	**18**	**Bold**
Dutch	**24**	**Bold**
Σψμβολ (Symbol)	10	Νορμαλ (Normal)
Courier	12	Normal

Figure 5.6: Sample Typefaces on the HP LaserJet

attribute setting. There's also an indicator where the text returns to normal. We'll call this code an *ending attribute setting*.

Even though you cannot see attribute settings on the screen, you can affect them (for instance, by cutting and pasting them) just as you can regular text. Therefore, you must be careful when you edit. Inadvertently removing an attribute setting will usually affect the text format.

For instance, should you delete an ending attribute setting, Ventura would have no flag to tell it where the text should return to normal, and the nonstandard font would continue past the intended ending spot. Note, however, that Ventura will allow an unusual effect to continue only to the end of the paragraph. Thus, a Paragraph End symbol (¶) acts as an automatic ending attribute setting.

If the attribute settings are invisible, how can you watch out for them? The answer is by looking in the Current box at the bottom of

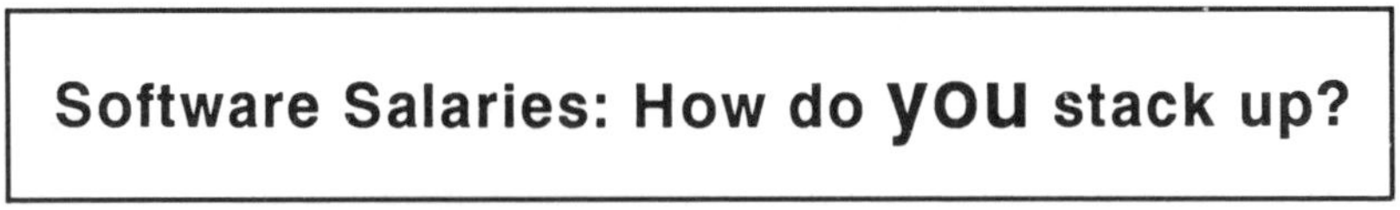

Software Salaries: How do **you** **stack up?**

Figure 5.7: Font Changes Within a Paragraph

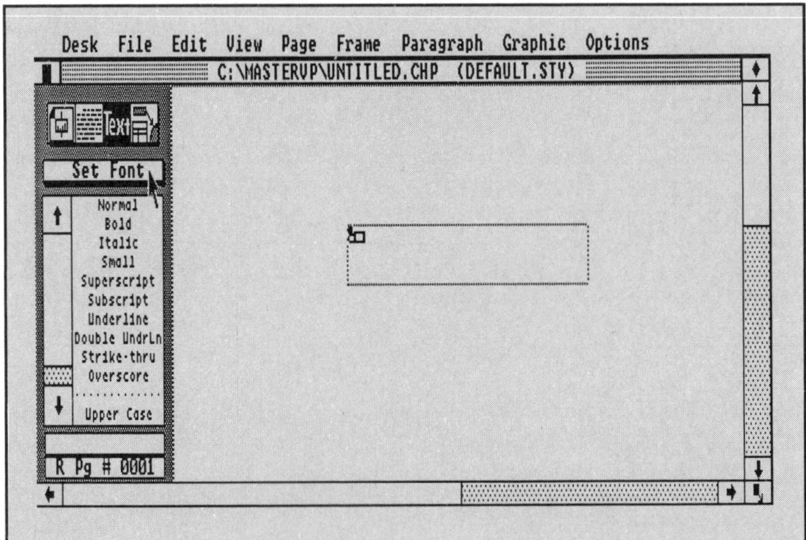

Figure 5.8: Clicking the Set Font Button

the Side-bar. In Text mode, it indicates the *current character*, the character that is to the immediate right of the blinking keyboard cursor in the working area. The Current box is often blank; nothing appears in it when the current character is a standard visible one, such as a letter of the alphabet or a number. (You don't need the box because you can see the character on the screen.)

If the character is an attribute setting code, however, the Current box will read

Attr. Setting

Obviously, this designation does not tell you which attribute setting is in place, but it's still quite useful. Usually you can tell the nature of the attribute by simply looking at the text that appears in the working area. In our example, for instance, it's obvious that there is a change in font size for the word *you*.

You can also check attributes by selecting the text in question and clicking the Set Font button. The Font dialog box thus displayed will show the current settings for the selected text. To leave the settings as they are, simply click Cancel.

Although attribute settings occupy a place in the text, they have no width on the screen. Thus, as you move the keyboard cursor across an attribute setting, the cursor will not move on the screen. However, the Current box will change to reflect the presence of these nondimensional codes.

Let's say, for instance, that you use the → key to move the keyboard cursor across the sample headline

How do you stack up?

As you approach *you*, set in a nonstandard font, the cursor passes over the space preceding that word. When it does, the beginning attribute setting is just to the right of the cursor, and the words

Attr. setting

appear in the Current box.

Pressing the Del key at that point would delete the setting, and the *you* would revert to normal type. If, however, you press the → key again at this point (instead of the Del key), the cursor moves past the setting. The *y* in *you* becomes the current character. As *y* is a standard character, nothing shows in the Current box. Pressing Del at this point deletes the *y*. Pressing Backspace deletes the invisible attribute setting.

Attribute settings may indicate where other text formats, such as italics and boldface, begin and end. We've seen how you can set font faces and sizes with either attribute settings or paragraph tags. You can use either approach to set italics and boldface, too.

ITALICS, BOLDFACE, AND SMALL

To begin our examination of italics and boldface, let's consider the Font dialog box again. In the Style category, you have a choice of Light, Normal, and Bold. You can also choose Italic versions of these three. Again, the styles you can use for a given font will vary; ghosting indicates those that are unavailable due to your printer or printing software. In Figure 5.4, Light, Light-Italic, and Bold-Italic versions of the indicated font are not available.

You can set italics and boldface in three ways. First, using the Paragraph mode, you can select a sample paragraph, pull down the Paragraph menu and click Font. This displays the Font dialog box. Italic and bold settings you implement in this way affect all similarly tagged paragraphs in the chapter you're working on, as well as in all other chapters using the same style sheet.

The second way to set italics and boldface is to activate the Text mode, use the mouse to darken your selected text, and click the Set Font button on the Side-bar. This also displays the Font dialog box, but only the selected text will change to italics or boldface. Attribute settings mark the beginning and ending points.

The third method of assigning boldface and italics also uses the Text mode and selected text. However, instead of displaying a dialog box, you use the Assignment list to apply formatting. This method is a little quicker to use. As with the second method, the resulting formats are local in nature, and attribute settings mark the beginning and ending points. The steps for assigning these text attributes are similar to those used for setting attributes with the Set Font button,

Using Italics

Use italics for the titles of books, newspapers, periodicals, plays, motion pictures, musical compositions, and works of art. Also use italics for the names of boats and trains. Use quotes rather than italics to indicate short stories, short poems, and sections of a book. For example:

> Consult Chapter 10, "Tables, Columns, and Boxes" in *Mastering Microsoft Word.*

Italicize foreign words but not foreign words that have been accepted into the English language. Consult a dictionary if you're unsure about a word's status in this regard.

Italicize words, letters, and numbers referred to as such (for example, the word *the*). Italicize technical terms when you introduce them. This especially holds true when you follow the term with its definition.

Although italics can be used effectively to attract the reader's attention, use them sparingly in this manner. Generally, only a few words at a time should be italicized and never as much as an entire passage. Since this use of italics is for providing emphasis, overdoing their use defeats the purpose.

except that you select them from the Assignment list rather than by displaying the Font dialog box. Here are the steps to follow:

1. Be sure that the Text mode is active.
2. Use the mouse to darken the text that you select for a special attribute.
3. Click the appropriate attribute name on the Assignment list, such as Bold or Italic.

Besides italics and boldface, you can set other formats with the Assignment list. For instance, you can quickly reduce the size of the font with the Assignment list. The Small assignment reduces font size from that specified by the tag to the next available size. (Custom settings are reduced by two points.) This feature is useful, for instance, in creating small caps. Select the text, change it to uppercase (as we'll see shortly) and click Small.

If you later change the size of the tag's font, text formatted with the Small text attribute will adjust to the next size smaller than that of the tag's new font size. Note that if you use the Set Font button to display the settings for text that you've formatted in this manner, you won't see the change reflected in the dialog box, which will still indicate the original size of font. Bold and Italic settings will be indicated correctly, however, and you may use the dialog box in Text mode to change them, even if you set them originally with the Assignment list.

You can use the Normal feature on the Assignment list to return selected text to the settings specified with the paragraph tag. (Simply deleting attribute setting codes can have the same effect.)

In the next few sections, we'll discuss the remaining text attributes that appear on the Text mode's Assignment list and/or in the Font dialog box. Note that not all settings in the Font dialog box are conveniently located on the Assignment list. For instance, the Color setting, which we'll study next, is not.

COLOR AND FONTS

If your printer is capable of printing in color, the Color category of the Font dialog box allows you to utilize that capability. However, you can also use a regular printer to create originals for conventional color duplication, such as offset printing. If you have a color printer, be careful if you use it to create an original for color duplication. Check with a printing professional for the best way to prepare color text for printing at a print shop. It's usually best to create multiple versions of the original in black and white, each one separating out various segments of the text according to the color that will be used. This printing technique is called *color separation*. The print shop runs the copies through the printer several times, once for each color. Each run uses a different version of the original.

You can perform color separation automatically for often-used style sheets. You do this by creating separate versions of your style sheet for each color you plan to use. For instance, if you want a headline in blue, create a new BLUE.STY style sheet that's a duplicate of the style sheet you're using for your newsletter. Then, change all tags to the White color setting *except* the Headline tag, which you set for black. When you apply this style sheet to your newsletter and print, no text other than that tagged as Headline will appear, due to the White settings. The print shop can use the resulting printout to create the blue separation. Repeat the process for each color involved.

In Chapter 13, you'll see how you can use the White setting to create reverse type and other effects.

SUPERSCRIPT AND SUBSCRIPT

The last two settings in the Font dialog box, Shift and Kern, will always ghost when you use the Paragraph mode to invoke the dialog box. They can be set only in the Text mode.

The term *Shift* refers to the position of the text relative to the normal position, above or below the imaginary line on which the text sits. This line is called the *baseline*. *Shift-up,* also called *superscript,* is used to raise text above the baseline, as in $E = mc^2$. *Shift-down,* also called *subscript,* is used to lower text below the baseline, as in H_2O. Notice that with the Font dialog box you can also set the amount you wish the selected characters to be shifted up or down.

As with other dialog boxes, you can change the system of measurement that Ventura uses to measure the amount of the shift. Just point the mouse arrow at the measurement name that's showing, such as inches, and click. You can use centimeters, picas, or points. Any existing measurements are converted to the newly selected system automatically.

The reason why Ventura won't allow you to set the Shift feature in the Paragraph mode is that formats that you set with paragraph tags affect the entire tagged paragraph. Because Shift alters the placement of one piece of text relative to another on the same line, it would be meaningless to specify Shift for an entire paragraph.

UNDERLINE, OVERSCORE, AND STRIKE-THRU

Underline, Overscore, Double Underline (UndrLn) and Strike-thru are text attributes that appear only on the Assignment list. You cannot use the Font dialog box in either the Paragraph mode or the Text mode to assign these attributes.

Underline is self-explanatory: you use this setting to underline the text that you've selected. You might not use it much in desktop publishing because underline is usually a substitute for italics on a typewriter or word processor. With Ventura, italics are easily available.

If you are engaging in accounting applications, however, you will probably use Underline, as well as two other text attributes that are new with Version 1.1: Double Underline and Overscore. You can now underline subtotals, for instance. Overscore draws a line *above* selected text. You can overscore or double underline net amounts. You can also use underscore and overscore to create a division line in a scientific formula.

Strike-thru draws a straight line through the center of a line of text. Typically, the legal profession makes use of strike-thru when revising contracts and other documents to designate text that's being suggested for deletion.

As with the other attributes, you can undo these by using the Assignment list to set the text to Normal. Alternatively, you can simply delete the invisible attribute-setting codes. Place the keyboard cursor just to the right of the invisible setting code.

Attr. Setting

should show in the Current box in the Side-bar. Then press the Del key to delete the code.

UPPER CASE, CAPITALIZE, AND LOWER CASE

Upper Case, Capitalize, and Lower Case operate on each other in a manner somewhat different from the others. They are not available in a dialog box. They are grouped together below the dotted line on the bottom of the Text mode Assignment list. To see all three, you need to scroll the Assignment list. Click the shaded area to the left of the Assignment list to move it in one step. Figure 5.9 shows the Assignment list just after scrolling.

The same rules apply to setting these as apply to other text attributes. The Text mode must be active, and you must have text selected (darkened). Although these attributes may be assigned when typing text at the keyboard, they are especially easy to implement when text is already selected for other formatting purposes. In our sample headline, for instance, after changing the font size, you might decide that it would be best to change *you* to uppercase.

When you click Upper Case on the Assignment list, all lowercase letters in the selected area change to uppercase letters. The sample would then look like Figure 5.10.

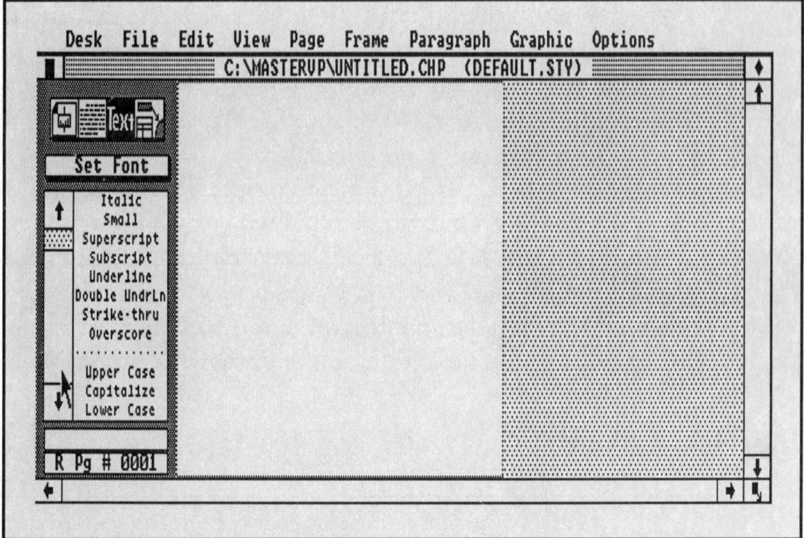

Figure 5.9: Upper Case, Capitalize, and Lower Case Attributes Revealed on the Assignment List

Software Salaries: How do YOU stack up?

Figure 5.10: Selected Word Changed to Uppercase

Choosing Capitalize will capitalize the initial letter of each word in the darkened area. You can use this effect to assist you in capitalizing titles and headings. Remember, though, that by convention, only the first word and other important words in a title are capitalized. Thus, you may need to adjust some letters individually when you use this feature. For instance, you shouldn't capitalize articles (a, an, the), conjunctions (and, but, or) or short prepositions (with, into, by) unless they occur at the beginning of the title.

Choosing Lower Case changes all the capital letters to lowercase letters. You can use this setting to undo text that you have capitalized in error. Be careful with it, too. It changes *all* characters to lowercase—even the first letter in a sentence if that letter appears in the darkened area.

The Normal setting at the top of the Assignment list will not reverse the effects of these items. Also, these features do not produce invisible attribute-setting codes before and after selected text, as the other items on the list do. Instead, they change the actual characters themselves.

This completes our examination of the items that appear on the Assignment list in the Text mode. We've seen how some choices appear only there, while others can be set in Text mode as well by clicking the Set Font button. In addition, we've looked at the Paragraph menu's Font dialog box. However, there are other paragraph commands below Font on the Paragraph pull-down menu. Each one contributes to the format that a tag provides to a paragraph. Let's examine some additional paragraph formatting commands by proceeding with the next item on the Paragraph menu, Alignment.

FLUSH LEFT AND RIGHT, CENTERING, AND JUSTIFICATION

Ventura groups a number of features together that control the way in which elements in a paragraph line up with one another. Generally, these features control where and how the edges of paragraphs appear. Chief among these features are justification (for text that's flush at the edges), centering, and automatic indenting of the first line in each paragraph. These features are collectively called *alignment*. Follow these steps to set them:

1. Activate the Paragraph mode.
2. Select a sample paragraph whose alignment you wish to change by clicking it with the mouse. Remember, all paragraphs similarly tagged will change as well.
3. Pull down the Paragraph menu.
4. Click the Alignment command. You'll see the Alignment dialog box, as shown in Figure 5.11.

The first category in the Alignment dialog box is Alignment.

ALIGNING FLUSH LEFT OR RIGHT

Figure 5.12 shows how the first column of the newsletter would look with left, right, centered, and justified alignment. (To emphasize the

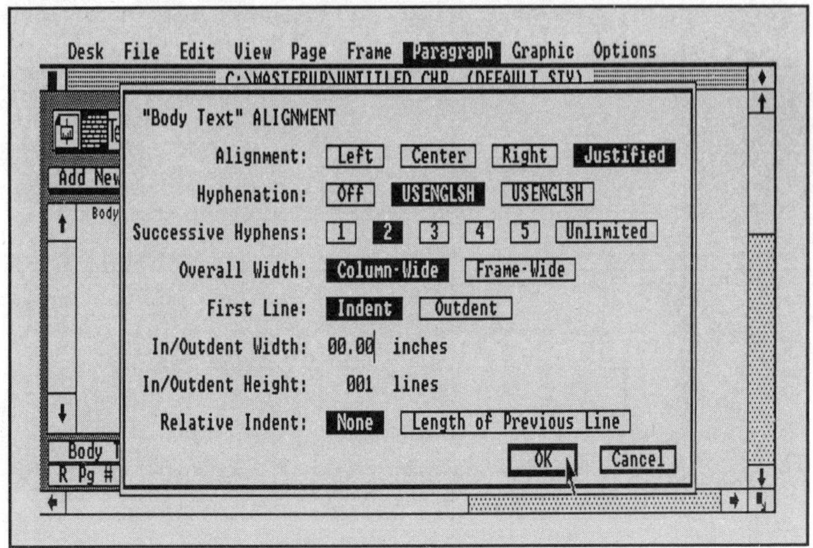

Figure 5.11: The Paragraph Menu's Alignment Dialog Box

Because of the dynamic growth of the software industry over the last decade, the demand for experienced, qualified programmers has greatly increased, thus leading to a spiraling of salaries.

But what causes managers to pay one programmer more than another? Does the type of organization, its size, or location make a difference? What career path or programming specialty leads to the most remuneration?

To answer these questions, Acme Magazine recently conducted its third annual compensation survey for software professionals. This newsletter article presents the results of this study and explores what the findings may mean to you.

Acme Magazine asked Joe Smith, a compensation consulting specialist for the software industry, to design and conduct the survey. Twenty-four positions, representing four programmer job families plus management, were included.

Data was collected for base pay, bonus and incentive payments, and whether nor not incumbents received stock options or other forms of equity.

Left Alignment

Because of the dynamic growth of the software industry over the last decade, the demand for experienced, qualified programmers has greatly increased, thus leading to a spiraling of salaries.

But what causes managers to pay one programmer more than another? Does the type of organization, its size, or location make a difference? What career path or programming specialty leads to the most remuneration?

To answer these questions, Acme Magazine recently conducted its third annual compensation survey for software professionals. This newsletter article presents the results of this study and explores what the findings may mean to you.

Acme Magazine asked Joe Smith, a compensation consulting specialist for the software industry, to design and conduct the survey. Twenty-four positions, representing four programmer job families plus management, were included.

Data was collected for base pay, bonus and incentive payments, and whether nor not incumbents received stock options or other forms of equity.

Center Alignment

Because of the dynamic growth of the software industry over the last decade, the demand for experienced, qualified programmers has greatly increased, thus leading to a spiraling of salaries.

But what causes managers to pay one programmer more than another? Does the type of organization, its size, or location make a difference? What career path or programming specialty leads to the most remuneration?

To answer these questions, Acme Magazine recently conducted its third annual compensation survey for software professionals. This newsletter article presents the results of this study and explores what the findings may mean to you.

Acme Magazine asked Joe Smith, a compensation consulting specialist for the software industry, to design and conduct the survey. Twenty-four positions, representing four programmer job families plus management, were included.

Data was collected for base pay, bonus and incentive payments, and whether nor not incumbents received stock options or other forms of equity.

Right Alignment

Because of the dynamic growth of the software industry over the last decade, the demand for experienced, qualified programmers has greatly increased, thus leading to a spiraling of salaries.

But what causes managers to pay one programmer more than another? Does the type of organization, its size, or location make a difference? What career path or programming specialty leads to the most remuneration?

To answer these questions, Acme Magazine recently conducted its third annual compensation survey for software professionals. This newsletter article presents the results of this study and explores what the findings may mean to you.

Acme Magazine asked Joe Smith, a compensation consulting specialist for the software industry, to design and conduct the survey. Twenty-four positions, representing four programmer job families plus management, were included.

Data was collected for base pay, bonus and incentive payments, and whether nor not incumbents received stock options or other forms of equity.

Justified Alignment

Figure 5.12: Four Types of Alignment

differences in alignment and make them more pronounced, we've eliminated the first-line indent, added spacing, and turned hyphenation off. We'll study each of these other paragraph features as we proceed in this chapter.)

Left alignment is rather like standard typewriter format. With left-aligned text, the left edge is flush; the right edge of the paragraph is *ragged*.

By setting alignment to Right, you get the opposite of left-aligned text; the right edge of the paragraph is flush and the left edge is ragged.

CENTERING TEXT

With center alignment, each line of text in the paragraph is centered. You can have the text centered within the column it appears in or, if the frame consists of more than one column, within the entire frame. We'll see how to do each of these shortly. Even when you have only one line to center, as is often the case with headings and titles, Ventura will center the one line. It considers the line to be a paragraph as long as it ends with a Return.

JUSTIFYING TEXT

Both left and right edges of justified text are flush. Ventura accomplishes justification by varying the amount of space that it inserts between letters and words (see Chapter 13).

Use justification judiciously; it may look snazzy at first glance, but the additional space can make text more difficult to read. It's a good idea to print some sample text before committing to justification to compare the sample with left-aligned text for readability.

HYPHENATION

With justified text, especially when working with narrow columns, it's standard practice to hyphenate. Otherwise, you may end up with *loose* lines—lines that contain big gaps as a result of the justification process. These gaps can bring about the undesirable appearance of "rivers" of white space that flow down the length of the page. Wide columns that are not justified may not need hyphenation. You may also wish to turn hyphenation off for paragraphs where it's not appropriate—in a table of contents or with headline text, for instance.

Version 1.1 of Ventura has numerous tools that provide the program with sophisticated hyphenation capabilities. Table 5.4 lists the tools that you can use to hyphenate text to exacting specifications.

SETTING THE HYPHENATION STATUS FOR A PARAGRAPH TAG

You may not need to concern yourself with many of the tools listed. For most applications, it is sufficient to set hyphenation on or off for a given paragraph tag. You can do this by following these steps:

1. Activate the Paragraph mode and select a sample paragraph, appropriately tagged.
2. Pull down the Paragraph menu and click Alignment. You'll see the dialog box shown in Figure 5.11.
3. In the Hyphenation grouping, click Off for no hyphenation. Click one of the USENGLSH buttons for Ventura's standard hyphenation.

To hyphenate text, Ventura uses computer *algorithms* (program procedures) to determine where to hyphenate. The standard algorithm Ventura uses to hyphenate according to American English usage is in the file USENGLSH.HY1. Ventura allows you to use a second algorithm for hyphenation as well. The second algorithm has an extension of HY2. However, when you install Ventura, USENGLSH is the only one available, so it appears on two of the Hyphenation buttons.

BILINGUAL HYPHENATION

If your documents contain text in a second language, you may wish to use a second hyphenation algorithm. If you do put a second

TOOL	LOCATION	DESCRIPTION	COMMENTS
USENGLISH.HY1	File on the Utilities disk (#11), copied into the VENTURA directory during installation	Standard hyphenation algorithm	This is the algorithm normally used to hyphenate.
SPANISH.HY2 FRENCH.HY2 ITALIAN.HY2 UKENGLSH.HY2 USENGLS2.HY2	Files on the Utilities disk (#11)	Second hyphenation algorithm	Copy one (and only one) of these into the VENTURA directory if you wish to have it available in addition to the standard algorithm.
Ctrl-hyphen	Keyboard	Discretionary hyphen	Type Ctrl-hyphen to add a hyphen to one particular word only. Ventura will not print the hyphen if subsequent editing causes it to fall within a line (rather than at the end).
Hyphen key	Keyboard	Standard hyphen	Avoid typing a standard hyphen in your documents except for words that should always be hyphenated, whether at the end of a line or within it.

Table 5.4: Tools Used for Hyphenating Text

TOOL	LOCATION	DESCRIPTION	COMMENTS
Hyphenation setting	Paragraph menu's Alignment dialog box	Off, or one of two algorithms	Click this setting off if you don't want hyphenation for paragraphs formatted with the selected tag. Click one of the other boxes if you want hyphenation performed using the indicated algorithm.
Successive Hyphens setting	Paragraph menu's Alignment dialog box	1 to 5 or Unlimited	Use this setting to limit the number of lines following one another that may be hyphenated.
HYPHEXPT.DIC	File on the Examples disk (#2), copied into the VENTURA directory during installation	Hyphenation Exception dictionary	This file contains a listing of hyphenated words that are exceptions to the algorithm rules. The listings override the algorithm on words for which the algorithm does not operate properly.
HYPHUSER.DIC	File on the Examples disk(#2), copied into the VENTURA directory during installation	Hyphenation User dictionary	Use this file to enter your own hyphenated words in ASCII. For a word you never want hyphenated, enter the word without a hyphen. The listings override both the algorithm and the Hyphenation Exception dictionary.

Table 5.4: Tools Used for Hyphenating Text (continued)

hyphenation algorithm into operation, the third Hyphenation button will show its name, such as SPANISH, as shown in Figure 5.13. Once an algorithm is operational and its name is showing on the button, clicking that button will cause the selected paragraphs to use that algorithm for hyphenation.

To place a second algorithm into operation, use the operating system to copy the algorithm to your hard disk. Follow these steps to do this:

1. At the system prompt for your hard disk, insert the Utilities disk (#11) into your floppy-disk drive.
2. Change to the VENTURA directory by typing

   cd \ventura

3. Type the word **copy**, a space, the letter **a**, a colon, and the name of the file as listed in Table 5.3. Thus, to copy the SPANISH.HY2 algorithm file, you'd enter

   copy a:spanish.hy2

You may have noticed that there is a second U.S. English file, USENGLS2.HY2. Although the original algorithm installed with

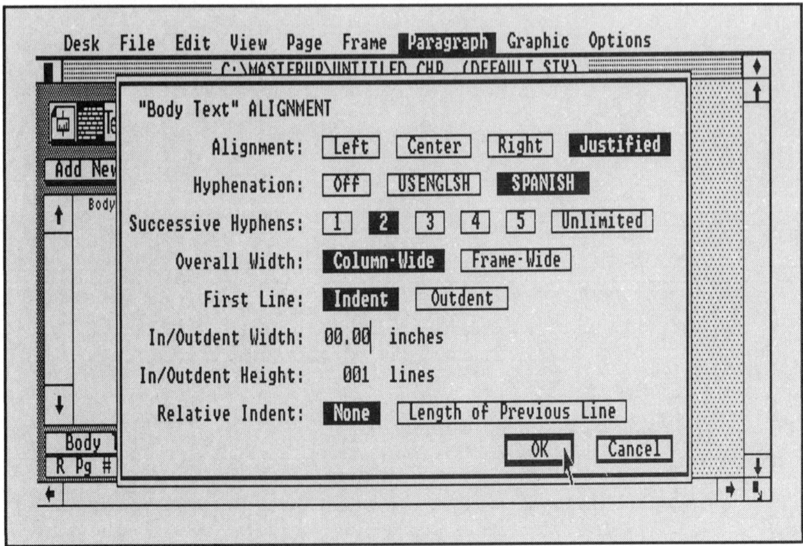

Figure 5.13: The Spanish Algorithm Available for Hyphenation

Ventura hyphenates words correctly, it is not as thorough as some people would like. It doesn't hyphenate some words at all, even when such hyphenation is permitted by standard usage. It does so to speed hyphenation. The algorithm seldom, if ever, hyphenates incorrectly and works fine with most applications. When documents have very narrow columns, however, insufficient hyphenation can cause unacceptable gaps in justified text (see Chapter 13).

The second American English algorithm, USENGLS2.HY2 is very thorough. It overlooks few opportunities for hyphenation, so it's better suited to use with narrow columns. However, it takes quite a bit longer to operate than the standard one, so only use it when truly necessary. Chiefly, the delay occurs when you are loading a chapter.

SPECIFYING THE NUMBER OF SUCCESSIVE HYPHENATIONS

Regardless of the algorithm you use, you can instruct Ventura to restrict the number of lines it hyphenates in a row. Just click a number (1 to 5) in the Successive Hyphens grouping. No more than 2 is ideal, but again the narrowness of the column is a key factor: the narrower the column, the more hyphenations you may need in order to avoid frequent gaps.

HYPHENATING INDIVIDUAL WORDS

You can also specify hyphenation in individual words that Ventura overlooks. The first line in the first example shown in Figure 5.14 is loose. This is because Ventura failed to hyphenate the word *keyboard* at

Correct unacceptably loose lines by using the keyboard to insert a discretionary hyphen.

Correct unacceptably loose lines by using the key-board to insert a discretionary hyphen.

Figure 5.14: Hyphenating a Word to Tighten the Previous Line

the beginning of the second line. As the second version of the sentence shows, hyphenating that word causes its first syllable to move to the preceding line, tightening the line. To tighten a given line, hyphenate the first word on the line following it, using one of the techniques we'll examine shortly.

Showing Loose Lines

Ventura can assist you in drawing your attention to such loose lines. Just pull down the Options menu and click Show Loose Lines. Loose lines will appear darkened, in reverse video.

IMPORTANT

It's a good idea to return this setting to normal (by pulling down the Options menu and clicking Hide Loose Lines) as soon as you're done. Loose lines that are shown look just like selected text and can be very confusing if left showing.

Using Discretionary Hyphens

There are two ways that you can hyphenate words that Ventura overlooks, such as *keyboard* in the previous example. Which method you use depends upon how often you expect to encounter a given word.

First, you can insert a *discretionary hyphen* into the overlooked word directly. You do this in Text mode by placing the text cursor at the point in the word where you want the hyphen to go and typing Ctrl-hyphen. You use a discretionary hyphen when the overlooked word is one that you don't expect to use often. For instance, if your newsletters are about corporate mergers and you usually don't write articles about keyboards, you would probably use this method to hyphenate *keyboard*.

A standard hyphen, obtained by hitting the Hyphen key, is used only for *hyphenated compounds*. These are words that are always hyphenated, regardless of where they appear, such as double-cross, long-winded, and ill-fated. If later editing or electronic paste-up should cause a word hyphenated with a standard hyphen to move to the center of the line, the standard hyphen would still appear. Thus, if you used a standard hyphen to hyphenate *keyboard* in the example, and later changed the margins, you might end up printing something like

> by using the key-board to insert

Typing Ctrl-hyphen to insert a discretionary hyphen allows you to avoid such an occurrence. If a discretionary hyphen falls in the middle of a line like this, Ventura will not print it. The discretionary hyphen appears only when the word straddles two lines.

You can display a discretionary hyphen on the screen, even when it falls in the middle of a line, if you use the Options menu and select Show Tabs & Returns (or type Ctrl-T). On the screen, a discretionary hyphen is slightly heftier than a standard hyphen. It's important to realize, however, that even though you may display discretionary hyphens on the screen, those appearing midline won't show up in the printed version of the document. Choose Hide Tabs & Returns to make midline discretionary hyphens disappear from the screen.

As with attribute-setting codes, which we discussed earlier in this chapter, you can use the Current box in Text mode to detect the presence of an invisible discretionary hyphen. When such a hyphen is located to the right of the keyboard cursor, the words

> Discr. Hyphen

appear in the Current box. If desired, you can then delete the hyphen by pressing the Del key.

Using Hyphenation Dictionaries

There is another way you can have Ventura hyphenate a word that it would otherwise miss. You can add the word to the Hyphenation User dictionary. Such words will then be hyphenated as necessary only at the end of lines.

As mentioned, Ventura uses an algorithm as its chief means of determining where to hyphenate words. There are words, however, that do not adhere to the rules that the algorithm follows. To hyphenate these words properly, Ventura lists them in the Hyphenation

Exception dictionary, which is contained in the HYPHEXPT.DIC file. These listings are checked automatically when Hyphenation is on and take precedence over the algorithm.

In addition, Ventura also consults the Hyphenation User dictionary, located in the HYPHUSER.DIC file in the VENTURA directory. This dictionary takes precedence over both the algorithm and the entries in the HYPHEXPT.DIC file. You can add entries to this dictionary yourself. (Ventura has some as samples in the file already.) Just use your word processor in ASCII mode to open this file (see Chapter 12). Type in your entries with standard hyphens in place. Enter each word on a separate line with a hard return at the end of the line. Save the file in ASCII format.

Use the Hyphenation User dictionary for words that you expect to use frequently in your desktop publishing applications. Thus, if you compose newsletters about pianos all the time, you may want to make the word *keyboard* a part of the HYPHUSER.DIC file.

Be aware, however, that each word you add will slow down the hyphenation process, however slightly. The effects are cumulative, so only add a word if you expect Ventura to encounter it in documents you later create. If you don't expect that Ventura will encounter the word again, insert a discretionary hyphen in the word as it appears in the working area.

Keeping Individual Words from Being Hyphenated

There may be words that you do not ever want Ventura to hyphenate, such as proper names or regular words used as proper names. You can prevent Ventura from hyphenating a given word by using either a discretionary hyphen or the Hyphenation User dictionary. Again, the frequency with which you expect the program to encounter the word should be the factor that determines which method you use.

To use a discretionary hyphen for this purpose, type Ctrl-hyphen at the *beginning* of the word. This will keep Ventura from hyphenating the particular word, no matter where it falls on the line.

To enter such a word into the HYPHUSER.DIC file, type the entire word *without* any hyphens. Ventura will never hyphenate a word that you designate in this manner.

HEADLINES THAT STRETCH ACROSS COLUMNS

Let's continue with our examination of the Paragraph menu's Alignment dialog box. Following the Successive Hyphens grouping, notice that the Overall Width of a tag can be set for Column-Wide or Frame-Wide.

If the frame you are working with is set for only one column, the Overall Width setting has no effect. However, if you are working with multiple columns in a frame, you have a choice: you can have your text occupy the width of one of the columns or have it as wide as the entire frame. Figures 5.15 and 5.16 show how the same headline can fill one column or stretch across two columns to fill the frame. In this way, you can make a headline appear above as many columns as the frame holds without creating a special frame just for the headline.

If the frame-wide heading is the first paragraph in the frame, Ventura will handle the entire procedure automatically. You need do nothing more than make the setting. There may be times, however, when you want to place such a heading in the middle of a frame. This would be the case, for instance, with two articles that follow each

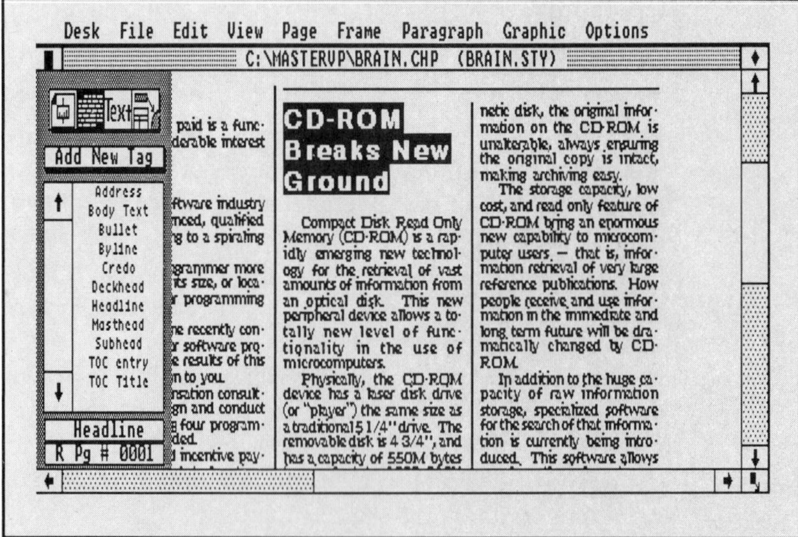

Figure 5.15: Column-Wide Heading

other, each with its own heading, or one article with a frame-wide subheading.

In Figure 5.17 the subheading

Theory of Operation

has a column-wide format. We've numbered the paragraphs in this article so you can easily follow along as we demonstrate. In Figure 5.18, we've given the same subheading a frame-wide format. Notice how the paragraphs rearrange themselves so that they still fall under the proper heading.

To make paragraphs fall correctly under frame-wide headings, *balance* the columns in that frame. Balancing columns makes the text end evenly for each column in the frame, as discussed in Chapter 3. To do that, activate the Frame mode, click the appropriate frame, and use the Frame menu's Sizing & Scaling command. For the Column Balance setting, click the On button. Failure to balance the columns could result in one of the following: large empty columns, as shown in Figure 5.19; text for the first heading appearing beneath the headline for the second article; or text on top of text, as shown in Figure 5.20.

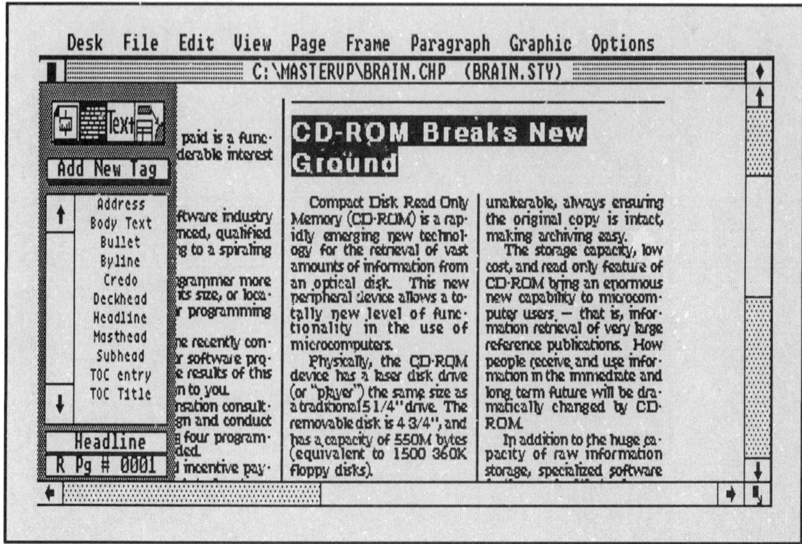

Figure 5.16: Frame-Wide Heading

CD-ROM Breaks New Ground

1) Compact Disk Read Only Memory (CD-ROM) is a rapidly emerging new technology for the retrieval of vast amounts of information from an optical disk. This new peripheral device allows a totally new level of functionality in the use of microcomputers.

2) Physically, the CD-ROM device has a laser disk drive (or "player") the same size as a traditional 5 1/4" drive. The removable disk is 4 3/4", and has a capacity of 550M bytes (equivalent to 1500 360K floppy disks).

Theory of Operation

3) Information stored on a CD-ROM can be loaded into memory (RAM), displayed and printed, as with other media. While that data in RAM may be altered and stored to a conventional magnetic disk, the original information on the CD-ROM is unalterable, always ensuring the original copy is intact, making archiving easy.

4) The storage capacity, low cost, and read only feature of CD-ROM bring an enormous new capability to microcomputer users – that is, information retrieval of very large reference publications. How people receive and use information in the immediate and long term future will be dramatically changed by CD-ROM.

5) In addition to the huge capacity of raw information storage, specialized software for the search of that information is currently being introduced. This software allows searching the information in areas, methods and speeds not previously feasible.

6) It now becomes possible to electronically publish reference material more economically than to print the same material in book form. That cost benefit, coupled with search and retrieval software, make an astonishing price/performance ratio.

Figure 5.17: Column-Wide Subheading

CD-ROM Breaks New Ground

1) Compact Disk Read Only Memory (CD-ROM) is a rapidly emerging new technology for the retrieval of vast amounts of information from an optical disk. This new peripheral device allows a totally new level of functionality in the use of microcomputers.

2) Physically, the CD-ROM device has a laser disk drive (or "player") the same size as a traditional 5 1/4" drive. The removable disk is 4 3/4", and has a capacity of 550M bytes (equivalent to 1500 360K floppy disks).

Theory of Operation

3) Information stored on a CD-ROM can be loaded into memory (RAM), displayed and printed, as with other media. While that data in RAM may be altered and stored to a conventional magnetic disk, the original information on the CD-ROM is unalterable, always ensuring the original copy is intact, making archiving easy.

4) The storage capacity, low cost, and read only feature of CD-ROM bring an enormous new capability to microcomputer users – that is, information retrieval of very large reference publications. How people receive and use information in the immediate and long term future will be dramatically changed by CD-ROM.

5) In addition to the huge capacity of raw information storage, specialized software for the search of that information is currently being introduced. This software allows searching the information in areas, methods and speeds not previously feasible.

6) It now becomes possible to electronically publish reference material more economically than to print the same material in book form. That cost benefit, coupled with search and retrieval software, make an astonishing price/performance ratio.

Figure 5.18: Frame-Wide Subheading

CD-ROM Breaks New Ground

1) Compact Disk Read Only Memory (CD-ROM) is a rapidly emerging new technology for the retrieval of vast amounts of information from an optical disk. This new peripheral device allows a totally new level of functionality in the use of microcomputers.

2) Physically, the CD-ROM device has a laser disk drive (or "player") the same size as a traditional 5 1/4" drive. The removable disk is 4 3/4", and has a capacity of 550M bytes (equivalent to 1500 360K floppy disks).

Theory of Operation

3) Information stored on a CD-ROM can be loaded into memory (RAM), displayed and printed, as with other media. While that data in RAM may be altered and stored to a conventional magnetic disk, the original information on the CD-ROM is unalterable, always ensuring the original copy is intact, making archiving easy.

4) The storage capacity, low cost, and read only feature of CD-ROM bring an enormous new capability to microcomputer users – that is, information retrieval of very large reference publications. How people receive and use information in the immediate and long term future will be dramatically changed by CD-ROM.

5) In addition to the huge capacity of raw information storage, specialized software for the search of that information is currently being introduced. This software allows searching the information in areas, methods and speeds not previously feasible.

6) It now becomes possible to electronically publish reference material more economically than to print the same material in book form. That cost benefit, coupled with search and retrieval software, make an astonishing price/performance ratio.

Figure 5.19: Empty Columns Due To Columns Not Being Balanced

CD-ROM Breaks New Ground

1) Compact Disk Read Only Memory (CD-ROM) is a rapidly emerging new technology for the retrieval of vast amounts of information from an optical disk. This new peripheral device allows a totally new level of functionality in the use of microcomputers.

2) Physically, the CD-ROM device has a laser disk drive (or "player") the same size as a traditional 5-1/4" drive. The removable disk is 4-3/4", and has a capacity of 550M bytes (equivalent to 1500 360K floppy disks).

3) Information stored on a CD-ROM can be loaded into memory (RAM), displayed and printed, as with other media. While that data in RAM may be altered and stored to a conventional magnetic disk, the original information on the CD-ROM is unalterable, always ensuring the original copy is intact, making archiving easy.

Theory of Operation

4) The storage capacity, low cost, and read only features of CD-ROM bring an enormous new capability to microcomputer users — that is information retrieval of very large reference publications. How people receive and use information in the immediate and long term future will be dramatically changed by CD-ROM.

5) In addition to the huge capacity of raw information storage, specialized software for the search of that information is currently being introduced. This software allows searching the information in areas, methods and speed not previously feasible.

6) It now becomes possible to electronically publish reference material more economically than to print the same material in book form. That cost benefit, coupled with search and retrieval software, make an astonishing price/performance ratio.

Figure 5.20: Text on Top of Text Due To Columns Not Being Balanced

INDENTING AND OUTDENTING THE FIRST LINES OF PARAGRAPHS

The last four settings in the Paragraph menu's Alignment dialog box (see Figure 5.13) regulate indenting of the first lines of all paragraphs that are tagged alike. Figure 5.21 shows two examples of indents as well as an example of an outdent.

This paragraph has a first-line indent of 1/2 inch. Notice how the first line sinks into the main body of text. To achieve this effect, use the Paragraph menu's Alignment command. Set First Line to Indent. For In/Outdent Width, specify .5 inches.

This paragraph has the first three lines indented 1/2 inch. Notice how the first three lines sink into the main body of text. To achieve this effect, use the Paragraph menu's Alignment command. Set First Line to Indent. For In/Outdent Width, specify .5 inches. For In/Outdent Height, specify 3 lines.

This paragraph has a first-line outdent of 1/2 inch. Notice how the first line protrudes from the main body of text. To achieve this effect, use the Paragraph menu's Alignment command. Set First Line to Outdent. For In/Outdent Width, specify .5 inches.

Figure 5.21: Indenting and Outdenting the First Lines of a Paragraph

As the First Line category in the dialog box and the examples indicate, you can choose between Indent and Outdent. A *first-line outdent* creates what is sometimes called a *hanging paragraph*. In this format, the first line of a paragraph protrudes beyond the main body of the paragraph, into the frame's left margin space.

To set an indent or outdent for a paragraph, proceed as follows:

1. Activate Paragraph mode and click a paragraph with the tag you wish to change.
2. Pull down the Paragraph menu and click Alignment.
3. In the Alignment dialog box, set First Line to Indent or Outdent as appropriate.
4. Enter a value for In/Outdent Width. (If you wish, you can change the system of measurement by clicking the unit name, initially inches.)
5. Move the keyboard cursor (with Tab, ↓, or the mouse) to the In/Outdent Height field. Enter a value for the number of lines that should be affected.

IMPORTANT

When using outdents, you may need to increase the frame's left margin to accommodate all the text. To do that, activate the Frame mode and click the appropriate frame. Then pull down the Frame menu and click Margins & Columns. As an alternative, you can increase the paragraph's In From Left value. In Paragraph mode, select the paragraph with the outdent, then use the Paragraph menu's Spacing command and increase the In From Left value.

The last setting in the Alignment dialog box is Relative Indent. This setting is used in conjunction with settings in other dialog boxes that you gain access to by way of the Paragraph menu. We'll study these later in this chapter (see "Multitag Paragraphs").

We've seen how the Paragraph menu's Alignment box controls the manner in which various aspects of a paragraph line up. Next, we'll see how to control the amount of blank space taken up by a paragraph as well as by similarly tagged paragraphs throughout the chapter.

LINE SPACING AND SET-IN PARAGRAPHS

The third item on the Paragraph pull-down menu is Spacing. This command controls the space between the lines of a paragraph, between paragraphs, and on either side of paragraphs. To set the spacing for a given paragraph tag, proceed as follows:

1. Activate the Paragraph mode and click a sample paragraph with the mouse.
2. Pull down the Paragraph menu and click Spacing. This displays the Spacing dialog box, shown in Figure 5.22.

VERTICAL PARAGRAPH SPACING

The four values at the top of the Spacing dialog box control a paragraph's vertical spacing, while the two values toward the bottom of the box control the horizontal spacing.

Use the Above and Below settings to add space above and below paragraphs. By placing a value in either of these fields, you guarantee at least that amount of space above or below the paragraph.

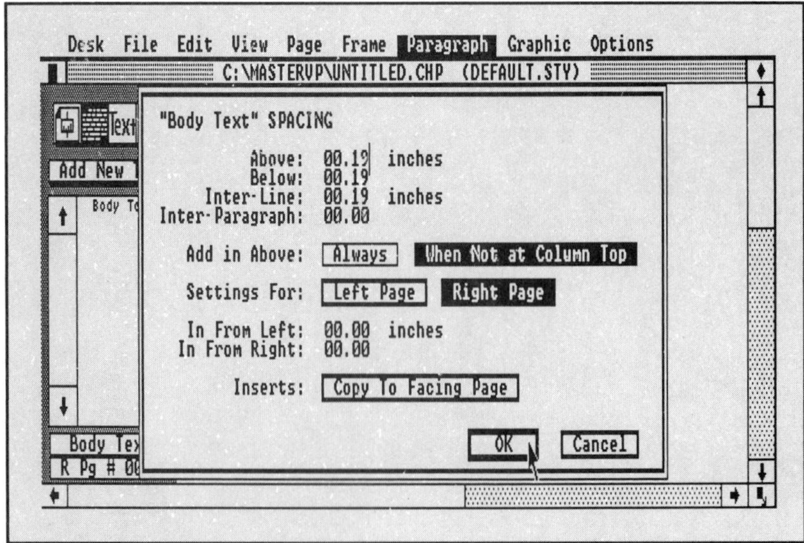

Figure 5.22: The Paragraph Menu's Spacing Dialog Box

The Inter-Line setting governs the amount of space between the lines. Typographers refer to this spacing as *leading*. The term is derived from lead slugs that fill the space between lines of manually set type. In Ventura, however, interline spacing is the distance from one spot on a line, say the top of a certain letter, to the top of the same letter on the next line. Ventura recommends an interline spacing of 1.2 times the size of the type that composes the paragraph. However, this may be a bit much by others' standards especially with larger fonts. Don't be afraid to experiment until you find spacing that makes the text seem most readable to you. We'll discuss spacing and Ventura's other typographic capabilities in greater detail in Chapter 13.

The Inter-Paragraph setting adds additional space between paragraphs with the same tag that follow one another. You can increase or decrease these values in order to fit the necessary amount of text on a page.

The Add in Above setting refers to the value you entered for the Above setting. Click Always when you want the Above value to apply in every situation. When Not at Column Top instructs Ventura not to add the Above value when a paragraph so tagged begins at the top of a column. Use this setting when you find that an inordinate amount of space occurs at the top of a column. (We'll see an example of this in Chapter 13.)

SETTING PARAGRAPHS IN FROM BOTH MARGINS

The In From Left and In From Right settings deal with horizontal spacing. You use them to set paragraphs further in from the margins. For instance, you may wish to create a tag for extended quotations that would cause the edges of paragraphs so tagged to be set in from those of regular text; that is, the paragraph will have wider margins than usual. These settings add the additional margin to any margin already set for the frame (with the Frame menu's Margins & Columns command).

The Settings For category, which has buttons for Left Page and Right Page, applies *only* to these horizontal measurements (In From Left and In From Right), not to other items in this dialog box. Clicking one button or the other allows you to see and set those measurements. If you adjust these settings for one page and then decide that you want the same settings for the opposite page, click Copy To Facing Page. Ventura registers the same horizontal values for the facing page. However, there will be no immediate feedback to let you know the transfer has occurred. You can make sure the values are registered by clicking the button for the opposite page.

CONTROLLING THE BREAKUP OF TEXT

The Paragraph menu's Breaks command displays a dialog box that deals with some sophisticated typographical concepts. Figure 5.23 shows the Breaks dialog box. The settings displayed in the figure are the default ones; if ever your paragraph breaks go awry, you can return to these settings and try again.

The categories in this dialog box are listed in order of priority. In other words, the effect each setting has on a paragraph so tagged nullifies the effect of any settings that follow.

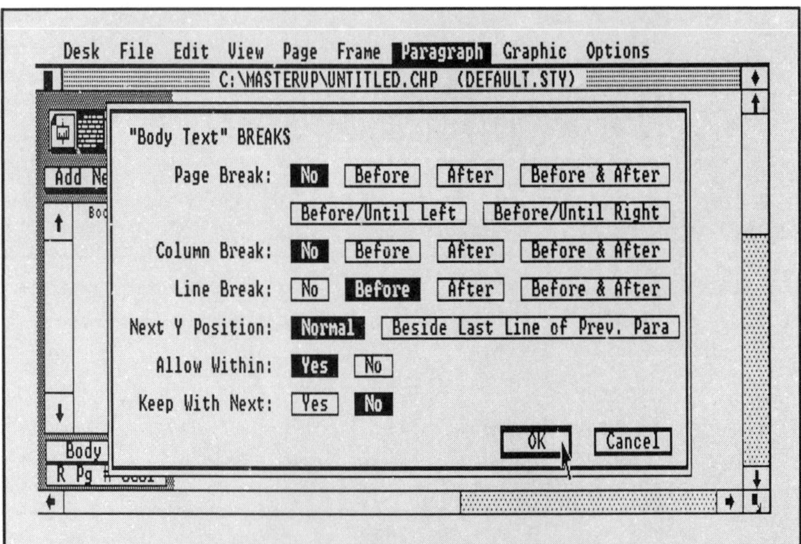

Figure 5.23: The Paragraph Menu's Breaks Dialog Box

Ventura describes a *break* as an "interruption in the flow of text at a paragraph boundary." That is, when a paragraph ends, you decide where the next paragraph resumes. It can start on the next page, at the top of the next column, or on the next line.

For instance, when a standard paragraph ends, you indicate this with a paragraph Return, and the text for the new paragraph begins on the next line. This arrangement constitutes a *line break*.

BREAKING FOR PAGES

You can, however, cause a tag to create a page break. You might use such tags on titles of sections that should always begin on a new page. When you set Page Break to Before, Ventura will start the tagged text on a new page. It will cause a page break to occur *before* the tagged paragraph. (It won't matter if there is blank space at the bottom of the previous page.)

If you set Page Break to After, the program will start the new page *after* a paragraph with such a tag. You might use this setting, for instance, for the final paragraph of the section. This setup is not usually used.

You can also have the page break before *and* after the tagged paragraph. You could use this arrangement for a table that you want on a separate page, even though it's embedded in the middle of text. Be aware, though, that the page before might have a large blank area at the bottom.

If it's important that a new section begin on a left page, click Before/Until Left. If the text for the previous section ends in the middle of a left page, Ventura will allow the bottom of that page to be blank. It will then skip the next (right) page, leaving it completely blank. The new section would begin on the following (left) page. Thus, it would leave 1½ blank pages before starting the new section. Similarly, you can click Before/Until Right if you want the new section to always begin on a right page.

BREAKING FOR COLUMNS

The Column Break category is similar in operation to Page Break. The Before setting, which is commonly used for column headings, causes Ventura to place that heading in a new column along with the text that follows it. After and Before & After work the same way as their page break counterparts, but with respect to columns.

MULTITAG PARAGRAPHS

Earlier, we examined how to use text attributes in order to change fonts and other formatting attributes within a paragraph. Using text attributes works fine for instances where a localized change is called for, within a specific paragraph only. Suppose, however, you have a format you need to apply repeatedly and identically within several paragraphs. Magazine interviews, for instance, will often precede a series of quotes with the interviewee's name set in boldface. Using the text attributes to achieve this effect, you'd run the risk of accidentally applying the wrong effect to a few of the paragraphs and ending up with a hodgepodge. By creating multitag paragraphs with the Breaks dialog box, you can be sure that effects are applied consistently, and you can later change them as a group, rather than one by one.

The Line Break setting for a given tag is usually set to Before. This causes a new paragraph to start on a new line. If, however, you set it to No, the new paragraph would begin on the same line as the paragraph before it. When used in combination with other settings in this dialog box, the result is a paragraph that actually contains more than one tag. You may wish to use such multitag paragraphs to accommodate explanatory text that begins several paragraphs in succession. Such material is often called a *lead-in*.

Figure 5.24 shows an example of a lead-in. The example is from the sample chapter and style sheet &PREL-P1. The text

LOS ANGELES, CA, July 17 —

ends with a Return and is formatted with one tag (the Dateline tag), while the rest of the paragraph is formatted with another (the Firstpar tag).

LOS ANGELES, CA, July 17 – XYZ Corp., the leading manufacturer of widgets for the automated widget supply industry, announced that it has shipped its 1000th Model 123-X enhanced widget. The customer is ABC Inc. of Livonia Hills, MI.

Figure 5.24: A Multitag Paragraph

To produce multitag paragraphs, text in the paragraph must meet the following conditions:

1. The first tag in the paragraph must not have a line break set to occur after it. Thus, Line Break must not be set for After or Before & After.
2. The second tag in the paragraph must not have a line break set to occur before it. Also, the Next Y Position should be set to Beside Last Line of Prev. Para (we'll discuss this setting presently).
3. The second tag must also have a *relative indent*. To set this, pull down the Paragraph menu and choose Alignment. For Relative Indent, click the Length of Previous Line button. This will cause the first line with the second tag to be indented the same amount as the length of the lead-in, which means the text of the second tag will follow on the heels of the text for the first.
4. If a third tag follows in the same paragraph, the second tag must not have a line break after it. The third tag must meet the same conditions as for the second tag.

The *Y position* is the distance for the tagged text down from the top of the previous paragraph. Setting it to Beside Last Line of Prev. Para will cause text with the second tag to begin on the same line as the end of the text with the first tag. We'll study the Y position more when we work with tables in Chapter 9.

IMPORTANT

Do not use multitag paragraphs in conjunction with justified text (as set with the Paragraph menu's Alignment command). Ventura will justify the second-tagged text, but not the first (the lead-in text). Thus, the first line of the second tag may well be unacceptably loose, while the lead-in text on the same line will be tight. For best results, use left-aligned text instead.

KEEPING PARAGRAPHS TOGETHER

The final two break settings regulate the cohesion of paragraphs. Ventura consults these settings as it is running out of room at the bottom of a page or a column.

When Allow Within is set for Yes, as it usually is, Ventura will fill as much of the page as possible before starting to fill the next page. It's OK if only a part of one paragraph ends up at the bottom of the first page, and the paragraph continues on the next page. In other words, the setting instructs the program to allow a break to occur within the paragraph.

There may be times, however, when you want Ventura to keep entire paragraphs on the same page. To guarantee that this is the case, regardless of editing, set Allow Within to No. If the paragraph will not fit at the bottom of one page in its entirety, the entire paragraph will go to the top of the next page, leaving some blank space at the bottom of the first page. For example, you'd want to keep a table all on the same page.

There are some paragraphs, such as headings, that you'll want to keep with the paragraph that follows them. Otherwise, for instance, you could end up with a heading by itself at the bottom of a page. To keep this from occurring, set Keep With Next for the heading's tag to Yes.

There are other tasks that you'll use tags to accomplish. In Chapter 8, you'll see how to draw lines that are associated with paragraphs. In Chapter 9, you'll learn how you can set tabs to create tables. For now, though, we need to consider how to manipulate the tags themselves.

ADDING, RENAMING, AND REMOVING TAGS

As you work with Ventura, you'll undoubtedly find that you want to customize the list of tags in your style sheets. To do that, Ventura allows you to add, rename, and remove tags. The procedures for these three operations are similar.

ADDING TAGS

To add a tag, you use a copy of an existing tag as the basis for a new tag. You can then format the new copy. To create a new tag, follow these steps:

1. Activate the Paragraph mode.

2. Click a paragraph for which you want the new tag. If you have no such paragraph, select any paragraph.
3. Click the Add New Tag button in the Side-bar. The Add New Tag dialog box appears, as shown in Figure 5.25.
4. Make up a name for the new tag and enter it into the Tag Name to Add field.
5. The Tag Name to Copy From setting is initially the same as the original tag of the selected paragraph. You can change it if you want Ventura to copy the formatting from another tag. To do that, move to the field (using the Tab key, the ↓ key, or the mouse), press Esc to clear the field, and enter a different tag's name.
6. Give the OK by pressing Return or clicking the mouse. The new tag name is added to the Assignment list.
7. Change the formatting for the new tag using the tools we've covered in this chapter.

Remember that names on the Assignment list appear in alphabetical order. Thus, to keep similar tags together, name them beginning

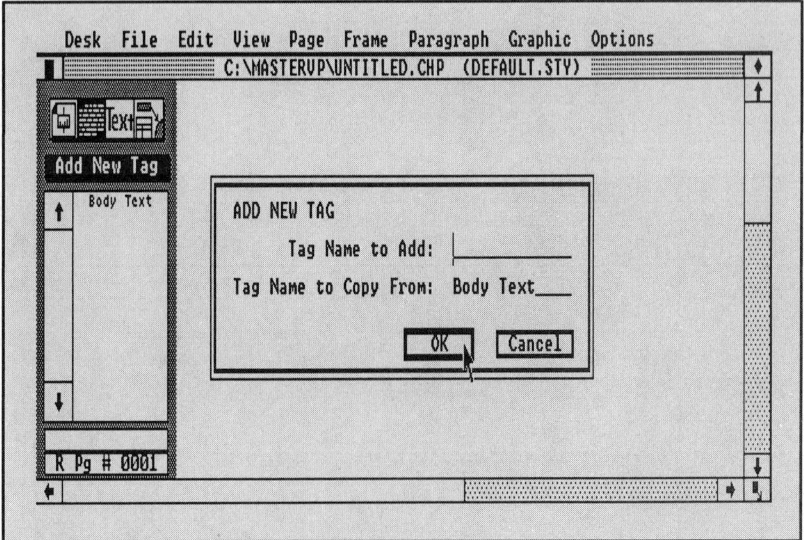

Figure 5.25: The Add New Tag Dialog Box

with the same general name rather than a specific one. Thus, names such as Column #1, Column #2, and Column #3 are better than First Column, Second Column, and Third Column.

RENAMING TAGS

If you find that the names of your tags are unorganized or inappropriate, you can easily rename them:

1. Activate Paragraph mode and select a paragraph tagged with the name you wish to change. If there's no such paragraph, any paragraph will do.
2. Pull down the Paragraph menu and click Rename Tag. The Rename Tag dialog box appears, as shown in Figure 5.26.
3. The Old Tag Name field in this dialog box initially displays the name of the tagged paragraph. If you want to change the name of some tag other than this one, erase the displayed name by pressing the Esc key and enter the other tag's name.
4. Enter a new name in the New Tag Name field and give the OK.

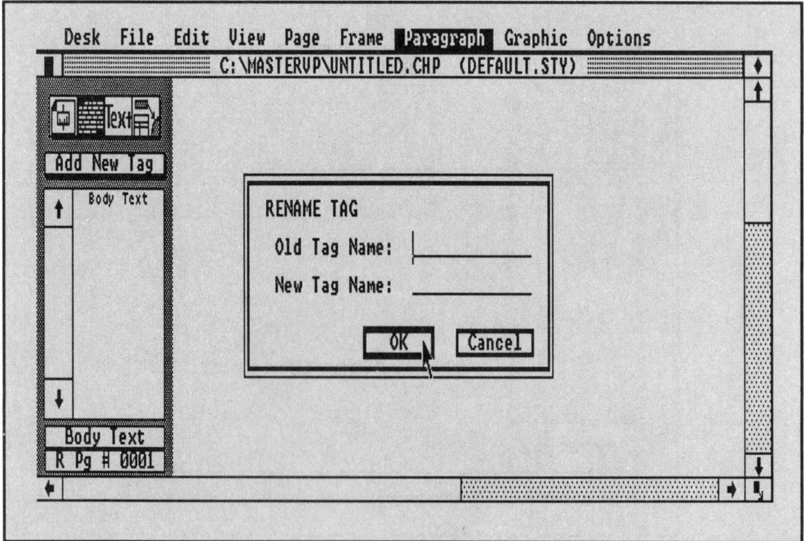

Figure 5.26: The Rename Tag Dialog Box

REMOVING TAGS

If you're not using a particular tag, it's wise to remove it from the Assignment list. Having fewer tags makes it easier to locate them, because you'll do less scrolling. In addition, fewer tags may improve the performance of the program and allow you to create larger chapters, because every tag uses memory even if you don't use the tag. Here's how to remove a tag:

1. Activate the Paragraph mode and select a paragraph tagged with the tag you wish to remove. If none of your paragraphs are tagged with the soon-to-be-discarded tag, click any paragraph.
2. Pull down the Paragraph menu and click Remove Tag. The Remove Tag dialog box, shown in Figure 5.27, appears.
3. The name indicated for Tag Name to Remove is initially the tag name of the selected paragraph. If you wish to remove the tag for a different kind of paragraph, press Esc and enter the appropriate name.

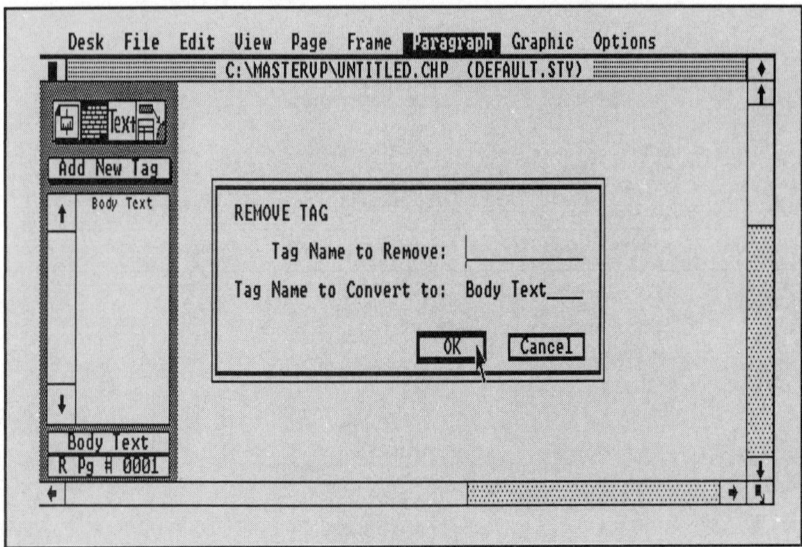

Figure 5.27: The Remove Tag Dialog Box

4. Tag Name to Convert to indicates how you want affected paragraphs to be retagged. The initial setting is Body Text, but you can change it if you wish.
5. Give the OK to remove the tag.

This concludes our initial examination of formatting. Although we will be discussing formatting throughout the book, you should now know enough to create your own well-formatted publication, such as a newsletter. In the next chapter, you'll see how to deliver the end product of desktop publishing: printed matter.

CHAPTER SIX

Start the Presses: Printing and Other Output

WITH THE ADVENT OF DESKTOP PUBLISHING, TYPE-set-quality printing is now available for many types of communications in the office. The move is on for paper communications of an increasingly higher caliber. Gone are notions of the "paperless office" of the future. Gone is the once widely entertained idea that communication strictly via computer screens is a desirable goal.

While printing and other output operations are simple to perform with Ventura, the program nevertheless permits you to make numerous choices. The program wisely provides for a great deal of flexibility in printing, as it does in other areas. You can print plain or fancy, now or later, all or some, forward or backward.

While for most operations, output from a computer means printed output, Ventura can also create another form of output: output to a computer file. Doing so allows you to print the document at another time and place, even without Ventura.

These capabilities, though, are icing on the cake. Printing can also be simple and straightforward. In this chapter, we'll first examine simple printing procedures. Then we'll look at Ventura's flexibility in output.

A PRINTING OVERVIEW

As mentioned above, printing with Ventura is a simple process. In most circumstances, you'll probably find that you can just issue the printing command. Here is a summary of the procedures we'll discuss in this chapter that you'll be utilizing to print a document:

- Loading the chapter that you wish to print
- Using the Options menu's Printer Info command to setup the appropriate printing configuration
- Indicating how much you want to print and commencing the operation with the File menu's To print command

Note that these procedures are geared to printing a single chapter. We'll see how to print multichapter publications in Chapter 11.

We'll also examine printers and other hardware you'll use in the printing process. If you don't have a printer yet, or you are considering the purchase of a new one, you'll be interested in reading "Which

Printer Is Best for Me?'' later in this chapter. If you already have one, you'll need to find out what it's capable of doing and not doing with Ventura. The next section describes the way to do this.

CHECKING YOUR PRINTER'S CAPABILITIES

To let you check the capabilities of your printer, Ventura provides you with a special chapter file called CAPABILI.CHP. It's located in the TYPESET directory. Figure 6.1 shows you two printouts of this test document.

To load this document in order to check your printer, pull down the File menu and click Open Chapter. Change to the C:\TYPESET*.CHP directory, if necessary. Remember, you can change directories by using the Backup button (the small square at the top of the Item Selector list), and you can use the scroll bar to see the files in the Item Selector list.

To print CAPABILI.CHP or any document for that matter, follow the procedure we are about to describe. If all is working properly, you should get a printout like those in Figure 6.1.

The capabilities that this document tests are described in the document. Among other features, your printout will show you the point sizes that are available for your printer. It will also indicate the area around the edges of the paper on which the printer is unable to print. Notice how the capabilities of the two printers tested in Figure 6.1 differ.

SETTING UP PRINTER INFO

To prepare Ventura for printing, you need to provide the program with information about your printer and printing needs. Proceed with the following steps (any of Ventura's four modes may be active):

1. Pull down the Options menu.
2. Click Set Printer Info.

The dialog box for Set Printer Info, which will look something like Figure 6.2, will appear. Its actual contents will vary, depending upon

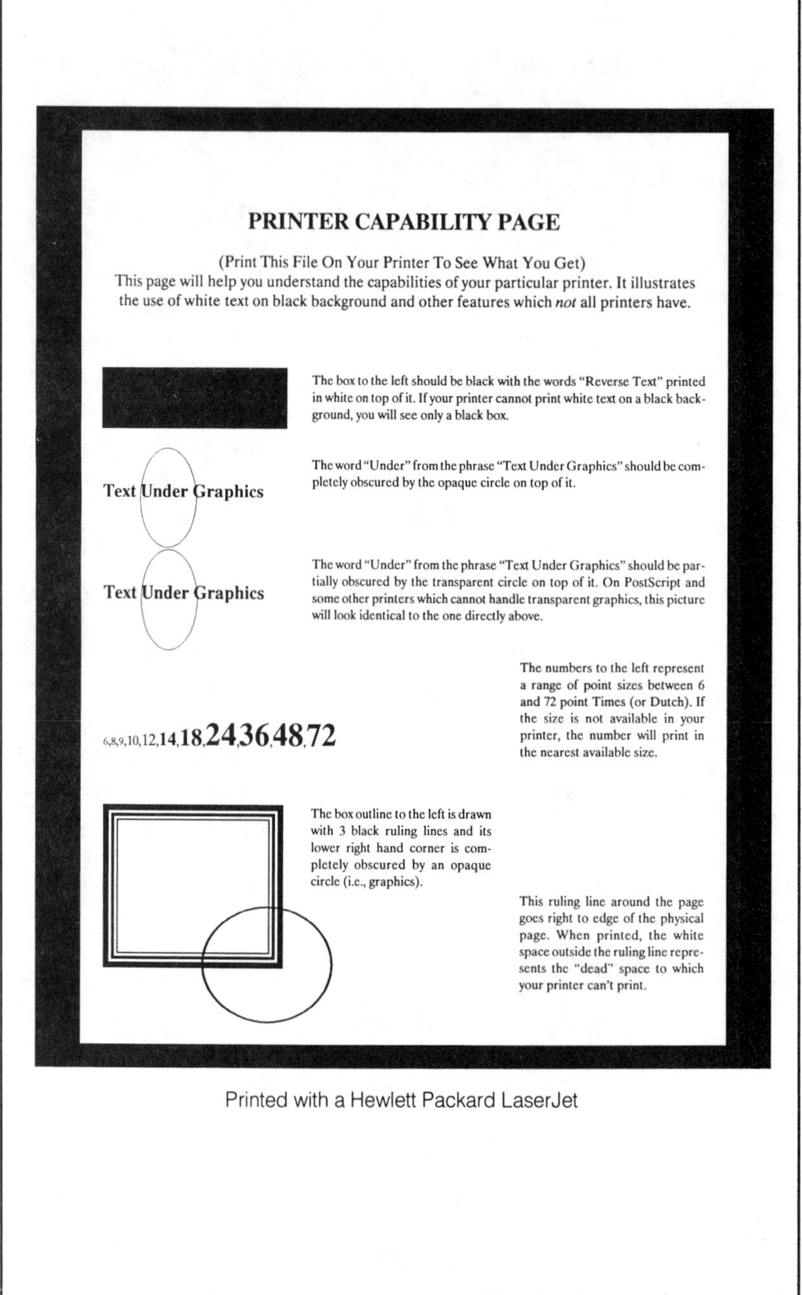

PRINTER CAPABILITY PAGE

(Print This File On Your Printer To See What You Get)
This page will help you understand the capabilities of your particular printer. It illustrates the use of white text on black background and other features which *not* all printers have.

The box to the left should be black with the words "Reverse Text" printed in white on top of it. If your printer cannot print white text on a black background, you will see only a black box.

Text Under Graphics

The word "Under" from the phrase "Text Under Graphics" should be completely obscured by the opaque circle on top of it.

Text Under Graphics

The word "Under" from the phrase "Text Under Graphics" should be partially obscured by the transparent circle on top of it. On PostScript and some other printers which cannot handle transparent graphics, this picture will look identical to the one directly above.

6,8,9,10,12,14,18,24,36,48,72

The numbers to the left represent a range of point sizes between 6 and 72 point Times (or Dutch). If the size is not available in your printer, the number will print in the nearest available size.

The box outline to the left is drawn with 3 black ruling lines and its lower right hand corner is completely obscured by an opaque circle (i.e., graphics).

This ruling line around the page goes right to edge of the physical page. When printed, the white space outside the ruling line represents the "dead" space to which your printer can't print.

Printed with a Hewlett Packard LaserJet

Figure 6.1: The Printer Capability Page Printed with Different Printers

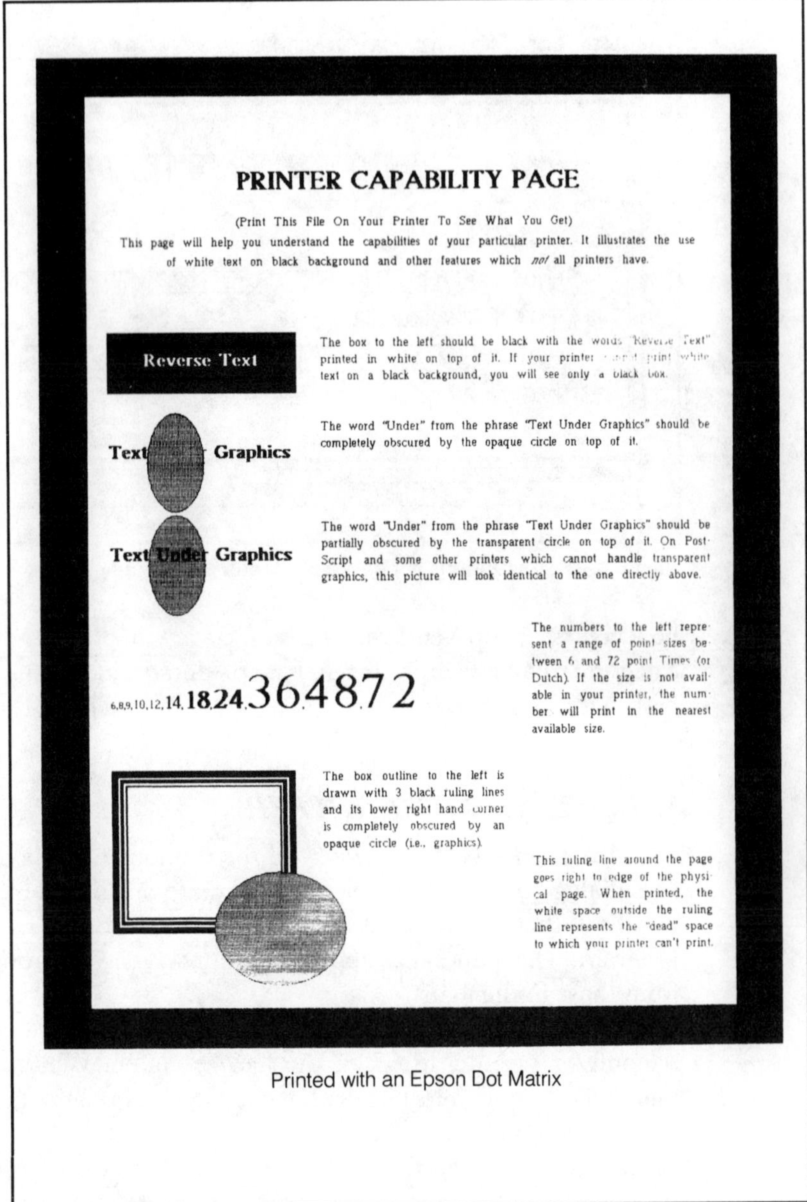

PRINTER CAPABILITY PAGE

(Print This File On Your Printer To See What You Get)

This page will help you understand the capabilities of your particular printer. It illustrates the use of white text on black background and other features which *not* all printers have.

Reverse Text

The box to the left should be black with the words "Reverse Text" printed in white on top of it. If your printer can't print white text on a black background, you will see only a black box.

Text Under Graphics

The word "Under" from the phrase "Text Under Graphics" should be completely obscured by the opaque circle on top of it.

Text Under Graphics

The word "Under" from the phrase "Text Under Graphics" should be partially obscured by the transparent circle on top of it. On PostScript and some other printers which cannot handle transparent graphics, this picture will look identical to the one directly above.

6,8,9,10,12,14,18,24,36,48,72

The numbers to the left represent a range of point sizes between 6 and 72 point Times (or Dutch). If the size is not available in your printer, the number will print in the nearest available size.

The box outline to the left is drawn with 3 black ruling lines and its lower right hand corner is completely obscured by an opaque circle (i.e., graphics).

This ruling line around the page goes right to edge of the physical page. When printed, the white space outside the ruling line represents the "dead" space to which your printer can't print.

Printed with an Epson Dot Matrix

Figure 6.1: The Printer Capability Page Printed with Different Printers (continued)

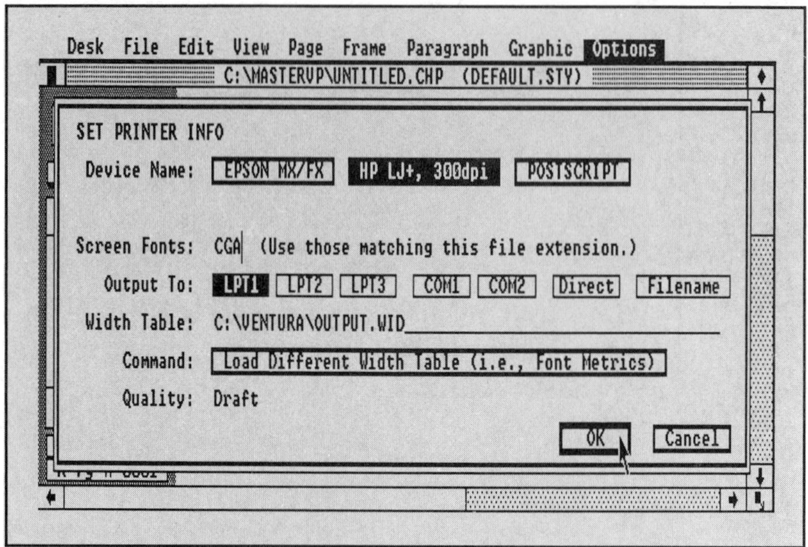

Figure 6.2: The Options Menu's Set Printer Info Dialog Box

how you've set up Ventura, as described in Chapter 1. Examine the categories that appear in this dialog box and decide on the setup that best meets your needs.

SELECTING THE PRINTER

In the Device Name category of the Options menu's Set Printer Info dialog box, you'll see the printers that you can use. The names are those that you specified with VPPREP, Ventura's installation program. The names that appear on your screen will probably differ from those in the figure.

You may have installed only one printer. In that case, you would see only one printer listed for the Device Name. Why install more than one? The answers usually have to do with quality and availability. You could use one printer to create rough drafts of your documents and another for the final versions. You could also install a color printer and a black-and-white one if you have access to both. However, you don't have to have a particular printer immediately available in order to use it later, as we'll see when we discuss the creation of output files.

The printer that you installed first will appear first in the list. Initially, this first printer will be darkened, indicating that it is selected. If you wish to use this printer, you need do nothing. If you wish to use a different printer, click the button with that printer's name, which will then darken.

As mentioned, if you installed only one printer, only that printer will appear, and it will always be darkened. If you acquire a new printer, you can add its name by running the VPPREP program again.

IMPORTANT

When you change printers, be careful. There is more to changing printers than just clicking the button for Device Name. You will also need to change the Width Table setting that is associated with the printer, which we'll discuss later in the chapter.

By the way, the VPPREP program also sets the Screen Fonts field, which appears next in the dialog box. This setting is determined by the monitor you specify when you run the VPPREP program. We'll examine this setting when we look at how to add fonts later in this chapter.

CHOOSING AN OUTPUT

Next, take a look at the Output To setting. There are seven buttons associated with it.

Serial versus Parallel Printers

The first five buttons begin with the letters LPT or COM. These five choices are usually called *ports*. They are provided by the operating system (DOS) and may be limited by your hardware. You may recognize these choices from other software packages with which you are familiar.

A computer port is simply one of the output connectors that your computer provides. Typically, one or more ports are located on the back of the computer. (Although DOS allows up to five ports on a computer, you probably have the hardware for only one or two.) You plug a cable from your printer into a port as you would a VCR or a cable-TV line into your television. Through this hookup, the signal travels from the computer to the printer. The port does not provide electrical power to the printer; it only directs the signals.

The two kinds of ports, LPT and COM, reflect the two ways in which computers can send signals to a printer. You use LPT settings for *parallel* printers. COM settings are for *serial* printers. As you can see by the Output To grouping, DOS allows up to three parallel and two serial printers (or other devices).

Computers send serial signals "bit by bit": the computer fires out bits of information single file. With serial printers, there are no control signals to ensure that accurate data transmission occurs, so you must set up a variety of parameters. Computers send parallel signals in a "side-by-side" fashion, which keeps the signals aligned and organized.

Installation of parallel printers is simpler than serial printers. However, you must keep parallel printers within about ten feet of the computer.

If you already have a printer, you must determine the signaling method it uses—parallel or serial. Usually, it's designated on the original box that the printer came in. Sometimes it's also specified in the printer operating manual or even on the sales receipt.

You can also tell the signal method by examining the connectors on the back of the printer. Figure 6.3 shows the two connectors.

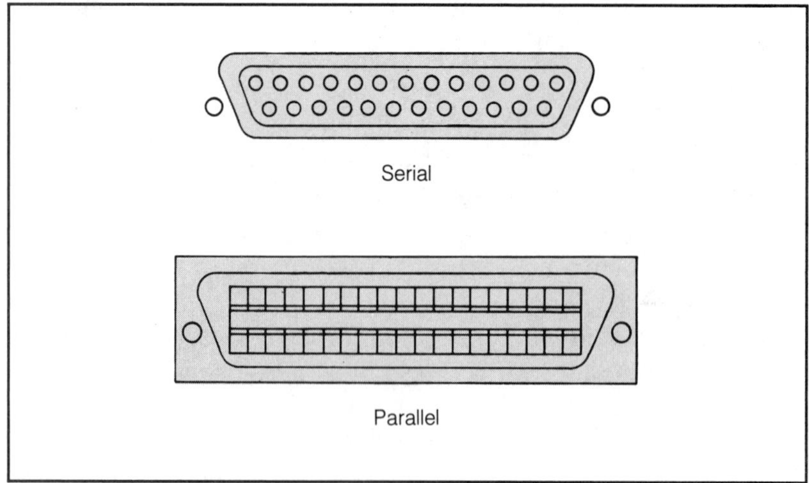

Figure 6.3: Parallel and Serial Connectors for Printers

Many printers are available in either parallel or serial models. Due to simplicity of installation and speed of printing, parallel printers are preferable. Some printers, like the Apple LaserWriter, are available only as serial. On the other hand, if you own an HP LaserJet, you can configure it to operate in either serial or parallel fashion.

Direct Connections

After the five LPT and COM settings is the Direct setting. You use the Direct setting in conjunction with printer configurations that do not use the ports. For instance, use this setting if your printer is operating via a JLaser card. The printer connects to the card, which plugs into a slot within the computer. This arrangement bypasses the ports altogether, and so the connection is direct.

Printing to Disk

The Filename button allows you to "print" the document to a file on the disk. Use this option to create output that you don't want to print just yet. Once you've created such a file, you no longer need Ventura to print it. The technique of printing to a file and the reasons for doing so are described in the section "Printing from Output Files," at the end of the chapter.

WIDTH TABLES

The next setting in the Options menu's Set Printer Info dialog box is entitled Width Table. By its name, you can see that it's associated with the big button labeled

Load Different Width Table (i.e., Font Metrics)

To understand these two settings, we need to know how Ventura works with fonts and printers.

How Ventura Links Fonts and Printers

In various files, Ventura has descriptions of the fonts it uses as well as particulars on the printers you have installed. However, it must associate these files in order to print your documents correctly. To link font and printer files meaningfully, Ventura uses *width tables*.

The names of the width tables match the names of the printers. There's also one we'll discuss shortly, called OUTPUT.WID, that's a copy of the default printer's width table. Let's say that you have installed Ventura for use with an Epson printer and an HP LaserJet Plus. In this case, the installation program will copy EPSON and HLJPLUS width tables from the original Ventura disks to your hard disk, making them available to print with.

Ultimate versus Draft Quality

You're probably wondering why Ventura doesn't simply keep the specifications for the font widths right along with the rest of the printer specifications. At first, such an arrangement seems to make sense. You wouldn't have to remember to change width tables whenever you change printers.

The reason is flexibility. Keeping the specifications in separate files allows you to mix printers and width tables. You'd do this, for instance, when you want to get a sample printout on one printer that approximates the final version, which you will print on a different printer.

Ventura uses the term *ultimate quality* to describe the final printout on the final printer. You achieve ultimate quality when you select a printer and a width table that match. When the width table doesn't match the printer in use, the resulting document is of *draft quality*.

Let's say that you want to create a company catalog on a LaserJet. The problem is, however, that you have only an Epson printer at your desk. Now assume that a department elsewhere in the building does have a LaserJet that they are willing to let you use. However, you want to do the bulk of your work at your desk, because all the information for the catalog is being channeled through you. Naturally, as you work, you'd like to get an idea of how the catalog will look when you print it.

If you were to set both the Device Name and Width Table to Epson, you'd get a good printout at your desk. However, when you took the files to the LaserJet station, you'd be in for some surprises. Different printers treat the same font differently; that is, the same font may print in different widths, depending on the printer. If the widths of the letters differ, the number of words on a line will differ as well. This affects the length of the paragraphs as well as the amount of text on a page. The items in your LaserJet catalog would be dislocated, and the catalog wouldn't look like the finely-tuned document that it was at your desk.

To approximate the LaserJet on the Epson, you wouldn't simply change the Device Name to LaserJet. The signals Ventura sends to a LaserJet would be meaningless to the Epson, and the resulting printout would be garbage. Rather, you'd set Device Name to Epson and set Width Table for the LaserJet. The result would be a draft quality document, as indicated by the Quality setting at the bottom of the dialog box. Normally, you wouldn't use the draft version for duplication and distribution. Spacing could be odd and letters may overlap. You could, however, use it to get an idea of how the ultimate quality version will look. You could tell, for instance, where each line ends, how much of an article will fit on a page, and how many pages a chapter will run.

Changing Width Tables

You cannot directly change the Width Table setting and the Command setting that follows it. Like the Quality setting, they are only display fields that show the system's current status. To change the width table, you must click the box that reads

Load Different Width Table (i.e., Font Metrics)

When you click this box, you see the Item Selector box shown in Figure 6.4. This Item Selector box displays various width tables from which you may choose. Those displayed for you may differ from those in the figure; the box shows the width tables that the VPPREP program copies onto your hard disk when you install Ventura. There will be one for each installed printer, each ending with a WID extension. There will also be a width table called OUTPUT.WID.

Using OUTPUT.WID

OUTPUT.WID is identical to the width table for the default printer, the first printer listed on the Device Name line in the Set Printer Info dialog box. If Epson, appearing first, is the default printer, as it is in our

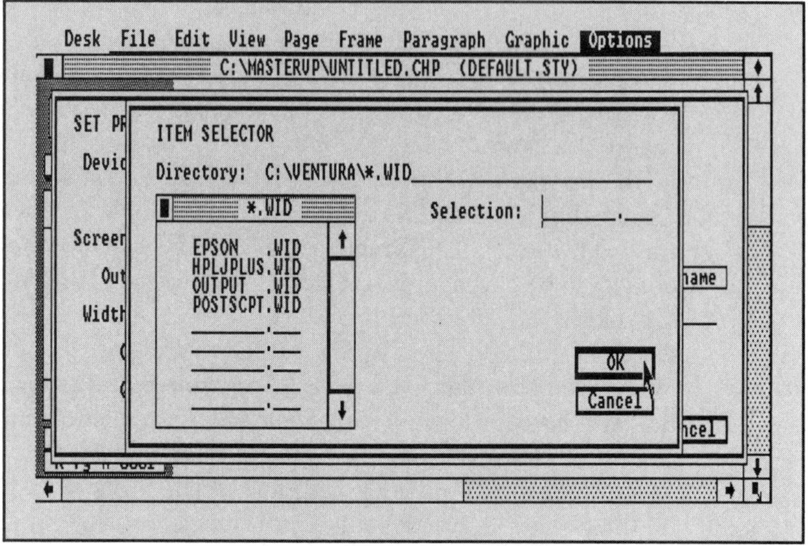

Figure 6.4: The Item Selector Box for Width Tables

example, OUTPUT.WID will match EPSON.WID. As a result, you could use either width table to achieve ultimate quality when you print with the Epson printer.

The style sheet stores your choice of width table. Those that Ventura initially provides are set to use the OUTPUT.WID width table. That way, you can print the samples with your default printer without having to change the width table.

If you are designing a style sheet that people will use for printing at various stations with various printers, choose OUTPUT.WID for the width table. As long as only one printer (or the default printer) is in use, the document will print correctly (that is, the printout will be of ultimate quality).

IMPORTANT

Switch printers with care when you are concerned about exact line, paragraph, and page endings. Always check the results. Mixing printers works best in book-style publications—not newsletters, in which placement and line endings are important.

If you'd like to use the width table for a printer you didn't originally install, you don't need to use the reinstall procedure. Simply copy the width table from one of Ventura's original floppy disks into the Ventura directory on your hard disk. You may have to hunt for your width table, though, since they are stored on various disks. You can use the DOS asterisk wild card to search by typing

```
dir a:*.wid
```

at the DOS prompt.

PRINTING

Once you've selected all the settings in the Options menu's Set Printer Info dialog box, you're ready to begin printing the displayed document. If you want to print the displayed document again, you don't need to use this dialog box unless you wish to change one of the settings.

To print a chapter, you'll need to use the Print Information dialog box, shown in Figure 6.5. To display it, follow these steps:

1. Pull down the File menu.
2. Point the mouse arrow at To Print and click.

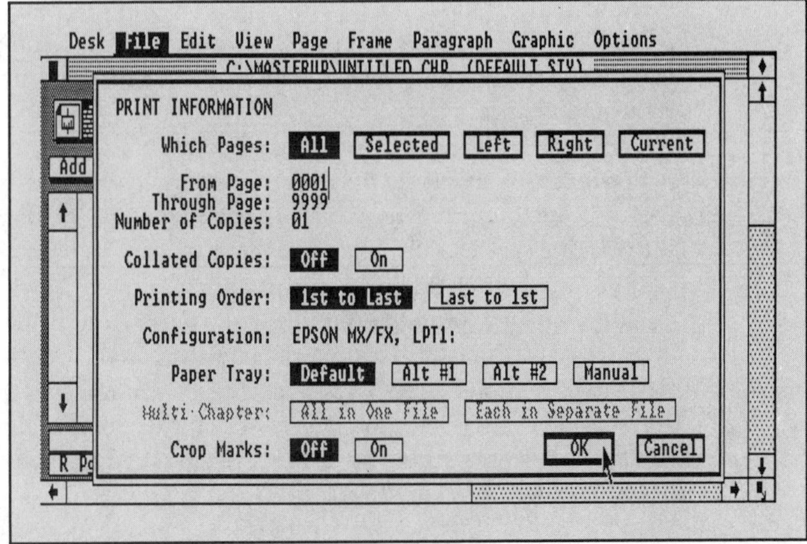

Figure 6.5: The Print Information Dialog Box

If you wish to print an entire chapter, you can just give the OK without changing anything in the dialog box.

Ventura does, however, allow you to control much of the printing process. The following sections show you how to customize your printout choices, if you so desire.

SELECTING PAGES TO PRINT

The first setting in the Print Information dialog box, Which Pages, asks you to indicate how much of the chapter you'd like to print. Choose All for normal printing of the entire chapter or Selected if you wish to indicate a range of pages to print. Click the Current button if you want to print only the page that's on the screen.

You may wish to use Selected if, for instance, there are last-minute changes made after you've printed an entire document. If you do make changes after printing, though, be certain to reprint *all* affected pages, including those that follow the revised page. This will occur when text spills from one page to another as a result of edits on an earlier page. On the other hand, there's no need to waste time reprinting pages that remain the same despite a change elsewhere in the document. So use this setting to your advantage.

The Left and Right buttons are new with Version 1.1. You use them to create double-sided printouts. First use the Left button and print all the left-hand pages in the document. Then, remove the stack from you printer's output tray, flip it over, reinsert it, and print the right-hand pages.

Now look at the next two settings, From Page and Through Page. When Which Pages is set for All, as it normally is, these two settings will indicate that printing goes from page 1 to page 9999. (Of course, the printing will actually stop with the final page of your document.)

If you choose Selected for Which Pages, use these two fields to indicate the pages you want to print. Type the number of the first page you desire into the From Page setting. Then use the mouse, tab, or ↓ key to move to the Through Page setting, and type the number of the last page you want to print. (Don't forget that once the cursor is in this field, you can erase the entire set of four 9's by pressing the Esc key.)

In Chapter 11, you'll see that you can use the Page menu's Page Counter command to change the page numbering that appears on the printed copy. If you do, the page numbers in the Side-bar (on the screen) will not agree with those in the document. In case of such a discrepancy, be aware that Ventura will always use the page numbers in the Side-bar when calculating the pages to print.

Finally, if you set Which Pages to Current, the From Page and Through Page fields will both reflect the same number; that is, they'll both show the number of the displayed page.

MAKING MULTIPLE COPIES

If you want Ventura to print more than one copy automatically, enter the number of copies you desire at the Number of Copies setting. You can print up to 99 copies in a run. Of course, consider whether using Ventura is the most efficient way to make copies. Usually, it's faster to use some other conventional means, such as a photocopier or an offset printer. However, if you want exceptional quality for all copies, or if other means are not available, you may find this setting useful.

If you want to print more than one copy of a document that's more than one page long, consider the next setting. Usually, Collated Copies is set to Off. This way, Ventura prints all copies of page 1 first. Only then does it go on to print all copies of page 2, then all page 3s, and so on. This means that once the chapter is printed, you must assemble the pages in proper sequence, which could be quite tedious, for instance, with a long operating manual.

If you turn this setting On, Ventura will print out one copy of the document in its entirety before proceeding to the next. So why shouldn't Ventura always collate as it prints? The reason is that when the pages you are printing contain pictures, printing with Collated Copies set to On is much slower than it is with the normal Off setting. Pictures require a large amount of memory, which means it takes a long time to load one. Once a page is loaded, it's more efficient to print as many copies as necessary, rather than load another page. If you're in no rush for the copies, and you don't need to free up the computer, it may be worth having Ventura collate for you. (Such a project may be a candidate for overnight printing.)

PRINTING FORWARD OR BACKWARD

When cut-sheet (individual page) printers eject a finished page, some scoot the new page behind or under those that are already printed, or stack the pages upside down, resulting in normal order, with page l followed by pages 2, 3, and so on. Other printers, however, lay the new page face up on top of pages already in the output tray; the resulting stack is in backward order.

Use the next setting, Printing Order, to compensate for such a backward printer. Usually, this setting should be on 1st to Last. With backward printers, such as the LaserJet and LaserJet Plus, you'll need to change this setting to Last to 1st for a normally ordered stack. However, Hewlett-Packard has corrected the problem with the new LaserJet Series II, so that you can now use the lst to Last setting. With continuous paper printers, there is no need to concern yourself with this setting.

OTHER PRINT INFORMATION

The Configuration setting is only an indicator of the settings you've made with the Options menu's Set Printer Info dialog box and cannot be changed. The Configuration field shows the name of the printer (Device Name) and the port or other output designation.

Use the Paper Tray grouping to specify how Ventura should feed the printer paper. If your printer has multiple feeder trays, you can use the grouping to indicate which tray Ventura should use for paper. Each of the first three buttons (Default, Alt #1, and Alt #2) could, for instance, correspond to a different size of paper. Use the fourth button, Manual, for envelopes that you insert one at a time. Printers that have this capability pause after each envelope and restart printing once you've inserted a fresh envelope.

When you gain access to the Print Information dialog box via the File menu's To Print command, the Multi-Chapter setting will ghost, indicating that it's not available. We'll examine the use of this setting when we study multichapter publications in Chapter 11.

Finally, the Crop Marks setting works only when you use the Page menu's Page Layout command to specify a paper type smaller than the size you're printing with. If that's the case, clicking Crop Marks On will cause Ventura to indicate the corners of the smaller page with *crop marks* (see Figure 6.6). Layout photographers use crop marks to position material for shooting accurately.

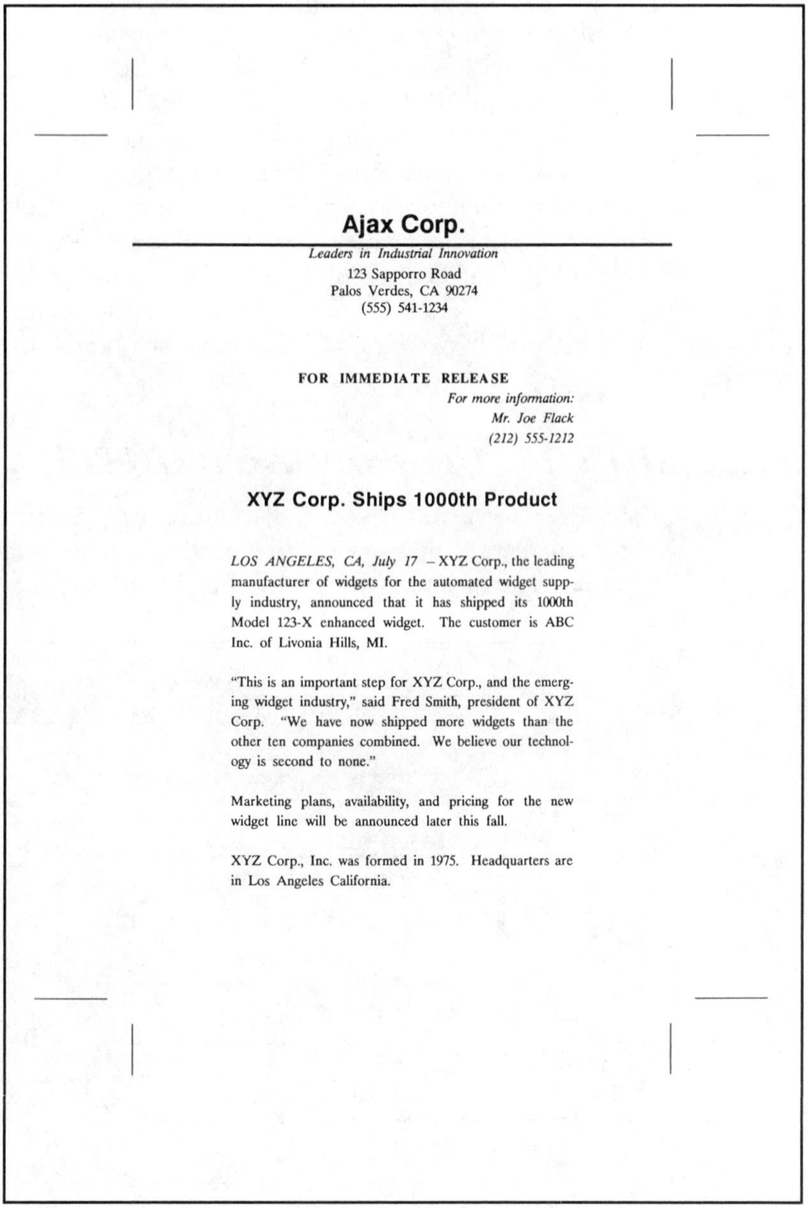

Ajax Corp.

Leaders in Industrial Innovation
123 Sapporro Road
Palos Verdes, CA 90274
(555) 541-1234

FOR IMMEDIATE RELEASE
For more information:
Mr. Joe Flack
(212) 555-1212

XYZ Corp. Ships 1000th Product

LOS ANGELES, CA, July 17 – XYZ Corp., the leading manufacturer of widgets for the automated widget supply industry, announced that it has shipped its 1000th Model 123-X enhanced widget. The customer is ABC Inc. of Livonia Hills, MI.

"This is an important step for XYZ Corp., and the emerging widget industry," said Fred Smith, president of XYZ Corp. "We have now shipped more widgets than the other ten companies combined. We believe our technology is second to none."

Marketing plans, availability, and pricing for the new widget line will be announced later this fall.

XYZ Corp., Inc. was formed in 1975. Headquarters are in Los Angeles California.

Figure 6.6: Crop Marks

PRINTING AND INTERRUPTING

Once you've completed your settings in the Print Information dialog box, click the OK box or press Return to commence printing. Normally, the printer will start to churn out the pages. Once printing begins, you'll see a message that indicates you can stop the printing process by pressing the Esc key (see Figure 6.7). If you press Esc (and confirm it), Ventura will finish printing the page it is working on and then stop, canceling the rest of the print job.

With what you know so far, you can do many print jobs; you can, for instance, print the Printer Capability Page. However, printing is a forte of Ventura. The rest of this chapter contains an in-depth look at printing as well as a brief look at the state of printing in the desktop publishing world. We begin with a discussion of serial printers.

SETTING UP A SERIAL PRINTER

With a serial printer, you must configure your serial port to accommodate it. To do so, you'll first need to find out some information about your printer. You should be able to get what you need

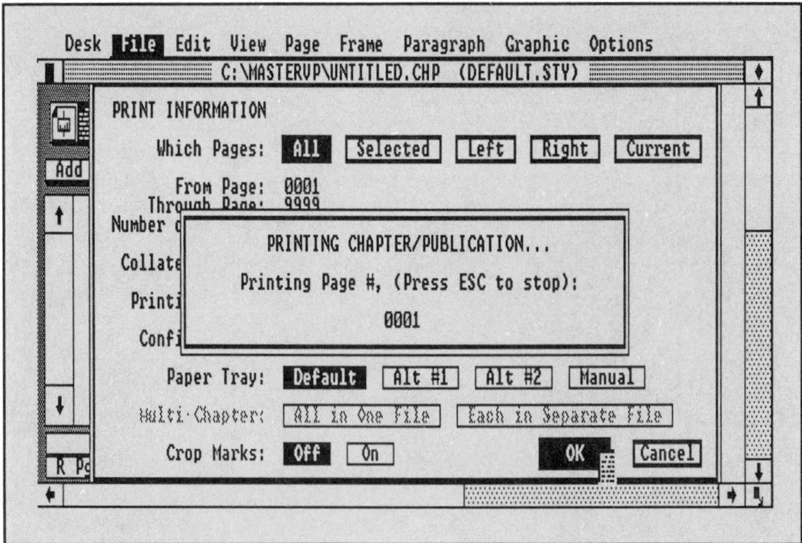

Figure 6.7: The Screen during Printing

from the documentation that came with your printer or from your dealer. Here's the information you'll need before you can proceed:

1. Baud rate. (Use the first two digits.)
2. Parity. (Use N for no parity, O for odd parity, E for even parity.)
3. Number of data bits. (Use the number 7 or 8.)
4. Number of stop bits. (Use the number 1 or 2.)

DETERMINING THE METHOD FOR CONFIGURATION

When using a serial printer, you must configure the port prior to printing every time you turn on the computer. To save time and energy, it's wise to automate the procedure. Generally, you do this by using your word processor to add the MODE command, which configures the port, to your AUTOEXEC.BAT file. We'll look at the exact syntax of this command in a moment. Alternatively, you may wish to add the command to your VP.BAT file or enter it in its own special batch file.

If you add the command to the AUTOEXEC.BAT file, the computer will configure the port automatically as soon as you turn it on. This is the best way to proceed if you have only the one serial printer and it is the only device for which you are using the port. (You could also use the port for a modem, for instance.)

You should add the command to your VP.BAT file if you want the computer to configure the port only when you start Ventura. This would be a good method if you are using the same port to accommodate more than one serial printer or another device. Assuming that you always use the same serial printer with Ventura, you can simply plug in the proper printer, and the port will be configured correctly when you start the program.

Lastly, if you use more than one serial printer with the same port and you plan to use either printer with Ventura, you'll need to set up a MODE command for each printer. Then, before you start Ventura, decide which printer to use, type in the command for the batch file corresponding to that printer, and then start the program. If you need to switch printers, you must exit from Ventura, run the new batch file, and start the program up again.

INSTALLING THE MODE PROGRAM

Whichever method you use to configure your port, you'll make use of DOS's MODE command. For it to work, you'll need to have the MODE.COM program on your root directory. The root directory is normally the first directory that is active when you turn on your computer. (This would not be the case if you or someone else configured the computer differently than usual, causing another directory to be activated automatically.) You can find out which DOS directory is active by typing

```
dir/p
```

and hitting the Return key. This command displays the contents of the current directory, pausing if the screen should fill up. Check the top of the display. If it's the root directory (and if, of course, you're using drive C to store Ventura), you'll see this message:

```
Directory of drive c:\
```

If you don't, type

```
cd\
```

and press Return to activate the root directory.

Once you have the root directory, you'll need to place a copy of the MODE program there. Insert your DOS disk into drive A, type

```
copy a:mode.com
```

and hit Return. Be sure to include a space after the word *copy* and use a colon (not a semicolon) after the letter a.

USING THE MODE COMMAND

Once the MODE program is on the root directory, you're ready to enter the appropriate MODE command in ASCII format. If necessary, check Chapter 12 for information on creating ASCII text.

Use the appropriate batch file name according to the method you've decided upon. The file name must have BAT as an extension (for instance, AUTOEXEC.BAT, VP.BAT, or LASER.BAT).

Here's how to create the command in the file. On a separate line, type the words

```
mode com1:
```

(assuming that you're using the com1 port), followed by a space, the first two digits of the baud rate, the parity, the number of data bits, and the number of stop bits. Follow each item with a comma. Lastly, type the letter **p** to indicate that you are configuring for a printer. Thus, if the documentation for your printer specifies 9600 baud, no parity, eight data bits, and one stop bit, you would enter

```
mode com1: 96,n,8,l,p
```

and press Return. This is the configuration that most popular laser printers, including the LaserWriter and the LaserJet, use.

PAGE DESCRIPTION LANGUAGES

As our discussion of serial printers shows, printing can become a complicated process, depending upon the hardware. To standardize procedures and minimize confusion caused by a variety of printers, programmers have begun developing *page description languages*.

Usually, when you install a piece of software, you must indicate the name of the specific printer you will be using. A page description language (PDL) standardizes the methods that computer systems use for printing. All printers that conform to a particular PDL's specifications will operate with that PDL. So instead of installing a specific printer, you simply install the PDL.

With good reason, interest in page description languages is on the increase. One reason is that PDLs are so useful with desktop publishing applications. The ability to use more than one printer is important as you go from draft to finished product or from station to station. A PDL makes it easy to switch printers without producing unexpected results. Of course, such printers cost more, because you must pay for the PDL as well.

Various PDLs have been vying for top position in the market place, hoping to become the standard of the industry. PostScript, created by Adobe Systems, is a PDL that Ventura supports. The program also supports the Interpress PDL. Recently, IBM announced the introduction of its own PostScript printer and endorsed PostScript as the only PDL that it plans to work with. With the Apple LaserWriter and numerous other printers already supporting this PDL, PostScript is certain to be the industry standard. As more printer manufacturers support PostScript, special software installation of printers may become a thing of the past.

By using the Options menu's Set Printer Info box you can specify a PostScript printer for Device Name (as long as you have installed PostScript with VPPREP). When you do, you can use any printer that adheres to the PostScript standard, and the output will be similar in design. In other words, lines of text will break at the same spot, the sizes of boxes will match, and so on. Depending upon the quality of the printer, the resolution on the printed page may differ, but that's about all. For example, you can use a less expensive printer for rough drafts and a higher quality printer for the final copy. You'll be certain of how the finished document will look, based on the appearance of the rough draft.

ADDING FONTS

Though a degree of page standardization is a real possibility due to the PDL, it's unlikely to happen in the area of fonts. The public's appetite for typefaces seems to be insatiable. Fortunately, you are not confined to using the fonts supplied with your printer, or even those provided by the printer's manufacturer. You can also use fonts that have been created by third-party vendors to work with Ventura and your particular printer (see Appendix D).

To use a new font, you can simply add it to the fonts you already use for the printer. Existing fonts are in the width table for the printer, and you can create a new width table that combines both old and new fonts. You can do this using the following steps:

1. For best results, acquire a font whose manufacturer provides a width table. More and more vendors are now providing these.

2. For safety, make a copy of the width tables for the fonts you are already using. Should something go wrong in the process of adding fonts (like erasing the fonts instead of adding to them), you can retrieve your old fonts.
3. Copy the new font along with its corresponding width table to the VENTURA directory, which is created when you install Ventura.
4. In Ventura, use the Options menu's Set Printer Info dialog box to load the width table for the printer you want to add fonts to.
5. Pull down the Options menu and click Add/Remove Fonts. You'll see the dialog box shown in Figure 6.8. This dialog box displays the fonts whose specifications are currently stored in the width table you just loaded. Your new font will join this listing.
6. Click Merge Width Tables. In the resulting Item Selector box, choose the width table that corresponds to your new font. This action will combine the old fonts, already loaded, with the new one you specify.
7. Click the Save As New Width Table button and make up a new width table name. Doing so will create a new table that contains the old fonts as well as the new one for the specified printer.

From now on, you can use any of the fonts for a given printer just by loading this new width table (using the Options menu's Set Printer Info dialog box). If you want to use only the old fonts, load the old width table.

Be aware that Ventura will not always show added fonts on the screen; instead, it may replace them with standard fonts of the same size. However, it does show the new font names on the appropriate menus for selection.

Ventura can display the fonts exactly as they will appear when printed if the font manufacturer provides specifications for doing so. These specifications are contained in *screen-font* files. If the fonts you acquire have matching screen-font files, you need not use the Add New Fonts dialog box to add them to Ventura's fonts. Instead, you

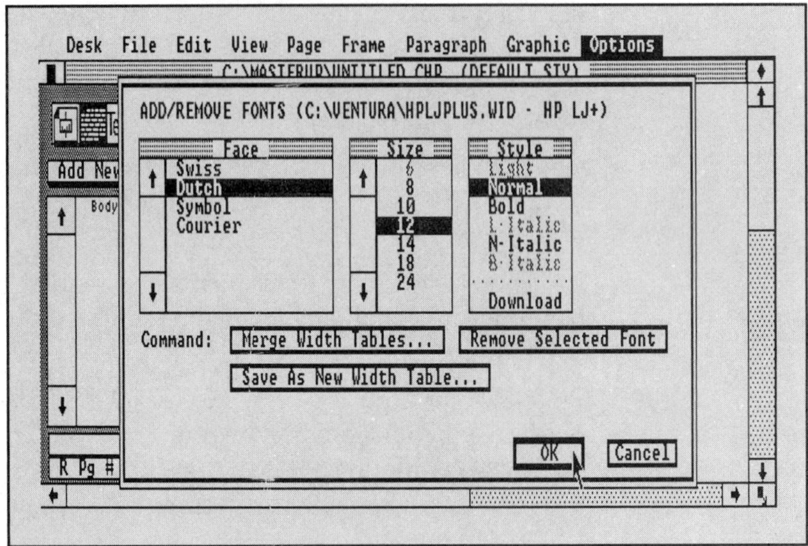

Figure 6.8: The Options Menu's Add/Remove Fonts Dialog Box

can simply use the Options menu's Set Printer Info dialog box (Figure 6.2). Click the Load Different Width Table button and select the new width table. Once you do, use the same dialog box's Screen Fonts field to enter the extension of the screen font you wish to use. The screen fonts will match their printed counterparts. If you need to change back to Ventura's screen fonts, be aware that Ventura uses the CGA extension for low-resolution screens and EGA for all high-resolution screens (including IBM's Enhanced Graphics Adapter, Hercules boards, Genius monitors, and so on).

DOWNLOADING FONTS

In the Add/Remove Fonts dialog box, notice the unusually placed setting at the bottom of the Style column, which will say either Resident or Download.

Downloading fonts refers to the process by which Ventura and some other programs make a copy of font specifications from the hard disk and load it into your printer's memory, using the following procedure:

1. Ventura goes to the hard disk to retrieve font specifications from the Width Table file.

2. It then sends those specifications to the printer.
3. The printer uses the font specifications to place the fonts on the page.

The Download setting on the Add/Remove Fonts dialog box causes Ventura to perform the download procedure automatically when it comes time to use the particular font indicated. Some printers, however, have font specifications built into them. To indicate that Ventura does not need to copy these font specifications from the disk, the setting for such fonts is Resident. Printing is much faster when the fonts you need are Resident.

Ventura's installation process sets the Download/Resident status for all fonts, and you usually don't have to make any changes. In fact, changing the status of a font without great care could cause problems if, for example, it causes Ventura to look for the font's specifications in the wrong location.

There may be times when it's desirable to change the setting—for instance, when using the Linotronic typesetter, which we'll examine in the next section. At those times, you may find it advantageous to use the printer's software to download fonts *before* using Ventura. For fonts that you download in this manner, change the setting to Resident. Doing so will save you the waiting time necessary to download the fonts a second time.

IMPORTANT

The Download/Resident setting applies to the particular combination of Face, Size, and Style indicated by the darkened bars in the dialog box. Ventura considers each such combination to be a font, and hence each combination has its own Download/Resident setting that you can change. Figure 6.8, for instance, indicates only that Dutch face, 12-point size, normal style is set for Download status. Other combinations may or may not be set for Download. So, if you want to change all sizes and styles for a particular face, you must change each combination of face, size, and style.

Note that the Add/Remove Fonts dialog box also allows you to remove font specifications from the width table you are using. You may wish to remove fonts you don't use so as to improve Ventura's performance. First, it's wise to make a copy of the width table's file. Then select the combination of face, size, and style you wish to remove and click the Remove Selected Font button. Note that if you have other fonts loaded that do not come with matching screen fonts, you must not remove the Swiss 10-point size font. Ventura uses this font to create substitute screen fonts when necessary.

Now let's look at how you can use Ventura with a typesetter, as mentioned earlier in the chapter.

PRINTING WITH A TYPESETTER

Printing with a computer consists of using typefaces, images, graphics, and so on, that are composed of numerous tiny dots. The concentration of dots determines the resolution of the images on the printed page. Laser printers print with resolutions of up to 300 dots per inch (dpi). For truly snazzy output—for instance, a report you're sending to upper management—you may want resolution better than 300 dpi. By using typesetting equipment, such as one of the Linotronic series of PostScript typesetters, you can print with resolutions up to 2000 dpi.

Fortunately, you don't need to own such a typesetter to use one: you can rent time on one. For instance, you can use your PostScript laser printer for rough drafts. Once your document is assembled, you can create an output file that you can print at a desktop publishing service center.

Alternatively, if the center has Ventura available at its stations, you can bring along the files that are associated with the document you want to print. If you anticipate that you will be going this route, you can create the document entirely on the floppy drive to begin with. That is, locate the style-sheet (.STY), text and picture, chapter (.CHP), and width table (.WID) files all on drive A. Then, all you have to do is insert the disk at the service center and you're ready to print.

If you initially create the document on a hard disk, use the Options menu's Multi-Chapter command to make a copy of a chapter file. Although the command is named Multi-Chapter, the copying procedure also works with individual chapters. We'll explain how to utilize the dialog box for multichapter operations in Chapter 11.

Using Ventura to copy your chapter files is preferable to using DOS's COPY command. In addition to copying, Ventura automatically adjusts the location references for the files a chapter utilizes, so that they can be located on the appropriate disk drive and directory. Using DOS's COPY command leaves the old location references in place, which may no longer be correct.

Be aware, though, that using typesetting equipment in conjunction with personal computers is a new art. You may need to spend quite a bit of time working out the kinks. Be sure that you work with a knowledgeable typesetter who's enthusiastic about desktop publishing, not threatened by it.

You can limit the time you spend at the typesetter's with your strategy for downloading fonts. Often, fonts will already be downloaded when you start to use the equipment. If so, you can save time (and hence money) by setting your fonts to Resident, as described in the previous section.

WHICH PRINTER IS BEST FOR ME?

Although we've been discussing how to use more than one printer with the same document, it is possible that you don't even have your first printer yet. If you have one printer, though, Ventura's capabilities may be causing you to consider the acquisition of another. In either case, you're probably wondering which printer is best for you. The route you take depends upon the quality of output you desire and the budget that you have available. In this section, we'll discuss some popular types and brands of printers.

DOT-MATRIX PRINTERS

If you're on a budget, you may be able to get by with a simple dot-matrix printer. With these printers Ventura can create output of a surprisingly acceptable quality. However, you probably wouldn't want to use a dot-matrix printer for final quality output, except under limited circumstances. For instance, you could use such a printer to print a small newsletter for a hobby club. You could also use it to print simple intraoffice forms, handout fliers, errata sheets, and other "quickie" publications.

Another reason to use dot-matrix printers only for short applications is their slow speed. The print head moves from side to side, printing only a narrow strip on each pass. Also, it must pass over the same area repeatedly.

Dot-matrix printers are also noisy. This is because they create printed copy by repeatedly firing tiny individual pins at the paper. This is an important factor to consider if your quarters are tight.

As discussed earlier, some people use these printers to create rough drafts. People who don't have a LaserJet available, for instance, can use one to get an idea of how the output will ultimately appear.

LASER PRINTERS

The availability and increasingly low cost of laser printers makes them ideal for most desktop publishing applications. For some people, in fact, printing with a laser printer is synonymous with desktop publishing. These printers are flexible in output, comparatively swift, and whisper quiet.

A laser printer is suited to the production of larger publications, such as well-circulated newsletters, technical manuals, catalogs, and booklets. You can also use them to print brochures, press kits, bulletins, and so forth.

You may wish to consider whether you should purchase a laser printer or do the work elsewhere. Some copying centers, for instance, will let you rent time on a laser printer.

Whether you purchase, lease, or rent time on a laser, you'll want to consider which brand is best suited to your needs. Let's examine two popular brands.

The Hewlett-Packard LaserJet

The Hewlett-Packard series of LaserJets are the most popular of laser printers. The LaserJet prints with a resolution of 75 dots per inch (dpi), while the LaserJet Plus prints at 150 dpi. You must purchase the F cartridge to use the original LaserJet with Ventura. (This is a piece of hardware that plugs into the printer.) However, there are a limited number of fonts available for both printers. The LaserJet

Plus provides the resolution necessary for graphics, and with the LaserJet Plus you can also load fonts from disk.

In either case, talk of the LaserJet and the LaserJet Plus will soon be moot. Hewlett-Packard is now shipping its new LaserJet Series II. The Series II replaces the LaserJet and the LaserJet Plus, both of which are being discontinued. The Series II is compatible with software designed to work with the first two LaserJets. It's smaller, quicker, and less expensive. With an optional plug-in card, you can achieve up to 300 dpi.

Be aware, though, that the LaserJet has some limitations, especially with regard to graphics. To see some of these, check the Printer Capability page shown in Figure 6.1.

The Apple LaserWriter

One advantage that the Apple LaserWriter has over the LaserJet is its ability to print in greater detail. In addition, it has 15 families of fonts built in. The Apple LaserWriter achieves printing resolution of 300 dpi. As discussed earlier, it also honors PostScript. Of course, the LaserWriter is more expensive as well.

PRINTING FROM OUTPUT FILES

As we've discussed, you can use the Options menu's Set Printer dialog box to direct the output of a print operation to a disk file, rather than a printer. Once you've created this file, you no longer need Ventura in order to print it. Printing from the disk is handy if a station has the printer you want but not the software (Ventura) you'd normally need for printing.

IMPORTANT

Before beginning, make sure you have enough disk space to create the output file. You will need at least the sum total of all the files that go into making up the document you want to print. This includes chapter files, text files, graphics files, and so on. Printing to disk combines them and creates one very long file (see Figure 6.9). Should

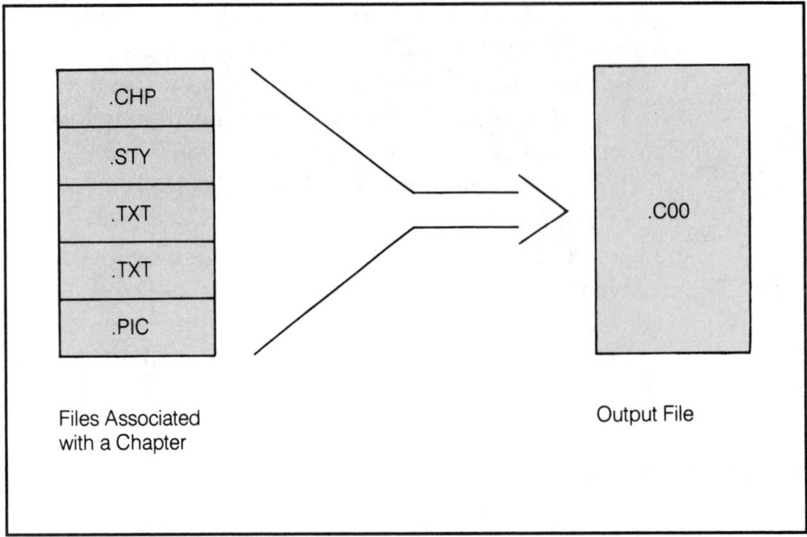

Figure 6.9: Using Files Associated with a Chapter to Create an Output File

Ventura run out of room, it provides no indication that the output was unsuccessful.

Follow these steps to create an output file:

1. Use the Options menu's Set Printer Info dialog box and click the Filename button.
2. Pull down the File menu and click To Print.
3. Choose the settings for the Print Information dialog box as usual and give the OK, just as you would to print normally.
4. Instead of the printer beginning to print, the Item Selector box will appear (see Figure 6.10). Use this box to specify the disk, directory, and name of a file in which to store the output. If you plan to transport the output file on a floppy disk, you'll probably want to specify drive A.
5. When you give the output file a name without providing an extension, Ventura adds the letter C and two zeros as an ending to the name you provide. Give the OK, and Ventura will begin to manufacture the output file.

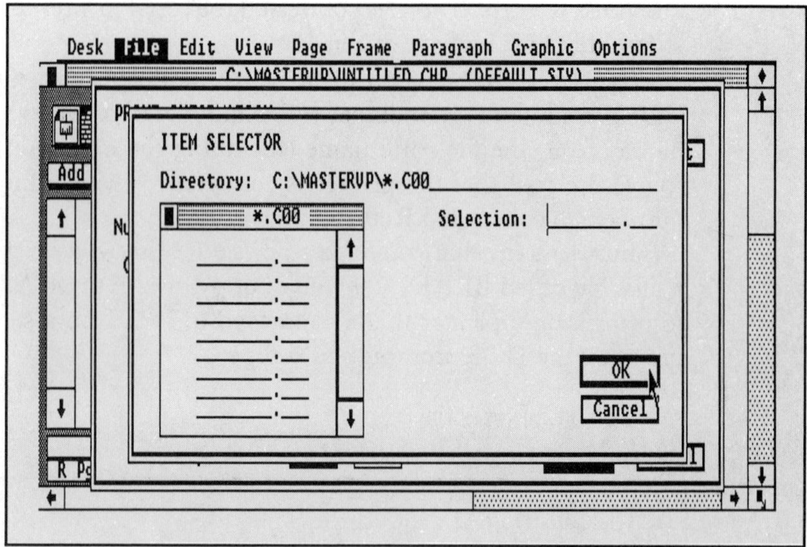

Figure 6.10: The Item Selector Box Used when Printing to a Disk File

Once you've created the output file, you can print the file just by using DOS. Of course, the printer you use must match the printer in effect when you created the output file.

You aren't restricted to transporting an output file on a floppy disk. For instance, you can transmit the file over the phone lines with a modem. If you have a network setup, you can send the output file to another computer on the network. In any case, whatever you do with it, make sure that there's enough room for the file wherever it's expected to land.

You will use DOS's COPY command to print the file. If, however, you have a serial printer, you must first perform the steps described in the next paragraph. (You can skip the next paragraph if you have a parallel printer.)

With a serial printer, of course, you must first issue DOS's MODE command, which specifies the baud rate, parity, and so on. Then, assuming the serial printer is connected to the COM1 port, type in the following command. (Be sure to type only one space after **mode**, and use colons, not semicolons, after the port numbers.) Type

```
mode lpt1: = com1:
```

and press Return. If you've connected the serial printer to com2 substitute that port in place of com1.

When you are ready to print from the output file, use DOS's COPY command. Remember to include the disk drive that has the file, a colon, the file's full name (including the extension), another space, the port that the printer is connected to (including the port number), a colon, and Return.

Thus, let's say that you have a newsletter that you've compiled in a disk file called BRAIN.C00 on a floppy disk in drive A. You want to print it on a printer that's connected to LPT1 on a second computer. At the DOS prompt, you'd type

```
copy a:brain.c00 lpt1:
```

Creating an Output File for a PostScript Printer

With a PostScript printer, you must perform an additional step when creating a disk file. Prior to printing, you must transmit the contents of a special file to your printer. The file's name is DTR.TXT, and it's located within the POSTSCPT directory on the Utilities disk (#11). To use this special file, perform these steps:

1. Make sure that your PostScript printer is on, connected, and online.
2. Insert disk #11 into drive A.
3. At the DOS prompt, type in the following (being certain to space correctly and use the backslash and the colon as indicated):

   ```
   copy a:\postscpt\dtr.txt lptl:
   ```

4. If you turn off the PostScript printer, repeat these steps before you print again.

If you print output files regularly, you may want to automate these procedures. Use a batch file (a file with a BAT extension) as discussed under "Setting Up a Serial Printer."

and press Return. If you're using the standard extension to the file name (as we have here), be sure to use zeros at the end of the extension, not the capital letter O.

If the file is contained in a directory, be sure to include that information. Thus, if you're printing the BRAIN.C00 file that's located in the MASTERVP directory on drive C, you'd type

```
copy c:\mastervp\brain.c00 lpt1:
```

and press Return to print at the LPTl port.

In this chapter we've seen how printing with Ventura Publisher can be simple and straightforward or tailored to your needs. But suppose your needs include the printing of graphics. Printing of text has been a capability of personal computers for a long time, as has the printing of graphics. The integration, though, of both text and graphics on the same page is an innovation of desktop publishing. We'll see how to do that with Ventura in the next chapter.

CHAPTER SEVEN

Adding Pictures from Lotus 1-2-3 and Other Sources

THE ABILITY TO ADD PICTURES TO EXISTING TEXT and vice versa is one of the most exciting features of desktop publishing and, in a sense, defines how desktop publishing is different from both word processing and graphics programs. With Ventura, you can make text-graphics combinations that are truly striking, and you can do it easily.

Ventura provides you with lots of freedom when combining text and graphics. As we've mentioned, you can use text files from a variety of word processors. Likewise, you can use the graphics you create with a variety of graphics packages. With some graphics formats, you use the pictures as is; Ventura references the original file. With others, Ventura converts the original file quickly and automatically, whenever you load a chapter. Either method means that you can continue to work with the original file using the graphics software, if necessary. All updates are reflected automatically in your Ventura documents.

Once you've loaded pictures in Ventura, you can place them anywhere on the page: between paragraphs, within paragraphs, in one column, or straddling columns. Wherever you position them, text already in place will automatically flow around the picture.

You can also manipulate pictures on the page. You can stretch them in one direction or another. You can use a certain area of a picture while ignoring the rest (this procedure is called *cropping*).

As with text, Ventura uses frames to hold pictures. The steps you can perform to incorporate a picture are similar to those you use with word processed text. Here is a summary of these familiar steps, along with a few that are new:

1. Create the picture with appropriate graphics software.
2. Load the picture. This process adds the graphic's file name to the Frame mode's Assignment list.
3. Create a frame, which demarcates the picture's position on the page.
4. Use the Frame mode's Assignment list to pull the picture into the frame.
5. Crop or stretch the picture as necessary.
6. Add a caption and other enhancements to the picture if desired.

We'll use a variation of this method—one that reverses steps 2 and 3—for assigning a file to a frame. Using this method allows us to skip step 4, as we'll see.

The spreadsheet program Lotus 1-2-3 is one of the most popular generators of business graphs. Business users are taking advantage of 1-2-3's ability to create graphs instantly from its spreadsheets, producing graphs of all kinds. In this chapter, we'll show how you can incorporate a 1-2-3 graph into an existing Ventura chapter. You'll also learn how to bring other kinds of pictures into your documents.

This chapter will describe in detail the two types of pictures with which Ventura operates: *images* and *line art*. You'll see the differences between them as well as the advantages and disadvantages of each. You'll also see how to move pictures around and change their size.

Our discussions of importing graphics will carry over into the next chapter. There, you'll see how you can enhance imported pictures by adding various graphic elements that come with Ventura.

INSERTING A 1-2-3 GRAPH

In this section, we'll see how easy it is to incorporate a graph created with Lotus 1-2-3 into a Ventura document. If you are unfamiliar with Lotus 1-2-3, you can use another spreadsheet program or a graphics package to create the chart we'll be working with.

Alternatively, you can practice with any chart or graphic, such as the nozzle graphic that comes with Ventura. It's in the TYPESET directory, which is created by Ventura during the installation process. The file is called NOZZLE.GEM, and it is stored in GEM line-art format. This format is an important factor, as we'll see later on. While almost any figure will do for purposes of demonstration, when you create graphics for your own documents the graphic and the accompanying text will be related, as they are in the example we will now develop.

CREATING A SAMPLE GRAPH WITH 1-2-3

We'll create a graph to illustrate the figures that appear in Ventura's sample table, TABLE.CHP, located in the TYPESET directory. Use the File menu's Open Chapter command to load the file.

The table is shown in Figure 7.1. We'll add the graphic to the same sample page, just below the table.

To create the graph, enter the values in 1-2-3 as you see them in Ventura's sample table (see Figure 7.2). Instead of the titles at the top, however, just enter the year over each column. (You may notice that Total Cost of Sales for 1984 shows an error in addition that the D10 cell formula in 1-2-3 caught. We'll ignore the error.)

Once you've entered the table in 1-2-3, use the / Graph command to display the / Graph menu. Then set the Type command to Bar.

	Year Ended December 31, 1985	Year Ended December 31, 1984
Income		
Sales	$1,234,567.00	$1,345,678.00
Other Income	12,678.00	24,677.00
Total Income	**$1,247,245.00**	**$1,370,355.00**
Cost of Sales		
Cost of Goods	$234,344.00	$456,765.00
Packaging	12,654.00	54,678.00
Other	12,232.00	56,567.00
Total Cost of Sales	**$259,230.00**	**$568,040.00**

Figure 7.1: Ventura's Sample Table

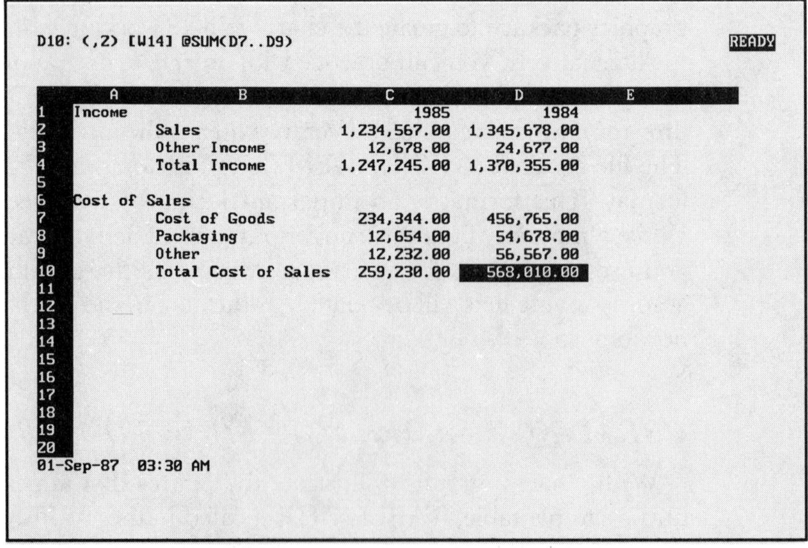

D10: (,2) [W14] @SUM(D7..D9) READY

	A	B	C	D	E
1	Income		1985	1984	
2		Sales	1,234,567.00	1,345,678.00	
3		Other Income	12,678.00	24,677.00	
4		Total Income	1,247,245.00	1,370,355.00	
5					
6	Cost of Sales				
7		Cost of Goods	234,344.00	456,765.00	
8		Packaging	12,654.00	54,678.00	
9		Other	12,232.00	56,567.00	
10		Total Cost of Sales	259,230.00	568,010.00	
11					
12					
13					
14					
15					
16					
17					
18					
19					
20					

01-Sep-87 03:30 AM

Figure 7.2: Creating a Sample Table in Lotus 1-2-3

For the X value, use the year labels at the top of each column. For the A value, specify the two cells that contain the values for Total Income. For the B value, indicate the cells that contain the amounts for Total Cost of Sales.

Because Ventura is so flexible with text and formatting, you can avoid extra effort by not entering too many labels while still in 1-2-3. It's unnecessary to enter a title for the chart, for instance. Should you desire such a title, you can always add one after you import the graph into Ventura.

For the sake of organization, however, it is wise to insert some labels with 1-2-3. Later, you can cover the 1-2-3 text with Ventura text, as long as your printer has the capability of completely obscuring text under graphics. (See Chapter 6 for more on printers and their capabilities.) Inserting the labels with 1-2-3, though, will allow you to keep from confusing labels. From the / Graph menu, use the Options Legend command. For the A legend, enter the words **Total Income**. For the B legend, enter **Total Cost of Sales**. It's best to at least insert labels for the axes and indicate the legend while still in 1-2-3.

From the / Graph menu, use the View command to check your results. Your screen should look like the graph in Figure 7.3.

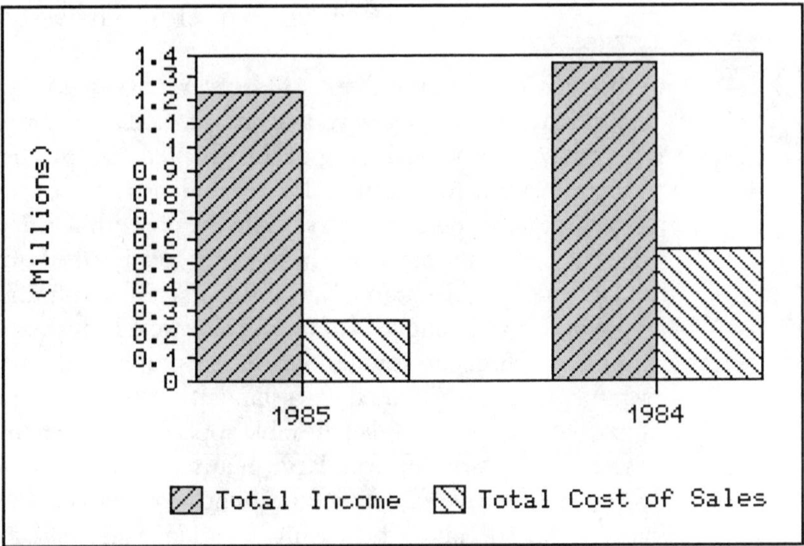

***Figure** 7.3:* A Graph Created with Lotus 1-2-3

Lastly, use the Save command from the / Graph menu to save the graph. (This is the command that you usually use to create graph files you expect to print using Lotus PrintGraph.) Save the file in your MASTERVP directory, which we created in Chapter 3 to hold exercises from this book. Simply call it TABLE; 1-2-3 will add its usual PIC extension.

CREATING A FRAME FOR THE GRAPH

Once you've created the 1-2-3 graph, you can place it in a Ventura chapter. In this example, we'll insert our chart below the sample table that we used to create the chart. To keep the original version of the table intact and free from alteration, first save it in the MASTERVP directory, using the File menu's Save As command. You can use the name TABLE or another name of your choice.

As we discussed in Chapter 3, this copying procedure does not make a copy of the text files used by the chapter file. Because you will usually want to replace these text files with your own anyway, this does not present a problem. However, if you intend to alter the text that makes up the document, rename those files with the Edit menu's File Type/Rename command, or use the Option menu's Multi-Chapter command to copy the chapter and its associated files (see Chapter 11).

Once you've saved the chapter file under a new name, you can add the graph to it. In Chapter 4, you saw how to add a text file to a chapter. As mentioned at the beginning of this chapter, you can use the same technique to add a graphic file. Also as mentioned, you'll use an alternative technique to display our sample graph within the document. Instead of loading the file first, you begin by creating the frame. You can then load the file and automatically assign it to the new frame. Note that this method of assigning files to frames also works with text files.

To create a frame to contain our sample graph, you'll need to scroll down the document (if you have a standard screen) to position the display so that only the bottom of the table appears, as shown in Figure 7.4.

When you're working with large pictures, as we are, you may find it necessary to turn off the Side-bar in the process (as we have done in Figure 7.4), especially when using a standard-size display. Start the Add Frame procedure before turning the Side-bar off, however, since you'll need the Side-bar to add a frame.

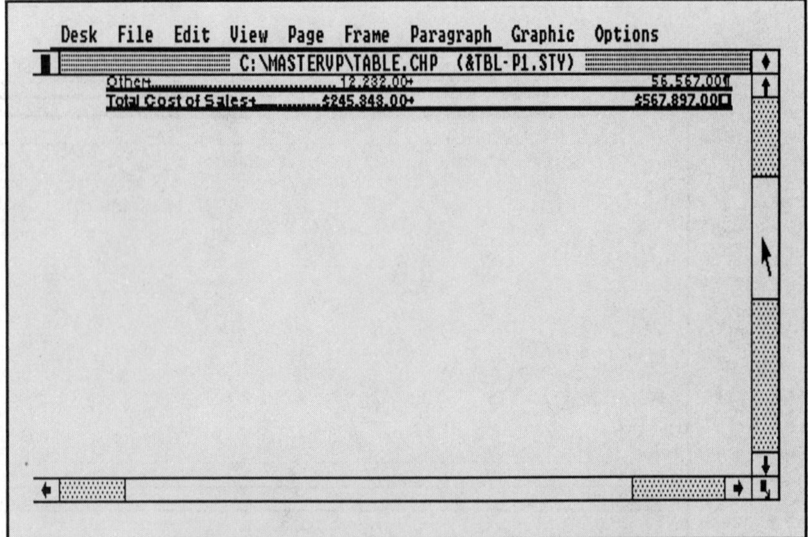

Figure 7.4: The Sample Table Positioned to Receive a Graph

Here then are the steps for placing a frame on a page. Use them to place a frame below the sample table.

1. Activate the Frame mode, if it's not yet active.
2. Click Add New Frame in the Side-bar. You can then turn off the Side-bar, if necessary. (Use the Options command or type Ctrl-W.)
3. Position the mouse cursor for the upper-left corner of the frame that is to hold the picture. The mouse cursor changes to the letters FR, housed within a corner bracket.
4. Press the mouse button and hold. The mouse cursor changes to a pointing finger.
5. While holding its button, drag the mouse cursor to the lower-right corner of the frame (see Figure 7.5).
6. Release the mouse button. This establishes the frame. The new frame is selected, as indicated by the eight black handles that appear along its periphery.

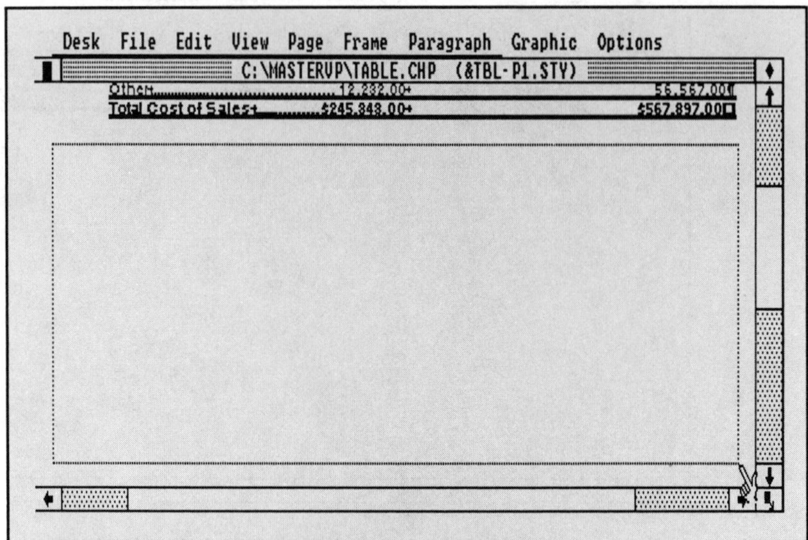

Figure 7.5: Creating the Frame to Hold the Graph

LOADING AND ASSIGNING A 1-2-3 GRAPH

Next, you can load the graph, adding it to the Assignment list and assigning it to the frame in the same step. This will only work if your frame is selected and *empty* at the time you load the file. (The word EMPTY appears in the Current box when the Side-bar is showing and the frame is selected.)

Follow the steps below to add the 1-2-3 graph to the frame. (In step 3, you'll specify the type of picture that you're using. We'll examine the types of pictures Ventura uses in the next section.)

1. Make sure that the Frame mode is active and that an empty frame is selected.
2. Pull down the File menu and click Load Text/Picture. You'll see the dialog box shown in Figure 7.6.
3. Click the box labeled Line-Art. This will make the Line-Art Format grouping available, as indicated by normal (not ghosting) buttons in that category.
4. Click the Lotus .PIC box.

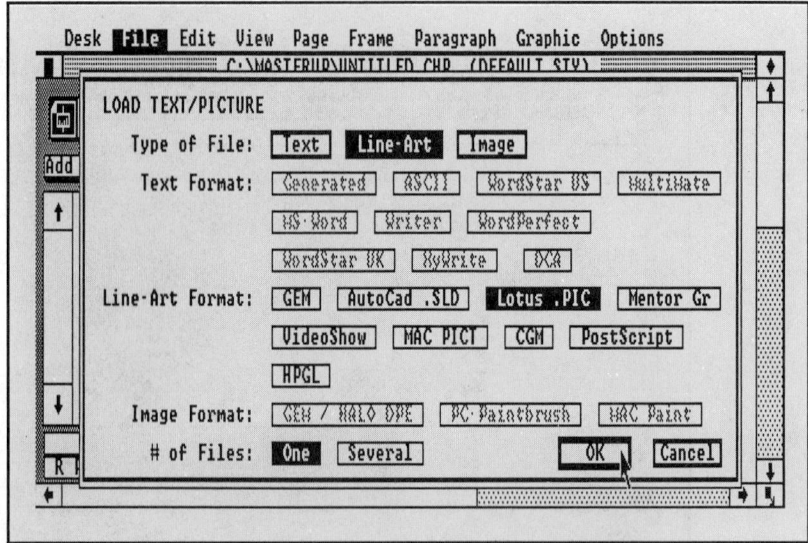

Figure 7.6: The File Menu's Load Text/Picture Dialog Box

5. Give the OK.
6. Use the Item Selector box that appears to indicate the PIC file you wish to use (our example is TABLE.PIC). Don't forget that you can use the Backup button (right under the D in Directory) to back out of directories or to change drives.
7. Give the OK for the Item Selector box. Once you have, Ventura adds the name of the picture file to the Assignment list (of course, you'll only see it when the Side-bar is showing). It also assigns the file to the frame.

If you've used these steps to add the graph to the sample table, your screen should look like Figure 7.7. Printed out, the page looks like Figure 7.8. Looking at these figures, you may notice that some aspects of the page could do with a little polishing; for instance, the positioning of the graph leaves a lot of space at the bottom of the page, and the text on the chart is rather small. Also, the LaserJet used to print Figure 7.8 was unable to print the sideways label *Millions*. We'll see how to fix these details as we proceed with this chapter and the next.

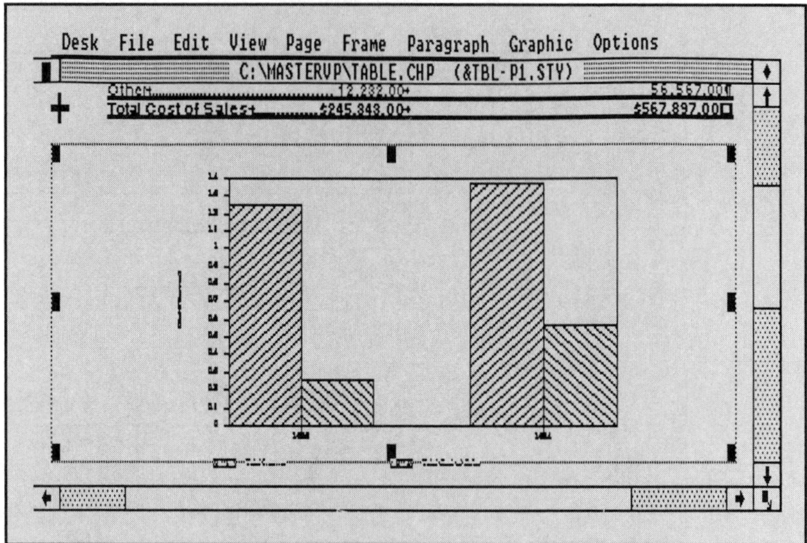

Figure 7.7: The Graph File Assigned to a Frame

VENTURA'S TWO PICTURE FORMATS

When you were loading the graph, you probably noticed that besides text, there are two categories listed on the File menu's Load Text/Picture dialog box (Figure 7.6). These are the types of pictures that Ventura can use. Table 7.1 summarizes the graphics terminology that Ventura uses, including these two formats. Refer to it as we examine the various graphics features.

HOW THE FORMATS ARE PRODUCED

As the Load Text/Picture dialog box shows, Ventura can use pictures classified as either *images* or *line art*. These names represent the different *formats* computer programs use to create graphics. The method that a particular picture file uses depends upon the software with which it was created. Let's take a look at each of these formats now.

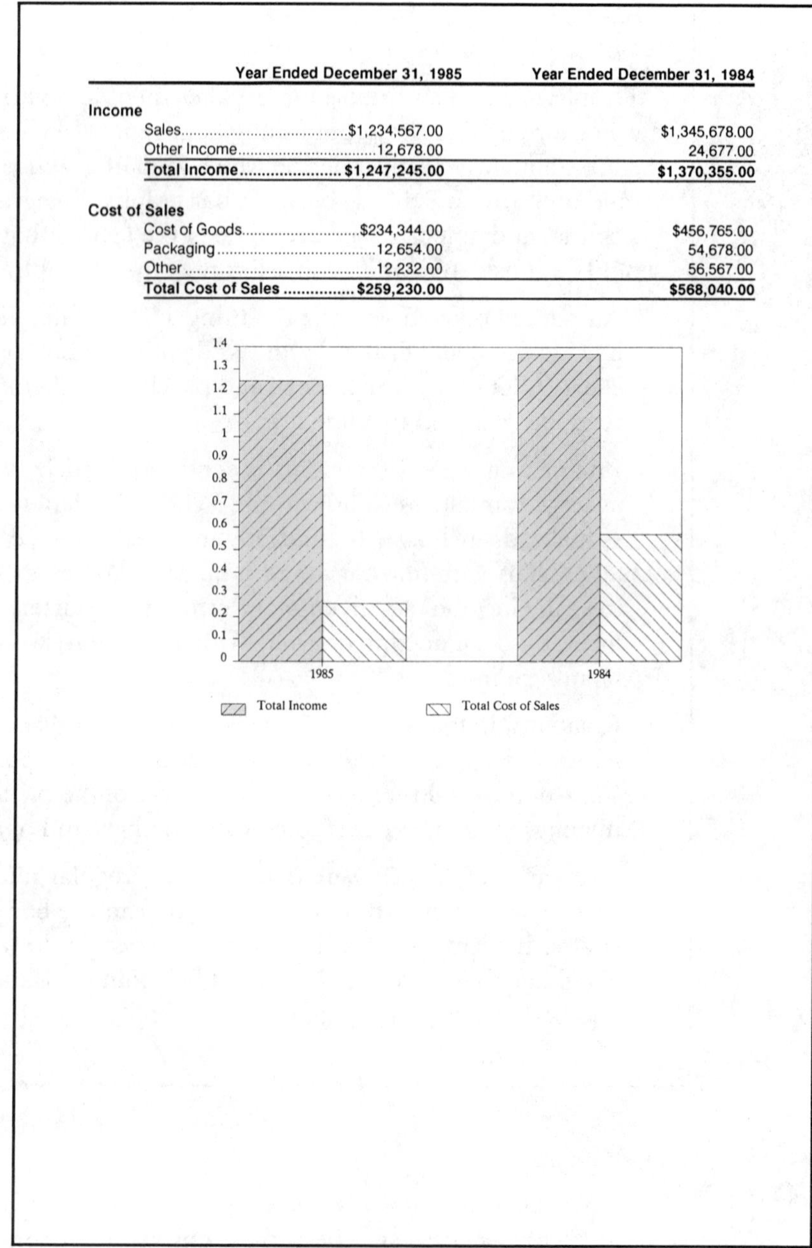

	Year Ended December 31, 1985	Year Ended December 31, 1984
Income		
Sales	$1,234,567.00	$1,345,678.00
Other Income	12,678.00	24,677.00
Total Income	**$1,247,245.00**	**$1,370,355.00**
Cost of Sales		
Cost of Goods	$234,344.00	$456,765.00
Packaging	12,654.00	54,678.00
Other	12,232.00	56,567.00
Total Cost of Sales	**$259,230.00**	**$568,040.00**

Figure 7.8: The Printed Version of the Sample Table and Its 1-2-3 Graph

Which Graph for the Job?

Graphs can add an important visual element to a variety of business-oriented desktop-publishing applications. Whatever the use, though, you must decide which kind of graph you should use. You can choose between bar graphs, line graphs, pie charts, and others. What are some of the factors that should be considered when you select the type of graph?

- Amount of data: If you're presenting a lot of data, you'll need to use a line graph. With less data, use a bar or pie chart. A lot of data makes bar and pie charts difficult to read, but can add to a line graph.
- Intervening data: Where data is continuous, such as with average rainfall, use a line graph. Where the data is individualized, such as with quarterly income for the year, use a bar chart with one bar for each quarter. You can't surmise the income of a given month from the quarterly income, so connecting quarters with a line chart would be misleading.
- Relationship to a whole: Pie charts are best for displaying a relationship of parts to the whole, such as a company's share of the total market. If critical pieces of the pie are missing, though, it's best to go with another kind of graph.
- Regularity of data: Where data occurs at regular intervals, such as with standard time periods, you can use bar or line charts. If events occur at irregular intervals, you'll want to avoid bar charts. A line chart would smooth the data out, and perhaps display a pattern.

Image Format

Programs that use the *image format* are sometimes called *paint programs* or *bit-mapped programs*. These programs create pictures by storing the settings for tiny dots (called *bits* or *pixels*) that the computer uses to display the picture on the screen or with the printer.

TYPE OF GRAPHIC	DESCRIPTION
Picture	Any illustration used with Ventura, be it image or line art.
Line Art	Picture produced and stored as a collection of objects, also known as object-oriented art. Created with a "draw" program such as AutoCAD or with the Lotus 1-2-3 Graph Save command.
Image	Picture composed of individual dots, or *pixels.* Created with a "paint" program, such as Publisher's Paintbrush, or with a scanner.
Graphic Elements	Line art that you create with Ventura by using the Graphics mode, as opposed to art you bring in from another program. Often, these graphic elements will supplement imported pictures.

Table 7.1: Graphics Terminology in Ventura

As an analogy, think of the big electric sign in New York's Times Square. It displays images in much the same manner as a paint program. Its many individual light bulbs turn on and off in various combinations, creating images you recognize to promote a product or service. Similarly, image programs store information about the screen's dots in image files. Displaying them on the screen switches the screen's dots on and off to create pictures that you recognize.

Typical uses for image format include reproducing photographs and simulating paintings and sketches. Image format works well with images in which objects tend to have soft edges, since arcs and diagonal lines are not smoothly formed in image format. You can use these programs to create brush-stroke, spray-paint, and air-brush effects.

Paint programs that Ventura supports include PC Paintbrush, GEM Paint, and MAC Paint (imported from a Macintosh). It will also support software that stores images in these formats. You should convert images obtained with a scanner (see Chapter 1) into PC Paintbrush format if they're initially in some other format.

Line-Art Format

Line art is sometimes called *drawn* or *object-oriented* artwork. With line art, the computer stores information on the drawing in terms of geometric formulas. For example, rather than telling the computer that certain pixels should be dark, which gives the impression of a line, the specifications simply indicate the starting measurements, the length, direction, ending measurement, and so on. The result is a cleaner looking line, especially when you print the picture. Lines and circles are sharp and smooth. Objects are layered one on top of another, allowing them to be manipulated individually.

Applications for line art include graphs such as the one that we created with Lotus 1-2-3. Ventura also supports graphs created with GEM Graph.

Other line-art applications are provided with drawing programs. You use drawing programs to create architectural diagrams, logos, and various other drawn objects. Supported programs include AutoCAD, the most popular computer-aided design program available. Ventura also accommodates drawings created with GEM Draw, a simpler drawing package, and other programs you see in the Load Text/Picture dialog box.

Most line-art files can be used as is, but some you will have to adapt. With AutoCAD, for example, you must use the optional ADE-2 package to store artwork in slide-file format. (You use this format to create computer slide shows for quick viewing.) To create a slide, load your drawing and issue the MSLIDE (Make Slide) command. Doing so creates a new file with an SLD extension, which Ventura can then load. As with images, Ventura will support any software whose artwork you can convert to one of the listed formats.

Also note that if you use an encapsulated PostScript file (one with an EPS extension), Ventura will not display its contents on the screen. Instead, a large X will show in the frame to which the file is assigned.

ADVANTAGES AND DISADVANTAGES OF EACH FORMAT

As you can see, the method Ventura uses depends upon the software you use to create your pictures. If you're committed to using pictures from one program or another, the method you use is determined for you. Suppose, however, you have yet to choose a graphics package, or you have access to several. Which technique should you use to create a picture? Let's look at the advantages each format has to offer.

With images, what you see on the computer screen is pretty much what you will get on the printer. That is, the resolution on the screen is the maximum you can expect to achieve with the printer. Generally, screen resolution is not so hot. Even though printer resolution is theoretically better, the printer merely copies the images, dot for dot, from the screen. Thus, image files do not allow you to use printers to their fullest capacity.

With line art, since the program stores drawings in terms of computations, not dots, you always get the maximum amount of detail that the output device has to offer. Thus, printed versions of pictures usually look better than their screen counterparts. If you use a Linotronic typesetter, pictures in line-art format will look better still. On the other hand, even on a Linotronic, pictures in image format look no better than they do on the screen.

With image programs, you can magnify an area of the picture and work on the pixels that make it up. This feature allows you to fine-tune the image bit-by-bit. Figure 7.9 shows how part of a circle created with PC Paintbrush looks when you enlarge it with that program. Notice how jagged the edge is. Some line-art programs, such as AutoCAD, also allow you to zoom in on an area. With a drawing program, however, a curve remains sharp, even in close-up (see Figure 7.10).

Because the dots that make up an image show up when you magnify it, it's important that you take care when constructing it. Always consider the way in which your image will finally be put to use. Don't paint an image smaller than you intend to use it, expecting to magnify, or you'll lose resolution. Rather, always draw the image big and reduce it later if necessary. Reducing will result in a cleaner image and fewer jagged edges.

Image files also tend to take more disk space than do line-art files, because they must store information on every tiny dot that goes to

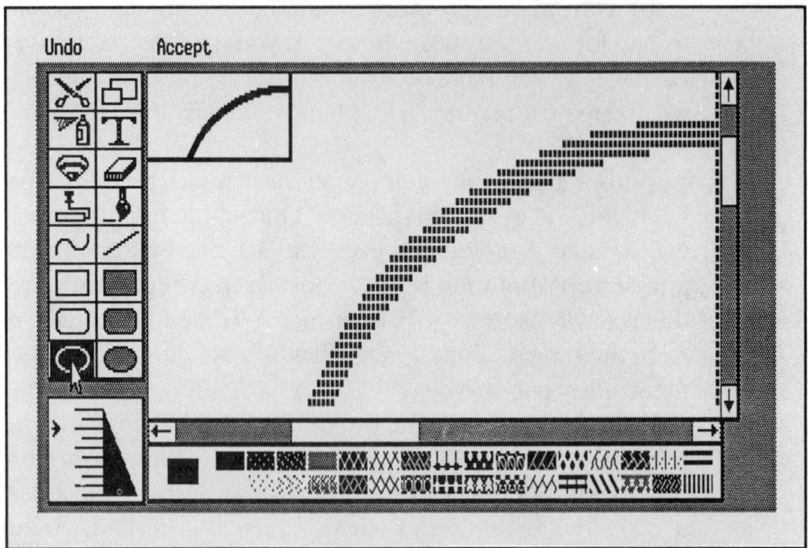

Figure 7.9: An Enlarged Portion of a Circle Created with PC Paintbrush

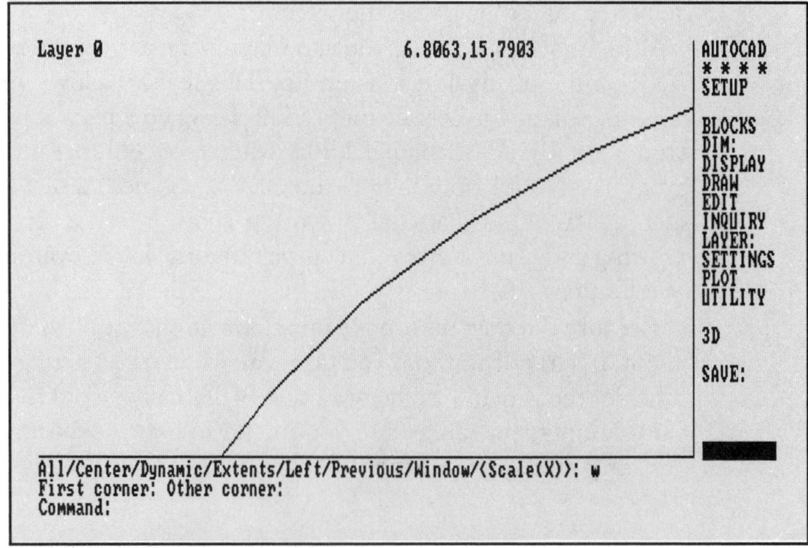

Figure 7.10: An Enlarged Portion of a Circle Created with AutoCAD

make them up. This consideration can be especially troublesome when you use a scanner to import an image, resulting in very big files. Although Ventura will crop very nicely, as we'll see, you should do some preliminary cropping yourself. To save disk space, only scan that portion of a picture that you are certain you will use.

To summarize, then, remember the effects you wish to achieve when selecting a graphics package. Image programs, by their nature, create soft-edged, "painted" pictures. Line-art programs create sharp, drawn, exacting pictures.

MANIPULATING PICTURES

Regardless of which technique you use to create a picture, once you've imported it into a Ventura document, you can manipulate it in many ways. With Version 1.1 you use the same techniques to manipulate either type. You can move the picture around on the page, change its size, delete it, or crop it. We'll study the techniques for performing these operations in this section.

Be aware, though, that you cannot use Ventura to rotate pictures. If you must rotate a picture (that is, change it to face horizontally or vertically), use your graphics software to do so.

TOOLS THAT SUPPLEMENT PICTURE MANIPULATION

Before we begin, let's examine some supplemental tools Ventura provides that can assist you in your manipulation of pictures. You'll need these tools as you work. These tools do not perform cut, copy, and paste operations per se, but they do expedite those procedures and make certain operations possible.

Hiding Pictures Temporarily

Pictures consume a lot of the computer's memory, because a lot of data goes into composing them. For this reason, working with pictures can really slow down the operation of the program. This especially holds true for image-format pictures.

Fortunately, Ventura provides a way for you to hide pictures in order to speed things up. Pull down the Options menu and click Hide Pictures. Hidden pictures are replaced with a solid block on the screen but they appear on paper when you print the document. Usually, the operation of the program is improved considerably by hiding pictures.

Generally, you'll want to keep pictures hidden, except when you really need to look at them—to crop, for instance. To display a hidden picture, use the flip side of the same command—the Options menu's Show Pictures command. When you're done, hide your pictures again right away.

Using Cross Hairs

With Version 1.1, you can also use cross hairs, as we discussed in Chapter 3, to help position frames. These are available when you've used the Options command to show rulers at the top and left edges of the working area.

Starting at the 0,0 box, drag the mouse onto the working area to see and use cross hairs (see Figure 7.11). Remember that releasing with the mouse cursor in the working area relocates the zero point of the rulers, while releasing on one of the rulers causes only that ruler to be affected.

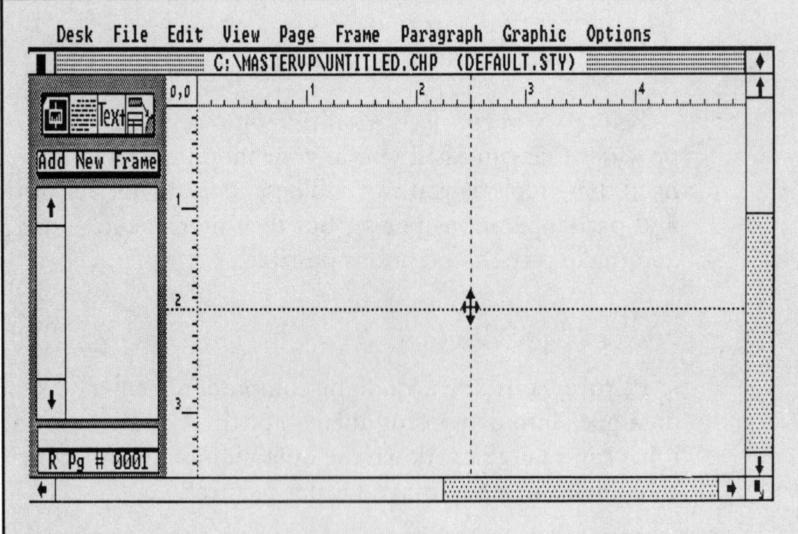

Figure 7.11: Cross Hairs

Changing Views

When manipulating frames, don't forget to change to a more general view, as necessary. The larger the frame, the more likely operations will be quickened by using Reduced or Facing Pages view. Be aware, though, that Facing Pages view has limitations. You cannot drag pictures across its page boundaries. However, you can use Facing Pages view in conjunction with cross hairs to check the alignment of frames on a two-page spread.

Selecting Techniques

To work with a picture frame, you must first select it with the mouse, just as you would a text frame. Selecting is discussed in Chapter 3. Remember you can use Shift-clicking to select multiple frames. With the mouse, you can manipulate the frames as a group; moving, copying, stretching them, and so on. Be aware, however, that you cannot use the menus to change the characteristics of multiple frames simultaneously. For instance, once multiple frames are selected you cannot pull down the Frame menu to set the margins for all selected frames. Only the settings for the first frame selected would be affected in this case.

Remember also that Ctrl-clicking allows you to select frames that are beneath other frames. For example, later in this chapter we'll see how to create a text run-around, which allows text to follow the contours of a picture. For this application, a picture frame must be on top of a frame that holds the text. You can Ctrl-click either frame as necessary to select the one that you need to work with.

MOVING PICTURES

Now that you have some basic tools under your belt, let's begin to examine picture manipulation. Some of the more straightforward operations you can perform include moving, cutting, and pasting frames. You move picture frames in the same way that you move other frames in Ventura. Just move the frame and you move the picture. The techniques are the same as those described in Chapter 4.

You'll probably find it desirable to have the edges of your frames line up with columns and lines. To do that, use the Options menu to turn column snap and line snap on, as discussed in Chapter 2.

You can also use the menus to move a frame. Once you've selected the appropriate frame, pull down the Frame menu and click Sizing & Scaling. In the resulting dialog box (Figure 7.12), adjust the Upper Left Y (top) and X (left) coordinates as discussed in Chapter 3.

In addition, you can use the other cut-and-paste procedures to manipulate pictures. Just activate the Frame mode and select the appropriate picture frame. Pull down the Edit menu to cut, copy, and paste the frames, just as you do with frames of text. Alternatively, use the Del and Ins keys, as noted on the Edit menu.

RESIZING PICTURES

With Ventura you can change the size of pictures that you've imported. One way to resize a picture is simply to resize the frame that contains it. Normally, the picture enlarges or reduces to accommodate the frame. Again, the techniques are the same as those we've already studied. That is, once you've selected a frame, you use the mouse to grab one of the frame's handles and stretch the frame in one

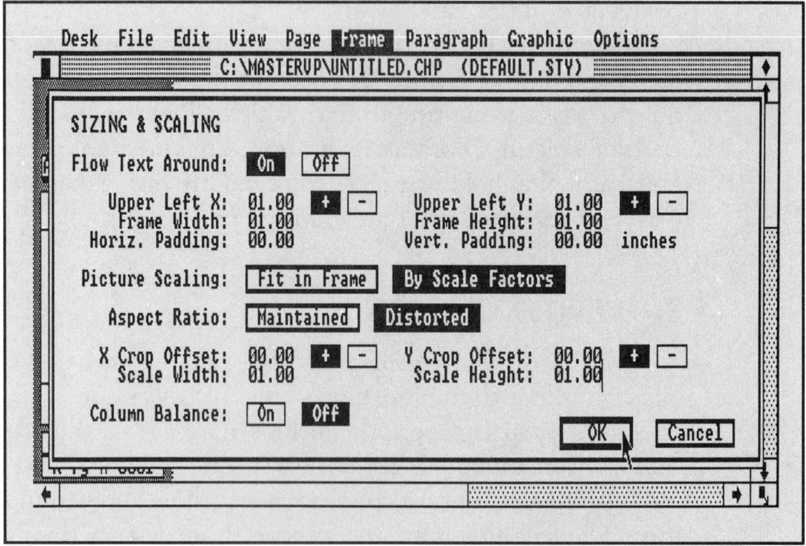

Figure 7.12: The Frame Menu's Sizing & Scaling Dialog Box

direction or another. Alternatively, you can use the Frame menu's Sizing & Scaling dialog box (Figure 7.12). Adjust the frame's settings for Upper Left Y and X and for Frame Width, Frame Height, and Padding as desired. As the frame changes size, the picture will too. For instance, Figure 7.13 shows how you could stretch the graph we worked with earlier in order to fill the remainder of an 8-1/2-by-11-inch page.

There may be times, though, when you want to resize a picture without changing the size of its frame. This dialog box also allows you to accomplish that. A picture will resize as you adjust the frame, as long as Picture Scaling is set to Fit in Frame. If you set Picture Scaling to By Scale Factors, Ventura will instead scale the picture according to the values you provide for settings in the bottom part of the dialog box. These settings scale with respect to the original size of the picture, independent of the size of the frame. We'll examine these settings in a moment.

Changing the Aspect Ratio

When resizing pictures in Ventura, we can make use of Ventura's ability to maintain or distort the aspect ratio of a picture. The *aspect ratio* is the ratio of a picture's height to its width. A picture that's 8 by 10 inches, reduced without distortion to 4 by 5, maintains the same aspect ratio, since these measurements have the same ratio.

Stretching pictures can produce some odd results, but it can also prove a useful tool in putting together your pages. To stretch the bar chart in order to fill the page, we had to allow its aspect ratio to be distorted. However, you probably wouldn't want to stretch a pie chart; because of the distortion in the aspect ratio, the pie would come out looking egg-shaped.

Now consider Figure 7.14. This is an image-type picture. It was created from a photo that was scanned using a Princeton scanner with Publisher's Paintbrush, then placed in a Ventura document. In the image on the left, the aspect ratio is normal. If you keep the Aspect Ratio set on Maintained, the picture will continue to resemble the original as you enlarge or reduce. Ventura will crop or add white space, if necessary, so as not to distort the picture.

In the same figure, the two images on the right have been scaled by scale factors, with the Aspect Ratio set to Distorted. To practice such

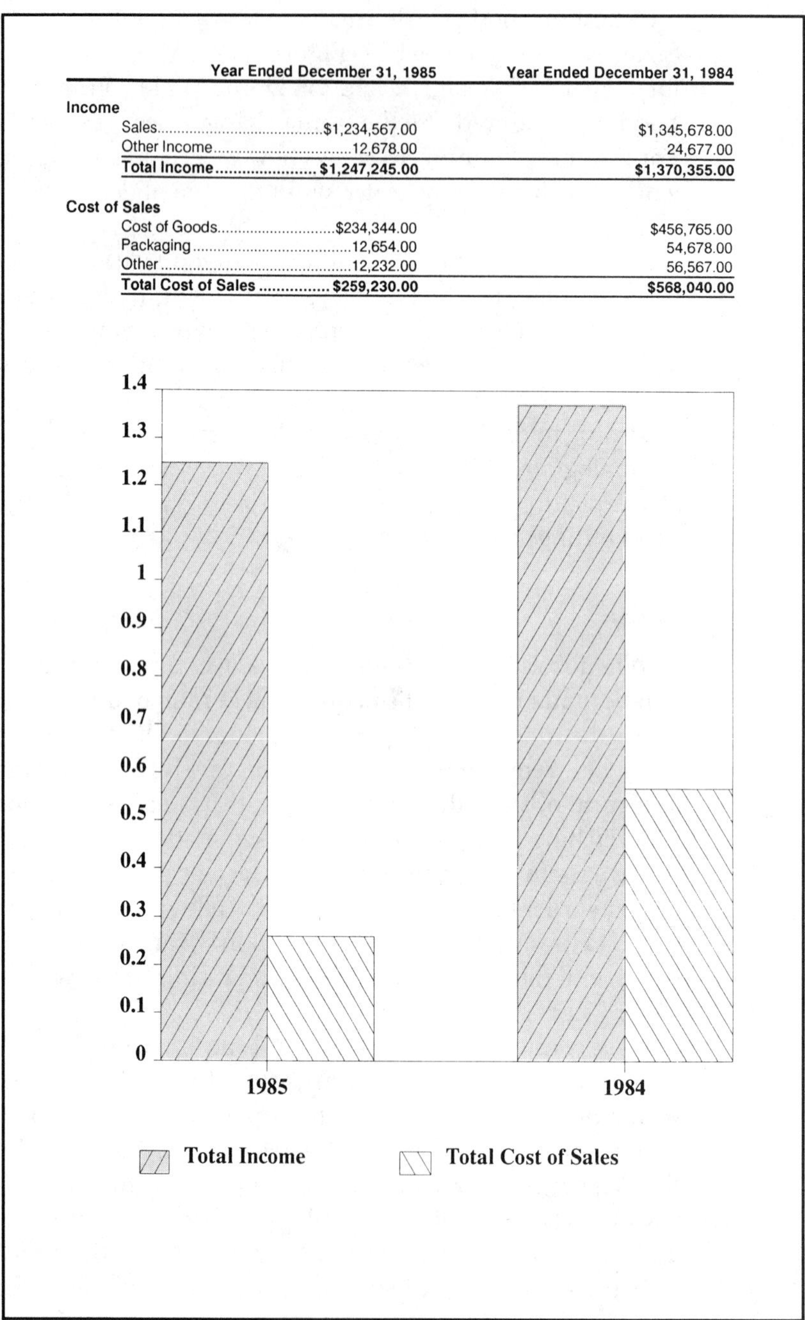

	Year Ended December 31, 1985	Year Ended December 31, 1984
Income		
Sales	$1,234,567.00	$1,345,678.00
Other Income	12,678.00	24,677.00
Total Income	**$1,247,245.00**	**$1,370,355.00**
Cost of Sales		
Cost of Goods	$234,344.00	$456,765.00
Packaging	12,654.00	54,678.00
Other	12,232.00	56,567.00
Total Cost of Sales	**$259,230.00**	**$568,040.00**

Figure 7.13: The Chart Stretched to Fill the Page

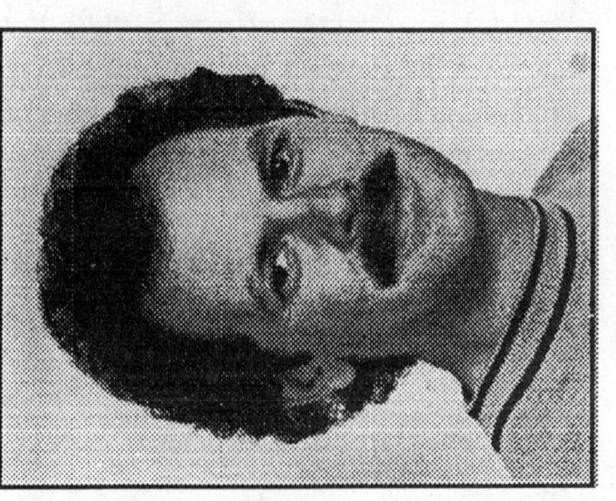

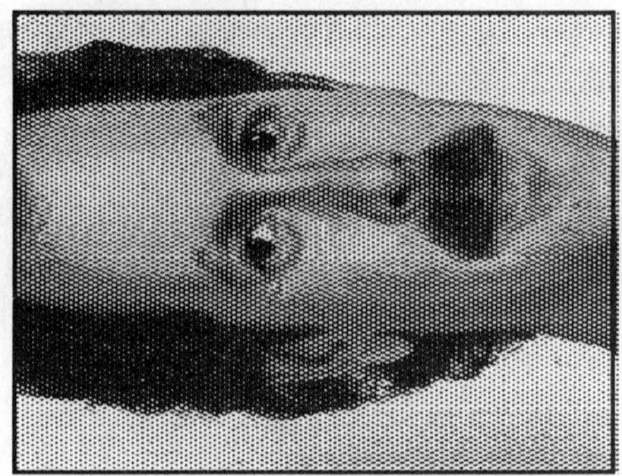

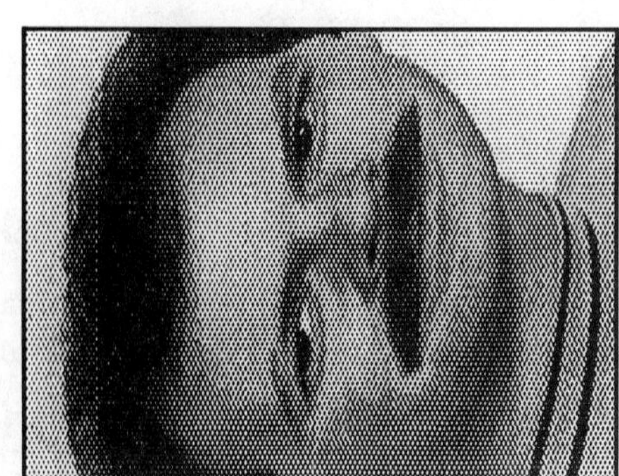

Figure 7.14: Distorting the Aspect Ratio

image distortion, you can use your own file or the CHANEL.IMG file that's located in the TYPESET directory. CHANEL.IMG is in GEM image format.

Setting Scale Factors

As mentioned, you can click the By Scale Factors button in order to adjust a picture's size independently of its frame. When Fit in Frame is selected, values will ghost for Scale Width and Scale Height toward the bottom of the dialog box. When By Scale Factors is selected, one or both of these Scale dimensions become available. The ghosting of Scale Height will change as you change the Aspect Ratio setting.

If Aspect Ratio is set to Distorted, both Scale Width and Scale Height become available. The values you see will change from the ghosting (frame size) values to the actual size of the picture, independent of its frame. You can then adjust these settings to increase or decrease the size of the picture. Adjusting the settings stretches the picture accordingly (see Figure 7.14).

The original size of the picture appears, just after clicking By Scale Factors. You may wish to bear this value in mind as you adjust picture size. Thus, for instance, if you want to double a picture that's initially 1.02 inches wide, change the scale width to 2.04 inches.

As you resize scanned images, you may see unexpected bars across the face of the picture. However, they will not be present in the printed version of the document. They're caused by differences in resolution between the screen and the image as it was scanned.

If you've selected By Scale Factors and have Aspect Ratio set to Maintained, the Scale Height setting will ghost. You will only be able to set Scale Width. Scale Height will adjust automatically in order to maintain the correct aspect ratio.

Above the Scale Width and Height settings you can see settings for Crop Offset. Let's discuss cropping and see how Ventura accomplishes it.

CROPPING

Cropping is the technique of cutting away parts of a picture or matting it so that only the desired portion appears. By displaying only what you want shown, Ventura allows you to edit your pictures. However, cropping only affects the picture as it's displayed by your chapter file. The original picture always remains intact, which means you can crop again later to show a different portion instead.

Using Alt-Mouse

As with other features we've studied, there is both a fast, easy way to crop and a more exacting method. The easy way to crop is by using the Alt key in conjunction with the mouse, as follows:

1. Set Picture Scaling to By Scale Factors. Fit-in-Frame pictures cannot be cropped; they always adjust to the frame.
2. Consider the frame size and the original scale dimensions of the picture you wish to crop. The frame values must be smaller than the scale values in order to crop the image with the mouse.
3. Point the mouse cursor anywhere on the picture in the frame. You will see only that portion of the original picture that can fit in the frame.
4. Press the Alt key and hold it down.
5. While holding the Alt key, press the mouse button and hold it down. The mouse cursor will change to the shape of a flattened hand (see Figure 7.15). Once you're holding the mouse button down, you may release the Alt key, if you wish.
6. While still pressing the mouse button, drag the picture as desired. You'll see the picture move beneath the frame.
7. When the picture is cropped to your liking, release the mouse button.

Watching Ventura crop for the first time is thrilling. It looks as though the flattened hand of the mouse cursor is moving a picture beneath a cutout in the page. It's a great visual example of the ingeniousness that went into the design of this program. You can also crop in a less visually dramatic fashion by using settings in the Frame menu's Sizing & Scaling dialog box.

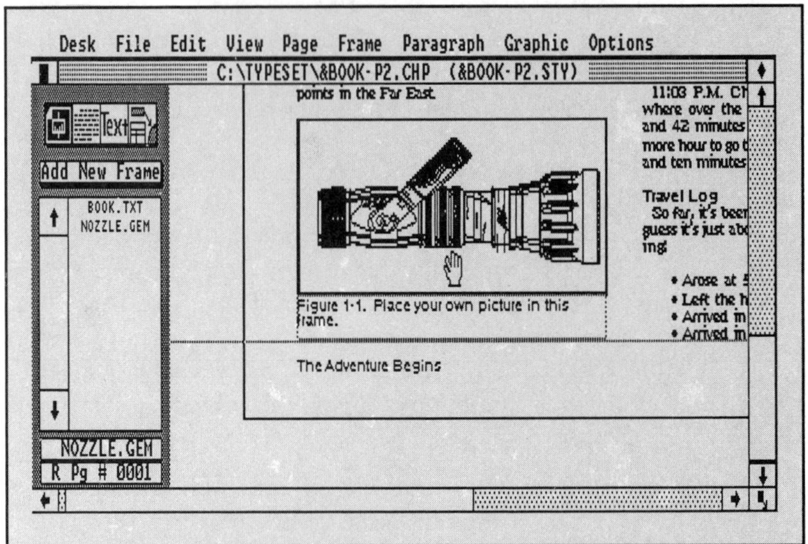

Figure 7.15: The Mouse Cursor in the Shape of a Flattened Hand for Cropping

Using Offset Settings

As we mentioned in the steps above, you can't use the mouse to crop if the size of the frame is greater than the size of the picture as scaled. However, you can use the Sizing & Scaling dialog box to crop under these circumstances. Adjust the values for X and Y Crop Offset and their accompanying Plus and Minus buttons. Use X Crop Offset to adjust the picture left (+) and right (–) with respect to the frame. Use Y Crop Offset to adjust the picture up (+) and down (–). For example, let's say you have a picture that's originally 3 inches high, with the middle third showing in the frame. You want to show the top third of it in a frame that's 1 inch high. To do this, you'd set the Y Crop Offset to 1 inch and click the Minus button. This would adjust the picture down the frame, thus showing the top third.

CHANGING FRAME MARGINS

We've seen how you can change the size of a picture and crop to control the portion of the picture that's seen. You can also limit the area within a frame that's available for the picture. When pictures are used with densely written material, for instance, you can use this technique to create white space for clearly setting off the image from the text. Do so by following these steps to increase the frame's margins.

1. Activate the Frame mode and select the frame with the image.
2. Pull down the Frame menu and click Margins and Columns.
3. Set the margins as desired and give the OK.

Once the display area is reduced, you can then crop to display the portion of the image you wish to show.

CREATING TEXT RUN-AROUNDS

So far, we've been manipulating frames to influence the display of pictures they contain. Now let's turn our attention to using frames in order to influence the text that surrounds a picture.

A *text run-around* is text that follows the contours of some graphic, such as a company logo (see Figure 7.16 for an example). Normally, Ventura diverts text around frames that you create for holding pictures. However, you can allow the text to flow beneath the frame that holds a picture. Then, by using a series of stepped frames, you can cause text to conform to the outline of the picture. Here are the steps for creating a text run-around with Ventura:

1. In Frame mode, use the Add New Frame button to create a frame on top of the text. Then load the picture into it. The text will flow around the frame as usual.
2. With this picture frame selected, use the Frame menu's Sizing & Scaling dialog box and set Flow Text Around to Off. Text will then flow beneath the frame and you'll see your picture superimposed on the text.
3. Within the picture's frame, create a series of small frames that cover those areas of the picture you want protected from

text. Hold down the Shift key while you position these frames and the Add New Frame button will remain operational, relieving you of the need to click repeatedly. Line by line, these small frames will nudge the text out from protected portions of the picture's frame, creating the type of text run-around shown in Figure 7.16.

Figure 7.17 shows the completed text run-around in print. As you can see, the logo is off to one side. This is the easiest placement to accommodate. If you position your picture in the middle of a column, with text on either side of it, you must create a separate small frame for each line of text. If the logo in the example is placed within a column, for instance, the single frame around the word SYBEX would have to be replaced with three smaller frames, one for each line of text. Otherwise, the text would first flow down the left side of the single frame and then down the right side, disrupting the reading pattern at that point.

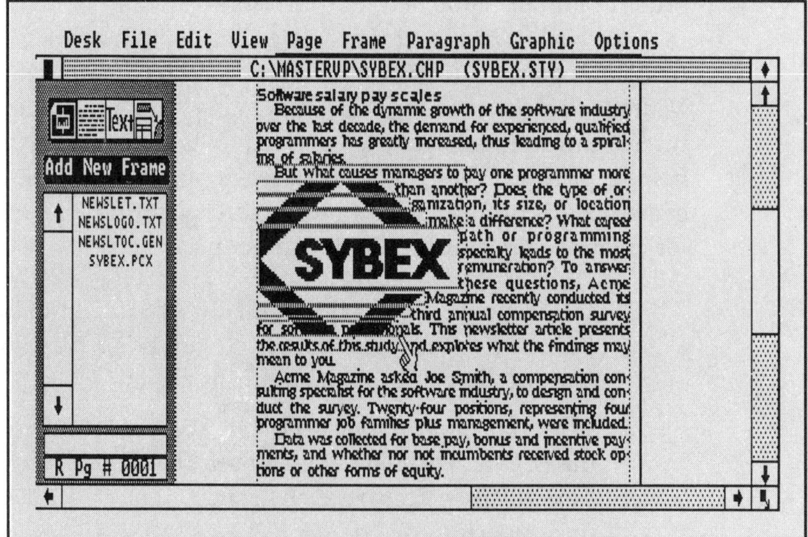

Figure 7.16: Using Small Frames to Create a Text Run-Around

Software salary pay scales

Because of the dynamic growth of the software industry over the last decade, the demand for experienced, qualified programmers has greatly increased, thus leading to a spiraling of salaries.

But what causes managers to pay one programmer more than another? Does the type of organization, its size, or location make a difference? What career path or programming specialty leads to the most remuneration? To answer these questions, Acme Magazine recently conducted its third annual compensation survey for software professionals. This newsletter article presents the results of this study and explores what the findings may mean to you.

Acme Magazine asked Joe Smith, a compensation consulting specialist for the software industry, to design and conduct the survey. Twenty-four positions, representing four programmer job families plus management, were included.

Data was collected for base pay, bonus and incentive payments, and whether nor not incumbents received stock options or other forms of equity.

SYBEX

***Figure** 7.17:* Text Run-Around in Print

ADDING CAPTIONS WITH AUTOMATIC FIGURE NUMBERS

Many applications that use pictures require that captions accompany the pictures. From short newsletters to book-length documents, captions allow the reader to associate the picture with related material in text. In addition, some documents require a figure number in the caption as well for text that directly references a picture. Ventura allows you to accomplish captioning with ease and dispatch. It also provides you with the means of automatically numbering the captions in a variety of styles.

CREATING CAPTION LABELS

To create a caption for a figure, you begin by creating a caption frame. A caption frame is a special frame that is associated with a particular standard frame—namely, the one holding the picture you wish to caption. The caption frame piggybacks onto the standard frame and the two stay together wherever you move them. To create a caption frame, display the dialog box for setting captions, as follows:

1. Activate the Frame mode and select the appropriate frame.
2. Pull down the Frame menu.
3. Click Anchors & Captions.

This action displays the dialog box in Figure 7.18.

Begin by considering the Caption setting. As you can see from this grouping, it's possible to place the caption frame on any one of the four sides of its host frame. Click the position that you desire.

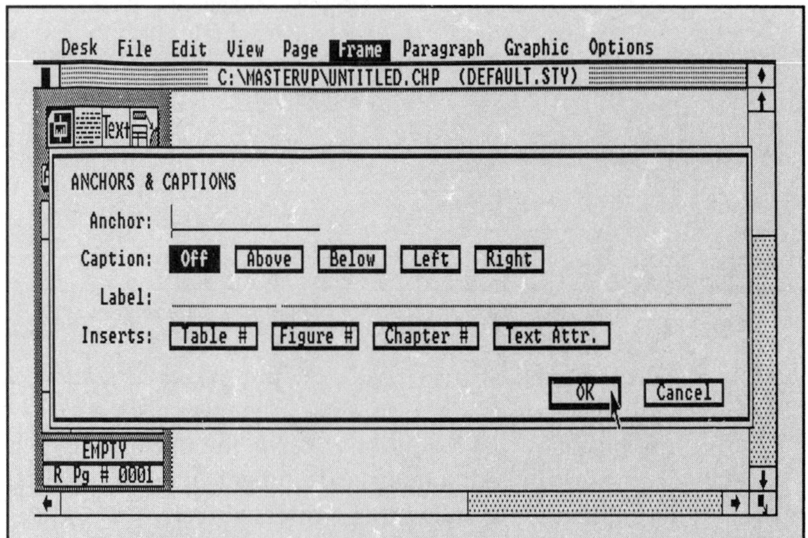

Figure 7.18: The Dialog Box for the Frame Menu's Anchors & Captions Command

Once you choose a position, you'll be able to enter a *caption label.* Note that there is only one line provided for you to type the label in. This does not mean, however, that your captions can be only one line long. Rather, this line in the dialog box is for earmarking the caption. The standard style for such earmarking uses the word *Figure*, a space, and then the figure number. This text becomes the caption label. Material that you enter as a caption label can only be edited in this dialog box in the Frame mode. However, you can add (and edit) additional explanatory material, if necessary, directly within the caption frame in Text mode. We'll see how to do this in the next section.

To create such a standard label, type in the word **Figure**, and then the space. Next, make use of Ventura's automatic figure numbering system. Click the button labeled Figure #. Doing so will cause Ventura to add a special bracketed code, [F#], to the label line. This code indicates that the automatic figure number should appear in that position. Thus, the finished label line will look like this:

```
Figure [F#]
```

When printed, this caption label would appear like so for the first figure:

```
Figure 1
```

Ventura inserts bracketed codes like this for your convenience, so that you can use the automatic numbering without having to remember the exact syntax for the codes. If you wish, though, you can simply type in the entire label line, including the bracketed code.

As you can see, Ventura also provides boxes for the automatic numbering of tables and chapters. These are each separate counters. You can use them separately or in conjunction with each other. Thus, let's say that you'd like tables to be numbered using the chapter number and the table number. For example, if you want the third table in Chapter 1 to be captioned

```
Table 1–3
```

here's what you'd enter on the label line:

```
Table [C#]–[T#]
```

Again, you can simply type it all in just as it appears above, or you can click boxes as appropriate. Here you would type the word **Table**, a space, then click the Chapter # box, type the hyphen, and finish by clicking the Table # box. Either method of entering the label is acceptable.

There is even a code that doesn't have a box counterpart. By typing

[P#]

you insert the page number into the caption label automatically. You can use this undocumented feature to position the page number in unusual places—along the edge of the page, for instance. We'll see how that's done when we work with pages in Chapter 10.

The Text Attr insert allows you to assign text attributes to the caption labels, such as font sizes, underlining, boldface, and so on. You then enter codes as you would with a word processor in a text file. We'll study these codes in Chapter 12.

Once you have the caption's label and position set, give the OK. You should see the label appear on the screen, along with the appropriate numbers. If you can't see it all, you may need to enlarge the caption frame. Do so as you would with any frame: use the frame's handles or the Frame menu's Sizing & Scaling command. Alternatively, you may wish to shorten the wording in the caption label.

FREE-FORM CAPTIONS

If the one line allowed for captions in the dialog box isn't sufficient, you can add a free-form caption. A free-form caption consists of one or more paragraphs that follow the caption label in the caption frame.

You create and edit a free-form caption just as you do normal text: directly in the frame, rather than in a dialog box. In Text mode, place the keyboard cursor directly in front of the square-shaped end box that terminates the caption and type in the additional text. Remember that you cannot use the Text mode to edit the caption label that precedes the free-form caption. To change a caption label, you must use the Frame mode and the Frame menu's Anchors & Captions dialog box.

TAGGING CAPTIONS

As soon as you create caption labels and free-form captions, Ventura automatically creates special tags that it assigns to them. These are part of the set of generated tags that we discussed in Chapter 5. Remember that you can display a list of the generated tags used in a document by using the Options menu's Set Preferences dialog box to change the Generated Tags setting to Shown.

Remember also that you can alter the format of generated tags just as you would any other tag. Figure 7.19 shows how you can change these tags to achieve a variety of captioning effects.

CAPTIONS AND YOUR WORD PROCESSOR

When you save your chapter, Ventura creates a file that holds all the captions. The caption file has the same name as its chapter file, except Ventura assigns a CAP extension to it.

If you're careful, you can use your word processor to edit this file. For precautions to use when doing so, see Chapter 12.

AUTOMATIC COUNTERS FOR CAPTIONS

Finally, let's look at how you can adjust the numbers that appear with your captions. Ventura provides two dialog boxes that allow you to change these numbers: one for tables and one for figures. With the exception of which caption they control, they are identical in look and operation. To display a dialog box, follow these steps:

1. Activate the Frame mode and select the caption frame (or its hosting frame) that has the figure or table reference you wish to adjust.
2. Pull down the Frame menu. If the selected caption frame contains a number reference for the figure or table it contains, its matching command (Figure Counter or Table Counter) will be available for you to click.
3. Click Figure Counter or Table Counter as appropriate. The dialog box shown in Figure 7.20 will appear.

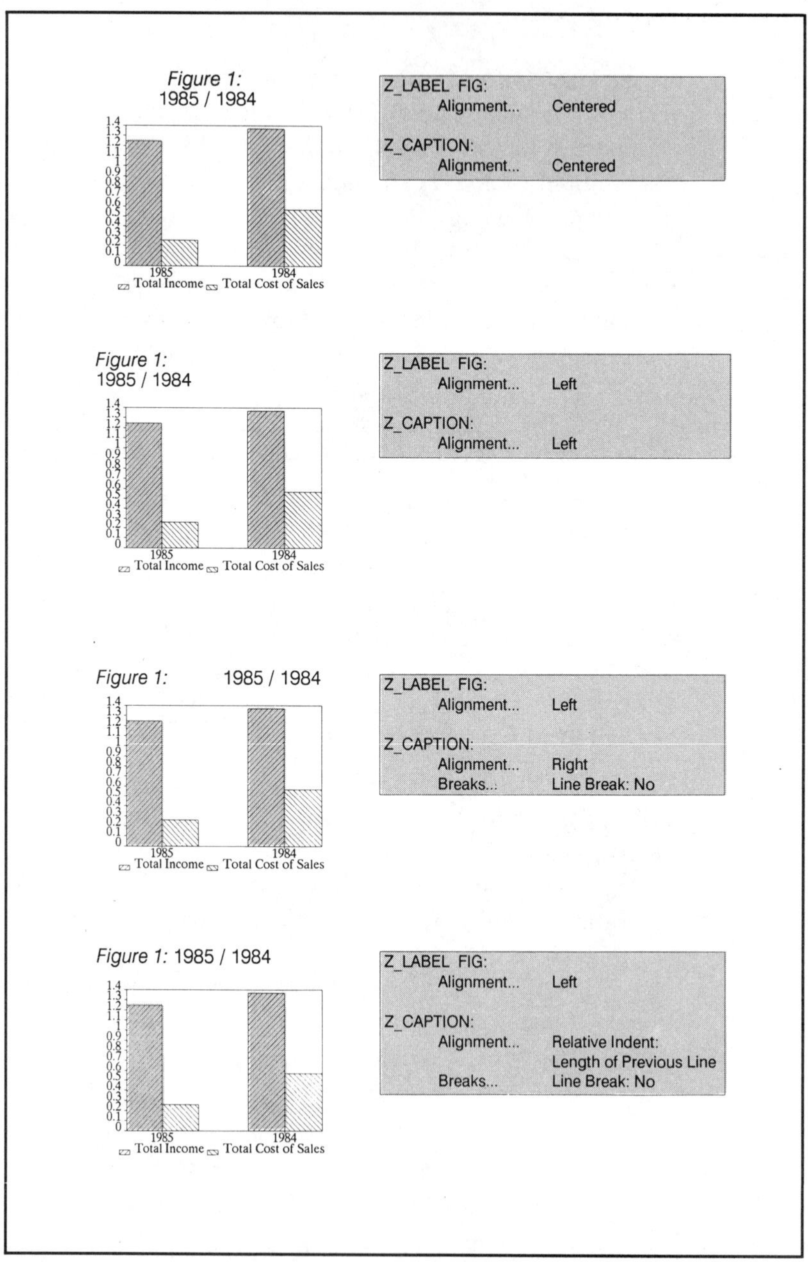

Figure 7.19: Formatting Caption Labels and Free-Form Captions

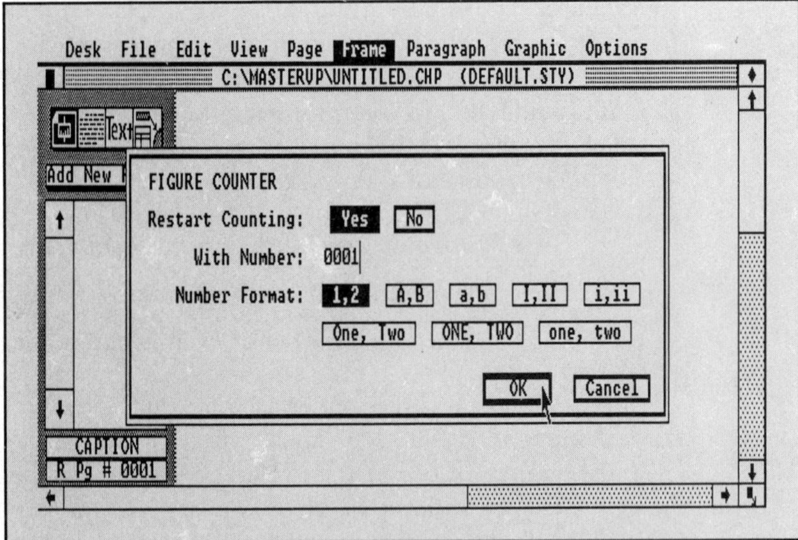

Figure 7.20: The Dialog Box for the Frame Menu's Figure Counter Command

Use this box to set the number for the caption should you need to adjust it. Specify Yes and the new starting number. The indicated caption will adjust and all those that follow it will increment automatically.

You can also use this dialog box to set the numbering format for your captions. As you can see, you have a variety of choices. You can number with Arabic and Roman numerals, with capital or lowercase letters, or even use numbers that are spelled out. Click the box that corresponds to your choice and give the OK when your settings are complete.

So far we haven't looked at the Anchors portion of the Anchors & Captions dialog box. Let's turn to these settings now.

ANCHORING PICTURES TO TEXT

People in the publishing world who work with figures know that during edits, figure placement requires constant attention. As editors revise material, there's always the possibility that pictures will become too far removed from the text they complement. Fortunately, with Version 1.1, Ventura provides the means to keep pictures with their associated text. By using an *anchor*, a specially coded flag at a critical spot in the text, you can have a picture frame (or any frame, for that matter) stay with related material. However, the process is not fully automatic, so you must still remain vigilant.

Anchor operations make use of three commands and the dialog boxes these commands give rise to:

- The Edit menu's Insert/Edit Anchor command
- The Frame menu's Anchors & Captions command
- The Page menu's Re-Anchor Frames command

Using anchors is a three-step procedure that corresponds to these three commands. First, you choose a frame you wish to anchor and give the frame an *anchor name* for reference. Then you pick out a spot in text and link it with the frame by way of the frame's anchor name. You repeat these two steps for all frames that you wish to anchor.

You can then proceed to work with your document as usual; this is where you must remain alert. As you edit, pictures may still drift from their anchors in the text. So before printing, you perform the third step, re-anchoring, which reunites wayward frames with their appropriate anchors in text. Let's examine these three procedures.

CREATING THE ANCHOR NAME FOR A FRAME

The first procedure in anchoring a frame is to assign an anchor name to the frame, using the following steps:

1. Activate the Frame mode and select the frame you wish to anchor.
2. Pull down the Frame menu and click Anchors & Captions. The dialog box we looked at in Figure 7.18 appears.
3. Enter an anchor name in the Anchor field and give the OK.

Use anchor names that are short yet unique. They should be descriptive and pertain to the contents of the frame. Be sure to take note of the name that you assign; you'll need it later to reference the frame.

Although you can click the Inserts buttons and enter bracketed codes, like the figure number used with captions, it's best not to. You may wish to relocate pictures, which could change the reference number of the frame. If so, the figure number of the anchor in text would no longer agree with that of the figure.

INSERTING ANCHORS

Once you've created an anchor name for your frame, you next create an anchor in text that's linked to the frame. (You can reverse the order of these first two procedures if you wish.)

When you create the anchor, you use a dialog box to specify where the anchored frame should be placed with respect to its corresponding anchor in text. You can have the frame placed in either of two relative locations: that is, below or above the anchor. Or you can have it placed in a fixed location: always in the same position that it occupies on the page, as long as it's on the same page as the anchor in text.

Here, then, are the steps for creating an anchor in text and specifying the frame's location with respect to it:

1. Activate the Text mode and click the spot in text where you wish to place the anchor. Usually this would be immediately after a reference made to the picture, such as *See Figure 1*.
2. Pull down the Edit menu and click Insert/Edit Anchor. The dialog box in Figure 7.21 appears.
3. Enter the reference name of the frame you wish to anchor. Make sure that you spell the name exactly as assigned to the frame.
4. Select one of the buttons for the frames location and give the OK.

When you give the OK, Ventura will relocate the frame to the location you've specified, if necessary.

To indicate an anchor in text, Ventura uses a small circle, like a temperature degree symbol (°). You won't be able to see anchors in text if the Options menu is set to Hide Tabs and Returns, although

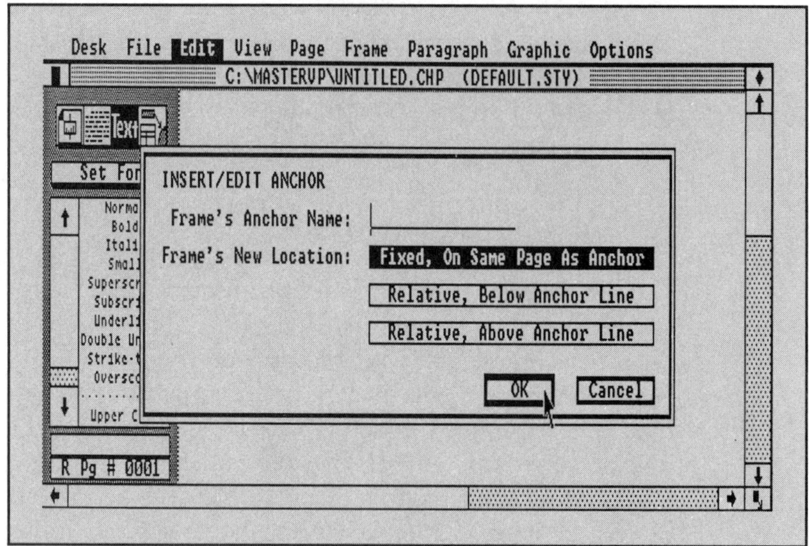

Figure 7.21: The Edit Menu's Insert/Edit Anchor Dialog Box

they'll still operate. These symbols will not appear in the printed version of your documents.

If you move the keyboard cursor so that this symbol is immediately to its right, the symbol is selected, and the word Anchor appears in the Current box. Pressing the Del key at this point would delete the anchor.

You use the same command to edit anchors as you do to create them. Just select the anchor in text, and issue the Edit menu's Insert/Edit Anchor command. Then make adjustments in the dialog box.

RE-ANCHORING FRAMES

Once you've given anchor names to frames and placed their corresponding anchors in text, you can properly reposition the frames whenever it's necessary. Use the Page menu and click Re-Anchor Frames. The atypical dialog box shown in Figure 7.22 appears. Respond by indicating whether you want to reanchor all the frames or just those on the page you're working with, and the reanchoring process will begin.

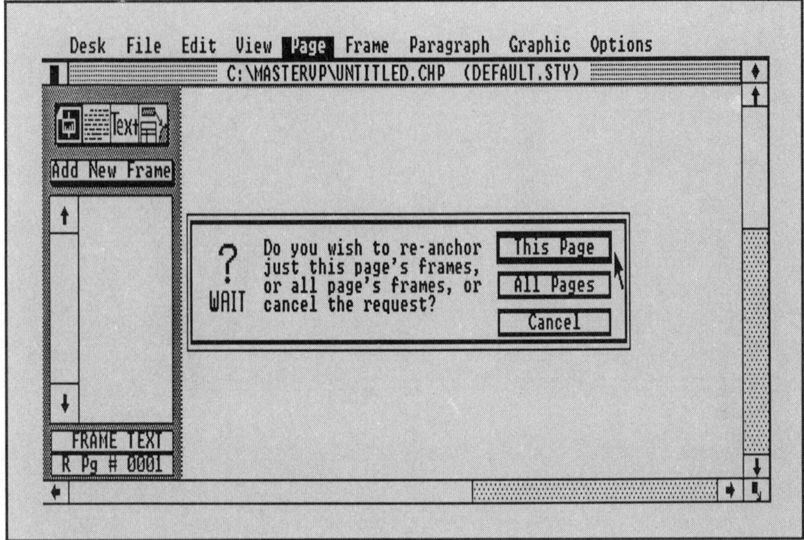

Figure 7.22: The Dialog Box Displayed by the Page Menu's Re-Anchor Frames Command

Once Ventura finishes reanchoring, you should check the results. Frames will be placed on the correct page, but you may need to do some manual fine-tuning in terms of positioning. For instance, reanchored frames may overlap each other, or Ventura may place a frame in a margin. So be sure to check the entire document after reanchoring and before printing.

Ventura Publisher has a variety of graphics capabilities you can use to enhance pictures you import from other programs. For instance, we can improve the legends that appear with our sample graph by assigning them better fonts. We can also add arrows to point at salient features, along with accompanying descriptions.

In the next chapter, we'll put these graphics tools to work by using them to improve the look of our chart. We'll also see how you can use Ventura to draw circles, lines, and rounded boxes.

CHAPTER EIGHT

Lines, Circles, and Boxes

LOOK AT ALMOST ANY PROFESSIONALLY PUBLISHED document and you're bound to see that it uses straight lines in some fashion. Such lines, also called *rules* or *ruling lines*, are a vital layout tool. For instance, the judicious use of lines can group related newspaper articles so they appear to be associated. Conversely, lines can separate items so that they are distinct on the page. You may see lines below or above titles, or between columns. In addition, the thickness, length, and placement of lines can contribute to the style of a document. Lines can also communicate ideas, indicating a flow of information, as they do with some diagrams. Some publishing applications call for lines connected to form boxes, or curved to form circles.

As we've seen, Ventura can import line art created with a variety of software. Graphics software is one way for you to create the lines you need. Sometimes, however, the imported graphic appears unfinished or stylistically ill-suited to your document; it needs to be touched up. In addition, it would be impractical to import lines for every need, such as when you want to associate lines with specific tagged paragraphs.

Fortunately, Ventura has the capability of creating its own graphics. Thus you can add lines, circles, and boxes to a document without using an external graphics package. The graphics you create with Ventura can stand on their own, or you can use them to enhance graphics that you import into your documents.

Ventura is very clever in the way it combines imported graphics and its own graphics. To display a graphic, it utilizes the original graphics file directly. Any enhancements you provide stay with the Ventura document and, although they affect the look of the file in the Ventura document, they do not alter the graphics file. Thus, the original remains fully functional; you can then use the original in a different application altogether, or you can use your graphics software to make changes in it as necessary. Any changes you make will be automatically reflected in your Ventura file.

By combining graphics files with the lines, circles, and boxes that Ventura draws, you can achieve just the right graphic look for your document. With the right fonts, the result is a document that's visually inviting and cohesive.

THREE METHODS OF CREATING GRAPHIC ELEMENTS

When we worked with fonts, you saw that Ventura provides several ways for you to set font attributes. Similarly, it provides you with three basic methods of drawing its graphic elements:

- You can draw straight lines horizontally and create boxes in conjunction with paragraph tags.
- You can draw straight lines horizontally or vertically and create boxes in conjunction with a frame.
- You can use the Graphics mode to draw in a more free-form manner. In conjunction with a frame, you can draw lines horizontally or vertically, at any angle, boxed or curved.

The first two techniques are similar in operation. Therefore, we'll study them together. Later in the chapter, we'll see how you can use the third method, Ventura's Graphics mode, to create free-form graphics.

Your choice of method is important, as it affects the subsequent line. Your choice can affect the line's relationship to elements on the page, the ease with which you create the line, and the speed with which the line adapts to changes you make in the document.

The paragraph tagging method works with paragraphs—that is, any unit of text ending with a Return. The paragraph tagging method is useful for adding lines to callouts or headlines, for instance. If you use the paragraph method, all paragraphs that you've tagged similarly will receive the same lines. Thus, if you use this method to add lines to chapter headings, all of your chapter headings will automatically have similar lines. Note that Ventura is not designed to create vertical lines with the paragraph method. However, you can trick the program into creating such lines, as we'll see when we study boxes.

With the Frame mode, you can create horizontal or vertical lines. The resulting lines are associated with the frame you've selected. For this reason, the Frame mode is useful with elements that are larger than paragraph size. Frames can, in fact, hold several paragraphs, and, of course, imported graphics are assigned to frames as well. As you use this technique, though, remember that the underlying-page frame is a special type of frame. Any graphics you add to it will appear on all pages with the same underlying-page frame; generally, this means throughout the entire document. We'll examine the underlying-page frame more closely in Chapter 10.

The third technique, which uses the Graphics mode, is actually an extension of the Frame method. That's because you must associate every element you create in Graphics mode with a standard frame, created in the Frame mode. Even so, you aren't forced to keep such graphics within the frame's perimeters. It's just that they always maintain the same position relative to the frame (and whatever it contains), no matter where you move the frame. Using Graphics mode provides you with more flexibility with the shape of graphics elements than either of the other two methods.

Let's begin our look at lines by studying vertical lines. As mentioned, the Frame mode is the primary means of creating vertical lines.

COLUMN RULES AND OTHER VERTICAL LINES

In the Frame mode, you can create vertical lines that are associated with any frame. This includes the underlying-page frame. When you create lines for the underlying-page frame, the settings you specify appear repeatedly on similar pages.

Ventura provides two methods of creating vertical lines directly associated with a frame. First, you can create *intercolumn rules*. These are lines that appear between columns of text. This application is perhaps the most common use for vertical lines. Adding lines between columns can give a more structured, formal feeling to a document. Sometimes it makes the text more readable as well.

Second, Ventura allows you to insert one or two freely placed vertical lines anywhere on the page. Regardless of the frame you use, you position these lines with respect to the underlying page. You might use these to create a wide line along the left edge of letterhead stationery, for example.

LINES BETWEEN COLUMNS

To create lines between columns, first decide which frame you want to use for the rules. Then follow these steps to display the dialog box that appears in Figure 8.1:

1. Activate the Frame mode and select the appropriate frame.
2. Establish columns for the frame using the Frame menu's Margins & Columns command (see Chapter 3).
3. Pull down the Frame menu.
4. Click Vertical Rules.

Be careful which frame you select for the column rule. Suppose, for example, that you set up a two-column format for the underlying-page frame of a newsletter. Next, you create two long frames in each column, because you want each to hold a different text file. To add intercolumn rules between the two articles, select the underlying-page frame, since that's the frame with the two-column format. Don't make the mistake of using one of the two smaller frames.

Once you have selected the appropriate frame and displayed the dialog box for Vertical Rules, you can create your lines. If you've used the Page menu's Page Layout command to set up double-sided pages for the document, first consider the Settings For setting. Click Left Page or Right Page to display the settings for these respective pages. Once

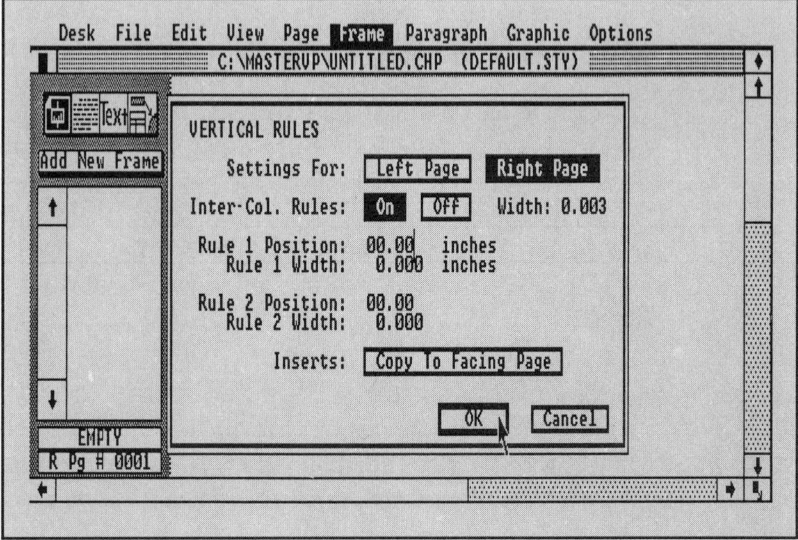

Figure 8.1: The Dialog Box for the Frame Menu's Vertical Rules Command

you've established the settings for one side, you can duplicate them for the other side, if desired. Just click the button labeled

Copy To Facing Page

at the bottom of the dialog box and Ventura transfers your settings to the opposite page.

Next, look at the Inter-Col. Rules category. Here you indicate that you want vertical lines to appear between columns within the selected frame. Click the appropriate box, On or Off, to turn the column lines on or off. If you click On, indicate the width you'd like for the line. (If Off is darkened, the Width setting has no effect, whether or not a value appears within it.) Ventura shows the values that appear here in terms of the units used for Rule 1 Width. To change the system of measurement for the width of intercolumn rules (from inches to fractional points, for instance) click the unit name that appears for Rule 1 Width. For greatest precision and speed of operation, you may want to use fractional points.

Note that the width of your gutters, as specified with the Frame menu's Margins & Columns command, will restrict the width of the intercolumn rule. Thus if you want to widen an intercolumn rule line, you may need to widen the gutter to do so.

VERTICAL PAGE BARS

Use the Rule 1 and Rule 2 settings to create what we'll call *vertical page bars*. Note that the values you enter into these settings have no effect whatever on intercolumn rules.

Vertical page bars are rather odd creatures. It's hard to know why for sure, but Ventura makes these lines operate in an unusual manner. Here are the points to bear in mind when you work with vertical page bars.

- You can create only one or two vertical page bars.
- The measurements you provide always position the bar from the left edge of the page. This is true even when you create the bar by using a frame smaller than the full page. Thus, as

you move such a frame around on the page, the bar appears to remain stationary relative to the page as it shows through the frame.

- Column-wide text does not automatically flow around these bars. To make the text do so, you must use the Frame menu's Margins & Columns command and provide a text-free margin for the bar. Otherwise, the bar will cover any text it encounters, hiding the text from the reader's view.
- There is no way to directly indicate the length of the bars themselves. They extend all to way from the top margin of the selected frame to its bottom margin.

Because of the peculiar way in which these lines operate with regard to smaller frames, it is wise to confine their use to the underlying-page frame.

Figure 8.2 shows a vertical page bar in use. This figure is an enhanced version of the table we worked with in the last chapter. If you created this example in the previous chapter, you may want to try your hand at making these enhancements as you work through the techniques in this chapter.

The vertical page bar shows along the left edge of the page. This enhancement serves to tie elements of the page together. As a result, the table and its accompanying chart seem to belong together and appear less disjointed. Notice that we used the same width for the vertical rule as that of the existing horizontal rule along the top. This choice serves to further unify the elements on the page.

As mentioned, sometimes a vertical page bar will cover existing text. Specifically, the bar will cover column-wide paragraphs but not frame-wide ones. To change this setting for a given tag, activate the Paragraph mode, select a sample paragraph, pull down the Paragraph menu, and click Alignment. Use the Overall Width setting to make the adjustment.

In our sample table, the Category tag was initially set for Column-Wide, so that the vertical page bar covered the beginning of the titles *Income* and *Cost of Sales*, both of which carry this tag. By changing the Category tag to Frame-Wide, the vertical page bar now breaks at these words, as you can see in the figure.

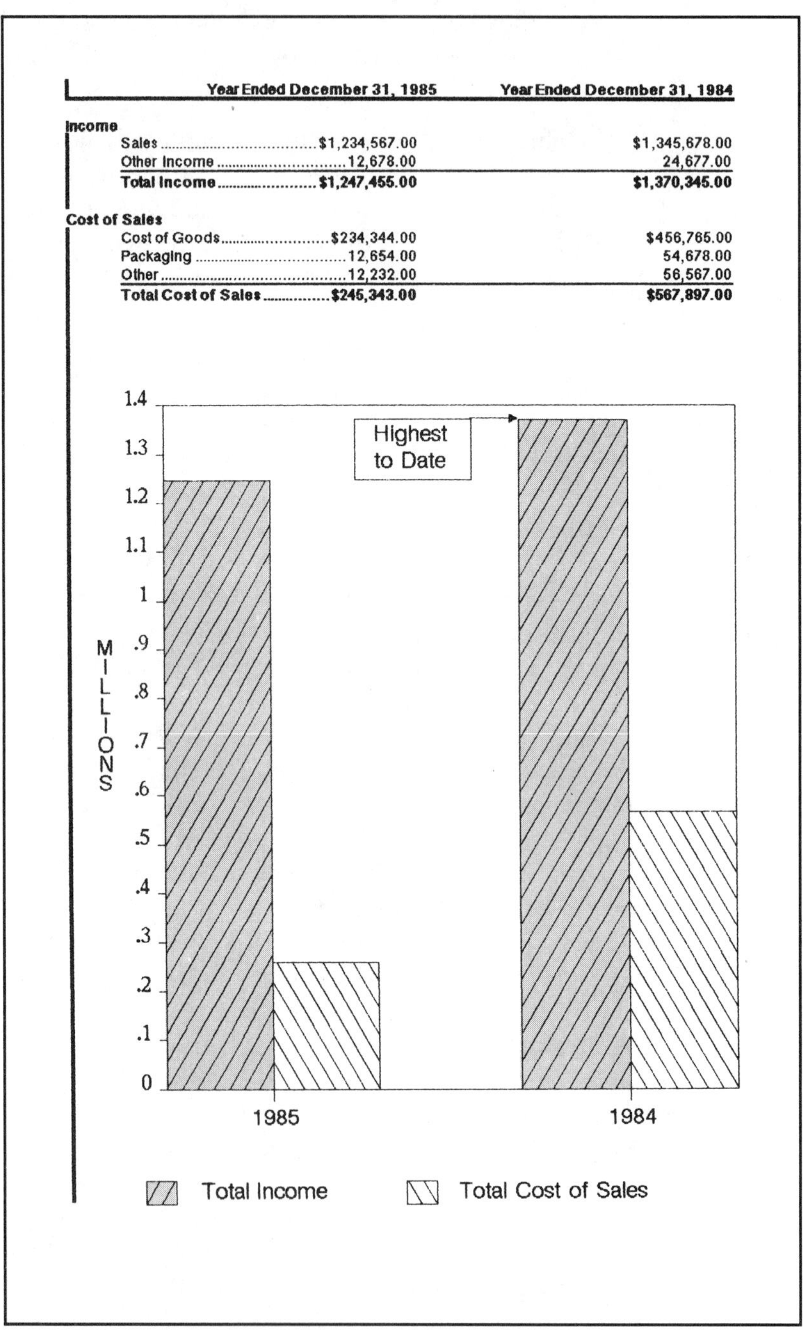

	Year Ended December 31, 1985	Year Ended December 31, 1984
Income		
Sales	$1,234,567.00	$1,345,678.00
Other Income	12,678.00	24,677.00
Total Income	**$1,247,455.00**	**$1,370,345.00**
Cost of Sales		
Cost of Goods	$234,344.00	$456,765.00
Packaging	12,654.00	54,678.00
Other	12,232.00	56,567.00
Total Cost of Sales	**$245,343.00**	**$567,897.00**

Figure 8.2: A Chart Enhanced with Line Graphics

Don't forget that the vertical lines you create are associated with the frame that's selected when you use the Frame menu's Vertical Rules command. Thus, they'll always be associated with that frame, no matter where you position it. You can also create horizontal lines that will stay with the frame they're a part of; we'll look at these next.

HORIZONTAL LINES

Ventura allows you to create horizontal rules that are positioned with respect to either frames or paragraphs. When you do, the lines stay with the frame or paragraph to which you've assigned them, regardless of where you move the frame or paragraph. In addition, should you widen or narrow the frame or paragraph, associated horizontal lines can be made to adjust automatically. Let's see first how horizontal ruling lines work with frames.

HORIZONTAL LINES FOR FRAMES

When you create horizontal lines in conjunction with frames, you can position them at the top or bottom of the frame. One typical use is in creating lines that set off pictures from text. You could also use horizontal lines to separate one newspaper article, contained within a frame, from the articles above or below it.

Rules at the Top of a Frame

To study horizontal frame lines, let's begin at the top. You can make rules appear at the top of any given frame by using the dialog box shown in Figure 8.3. Follow these steps to display the dialog box:

1. Activate the Frame mode and select the frame or frames for which you want lines at the top.
2. Pull down the Frame menu.
3. Click Ruling Line Above.

IMPORTANT

The name for this dialog box, Ruling Lines Above, is actually misleading. The name implies that ruling lines will appear above the frame in question. This is not the case. A frame's ruling lines actually appear *within* the frame. Thus, a more appropriate name for this dialog box might instead be Ruling Lines at Top. When we look at paragraphs shortly, you'll see that ruling lines for paragraphs can be made to appear above the selected paragraph using Paragraph mode. Since this latter procedure uses this same dialog box, the box's name is appropriate for paragraph tagging.

To create a ruling line at the top of a frame, set the first category of the dialog box, Width, to Frame. To remove existing ruling lines, click None. Notice that these two settings are the only ones available for Width; the others ghost. The other four choices are not used for frames; they are used only for horizontal lines you create in Paragraph mode.

Next, look at the Color category. Normally, Black is selected. If you have a color printer, you can make use of the other boxes to color your ruling lines. With some printers, you can use the White setting. For white to appear, though, it must be against a dark background, usually black. Create such a background for the same frame, using the Frame menu's Frame Background command.

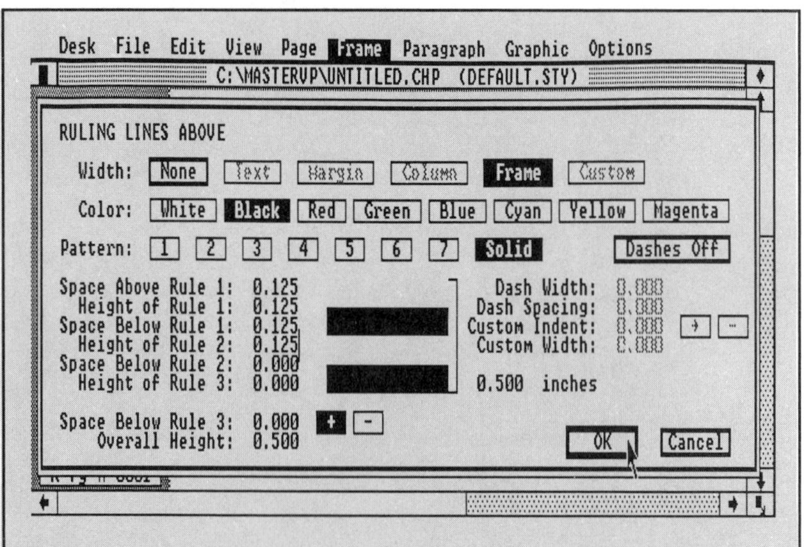

Figure 8.3: The Dialog Box for Creating Rules at the Top of a Frame

Next, you can choose a pattern for the ruling line. The chart we've created in Figure 8.4 shows the patterns that Ventura provides. Once you've indicated the height (that is, the thickness) of the ruling line, the pattern you've selected will appear in the dialog box. Thus you can try out various patterns to see which you like. Ventura makes these patterns available for a variety of lines and boxes, including frame backgrounds.

Use the next group of settings to specify the thickness of your ruling lines and the amount of space between them. Figure 8.5 shows how these settings determine the spacing for ruling lines. (This figure also contains an example of spacing for boxes, which we'll look at in more detail later in the chapter.) Note that with the dialog box for Ruling Lines Above, the last setting, Space Below Rule 3, does not apply. (This setting does apply when the dialog box is used elsewhere, such as with Ruling Lines Below.) Don't make the mistake of thinking that this space will be the distance before the text in the frame appears. Text and pictures in a frame are completely independent of the ruling lines. To keep collisions from occurring, you must use the Frame menu's Margins & Columns command and create adequate text margins to hold the rules. The ruling lines will then rest within those margins and not interfere with the text.

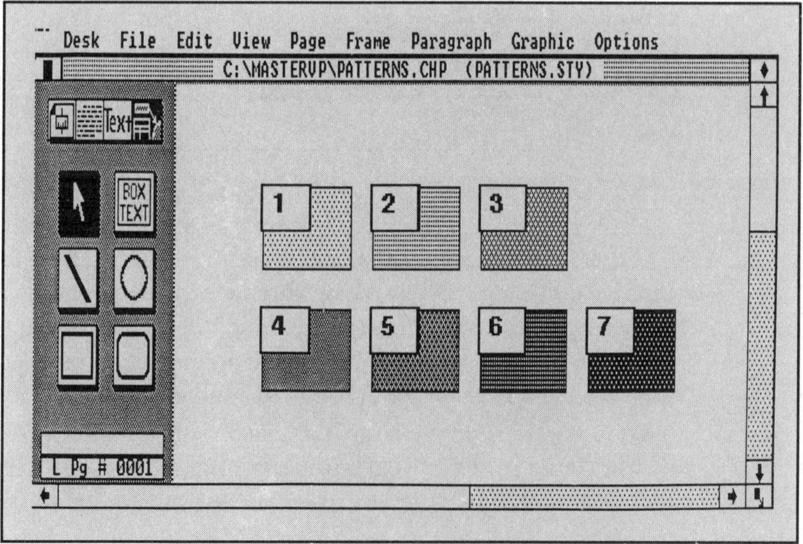

Figure 8.4: Patterns Available for Ruling Lines and Other Formats

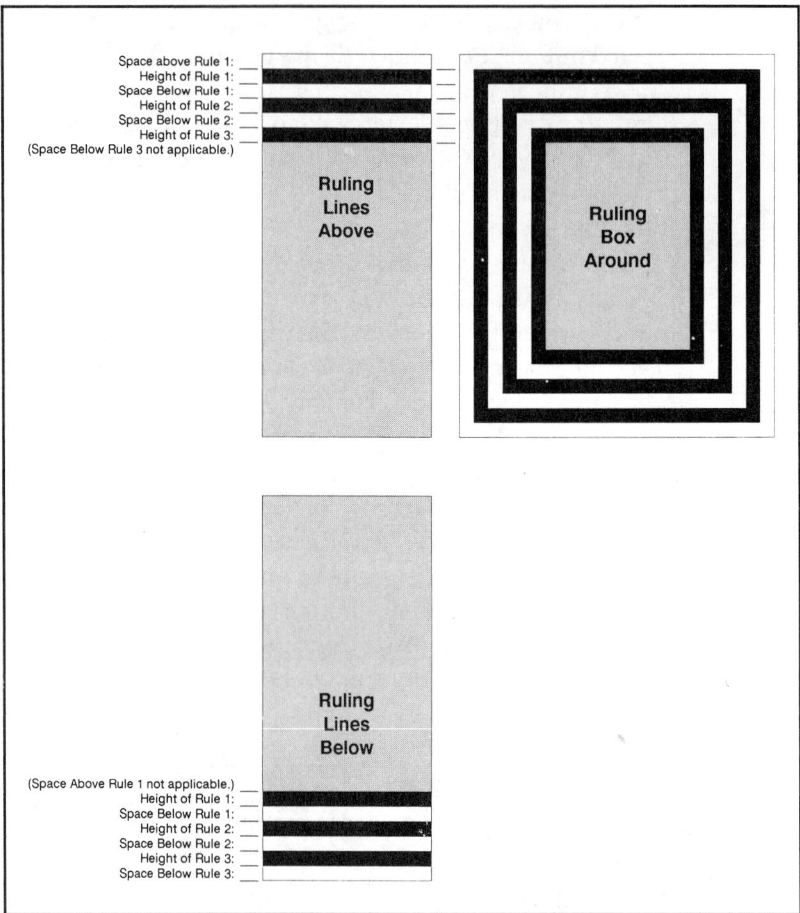

Figure 8.5: Ruling Measurements for Frames

To the right of the Space and Height settings there is a bracketed area. As you specify heights (thickness) for the rules, you'll see blown-up thickness samples of the first half inch of ruling lines within this area. These samples will appear in the same color and pattern that you've specified with the settings above them. Be aware, however, that the samples shown are *double* the thickness of their true counterparts in the actual frame. That is, although the bracket displays one-half inch of ruling area, the bracket is one inch long.

Be careful with regard to the half-inch limit of this display. If you've specified heights and spacing totaling more than one-half inch, you won't see samples for the area beyond the half-inch bracket. However, your settings will still take effect and display the rules you've specified in the frame.

If you're uncertain about the amount of space your rules occupy, you can see a measurement of their total area by checking the Overall Height setting at the bottom of the dialog box. Note that you cannot enter a value directly into this setting. It is simply a display that provides you with a sum of the values above it.

Turning our attention to the right side of the dialog box, we see settings concerned with dashes. Ruling lines are normally unbroken. However, you can create rules made up of dashes (often called dotted lines). Such broken lines are useful for such applications as creating lines around coupons. To create dashes, click the box that says Dashes Off; when you do, it changes to read Dashes On. You can then enter values into the two settings below this box. Use them to specify the width of a dash and the amount of space between it and the next dash.

On the right and just above the OK is a measurement unit indicating the system of measurement that Ventura is using to display values in this dialog box. Initially, it uses inches. If you wish to change the system of measurement in use (to centimeters, picas and points, or fractional points), successively click this name until the name of the desired units appears. If you want to use picas and points as your system of measurement, remember that 12 points make up 1 pica and that approximately 6 picas make up an inch. Thus, 5 picas and 12 points (written as *5,12*, with a comma between the pica and point quantities) is the same as 6 picas (6,00) which is the same as 1 inch.

IMPORTANT

The notation for picas and points can be confusing if you are used to working with different units. For example, in centimeters or inches, 5.1 is very close to 5.0—just one tenth of a unit greater. 5,1 picas, however, is interpreted by Ventura as 5 picas, 10 points, which is closer to 6 picas that 5. Be sure you understand the picas and points system before working with these units.

The value displayed before the measurement unit is always equal to one-half inch, the size of the bracketed area. You cannot change this value. You can only change the measurement units in which it is expressed.

This completes our look at the dialog box for Ruling Lines Above. As we turn to the box for Ruling Lines Below, you'll see that it's quite similar to this box.

Rules at the Bottom of a Frame

Creating ruling lines at the bottom of a frame is similar to the process used to create them at the top. To specify rules for the bottom of a frame, display the dialog box for Ruling Lines Below with these steps:

1. Activate the Frame mode and select the appropriate frame(s).
2. Pull down the Frame menu and click Ruling Line Below.

When you do this, a dialog box very similar to the one for Ruling Lines Above will appear. The only difference, in fact, lies in the name at the top of the box, with *Below* replacing *Above*.

Note that as with the Above box, this dialog box is misnamed as well. The ruling lines do not appear below the frame; rather, they appear within the frame, but at the bottom of it.

Here are some additional points to remember with regard to ruling lines at the bottom of a frame. In the dialog box for Ruling Lines Below, the setting for Space Above Rule 1 has no effect. Remember, text or graphics that appear within the box (and hence above these rules) are not controlled by the rules. These elements are controlled by the Frame menu's Margins & Columns command. Thus, there is nothing regulated above Rule 1 from which the rule can be spaced.

On the other hand, Space Below Rule 3 does have an effect. As you can see in Figure 8.5, it governs the distance between the third rule and the bottom edge of the frame. Be aware that if the frame does not have three rules, this value controls whichever rule is last in the frame. In other words, it controls rule 2 if there are 2 rules, rule 1 if there's only 1 rule.

In addition, you can use the small Plus (+) and Minus (–) buttons that appear to the right of the value for Space Below Rule 3.

These buttons regulate the vertical placement of the last rule with regard to the frame. Normally, the Plus button is selected, resulting in ruling lines placed within the frame. By using the Minus button, the Ruling Lines Below can be made to appear below the frame. This feature is put to best use by creating reverse text in the Paragraph mode, as we'll see in Chapter 13.

Otherwise, the rules for ruling lines at the bottom of a frame follow those for rules at the top. Use the earlier discussion of the dialog box to set rules at the bottom of a frame.

HORIZONTAL PARAGRAPH RULES

As we discussed, the same dialog box appears for both the Frame menu's Ruling Line Above command and the Ruling Line Below command. This same dialog box also appears when you set the ruling lines for a paragraph tag. In many ways, it operates in the same fashion. There are, however, some key ways in which paragraph rules differ from frame rules:

- Paragraph rules work with paragraphs. As such they are usually best used when your application contains a small amount of text, or even none at all.
- You set paragraph rules with tags. As such, they affect all paragraphs tagged with the same tag. By contrast, what you do to one frame will not affect other frames, except when you're working with the underlying-page frame.
- Unlike frames, paragraph rules above and below are, indeed, above and below the paragraph. They do not normally cover the text. With paragraph rules, there is no need to set aside margins for text as you must with frames.
- You can set paragraph rules for a variety of horizontal widths, independent of the paragraph. The widths of frame rules are controlled by the width of the frame.

The sample style sheets provided with Ventura use horizontal paragraph rules for many effects. Table 8.1 shows some of the style sheets that include tags with horizontal ruling lines. You can compare them by loading a sample chapter or checking Appendix A.

STYLE (.STY) AND CHAPTER (.CHP)	TAG	RULING LINE	WIDTH
&BOOK-P1	Chapter #	Above	Margin
		Below	Margin
&BOOK-P2	Major heading	Below	Column
&BRO-L2	Title	Above	Column
		Below	Column
	Setting	Below	Text
&BRO-P3*	Table header	Below	Margin
&INV-P1**	Address	Above	Margin
	Invoice	Above	Margin
	Column heads	Below	Margin
	Total	Above	Margin
&LSTG-P2	Category	Below	Column
<R1-P1	Name	Below	Frame
&MAG-P3	Lift	Above	Frame
		Below	Frame

* Table item heading was made with the Underline text attribute.
** This tag uses Pattern 1. It has a negative value for Space Below Rule 3 that's equal to the height of Rule 1.

Table 8.1: Sample Style Sheets with Ruling Line Tags

Notice that this table lists a variety of widths for the sample tags. To set a ruling-line tag, begin by following these steps to display the dialog box for Ruling Lines Above or Below (Figure 8.6).

1. Activate the Paragraph mode and select a sample paragraph.
2. Pull down the Paragraph menu.
3. Click Ruling Line Above or Ruling Line Below, as appropriate.

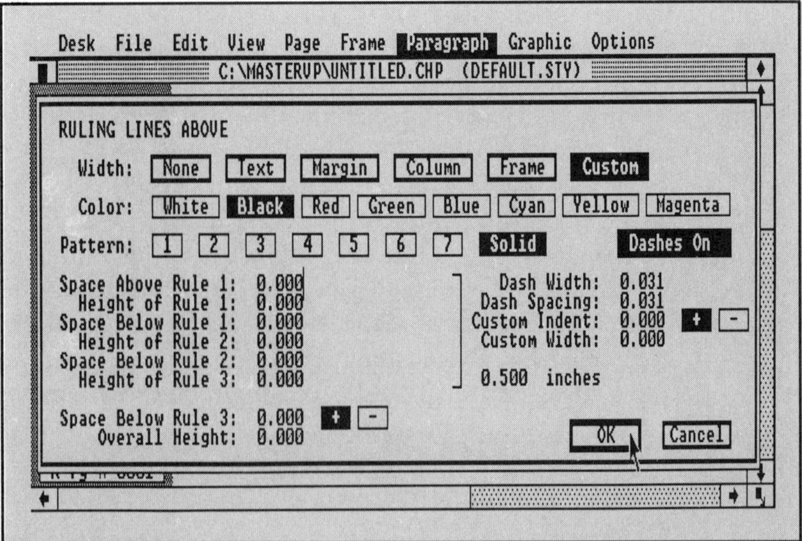

Figure 8.6: The Ruling Lines Above Dialog Box

Although the dialog box that appears looks almost identical to the box the Frame mode uses, there is an important difference. The Width category for the Paragraph version has four additional buttons (Text, Margin, Column, and Custom) available for your use. These four buttons ghost in the Frame version.

Select Text if you want the ruling line to be the same width as the text in the paragraph. If lines of the tagged paragraph are of varying lengths, Ventura uses the length of the line closest to the rule to determine its length. That is, if you're using Ruling Lines Above, the program will use the paragraph's first line of text to determine the width of the rule. If you're using Ruling Lines Below, it uses the last line of text. For a example of how this looks, see the &BRO-L2 sample chapter and style sheet, and look at the Setting tag.

Set the Width to Margin if you want the program to set the rule according to the paragraph's In From Left and In From Right settings. (These settings appear in the Paragraph menu's Spacing dialog box.) The rule will begin at the paragraph's In From Left position and end at its In From Right position.

The last two settings, Column and Frame, seem to indicate that the makers of Ventura originally hoped to provide flexibility with regard to placement of ruling lines when such placement differs from the paragraph's alignment. However, at this writing a little experimentation reveals that the program ignores these settings. Instead, it takes its cues for the width of ruling lines from the Paragraph menu's Alignment dialog box, using the Overall Width setting as the determining factor.

The last button, Custom, is new with Version 1.1. It allows you to create paragraph rules with a great deal of flexibility. Once you choose Custom, you must provide a Custom Width in order for the line to appear. Optionally, you can provide a Custom Indent, which determines how far from the left edge of the paragraph the left end of the line begins. By clicking the Minus button to the right of Custom Indent, you create an outdented line—one which protrudes beyond the left edge of the paragraph.

CREATING BOXES

In much the same way that you create ruling lines, you can create ruling boxes. Except for the name—Ruling Box Around—the dialog box you use is identical to the one used for ruling lines.

BOXES FOR FRAMES AND PARAGRAPHS

You can make ruling boxes for frames or for paragraphs. Typically, you might place frame boxes around pictures to set them off from text. You might use a paragraph box around a liftout in a magazine article. (A *liftout* is an important paragraph or sentence that's copied from the text and set in a larger type. Its purpose is usually to draw readers' attention and interest them in the article.) The sample document &MAG-P3 uses a liftout (the Lift tag) but sets it off with ruling lines above and below, an alternative method.

Ruling boxes follow the same rules as Ruling Lines Above. Look back at Figure 8.5 and notice how ruling boxes for frames use the same settings as Ruling Lines Above.

Ruling boxes around paragraphs are generally used for short amounts of text only, such as a heading. If you use them for long paragraphs, be careful with paragraphs that start in one column and continue in the next. Ventura will only place a box around the first part of the paragraph. It will ignore the second half of the paragraph at the top of the next column. To prevent a boxed paragraph from straddling columns in this fashion, pull down the Paragraph menu and click Breaks. Set Allow Within to No, which causes the entire paragraph to move to the next column rather than allowing it to break within.

For the same reason, ruling boxes around paragraphs must not be interrupted with an overlayed frame, containing a picture, for example. However, not allowing a break within to occur will not prevent this from happening. If a frame interrupts such a paragraph box, you must reposition the frame manually.

CREATING VERTICAL RULES WITH THE BOX FEATURE

As we mentioned, you can use the Ruling Box Around feature to create a vertical line that's associated with a paragraph. A typical use for such a line is in creating a *change bar*. Some editors use change bars to flag material that they have altered in some way. The change bar is placed to the left of any paragraph that's been revised since the previous version of a document. The sample chapter and style sheet &BOOK-P1 has a tag labeled Change Bar with this feature in place (see Appendix A).

To create a change bar, proceed as follows:

1. In Paragraph mode, select a paragraph for which you want to create a change bar.
2. Click Add New Tag on the Side-bar. Make up a name for the new tag (Change Bar, for example) and give the OK.
3. Pull down the Paragraph menu and click Ruling Box Around. Specify a negative Custom Width (click the Minus button) for the rule and give *the same value* for Height of Rule 1.

Thus, the sample change bar has a custom width of – 1.98 fractional points and a height of 1.98 as well. Since the width of the box is the same as the thickness of its rules, all you see is the box's left and right rules, superimposed. Any paragraph you format with such a Change

Bar tag will have a line along its left edge that extends the length of the paragraph.

Be aware that the same restrictions that apply to boxes apply to change bars; you must keep the paragraph with the change bar together.

USING BUILT-IN GRAPHICS

So far, we've seen how you can create lines and boxes in a structured format that relates directly to frames and paragraphs. With Ventura, you can also create lines and boxes, as well as other shapes, in a more free-form fashion. You gain this additional flexibility by using the Graphics mode.

With Graphics mode you can create boxes and lines, circles and ovals, and arrows as well. You can even create round-edged boxes.

The shapes you create can come in a variety of sizes. You can vary thicknesses and fill patterns, too. What's more, by combining these shapes and masking parts of them, you can create a greater variety of forms.

Don't overestimate these graphics capabilities, though. Ventura's graphics are not a substitute for a complete graphics package, any more than its ability to edit text is a substitute for a full-fledged word processor. However, the Graphics mode may allow you to create just the shapes that your documents need. You can also use the Graphics mode to spruce up graphics that you import into Ventura. That way, your text and graphics may blend better on the page. They'll look like they belong together, rather than having a patchwork-quilt appearance of input from various sources.

Graphics that you create are always tied to one of the document's frames. As such, they stay with the frame wherever you place it. However, there are no restrictions on their placement with respect to the associated frame. They can be inside the frame, outside it, or both. A graphic can be at one corner of the page even though its host frame is at the opposite corner.

ACTIVATING THE GRAPHICS MODE

Before activating the Graphics mode, you must first decide which frame will play host to the graphic. Whichever frame is selected when you activate the Graphics mode is the frame to which the graphic will be tied when you create it. Thus, the broad steps for creating a graphic always consist of the following:

1. Activate the Frame mode first, and select the frame to which the graphic will be tied.
2. Activate the Graphics mode.
3. Draw the graphic, and set its characteristics.

IMPORTANT

All graphics that you create are assigned to the frame that you selected just before activating the Graphics mode. To assign graphics to another frame, you must activate the Frame mode, select the appropriate frame, and then reactivate the Graphics mode.

Once you've set the frame which will host the graphic, activate the Graphics mode using one of these three methods. All three methods are equivalent; use the one with which you feel most comfortable.

- Pull down the View menu and click Graphic Drawing, or
- Click the Graphic button at the top-right corner of the Side-bar, or
- Type Ctrl-P.

Once you've activated the Graphics mode, you'll see the Side-bar change to the format shown in Figure 8.7. The standard assignment list that is usually on the Side-bar disappears and these six icons replace it.

The first icon, with the arrow, is different from the other five. This is the graphics selection icon. You use it to select a shape you've previously created with one of the other five icons. Like frames, selected graphics are indicated with handles. Don't make the mistake of thinking that you use this arrow icon to create arrows. In fact, to create an arrow you use the icon right below it containing the diagonal line, which is also used to create lines.

USING THE GRAPHICS GRID

Regardless of the icon, you should first decide if you wish to use Ventura's graphics grid. By using this invisible grid, the points of your graphics snap to meet and line up at predetermined intervals. Generally, this arrangement results in cleaner, more precise graphics. Set up the graphics grid as follows:

1. Activate the Graphics mode.
2. Pull down the Graphic menu.
3. Click Grid Setting. The dialog box shown in Figure 8.8 will appear.

In the dialog box, click On to make the graphics grid operational. Then insert values for the horizontal and vertical spacing of the grid and give the OK.

DRAWING WITH GRAPHICS ICONS

Once you've set the graphics grid as you desire, you can draw with Ventura. To draw with one of the graphics icons, follow these steps:

1. Click the icon that represents the shape you wish to use.
2. Move the mouse cursor onto the working area. The cursor changes into a shape representing the graphic shape you've chosen. Figure 8.9 shows how the mouse cursor shapes correspond to the various graphic shapes.
3. Position the mouse cursor at the spot for the top-left corner of the graphic. Press the mouse button and hold it down.
4. Still pressing the mouse button, drag the mouse to the bottom-right corner for the graphic.
5. Release the mouse button when the mouse cursor is at the spot you desire for the bottom-right corner. The graphic corresponding to the icon appears.

Once the graphic is created, it is also selected, as indicated by handles that appear around it. Its name appears in the Current box.

With the Selection icon active (the one with the arrow on it) you can grab one of the handles and stretch or shrink the graphic, just as you do with frames.

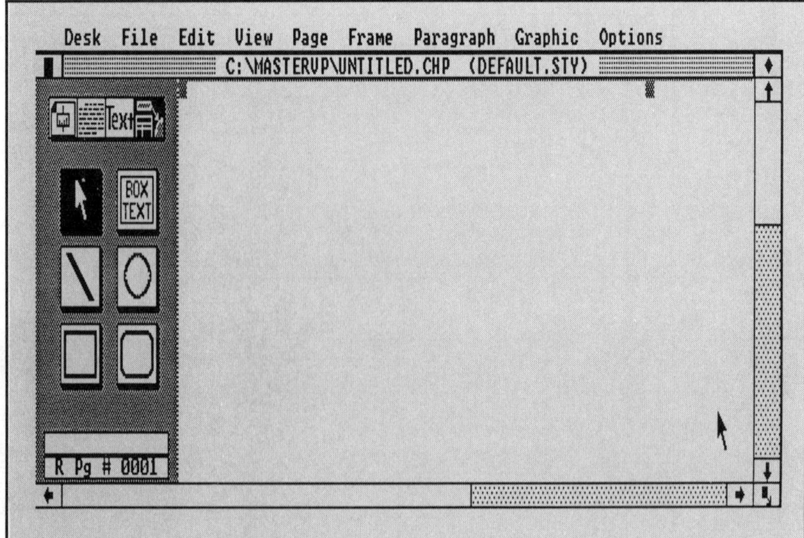

Figure 8.7: The Side-Bar in the Graphics Mode

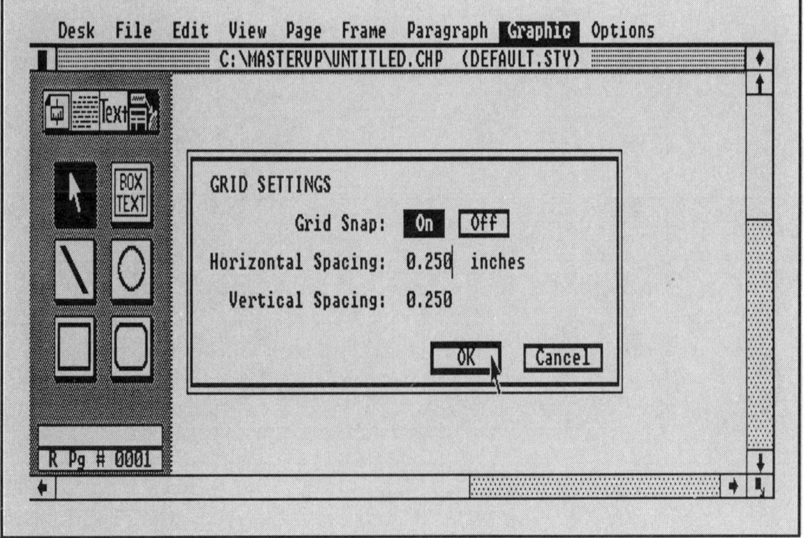

Figure 8.8: The Dialog Box for the Graphic Menu's Grid Setting Command

GRAPHIC NAME	SIDE-BAR MENU	MOUSE CURSOR SHAPE
Box Text	BOX TEXT	Te
Line		
Circle		
Rectangle		
Rounded Rectangle		

Figure 8.9: Graphic Icons and Their Corresponding Mouse Cursor Shapes

Figure 8.10 shows some graphics shapes that you can create using the Graphics mode. For each shape, the figure indicates the icon(s) that you use to create the shape. As the bottom row shows, you can

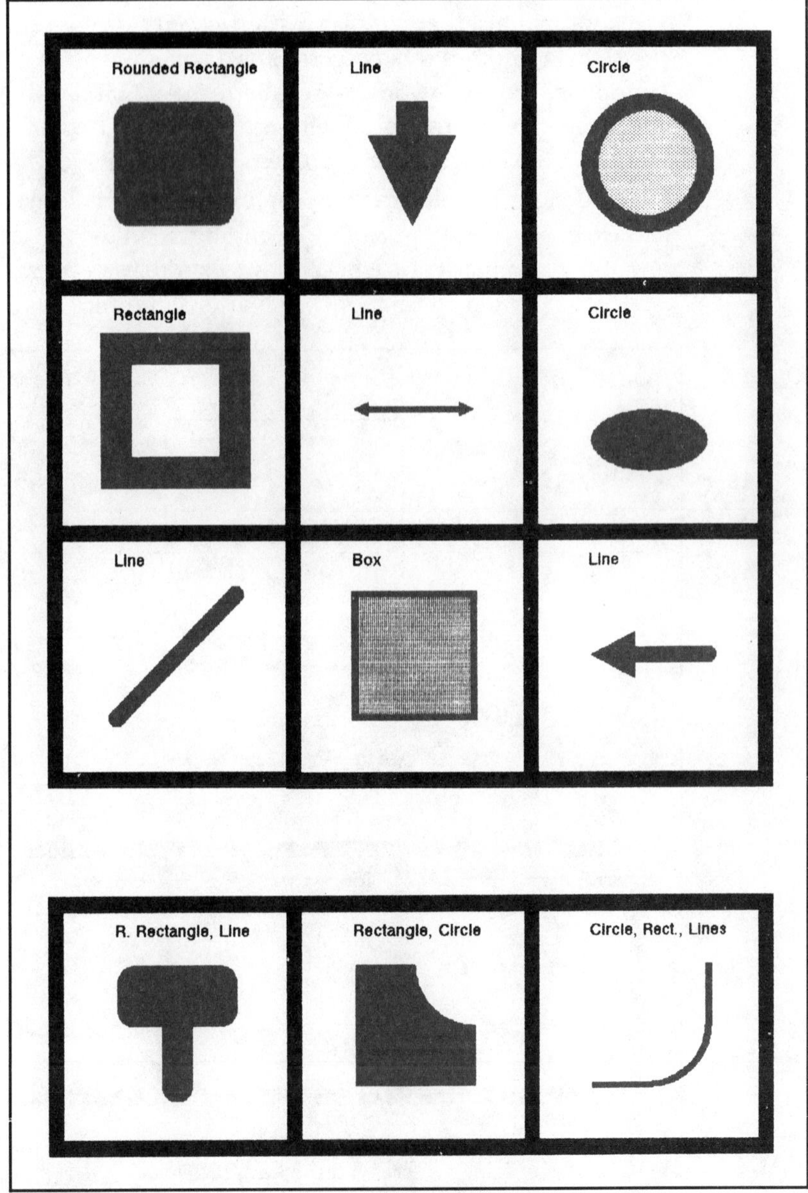

Figure 8.10: Shapes Created with the Graphics Mode

create additional shapes by combining two or more of the standard shapes. You can create the shape in the lower-right corner, for instance, by first drawing a circle, then drawing (or moving) two opaque boxes over it to cover three-fourths of it. On top of those boxes, draw lines that connect with each end of the remaining arc. Figure 8.11 outlines this process. For display purposes, the boxes at the top have edges so you can see them. In actual use they would be simply opaque white blocks whose presence you could tell only by handles that would appear should you select them.

Up to eight handles can appear to stake out a selected graphic. There can be fewer than eight, depending upon the size and orientation of the graphic. Figure 8.12 shows examples of selection handles as they appear in conjunction with various graphics.

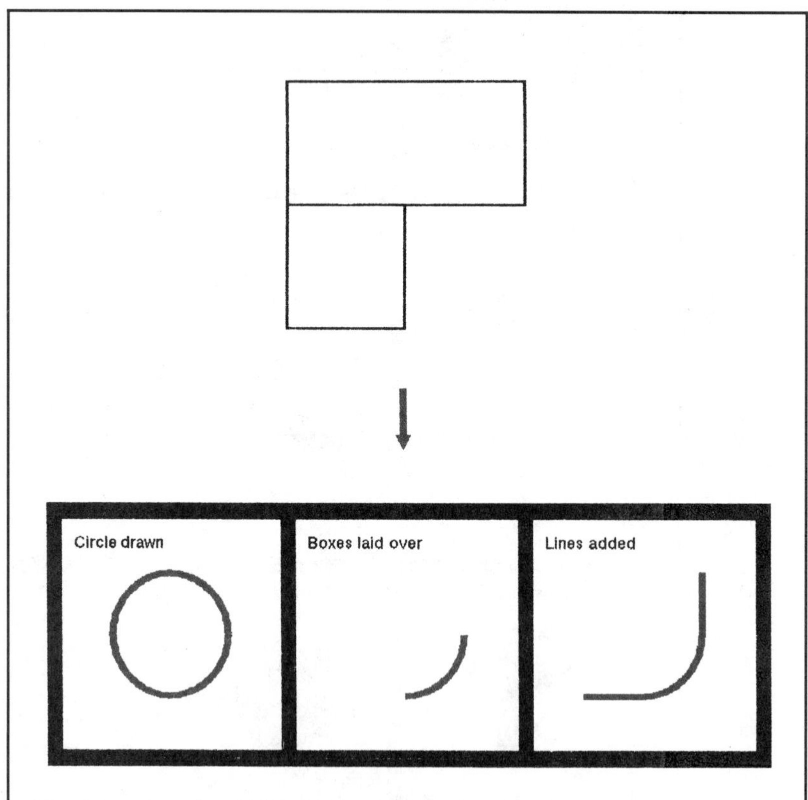

Figure 8.11: Creating an Arc with the Graphics Mode

Although moving graphics is generally straightforward, moving a horizontal or vertical line (or arrow) can be tricky, due to the placement of its selection handles. Figure 8.13 gives some tips for doing so.

Unfortunately, you cannot save graphics independent of your document. However, you can cut and paste them, just as you do frames. Press Del, Shift-Del, and Ins to cut, copy, and paste, respectively, or

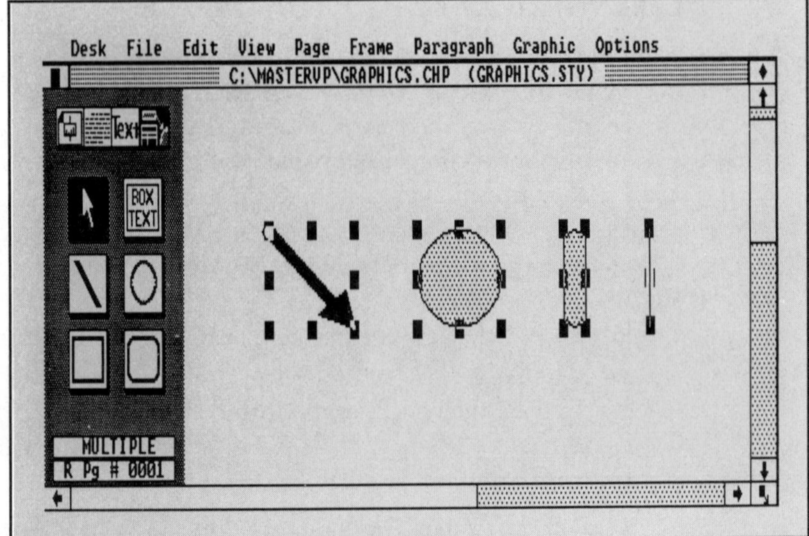

Figure 8.12: Selection Handles for Graphics

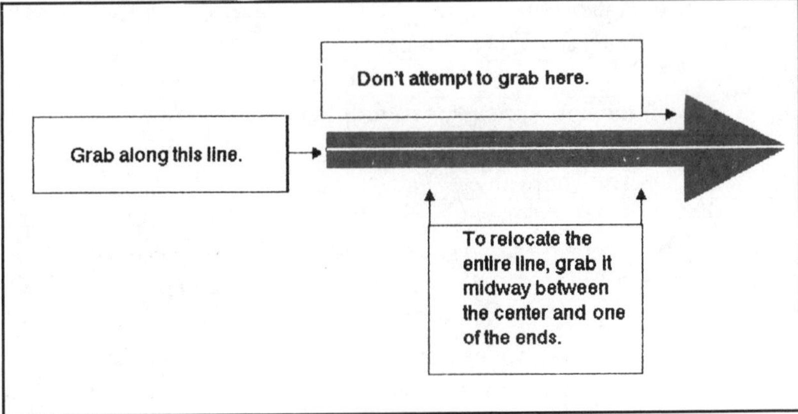

Figure 8.13: Moving a Line or Arrow

use the Edit menu to perform these procedures. Graphics that are cut or copied are placed on a graphics clipboard for later pasting, separate from material on the clipboards for frames and text. The clipboard is not cleared when you load a new chapter, so you can use it to move graphics from one chapter to another.

CHANGING LINE ATTRIBUTES

As we've discussed, graphics can vary in size and shape. In addition, you can control two other characteristics of graphics. These characteristics are called *line attributes* and *fill attributes*.

Line attributes control lines that you create with the Line icon. They also control lines that make up the outline of other graphic shapes. To set line attributes for a given graphic, you must display the dialog box for the Line Attributes command as follows:

1. Be sure that the frame that's attached to the graphic is selected in the Frame mode.
2. Activate the Graphics mode and select the graphic you wish to change (that is, click the graphic you've created in the working area).
3. Pull down the Graphic menu and click Line Attributes, or type Ctrl-L.

This procedure should display the dialog box shown in Figure 8.14.

With the Thickness category, you can set the selected line to Thin, Thick, or one of the standard settings in between. When you do, its dimension appears, ranging between 0.06 points and 18 points. To create an exact specification, click Custom Width and enter the appropriate value.

Set the color you desire by clicking the appropriate box. With some printers, you can use the White setting to create a white arrow against a black background. As you adjust the colors, the End Styles grouping will reflect your choice. White causes the grouping to disappear.

The End Styles settings dictate the manner in which a line terminates. Click these settings to create arrowhead and rounded endings, as well as the standard flat ends. The current settings have a check

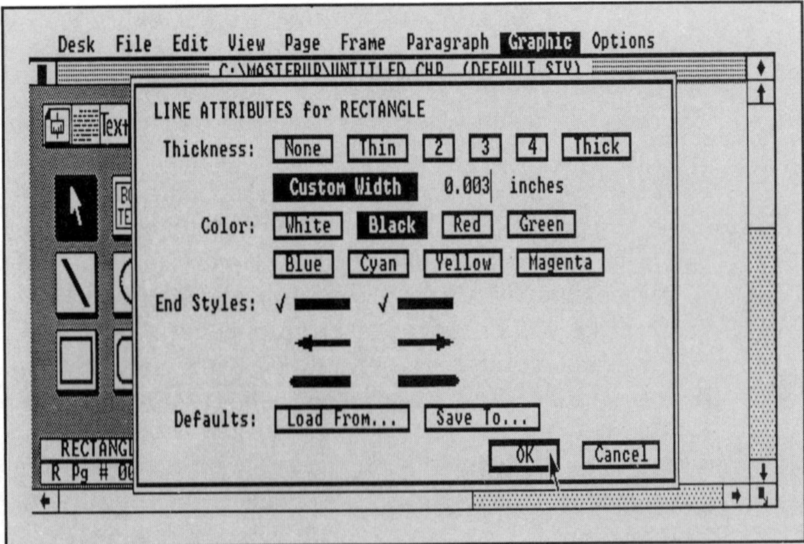

Figure 8.14: The Dialog Box for the Graphic Menu's Line Attributes Command

mark next to them. The left column corresponds to whichever end you created first, the right column to the other end. Note that they do not necessarily correlate with the left and right ends of the line.

Once you've created the settings you desire, you can set them aside for use with a similar graphic. Do this by clicking the Save To button. This copies the settings to a kind of holding area, similar to the clipboard. To duplicate the settings with another graphic of the same icon, display its Line Attributes dialog box and click Load From. These values also become the default settings for newly created graphics.

SPECIFYING FILL ATTRIBUTES

The other attribute of a graphic you can control is the fill attribute. This setting controls the manner in which Ventura treats the interior space of the graphic, including color and pattern. Note that you cannot set fill attributes for the graphics lines themselves; they're always solid. This differs from the way you can set interior line patterns with the Frame or Paragraph menu's Ruling Line commands.

To specify fill attributes for a selected graphic, follow the same procedure as that of line attributes, but use the Graphic menu's Fill Attributes command. Alternatively, after selecting the appropriate graphic, you can type Ctrl-F. You will see the dialog box shown in Figure 8.15.

Use this dialog box to specify the graphics color and pattern. A preview of your choices will appear in the Result box.

One setting that cannot be previewed is the choice of Opaque or Transparent. This setting is meaningful only when a graphic is to be placed on top of text or other graphics. It governs the manner in which that graphic treats the underlying material. If opaque, the graphic will hide all material beneath it from view. If transparent, it will allow the material to bleed through the graphic. The printer capability page that we created in Chapter 6 has examples of both opaque and transparent circles. Check your printout to see if your printer has the capacity to create transparent graphics.

The Load From and Save To buttons operate the same way they do for the Graphic menu's Line Attributes command. Use them to transfer fill attributes easily from one graphic to another and to set the default values.

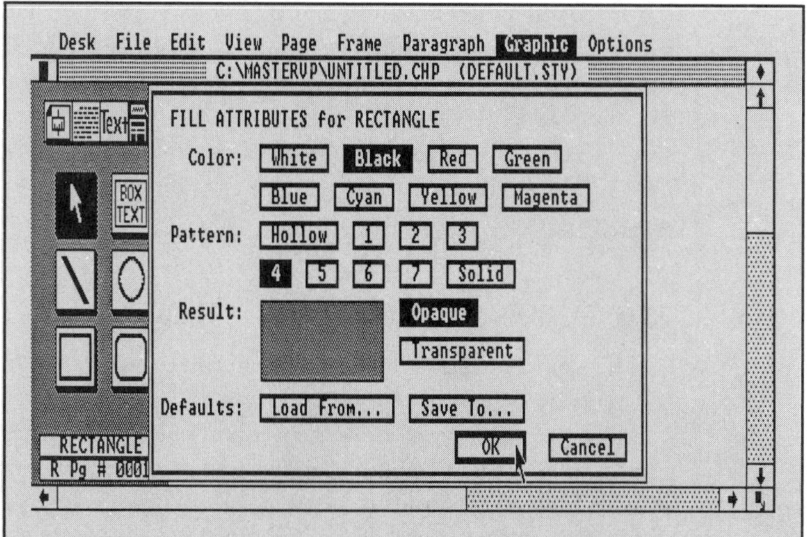

Figure 8.15: The Dialog Box for the Graphic Menu's Fill Attributes Command

USING BOX TEXT

One important use of opaque graphics is covering portions of an imported picture, such as the labels in our Lotus 1-2-3 graph. Once you've hidden the imported labels, you can add Ventura labels that use fonts similar to those you're using elsewhere on the page. Doing so lets you make the new graphic conform to the rest of the document.

The graphic feature called *box text* provides the means to accomplish both of these operations simultaneously. Use the Box Text icon to create a box just as you would use the other icons to create other graphic elements: click the icon, position the mouse cursor, and then drag and release. When you do, the box you initially create will display the words

Box Text

within it. Simply use the Text mode to delete these words and insert your own text in the box.

At first, box text may seem to be quite similar to a standard frame filled with a text file. There are, however, several ways in which the two differ:

- As with other elements you create with the Graphics mode, box text is tied to a frame. Thus, should you move its host frame to another location, box text will move right along with it. At the new location, box text will occupy the same position relative to the frame that it held at the old location.
- With box text you can't specify a text file to store the text as you can with a standard frame. All box text is stored in the chapter's CAP file, making it well-suited to covering numerous labels.
- As a graphic, you can use box text as you would other Ventura graphics. You can move other graphics above or beneath it. You can place it on the underlying-page frame and it will repeat on every page, as other graphics do.

Several box text boxes are used to cover the labels on the sample 1-2-3 graph shown in Figure 8.2 and replace them with a better font.

In this figure the Graphic menu's Fill Attributes are set for solid, opaque white. Box text is used to cover the sideways label *Millions* and replace it with our own vertical label. The same opaque box also covers the unnecessary and distracting zeros that appear in the scale. Figure 8.16 shows the underpinnings of the reformatted graph. (For the purpose of demonstration, we have changed this box to transparent and given it a thin outline.) Each letter in the word *MILLIONS* has a Return following it and is thus a separate paragraph. The alignment for these paragraph/letters, specified with the Paragraph menu's Alignment command, is Centered.

MANIPULATING MULTIPLE GRAPHICS

As you create graphics that are more and more sophisticated, you will find it necessary to place graphics on top of one another more and more often. When you do this, you will need to reorder the various layers. To do this, select a graphic and use the Graphic menu's Send To Back (Ctrl-Z) or Bring To Front (Ctrl-A) commands. To select a graphic that's behind another (so you can bring it forward, for instance), hold down the Ctrl key when clicking the graphic with the mouse. The procedure is the same as that used to select piled frames (see Chapter 3). Figure 8.17 shows how the circle, at the back of the custom graphic we created in Figure 8.11, changes the graphic when brought forward with Ctrl-click, then Ctrl-A. One use of these commands is to display a graphic that has been inadvertently obscured by another.

Sophisticated graphics may also require that you select several elements at once. Doing so allows you to move all selected graphics as a unit. To select several graphics in succession, hold down the Shift key as you click each with the mouse.

To select all the graphics tied to a frame in one step, pull down the Graphic menu and click Select All (or use Ctrl-Q). You can use either technique to move the graphics around on a page, while keeping them equidistant with respect to each other. You can also use them to cut or copy the graphics all at once. Of course, you could move the graphics' associated frame in order to move them as a group. The Select All command, however, allows you to relocate the graphics with respect to their host frame. It also allows you to move all graphics that are tied to the

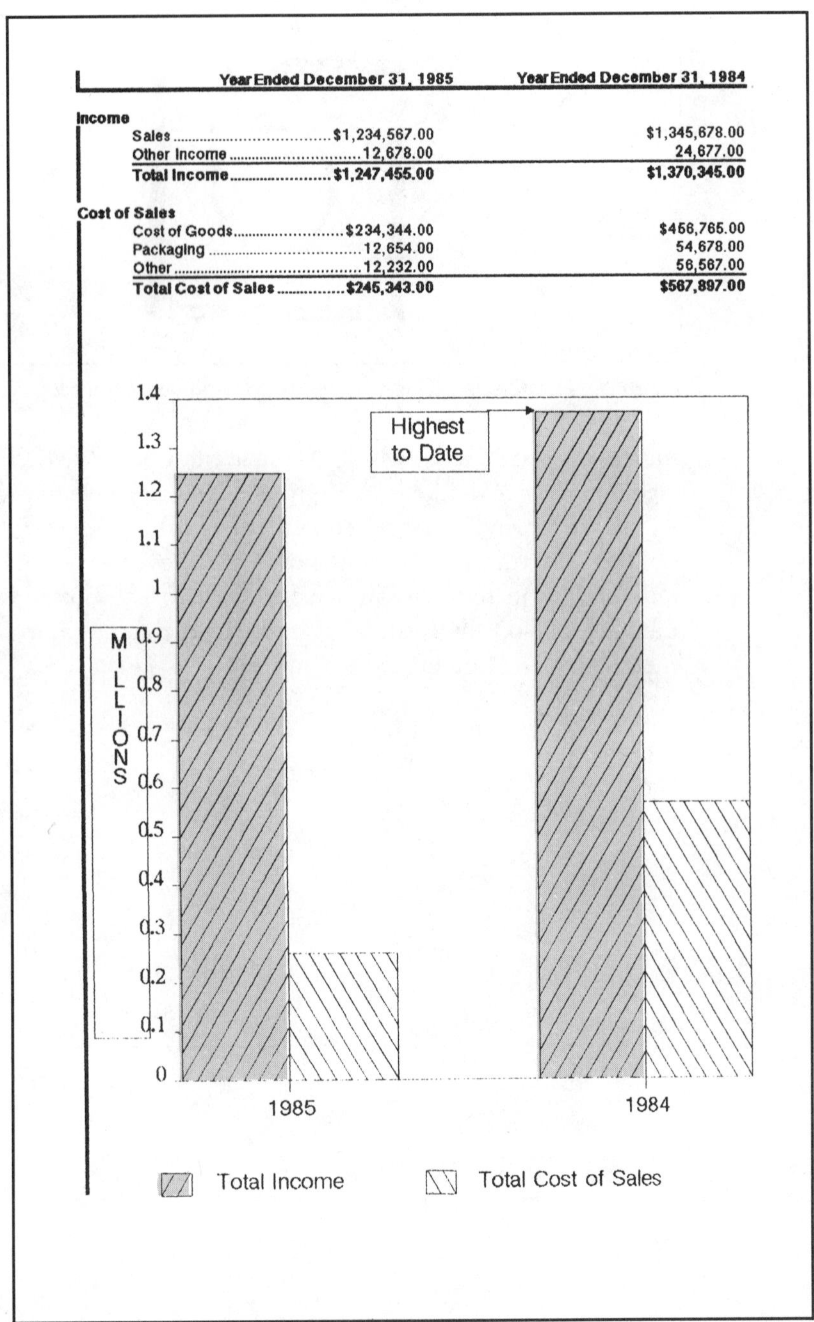

	Year Ended December 31, 1985	Year Ended December 31, 1984
Income		
Sales	$1,234,567.00	$1,345,678.00
Other Income	12,678.00	24,677.00
Total Income	**$1,247,455.00**	**$1,370,345.00**
Cost of Sales		
Cost of Goods	$234,344.00	$456,765.00
Packaging	12,654.00	54,678.00
Other	12,232.00	56,567.00
Total Cost of Sales	**$245,343.00**	**$567,897.00**

Figure 8.16: Using Box Text to Enhance the 1-2-3 Graph

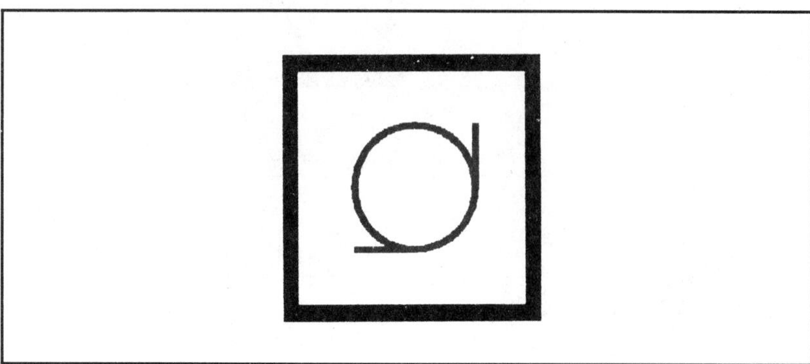

Figure 8.17: A Circle Brought Forward to Change a Graphic

underlying-page frame, which of course can't be moved. Once we created the boxes of shadings in Figure 8.4, we were able to position them within the screen by first selecting them as a unit.

Our study of box text has shown you how to use this feature to enhance imported graphics. You can also use box text to create tables. We'll look at this feature in the next chapter, along with other methods of creating tables in Ventura.

CHAPTER NINE

Creating Tables

AS WITH SO MANY OTHER FEATURES OF VENTURA, there are several approaches you can use to make tables. Naturally, you'll want to examine all the methods that are available. Then you'll be able to decide which technique is the best to use under the circumstances.

There are four basic ways to construct tables. The method you choose will dictate what you can enter into the table, how you enter it, and how your table will look. Let's look at the four methods, examine how they differ, and discuss the circumstances in which each is appropriate.

Table 9.1 summarizes the methods of creating tables. Although the methods are listed separately, be aware that one table can mix several techniques. For instance, box text can contain paragraphs that are formatted with tab settings.

Before we examine these methods, let's agree on some terminology. *Table entries* are the individual items that collectively create the table. Table entries combine to create *rows* and *columns* and so make up a table. Rows of table entries go across the table horizontally; columns span table entries that line up vertically. A row or column can consist of a single entry.

Regardless of which of the four techniques you use, creating a table consists of two fundamental operations: setting up the structure of the table and making entries into it. Usually, you set up the structure of the table before making entries into it, but some methods allow you to do either operation first.

With some methods, you can use your word processor or other programs, such as an electronic spreadsheet, to input entries. Under most circumstances, however, you'll probably find that it's easiest to use Ventura to make the entries into tables you create. This is because it's difficult, and in fact unnecessary, to get your word processor's settings to match those you create with Ventura. Thus, the word processor version of the table file generally bears little resemblance to the final Ventura version. However, if you want to use your word processor to make entries, you should check the procedures discussed in Chapter 12.

Let's begin by studying the method that is closest to using the typewriter and to word processing—using tabs.

METHOD	COMMENTS
Tabs	Table entries must be on one line each.
	Provides decimal tabs.
	Can use leader characters.
	Resetting can be difficult.
Paragraph Tags	Tricky to set up.
	Accommodates descriptive text of varying lengths automatically.
	Makes changing column widths an involved process. Usually necessitates changing other columns as well.
Box Text	Very visual. Easy to set up.
	Each item requires a separate box.
	Useful when the shape of table is important, such as with invoices.
	Does not use imported word processed text.
	Easy to surround table items with outlines and backgrounds.
	Easy to make changes because of visual orientation.
	Must adjust format manually if text length is too great.
Space Characters	Should generally be avoided due to lack of flexibility.
	May be used with nonproportional fonts only.

Table 9.1: Techniques for Creating Tables

SETTING TABS TO CREATE TABLES

Each method of creating tables has advantages and limitations, and each is best suited to a particular kind of task. One advantage of using tabs is that each tab setting offers you a variety of alignments.

Depending on which you choose, you can have the columns of your table line up in various ways, including along decimal points. The limitation, however, is that it's only practical to use tabs when each entry in the table is no longer than one line.

Setting up a table consists of assigning *tab settings* by using paragraph tags. Tab settings affect only that paragraph (or those paragraphs) that you format with this same tag. Thus, to assign tabs to a paragraph, you assign the tab settings for a paragraph tag, and assign that tag to the paragraph. Remember, though, that paragraph tagging is stored with the style sheet. Thus, any Ventura chapter that references the same style sheet can use tags with the same tab settings. That way, you can use your tab settings in various documents.

Tabs you set for a tag operate very much like tabs that you set when you use a typewriter. With a typewriter, you set a tab stop. When you press the typewriter tab key, the carriage jumps to the tab stop. Then you continue typing from the new position.

Ventura's tab settings operate like the tab stops of a typewriter, but in a more sophisticated fashion. When you type in your entries, you press the Tab key after each entry. Doing so inserts a *Tab character* into the text. The Tab character extends from the end of one entry to the next tab setting to the right. Text that follows the Tab character is then located with respect to the tab setting.

You can work with tabs in Ventura using one of two approaches: you can either type in your text first and then set up the structure of the table (by setting tabs), or you can set the tabs first and then type in the table entries. If you press the Tab key before you set the tabs, Ventura will insert a Tab character into the text nonetheless. However, the Tab character will not affect positioning of the text until you set the tab, at which time the tab effect will take place retroactively.

Usually it's best to set the tabs first, even if you have only a ballpark idea of their actual positions. That way, as you make the entries, you'll be able to see the table take some shape. If, when you add text, your entries don't fit between the your tab settings, you can fine-tune the tab settings as necessary. Ventura will automatically adjust the table entries to conform to the new settings.

To display the dialog box that allows you to set tabs, follow these steps:

1. With Paragraph mode active, click a paragraph to provide it (and similarly tagged paragraphs) with tabs as part of its format.
2. Pull down the Paragraph menu and click Tab Settings. The dialog box you see in Figure 9.1 appears.

As you can see from this dialog box, a paragraph tag can contain up to 16 tab settings, identified by a Tab Number. By clicking any one of the identifying buttons in the Tab Number grouping, you'll cause the dialog box to display settings that are in place for the particular tab. In this way, the Tab Number setting regulates all of the other settings in the dialog box.

Let's say that your paragraph tag has 3 tab settings associated with it. They would probably be numbered with Tab Numbers 1, 2, and 3. With 1 darkened in the Tab Number grouping, you'd see the characteristics of Tab Number 1 displayed in the dialog box, and you could adjust these characteristics as necessary. By clicking 2 to darken it, you could see and adjust the characteristics of Tab Number 2. Likewise, clicking the 3 button would allow you to work with Tab Number 3.

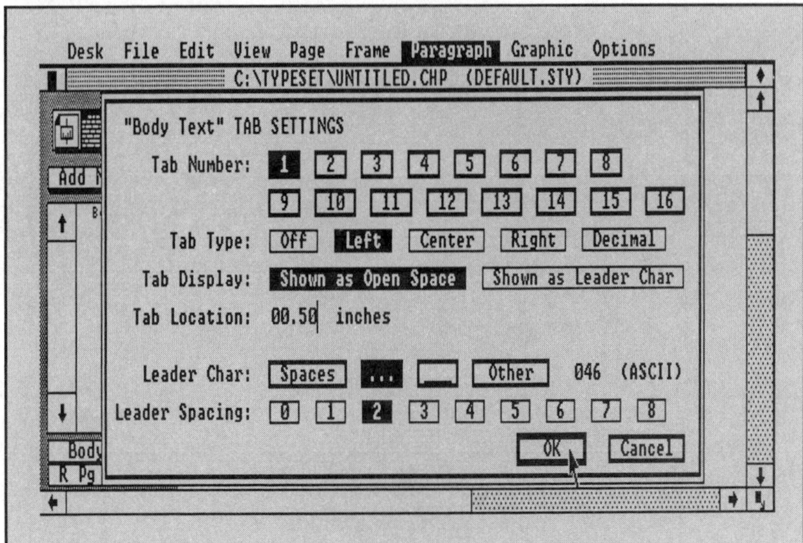

Figure 9.1: The Paragraph Menu's Dialog Box for Tab Settings

TURNING TABS ON AND OFF

The Tab Type category has five buttons. They are labeled Off, Left, Center, Right, and Decimal.

Once you've selected a tab setting by number, click Off if you want to make the indicated Tab setting nonoperational. If you click Off, none of the other settings in the dialog box will affect that tab setting. To turn a tab on, choose one of the four alignments available.

Left alignment is the standard type of alignment. When a tab setting is left-aligned, the table entries associated with the tab setting (that is, text that follows the corresponding Tab character) will begin at the tab location. Tab Location is a field setting that appears about midway in the dialog box. It shows the distance from the left edge of the table to the tab setting in question. When they are left-aligned, table entries have their left edge even with the tab location. The location of the right edge of such entries will vary, depending upon the amount of text in the entry, similar to the "ragged right" text format we saw in Chapter 5.

Figure 9.2 shows part of a sample chapter that's included with Ventura. The name of the file containing this chapter, and its associated style

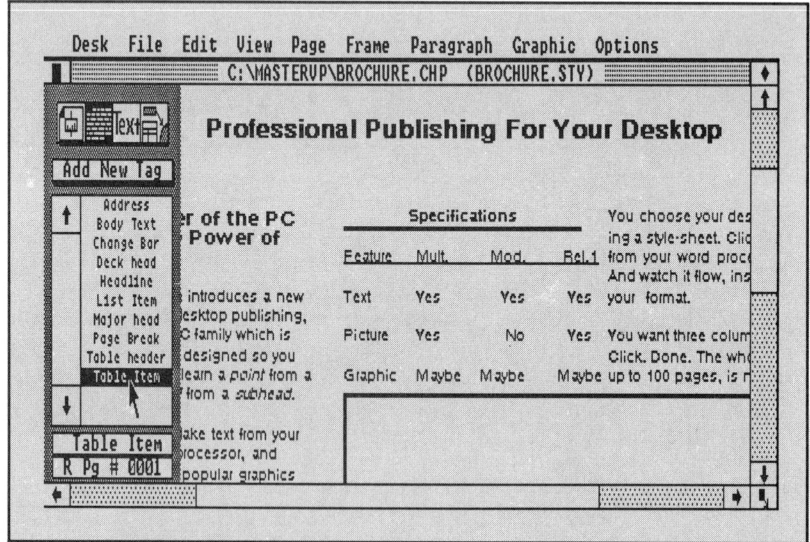

Figure 9.2: A Small Table in a Document

sheets, is &BRO-P3. To more fully examine tabs, we've made some changes in this file and saved it in the MASTERVP directory.

Look at the small table in the center of the screen. Better to demonstrate the types of alignment used in these columns, we've changed the last entries in the columns to *Maybe*.

Now examine Figure 9.3. In it you'll see the same table, but in this figure you can see the Tab characters between each table entry, in the form of → characters. In the Current box, these characters are referred to as Horizontal Tab codes when their presence is detected by the keyboard cursor. To display these codes, press Ctrl-T or pull down the Options menu and click Show Tabs and Returns. If the menu says Hide Tabs and Returns, then the tabs are already showing; clicking this command or typing Ctrl-T will turn them off.

The first tab in this example—the one set up for the *Mult.* heading—is left aligned. Notice how the first letter of each word in the column starts at the same spot. Each word begins at the tab location of the first tab and ends on the right according to the length of the entry. Thus, the word *Maybe* protrudes further to the right than the *Yes* entries above it.

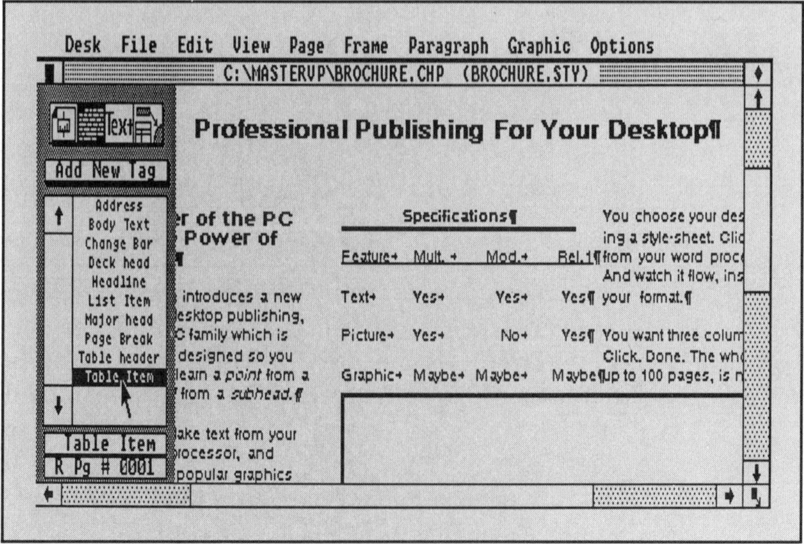

Figure 9.3: The Table with Tab Characters Displayed

IMPORTANT

Tab numbers usually do not correspond to the columns they control: Tab Number 1 governs the alignment of the second column, Tab Number 2 governs the alignment of the third column, and so on. This occurs because the first column of a table is not usually offset by a tab. Generally, the first column is aligned with the left edge of the table, as it is in the example.

You may find this arrangement confusing. If so, you can remedy the situation with any table by simply setting the Tab Location for Tab Number 1 to zero. If you do that, Tab Number 2 will control column 2, Tab Number 3 will control column 3, and so on. However, we'll leave our example as it has been set by the makers of Ventura.

The second Tab setting in the example controls the column under *Mod.* This column is right-aligned. Notice how the last letter of each entry in this column ends at the same spot, causing the column to be even on the right. The tab position is the spot where the last letter in these entries ends.

We've changed the setting of the third tab, which controls the fourth column, to center alignment. Notice how each entry in this column (*Rel. 1*) is centered on either side of a common invisible vertical line. The position of this line corresponds to the Tab Location of the third tab.

This example shows only three of the four types of tab settings. In a moment, we'll look at the last type of tab, Decimal.

PRECAUTIONS FOR SETTING TABS

Besides taking care that Tab numbers correspond to column numbers, as mentioned above, there are several other possible table traps you should watch out for. First, when you use tabs, always assign your tab settings by Tab Number in the same order they occur on the page, from left to right. Ventura ignores any tab settings that are out of order.

If you wish to use the same tab setting with a different tag, you can add a tag that initially has the same tab settings. In the Paragraph mode, select the paragraph with the original tab settings and click the

Add New Tag button on the Side-bar. You can add or remove tab settings of the new tag. They cannot be rearranged, however; you can only adjust existing tabs.

Be sure each Tab setting is wide enough. It must accommodate the widest entry in any column that precedes it in this or any other table using the same tag. In the case of right-aligned tabs, the tab must accommodate the widest entry in the column it controls. Any text from a previous column that extends past the position of a tab will move to the right, to the next Tab setting, when you insert a Tab character after the entry. In the example, if you were to replace the word *Picture* with a longer entry, such as *Reproduction*, that extended beyond the Tab setting for the *Mult.* column, the *Yes* under *Mult.* would be bumped into the *Mod.* column. The *No* under *Mod.*, in turn, would be repositioned under *Rel. 1*. The results appear in Figure 9.4.

Notice that the final *Yes* in the line has been moved out of the column. A line with tab characters in it still accepts as much text as it would without the tab characters. This holds true even if it means that text may be pushed past the edge of the column, or even past the edge of the page, causing some text to disappear. If you're working

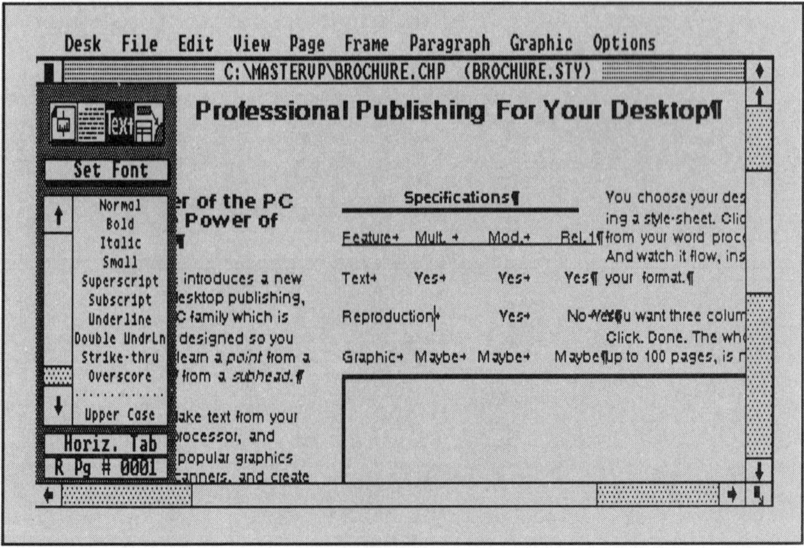

Figure 9.4: Displaced Table Entries

with a left-aligned Tab setting, Ventura could push text past the right edge of the page. If the Tab setting is right-aligned, additional text will be pushed to the left, past the left edge of the column or off the page to the left.

Note also that the paragraph tag for a table entry must not be set for Justified in order for tabs to show up. To check and change the alignment setting for a tag, pull down the Paragraph menu and click Alignment.

Finally, note that when you insert values into the Tab Location setting, Ventura does not consider a tag's In From Left value, as specified with the Paragraph menu's Spacing dialog box. For the tab position, Ventura always measures from the left edge of the paragraph, as if the paragraph has no In From Left indent.

SETTING DECIMAL TABS

Let's turn to another example for our look at decimal tabs. The sample Lotus 1-2-3 table that we've been working with in the past couple of chapters contains examples of decimal alignment. Figure 9.5 shows these examples. Notice how the decimal point in each column is lined up, one under another. The location of the decimal tab determines where the decimal points line up.

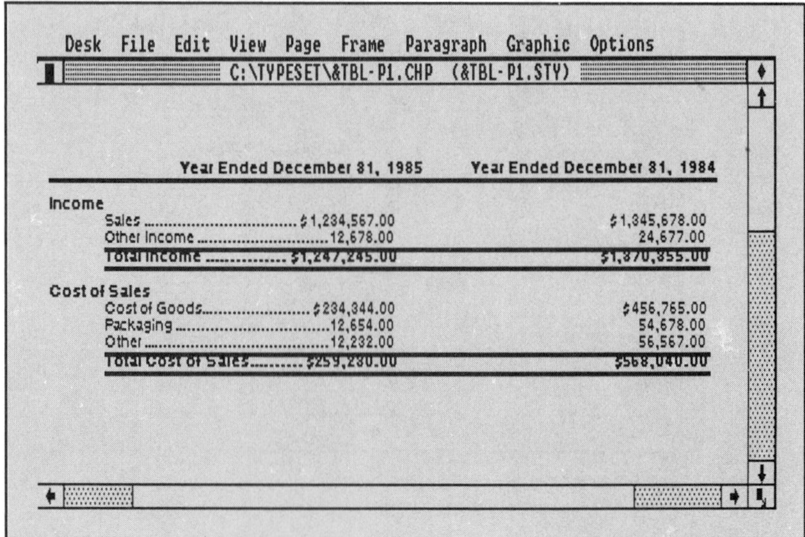

Figure 9.5: Decimal-Aligned Tabs

This alignment by decimal point operates regardless of the number of digits that a table entry contains. Even if you were using 5 or more decimal places for scientific work, the decimal points would always line up.

When typing currency amounts utilizing decimal-aligned Tab settings, begin with the cursor initially to the left of the tab location. When you hit the Tab key, the cursor moves to the decimal tab location. Then type in your dollar sign, if desired, and the whole dollar values.

As you type, the characters push backwards, to the left. When you press the period, the decimal point freezes at the tab location. Then, as you type in the cents, typing proceeds normally, moving to the right.

For example, let's say that you wanted to type in $125.35. Here's how the screen would look at each successive keystroke, as you entered this value:

```
(press Tab)
     $
    $1
   $12
  $125
  $125.
  $125.3
  $125.35
```

The result is that the decimal point remains at the location of the decimal tab, and other characters adjust accordingly.

There's one final point to mention about decimal-aligned Tab settings that that should be of interest to international users of Ventura. Normally, Ventura recognizes the period character as a decimal point when determining the placement of numbers associated with a decimal tab. However, you can direct Ventura to use any character of your choosing for this purpose. To change the default decimal point, pull down the Options menu and click Set Preferences. In the resulting dialog box, provide the ASCII value for the character you prefer in the Decimal Tab Char field. Appendix E lists the ASCII characters, along with their code number equivalents. Those who wish to use European style and set the comma character as the decimal point should specify a value of 44.

USING LEADER CHARACTERS

Besides decimal tabs, the table shown in Figure 9.5 also provides us with an example of *leader characters*. You can have leader characters automatically fill in the space occupied by a Tab character. They lead up to the entry controlled by the next tab setting using a specified leader character. (The alternative, as shown in the Tab Display setting in the Tab Settings dialog box, is to have the Tab character displayed as open space.)

Figure 9.5 shows periods used as leader characters for tab setting number 1 (the 1985 column). There is a Tab character following the word *Sales* and leading up to the decimal-aligned value $1,234,567.00. The space occupied by that Tab character is automatically filled in with periods.

Periods are the most common type of leader character. For this reason, Ventura provides a button for periods, as well as one each for spaces and underlines, in the Leader Char grouping of the Tab Settings dialog box (Figure 9.1). However, you can choose any character you'd like as a leader, by clicking the Other button and then entering the ASCII value for the character of your choosing (see Appendix E).

The last category in the Tab Settings dialog box is Leader Spacing. This setting controls the number of character spaces Ventura inserts between each leader character. For short tab distances, you'll want to insert fewer spaces. Figure 9.5 has leader spacing set for zero. If the tab is traveling across greater expanses of the page, you may wish to spread out the leader characters by using a larger number.

COLUMN TAGS

Now that you've seen how to set tabs to create tables, let's look at Ventura's second method for making tables: *column tags*. The column tag method is sometimes called *vertical tabs* or *side-by-side paragraphs*. Be aware, however, that this method does not have anything to do with columns as specified in the Frame menu's Margins & Columns dialog box. When you use column tags, each column in the table has a corresponding paragraph tag. Thus, if your table has four columns in it, you would create four tags with indicative names, such as Col 1, Col 2, Col 3, Col 4.

Figure 9.6 shows a sample chapter, &TBL2-L1, that takes just such an approach. Note that you could not create this table by using tabs. Tabs only operate with table entries that are no more that one line; most of the entries shown in the second and third columns are several lines long.

Instead, you set up tags for each column. Each table entry is a separate paragraph, tagged with the appropriate column tag. Thus, the table entries in the first column—*First Entry*, *Second model.*, and *Entry #3*—are each separate paragraphs and each tagged with Col 1. The paragraphs in the next column are each tagged with the Col 2 format. Likewise, each entry in the third column is a separate paragraph, tagged with Col 3, and each price in the last column is tagged with the Col 4 format.

FORMATTING COLUMN TAGS

For these four paragraph tags to operate, they must receive some special, unusual formats. First, in order to position each paragraph correctly, you must use the Paragraph menu's Spacing command. In the dialog box that this command displays, you set the In From Left and In From Right values so that each column entry is positioned properly from left to right. Figure 9.6 shows the values that are set for Col 2 and Col 3.

There are also some adjustments you must make in the Breaks dialog box, shown in Figure 9.7. To display this dialog box, pull down the Paragraph menu and click the Breaks command. Figure 9.8 summarizes the settings in the Paragraph menu's Spacing and Breaks dialog boxes that affect column tags.

In order to understand the Paragraph Breaks settings, let's first consider the standard paragraph. When you finish typing a regular paragraph into a document and hit Return, the cursor moves down to the line below the paragraph you've just completed. This action constitutes a *line break*. You then type in your text, beginning at the new spot.

For the Col 1 tag, Line Break is set to Before. This will cause the Column 1 entries—the first table entries in each row of entries— to begin on a new line, just as a standard paragraph does.

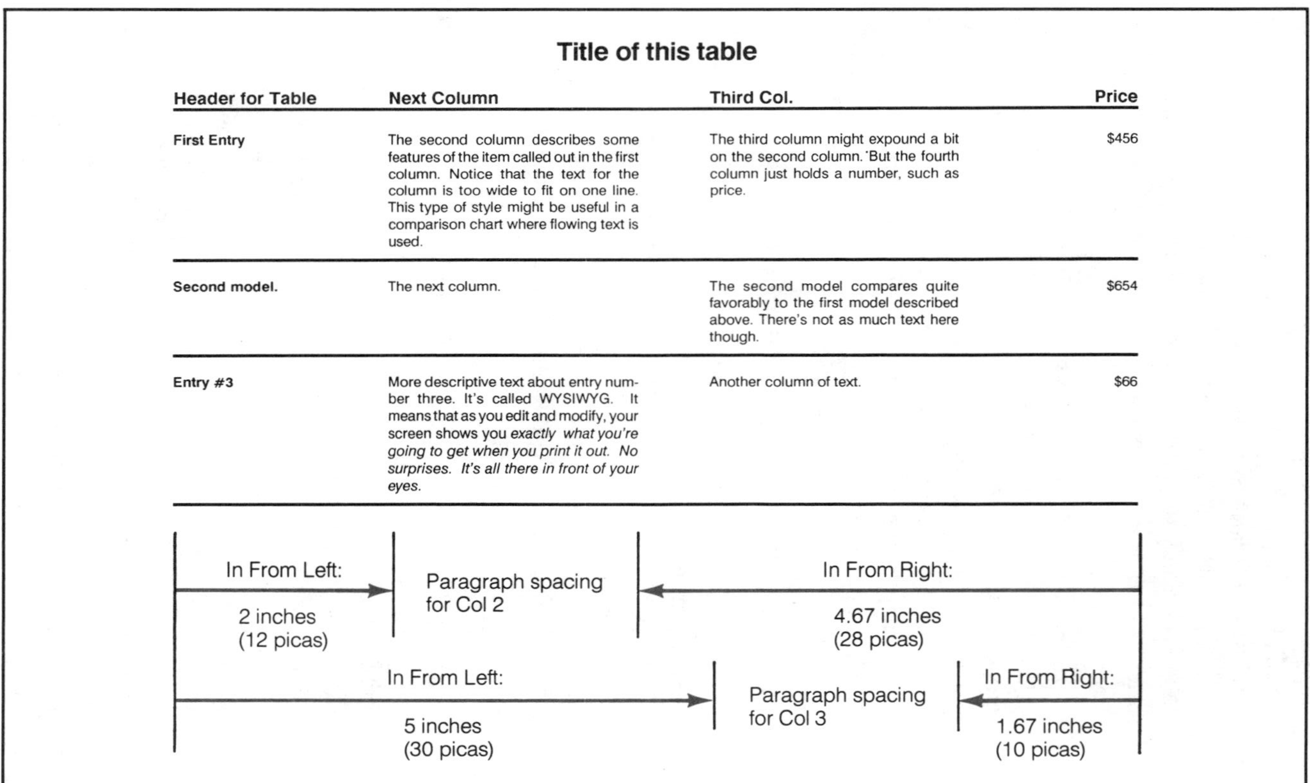

Title of this table

Header for Table	Next Column	Third Col.	Price
First Entry	The second column describes some features of the item called out in the first column. Notice that the text for the column is too wide to fit on one line. This type of style might be useful in a comparison chart where flowing text is used.	The third column might expound a bit on the second column. But the fourth column just holds a number, such as price.	$456
Second model.	The next column.	The second model compares quite favorably to the first model described above. There's not as much text here though.	$654
Entry #3	More descriptive text about entry number three. It's called WYSIWYG. It means that as you edit and modify, your screen shows you *exactly what you're going to get when you print it out. No surprises. It's all there in front of your eyes.*	Another column of text.	$66

Figure 9.6: A Table Created with Column Tags

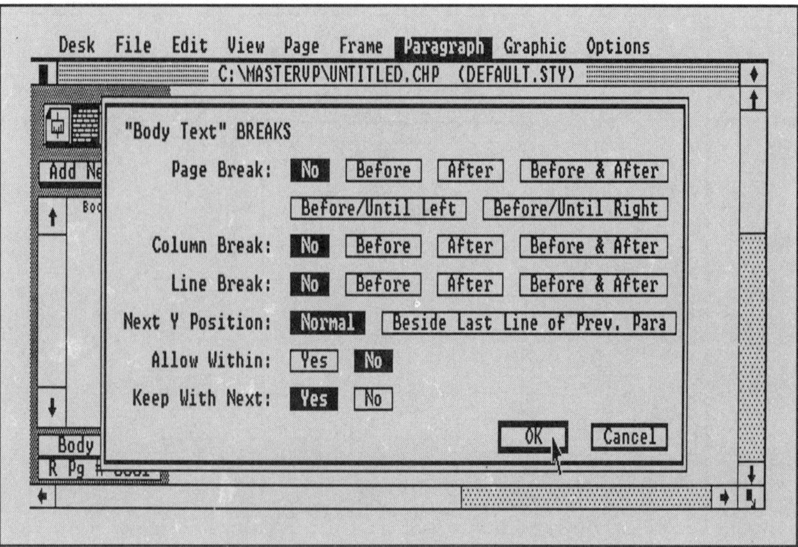

Figure 9.7: The Paragraph Menu's Breaks Dialog Box, with Tag Settings for Columns 2 and 3

For the intermediate tags, Col 2 and Col 3, paragraphs must appear to the *right* of the previous paragraph, rather than below it. The second entry in a table is the paragraph which should be placed to the *right* of the first entry, not below the first entry. Thus, rather than breaking to the next line, you want the text to move back up to the *same* line that the previous paragraph began on. This arrangement allows paragraphs to line up horizontally on the page. By adjusting the Line Break setting, you control placement of the new paragraph in this manner.

For Col 2 and Col 3, click the No button for Line Break. This will make these table entries begin on the same line as the table entry before them. Normally, because this setting controls only vertical placement, returning to the same line as the previous paragraph would cause a new paragraph to be superimposed on the previous paragraph. However, the new paragraphs in this case have In From Left and In From Right values different from those of the preceding paragraph. The new paragraph will be offset to the right of the previous paragraph, rather than placed squarely on top of it.

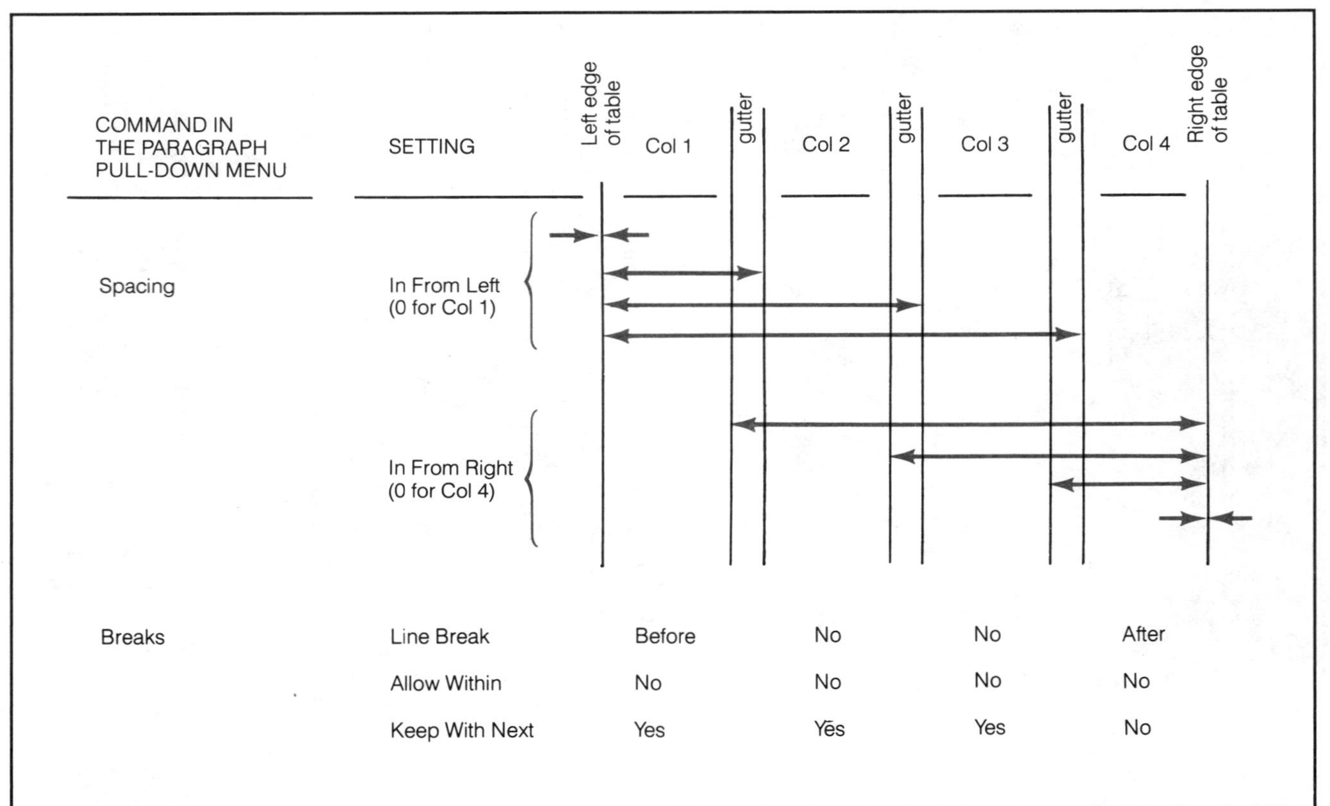

Figure 9.8: Settings That Affect Column Tags

Once you affix column tags to your text, you must never press Return to begin a new paragraph within interior columns (that is, Col 2 and Col 3). Doing so will start a new paragraph, to be sure, but the new paragraph will be tagged the same as the previous paragraph. Because there would be no break between the paragraphs, the new paragraph would begin *at the same spot* as the previous paragraph. Ventura would superimpose the text of the new paragraph on that of the previous paragraph. If you should accidentally hit Return like this, immediately press the Backspace key to delete the Return.

SINGLE COLUMN ENTRIES

If you want to create a single entry for a row, there are two ways you can do so. First, you can insert a Line Break code in the paragraph above the prospective entry by pressing Ctrl-Return. This character looks like a broken arrow pointing to the left (see Figure 9.9). The text will start on a new line, giving the appearance of a new paragraph.

In Figure 9.10, the paragraph beginning with *Notice that the text* has received this treatment. Since it isn't a new paragraph as Ventura defines it (one created with Return), the Line Break settings in the Paragraph menu's Break dialog box do not take effect.

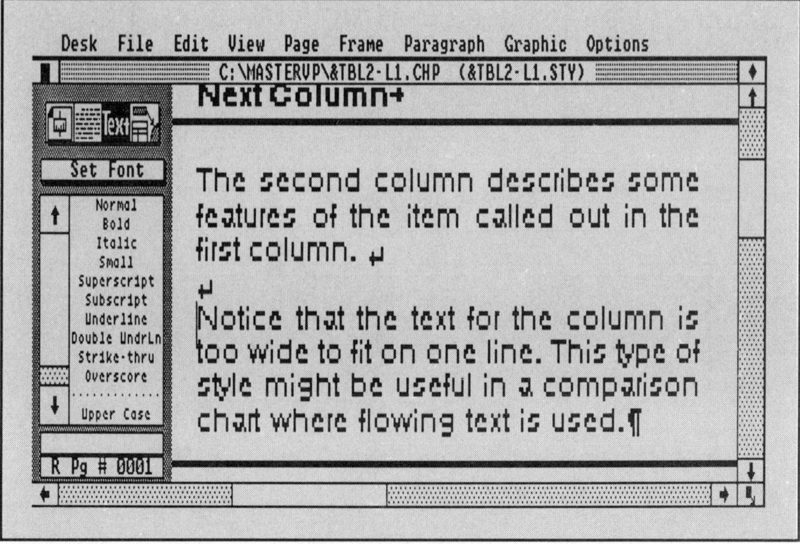

Figure 9.9: Creating a New Paragraph with Line Break Codes (Ctrl-Return)

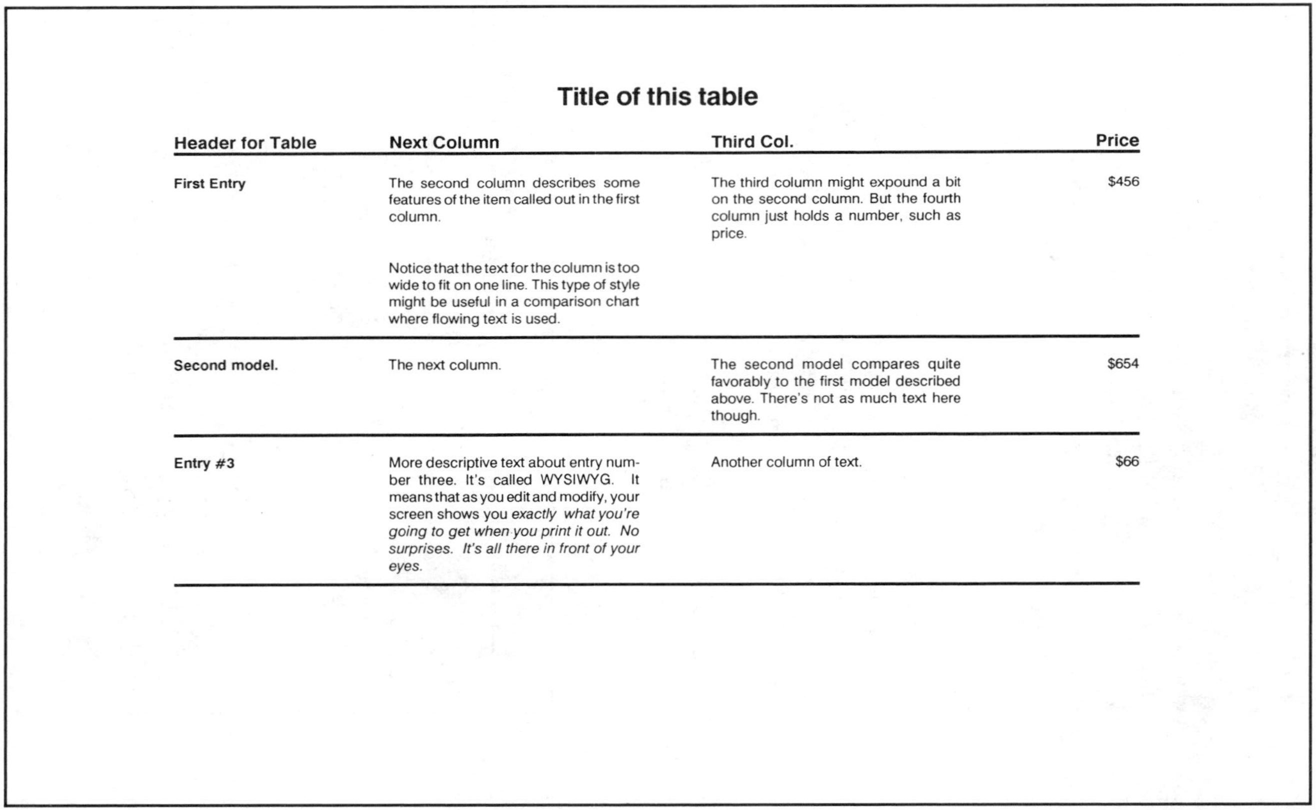

Title of this table

Header for Table	Next Column	Third Col.	Price
First Entry	The second column describes some features of the item called out in the first column. Notice that the text for the column is too wide to fit on one line. This type of style might be useful in a comparison chart where flowing text is used.	The third column might expound a bit on the second column. But the fourth column just holds a number, such as price.	$456
Second model.	The next column.	The second model compares quite favorably to the first model described above. There's not as much text here though.	$654
Entry #3	More descriptive text about entry number three. It's called WYSIWYG. It means that as you edit and modify, your screen shows you *exactly what you're going to get when you print it out. No surprises. It's all there in front of your eyes.*	Another column of text.	$66

Figure 9.10: Creating a Row Containing a Single Entry

Unfortunately, other characteristics of the various Paragraph commands won't take effect either. For instance, if you're using the Paragraph menu's Spacing command to set Inter-Paragraph space, it won't apply to the space between paragraphs created with Ctrl-Return. However, you can add space between such paragraphs by using Ctrl-Return repeatedly to insert additional Line Break codes, as was done in this example.

The other way to create a single entry is to enter it after the last entry of the previous row of entries. After making the entry, tag it with the appropriate column format.

Note that this method in fact creates a new row. As such, the entry in the new row will begin after the entry of the previous row with the most lines. When used with our example, the result of this technique is identical to Figure 9.10. You can insert one or more individual entries like this as long as the entry at the end of the previous row is set to have a line break after it. If you can't use either of these techniques—if, for instance, the lines aren't breaking correctly—you can create an entirely new row of blank table entries.

ADDING A NEW ROW OF ENTRIES

If you need to add a new row of table entries, copying is probably the easiest way to accomplish that. Just copy the text of an existing row using the cut-and-paste techniques we discussed in Chapter 5. Then replace the text for each entry with the new text as required.

Figure 9.11 shows the table we've been studying in Reduced view. Here the third row of the table has been copied, creating a new fourth row that's identical to the third. The new fourth row is darkened, since it has just been pasted in position. Text in the fourth row, except for the Return characters (or Paragraph End codes) would be deleted and replaced with appropriate entries for the fourth row.

Although this technique is easy to understand and perform, it usually results in a lot of unnecessary text that you must delete. If you'd prefer to begin with a clean slate, try the following method using our example:

1. Start in the Text mode. Position the keyboard cursor at the beginning of the row of table entries that you wish to place the new row *above*. Press Return the required number of

times to create the appropriate number of Paragraph End codes (one for each column plus others for formatting intervening paragraphs, such as rule paragraphs).

2. Change to Paragraph mode. Tag each Paragraph End code appropriately (for example, Rule, Col 1, Col 2, and so on). The Paragraph End code will in turn position itself in the appropriate column.
3. Change back to the Text mode. Position the cursor before each Paragraph End code in turn and type in your text.

In our example, let us assume that we wish to create an empty row before the row that begins with *Second model*. Consider that a row of table entries consists first of the Paragraph End code formatted with the Rule tag. There's no text in this "paragraph," only the code. The only purpose of this tag is to create the horizontal line that separates each row of entries. So for the first step, make sure you are in Text mode, position the cursor just before the code formatted with the Rule tag, and press Return five times. Since all the Paragraph End codes will initially have the Rule tag, this action creates five additional horizontal lines (see Figure 9.12).

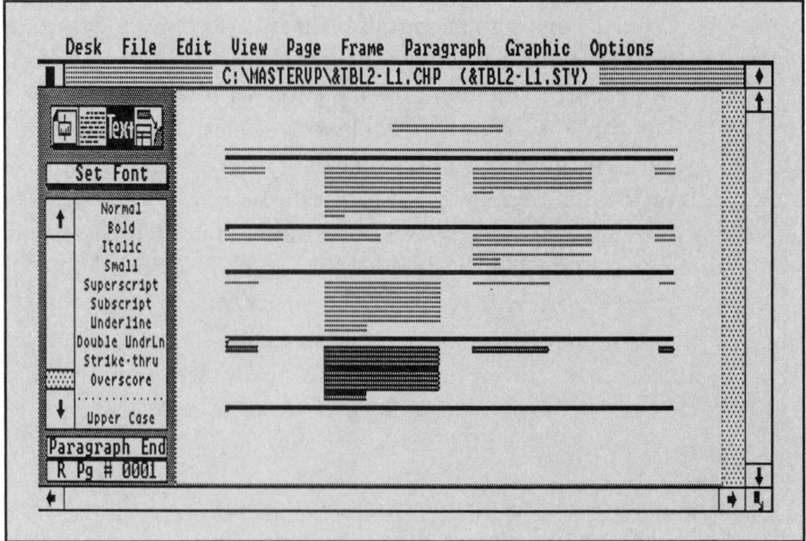

Figure 9.11: Copying to Create a New Row

Next, tag the codes appropriately. Leave the first code tagged with the Rule format. Tag the code right below it as Col 1. When you do, the horizontal line above that code disappears as it takes on its new format, that of Col 1. Next, tag the code below Col 1 as Col 2, which causes this code to lose its rule and move up and over to column 2 (see Figure 9.13). Repeat the process for the last two Paragraph End codes and your four columns are formatted and ready for text.

ADJUSTING THE SAMPLE FOR USE

Before we finish with our discussion of column tags and our work with the sample table shown in Figure 9.5, there is one last point we need to make about the sample. The discussion that follows is for those who wish to change the text and use the sample for their own purposes.

Notice that column 1 and column 4 each have very short table entries in them. Specifically, there is a short "header" in column 1 and a price in column 4. If you wish to use these two columns for longer entries, like those you see in columns 2 and 3, you'll have to make some changes in paragraph spacing. Apparently, columns 1

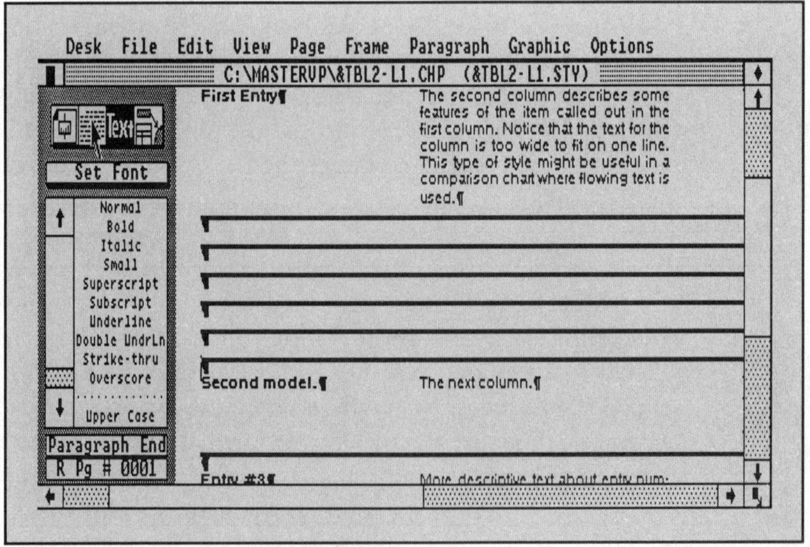

Figure 9.12: Creating Paragraph End Codes to Be Formatted As Columns

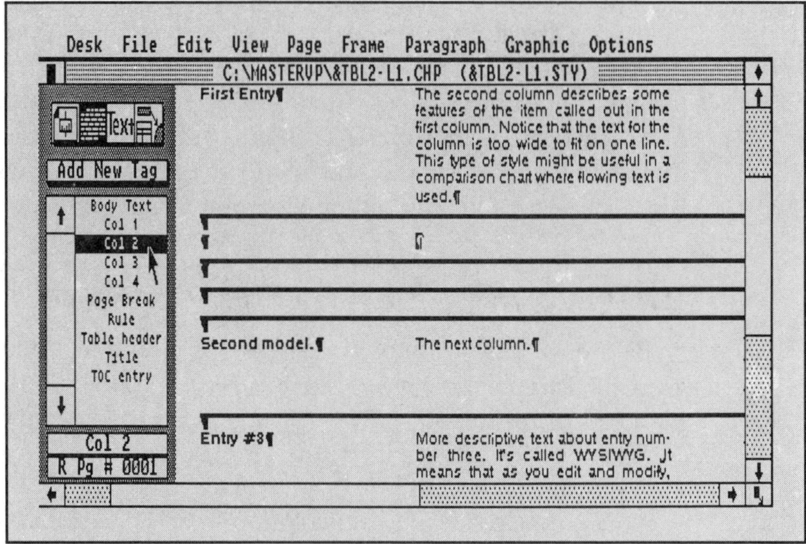

Figure 9.13: Tagging a Paragraph End Code to Position It in the Second Column

and 4 weren't designed for long entries. If you start to type into these columns without making adjustments, the text you enter will overlap parts of columns 2 and 3.

To properly space these columns so that the distance between each column matches the space currently between columns 2 and 3, change the Paragraph menu's Spacing dialog box as follows. For the Col 1 tag, change the In From Right setting to 7.67 inches (or 46 picas). For the Col 4 tag, change the In From Left setting to 8 inches (or 48 picas).

As you can see, using column tags can become quite complex as the various properties of the tags interact with each other. However, once you set up a format, you can use it with any document that references the same style sheet. Using column tags is especially helpful when you have long columns, with lots of descriptive or narrative text. Because the table length (that is, the number of lines the table occupies) adjusts automatically, the form of the table is dictated by its contents. If, on the other hand, the form of your document should control the length of its contents, you may want to use the third method of creating tables: box text.

BOX TEXT

With box text, you decide the shape of the table in a way that's independent of its contents. If the shape of your table must conform to a predetermined, highly structured format, such as that of an invoice, Box Text may be the most appropriate way to produce it. Figure 9.14 shows a sample table using this method. The shape of a box text table does not adjust automatically as its contents change. If it becomes necessary to change the shape of such a table, you must do so as a separate operation.

We examined box text in the previous chapter, using it to create labels for a graph. Remember that the contents of box text are stored in the chapter's caption file: that is, the file with the same name as the chapter, except with a CAP extension. This means that you do not bring in word processed files to use with box text.

This also means that when you use box text, you must set up the structure of the table before you can make any entries in it. You cannot create the table entries first and then shape those entries into a table, as you can with the previous methods.

Remember, too, that box text, like any graphic, is tied to a frame. In the Frame mode, you must first select the appropriate frame

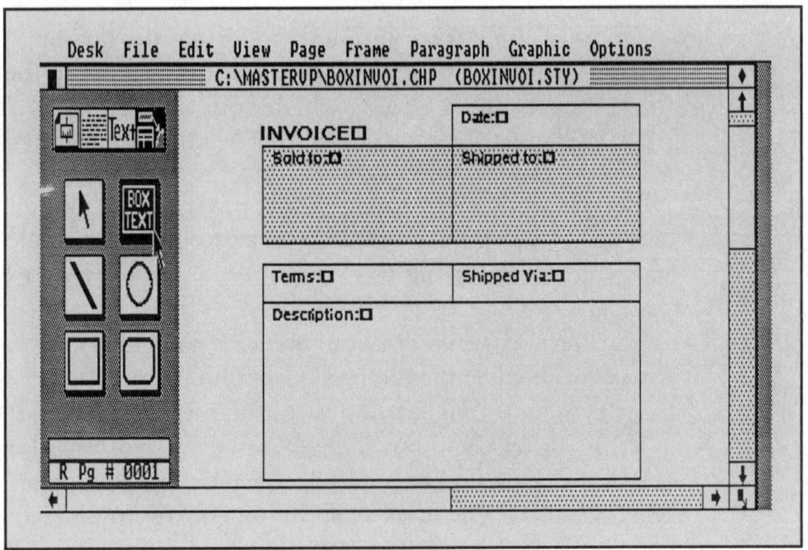

Figure 9.14: Creating a Table with Box Text

before you can use the Graphics mode to select a given text box for alteration.

Here are the steps to create a table, such as the Invoice shown in Figure 9.14, using box text:

1. In Frame mode, select the frame to which you want the box text tied.
2. Activate the Graphics mode. If you want your boxes positioned at regular intervals, use the Graphic menu's Grid Settings command to indicate Grid Snap.
3. To create box text, click the Box Text icon. Position and stretch each box into place. If you wish to create multiple boxes, hold down the Shift key as you create and size each one. That way, you won't have to click the Box Text icon for each box.
4. Replace the words *Box Text* that appear in each box with the appropriate text for the box. (Use the Text mode to create and edit this text.)
5. Format the boxes as desired, using the Graphic menu's commands.
6. Use the Paragraph mode to format the box text paragraphs as necessary. Initially, box text is tagged with the generated tag Z_BOXTEXT, which you can change as desired (see Chapter 5 for a discussion of Ventura's generated tags).

When first created, each box text entry usually has a thin outline around it. As we have seen, however, you can eliminate or modify such outlines by using the Graphic menu's Line Attributes command (or typing Ctrl-L).

You can add backgrounds to box text, too. This makes special formats possible, like the address backgrounds in Figure 9.14. Use the Graphic menu's Fill Attributes command (or type Ctrl-F).

With box text, you can change formatting attributes for more than one box at a time. Once you select one box, pressing the Shift key as you click allows you to select additional boxes simultaneously. Multiple selected boxes can then be formatted together, as well as moved, stretched, and shrunk with the mouse and cut or copied with the Del key. For instance, you may wish to move the bottom three boxes in Figure 9.14 away from the others. Select these three as a group and move any one of them; the other two will move with it. Note that this capability differs from that available to multiple frames, which can be cut, copied, and moved as a unit, but cannot incorporate formatting changes to all of them at one time.

We've now examined the three most common and effective ways to create tables. There is a fourth way, however, that you may need to consider.

USING SPACES TO CREATE TABLES

You can also use spaces, created by pressing the Space bar, to separate the entries in a table. It's undesirable to do so, however, because of the limitations that using spaces imposes.

First, you can only print tables created with spaces if you use a nonproportional font. With proportional fonts, characters vary in width, making it hard—often impossible—to line up columns containing different characters.

In addition, it's difficult to make changes to a table created with spaces. To move columns, you have to add or remove spaces for each line of text involved.

Unfortunately, tables you import will often use spaces between entries. For instance, if you use the Lotus 1-2-3 / Print File command to export a table, the resulting table has spaces between entries. In addition, people preparing tables with a word processor often make the mistake of using spaces to separate entries. In a word processor, where proportional fonts are not displayed, columns separated by spaces may line up very nicely—not so once the text is transferred to Ventura.

If you should acquire a table that uses spaces, you have two basic options for dealing with it. You can use it as is and print the table with a nonproportional font, if your printer has one. (Of course, only the table needs the nonproportional font. Text above or below the table can use proportional fonts.)

Alternatively, you can go through the table, with Ventura or your word processor, and strip away the spaces between entries, replacing them with tabs. Then you could use Tab settings to align the columns properly. There are other methods available, but unfortunately none are especially effective.

Placement of the items in a table is important in determining how the table looks and communicates its subject matter. In Chapter 10, we'll see how placement of items on the page is just as important in determining how the page looks and communicates.

CHAPTER TEN

Working with Pages: Formats and Page Headings

GENERALLY, DESKTOP-PUBLISHING DOCUMENTS THAT you create with a computer fall into two basic categories. The first type of document emphasizes elements on the page. It's created with the computer equivalent of a layout artist's pasteup board. Individual pages are important in this type of document. Each page is carefully composed and the elements on the page are strategically positioned. This kind of document is often deemed *layout intensive*, or *pasteup oriented*. Sometimes it is called a *complex document*. Newsletters and magazines are examples of layout-intensive documents.

The second type of document emphasizes one long section of text; books and manuals both fall within this category. The strategy for creating these documents lies in setting up general parameters for pages. Pages are not individually crafted (although they are usually fine-tuned). Instead, the computer constructs the document more or less automatically, guided by the parameters you set. Sometimes the resulting document is called a *batch-processed document* or a *simple document*. Perhaps *book-style document* is the most direct term.

Fortunately, Ventura has the ability to create and handle both types of documents. With Ventura, it's as easy to paste up individual pages as it is to set up the parameters for a book. And regardless of the method, Ventura allows you to see on the screen what you'll get when you print (which is not the case with other programs, especially those that create book-style documents).

To create book-style publications with Ventura, you assign a word processed file to the underlying-page frame. The amount of material in the file initially determines the number of pages in the document. This is because Ventura automatically creates as many pages as necessary to accommodate all the text in the assigned file. To create layout-intensive documents, on the other hand, you generally use numerous standard frames that are placed on top of the underlying-page frame. Sometimes, the underlying-page frame holds little or no material.

For both types of documents, you use a variety of Ventura commands to set up their respective formats. Be aware, however, that most formatting commands do not apply strictly to one type of document or the other; most are used with either type. Also be aware that not all documents fall neatly into one of these two categories. Many documents possess properties of both types.

Bearing this in mind, in this chapter we'll examine Ventura commands chiefly as they apply to layout-intensive documents. Even so, we must examine the underlying-page frame, as it forms the substratum of both kinds of documents in Ventura. In Chapter 11, we'll focus on commands that are more generally utilized with book-style documents.

The newsletter we studied earlier in this book is an example of a layout-intensive document. As constructed, it has numerous standard frames that hold text and pictures. However, there is no material in its underlying-page frame; all its material is placed in the various standard frames that sit on top of the underlying-page frame.

Text for standard frames may be stored in either of two ways. You can use word processed text in files that you assign to the frame with the Assignment list. Or, in Text mode, you can click the frame and simply type your text directly into the standard frame. Such directly entered text is called *Frame Text.* When you select such a frame in Frame mode, this is the designation that appears in the Current box. Ventura stores Frame Text in the chapter's CAP file. (Note that you cannot type and store text directly in the underlying-page frame; such text must be stored in a file.)

ADDING AND REMOVING PAGES

With layout-intensive documents, you carefully construct each page. Initially, a Ventura document has only one page. So work with layout-intensive documents usually means crafting the first page and adding additional pages, laying each out as you go.

CUSTOM PAGES

The usual way to add pages is with the Page menu's Insert/Remove Page dialog box (see Figure 10.1). As indicated by the darkened button in this dialog box, the default choice inserts a new page after the page that is current when you invoke the dialog box. You can also insert a page before the current page by using the first button in the dialog box.

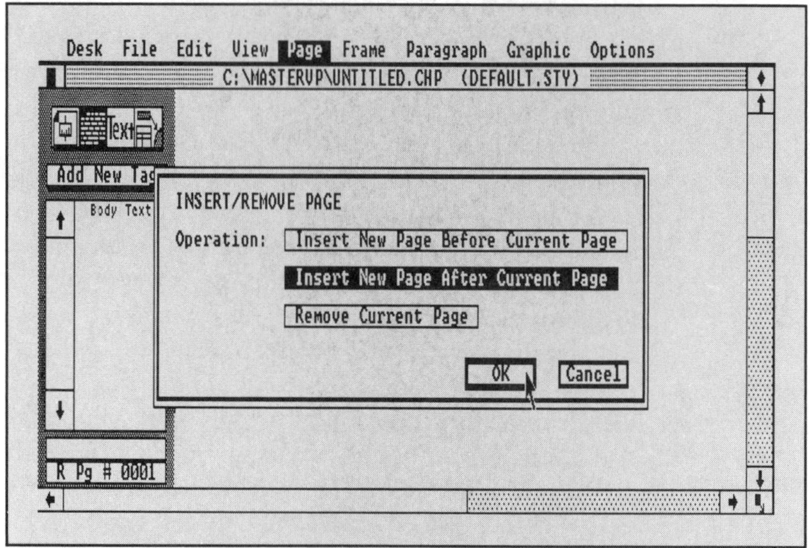

Figure 10.1: Page Menu's Insert/Remove Page Dialog Box

When using this dialog box, however, be aware that the page you insert differs from other pages that may have been automatically generated to accommodate text in the underlying-page frame. With pages that are automatically generated, underlying-frame attributes that you set for one page, such as margins and columns, ruling lines and boxes, and frame background, affect all the pages. However, when you insert a page using the Page menu, these frame attributes are handled separately for the new page. Likewise, graphics elements, which repeat on the underlying-page frame, will not appear on the inserted page. (In fact, inserting a page creates a second underlying-page frame. As we'll see shortly, this new underlying-page frame can generate additional pages which share its attributes.)

The fact that an inserted page can have margins, columns, and other attributes different from those of other pages makes inserted pages useful when creating layout-intensive documents. With such documents, it's often necessary for each page to be set up differently. Using inserted pages you can have, for instance, page 1 set up for 2 columns and page 2 set up for 3 columns. Even if you do not use the columns to hold text directly, you can then use them to snap standard frames into place.

The underlying-page frame of a newly created page has the same initial format as the page that comes before it in the chapter. This holds true whether the previous page was automatically generated or custom created by inserting. It also holds true whether you created the page by inserting it before or after the current page. This format can be changed, as we'll see in a moment.

In addition to creating pages, you use the Page menu's Insert/Remove Page dialog box to remove the currently displayed page. Be very careful when you remove a page. Once you do, it cannot be retrieved. There is no clipboard that stores the removed page. If you wish to save the contents of the current page for later use, you can effectively move the page items as a group by moving multiple frames. Use the Frame mode to select all the frames (by Shift-clicking each one) and delete them as a group (with the Del key or the File menu's Cut Frame command). Once you've created a new page, you can use the Ins key (or the Edit menu's Paste Frame command) to place the group of frames in their same relative positions on the new page.

AUTOMATICALLY GENERATED PAGES

As mentioned, when you assign a file to the underlying-page frame, Ventura will automatically generate as many pages as necessary to accommodate the text that is in that file. In addition, you can trick Ventura into generating additional pages, even when you don't use the underlying-page frame to accommodate a file. To do so, you fill each page with standard frames; as you do, Ventura automatically generates additional pages. The resulting pages, because they are automatically generated, all share the same underlying-page frame and hence the same format. This holds true even if you later change the format of any page. Use this technique when you want features of the underlying-page frame to be similar throughout the document and remain similar, even though the standard frames on top may differ. Here's how you get Ventura to automatically create pages without text:

1. In Text mode, click the underlying-page frame as if you were placing the keyboard cursor into position. The End of File marker (□) will appear and Ventura will inform you that you

need to create a new file to hold text for the underlying-page frame.

2. Click New File. In the Item Selector box that appears, provide a new name for the file. The name is not important because the file will hold no text. Only the End of File marker will appear in the working area.
3. Place your frames on the underlying-page frame as usual.
4. When you fill up an entire page with frames, these frames will push the End of File marker off the page, causing it to create a new page. The new page will share the same underlying-page frame as the page from which it was generated.

Once created, new pages will be similarly formatted and will adjust as you make changes to the underlying-page frame on any page. Use this method if, for instance, you expect to have three columns of frames and constant margins throughout. If you want to be able to mix formats on the underlying-page frame, use the method outlined earlier to create additional frames.

Even with layout-intensive documents, you may wish to use the underlying-page frame if your document addresses one main text file at a time and you want to use the entirety of that file in sequence. Thus, a magazine that uses a lot of frames would usually be considered a layout-intensive document. If there is one main article at a time, however, you would probably want to assign that article to the underlying-page frame. Because Ventura creates as many pages as necessary to hold the contents of the underlying-page frame, all the material in the assigned file will always be displayed. Removing a page that is automatically generated will not decrease the number of pages; Ventura will immediately recreate the page to accommodate the text.

COMBINING TEXT FILES

When, in the course of the magazine, a new article becomes the main article, there are two ways you can accommodate the new article. Obviously, you can place the second article in the same word processed file as the first article, assuming they each use the same word processing format. If they don't, you must change the word processing format of one or the other before combining them in the same file. (Use the Edit menu's File/Type Rename command and then save the chapter.) With the articles in the same file, the second article will naturally follow right on the heels of the first. Of course, you'll want to tag the article's title to set it off from body text and separate the articles. If you want the second article to begin on a new page, create a title tag that has the Paragraph menu's Breaks dialog box set for Page Break Before. Follow a similar strategy with Column Break Before if you want the second article to start at the top of a new column.

Another way to deal with the second article is to keep it in a separate file. You won't be able to assign it to the same underlying-page frame as the first article; doing so would cause the second article to replace the first on all pages the first article appears on. Instead, use the Page menu's Insert/Remove Page command to insert a new page. The newly inserted page will initially be blank. Assign the second article to the inserted page. Doing so creates a new underlying-page frame. As such, Ventura will generate as many additional pages as necessary to accommodate the second article.

When you insert the additional page, you can do so at the beginning, middle, or end of existing pages. Ventura will cause newly generated pages to immediately follow the page you originally inserted. For example, assume you insert a page in the middle of the first article. When you assign the second article to it, Ventura will generate as many pages as necessary to accommodate the second article and push the last half of the first article back. The first article will continue on its pages after the second article is complete (see Figure 10.2).

If you want the second article (in a separate file) to appear on the same page where the first article ends, create a standard frame on the page, after the end of the first article. Assign the second article to that frame. Figure 10.3 shows such a frame, indicated by the selection handles. The frame holds the beginning of the second article. The left-hand page has the first article assigned to it, which ends just above the standard frame. The right-hand page, created with the Page menu's Insert/Remove Page, commonly has the second article assigned to it; because of how it's created, this page has a new underlying-page frame. The article picks up at the top of the right-hand page from where it left off at the bottom of the standard frame on the lower left.

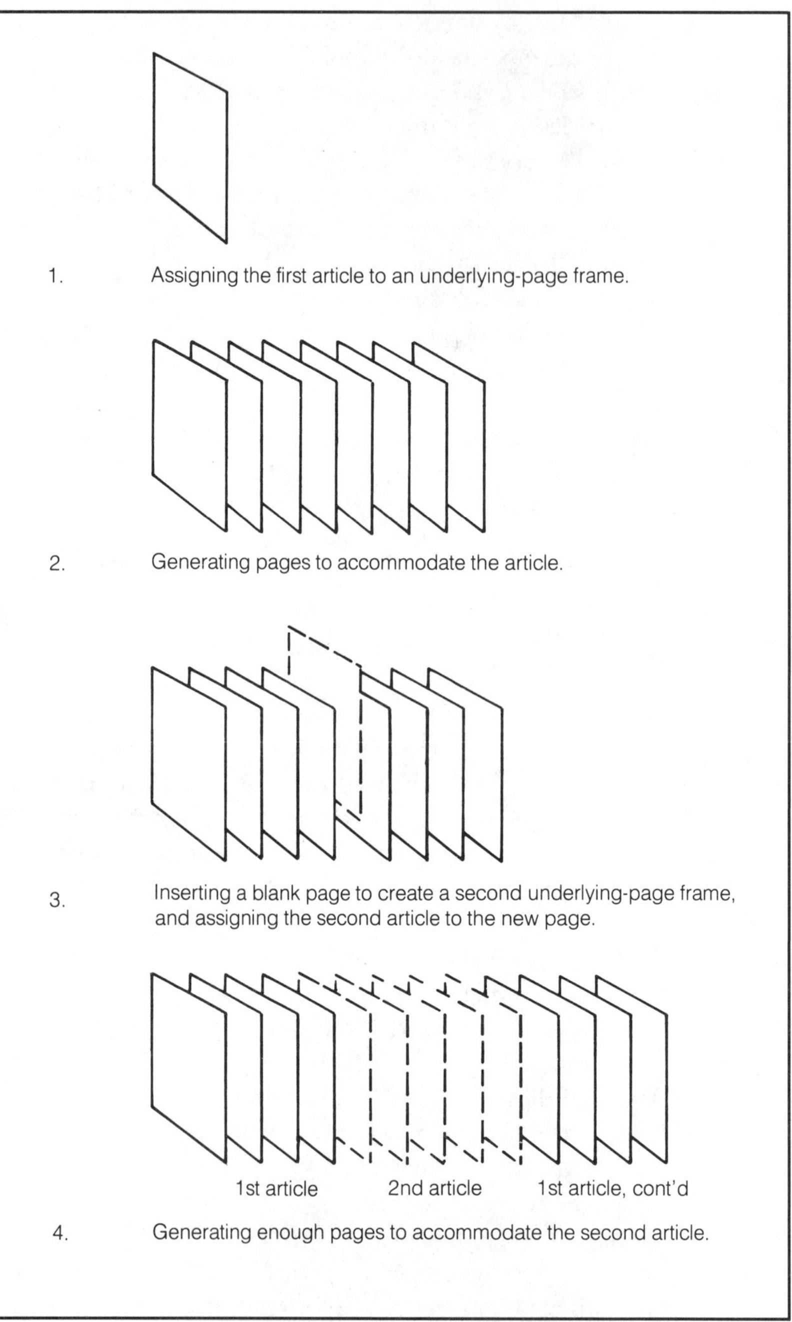

1. Assigning the first article to an underlying-page frame.
2. Generating pages to accommodate the article.
3. Inserting a blank page to create a second underlying-page frame, and assigning the second article to the new page.
1st article
2nd article
1st article, cont'd
4. Generating enough pages to accommodate the second article.

Figure 10.2: Inserting a Page to Create a Second Underlying-Page Frame

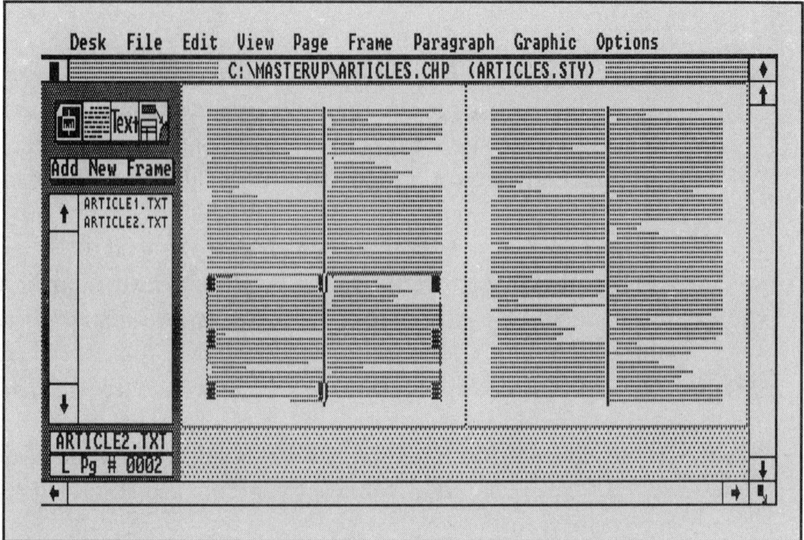

Figure 10.3: A Second File's Article Beginning on the Same Page

Now that we have an understanding of underlying-page frames, let's look at another feature for page layouts: frames that repeat on every page.

REPEATING FRAMES

Ventura's repeating-frame feature allows you to create a frame which is repeated on every page in the chapter. With this feature, you can make any frame and its contents, such as your company logo and slogan, appear on every page. The entire frame will be repeated in the same size and position on every page, whether automatically generated or custom inserted. Other attributes assigned to the frame, including vertical rules, ruling lines, and frame background, also repeat. There are some restrictions, however. Repeating frames cannot be cut, copied, or pasted, and they cannot have a caption.

CREATING REPEATING FRAMES

To make a repeating frame, begin by creating a standard frame on any page of the document.

If you are using pages with double sides (as specified with the Page menu's Page Layout command) you can create a repeating frame on the left- or right-hand pages or both. If you plan to create a frame that repeats on the left-hand pages only, create the initial standard frame on a left-hand page for the most predictable results. Likewise, create a standard frame on a right-hand page if you want it to repeat on right-hand pages only.

Once the standard frame is created, select it in the Frame mode to assign a text or picture file to it. Or place the keyboard cursor in the frame and type in frame text. Add any decorating attributes, such as ruling lines and frame background, that you desire. Use Graphics mode to create graphics tied to the frame if you wish. (You can also change or add to frame attributes or graphics after the repeating frame is created.) Once you've fashioned the standard frame to your satisfaction, proceed as follows to change the standard frame into a repeating frame:

1. Activate the Frame mode and select the standard frame you wish to change into a repeating frame.
2. Pull down the Frame menu and click Repeating Frame. You'll see the dialog box shown in Figure 10.4.
3. In the For All Pages grouping, click the Left, Right, or Left & Right button to indicate where you want the repeating frame to appear.
4. Give the OK to create the repeating frame.

If you designate the frame to repeat on both left- and right-hand pages, the frame will be reflected on the page opposite the one it is created on (see Figure 10.5). If you don't want the frame on the opposite page to reflect but rather copy *exactly* the original, copy the original to one of the facing pages before changing the standard frame into a repeating frame. Make the version on the left-hand page a repeating frame for left pages. Make the frame on the right-hand page a repeating frame for right pages.

You can click a repeating frame in the working area to select it. You can then change various characteristics of the selected repeating frame and move or resize it. Changes that you make to a repeating frame on any page affect its clones on all other pages. When you select a frame, handles appear along the frame's edges, just as they do when you select a standard frame. However, the handles for

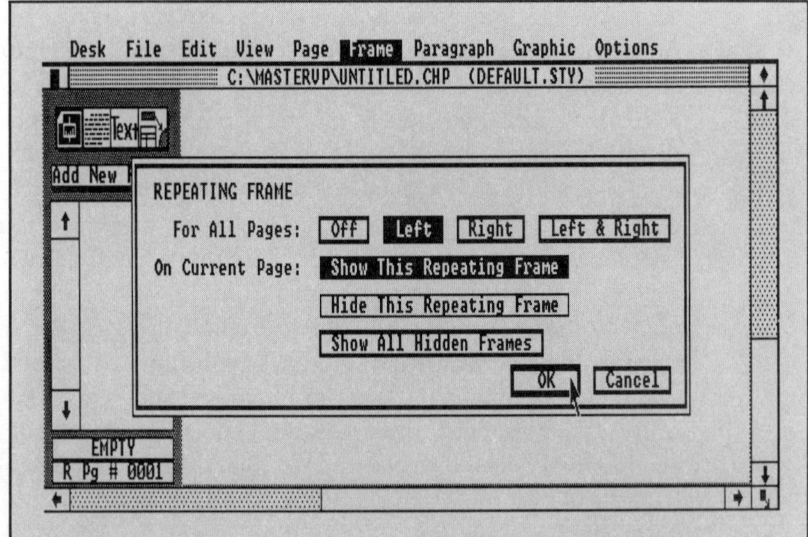

Figure 10.4: The Frame Menu's Repeating Frame Dialog Box

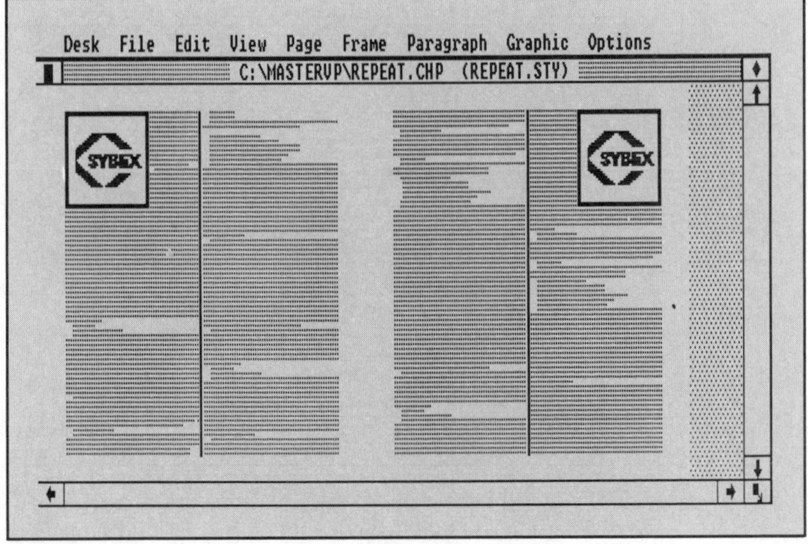

Figure 10.5: A Repeating Frame Reflected on the Facing Page

repeating frames are shaded instead of black, indicating they're attached to a repeating frame (see Figure 10.6).

You can create up to six repeating frames in a chapter. However, you cannot change standard frames into repeating frames simultaneously by selecting them as multiple. Likewise, you cannot change repeating frames that are selected as multiple back to standard frames simultaneously.

If you need to change a repeating frame back to a standard frame, display the page where you want the standard frame to appear. For instance, if you have placed a company logo on each page of a document using a repeating frame, and then decide that you want the logo on the first page only, you would call up this page. Once you change a repeating frame back to a standard frame, it will appear on this page and no others. If you plan to delete the frame, choose any page. (You must change a repeating frame back to a standard frame before you can delete it.) Activate the Frame mode and select the repeating frame. Then use the Frame menu's Repeating Frame dialog box and change the For All Pages setting to Off. When you give the OK, the frame will become a standard frame, which you can cut or copy as you wish.

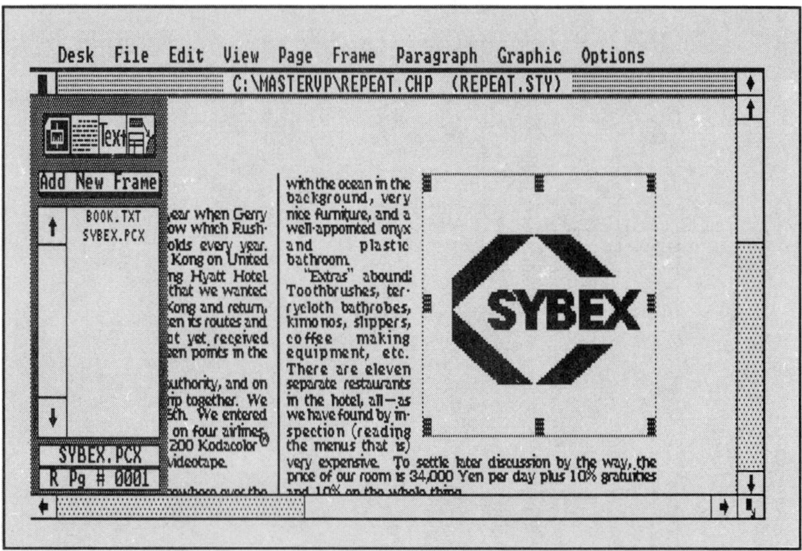

Figure 10.6: Shaded Handles Indicating a Repeating Frame

HIDING AND SHOWING INDIVIDUAL REPEATING FRAMES

You can use the Repeating Frame dialog box to keep a repeating frame from displaying on any given page. You may wish to do this if the repeating frame would disrupt the contents of a given page, such as a table occupying an entire page. To prevent a repeating frame from displaying, display the page with the repeating frame that you wish to remove. Select the repeating frame on that page. Then use the Frame menu's Repeating Frame dialog box and click Hide This Repeating Frame.

Once you hide a repeating frame, you can redisplay it in one of two ways, depending upon when you decide to do so. Right after hiding a frame, it remains selected and continues to appear on the page, though ghosting. If you change your mind at this point and decide that the repeating frame should be displayed, use the Repeating Frame dialog box and click Show This Repeating Frame. If, after hiding a repeating frame, you should choose some other frame or change operating modes, the hidden repeating frame will disappear. To redisplay it, you must click the button labeled Show All Hidden Frames. When you give the OK, the hidden repeating frame will appear along with any other repeating frames you've hidden on that page. You must then hide again those repeating frames that you don't want shown.

CREATING ADDITIONAL COLUMNS

As you know, all frames can accommodate up to eight columns. Since this includes the underlying-page frame, this means that you should normally be able to get eight columns of text per page as well. Yet when you attempt to use eight columns, Ventura often displays an error message saying that the frame is too complex to format. By utilizing repeating frames on top of the underlying-page frame, you can eliminate the error message and still use eight or more columns. To make the text flow unnoticeably from frame to frame, you assign the same text file to the repeating frames as the one assigned to the underlying-page frame.

Be aware, however, that applying these techniques can be tricky. Creating columns of equal width, keeping underlying text from appearing between frames, and avoiding frames that are too complex in the process all require a considerable understanding of how Ventura operates.

Consider the nine columns we have created in Figure 10.7 on a letter-size page. All displayed columns are .63 inches wide and all gutters are .17 inches wide. (In addition, the underlying-page frame has margins of .75 inches all around.) The selection handles indicate the positions of two repeating frames placed over the underlying-page frame. Each of these repeating frames contains three columns. Although the underlying-page frame appears to have three columns as well (the first three on the left), it actually has five columns. The two additional columns are under each of the two repeating frames. They are each 2.22 inches wide. No text, however, flows into these two additional columns, because they are fully covered by the two repeating frames. Note that we had to create two additional columns rather than one; with only one additional column, underlying text would show between the two repeating frames.

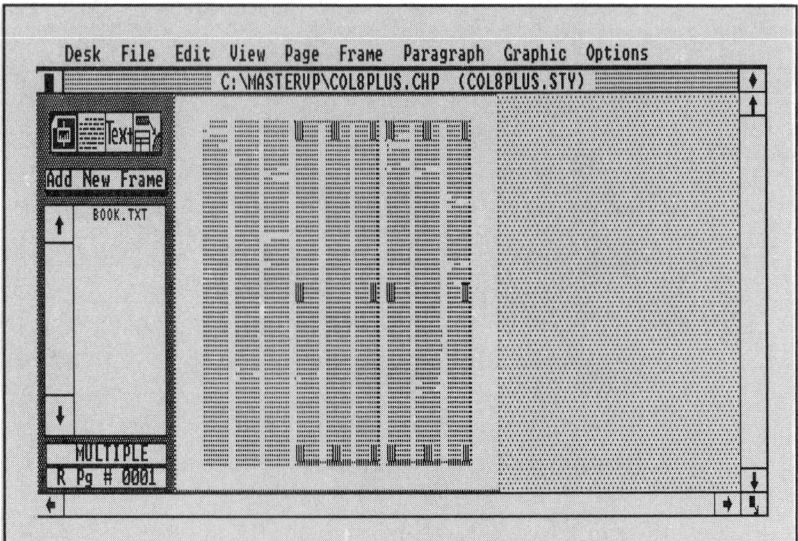

Figure 10.7: Repeating Frames Used to Create Additional Columns

So far we've looked at commands that control the layout of frames on the page. Now let's look at how Ventura's widow and orphan control affects where lines of text are placed.

WIDOWS AND ORPHANS

When filling a page with text, Ventura encounters situations at the bottom of the page where it is necessary to split a paragraph between the bottom of one page and the top of the next. Ventura allows you to specify how many lines may be separated from the bulk of the paragraph by such a split. Lines separated from a paragraph and placed at the top of the new page are called *widows*. *Orphans* are lines at the bottom of a page that begin a paragraph but are separated from the bulk of the paragraph, which is placed at the top of the next page.

A single such isolated line is generally considered undesirable. Consider that as you read text, you usually have an idea of where a paragraph is going to end. You sense the size of a paragraph in order to judge the amount of thought in it. So when you turn the page on a split paragraph, a single line can be jolting when you suddenly realize that the paragraph is ending. This draws your mind to the mechanics of the document and away from the subject matter.

Normally, widow control is set for two lines. This setting means that a minimum of two lines must be carried over to the next page when a paragraph runs out of room. So, when necessary, instead of filling in the first page with all but one line, Ventura will fill in with all but two lines and then place those two lines at the top of the next page. Orphan control is usually set for two lines as well.

Figure 10.8 shows the dialog box which regulates widows and orphans. To display this dialog box, pull down the Page menu and click Widows & Orphans. Notice that it doesn't matter which mode is active.

For the Widow grouping, this dialog box indicates that you can have between 1 and 5 isolated lines. Clicking 1 essentially turns widow control off. It allows single lines to be isolated at the top of the page should that condition arise. When the dialog box is set at 2, the default setting, widows will not be allowed. A single line at the top

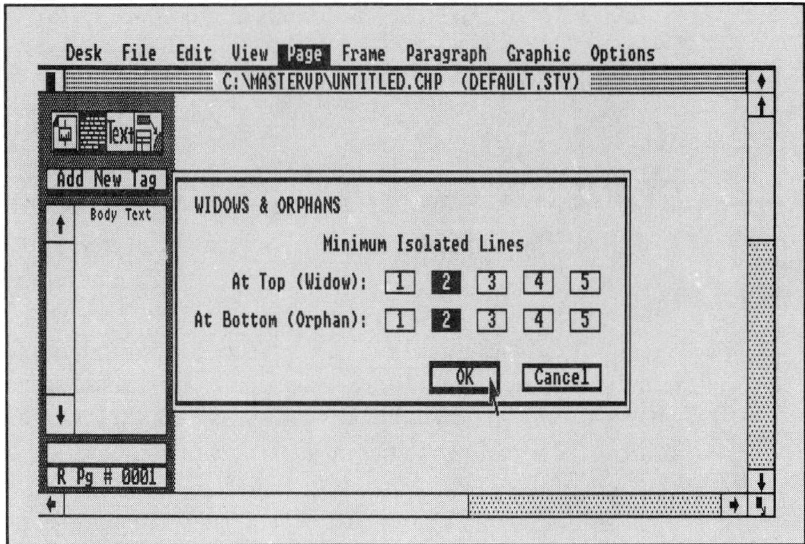

Figure 10.8: The Page Menu's Widows & Orphans Dialog Box

of a page will always be joined by another line pulled from the bottom of the previous page. Doing so, of course, adds a blank line to the bottom of the previous page. Such an additional blank line is generally acceptable, unless you are creating a document with facing pages, in which case text on the facing pages should end at the same place. You can adjust page depth by using a thin frame, as we'll see in the next section.

By providing numbers larger than 2 for Minimum Isolated Lines, Ventura provides additional flexibility. If you change the setting to 3, the program will not allow two lines to be widowed. Assume, for instance, that you're creating a catalog and each paragraph describes a product. Let's say that the last two lines of each paragraph list the prices of the item described in the paragraph. It would confuse the reader to allow these prices to be removed from at least some of the description. By changing the At Top setting to 3 you would guarantee that at least one line of descriptive text would precede the two lines of prices.

However, the one line of descriptive text could itself be considered undesirable. By changing this setting to 4, you would insure that at least two lines of description would always precede the two lines of prices.

Now let's consider orphans. By changing the Orphan setting in the dialog box, you can control the minimum number of lines required at the bottom of the page. Setting At Bottom to 1 allows for no control of orphan lines. The default setting is 2.

It is especially important to use orphan control when you are using *dropped capitals*. This effect creates a large character at the beginning of a paragraph; we'll see how to create it in Chapter 13. For an example, look at the first paragraph of the first article in Figure 10.9. If you have a tag that uses dropped capitals, be sure to set the number of Minimum Isolated Lines to match at least the number of lines dislocated by the dropped capital. To be certain of seeing the indented lines followed by at least one regular line, set the number of minimum isolated lines to at least one more than the number of lines the dropped capital dislocates.

Although widow and orphan control is usually considered with regard to pages, Ventura's controls operate with respect to columns as well. The settings in this dialog box control the amount of text that can be separated from a paragraph at the top or bottom of a column. Of course, they only take effect when you're using multiple columns.

ENDING COLUMNS EVENLY

As we mentioned, widow and orphan control can sometimes cause pages or columns to end in slightly different places. It's best if facing pages and especially columns on the same page end evenly. To correct such a problem, judiciously place a thin frame into short columns. The thin frame, often the equivalent depth of one line, will push material down so that text at the bottom of the page is flush with text on a facing page or in a matching column.

Ventura's sample document &MAG-P3 has this problem when printed with the HP LaserJet and some other printers. Examine the document in Figure A.8 in Appendix A. Figure 10.9 shows this document with thin frames added to correct the problem by pushing down text in the second and third columns. Selection handles indicate the thin frames. We've shown this document with a full-page display so that you can see the thin frames and their effect at the same time.

Now let's look at another design element that affects the tops and bottoms of pages.

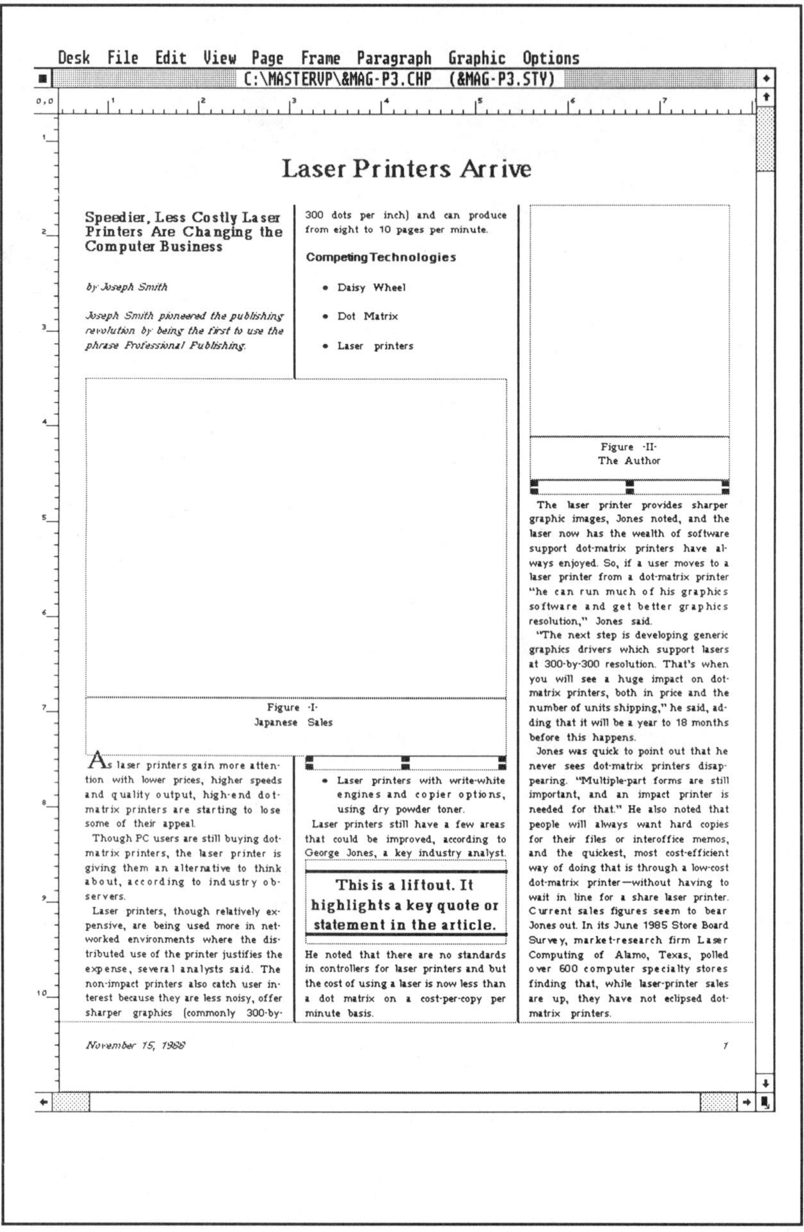

Desk File Edit View Page Frame Paragraph Graphic Options

C:\MASTERVP\&MAG-P3.CHP (&MAG-P3.STY)

Laser Printers Arrive

Speedier, Less Costly Laser Printers Are Changing the Computer Business

by Joseph Smith

Joseph Smith pioneered the publishing revolution by being the first to use the phrase Professional Publishing.

Figure -I-
Japanese Sales

As laser printers gain more attention with lower prices, higher speeds and quality output, high-end dot-matrix printers are starting to lose some of their appeal.

Though PC users are still buying dot-matrix printers, the laser printer is giving them an alternative to think about, according to industry observers.

Laser printers, though relatively expensive, are being used more in networked environments where the distributed use of the printer justifies the expense, several analysts said. The non-impact printers also catch user interest because they are less noisy, offer sharper graphics (commonly 300-by-300 dots per inch) and can produce from eight to 10 pages per minute.

Competing Technologies

- Daisy Wheel
- Dot Matrix
- Laser printers
- Laser printers with write-white engines and copier options, using dry powder toner.

Laser printers still have a few areas that could be improved, according to George Jones, a key industry analyst.

This is a liftout. It highlights a key quote or statement in the article.

He noted that there are no standards in controllers for laser printers and but the cost of using a laser is now less than a dot matrix on a cost-per-copy per minute basis.

Figure -II-
The Author

The laser printer provides sharper graphic images, Jones noted, and the laser now has the wealth of software support dot-matrix printers have always enjoyed. So, if a user moves to a laser printer from a dot-matrix printer "he can run much of his graphics software and get better graphics resolution," Jones said.

"The next step is developing generic graphics drivers which support lasers at 300-by-300 resolution. That's when you will see a huge impact on dot-matrix printers, both in price and the number of units shipping," he said, adding that it will be a year to 18 months before this happens.

Jones was quick to point out that he never sees dot-matrix printers disappearing. "Multiple-part forms are still important, and an impact printer is needed for that." He also noted that people will always want hard copies for their files or interoffice memos, and the quickest, most cost-efficient way of doing that is through a low-cost dot-matrix printer—without having to wait in line for a share laser printer. Current sales figures seem to bear Jones out. In its June 1985 Store Board Survey, market-research firm Laser Computing of Alamo, Texas, polled over 600 computer specialty stores finding that, while laser-printer sales are up, they have not eclipsed dot-matrix printers.

November 15, 1988 7

Figure 10.9: Dropped Capital and Thin Frames

HEADERS AND FOOTERS

A *header* is textual material that appears repeatedly at the top of each page in a document. Typically, it consists of information about the chapter or about material on the page where it appears. Headers are also called *running heads*. A *footer* is similar material that appears at the bottom of the page.

Using Ventura's standard header and footer mechanisms, you can create headers and footers of one or two lines each. Each header and footer makes material appear at the left, center, or right of the page. Unless you indicate otherwise, headers and footers appear on all pages in a document, whether custom inserted or automatically generated.

If necessary, Ventura moves standard text out of the way in order to accommodate headers and footers. Of course, Ventura won't need to move text if you've set top or bottom margins large enough to accommodate the extra text. If the margin is greater than necessary, Ventura will center the header or footer vertically between the top or bottom edge of the page and the top or bottom of the text (see Figure 10.10). Headers and footers appear above or below the text area only: never above or below the left or right margins.

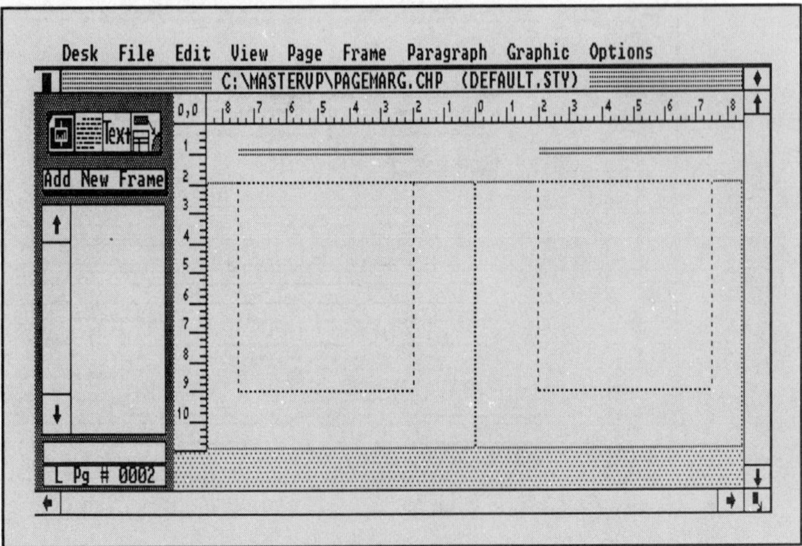

Figure 10.10: A Header Centered Vertically Within the Top Margin

Besides standard text, you can have the chapter number or page number appear automatically, and you can even have the header or footer display text that's on the page. This last option is used to create *catch phrases:* indicative entries similar to the first and final names that appear at the top of pages in a phone directory. The results usually change with each page; for this reason they are sometimes called *live* headers or footers.

You can also use repeating frames to supplement Ventura's standard header and footer capabilities. With repeating frames you can provide more material, so your headers and footers can be more than two lines long and even contain pictures. Likewise you can use Ventura graphics to enhance headers and footers. Graphics, when tied to an underlying-page frame, repeat on all similarly formatted pages.

To create a header or footer for any chapter, pull down the Page menu and click Headers & Footers. You can have any page in the chapter displayed when you do. The dialog box you see in Figure 10.11 will appear.

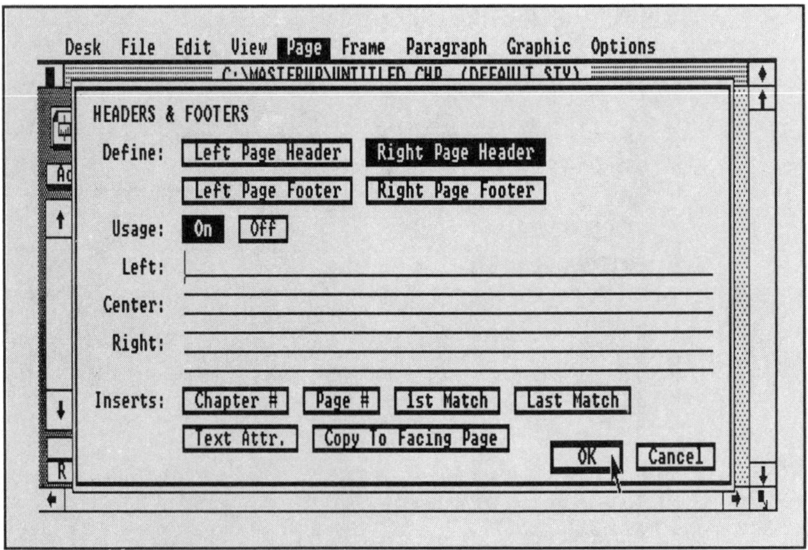

Figure 10.11: The Page Menu's Headers & Footers Dialog Box

DEFINING USAGE

To set up a header or footer, begin by clicking a button in the Define grouping to indicate its position on the page. Left Page and Right Page distinctions will only operate if you've used the Page menu's Page Layout command to specify Double Sides.

Once you select a Define button, the current settings that apply to that button will appear within the dialog box. (For new documents, of course, there will be nothing on the lines.) You can change the settings as you wish. Then, if desired, click another button in the Define grouping. The settings that define that button will then appear and you can adjust them as well.

Next, you'll want to consider the Usage setting. Click On or Off as appropriate to indicate whether you want the selected header or footer in the Define grouping to appear. When Usage is On, the entries you make into the field lines below (labeled Left, Center, and Right) will appear at the left, center, or right of pages in the Define location. Each location has two lines available. Unless you make an entry, Ventura does not set aside space for the header or footer, even though Usage is On.

When you click Usage Off, any text entered on the field lines will ghost. However, the entries remain available. Should you later turn Usage On, the entries will fully reappear.

ADDING INSERTS

At the bottom of the dialog box, notice the Inserts buttons. The buttons operate similarly to those we examined in the Frame menu's Anchors & Captions dialog box. Besides the Inserts we examined there, there are two additional Insert buttons, 1st Match and Last Match. These buttons allow you to specify catch phrases and thus create live headers and footers. We'll examine these buttons in a moment.

The Copy To Facing Page button allows you to make the settings for the facing page automatically reflect the settings that are displayed in the dialog box. Because this button creates a mirror image, entries you make on the Right field lines will appear on the Left lines for the facing page, and vice versa. To create headers and footers on the left-hand page and copy them to the right, proceed as follows:

1. Click Left Page Header. If the Usage is set to Off, the Left, Center, and Right settings (if any) will ghost.
2. Click Usage On. The Left, Center, and Right settings will appear in normal intensity.
3. Enter material for Left, Center, and Right to appear in those locations at the top of the left-hand page. Use the mouse, Tab key, or the ↓ key to move between the fields. Use the Esc key to delete an entire entry. Use the Inserts buttons as necessary (don't use the Copy To Facing Page button just yet).
4. When your settings for Left Page Header are complete, click Left Page Footer, set Usage On for the footer, and make entries into the Left, Center, and Right fields for the bottom of the left-hand page.
5. When both header and footer settings are complete for the left-hand page, click the Copy to Facing Page button. The left-hand page settings you provided will be mirrored on the right-hand page. You won't get any immediate feedback that the transfer has taken place, but you can see that the settings are in place by clicking the Right Page Header or Right Page Footer buttons.
6. Give the OK to register the settings.

Let's say that you wanted to place the newsletter title *The Brainstorm* in the top center of each page in our sample newsletter. In addition, on the outside edges at the top, you wanted the word *Page* followed by the page number.

To create this setup, begin by clicking the Left Page Header. (Of course, you could begin with the right and just reverse the instructions.) Position the keyboard cursor in the Center field. Enter the newsletter's title, **The Brainstorm**, next to the word *Center:*

```
Center: The Brainstorm
```

Then, to have the page number displayed on the outside edge of the left page, position the keyboard cursor next to the Left setting. Type in the word **Page** and then click the Page # button. The code for page numbers will appear, so that the completed setting should look like this:

Left: Page [P#]

Finally, click the Copy To Facing Page button. This causes the settings to be reflected on the facing page. You can check by clicking the Right Page Header button. When you do, you'll see

Center: The Brainstorm
Right: Page [P#]

Figure 10.12 shows the results of these maneuvers. It's a Facing Pages view of pages 2 and 3 of the document.

Normally, Ventura numbers the pages with Arabic numbers, beginning with the number 1. In Chapter 11 we'll see how you can adjust the page numbering system.

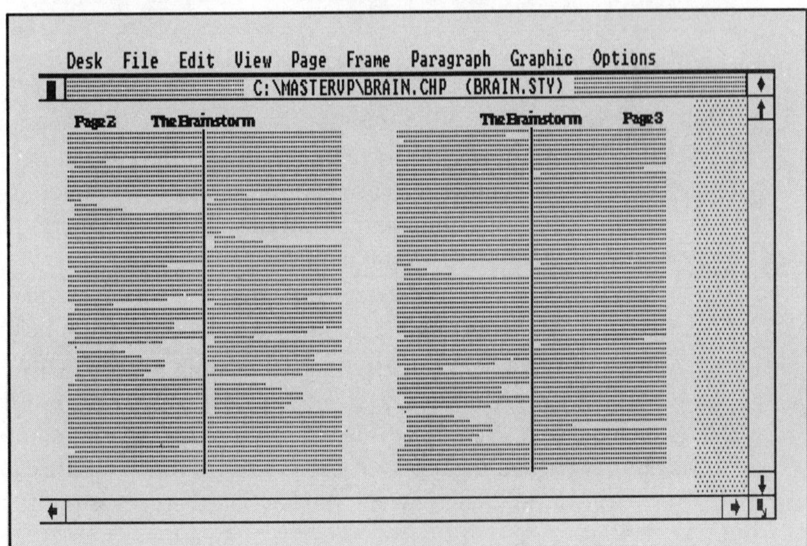

Figure 10.12: Facing Pages View of Headers and Footers

FORMATTING HEADERS AND FOOTERS

You can format headers and footers just as you do any paragraphs in the document. Activate the Paragraph mode and click the header or footer as it appears in the working area of the screen. For headers, you'll then see the tag name

Z_HEADER

appear in the Current box. This is a generated tag that Ventura automatically assigns to headers (see Chapter 5). You can format this tag by pulling down the Paragraph menu and clicking commands of your choice. For footers, you'll see the tag name

Z_FOOTER

which you can format as well. The names of these tags will not appear on the Assignment list unless you use the Options menu's Set Preferences dialog box to set Generated Tags to Shown. Regardless of whether they appear on the Assignment list, however, you can format them just as you do any other tag.

CREATING CATCH PHRASES

As we mentioned, there are two buttons, 1st Match and Last Match, that allow you to create catch phrases in your headers and footers. You may wish to use catch phrases in a catalog to show item numbers or in a technical manual to show the name of the manual's section that appears on the page.

As with the other inserts, you can either type in the entire entry that you desire or click the applicable insert button. Clicking the button guarantees that the appropriate syntax appears, but you'll have to adjust the resulting entry.

If you want Ventura to use the first paragraph on the page tagged with a particular tag, click the 1st Match button. You'll see the following text appear on the line where the keyboard cursor is positioned:

[<tag name]

You then replace the words *tag name* with the name of the tag used to tag the material you want for the catch phrase.

Let's assume that at the top left of the left-hand page you want Ventura to show the heading of the first subsection appearing on the page. You select Left Page Header, click Usage On, and then click 1st Match. The entry shown above will appear on the field line, with the keyboard cursor positioned just to the right of this entry. You then use the ← key to float the keyboard cursor over the bracket on the right and the Backspace key to delete the words *tag name*. In their place, type the tag name you use for subsection headings. Assuming that this tag name is Head Subsect, here is how the entry would look, next to the Left setting:

[<Head Subsect]

If you wish, you can simply type in this entire entry just like this, rather than clicking the 1st Match button and replacing the words.

If you want to display the last paragraph tagged with a certain tag, click the Last Match button. This displays the entry

[>tag name]

where the keyboard cursor is positioned. Again, you replace the words *tag name* with the name of the tag. You can use the Last Match button to have Ventura display the last subsection on a page. As a counterpart to the earlier catch phrase, you might want to do this on the top right of the right-hand page, as is often done in dictionaries.

You may wonder what happens if a tag that's used to designate a catch phrase does not appear on a given page. In that case, Ventura uses the previous occurrence of the tag. Let's say, for instance, that you set a header for Ventura's sample technical document &TDOC-P1 (see Appendix A). Within that header you set up a 1st Match that uses the Major Heading tag, like so:

[<Major Heading]

On page 1 of the document, there are two headings that use this tag: WYSIWYG and ITEM SELECTOR. As such, the header on the page would display WYSIWYG because it is the first match of the tag. On page 2, though, no paragraphs are tagged with the Major Heading tag. The header for page 2 would therefore display ITEM SELECTOR, the previous use of this tag, appropriately describing the material on the page.

TURNING HEADERS AND FOOTERS OFF AND ON PAGE BY PAGE

When you establish headers or footers for a chapter, the header or footer you indicate will initially appear on every page of the document. However, you can turn headers and footers off for any given page, if you choose. Doing so will not affect the headers and footers on the other pages. Many applications require that you suppress headers and footers on the first page, for instance. Some magazines suppress headers and footers on those pages that contain full-page ads.

To suppress the header or footer for a given page, follow these steps:

1. Display the chosen page on the screen.
2. Pull down the Page menu.
3. Click Turn Header Off or Turn Footer Off as appropriate.

Do not use these commands to turn headers or footers off for the entire document. To do that, use the Page menu's Headers & Footers command.

Once you turn the header or footer off for a given page, should you change your mind you can turn it back on. If the page you've displayed on the screen has the header or footer turned off, pulling down the Page menu will display the command

Turn Header On

or

Turn Footer On

as applicable. Clicking one of these commands turns the header or footer for the page back on.

CREATING OVERSIZED HEADERS AND FOOTERS

You can create headers and footers larger than the two lines allowed by the Page menu's Headers & Footers dialog box by using repeating frames. Just place a standard frame with the contents you desire in position near the top or bottom of the page and use the Frame menu's Repeating Frame command.

Unfortunately, you can't place an automatic page number, chapter number, or other insert into a repeating frame. However, you can use a standard header or footer to serve that purpose, and augment the header or footer with the repeating frame.

Ventura will not allow the contents within a repeating frame to cover a standard header or footer, so your page number or other counters will not collide with text in the frame. However, frame attributes (such as ruling lines and frame background) are not affected. Thus you can enhance standard headers and footers by framing them with repeating frames. The same holds true for a standard (nonrepeating) frame, but of course it would appear on only one page.

SPECIALLY POSITIONED PAGE NUMBERS

By using a frame caption, you can position automatic page numbers where conventional Ventura techniques would not otherwise allow, such as along the edge of the page. Unfortunately, you must place these frames on each page one by one, because Ventura will not allow repeating frames to have captions. However, frame captions are not difficult to create, so unless the document is very long, this technique should be quite efficient.

Begin by creating a frame on the first page in the approximate place where you want the page number to appear. Use the Frame menu's Anchors & Captions dialog box to give the frame a caption. In that dialog box, there is no insert for a page number. However, if you type in the entry

```
[P#]
```

on the field line for Label, Ventura will automatically replace this code with the page number in the caption.

Once the standard frame and caption are created, fine-tune the frame's position on the first page if necessary. Then copy the frame to every page. To do that, select the frame and press Shift-Del to copy it to the clipboard. Then press the PgDn key and the Ins key to copy the frame to page 2. Alternate pressing PgDn and Ins to copy the frame to each page in the document. If you're using double-sided pages and you want the page numbers on the outside edges, you must create and copy separately placed versions of the frame for left- and right-hand pages.

SPEED TECHNIQUES FOR LAYOUT-INTENSIVE DOCUMENTS

Now let's look at some techniques that will allow you to work with Ventura quickly and efficiently. These techniques are especially useful when working with layout-intensive documents. Such documents can have numerous frames and files; efficient use of the mouse and the keyboard allows you to combine these elements quickly. We've discussed most of these techniques previously, so we'll just mention each briefly.

- Load several files of the same type in succession. When you use the File menu's Load Text/Picture dialog box, specify Several for the # of Files setting. As you load files, Ventura will repeatedly display the Item Selector Box, so you can easily choose successive files. When you're done, click the Cancel button.
- Add several frames in succession. When you click the Add New Frame button in the Frame mode, hold down the Shift key as you add successive frames. The Add New Frame button will remain selected allowing you to add frames in succession. Release the Shift key before you add the last frame.
- Format all applicable paragraphs on a page with the same tag simultaneously. To do that, select multiple paragraphs. Hold down the Shift key as you click paragraphs in succession. With the paragraphs selected, click the proper tag name in the Assignment list to assign that tag's attributes to all

selected paragraphs. To deselect the paragraphs, simply click some other paragraph without the Shift key or change operating modes. Remember, you can only use this technique to assign tags. You can't use it to simultaneously change the attributes of paragraphs formatted with a variety of tags.

- Select multiple frames or graphics to cut, copy, move, or size them as a group. Shift-click frames or graphics in succession. You can then perform all these operations with the mouse. Cutting all the frames on one page and pasting them on another allows you to rearrange layout-intensive pages. And although you can't change attributes such as frame background and ruling lines for a selected group of frames, you can change attributes for graphics, such as line attributes and fill attributes. Once the multiple graphics are selected, just use the Graphic menu's various commands.

- Copy frames or graphics with similar characteristics, even if some characteristics differ. Even if you are creating frames or graphics that don't share all characteristics, it's usually helpful to copy rather than create each from scratch. For example, it's a good idea to copy frames with similar ruling lines and frame backgrounds, even if you intend them to have different sizes. Likewise, it's beneficial to copy frames that are to have the same size even if you intend to provide them with other attributes that differ.

- Hide pictures to speed screen processing. Use the Options command to do this. Display pictures only when you truly need to work with them. When you're about to begin working with one picture, you may find it helpful to move a neighboring picture off the screen temporarily before clicking Show Pictures. That way, Ventura won't have to redraw the additional picture unnecessarily. Hide pictures as soon as you're finished working with them. Hide before saving, loading, setting options, and scrolling rather than after, as Ventura redraws pictures after each of these procedures.

- Greek larger-size text to speed screen processing in Reduced or Facing Pages view. Use the Options menu's Set Preferences dialog box. Greeking all text makes for a turbo-charged screen, rather than the sluggish performance these views sometimes create.

- To speed the location of Ventura-related materials, keep the names of your directories low in alphabetical order. Doing so will minimize scrolling of Item Selector lists and you'll be able to select Ventura directories more quickly. You may wish to reverse the trick that Ventura uses with names of its generated tags and begin your Ventura-related directories with A_, as in A_BRAIN.
- Preassign tags and other attributes in word processed files. Doing so means you don't have to tag paragraphs in Ventura. The techniques for doing this (and their limitations) are discussed in Chapter 12.
- Create a template for documents that are repeatedly laid out in a similar fashion. Once you finish with the first volume of a document, such as a monthly newsletter, use the Edit menu's Remove Text/File command and remove most of the files that appear on the Assignment list. Keep only those that you plan to reuse in the next issue, such as the masthead. (Initially, you could instead place such material within a frame without assigning it to a file.) Save the resulting empty *template* or *shell* under a name designating it as such. Next month, load the template, and save it under a name designating that month's issue. Then load it with that issue's files and otherwise alter it as necessary.
- Use the Page menu's Go To Page command when you need to follow a selected frame's text from page to page. In this command's dialog box, click File for Relative to. Then click the Next button and give the OK. Ventura quickly displays the next frame that the selected frame's material continues in, even when the next frame is on a far-flung page.
- To reformat quickly, standardize the tag names in all your style sheets. For instance, if you use Heading 1 for major headings in one style sheet, use the same tag name for major headings in all style sheets. With standardized tag names, you can quickly apply any style sheet to any document. New

attributes will be automatically applied to all appropriately tagged paragraphs. Without similar tag names, Ventura will not apply the new tag's format automatically.

- To change all similarly tagged paragraphs to a different tag, remove the tag they're assigned to. When switching style sheets as just described, if tag names do not agree, many people think they must retag the paragraphs one by one. Instead, remove the tag name carried over from the old style sheet. Use the Paragraph menu's Remove Tag command to do that. When you do, the command's dialog box will allow you to specify a tag name to convert to. Specify the appropriate tag name as it appears on the newly assigned style sheet. The paragraphs will convert and all formats will be applied automatically.
- Assign and use the Function keys for tagging. Here, too, it's a good idea to standardize. As much as possible, the same function key should be use for the same tag. F10 should always be assigned to Body Text, following Ventura's convention. F1, F2, and F3 should be used for Heading 1, 2, and 3, respectively. If you forget which tags are assigned to the keys, the quickest way to check is to type Ctrl-K.

In this chapter, we've focused on Ventura features chiefly as they work with layout-intensive documents. In the next chapter, we'll examine features that are often used with book-style documents, including Ventura's ability to print multi-chapter documents.

CHAPTER ELEVEN

Multichapter Features: Tables of Contents, Indexes, Footnotes, and Numbering

JUST AS CHAPTER FILES COORDINATE PICTURES, TEXT files, and other elements, Ventura provides you with the means to coordinate various chapter files to create multichapter documents. A *publication* file is simply a listing of one or more chapters that you want treated as a unit. Ventura can use this listing to prepare an index and a table of contents for the entire multichapter publication and to print material in succession. Little else, however, is carried over from chapter to chapter; page formats, such as margins and columns, and even standard page numbering are not coordinated on a publication-wide basis.

To create a publication and manipulate it, you use the Options menu's Multi-Chapter command. Although you can use this command to handle multichapter operations, it also performs some operations for single chapters. With this command you can do the following:

- Display a listing of the files that are associated with a chapter. This is the easiest way to see which files the chapter references.
- Copy a chapter from one disk or directory to another. This procedure copies the chapter file and all files that are associated with it, including width tables but not including hyphenation dictionaries.

You can also use commands to display a listing of the files associated with a multichapter publication or make a copy of a publication file and all files associated with it.

To work with publications or individual chapters in this fashion, proceed as follows:

1. Click Options on the menu line.
2. Click Multi-Chapter.
3. If you didn't save your document just prior to selecting this command, Ventura will ask you if you wish to save it. Ventura makes this request because some of its multichapter operations make and save changes in files that are referenced by the displayed chapter. Normally, of course, you should specify Save. Ventura will then display the Multi-Chapter Operations dialog

box, shown in Figure 11.1. As you work with this dialog box, Ventura will redisplay it after each operation.

4. When you're finished with the Multi-Chapter Operations dialog box, click the Done button or press Return.

When you first display this dialog box, Ventura will list the chapter that's showing in the working area. The chapter name is selected, as indicated by the darkened bar that surrounds the name.

Work in the Multi-Chapter Operations dialog box is directed at the selected file. For example, if you've been working with the chapter C:\TYPESET\&TDOC-P1.CHP, Ventura will list that chapter and display it as selected. The program is assuming that you would like to construct a publication that includes this chapter or to use the file for a single-chapter operation.

However, if the dialog box has been used before, the name of the publication last used may be displayed instead of the current chapter. If so, you can click New (which clears the publication) and Done (which redisplays the document). If you use the Options menu's Multi-Chapter command again (immediately or later), the current document's name will then appear and will be selected.

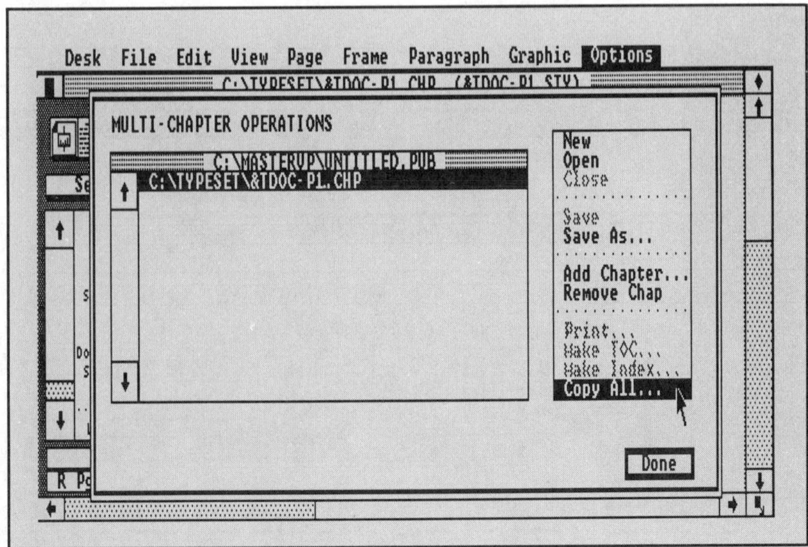

Figure 11.1: The Dialog Box Displayed with the Options Menu's Multi-Chapter Command

COPYING CHAPTERS AND PUBLICATIONS

You can use the Multi-Chapter Operations dialog box to make a copy (or *archive* as Ventura calls it) of a document. Doing so allows you to copy all material associated with a publication or with just one chapter, even if it's not part of a larger publication. To do either you use the Copy All command. If a single chapter is selected, you will copy the chapter and its related files. When you use this command, you'll see the dialog box shown in Figure 11.2. You can use this dialog box to copy all the material to the same directory, or you can split the material, according to type of file, among several directories.

The SOURCE file listed in this dialog box merely indicates the publication or chapter specified in the Multi-Chapter Operations dialog box and cannot be changed here. This is the file that Ventura will use as its guide to copying related material from the disk. Below, under DESTINATION, are categories specifying various directories for Ventura to use for the new copy of the publication or chapter. You can alter these directories to send the files to various locations if you wish. Notice that publications and chapters go together in the same directory, style sheets and printer width tables go to the same directory, and text, graphic, and image files can each go to separate directories.

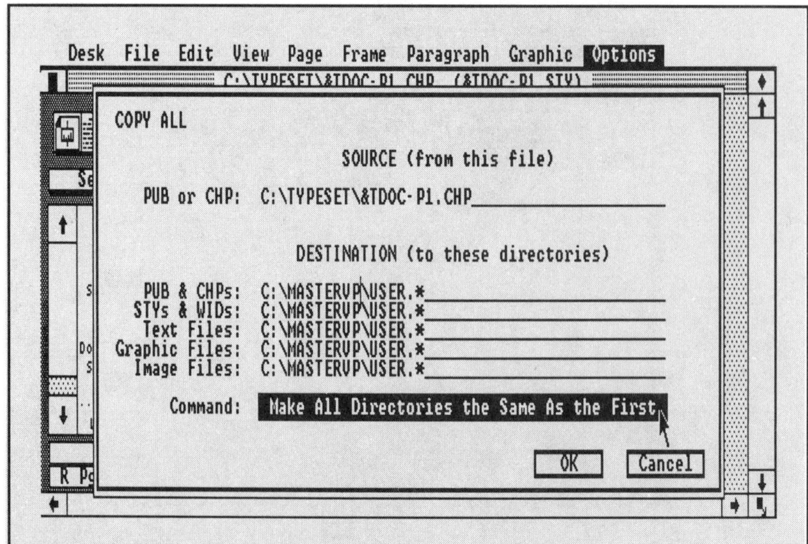

Figure 11.2: The Copy All Dialog Box

If you wish to copy all material for a chapter to the same directory, simply adjust the directory name for the first field (PUB & CHPs). Then click the box labeled

Make All Directories the Same As the First

Ventura will immediately duplicate the name of that directory in the other four fields.

If you'd like to work through the process as we create the material in this chapter, make a copy of the sample file &TDOC-P1.CHP. As we'll see, it's a good idea to use file names of fewer than five letters if you plan to create an index and a table of contents. Since the first title appearing on this sample is *USER INTERFACE*, we'll use the file name USER, as we have in Figure 11.2.

To trigger the copy process, you must click the OK button. With this dialog box, and others that spring from the Multi-Chapter dialog box, you cannot use the Return key to give the OK. This is to keep you from beginning the procedure accidentally, which could copy over existing files (although you would be warned before it did so).

As it copies, Ventura will display messages that show which files are being copied. At the same time, it adjusts all the unseen pointers, contained within the chapter, indicating the disk and directory location of each related file. If Ventura can't find a referenced file—if, for example, it was erased from the disk—you'll see a message that notifies you and asks if copying should proceed.

You can use the Copy All dialog box to copy a chapter or publication to one or more floppy disks and then copy the material from the floppies to another hard disk. When copying to floppies, specify drive A for all the destinations. If Ventura fills up one disk it will pause, giving you the opportunity to insert a different disk. Likewise, Ventura will pause when you copy back from the floppies, allowing you to insert as necessary.

OPENING PUBLICATIONS AND OTHER FILE OPERATIONS

Once you have copied your publication files and are ready to work with them, Ventura offers a series of commands for adding, moving, and generally reorganizing chapters in your publication. Perhaps the most important of these is the Open command, which we'll look at next.

OPENING PUBLICATIONS AND CHAPTERS

Just as the Copy All command can make copies of either publications or individual chapters, the Open command provides two services for publications or chapters. You can use the Open command to open a publication and list the chapter files that the publication coordinates, or you can open a chapter and see a listing of the various files the chapter orchestrates.

Ventura includes one sample publication file in the TYPESET directory. When you click the Open command, you'll see the Item Selector box screened for PUB files, so that only files ending with PUB appear. You can use this dialog box to open the file called &EXAMPLE.PUB. Once you do, you'll see the listing shown in

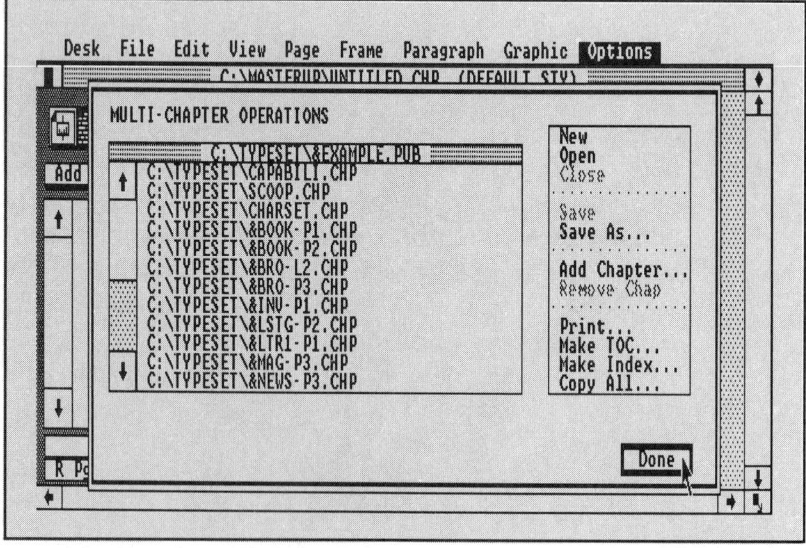

Figure 11.3: Listing of Chapters Referenced with &EXAMPLE.PUB Publication File

Figure 11.3. As you may be able to tell, this publication file is a compilation of all the samples provided with Ventura. Printing it out would simply print each sample document, one after another, in the order listed.

This sort of hodgepodge collection of chapters is not how you'll usually use a publication file. Figure 11.4 shows a chapter listing for a more typical publication. As you can see, all the files are in the same directory (MASTERVP). In addition, they each begin with the same four letters, which in turn serve as the name of the publication (indicated at the top of the listing). The next three letters in each chapter name designate the specific contents of the chapter. Thus, TOC indicates the table of contents file, followed by the introduction (INT). Each of the publication's (conventional) chapters is then listed in order (CH1 to CH5). At the end of the chapter listing is the appendix (APX) followed by the index (IDX). We'll see how you can generate the material for an index and a table of contents later in this chapter.

Once the chapter files for a publication are listed with the Open command, you can open in turn one of the listed chapters to see the names of the files that are associated with it. To open a chapter, use

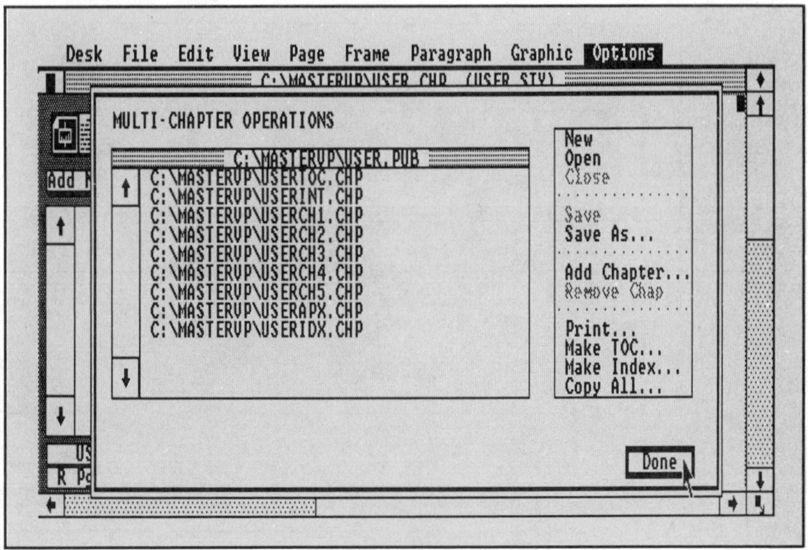

Figure 11.4: A Typical Publication Listing

the following steps:

1. Select the chapter of your choice by clicking it, as shown in Figure 11.5.
2. Click Open. You'll see those files listed that compose the selected chapter (see Figure 11.6).

IMPORTANT

Be aware that the dialog box that appears in Figure 11.6 does not show two important additional files that are associated with every chapter file. These are the CAP (caption) file and the CIF (chapter information) file.

Once a chapter is opened, only one command is available: Close. (You can also click the Done button.) In point of fact, this command is only available when you are examining a chapter (not a publication). When you finish examining the file names associated with a chapter, click Close to redisplay the publication listing, or Done to complete your multichapter work and go back to the document in the working area.

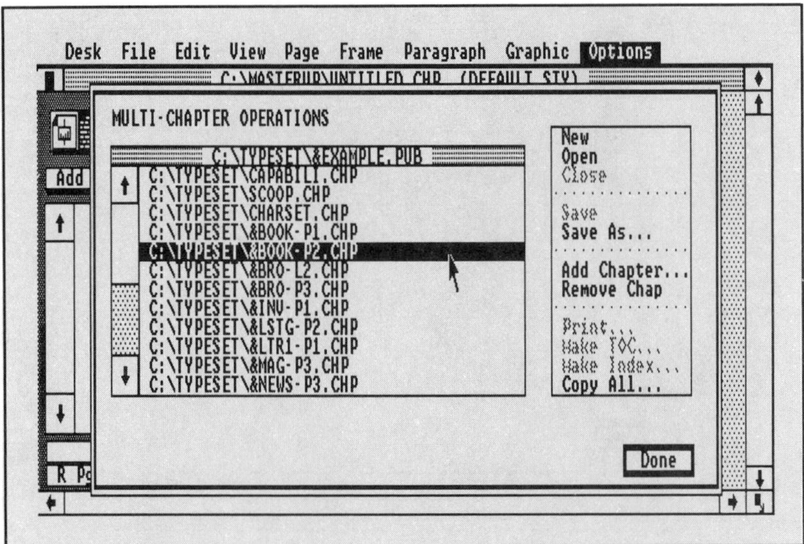

Figure 11.5: Selecting a Chapter in a Publication

OTHER FILE COMMANDS

Other filing commands work for publications just as they do for chapters with the File menu. Use the Save command to save your work on the publication file. Use the Save As command to save your publication work under a different name or to assign a name to a new publication. You must save a publication file at least once before you can make a table of contents or an index for it. Use the New command when you want to begin work on an entirely new publication.

ADDING, MOVING, AND REMOVING CHAPTERS

With the Add Chapter command you can add a chapter to the publication. When you use this command, the resulting Item Selector box allows you to add the chapter. If you've been consistent in naming chapters associated with a publication, you can use Ventura's filtering capability to display only chapter names that match your system of naming. Figure 11.7 shows the technique in operation. By using the DOS asterisk wild card (*), the Directory field is

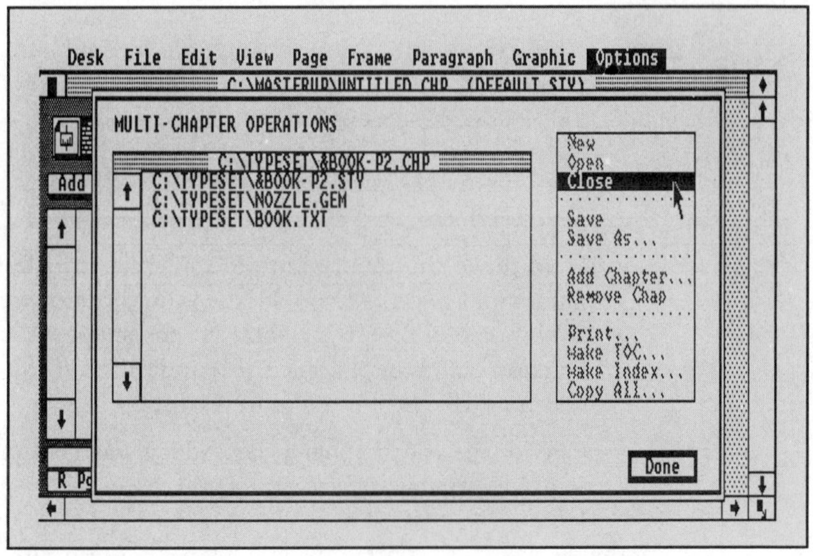

Figure 11.6: An Open Chapter

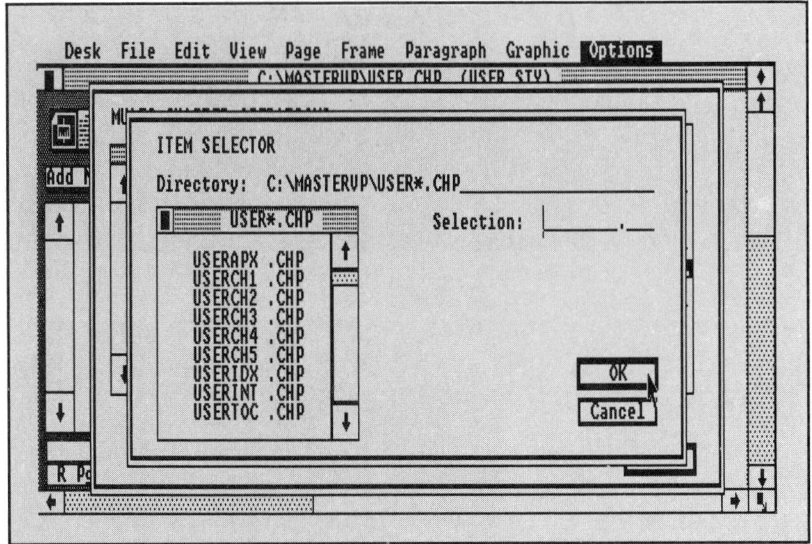

Figure 11.7: A DOS Wild Card Used to Filter Chapter Names

set up to display only files that begin with *USER*. (See Appendix C for more on DOS wild cards.) This approach is not so important if you store the files for only one publication in each directory.

You can move chapters from one position in the publication to another. Remember, the order in which the chapters are listed dictates their order in the publication. To rearrange chapters within a publication, follow these steps:

1. Place the mouse cursor on the name of the chapter that you wish to relocate.
2. Hold down the mouse button and drag the file name to a different location. As you do, the mouse cursor will turn into the shape of a flattened hand (like the shape we saw in conjunction with cropping pictures) and the bar indicating your selection will ghost (see Figure 11.8).
3. Position the selection bar so it straddles the files that you want to place the chapter between, and release the mouse button.

If the displayed list represents only a portion of the chapter names for the publication, you might not be able to reposition the chapter

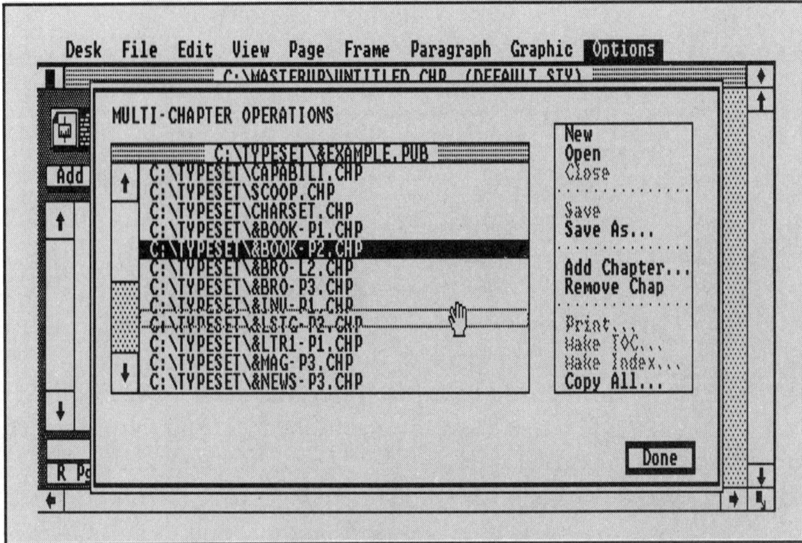

Figure 11.8: Moving a Chapter within a Publication

with one drag. In that case, drag the chapter name as far down or up the list as possible. When you release the mouse button, Ventura will obligingly scroll the list of file names in the direction you are headed. You can then drag the chapter name again and repeat the procedure if necessary.

Chapters that you need to dissociate from the displayed publication may be removed with the Remove Chap command. Use this command if you mistakenly add a chapter to the publication, if circumstances have made the chapter obsolete, or if you decide to use the chapter in a different publication. Removal is immediate upon clicking the command. Ventura does not ask for verification before removing because removed files are not erased from the disk and can easily be added again.

CREATING A TABLE OF CONTENTS

Once your chapters are properly organized, you can create a table of contents. Ventura makes it quite easy to create a table of contents for a multichapter publication. If you want one for a single chapter, however, you must create a single-chapter "publication" by saving the chapter as a publication.

Once you have a publication, click the Make TOC command. You'll see the dialog box called Generate Table of Contents (Figure 11.9). You use the buttons in the Inserts grouping at the bottom of the dialog box to insert various codes into the field lines that you see above them. Clicking them insures the correct syntax for codes representing page numbers, tags, and other features.

At the top of the dialog box is a field labeled TOC File. When Ventura creates the table of contents, it places the output into a text file, which is much like the word processor files you create for documents. You can assign this *generated file*, as Ventura calls it, to any document just as you do other text files.

The name that Ventura inserts into the TOC File field line consists of the first five letters of the publication and the letters TOC, indicating a table of contents file. The GEN extension identifies the file as a generated file. Although you can change the name, it's best to use it as is. When loading generated files, Ventura automatically filters for this extension.

The next line in the dialog box is the Title String. This is simply the name that appears at the top of the table of contents. Normally, this consists of the words *Table of Contents*. You can change the string; for example, you can shorten it to simply *Contents*.

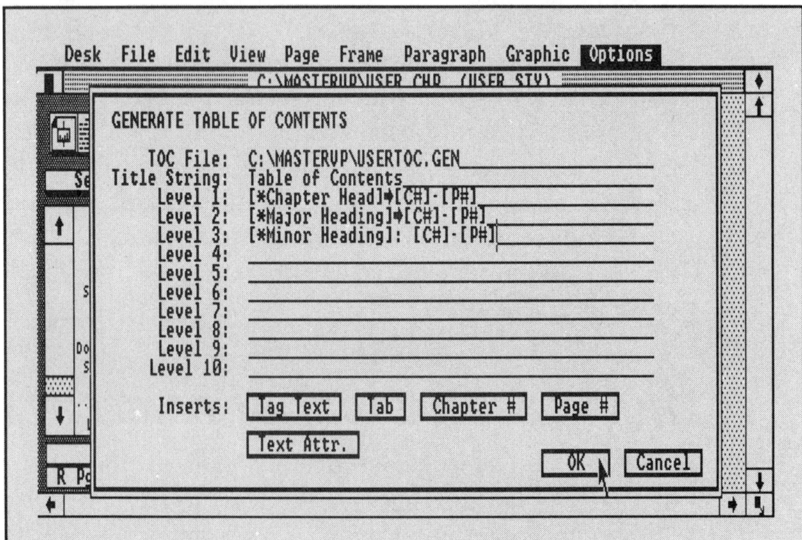

Figure 11.9: The Generate Table of Contents Dialog Box

Next are the ten levels to be displayed in the table of contents. These are simply the categories and categories within categories that will be included. Level 1 is the broadest category. Ten levels provide more levels of organization than you will ever use, except perhaps in extremely technical and highly organized material. For the most part, you probably won't want to use more than two or three levels.

We have created the entries shown in order to generate the table of contents for the USER document (see Figure 11.10). Notice that the document uses chapter numbers and a letter of the alphabet to number pages. We'll see how to set up page numbering formats later in this chapter.

Before we examine the exact entries we used, it's important to understand how Ventura generates a table of contents. Ventura uses two sets of tags to make a table of contents. The first set is made up of the various headings that appear throughout your document. In the case of the sample style sheet, the Level 1 heading is the tag named

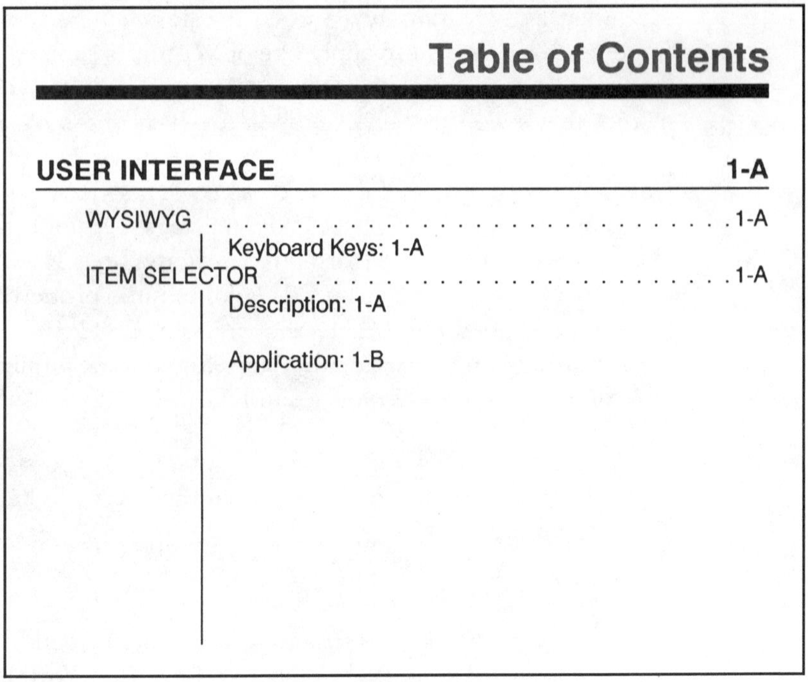

Table of Contents

USER INTERFACE 1-A

WYSIWYG 1-A

Keyboard Keys: 1-A

ITEM SELECTOR 1-A

Description: 1-A

Application: 1-B

Figure 11.10: The Generated Table of Contents

Chapter Head, Level 2 has the name Major Heading, and Level 3 is labeled Minor Heading. When creating the table of contents, Ventura scans your document, examining it for text formatted with the specified tags. When it finds them, it extracts the contents of the paragraphs so tagged, along with the corresponding page numbers. This information is placed in the TOC file specified at the top of the dialog box.

The second set of tags are applied to text in the table of contents as it is generated. The tags include Z_TOC TITLE for the title, Z_TOC LVL 1 for Level 1 text, Z_TOC LVL 2 for Level 2 text, and so on. Once the table of contents is generated, you can create a Ventura chapter file and load the generated TOC file. You can then format these generated tags just as you would any tags. If you make changes in the document and need to regenerate the table of contents, all entry placement and formatting is handled automatically when you give the OK in the Generate Table of Contents box. When you look at the table of contents, the new material is fully incorporated.

Rather than creating the entire format for elements in the table of contents, you can simply apply one of Ventura's sample style sheets that includes tags for generated index text. Of course, you can then modify that style sheet if desired. If you have the table of contents chapter referencing the USER.STY style sheet, the table of contents will not come out formatted, since this style sheet (originally named &TDOC-P1.STY) does not have tags for a table of contents; all the generated tags were formatted as Body Text. However, if you apply &TCHD-P1.STY, which does contain the properly formatted tags, you will obtain the results shown in Figure 11.10.

In summary, then, here are the steps for creating a fully formatted table of contents, such as you see in Figure 11.10:

1. Using the Generate Table of Contents dialog box, specify the format and tags for each level in the Table of Contents.
2. Give the OK to initiate the generating process.
3. Open a chapter file for the table of contents.
4. Within the chapter, use the File menu's Load Text/Picture command to indicate Generated for Text Format and load the table of contents text file.

5. Format the table of contents chapter file or apply a sample style sheet to format it for you.

Now let's examine the various field lines that allow Ventura to create this format. To indicate that Ventura should use a certain tag for a given level, click the Tag Text button in the Inserts grouping. Ventura will display the code

```
[*tag name]
```

on the line where the keyboard cursor is positioned. You then remove the words *tag name* and replace them with the actual name of the tag. For instance, on Level 1 you can see that the tag name *Chapter Head* is inserted. As with other inserts, you can type in the insert rather than clicking its button.

After the Chapter Head, we want Ventura to insert a tab character. To get a tab, you must click the Tab button on the screen. You cannot insert a tab by pressing the Tab key, because that moves the cursor to the next line. The presence of a tab is indicated by the left pointing arrow following Chapter Head.

After the tab character, we needed to have Ventura insert the Chapter # (indicated with [C#]), a dash, and the Page # (indicated with [P#]). This format is required by the unusual manner in which the document is numbered. The result is the words *USER INTERFACE*, followed by a tab, and then the page number. (The Z_TOC LVL 1 tag is formatted with a ruling line below, which creates the line below this entry.)

The titles WYSIWYG and ITEM SELECTOR are both tagged as Major Heading in the main document and as Z_TOC LVL 2 in the table of contents. This tag has leader dots that fill in the space where the tab character occurs.

Once Ventura generates the table of contents file and you load it into a document, the document is just like any other: you can edit it as you wish. Thus, although Ventura does not provide the means of making multiple entries on the same line, once generated you could edit the file to provide that. Be aware, though, that if you make changes in your document and have to regenerate the table of contents, you'll have to repeat each individual enhancement.

If possible, leave the table of contents as Ventura creates it. This is especially true if you expect to make changes to your document later on, thus necessitating a regeneration of the table of contents. The beauty of following Ventura's lead is that the table of contents is fully recreated and formatted automatically at your command. Just redisplay the Generate Table of Contents dialog box and give the OK. With no additional effort on your part, any changes you make in the document are reflected in the table of contents, including page numbers and headings. Ventura creates the text file, applies the tags, and formats the text accordingly, all automatically.

MAKING AN INDEX

Some of the processes involved in creating an index are similar to those used to create a table of contents. Be aware, however, that the process is not so straightforward and automatic. As it does when generating a table of contents, Ventura scans your document to make the entries for an index. Unlike the process involved in creating a table of contents, though, Ventura's indexing process doesn't make use of tags and text that are already in place as a result of standard editing and formatting. Instead, you must perform these initial steps before generating the index. You must insert index entries into the document and provide the text for those entries as well.

The simplest method available for creating an index is unfortunately quite time consuming. It involves using a dialog box to type in index entries one by one, for every page an entry should indicate. However, there are two main ways you can speed up the indexing process, and you will probably want to use them for any extensive indexing. One is by using a word processor (see Chapter 12). The other is by incorporating index entries into headers or footers. Using headers and footers, Ventura can be made to list a range of pages that a section of text covers. The simplest method should be used only for very short documents or to add overlooked entries. Let's look at how this method works, though, since doing so will provide us with an understanding of the indexing process.

MAKING INDEX ENTRIES

The first part to creating an index with Ventura is to insert index entries in the document. These are positioned at those points where you want Ventura to check the page number and generate entries for the index accordingly.

You can provide two levels of entries within the index—primary and secondary—but no more than that. *Primary* entries are the major alphabetized entries in the index, representing the general topics covered in text. *Secondary* entries are generally indented below primary entries, representing topics subordinate to a broader general topic. Often entries can be used as both primary and secondary entries within the same index. Once we create the sample index, for example, you'll be able to see how the entry *Cursor keys* is used alone as a primary entry. There is also an entry that uses *Text editing* as a primary entry and *Cursor keys* as a secondary entry under that. There are a few other operations, such as making cross references, that add greater flexibility to your indexing. Here, however, are the steps for making most simple entries:

1. Activate the Text mode and insert the keyboard cursor at the spot in text where you wish to place the index reference. This is the spot Ventura will use to determine the page number for the entry.
2. Pull down the Edit menu and click Insert/Edit Index. You'll see the dialog box displayed in Figure 11.11.
3. With Type of Entry set to Index, enter a Primary Entry and a Secondary Entry if desired.
4. Give the OK. Ventura inserts an Index Entry mark into the document at the position of the keyboard cursor.

The Index Entry mark is only visible if you've set the Options command to Show Tabs and Returns. The mark looks like a temperature degree symbol (°). When it's to the right of the keyboard cursor, the words *Index Entry* appear in the Current box.

The USER sample document has various index entries. Figure 11.12, in Enlarged View, shows several of the entries in place. Notice how one of the entries is to the right of the keyboard cursor and hence *Index Entry* appears in the Current box.

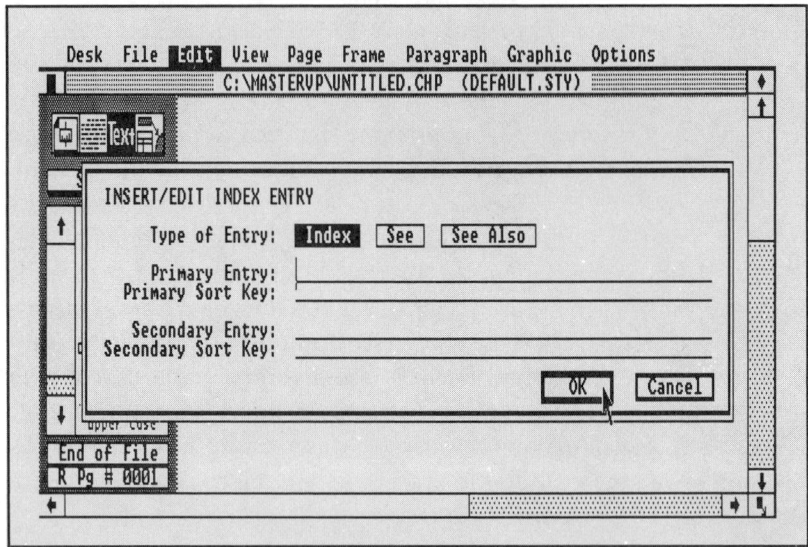

Figure 11.11: The Dialog Box Displayed with the Edit Menu's Insert/Edit Index Command

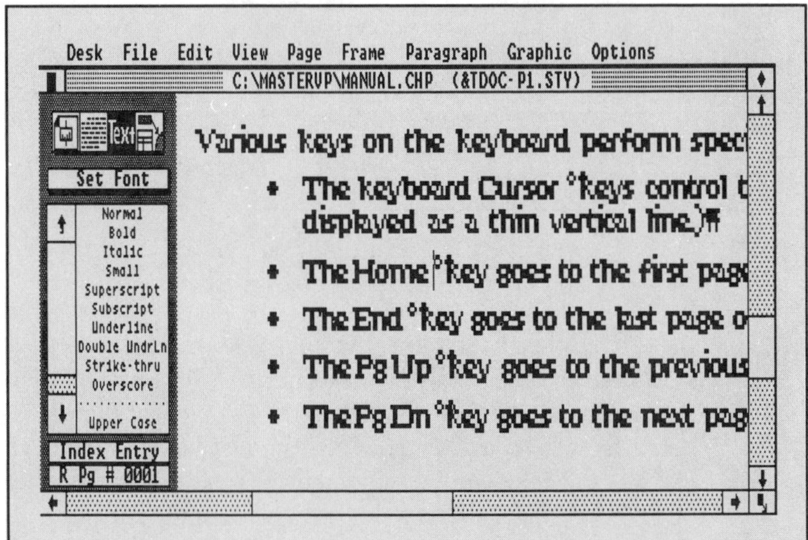

Figure 11.12: Index Entry Marks in a Document

If you want Ventura to indicate a range of page numbers in the index for any given entry, you must insert identical index entries on each page of the range. For such consecutive page entries, Ventura will show only the beginning and ending entries according to a format you specify, as we'll see shortly.

If you create more than one reference for the same index entry, be certain to spell the index entry exactly the same each time. Different singular and plural usage, for instance, will result in multiple entries. On the screen sample, there is an index reference for the PgUp key. In the dialog box that created this reference, the Primary Entry specifies the *Page Up key*. Therefore, even though *PgUp* appears in the text of the document, if you use *Page Up* as the entry in the dialog box, you would have to be certain to spell out all such entries, or you would have some entries listed under *PgUp* and some under *Page Up*. Be sure to proof your index printout for inconsistencies like this. Correct erroneous entries and regenerate the index as necessary.

To correct an entry, place the keyboard cursor to the left of the Index Entry mark whose settings you wish to adjust. Then pull down the Edit menu and click Insert/Edit Index, just as you do when creating the entry. You'll see the dialog box with the current settings for the selected mark. Adjust them as necessary and give the OK to register the new settings.

SPECIFYING SORTING EXCEPTIONS

To alphabetize your index, Ventura normally uses the Primary Entry and Secondary Entry fields. Some entries, however, need to be spelled one way and alphabetized another. If so, you can use the Primary Sort Key and Secondary Sort Key fields to indicate how Ventura should sort the entry. Thus, since an index should be alphabetized without regard to prepositions, a Primary Entry such as *Home key* that has a Secondary Entry *with Ctrl key* should have *Ctrl key* specified for Secondary Sort Key. Otherwise, the secondary entry would be sorted using the word *with*. Other common applications for sort keys include titles that begin with *The* or *An* (although it's probably best to form the entry using the main title followed by a comma and then the article). In Ventura, numbers are grouped together separately from letters of the alphabet. To alphabetize a number, spell the number out in the appropriate Sort Key field.

For the majority of your work, however, you won't need to make any entries into the fields for Primary Sort Key and Secondary Sort Key.

CREATING CROSS REFERENCES

As you can probably surmise from the See and See Also buttons, you use these to create cross references for your index. These entries do not indicate page numbers, so you may wish to group them in one place: the end of the chapter, for instance. That way you can find and consider them together, and so be sure that all appropriate cross references have been made. This works especially well when you use a word processor to create the index.

When you use these buttons, the text you enter into the Secondary Entry field will not be used as a regular subordinate entry. Rather, it will be another Primary Entry that you wish to point the reader to. You cannot make See and See Also entries for secondary entries.

Suppose, for instance, you want the reader looking under *Revising* to consult *Editing*. You'd click the See button and specify Revising for the Primary Entry and Editing (which is actually another primary entry, cross referenced) as the Secondary Entry.

Use the See button when there are no secondary entries elsewhere in the document for the primary entry specified. Use the See Also button when the primary entry does have secondary entries elsewhere. Since you may have a difficult time keeping track of which ones do and which do not, be certain to proof your index carefully, make corrections, and regenerate it as necessary.

DELETING AND MOVING INDEX ENTRIES

To delete an index entry, select it with the keyboard cursor by positioning that cursor to the left of the reference mark. The words *Index Entry* should appear in the Current box. Then press the Del key.

Once you delete the Index Entry mark in this fashion, it's placed on the text clipboard along with its entries, sort keys, See button status, and so on. You can insert the mark in a different location to effect

Compiling Index Entries

When compiling an index, look at the individual entries from the intelligent reader's point of view. The reader will look for the more general entry first, then for more specific topics under that entry. If readers cannot find the topic they are looking for, they consider synonymous terms. Make the index as extensive as possible, but do not include items that no reader would ever think of searching for.

When selecting terms and phrases in your document from which to create index entries, follow these basic rules of indexing:

- Index by significant words or phrases.
- Choose concrete nouns rather than general descriptive nouns as entries—use *Printers, types of,* not *Types of printers.*
- List entries under the key word of a phrase—*Commands, miscellaneous,* not *Miscellaneous commands.*
- Never use an adjective alone as an entry.
- When an adjective is part of several entries, repeat the adjective for each entry. For example, use

  Error message, 23-24
  Error tracing, 136-137

  rather than

  Error
  message, 23-24
  tracing, 136-137

- Entries should be alphabetized by their major words, disregarding prepositions and conjunctions.
- Page numbers should appear in ascending order.

a move. Simply place the keyboard cursor where you want the mark to go, and press the Ins key. (Note that this method of moving works only for special text entry characters, like Index Entry, Footnote, and Frame Anchor marks. Ventura will not move standard characters, such as letters and numbers, in this way. Standard characters individually deleted are not sent to the clipboard.)

If you use the Insert/Edit Index Entry dialog box and remove the entries from the field lines (with the Esc key, for instance), Ventura will remove the corresponding index mark when you give the OK. Therefore, when you first use this dialog box to insert an entry, you must provide some entry in the field or Ventura will not create the reference mark.

GENERATING THE INDEX

To generate the index, use the Options menu to display the dialog box for Multi-Chapter Operations. Open the appropriate publication and use the Make Index command. If you wish to index a single chapter, you must make and save a publication file for it.

When you commence generation of the index, the dialog box shown in Figure 11.13 appears. As we saw when creating a table of contents,

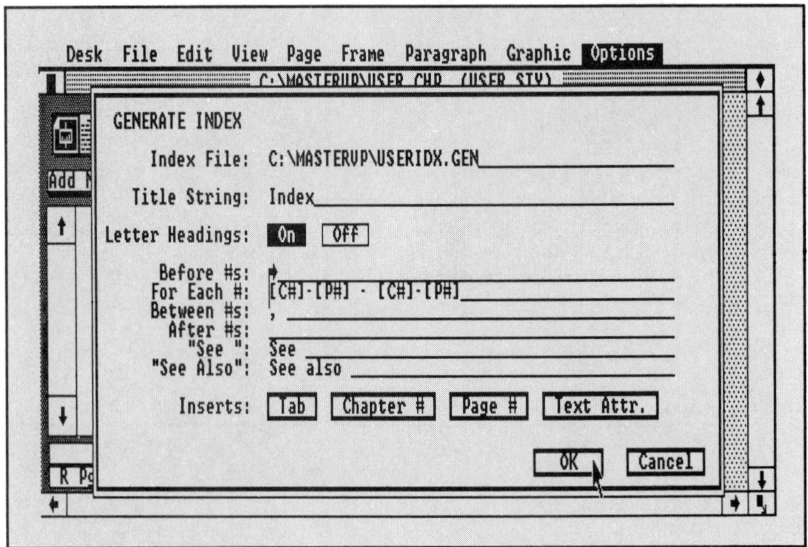

Figure 11.13: The Generate Index Dialog Box

you use this dialog box to create a text file of entries. You can then incorporate this generated text file into any Ventura chapter file.

The settings displayed are Ventura's defaults, except for the Index File name which will vary to correspond with the associated publication file. This field indicates the name given to the text file that will store the generated index. As with the table of contents generator, this setting will display the first five characters in the name of the publication file. It adds the letters IDX to those five, indicating that it is an index file, and the extension GEN to indicate that the file is automatically generated by Ventura.

Title String sets the title that Ventura places at the top of the index. The title is formatted with the tag Z_INDEX TITLE. The Letter Headings setting, when turned On, inserts the appropriate letter of the alphabet before each group of entries beginning with the same letter. Letter headings receive the tag Z_INDEX LTR.

The main grouping of field lines in the dialog box sets up the format for the index entries. Index entries are formatted with the tag Z_INDEX MAIN. The Before #s setting shows that a tab insert is the default before numbers in the index. The For Each # setting shows how numbers that indicate a range will be displayed. The default shows numbers as the chapter number, a hyphen, and the page number. The beginning and ending page numbers are separated by a space, a hyphen, and another space. The Between #s setting shows that a comma and a space will separate successive page numbers when more than one page number appears for the same entry. After #s shows that nothing special will be added after the page numbers. (You could specify a period here.)

You use the See and See Also settings when you want to change the wording for cross-referenced entries. For instance, rather than *See Editing* you may want the entry to read *Refer to Editing*.

Figure 11.14 shows an index created with the entries provided in the USER sample. We did, however, enhance it. First, we used the style sheet &TCHD-P1.STY, which has index tags (those beginning with Z_INDEX) that create the paragraph formats you see. The USER.STY style sheet (originally &TDOC-P1.STY) does not contain any of the special index tags. When this style sheet is used in conjunction with the index, all of the index comes out looking like body text.

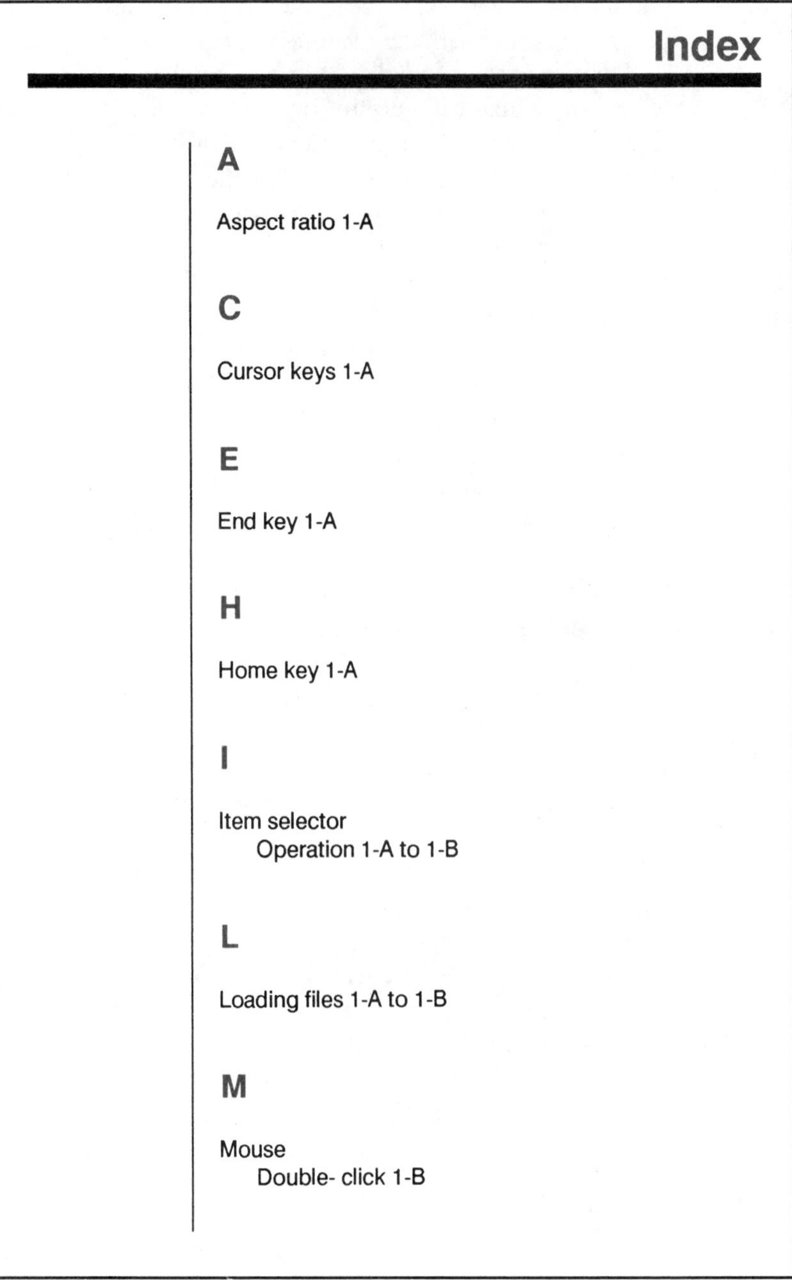

Index

A

Aspect ratio 1-A

C

Cursor keys 1-A

E

End key 1-A

H

Home key 1-A

I

Item selector
    Operation 1-A to 1-B

L

Loading files 1-A to 1-B

M

Mouse
    Double- click 1-B

Figure 11.14: A Generated Index

Figure 11.14: A Generated Index (continued)

We have also changed the Before #s and For Each # fields in the Generate Index dialog box. We've changed the default tab for Before #s to a space, and changed the hyphen indicating a number range in the For Each # setting to the word *to*. The default hyphen in the range proves too confusing when used in conjunction with hyphens between chapter and page numbers as well.

EXPEDITING INDEXING

As we mentioned at the start of the chapter, there are two ways to expedite the creation of index entries that you'll probably want to use for extensive index creation. One is to make the entries with your word processor in the text files. When used in conjunction with a keyboard enhancer or macro generating feature, the results are quite a bit less arduous. We'll examine the codes you enter into word processed text in Chapter 12.

The other technique uses the section headings of text in your document in conjunction with headers or footers. This is a very useful feature for creating references to page numbers in succession. What you do is create the index entry in a section title, which is referenced by a header or footer (using the 1st Match or Last Match insert). The header or footer repeats, showing index entries on every page until the next section title. When Ventura compiles the index, it sees references on each page, and so creates a range of page numbers.

For instance, if the words *Item Selector* are the title of a section, and you want Ventura to index the entire section as a range, you could insert an index entry into that title. For Primary Entry, you'd type in the words *Item Selector*. In the header or footer, you'd make a match reference to the tag with which *Item Selector* is formatted.

You don't even have to insert section titles into the headers and footers (or even use headers and footers that actually appear) to use this technique. The section title can consist of nothing other than the index reference, and the header and footer can contain just the match reference. The operation consists of several steps:

1. In Text mode, create text for the section title (if any) and insert the index reference into it. This material must be in a paragraph separate from any others. It must also be in the underlying-page Frame; standard Frame text does not work.

2. In Paragraph mode, format the paragraph with the tag for section titles. This will create a starting point for the index entry, which will continue until the next paragraph formatted with the same tag.

3. Use the Page menu's Headers & Footers command and reference the section title tag. Use the 1st Match or Last Match buttons.

Be sure to provide a paragraph later using the same tag in order to provide an ending page for the index entry. The ending paragraph can contain an index entry if you wish (to end the current reference and begin another) or not (to end the current one only).

AUTOMATIC NUMBERING OF SECTIONS

Another feature that is useful in organizing long documents is Ventura's ability to number the sections of your documents automatically. It can number sections, and sections within sections, up to ten levels deep. The key to numbering lies in two paragraph tags for each level. One tag is the standard one for a specific type of text in the document (usually headings), while the other tag is one of Ventura's generated tags.

The process of section numbering is quite similar to the one Ventura uses for captioning pictures. You may recall that to caption pictures, you work with two tags as well. You create a label tag for the caption text, such as *Figure 1.1:*, and then you can create a free-form caption that follows the caption label.

There are two parts to section numbering. For all items that are numbered, there is a label, such as *Section 1.1:*, that contains the automatic number. Other than the number, which increments automatically, labels can contain only text that is the same for all items with the same level of importance. This label precedes the free-form paragraph (in this case the heading), which contains information that varies for each section. Paragraph tags are used to combine these two elements. Once you indicate which tag you wish to use for each level, all heading paragraphs formatted with that tag receive the same numbering label. The numbers for paragraphs similarly tagged increment automatically.

To set up automatic numbering, pull down the Page menu and click Auto-Numbering. You now see the dialog box shown in Figure 11.15. With this dialog box, you create and control section numbering. To make numbering operational, click the On button in the Usage category.

CREATING SECTION LABELS

The Auto-Numbering dialog box works in a way similar to the box we studied when creating captions. On each line, you indicate the label with which you wish to precede paragraphs tagged with the specified tag. This label consists of a combination of standard text, which is the same from paragraph to paragraph, and variable inserts, set using the Inserts grouping at the bottom of the screen. In order to click any of these buttons, you must first set Usage to On.

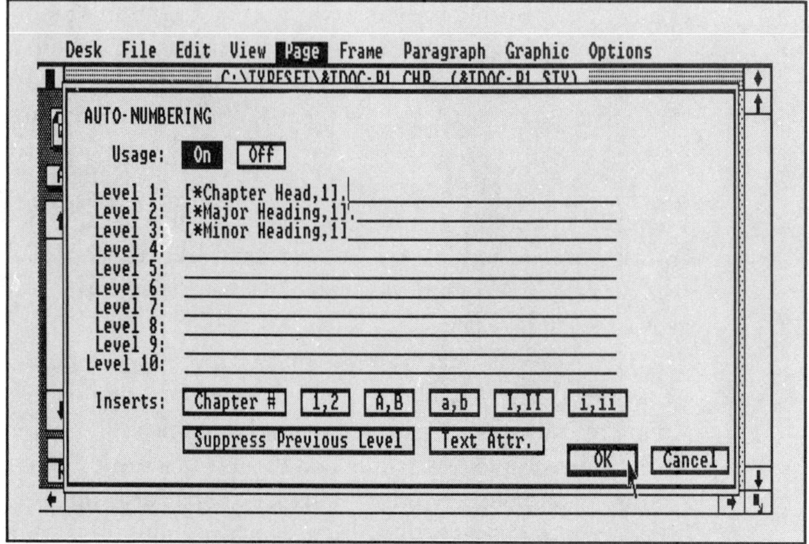

Figure 11.15: The Page Menu's Auto-Numbering Dialog Box

Labels with Numbers Only

The USER sample chapter and style sheet that we have been working with contain an example of auto-numbering, using variable inserts only. In Figure 11.15, the dialog box indicates the auto-numbering settings that are in place for the USER style sheet. With these settings in place, Ventura numbers all paragraphs that are tagged as Chapter Head, Major Heading, and Minor Heading. The Chapter Head tag receives Level 1 format, Major Heading receives Level 2, and Minor Heading is formatted according to Level 3. Figure 11.16 shows the printed chapter with the numbered headings set in place.

In the sample, the heading *USER INTERFACE*, tagged as Chapter Head, is numbered for Level 1. The headings *WYSIWYG* and *ITEM SELECTOR*, tagged as Major Heading, are numbered for Level 2. The headings *Keyboard Keys* and *Description*, tagged as Minor Headings, are both numbered as Level 3.

To create the settings for each of these levels, you can insert variable codes in the relevant field by clicking the button in the Inserts grouping that displays the style of numbering (or lettering) that you want to use. A corresponding code will appear for the level field that contains the keyboard cursor. Table 11.1 lists the insert buttons along with the matching codes that each creates.

Notice that many of the Insert codes contain the words *tag name*. As with previous features we've examined, you substitute the names of the tags that you want Ventura to use in place of these words. Thus, to create the setting shown in the Level 1 field, follow these steps:

1. Place the keyboard cursor in the Level 1 field.
2. Click the 1,2 button in the Inserts grouping.
3. Replace the words *tag name* by typing in **Chapter Head**.

Adding Text to Labels

As mentioned, you can use constant text in a numbering label. To use constant text, you simply type it into the field that corresponds to the level you wish to use. You can also use the keypad in conjunction with the Alt key to create characters from the international font to be used in the text portion of the label (see Appendix E).

1. USER INTERFACE

1.1. WYSIWYG

Figure 1-1
This is the caption for the figure. It is anchored below **WYSIWYG**

Ventura Publisher is designed to provide What You See (on the screen) Is What You Get printed (WYSIWYG). This means that the computer display should match as closely as possible, at all times, what you will see on the final printed page. Of course, the difference between the technology used to display a page on a CRT screen, and the technologies used to print a page on a laser printer or typesetter, do create some unavoidable differences. In particular, because the computer CRT screen cannot produce anywhere near the same resolution of a printer or typesetter, and because what is displayed is shown in a different aspect ratio (height to width ratio), the space between words and between lines may appear to be bigger or smaller than the printed page under certain circumstances. Several thin ruling lines, with little space between, may show on the screen as one thick line.

1.1.1 Keyboard Keys

Various keys on the keyboard perform special functions:

- The keyboard Cursor keys control the Text Cursor (The text cursor is displayed as a thin vertical line.)
- The Home key goes to the first page of the document.
- The End key goes to the last page of the document.
- The Pg Up key goes to the previous page.
- The Pg Dn key goes to the next page.

1.2. ITEM SELECTOR

1.2.1 Description

The display shown in Figure 10-2 is called an Item Selector. The Item Selector is used for saving and retrieving files.

1-A WYSIWYG

Figure 11.16: A Sample Chapter Using Auto-Numbering

INSERT BUTTON	INSERT CODE
Chapter #	[C#]
1,2	[*tag name,1]
A,B	[*tag name,A]
a,b	[*tag name,a]
I,II	[*tag name,I]
i,ii	[*tag name,i]
Suppress Previous Level	[-]
Text Attr.	<D>

Table 11.1: Insert Buttons and Codes for Auto-Numbering

For example, let's say that you want to create a label that has a bullet, then the word *Part* followed by a space and the chapter number. Then you want the word *Section* followed by a space and the section letter. After the section letter you want a colon. To create this format, proceed as follows:

1. Type in Alt-195 for the bullet, then the word **Part**, then click the Chapter # insert, and type a comma and a space.
2. Type the word **Section** and a space, and then click the A,B button.
3. Type a colon.

The result would be an entry that looks like this:

- Part [C#], Section [*tag name, A]:

Let's say that you want to put this effect into place for every paragraph formatted with the Chapter Head tag. You would substitute *Chapter Head* for the tag name as follows:

- Part [C#], Section [*Chapter Head, A]:

SUPPRESSING SECTION NUMBERING

When numbering sections and subsections, Ventura usually includes the section number as part of the subsection number. Ventura does, however, provide you with the means of showing only the subsection number. Use the Suppress Previous Level button with any given level to keep the previous level's number from appearing.

When you click this button, a bracketed minus sign ([–]) appears at the location of the keyboard cursor. Usually, it's kept at the end of the field for easy editing. Thus, in the USER document, to suppress the previous level for Level 2, you'd use this entry:

[*Major Heading, 1].[–]

To suppress for Level 3, you'd use this entry:

[*Minor Heading,1][–]

Figure 11.17 shows the results of suppressing these levels. Notice how the headings WYSIWYG and ITEM SELECTOR no longer carry the number 1 belonging to the previous level, USER INTERFACE.

RENUMBERING SECTIONS

When you finish using this dialog box, Ventura automatically renumbers the tagged material appropriately. If, however, you make changes in the free-form text as it appears in the working area, such as deleting a heading, Ventura will not renumber immediately. Instead, you must instruct it specifically to do so. To do this, pull down the Page menu and click Renumber Chapter, or type Ctrl-B. The numbers will be adjusted correctly.

For instance, let's say that upon examining the document, we wish to adjust the heading *Keyboard Keys*. The heading really has nothing to do with WYSIWYG, so it should receive the Level 2 tag, Major Heading. Upon applying the Major Heading tag, the document would look like Figure 11.18. Then upon renumbering (and using the Text mode's Assignment list to change the heading to uppercase letters), the document would look like Figure 11.19.

1. USER INTERFACE

1. WYSIWYG

Figure 1-1
This is the caption for the figure. It is anchored below **WYSIWYG**

Ventura Publisher is designed to provide What You See (on the screen) Is What You Get printed (WYSIWYG). This means that the computer display should match as closely as possible, at all times, what you will see on the final printed page. Of course, the difference between the technology used to display a page on a CRT screen, and the technologies used to print a page on a laser printer or typesetter, do create some unavoidable differences. In particular, because the computer CRT screen cannot produce anywhere near the same resolution of a printer or typesetter, and because what is displayed is shown in a different aspect ratio (height to width ratio), the space between words and between lines may appear to be bigger or smaller than the printed page under certain circumstances. Several thin ruling lines, with little space between, may show on the screen as one thick line.

1 Keyboard Keys

Various keys on the keyboard perform special functions:

- The keyboard Cursor keys control the Text Cursor (The text cursor is displayed as a thin vertical line.)
- The Home key goes to the first page of the document.
- The End key goes to the last page of the document.
- The Pg Up key goes to the previous page.
- The Pg Dn key goes to the next page.

2. ITEM SELECTOR

1 Description

The display shown in Figure 10-2 is called an Item Selector. The Item Selector is used for saving and retrieving files.

Figure 11.17: Suppressing the Previous Level Numbering

1. USER INTERFACE

1.1. WYSIWYG

Figure 1-1
This is the caption for the figure. It is anchored below **WYSIWYG**

Ventura Publisher is designed to provide What You See (on the screen) Is What You Get printed (WYSIWYG). This means that the computer display should match as closely as possible, at all times, what you will see on the final printed page. Of course, the difference between the technology used to display a page on a CRT screen, and the technologies used to print a page on a laser printer or typesetter, do create some unavoidable differences. In particular, because the computer CRT screen cannot produce anywhere near the same resolution of a printer or typesetter, and because what is displayed is shown in a different aspect ratio (height to width ratio), the space between words and between lines may appear to be bigger or smaller than the printed page under certain circumstances. Several thin ruling lines, with little space between, may show on the screen as one thick line.

1.1.1 Keyboard Keys

Various keys on the keyboard perform special functions:

- The keyboard Cursor keys control the Text Cursor (The text cursor is displayed as a thin vertical line.)
- The Home key goes to the first page of the document.
- The End key goes to the last page of the document.
- The Pg Up key goes to the previous page.
- The Pg Dn key goes to the next page.

1.2. ITEM SELECTOR

1.2.1 Description

The display shown in Figure 10-2 is called an Item Selector. The Item Selector is used for saving and retrieving files.

Figure 11.18: The Document with a New Heading Tag before Renumbering

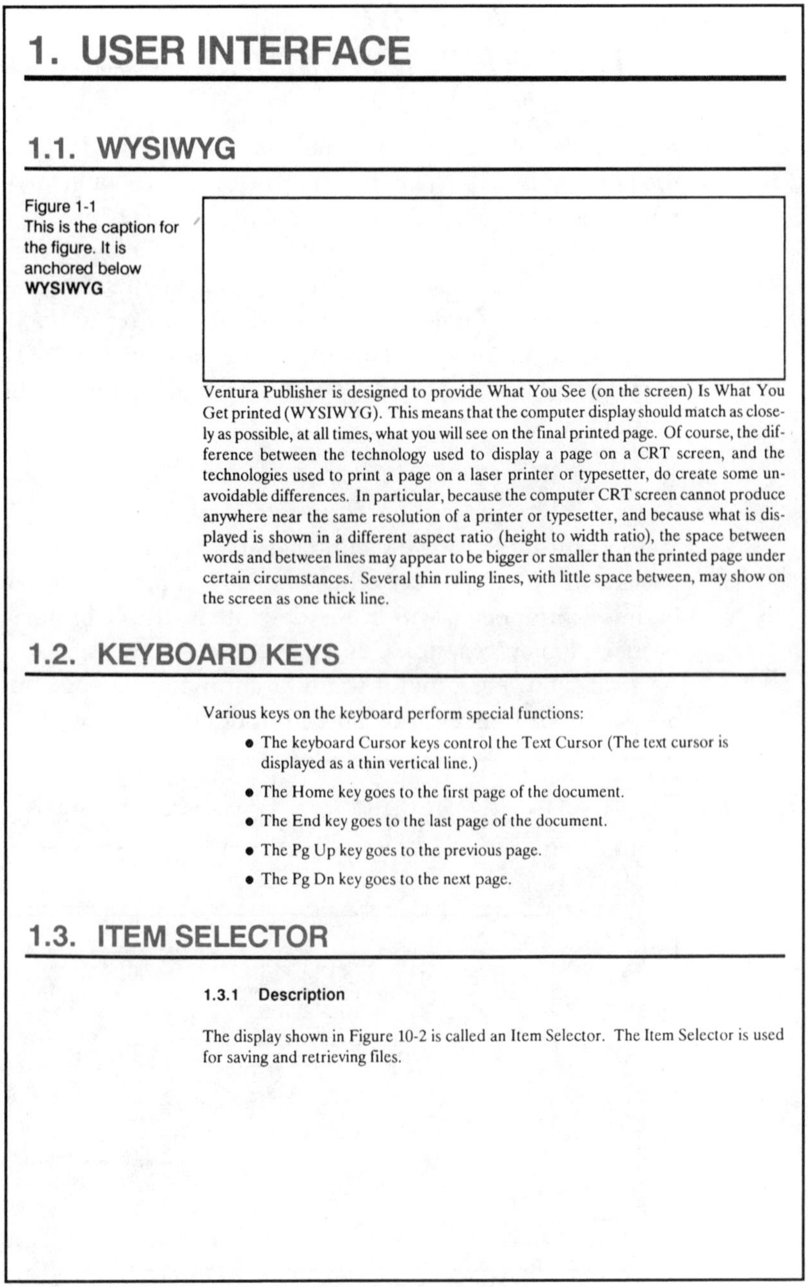

1. USER INTERFACE

1.1. WYSIWYG

Figure 1-1
This is the caption for the figure. It is anchored below **WYSIWYG**

Ventura Publisher is designed to provide What You See (on the screen) Is What You Get printed (WYSIWYG). This means that the computer display should match as closely as possible, at all times, what you will see on the final printed page. Of course, the difference between the technology used to display a page on a CRT screen, and the technologies used to print a page on a laser printer or typesetter, do create some unavoidable differences. In particular, because the computer CRT screen cannot produce anywhere near the same resolution of a printer or typesetter, and because what is displayed is shown in a different aspect ratio (height to width ratio), the space between words and between lines may appear to be bigger or smaller than the printed page under certain circumstances. Several thin ruling lines, with little space between, may show on the screen as one thick line.

1.2. KEYBOARD KEYS

Various keys on the keyboard perform special functions:

- The keyboard Cursor keys control the Text Cursor (The text cursor is displayed as a thin vertical line.)
- The Home key goes to the first page of the document.
- The End key goes to the last page of the document.
- The Pg Up key goes to the previous page.
- The Pg Dn key goes to the next page.

1.3. ITEM SELECTOR

1.3.1 Description

The display shown in Figure 10-2 is called an Item Selector. The Item Selector is used for saving and retrieving files.

Figure 11.19: The Document after Renumbering

CHANGING PAGE AND CHAPTER NUMBERS

In several of the dialog boxes we've examined in this chapter, we've seen the use of chapter- and page-number inserts. In Chapter 10 we used such numbers in headers and footers. You can adjust Ventura page numbers and chapter numbers through the use of *counters*.

The Page Counter and Chapter Counter dialog boxes are similar in look and, in some ways, operation (see Figures 11.20 and 11.21). To display one of these dialog boxes, pull down the Page menu and click Page Counter or Chapter Counter as appropriate. Let's look at how these counters operate, and then we'll examine some strategies for their use.

THE PAGE COUNTER

You can use the Page Counter dialog box to start numbering the pages with some number other than one. This counter affects numbering as it appears within the document, as set by insert codes in headers, footers, captions, and section headings, using the [P#] code. Be aware, however, that it will not renumber the page numbers that appear in the Current box at the bottom of the Side-bar.

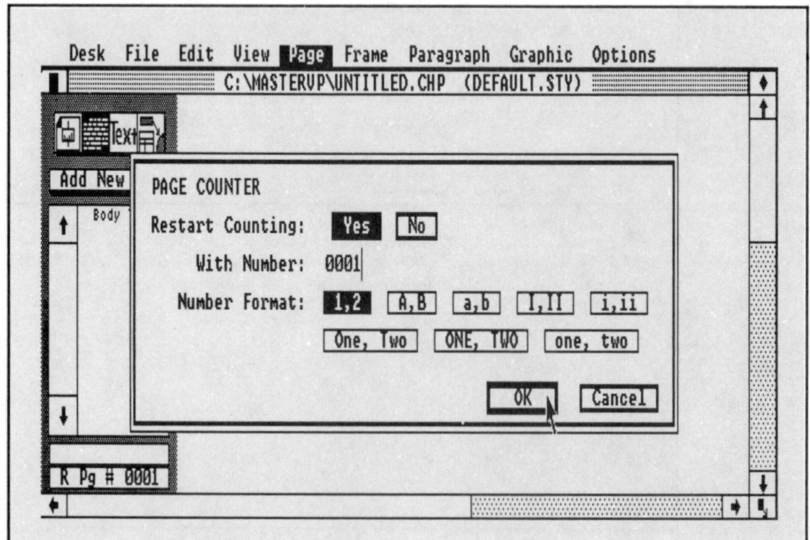

Figure 11.20: The Page Menu's Page Counter Dialog Box

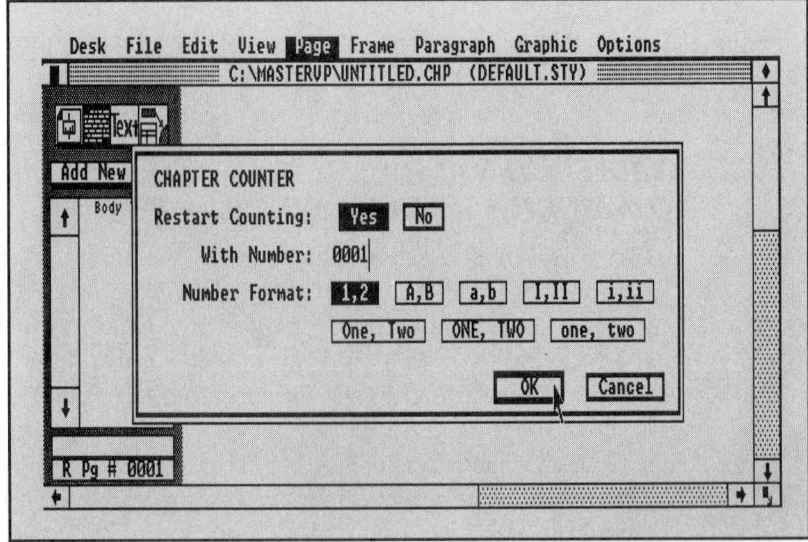

Figure 11.21: The Page Menu's Chapter Counter Dialog Box

IMPORTANT

When you use the Page menu's Go To Page command, Ventura always uses the page number displayed in the Side-bar as its reference. This number may not agree with those appearing on the page if you have adjusted them with the page counter.

There is one page counter for each page of the chapter. By changing the page counter for any given page you change that page's number and all pages that follow it.

By clicking Number Format buttons, you can also use the page counter to adjust the formatting style that the page numbers use. Normally, the format is Arabic numerals, as indicated with the 1,2 button. You may wish to use different numbering formats for different parts of a publication, such as small Roman numerals for the front matter.

THE CHAPTER COUNTER

The chapter counter operates like the page counter with two exceptions. First, it regulates chapter number inserts, indicated by the [C#] insert code. Second, there is only one chapter counter to a chapter. Adjusting that counter on any page in the chapter changes the chapter number throughout the chapter.

STRATEGIES FOR NUMBERING PAGES AND CHAPTERS

As we examine how to use the page and chapter counters, there is one important point to bear in mind. Ventura does not remember page or chapter numbers from chapter to chapter, even when those chapters are linked with a publication file. For this reason, the more you can avoid carrying these numbers from chapter to chapter, the easier it will be to print a publication and make adjustments to it later, and the less chance there will be for error.

If your document uses multiple Ventura chapters and you want fully sequential page numbers, you must use the Page Counter dialog box to sequence them. Since Ventura does not remember page numbers as it loads and prints, you must do the thinking for it. Just before printing a publication, you must set starting numbers chapter by chapter. Follow these steps to number the pages of multiple chapters:

1. Begin by loading the first chapter.
2. Use the End key to go to the last page and make a mental note of the page number.
3. Load the second chapter
4. Use the Page menu's Page Counter command to start the counting for the new chapter's first page at one after the last page number in the first chapter. Thus, if the first chapter ends with page 30, the second chapter should start with page 31.
5. Use the End key to go to the end of the second chapter and check the page number that it ends on, but be careful. Since you've adjusted the page numbers, you must check some page number that's displayed in the document. Do not use the page number appearing in the Side-bar.
6. Save the second chapter, open the third chapter, and repeat the process.

Manuals that restart page numbering with each chapter do not need to use the page counter. Such manuals typically include the number of the chapter as part of the page-numbering scheme. Thus, pages in the first chapter might be numbered 1-1, 1-2, 1-3, and so on; the second chapter would be numbered 2-1, 2-2, 2-3, and so on. (Our sample document, USER, uses numbers for chapters and letters for pages: 1-A, 1-B, and so on.)

Such manuals, however, still need to use the chapter counter if they use the [C#] code in headers, caption, and so on. Chapter numbers do not increment automatically from chapter to chapter any more than page numbers do. As such, the No setting for Restart Counting in the Chapter Counter box, which implies that chapter numbers do increment automatically, is rather misleading. Rather than Restart Counting, it would be more accurate to call the option Change the Chapter Number. Since there's only one chapter number to a chapter and numbering does not carry from chapter to chapter, the chapter number is always 1 unless you change it with the Chapter Counter dialog box.

Always be certain to use the Chapter Counter dialog box for all chapters other than chapter 1. If you rearrange chapters in a publication (by dragging with the flattened hand in the Multi-Chapter Operations dialog box), be certain to adjust the numbers of all affected chapters.

As you can see, Ventura's numbering limitations can add time to the process of revising documents and increase the chance of errors creeping in (which is devastating where page numbers are concerned.) Is there any way to automate the process more fully? The answer is yes, if you keep your chapters small enough and you don't need to use the [C#] code for displayed material such as figure captions.

Using this alternative approach, you keep all conventional chapters, not including front matter, together in one Ventura chapter. If all your conventional chapters are in one Ventura chapter, you can use the auto-numbering feature to number the chapters. With this approach, should you rearrange chapters, you would have to renumber with the Page menu's Renumber Chapter command (or Ctrl-B).

Put your front matter in a different Ventura chapter file and use lowercase Roman numerals for the page numbers. Use Arabic numerals for the main body of the publication and the first conventional chapter will begin with page 1. You won't need to number it specially.

This strategy will work only with small documents. The size of the Ventura chapter you can create will be affected by various features within the program. If you see an error message that says that you're out of memory, decrease the number of tags, if possible. Use the Paragraph menu's Remove Tag command to eliminate tags you're not using. Also, use the Paragraph menu's Tab Setting command and turn off tabs that you don't need. Eliminate leaders by changing the Tab Display setting in that same dialog box to Shown as Open Space (rather than Shown as Leader Char) to create larger Ventura chapters.

You can also eliminate resident programs that may be operating when you use Ventura. There may be resident programs that are set in place when you start the computer. If so, check your AUTOEXEC.BAT file to dismantle them. It would also be helpful to acquire additional memory. Increase the standard DOS memory to the maximum 640K and add additional memory with a RAM drive (see Appendix B).

As you can see, increasing the size of Ventura chapters to automate page numbering can come at a price. Be aware, too, that the larger the chapter, the more cumbersome it becomes to manipulate (and for you to remember where material is located). Weigh all these factors carefully as you decide how to construct your documents.

USING FOOTNOTES

Compared to its handling of page numbering, Ventura's handling of footnotes is quite simple and straightforward. There are three steps to creating footnotes. First you turn the footnote system on and indicate how you want the footnotes to appear. Then, you must insert *footnote references* into the text of your document. Finally, for each footnote, you provide the *text of footnote* as it appears at the bottom of the page. Ventura places the footnote text below the standard text and above any footer that you specify.

SETTING FOOTNOTES ON

To turn on footnote operations, use the Page menu and click Footnote Settings. You'll see the dialog box displayed in Figure 11.22.

Using the Usage & Format grouping, indicate whether you want Ventura to number the footnotes from the start of each page, using numbers or user-defined strings, or from the start of each chapter. *User-defined strings* are symbols that you provide for indicating footnotes. In the User-Defined Strings grouping, you specify the symbols you want Ventura to use. Defaults are the asterisks and plus signs indicated in Figure 11.22.

For the Start With # setting, you can regulate the number Ventura should start footnotes with. Normally, you would use 1. Even if you link chapters into a publication, footnote numbering usually begins with 1 for each chapter, so there would be no need to adjust this setting.

The Number Template indicates how Ventura should display the number at the bottom of the page. You can type in three characters, using the number symbol to represent the footnote number (or other reference mark). For instance, if you enter

```
#.
```

for Number Template, Ventura will print the number at the bottom followed by a period. Thus the first footnote number would appear as

```
1.
```

If you enter

```
(#)
```

for Number Template, Ventura would print the first number at the bottom as

```
(1)
```

Note that this template only affects the number at the bottom of the page. It has no effect on the number as it appears in the text of the document.

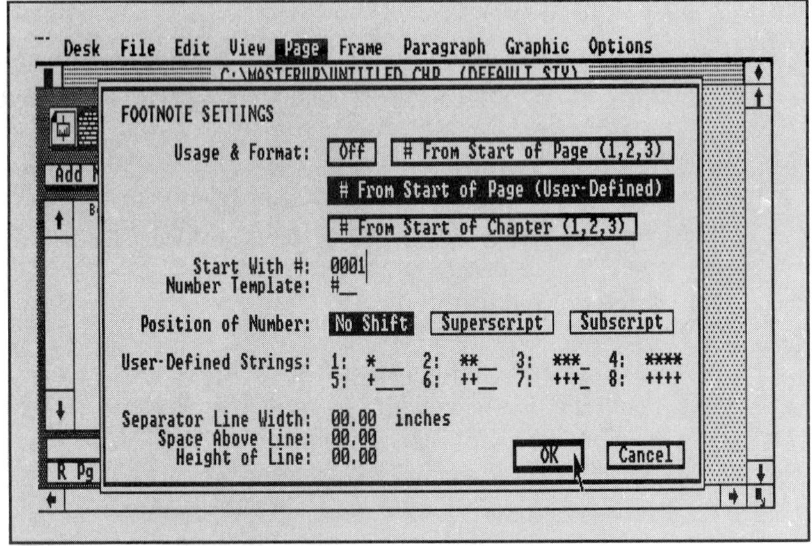

Figure 11.22: The Page Menu's Footnote Settings Dialog Box

The next setting, Position of Number, controls only the number in the text and has no effect on the number at the bottom. By clicking Superscript or Subscript you can position the number shifted above or below other text, respectively.

A *separator line* is a horizontal rule which separates the text of footnotes at the bottom of the page from the rest of the text on the page. By inserting values you create the line. Separator Line Width specifies the length of the line from left to right. Space Above Line is the distance from the text area to the line. Height of Line represents the line's thickness from top to bottom.

INSERTING FOOTNOTES

Once you've provided the footnote settings you can insert footnotes into the text. To do that, activate the Text mode and position the keyboard cursor at the proper spot in the text. Then use the Edit menu and click Insert Footnote. When you do, no dialog box will appear. Instead, Ventura will immediately insert the footnote number or other reference mark into position. At the same time, the corresponding reference mark will appear at the bottom of the page, as will any separator line that you've specified along with the words

Text of Footnote

Simply delete these words just as you would any normal text, and replace them with the text you want for your footnote.

Figure 11.23 shows how the screen looks after inserting a footnote and moving the keyboard cursor to the left one character. Since the cursor is to the left of the footnote reference, the word

Footnote

appears in the Current box on the Side-bar. The text of footnote appears in conjunction with a separator line.

The words *Text of Footnote* should be replaced with the actual footnote text: for example, *Also known as the File Selector.* To do this, follow these steps:

1. Drag the mouse across *Text of footnote*, thus darkening it.
2. Press the Del key.
3. Type in the actual footnote text.

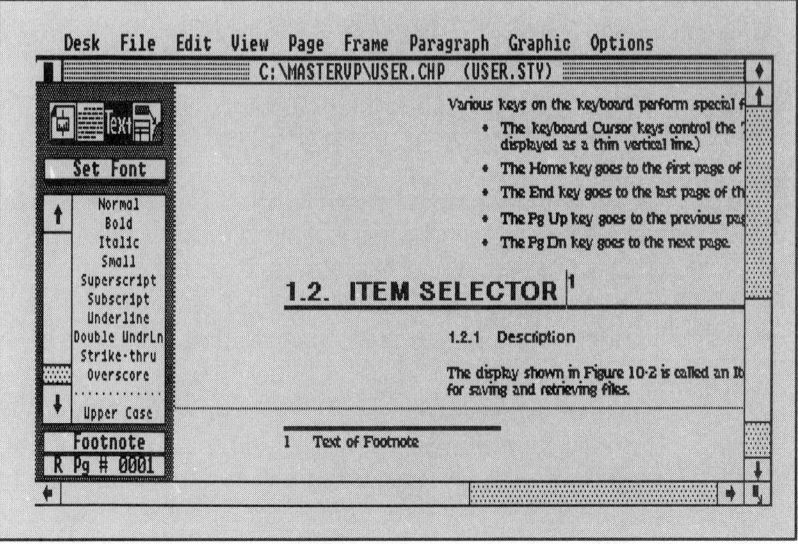

Figure 11.23: A Footnote Inserted in Text

The text of the footnote is automatically tagged as Z_FNOT ENTRY. The reference number at the bottom is tagged as Z_FNOT #. These are both generated tags. To change their settings, use the Paragraph mode and select their paragraphs at the bottom of the page. For instance, to lessen the distance that the text of footnote is displaced from the number, use the Paragraph menu's Spacing command and decrease the In From Left setting.

PRINTING A PUBLICATION

Once you've created a publication you can print it. The printing procedure for publications is very similar to that used for printing an individual chapter. Be careful if your publication has special needs such as page numbers, an index, or a table of contents. Before you print, be sure to check the sections in this chapter that cover those features.

To print a publication, follow these steps:

1. Use the Multi-Chapter Operations dialog box.
2. Open the appropriate publication file. (&EXAMPLE.PUB is the only sample publication file Ventura provides.)
3. Click the Print command. You'll see the Print Information dialog box, which looks just like it does when displayed with the File menu's To Print command (see Figure 11.24).
4. Set the print information you desire and click OK to print the publication.

The Multi-Chapter category in this dialog box will usually ghost with multichapters, just as it does with a single chapter. It will only appear fully when you've used the Options menu's Set Printer Info and specified Output To Filename. (Chapter 6 examines this procedure.) If so, you have a choice of combining all chapters in one output file or locating each chapter in a separate output file. Once you give the OK, Ventura will ask you to provide a name for the output. If you click Each in Separate File, Ventura will add sequential extensions to the name you specify for the output. The first file is labeled with C00 and the others in turn with C01, C02, C03, and so on. If

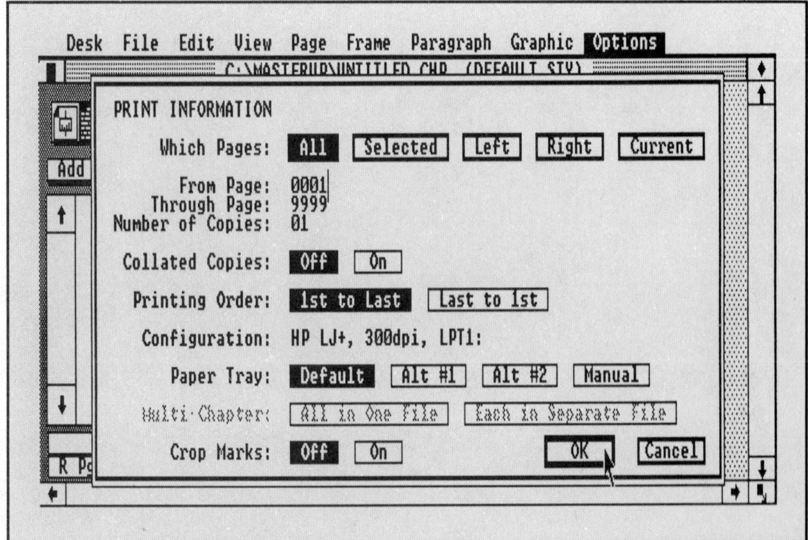

Figure 11.24: The Dialog Box Displayed Using the Multi-Chapter Print Command

you plan to output to disk in this fashion, it would be wise to place all your publication's front matter into one chapter, which would become the C00 file. Then chapter numbers will agree with output file numbers; Chapter 1 would become the C01 file, Chapter 2 would become the C02 file, and so on.

Effective use of other programs with Ventura can expedite the work you perform on extensive projects. In the next chapter we'll look at how other programs work with Ventura.

CHAPTER TWELVE

Using Other Programs with Ventura

ONE OF THE KEY FEATURES OF VENTURA IS ITS ABILITY to work with a wide variety of software—especially word processors—for entering text. Rather than attempting to do all things for all people with its text editor, Ventura's creators instead chose to coordinate many word processing standards. That way, you can choose the best word processing package for your job or continue to use the software that you are used to. With Version 1.1 in particular, Ventura's support is so extensive that most users find themselves immediately comfortable using their own familiar software.

Traditional publishing involves the talents of at least three types of persons: writers, editors, and typographers. With Ventura, you can perform all three of these jobs yourself. On the other hand, you may find it helpful to separate all three tasks or combine one or two. As we examine the work you do with text in this chapter, we'll see how people working in these different roles can use Ventura and supported programs.

Ventura's support of the major word processors means that it is possible to have the power of a full-featured word processor of your choice as you enter and revise the material. At the same time, you can have the material carry immediately over to Ventura. Much of the current desktop-publishing software has the ability to use text that has been saved in various word processed formats; once it enters the desktop-publishing system, however, there's no going back. You can no longer use the original word processing package to examine the text or to edit it.

Ventura, however, is quite a pioneer in creating a system that not only recognizes a variety of formats, but *saves* the original text in the original file in the same word processing format with which it was created. What's more, if you don't like that format, you can change it to another.

Even if Ventura does not fully support your word processor, you can still enter and edit text using ASCII format. The rules for this format differ from the rules for standard text in supported word processors. We'll look first at using supported word processors, then we'll examine the ASCII method.

USING SUPPORTED WORD PROCESSORS

As you compose your document, there are two ways that you can format it. As we've seen, you can use the various Ventura commands to specify text attributes, apply paragraph tags, lay out pages, create frames, and so on. Although page layout and frame manipulation must be handled with Ventura, there is another way to format text and paragraphs: you can use your word processor to provide the format information. This technique is known as *preformatting.*

METHODS OF PREFORMATTING

When you enter the text for a document, there are two ways that you can preformat it. First, if Ventura supports your word processor, you can preformat some text attributes by using the formatting operations that are built into your word processor. For italics, boldface, underlines, and some other straightforward text attributes, this means that you can create them using the same system or user interface (the word processor) that you've already mastered.

When you use Ventura to make alterations in the word processed files you create, Ventura uses the word processor's own codes to enter the formats into the text. This means that when you look again at the text file with the word processor, you'll see those features that you formatted with Ventura incorporated.

Be aware, however, that you should only use this approach with effects that are to be local in nature. Use them only on short passages, no more than a paragraph long. For more lasting effects or those that are to be repeated regularly, enter codes for paragraph tags.

This point brings us to the other way you can specify formatting in the word processor: you can enter Ventura code words and symbols directly into the word processed text. Once these codes are entered, Ventura will recognize them and understand the information they contain. You can use these codes for local effects just as you do your word processor's commands.

More importantly, though, you can use codes to tag paragraphs as you do in Ventura. Assign a tag name with the word processor and, once the paragraph is in a Ventura chapter, it will receive the attributes that you set up for the corresponding tag on the style sheet. In addition, you can use codes to enter special kinds of text, such as index references and footnote text.

ENTERING TEXT WITH A WORD PROCESSOR

When using your word processor to create Ventura files, you may find it helpful to think of your word processor in a different way. Rather than the fully functional formatting and layout software that it usually is, think of your word processor simply as a data entry device. You will use it primarily to indicate the text for a document. You don't lay out and format displayed material. The formatting that you do indicate is in the form of directions and codes that Ventura translates into the real thing.

Keep your text as simple as possible. For example, do not press the Tab key to indent the first line of your paragraphs. Let Ventura shape the paragraph by providing a first line indent when you specify that for the paragraph's tag. Likewise, don't use the word processor to create indented paragraphs, as is the practice for extended quotations. Handle that format within Ventura.

Do not attempt to right-justify text. Depending on the word processor, doing so could cause you to waste your time or wreak havoc on the Ventura document that contains the file. The same is true for centering. Don't center text; let a Ventura tag accomplish that.

If you will be entering tables, don't attempt to format them with your word processor. Be certain that you understand the different kinds of tables you can create with Ventura (see Chapter 9), and read the section on tables later in this chapter.

When entering text, you need only press the Space bar once after a period or colon. In most typing and word processing applications, there are usually two spaces after a sentence or a colon. When typesetting, however, two spaces create too much space, making for loose lines of text. When Ventura imports text with two spaces like this, it will display the second space as a nonstandard space. This is indicated by a lazy (upward-pointing) bracket (␣). This conversion also takes place when you save and retrieve a document with Ventura. When you see this symbol after the end of a sentence, it's wise to delete it.

With text at the end of a paragraph, place the Return that ends the paragraph immediately after the period or other visible character that ends the sentence. Do not place a space after the period and then enter the Return. Doing so sometimes causes Ventura to create an unnecessary additional line in the paragraph.

Press the Return key only once between each paragraph. Once you provide a tag for the paragraph, you will be able to indicate the amount of space between paragraphs. Suppose, however, that as an editor you receive material from a writer that has two Returns between paragraphs. Fortunately, you don't have to go through the file and remove the extra Returns one by one. Ventura has a special code that will perform that tedious job for you. At the very beginning of the file, type

```
@PARAFILTR ON
```

which stands for Paragraph Filter On. This instruction will cause Ventura to remove the extra Return when two follow in succession. Be aware, however, that when you save your document in Ventura, it will be saved without the extra return; that is, it will be saved with only one return between each paragraph. If you then view the file with your word processor, you may have trouble telling one paragraph from the next.

This brings us to another important point about text files. Once you create a text file for use with Ventura, you turn it over to Ventura. When you save Ventura documents, the program may perform all sorts of unusual acts to the related text file. The word processor margins may change, character attributes may disappear, and new code words may show up. Therefore, if you want to use the material that's in your document for some other application, don't assign the original file to Ventura. Instead, use a copy of the file.

To recap, here are the important points to bear in mind when you use a word processor to enter text for Ventura:

- Do not set up margins and other page formats.
- Do not indent paragraphs.
- Do not center or justify text.
- Do not format tables completely.

- Insert only one space after a period or colon.
- Hit Return only once after each paragraph.
- Enter only local formatting, no longer than a paragraph.

Figure 12.1 shows how you would enter the initial text for the USER.CHP document (originally called &TDOC-P1.CHP) that we've been examining in the last few chapters. (Of course, the text for this document has already been entered.) Each paragraph symbol (¶) indicates where you would press the Return key.

ENTERING CODES FOR PARAGRAPH TAGS

As you can see from Figure 12.1, all the text is the same. How does Ventura know which text is a headline, subheading, and so on? The answer is that, as the text file stands, Ventura wouldn't. If you were to load the file into Ventura in this condition, you'd see it all formatted as body text. You could then apply tags to format the paragraphs. Doing so would insert special codes into the text file, which is how Ventura keeps track of which tags have been assigned to which paragraphs. However, you can assign the same codes using your word processor.

Paragraph tagging codes are placed at the beginning of the paragraph that they apply to. They begin with the At symbol (@), followed by the name of the tag, a space, an equal sign (=), and another space. The name of the tag is usually in uppercase, but this convention is not required by Ventura.

Thus, for instance, the first paragraph in our example consists of the heading *USER INTERFACE*. It should be tagged as a Chapter Head. To apply this tag, you'd type

```
@CHAPTER HEAD = USER INTERFACE
```

If you then looked at the file in Ventura, you'd see *USER INTERFACE* formatted with the Chapter Head tag. Any paragraph attributes you set up for that tag would be applied to the heading.

```
USER INTERFACE¶
WYSIWYG¶
Ventura Publisher is designed to provide What You See (on
the screen) Is What You Get printed (WYSIWYG).  This means
that the computer display should match as closely as
possible, at all times, what you will see on the final
printed page.  Of course, the difference between the
technology used to display a page on a CRT screen, and the
technologies used to print a page on a laser printer or
typesetter, do create some unavoidable differences.  In
particular, because the computer CRT screen cannot produce
anywhere near the same resolution of a printer or
typesetter, and because what is displayed is shown in a
different aspect ratio (height to width ratio), the space
between words and between lines may appear to be bigger or
smaller than the printed page under certain circumstances.
Several thin ruling lines, with little space between, may
show on the screen as one thick line.¶
Keyboard Keys¶
Various keys on the keyboard perform special functions:¶
The keyboard Cursor keys control the Text Cursor (The text
cursor is displayed as a thin vertical line.)¶
The Home key goes to the first page of the document.¶
The End key goes to the last page of the document.¶
The Pg Up key goes to the previous page.¶
The Pg Dn key goes to the next page.¶
ITEM SELECTOR ¶
Description¶
The display shown in Figure 10-2 is called an Item Selector.
The Item Selector is used for saving and retrieving files.¶
Application¶
The Item Selector allows you to save and retrieve files by
pointing to the file name, or by typing the file name.¶
The Item Selector also provides a simple way to move between
various DOS subdirectories (sometimes called folders) where
text, Line Art, Image, chapter, and publication files may be
stored.¶
Finally, the Item Selector automatically filters the files
displayed so that you need only search for files which match
specified criteria.  For instance, only chapter files (which
are stored with a file extension CHP) are displayed when
loading or saving chapters.  The method for filtering the
files to be displayed follows standard DOS conventions,
including wildcard characters (e.g. * and ?).  These filters
can be changed by placing the text cursor on the Directory
line and typing a new filter name.  Figure 10-2 shows the
filter set to only display chapter (CHP) files that are
contained in the subdirectory called TYPESET.¶
Pointing to the desired file name, holding the mouse
stationary, and pressing the mouse button twice, with little
hesitation between each depression double-click, is
equivalent to selecting the file name and then selecting
OK.¶

If you only need one or two symbols within a paragraph, then
Tag the paragraph with a non-symbol typeface, and select the
one or two characters you wish to change to a symbol, and
change them using the Font Settings button.  For instance,
to put a p in the formula¶
pr2¶
type the letter p, then select this letter and use the Font
Settings button to change this one letter to a symbol font.¶
Function  Key¶
Bring to Front        ^A¶
Copy           Shift Del¶
Cut            Del¶
Enlarged View         ^E¶
Fill Attributes          ^F¶
Frame Setting Function   ^U ¶
```

Figure 12.1: An Unformatted Document Entered with a Word Processor

IMPORTANT

When you enter a tag name to preformat like this, the At symbol must be the first character in the paragraph. Do not place anything, including space or tab characters, before the At symbol.

Since the At symbol is a special flag to Ventura, you must use a special approach if you ever need to use an At symbol as a literal at the beginning of a paragraph. To have one At symbol actually appear in text, you must type *two* At symbols together (@@).

Now consider what happens when you don't insert tag codes with a word processor. If you simply left the paragraph alone in the word processor and then applied the tag within the Ventura document, the effect on the text file would be the same as preformatting. Upon opening the file with your word processor you would see the same code in place, just as if you had typed it in yourself.

If you look at Figure 12.2, you can see how the file is coded on your disk. Look at the first line and you see the tag code and then the text that appears in that paragraph: USER INTERFACE. Other tag names appear along the left edge: MAJOR HEADING, MINOR HEADING, BULLET, WARNING, and so on. These are the same tag names that you would see in the Side-bar's Assignment list when the Paragraph mode is active.

After the text for the first heading, there is another code. This is a code for an index entry. The less than symbol (<) indicates the beginning of the code. This is followed by $I, the code that flags index entries. The words that follow, *User interface*, are the entry for the index, as discussed in Chapter 11. These are the words you would enter in the Primary Key field with the Edit menu's Insert/Edit Index command.

Table 12.1 shows the codes you can use with your word processor to insert special text for various Ventura formatting features. Likewise, these are the codes that are inserted in your word processed text file when you use their equivalent commands in Ventura.

Note that there is a code for Hidden text. Use this code for text that you want to see with the word processor but that you don't want to appear in the Ventura document. Such text is used primarily by writers to leave themselves notes. It can also be used to send notes back and forth between writers and editors.

```
@CHAPTER HEAD = USER INTERFACE<$Iuser interface>
@MAJOR HEADING = <$&WYSIWYG[v]>WYSIWYG
<$IProblem;Can't print what's on
screen><$IWYSIWYG;Defined>Ventura Publisher is designed to
provide What You See (on the screen) Is What You Get printed
(WYSIWYG).  This means that the computer display should
match as closely as possible, at all times, what you will
see on the final printed page.  Of course, the difference
between the technology used to display a page on a CRT
screen, and the technologies used to print a page on a laser
printer or typesetter, do create some unavoidable
differences.  In particular, because the computer CRT screen
cannot produce anywhere near the same resolution of a
printer or typesetter, and because what is displayed is
shown in a different <$IAspect ratio>aspect ratio (height to
width ratio), the space between words and between lines may
appear to be bigger or smaller than the printed page under
certain circumstances.  Several thin ruling lines, with
little space between, may show on the screen as one thick
line.
@MINOR HEADING = Keyboard Keys
Various keys on the keyboard perform special functions:
@BULLET = The keyboard Cursor <$ICursor keys><$IText
editing;Cursor keys>keys control the Text Cursor (The text
cursor is displayed as a thin vertical line.)
@BULLET = The Home <$IHome key><$IText editing;Home key>key
goes to the first page of the document.
@BULLET = The End <$IEnd key><$IText editing;End key>key
goes to the last page of the document.
@BULLET = The Pg Up <$IPage up key><$IText editing;Page up
key>key goes to the previous page.
@BULLET = The Pg Dn <$IPage down key><$IText editing;Page
down key>key goes to the next page.
@MAJOR HEADING = ITEM SELECTOR <$IItem
selector;Operation><$ISaving files><$ILoading files>
@MINOR HEADING = Description
The display shown in Figure 10-2 is called an Item Selector.
The Item Selector is used for saving and retrieving files.
@MINOR HEADING = Application
The Item Selector allows you to save and retrieve files by
pointing to the file name, or by typing the file name.
The Item Selector also provides a simple way to move between
various DOS subdirectories (sometimes called folders) where
text, Line Art, Image, chapter, and publication files may be
stored.
Finally, the Item Selector automatically <169>filters<170>
the files displayed so that you need only search for files
which match specified criteria.  For instance, only chapter
files (which are stored with a file extension CHP) are
displayed when loading or saving chapters.  The method for
filtering the files to be displayed follows standard DOS
conventions, including wildcard characters (e.g. * and ?).
These filters can be changed by placing the text cursor on
the Directory line and typing a new filter name.  Figure 10-
2 shows the filter set to only display chapter (CHP) files
that are contained in the subdirectory called TYPESET.
@WARNING = <$IShortcut;Mouse double-click><$IMouse;Double-
click>Pointing to the desired file name, holding the mouse
stationary, and pressing the mouse button twice, with little
hesitation between each depression <169>double-click<170>,
is equivalent to selecting the file name and then selecting
OK.
If you only need one or two symbols within a paragraph, then
Tag the paragraph with a non-symbol typeface, and select the
one or two characters you wish to change to a symbol, and
change them using the Font Settings button.  For instance,
to put a <F128M>p<F255D> in the formula
@SYSTEM PROMPT = <F128M>p<F255D>r2
type the letter p, then select this letter and use the Font
Settings button to change this one letter to a symbol font.
@TABLE HEAD = Function   Key
@TABLE ITEM = Bring to Front         ^A
@TABLE ITEM = Copy              Shift Del
@TABLE ITEM = Cut               Del
@TABLE ITEM = Enlarged View          ^E
@TABLE ITEM = Fill Attributes        ^F
@TABLE ITEM = Frame Setting Function     ^U
```

Figure 12.2: The Text File with Paragraph Tags

FORMAT	**EQUIVALENT VENTURA MENU**	**COMMAND/ DIALOG BOX**	**TEXT INSERT**
Anchor for Frame—Fixed, On Same Page As Anchor	Edit	Insert/Edit Anchor	<&$*Anchor name*>
Anchor for Frame—Relative, Below Anchor Line			<&$*Anchor name*[v]>
Anchor for Frame—Relative, Above Anchor Line			<&$*Anchor name*[^]>
Footnote	Edit	Insert Footnote	<&F *Text of footnote*>
Index Entry with Primary Entry Only	Edit	Insert/Edit Index	<&I*Primary entry*>
Index Entry with Secondary Entry Too			<&I*Primary entry;Secondary entry*>

Table 12.1: Codes for Inserting Text

FORMAT	EQUIVALENT VENTURA MENU	COMMAND/ DIALOG BOX	TEXT INSERT
Index Entry with Sort Keys Specified			<$I*Primary entry*[*Primary sort key*]; *Secondary entry*[*Secondary sort key*]>
Index Entry with See			<$S*Primary entry*[*Primary sort key*]; *Secondary entry*[*Secondary sort key*]>
Index Entry with See Also			<$A*Primary entry*[*Primary sort key*]; *Secondary entry*[*Secondary sort key*]>
Hidden Text (for display in the word processor but not in Ventura)	(None)		<$!*Hidden text*>

Table 12.1: Codes for Inserting Text (continued)

When tabs and returns are showing, Ventura marks the location of hidden text by displaying a small temperature degree symbol, as it does with index entries and footnotes. This mark does not show in the printed version of a document. When the keyboard cursor is positioned to the left of this marker, Ventura displays the words *Hidden Text* in the Current box. There is no equivalent means of entering this code with Ventura.

Also be aware that, because of Ventura's special use of the < and > characters, the same "two-for-one" rule mentioned for the At symbol applies to them. That is, if you want one < to appear, you must type << when entering the symbol with your word processor.

ENTERING TEXT ATTRIBUTES

You can also enter and see codes for text attributes. In fact, all text attributes that appear on the Side-bar in the Text mode have equivalent corresponding codes (except, of course, Upper Case, Capitalize, and Lower Case.) Even attributes that you assign with the Set Font button can be duplicated.

Table 12.2 shows the codes for the various items on the Text mode's Assignment list and elsewhere. It also shows how to insert the codes using the three word processors we'll examine in this chapter. Note that you can insert the Ventura codes in the first column with your word processor even if the effect you desire is not supported by the word processor you're using.

If you use Ventura to create one of these effects and you're using a supported word processor, the codes won't appear in the word processed document. Instead, they'll be converted into the word processor's version of the effect. Thus if your supported word processor shows underlining, text you underline with the Text mode's Assignment list will appear underlined when you look at it with your word processor. You will only see the <U> code, beginning the underlining, if your word processor can't produce the effect.

The code you enter has two purposes: it indicates what the effect is and starts the effect. Text attribute effects continue in the text until the end of the paragraph or until they encounter the Normal code, <D>, whichever comes first.

There are other codes that can be entered and stored in text files, affecting the specialized typographical features available in the Edit mode. We'll examine typography and these codes in Chapter 13 and Appendix E.

USING SEARCH AND REPLACE

You can use your word processor's search and replace capabilities to correct a variety of problems you may encounter with text files. Using these commands can be especially helpful to an editor, for example, who is receiving text from other sources. Consider the problem cited earlier in which a writer inserts two spaces at the end of

Code	**Name on Assignment List**	**Microsoft Word**	**WordStar**	**WordPerfect**
<D>	Normal	Alt-Spacebar		
<B>	Bold	Alt-B	Ctrl-PB	F6
<I>	Italic	Alt-I		
<S>	Small			
< ^ >	Superscript	Alt-Plus	Ctrl-PT	Shift-F1, 1
<v>	Subscript	Alt-Minus	Ctrl-PV	Shift-F2, 2
<U>	Underline	Alt-U	Ctrl-PS	F8
< = >	Double Underline			
<X>	Strike-thru	Alt-S	Ctrl-PX	Alt F5, 4
<O>	Overscore			
<->	Discretionary Hypen (Ctrl-Hyphen)	Ctrl-Hyphen	Ctrl-OE	Ctrl-Hyphen
<N>	NoBreak Space (Ctrl-Spacebar)	Ctrl-Spacebar	Ctrl-PO	Home, Spacebar
<R>	Line Break (Ctrl-Return)	Shift-Return		

Table 12.2: Code Equivalents of Text Attributes on the Text Mode's Assignment List

a sentence instead of one. You could have your word processor find all occurrences of two spaces and replace them with one.

You can also use the word processor to replace text characters entered from the keyboard with codes for special typographical characters. Appendix E contains a list of these codes. In Ventura, you can use the Alt key in combination with one of these codes to enter characters that are unavailable on the keyboard. To enter these codes in your word processor, enclose them in the less than and greater than characters. For instance, the typewriter method of typing a dash is to press the hyphen twice. In typography, however, it's preferable to enter an *em dash*. Use your word processor to search for two dashes and replace them with a single em dash (code <197>).

Another use for the search and replace feature is inserting typographical quotation marks. The characters on the PC keyboard duplicate that of a typewriter. Thus, the same character is used for a beginning quotation mark as for ending. Ventura, however, has the ability to display true typographic quotation marks, in which the opening mark points upward (“) and the closing quote points down (”). Entering the codes <169> and <170>, respectively, in the word processor will cause Ventura to display these quotes.

If a writer has used the double quote key for beginning and ending quotes, clean up the problem first by having the word processor search for a space followed by a quote and replace these two characters with a space followed by the code <169>. This will replace all the opening quotes. Only closing quotes will then be left. Use the search and replace feature again to find all remaining quotes and replace each with code <170>.

You can also use search and replace to recreate some spacing in order to make the text more readable in the word processor, after Ventura's @PARAFILTR ON feature has stripped away the second Return between each paragraph. Use your word processor to search for one Return and replace it with two Returns.

MACRO GENERATORS

If you're inserting a lot of coding in a word processed file, you will undoubtedly wish to use some kind of macro-generating capability to enter the codes. When using such a facility, you simply issue some quick keystrokes (defined by you), and the macro program enters the entire code in its place. The result is increased efficiency and accuracy.

Macros are especially helpful in tagging paragraphs. Thus, assume that you have a tag for Chapter Head. Rather than typing in *@CHAPTER HEAD* = each time you need to tag a paragraph, you might set up a macro to insert it by typing Alt-CH, or Esc C, or Ctrl-C, depending on the system.

Most popular word processors now possess some ability to create macros. Besides being called a macro generator, this feature goes by a wide variety of names: a keyboard enhancer, a glossary, a key code, or shorthand.

There are also resident programs like SmartKey that perform the same function but with greater ability. Even if your word processor does have a macro generator, you may wish to consider a keyboard utility. Because the program is resident, you can use it with Ventura as well as your word processor. Of course, you wouldn't use it to insert tag names in Ventura, where you simply use the mouse or function keys to tag. However, such programs can be handy for inserting repeated text, such as a company letterhead.

Be aware that resident programs use computer memory, which can decrease the size of Ventura chapters. As such, it's important to use one that goes easy on the memory; SmartKey is good in this regard.

USING ASCII TEXT FOR NONSUPPORTED WORD PROCESSORS

Even if your word processor isn't supported by Ventura, you can use it by creating ASCII text. ASCII stands for the American Standard Code for Information Interchange. It's a standard that is supported not only by almost all word processors, but also by database management systems, electronic spreadsheets, and other programs. ASCII text is sometimes known as unformatted text, print-to-disk files, nondocuments, and DOS text files.

Usually, entering text in ASCII format requires that you press the Return key at the end of each line. This being the case, how does Ventura differentiate between the end of an ASCII line and the end of an ASCII paragraph? The answer is that Ventura looks for and expects two Returns between paragraphs. It only does this with ASCII text. Therefore, if you want to use ASCII format, you must place two Returns between each paragraph.

Unlike supported word processors, though, using ASCII is generally a one way operation. If your text doesn't have a Return at the end of each line, once you start to edit and save it with Ventura, Ventura will go ahead and add the format. The resulting text is hard to work with in the word processor.

WordStar format is closely akin to ASCII. However, when importing files in WordStar format, Ventura doesn't look for two Returns to signal the end of a paragraph and doesn't insert Returns at the end of each line. Therefore, you may be able to import text to Ventura in WordStar format when it's in ASCII style except for the two Returns at the ends of paragraphs. Doing so would keep Ventura from adding the unwanted Returns at the ends of lines.

POPULAR WORD PROCESSORS

Now let's examine some of the most popular word processing systems and see how they operate with Ventura. We won't look at all of those that operate with Ventura, but by examining these few, you should get an idea of the various ways that word processors may work with Ventura text files.

MICROSOFT WORD

Among popular word processors, Microsoft Word may be the one best suited for use with Ventura. Word's approach to formatting text is similar to that used by Ventura, allowing you to prepare text efficiently for use in Ventura. You can enter text into Word in ways that allow you to work easily with the text as you're preparing it. Additionally, Word has a Glossary feature that you can use to insert paragraph tags.

Some of Word's formatting is applied to text by the paragraph, similar to the way tags operate in Ventura. In addition, Word has its own style sheets that operate like Ventura's to coordinate documents and apply formatting consistently. Although you cannot convert Word's style sheets to Ventura format, they make it easier to enter and format text in Word.

For instance, we mentioned how conforming to Ventura's formatting can make your word processed text difficult to read. First, Ventura prefers text paragraphs formatted without a tab character in the first line. Second, although you can put two Returns after a paragraph in your original text file and then place the @ PARAFILTR ON code at the beginning of the file, when you save the document with Ventura, the extra Return will be gone. Without a first-line indent or an extra blank line between paragraphs, paragraphs appear to run together.

How, then, can you keep paragraphs visually distinct in the word processing file? Word provides an answer with its style sheet. You can create a style sheet called NORMAL.STY that's applied to documents in the same directory automatically. After inserting a Standard Paragraph style (the default style for paragraphs) into the style sheet, you can specify the format, and it will be applied to paragraphs in Word automatically, just as Body Text is applied in Ventura documents. You can thus make the format add a first-line indent or additional space between paragraphs.

Word also has a feature called *hidden text*. Text formatted as hidden can be either seen or made temporarily invisible. As you prepare text files in Word, you can format Ventura commands as hidden text. That way you can see the text with or without the embedded Ventura commands. Unfortunately, once Ventura starts to work with the hidden text, it strips away the hidden format, so that if you use Word to examine the text later, you won't be able to hide the codes.

Figure 12.3 shows the sample file in Word, with Ventura commands formatted as hidden text. Notice how you can distinguish standard text, in bold, from the Ventura codes. Also notice, as the paragraph marks indicate, there is only one Return after each paragraph. Nonetheless, there is still space between the paragraphs, making them readable. In addition, each paragraph has the first line indented. Since this indent is created with a Word style sheet, and not the Tab key, there'll be no surprises when you load the text file in Ventura.

Figure 12.4 shows the same file, but with the command codes hidden. The small double-headed arrow indicates the location of the hidden text. Displaying these arrows, as well as the paragraph marks, is optional.

You can use Word's Glossary feature—a version of the macro generators discussed earlier—to enter the codes for tagging paragraphs and making special text entries. The glossary entries can be

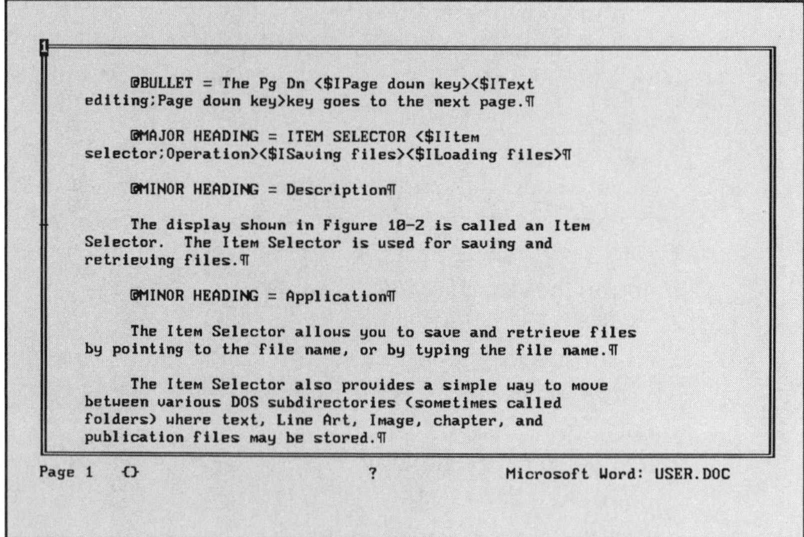

```
     @BULLET = The Pg Dn <$IPage down key><$IText
editing;Page down key>key goes to the next page.¶

     @MAJOR HEADING = ITEM SELECTOR <$IItem
selector;Operation><$ISaving files><$ILoading files>¶

     @MINOR HEADING = Description¶

     The display shown in Figure 10-2 is called an Item
Selector.  The Item Selector is used for saving and
retrieving files.¶

     @MINOR HEADING = Application¶

     The Item Selector allows you to save and retrieve files
by pointing to the file name, or by typing the file name.¶

     The Item Selector also provides a simple way to move
between various DOS subdirectories (sometimes called
folders) where text, Line Art, Image, chapter, and
publication files may be stored.¶
Page 1   {}                    ?             Microsoft Word: USER.DOC
```

Figure 12.3: Ventura Codes in a Word Text File

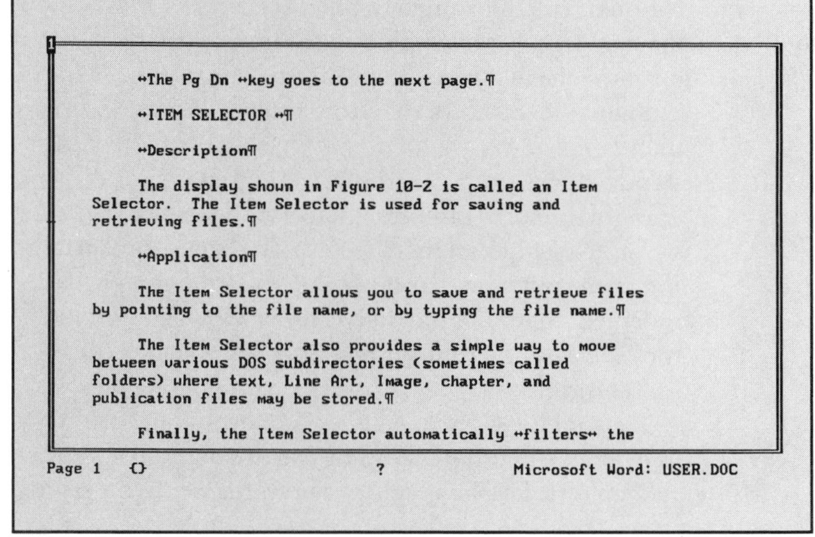

```
     ↔The Pg Dn ↔key goes to the next page.¶

     ↔ITEM SELECTOR ↔¶

     ↔Description¶

     The display shown in Figure 10-2 is called an Item
Selector.  The Item Selector is used for saving and
retrieving files.¶

     ↔Application¶

     The Item Selector allows you to save and retrieve files
by pointing to the file name, or by typing the file name.¶

     The Item Selector also provides a simple way to move
between various DOS subdirectories (sometimes called
folders) where text, Line Art, Image, chapter, and
publication files may be stored.¶

     Finally, the Item Selector automatically ↔filters↔ the
Page 1   {}                    ?             Microsoft Word: USER.DOC
```

Figure 12.4: A Word File with Ventura Codes Hidden

formatted as well, allowing you to apply the hidden text feature automatically. Another advantage of Word is that the glossary abbreviation you use to represent the Ventura code can be as short or as long as you like. Thus you can use abbreviations that make sense to you; for instance, you can use H1 for main headings, H2 for secondary headings, and so on. Or, if you prefer, you can use HEAD1, HEAD2, and HEAD3.

To create an ASCII text file with Word, save the file and when you do, indicate No for the Formatted setting. If the file was originally created as a standard Word document, this action will convert it to ASCII.

WORDSTAR

WordStar files have some peculiarities in dealing with Ventura. WordStar does not insert true tabs when you press the Tab key. Instead, it inserts five spaces. To insert true tabs with WordStar 4.0, you type Ctrl-PI or Ctrl-P Tab. With earlier versions, turn vari-tabs off by typing Ctrl-OV at the beginning of each work session and then use the Tab key. Also, with earlier versions you must remember to turn hyphen help off (with Ctrl-OH) before you start to edit. Likewise, turn justification off (with Ctrl-OJ) or WordStar will insert additional spaces into the document, making quite a mess. These last two procedures are unnecessary with WordStar 4.0, because the desirable settings are already in place by default.

Don't enter dot commands with WordStar. Ventura doesn't use them so they'll appear "as is" in your document, just like any other text.

WordStar 4.0 has a macro capability, called *shorthand,* which works quickly and efficiently. You gain access to it by pressing the Esc key within a document.

To create ASCII text in WordStar, open a new file by typing N for Nondocument at the opening menu. Be aware that opening an existing WordStar document in this manner will not convert it to ASCII format. To do that, you must "print" the output to a disk file. With WordStar 4.0 you do this by printing and entering the word ASCII as the name of the printer. This creates a file called ASCII.WS, which is the ASCII version of the file you specified.

WORDPERFECT

WordPerfect is straightforward in its use with Ventura. The general principles we discussed with regard to word processors apply to work you do with WordPerfect.

To create an ASCII file, use Text In/Out (Ctrl-F5). Use the resulting menu to save the file in DOS text file format.

DATABASE PROGRAMS

You can use Ventura's ability to work with ASCII text in conjunction with a database. Database management programs, such as dBASE III PLUS, can store large amounts of information in a highly structured fashion. A common desktop publishing operation is to use the records stored in such a system to publish a directory: for example, a listing of names and phone numbers. Ventura's ability to use codes embedded in ASCII text makes its use with a database program a natural, since most database programs can create ASCII text files, inserting the codes automatically.

To use an existing database with Ventura, proceed as follows:

1. Create and run a *report*, a database feature that processes information and creates output. The report should be designed to send its output into a text file.
2. Use Ventura to create a chapter.
3. Load and use the text file in the Ventura chapter just as you do any text file.
4. Print the Ventura chapter to obtain the final directory.

When you load the file, specify either ASCII or WordStar format, depending on how you want the returns formatted (as discussed earlier in the section "Using ASCII Text for Nonsupported Word Processors").

In the report design, specify codes for tags and other kinds of formatting as *constant* or *background* text within the layout of the report. This is text that doesn't change as the data is processed. Place *variables*, which indicate material that may change from one use to the next, where appropriate amidst the codes and other text.

Let's say that you are using the dBASE label generator to create a client directory (Figure 12.5). On the first line of each listing you want to have the client's first name (which you've assigned to the fname field), followed by the last name (assigned to lname). You want this line formatted with the tag called CLIENT NAME. In addition, you want the last name to appear in bold.

For the contents of this line in the label, you'd enter

'@CLIENT NAME = '+trim(fname)+' <B>',
trim(lname)+'<D>'

The Trim command keeps unwanted spaces from appearing when the names don't fill the field. The <B> starts the bold effect for the last name and the <D> discontinues it.

Eliminate blank lines between records on the report and set the left margin at zero. Remember, however, that you're only using the report to create a text file. Formatting effects such as spacing between paragraphs and indents from the left are created with tags with the Ventura chapter file.

When dealing with a large database, you may find it beneficial to restrict the number of paragraphs contained in the text file in order to

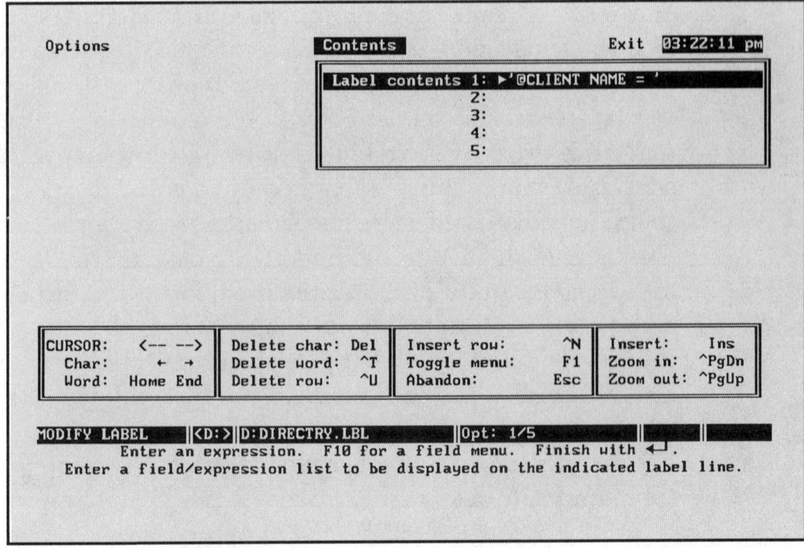

Figure 12.5: Using the dBASE Label Generator to Enter a Ventura Tag

speed operations. In Version 1.1, Ventura can accommodate approximately 48,000 paragraphs. Still, the fewer paragraphs you use, the better Ventura's performance will be.

To decrease the number of lines, insert a Line Break between information that you want on separate lines in the Ventura document but which is to receive the same paragraph tag. Then combine the information on the same line in your report. A Line Break is indicated by the code

<R>

Thus, let's say that you want a person's name, street address, and city on separate lines but similarly formatted. You want Ventura to consider these three items as a unit so you can change the spacing between one person's information and the next. To do that, you'd first enter the tag code for the paragraph (unless you want the paragraph treated as Body Text, in which case no code is necessary). Then you'd place the field for the first name, then the Line Break code, the street address field, another Line Break code, and the city field on the same line, with Return only at the end.

You can also use Ventura with a database for some mail-merge applications, such as personalized form letters. The general procedure for this involves making each page of a chapter hold a copy of an identical letter addressed to different people. To make the identical material appear on each page, create repeating frames to hold the constant text, such as the body of the letter. For the personalized material, create a text file containing alternating names and addresses, with each line separated by a return. Use the file-output techniques discussed earlier to create this file from the database. Then assign this file to the underlying-page frame. To cause each form letter to appear on a separate page, format the last paragraph of each person's information with a tag that has the Paragraph menu's Breaks command set for Page Break After. By using the techniques discussed earlier, you can automatically apply this tag to the each person's last paragraph as the output file is being created.

Now let's examine another type of data application: entering the text for a Ventura table.

ENTERING TEXT FOR TABLES USING A WORD PROCESSOR

Entering text for tables is easiest and surest if you simply use Ventura to do so. However, you can enter the text for your tables by using your word processor. The technique you use varies depending upon which method you use to create the table (see Chapter 9).

IMPORTANT

Entering table text with a word processor is very tricky, regardless of the technique you use to set up the table's format. If you must use the word processor, be very careful. Allow yourself enough time to proceed with care. Chapter 9 contains a detailed discussion of formatting tables.

USING TABS FOR TABLES

When you use the tab method for creating tables, each item in the table has a tab character between it and the next item on the same line. When you use the word processor to make table entries, you must insert tabs between each item in the table and the next item on the same line. Do not insert spaces and attempt to line up columns in the word processor that way. The distance a tab is set to travel in Ventura will undoubtedly be different from that set in your word processor, and the width of the spaces will probably be different as well. So these blank spaces will come back to haunt you when you work on tables in Ventura.

You don't need to adjust tab settings in your word processor at all. Just be certain to type in a Tab character between each table item. Most likely, the text in your word processor won't even line up in columns. This doesn't matter. As long as you insert the Tab characters correctly, you will be able to line up the columns in Ventura. For example, notice how the table at the end of Figures 12.1 and 12.2 appears, as shown in a text file. Compare these with how the table looks in the Ventura sample chapter, &TDOC-P1, shown in Appendix A.

Similarly, if you want to use leaders, do not enter leader characters, such as periods, between the items in the table; just enter the

Tab character. As long as you properly specify the leader in the paragraph's tag, leaders will appear in the Ventura document even though they don't show in the word processor.

When you insert a tab, you must be certain that your word processor is truly inserting a Tab character. Some, as we saw with WordStar, do not normally insert a Tab character, but instead simulate a Tab character by inserting multiple spaces. Spaces won't do for Tab characters in Ventura.

You can test your word processor on Tab character creation. To do this, enter the questionable Tab character with the word processor. Make the tab setting long enough so that it covers the distance of several spaces. Then, using the keys that move the cursor (probably the ← and → keys), move the cursor over the area covered by the tab. As you do so, if the cursor jumps from one side of the tab area to the other with one keystroke, it means the word processor is inserting one character, the Tab character. On the other hand, if each keystroke moves the cursor the distance of only one space, the word processor is inserting spaces to simulate a Tab character.

If you cannot get Tab characters into the word processed version of your text file, you must perform major surgery once the file is in Ventura. To make use of Ventura's ability to work with tabs, you must delete all the inappropriate spaces and replace them with Tab characters by pressing the Tab key.

Some other programs that "print" to disk, such as the / Print File command in Lotus 1-2-3, insert spaces as well. If you want to use the output in a Ventura tab table, you must replace the spaces as discussed. The only way you can use spaces as they are is by printing the table with a nonproportional font. In this case, you can't use Ventura to change various characteristics of the table, such as the width of columns, other than by inserting and removing spaces up and down the table.

USING COLUMN TAGS

If you enter the text for column tags in your word processor, don't attempt to create anything that resembles a table. Instead, just enter one standard paragraph after another, following the order of the table entries. Remember, table entries go left to right across the first row of entries, then down to the first item in the next row, then across that row from left to right, and so on.

Figure 12.6 shows the order of the paragraphs in the sample table we examined in Chapter 9. Remember, this table also has a Paragraph End character (that is, a Return character) tagged to create the horizontal lines. As indicated by the numbering in the figure, you must press a Return for each Return your file needs. Let's take a closer look at the sample's text file, shown in Figure 12.7.

Once you have entered your text for the table, you can use Ventura to tag it and so create a table by way of column tags. If, however, you use your word processor to assign tags to the paragraphs, the tag names must follow the same strict order as they do in the table. Thus, in the example, the first column entry is tagged as Col 1. So if you were to enter the first entry with your word processor, you'd begin by entering the tag code

```
@ COL 1 =
```

Then, you'd follow this code with the text for the first column. Hit Return only at the very end of the entire entry for the first row of the first column.

Note that this table is created using ASCII format. As such, you would enter a blank line between the paragraphs. In word processor format, the paragraph would have one Return only at the end, unless you used the @PARAFILTR ON feature at the beginning of the file.

Continuing with the demonstration, once you complete the first entry, on the next line you'd insert the tag code

```
@ COL 2 =
```

followed by text for the second entry in the first row of the table. In ASCII, the paragraph would again have two Returns at the end. You'd then continue in kind for the remaining columns.

In the sample printout, notice that the file has the code

```
@RULE =
```

This is the tag for the Paragraph End symbol with the Rule format. There's no text for the paragraph, but by itself the formatted Paragraph End symbol will create the horizontal line.

Title of this table

Header for Table	Next Column	Third Col.	Price
First Entry	The second column describes some features of the item called out in the first column. Notice that the text for the column is too wide to fit on one line. This type of style might be useful in a comparison chart where flowing text is used.	The third column might expound a bit on the second column. But the fourth column just holds a number, such as price.	$456
Second model.	The next column.	The second model compares quite favorably to the first model described above. There's not as much text here though.	$654
Entry #3	More descriptive text about entry number three. It's called WYSIWYG. It means that as you edit and modify, your screen shows you *exactly what you're going to get when you print it out. No surprises. It's all there in front of your eyes.*	Another column of text.	$66

Figure 12.6: The Order of Paragraphs Using Column Tags

```
@TITLE = Title of this table

@TABLE HEADER = Header for Table        Next Column      Third Col.       Price

@COL 1 = First Entry

@COL 2 = The second column describes some features of the item called
out in the first column. Notice that the text for the column is too
wide to fit on one line. This type of style might be useful in a comparison
chart where flowing text is used.

@COL 3 = The third column might expound a bit on the second column.
But the fourth column just holds a number, such as price.

@COL 4 = $456

@RULE =

@COL 1 = Second model.

@COL 2 = The next column.

@COL 3 = The second model compares quite favorably to the first model
described above. There's not as much text here though.

@COL 4 = $654

@RULE =

@COL 1 = Entry #3

@COL 2 = More descriptive text about entry number three. It's called
WYSIWYG.  It means that as you edit and modify, your screen shows
you <MI>exactly<N> what you're going to get when you print it out.  No
surprises.  It's all there in front of your eyes.

@COL 3 = Another column of text.

@COL 4 = $66

@RULE =
```

Figure 12.6: The Order of Paragraphs Using Column Tags

The Table Header tag uses tab settings to place a heading at the top of each column. One tab separates each of these items.

FRAME TEXT, BOX TEXT, AND FIGURE CAPTIONS

Lastly, let's look at using a word processor with CAP files. A chapter's CAP file has the same name as the chapter, but with a CAP extension. Ventura creates this file to hold all entries you make for the chapter's Frame Text, Box Text, and figure captions. As you may recall, Frame Text is text that you enter into a empty standard frame with the Text mode active. Frame Text, however, is not assigned to a standard file and displayed on the Assignment list when the Frame mode is active. Text for Box Text is also entered in Text mode. Boxes for Box Text are created in the Graphics mode.

You can work with a chapter's CAP file in your word processor, with two stipulations. First, always save it in ASCII format. For instance, you could use a spelling checker to check the CAP file and make corrections as long as the file is ASCII text when you are done. Ventura does not deal with other formats for the CAP file.

Second, when working with the CAP file, it's important not to mess with the Returns. Ventura uses the Returns it inserts to keep track of which entries go where in the document. So don't add any Returns and don't delete any. Changing them in the CAP file will cause incorrect placement of your entries in the chapter.

In the next and final chapter, we'll see how you can use advanced features of Ventura, many of them new with Ventura 1.1, to work with typographical elements in your documents.

CHAPTER THIRTEEN

Typographical Elements and Effects

TYPOGRAPHY IS THE CRAFT AND ART OF PLACING type and its equally important counterpart, spacing, on the printed page. As a craft, typography is utilitarian. You use it to disseminate information. Correct use of typography clues the reader in on the organization of the reading matter. It allows the reader to perceive the hierarchy of various subjects that are covered and the relation of text to pictures. As an art, typography makes the page aesthetically appealing and hence inviting. When typography is properly used, the reader learns with pleasure and ease.

Space is as much an element in a page's design as the type. Insufficient or poorly placed spacing may make the reader feel that the material is too dense to penetrate, and hence not worth the effort of reading. An inordinate amount of space, on the other hand, can cause text to appear to be lost on the page. As such, the material may seem to be without substance, causing the reader to question it even before reading it, or to assume the document is geared toward youngsters.

To disseminate information effectively, text on a page must remain readable. Do not allow design choices to thwart this end. Lines of text should be of an appropriate length, so that the eye does not lose its place when scanning the line. Text should not contain an inordinate amount of boldface or italics, making the page look heavy and defeating the purpose of these emphasizing elements.

IMPROVING A SAMPLE DOCUMENT

Ventura has some extraordinary typographic capabilities, but even a simple document can be enhanced using typographical elements properly. Consider the sample document and style sheet in the TYPESET directory, &NEWS-P3. The printed version of the document, as printed with the HP LaserJet, appears in Appendix A. It also appears as a full-page display in Figure 13.1. In this chapter, we'll see how we can improve this document using the various typographical elements available in Ventura.

First, let's look at the darkened text that appears on the screen. The text in the document is justified: the right edge of the text is flush

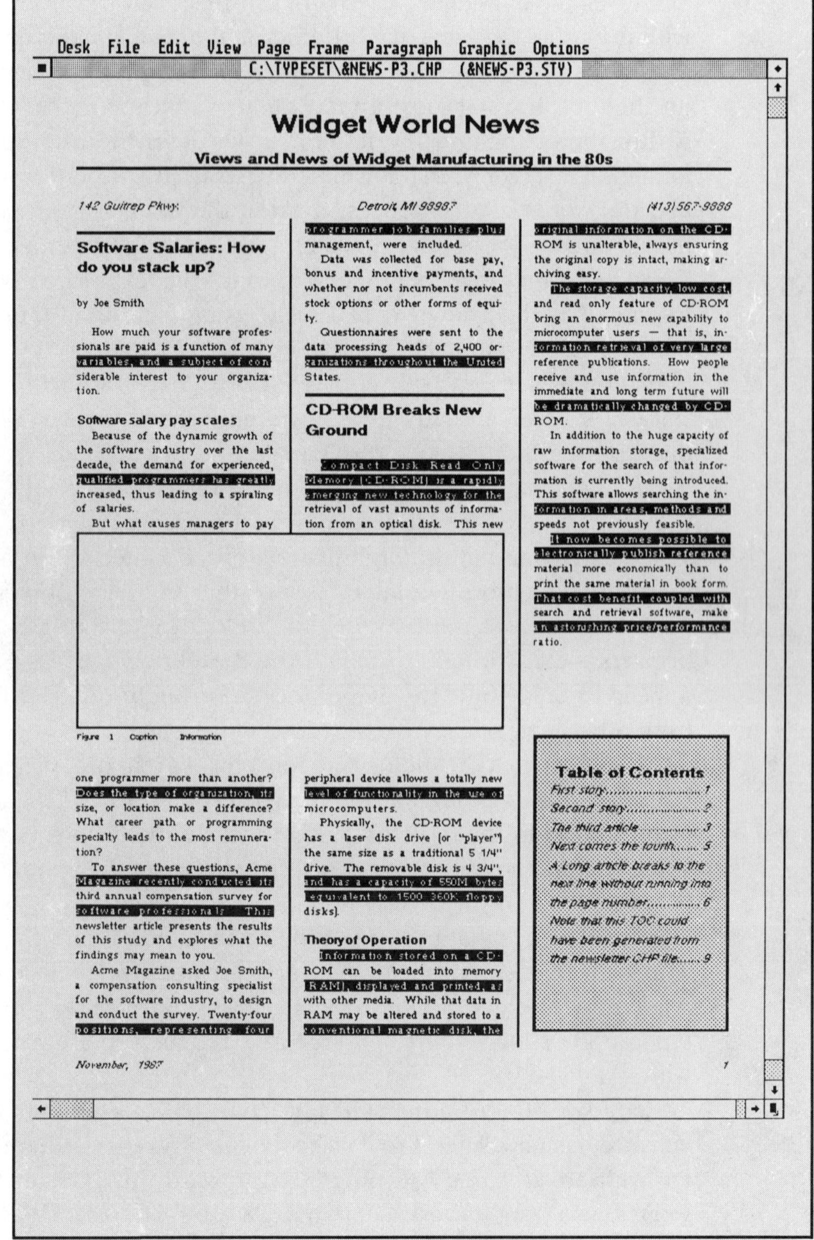

Widget World News

Views and News of Widget Manufacturing in the 80s

142 Guitrep Pkwy. Detroit, MI 98987 (413) 567-9888

Software Salaries: How do you stack up?

by Joe Smith

How much your software professionals are paid is a function of many variables, and a subject of considerable interest to your organization.

Software salary pay scales

Because of the dynamic growth of the software industry over the last decade, the demand for experienced, qualified programmers has greatly increased, thus leading to a spiraling of salaries.

But what causes managers to pay one programmer more than another? Does the type of organization, its size, or location make a difference? What career path or programming specialty leads to the most remuneration?

To answer these questions, Acme Magazine recently conducted its third annual compensation survey for software professionals. This newsletter article presents the results of this study and explores what the findings may mean to you.

Acme Magazine asked Joe Smith, a compensation consulting specialist for the software industry, to design and conduct the survey. Twenty-four positions, representing four programmer job families plus management, were included.

Data was collected for base pay, bonus and incentive payments, and whether nor not incumbents received stock options or other forms of equity.

Questionnaires were sent to the data processing heads of 2,400 organizations throughout the United States.

Figure 1 Caption Information

CD-ROM Breaks New Ground

Compact Disk Read Only Memory (CD-ROM) is a rapidly emerging new technology for the retrieval of vast amounts of information from an optical disk. This new peripheral device allows a totally new level of functionality in the use of microcomputers.

Physically, the CD-ROM device has a laser disk drive (or "player") the same size as a traditional 5 1/4" drive. The removable disk is 4 3/4", and has a capacity of 550M bytes equivalent to 1500 360K floppy disks).

Theory of Operation

Information stored on a CD-ROM can be loaded into memory (RAM), displayed and printed, as with other media. While that data in RAM may be altered and stored to a conventional magnetic disk, the original information on the CD-ROM is unalterable, always ensuring the original copy is intact, making archiving easy.

The storage capacity, low cost, and read only feature of CD-ROM bring an enormous new capability to microcomputer users — that is, information retrieval of very large reference publications. How people receive and use information in the immediate and long term future will be dramatically changed by CD-ROM.

In addition to the huge capacity of raw information storage, specialized software for the search of that information is currently being introduced. This software allows searching the information in areas, methods and speeds not previously feasible.

It now becomes possible to electronically publish reference material more economically than to print the same material in book form. That cost benefit, coupled with search and retrieval software, make an astonishing price/performance ratio.

Table of Contents

November, 1987 1

Figure 13.1: The &NEWS-P3 Sample Document as It Appears on a Full-Page Display

as well as the left edge. To accomplish this, Ventura inserts spacing within lines: space that would otherwise appear at the end of each line, if the document were unjustified (left-aligned). When Ventura justifies, it can create loose lines. *Loose lines* have too much white space within them, making the letters or words in the line appear disjointed. The reader can have difficulty stringing the letters into words and the words into sentences, making the writer's train of thought hard to follow. Proper use of typography can help minimize the number of loose lines in a document and make the text more readable. In Figure 13.1, the Show Loose Lines setting from the Options menu has been used to indicate loose lines with darkened text.

Now consider the document as a whole. Is it inviting? If you saw a stack of such documents in the company cafeteria, would you pick one up even though you were carrying a tray of food? Or does the material appear to be too difficult or boring to bother with? Tightening up the loose lines can make the text more inviting.

A clearer sense of the organization of the material can also make the document more readable. Notice that the page obviously contains two articles; the two headlines clearly indicate this. Further organization, though, is not immediately apparent. Subheads appear in bold, but this alone doesn't strongly differentiate them from other text, so they become lost on the page.

Also notice that the table of contents has a great deal of space at the bottom, but not enough at the top (below its title and the first story listing). Also in the table of contents, multiline listings (such as the entry beginning with *A Long article*) seem at first to be several separate listings.

Finally, notice that the text of the newsletter does not fill the page. The second article ends with the words *astonishing price/performance ratio*. After that, there's just leftover space on the page. Proper use of typography allows you to enlarge and reduce text in order to fit it within a given space.

Let's see how to adjust these typographical elements and thus enhance this newsletter. We'll correct these problems and others, starting with broad stokes and progressing toward more detailed kinds of work. If you want to work along, make a copy of the &NEWS-P3 document before beginning (using the Copy All command).

PARAGRAPHS BEGINNING WITH SPECIAL EFFECTS

Let's start with paragraph beginnings. By changing the way a paragraph begins, you can draw attention it. One use of unusual paragraph beginnings is to signal the onset of a new idea. As such, special effects at the beginning of paragraphs can help to organize material visually.

Ventura provides two explicit effects for paragraph beginnings. (It also provides the means to create others.) These two *special effects*, as they are referred to in Ventura, are the *bullet* and the *big first character* or *dropped capital*. Both are features that typesetters use frequently and that you've no doubt seen in print. To set either effect for a particular paragraph tag, display the Special Effects dialog box shown in Figure 13.2:

1. Activate the Paragraph mode and click a paragraph whose tag you wish to affect.
2. Pull down the Paragraph menu and click Special Effects.

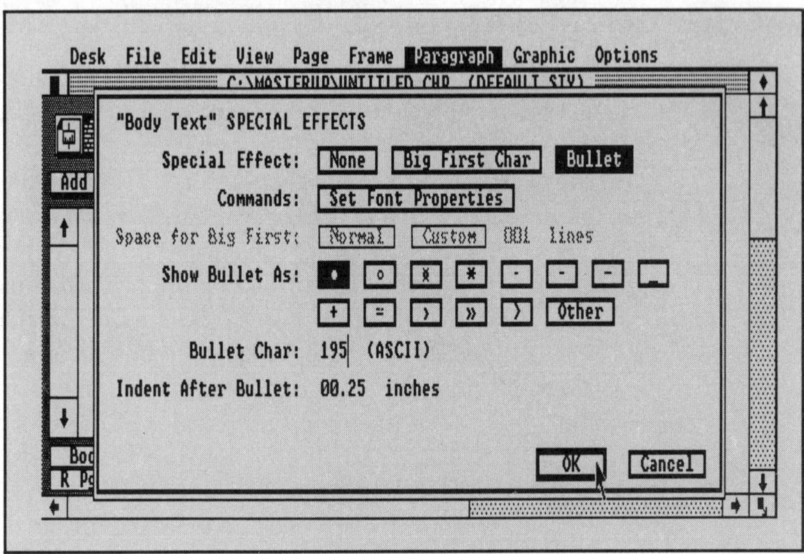

Figure 13.2: The Paragraph Menu's Special Effects Dialog Box

DROPPED CAPITALS

The first special effect button is labeled Big First Char. Click it to create a dropped capital. A *dropped capital*—a large letter at the beginning of a line that drops below the regular base of the line, thus drawing attention to the line—often appears in the first paragraph of a chapter or a magazine article. If you choose this effect, Ventura will automatically convert the first character in each paragraph appropriately tagged.

Dropped capitals aren't confined to the paragraphs that begin an article, however. Often, they can be used in the middle of an article to show a slight shift in thought—one not strong enough to warrant a new heading.

Figure 13.3 shows dropped capitals placed in our newsletter. This simple change makes the material more inviting.

You can specify the format that the dropped capital takes. This includes all font features, such as Face, Size, Style, and so on. Once you click the Big First Char button, click Set Font Properties in the dialog box. You'll see the Font Setting dialog box, like the dialog boxes we examined in conjunction with paragraph tags and text attributes in Chapter 5. You must use this dialog box to set the size of the dropped capital. If you don't, the character will remain the same size as standard characters in the paragraph. Set the size and other characteristics and give the OK. Ventura will then redisplay the Special Effects dialog box.

You can also use the Special Effects dialog box to set the number of lines that this effect occupies. Do so to create a *stickup initial:* a character that rises above the first line of the paragraph (see Figure 13.4). In the Space for Big First setting, click Custom and then enter the number of lines you desire. (These settings ghost in the dialog box shown in Figure 13.2 because the Big First Char button is not selected.) When set to Normal, Ventura automatically displaces just enough lines to fully sink the character in the paragraph. In order to raise the character up level with the base of the line, use a number smaller than the amount Ventura allocates. For the example shown in Figure 13.4, the big first character that displaced two lines as a dropped capital has been converted to a stickup initial by setting Custom to 1 line.

Widget World News

Views and News of Widget Manufacturing in the 80s

142 Guitrep Pkwy. *Detroit, MI 98987* *(413) 567-9888*

Software Salaries: How do you stack up?

by Joe Smith

How much your software professionals are paid is a function of many variables, and a subject of considerable interest to your organization.

Software salary pay scales

Because of the dynamic growth of the software industry over the last decade, the demand for experienced, qualified programmers has greatly increased, thus leading to a spiraling of salaries.

But what causes managers to pay one programmer more than another? Does the type of organization, its size, or location make a difference? What career path or programming specialty leads to the most remuneration?

To answer these questions, Acme Magazine recently conducted its third annual compensation survey for software professionals. This newsletter article presents the results of this study and explores what the findings may mean to you.

Acme Magazine asked Joe Smith, a compensation consulting specialist for the software industry, to design and conduct the survey. Twenty-four positions, representing four programmer job families plus management, were included.

Data was collected for base pay, bonus and incentive payments, and whether nor not incumbents received stock options or other forms of equity.

Questionnaires were sent to the data processing heads of 2,400 organizations throughout the United States.

CD-ROM Breaks New Ground

Compact Disk Read Only Memory (CD-ROM) is a rapidly emerging new technology for the retrieval of vast amounts of information from an optical disk. This new peripheral device allows a totally new level of functionality in the use of microcomputers.

Physically, the CD-ROM device has a laser disk drive (or "player") the same size as a traditional 5 1/4" drive. The removable disk is 4 3/4", and has a capacity of 550M bytes (equivalent to 1500 360K floppy disks).

Theory of Operation

Information stored on a CD-ROM can be loaded into memory (RAM), displayed and printed, as with other media. While that data in RAM may be altered and stored to a conventional magnetic disk, the original information on the CD-ROM is unalterable, always ensuring the original copy is intact, making archiving easy.

The storage capacity, low cost, and read only feature of CD-ROM bring an enormous new capability to microcomputer users – that is, information retrieval of very large reference publications. How people receive and use information in the immediate and long term future will be dramatically changed by CD-ROM.

In addition to the huge capacity of raw information storage, specialized software for the search of that information is currently being introduced. This software allows searching the information in areas, methods and speeds not previously feasible.

It now becomes possible to electronically publish reference material more economically than to print the same material in book form. That cost benefit, coupled with search and retrieval software, make an astonishing price/performance ratio.

Figure 1 Caption Information

Table of Contents

November, 1987 1

Figure 13.3: Dropped Capitals

Once your settings are in place, give the OK again. You'll see dropped capitals or stickup initials appear in all appropriately tagged paragraphs.

Should you change your mind, you can neutralize the effect. Use the Paragraph menu's Special Effects box and click the None button. Give the OK, and the effect will be undone.

When using Ventura's special effects, you may need to make adjustments if you switch printers. For example, when printed with the Hewlett-Packard LaserJet, the sample document and style sheet &BOOK-P1 sinks the dropped capital too far into the first paragraph. The result appears in Figure 13.5. Dropped capitals in another sample, &BOOK-P2, have the same problem. Apparently, this occurs because Ventura's samples were prepared initially with a PostScript printer.

Software Salaries: How do you stack up?

by Joe Smith

How much your software professionals are paid is a function of many variables, and a subject of considerable interest to your organization.

Figure 13.4: A Stickup Initial

This trip really began in September last year when Gerry won first prize in a raffle at the fashion show which Rush-Presbyterian-St. Luke's Medical Center holds every year. The prize was two round trip tickets to Hong Kong on United Airlines, and ten nights in the Hong Kong Hyatt Hotel. Analyzing our good fortune, we concluded that we wanted to do more than spend ten days in Hong Kong and return, but at the same time, United, having just gotten its routes and equipment from Pan American, had not yet received authority to fly to other destinations or between points in the Far East.

Figure 13.5: A Dropped Capital Set Too Low

However, we can fix the effect. By clicking the Set Font Properties button, we can change the settings to shift the dropped capital up. In Figure 13.6, we've raised the drop capital to an acceptable level by shifting it up six points. This is the paragraph display we have used in the document as it appears in Appendix A.

BULLETS

The second special effect Ventura provides is bulleted paragraphs. A *bullet* is a character that sets off items in a list, usually appearing to the left of each item that's listed as a separate paragraph. Generally, a bullet is displayed as a dot. In Figure 13.7 you can see how we've used bullets to clear up the confusion within items in the table of contents.

Ventura allows you to display bullets as a variety of other shapes. Once you click the Bullet button, 13 choices appear in the Show Bullet As grouping. If these choices aren't enough, click Other. This will allow you to type the ASCII code for any character into the Bullet Char field. (See Appendix E for a listing of the ASCII codes.)

Regardless of the character you choose for your bullet, you can set its formatting characteristics, such as font size, color, and so on, with a great deal of flexibility, just as you can with dropped capitals. You need only change the settings if you want the bullet to be formatted differently than the rest of the paragraph. Just as you do when working with Big First Char, click Set Font Properties and proceed.

> This trip really began in September last year when Gerry won first prize in a raffle at the fashion show which Rush-Presbyterian-St. Luke's Medical Center holds every year. The prize was two round trip tickets to Hong Kong on United Airlines, and ten nights in the Hong Kong Hyatt Hotel. Analyzing our good fortune, we concluded that we wanted to do more than spend ten days in Hong Kong and return, but at the same time, United, having just gotten its routes and equipment from Pan American, had not yet received authority to fly to other destinations or between points in the Far East.

Figure 13.6: A Dropped Capital Shifted Up

When using the bullet special effect, you must enter a value for Indent After Bullet. This value controls the amount of indent for the left edge of the entire bulleted paragraph. This indent is in addition to any other margin or indent you may set. Figure 13.8 diagrams the values you must consider in determining the placement of the left edge of a bulleted paragraph from the left edge of the page. Note that the first paragraph in the figure has the same indent settings as the second, except that the first has no bullet specified. We've increased some of the values from those of the &NEWS-P3 sample document to make the relationships clear.

As with dropped capitals, should you switch printers, you may need to make adjustments. For example, Figure 13.9 shows how the bulleted material in the &BOOK-P1 sample document appears when printed with the HP LaserJet. In Figure 13.10 we have increased the Indent After Bullet value to compensate for the change in printers. These results have been used to print the sample in Appendix A.

Table of Contents

- *First story 1*
- *Second story 2*
- *The third article 3*
- *Next comes the fourth.. 5*
- *A Long article breaks to the next line without running into the page number 6*
- *Note that this TOC could have been generated from the newsletter CHP file. 9*

Figure 13.7: Bullets Used to Differentiate List Items

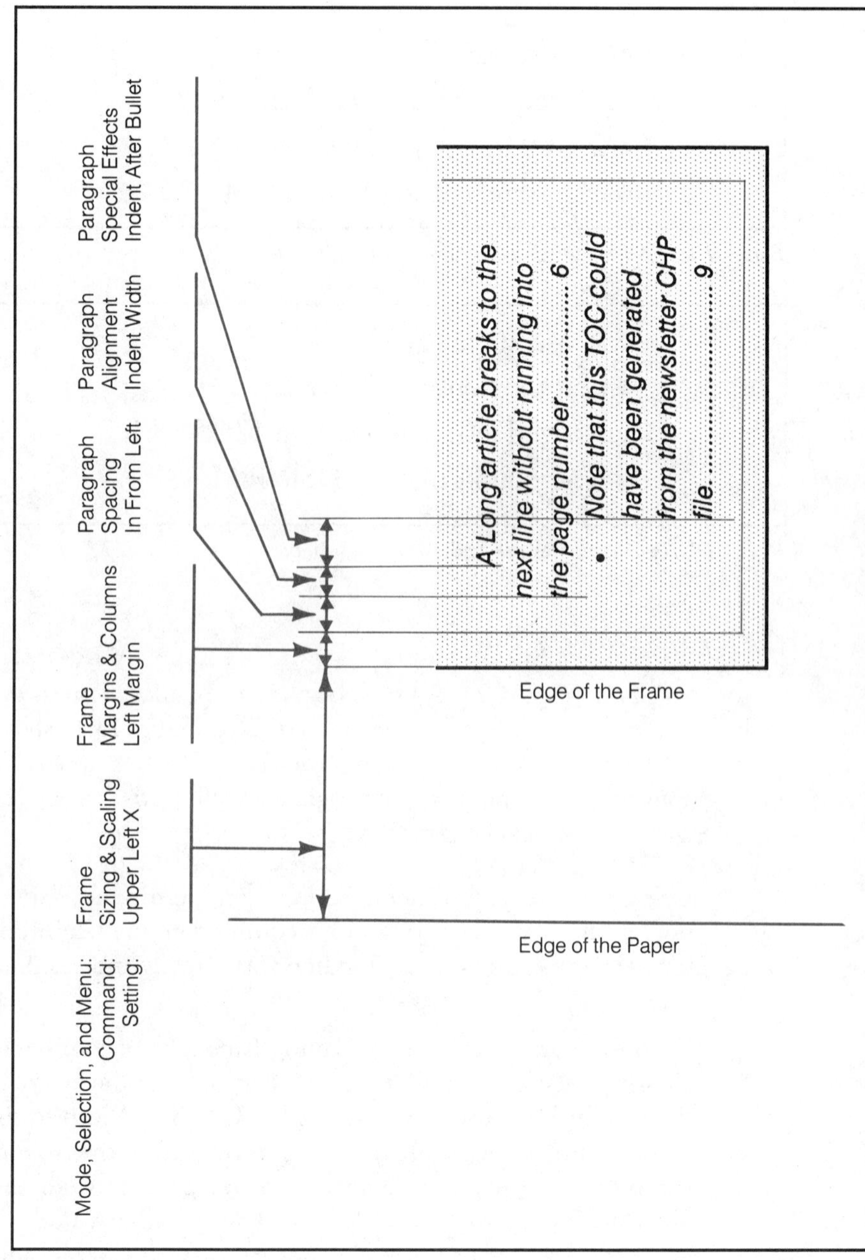

Figure 13.8: Indent Settings for a Bulleted Paragraph

•Arose at 5:30 A.M.
•Left the house at 7:00 A.M.
•Arrived in Los Angeles at 12:35 P.M.
•Arrived in Tokyo at 11:46 P.M.

Figure 13.9: An Insufficient Indent after Bullets

• Arose at 5:30 A.M.
• Left the house at 7:00 A.M.
• Arrived in Los Angeles at 12:35 P.M.
• Arrived in Tokyo at 11:46 P.M.

Figure 13.10: Increasing the Indent after Bullets

OTHER EFFECTS

You can create effects for paragraph beginnings besides those shown in the Paragraph menu's Special Effects dialog box. Figure 13.11 shows paragraphs formatted with a beginning black box. The box appears at the beginning of paragraphs that occur right after subheads. To create a box like this, use the following steps:

1. Using the Paragraph menu's Alignment command, indent the first line or lines enough to accommodate the beginning box. (In the example, the first line was already indented, so we actually skipped this step.)
2. With the Paragraph menu's Ruling Line Above command, click the Custom button. Then insert a value for the height of the rule in Height of Rule 1. Set the Custom Width to the same value. The value you use determines the size of the box. Also insert a negative value, greater than this amount, for Space Below Rule 3. The negative value will lower the rule, which normally appears above the paragraph, into the body of the paragraph.

3. Using the Paragraph menu's Spacing command, increase the Above setting. Creating the rule upsets the paragraph's spacing above; this setting restores the original spacing. (We'll examine such spacing later in this chapter.)

Widget World News

Views and News of Widget Manufacturing in the 80s

142 Guitrep Pkwy. *Detroit, MI 98987* *(413) 567-9888*

Software Salaries: How do you stack up?

by Joe Smith

How much your software professionals are paid is a function of many variables, and a subject of considerable interest to your organization.

Software salary pay scales

■ Because of the dynamic growth of the software industry over the last decade, the demand for experienced, qualified programmers has greatly increased, thus leading to a spiraling of salaries.

But what causes managers to pay one programmer more than another? Does the type of organization, its size, or location make a difference? What career path or programming specialty leads to the most remuneration?

To answer these questions, Acme Magazine recently conducted its third annual compensation survey for software professionals. This newsletter article presents the results of this study and explores what the findings may mean to you.

Acme Magazine asked Joe Smith, a compensation consulting specialist for the software industry, to design and conduct the survey. Twenty-four positions, representing four programmer job families plus management, were included.

Data was collected for base pay, bonus and incentive payments, and whether nor not incumbents received stock options or other forms of equity.

Questionnaires were sent to the data processing heads of 2,400 organizations throughout the United States.

CD-ROM Breaks New Ground

Compact Disk Read Only Memory (CD-ROM) is a rapidly emerging new technology for the retrieval of vast amounts of information from an optical disk. This new peripheral device allows a totally new level of functionality in the use of microcomputers.

Physically, the CD-ROM device has a laser disk drive (or "player") the same size as a traditional 5 1/4" drive. The removable disk is 4 3/4", and has a capacity of 550M bytes (equivalent to 1500 360K floppy disks).

Theory of Operation

■ Information stored on a CD-ROM can be loaded into memory (RAM), displayed and printed, as with other media. While that data in RAM may be altered and stored to a conventional magnetic disk, the original information on the CD-ROM is unalterable, always ensuring the original copy is intact, making archiving easy.

The storage capacity, low cost, and read only feature of CD-ROM bring an enormous new capability to microcomputer users – that is, information retrieval of very large reference publications. How people receive and use information in the immediate and long term future will be dramatically changed by CD-ROM.

In addition to the huge capacity of raw information storage, specialized software for the search of that information is currently being introduced. This software allows searching the information in areas, methods and speeds not previously feasible.

It now becomes possible to electronically publish reference material more economically than to print the same material in book form. That cost benefit, coupled with search and retrieval software, make an astonishing price/performance ratio.

Figure 1 Caption Information

Table of Contents

November, 1987 1

Figure 13.11: Paragraphs with Beginning Black Boxes

In our example, we inserted the following settings into the Paragraph menu's Ruling Line Above dialog box. Measurements are in picas & points.

Height of Rule 1: 00,06
Custom Width: 00,06
Space Below Rule 3: 00,09 -

In the Paragraph menu's Spacing dialog box, we entered the following value:

Above: 00,04

The beginning black box can vary in size. You can also create bars within the black box by turning dashes on.

Another effect used at the beginning of paragraphs is the hanging indent, or *outdent*. We examined this effect in Chapter 5. To create it you use the Paragraph menu's Alignment command. Figure 13.12 shows the table of contents given the outdent treatment.

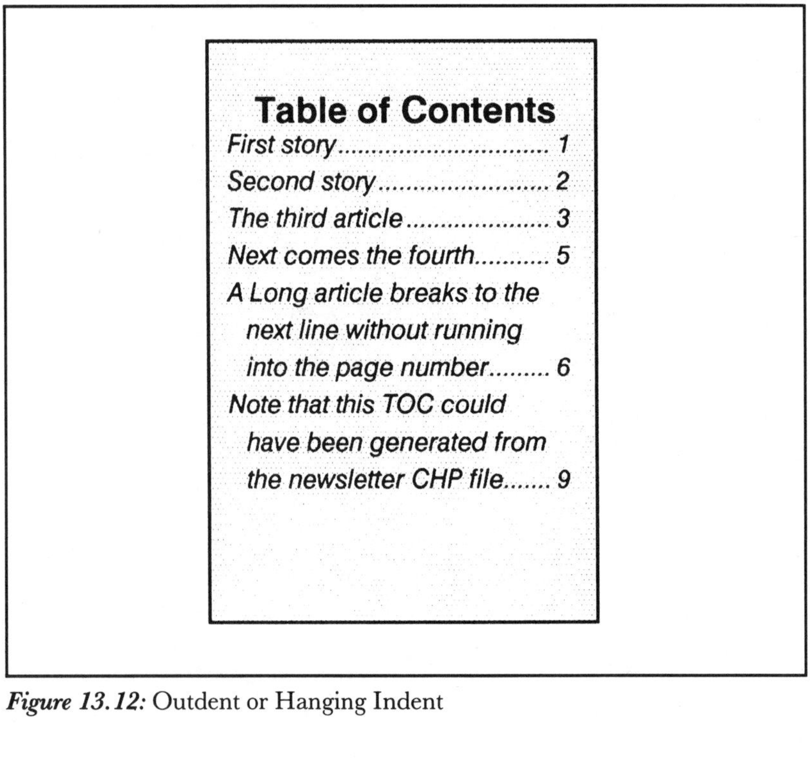

Table of Contents

First story.............................. 1
Second story......................... 2
The third article..................... 3
Next comes the fourth........... 5
A Long article breaks to the next line without running into the page number......... 6
Note that this TOC could have been generated from the newsletter CHP file....... 9

Figure 13.12: Outdent or Hanging Indent

Now let's examine another effect that makes text distinctive: reverse type.

REVERSE TYPE AND RELATED EFFECTS

Reverse text is a technique that typographers sometimes use to gain the reader's attention. Reverse text is created by placing white letters on a black background. You may want to use this effect to draw attention to the table of contents, for instance.

To use reverse type, your printer must be capable of creating white letters on a black background. The HP LaserJet does not have this capability, so our examples will appear only on the screen. To determine if your printer has this capacity, check your printout of the Printer Capability page, as discussed in Chapter 6.

REVERSE TEXT IN FRAMES AND BOXES

One way to create reverse text is by using frames. You can change the background of the frame to black; when you do, all text inside the frame changes to white automatically. This treatment even works with the underlying-page frame.

To achieve the effect, use the Frame mode and select the frame. Then use the Frame menu's Frame Background command. In the resulting dialog box, set Color to Black and Pattern to Solid. Figure 13.13 shows the table of contents frame presented in reverse type.

If you use this effect, remember that various screen effects Ventura uses to catch your attention will also be reversed. Thus, selected text will appear in white instead of black, and the handles on a frame you've selected will be white, too.

A variation on the black background is achieved by using one of the patterns in the Frame Background dialog box. The table of contents frame shown in Figure 13.1 uses a shaded background.

When you use a pattern, the text will not change to white automatically. You can, however, use the Paragraph menu's Font command to change the font color for paragraphs appearing within the frame.

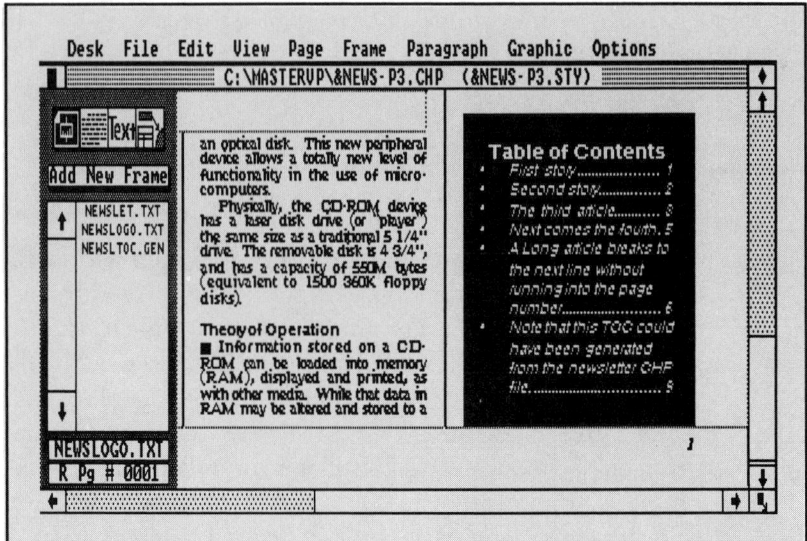

Figure 13.13: Reverse Type

You can also use Box Text to create reverse and shaded text. Use the Graphic menu's Fill Attributes command. Box Text produces the same effects as frames: Ventura changes text to white, but only when you indicate solid black. If you change back and forth from one effect to another, you may find it necessary to re-ink the screen by pressing the Esc key, in order to see the effect take place.

USING RULES TO CREATE REVERSE TEXT

Creating reverse text with frames is easy and quick. However, if you plan to repeat the effect regularly throughout your document, you may prefer to associate reverse text with a tag. Be aware, though, that these steps will only create reverse text for paragraphs that contain no more than one line.

This technique uses the Space Below Rule 3 setting to achieve reverse type with titles or headings. The process involves changing the font to white, then creating a black Ruling Line Above with a negative space below it. This negative space moves the ruling line down into line with the text. The result is a black bar with white text across it. Here are the steps for creating reverse text with a tag:

1. Activate the Paragraph mode and select a sample (one line) paragraph.
2. Pull down the Paragraph menu and click Font.
3. Set Color for the paragraph's font to White. Make a mental note of the font size you're using and give the OK. The text will seem to disappear, but don't be alarmed. It's still there, but its font is the same color at the background.
4. Pull down the Paragraph menu again and click Ruling Line Above.
5. Set the Width that you desire for the darkened bar against which the type will appear.
6. Click the Color setting to Black and the Pattern setting to Solid. (You can vary these choices.)
7. Set the units of measurement to fractional points or picas & points.
8. For Height of Rule 1, specify an amount equal to the font size or larger. If you're using fractional points, insert the point value to the left of the period. If you use picas & points, insert it to the right of the comma.
9. For Space Below Rule 3, insert a value determined using the following formula: add the point size of the font to the value you've specified for Height of Rule 1; divide the result by 2; then insert a value that is slightly more than this amount—2 points more seems to work well.
10. Click the Minus (–) box, so that the value is a negative one. Then give the OK.

Figure 13.14 shows the Table of Contents heading in reverse against a frame-wide band. Notice in this case that no characters descend below the line of text and thus out of the reverse band. If your heading contains descending characters, such as g or y, you will have to add extra points in step 9 above, to lower the reverse band further.

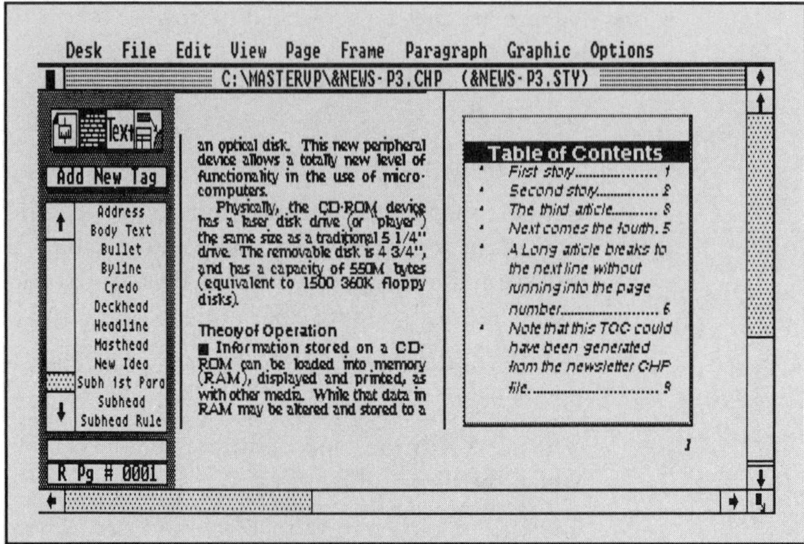

Figure 13.14: Reverse Text Created with a Paragraph Tag

As mentioned in step 5, you can vary the settings for the ruling line's color and pattern. If you do, be careful to consider the paragraph font's color. For the sake of readability, always use a font that will provide your readers with a sharp contrast to the background.

If you set the Width of the rule to Text, you may find that it's a good idea to add space before and after the text. Doing so increases the ends of the frame the rule creates, insuring that the white text doesn't bleed into the white background. Use one of the solid spaces that we'll examine shortly, such as an en space, to do this. Do not use a regular space (obtained by pressing the Spacebar). Ventura will erase such a space at the beginning of the paragraph.

Now that we've examined some type effects, let's examine spacing effects. Ventura has several ways to handle spacing.

KERNING TEXT

Kerning refers to the technique of moving a character closer to the previous character on the same line. Normally, as with a typewriter, when Ventura places characters side-by-side, the leftmost part of a character is positioned after the rightmost part of the character before it. With certain combinations of characters, such as when a *V* follows an *A*, there may be an inappropriate amount of space between the letters. This can make the text loose and difficult to read. By kerning, you draw characters closer to one another, and hence the text becomes more readable.

Kerning with Ventura means moving a character slightly to the left, and thus closer to the character before it. You can also kern strictly for effect—to join two characters together, for instance.

KERNING INDIVIDUAL LETTERS

With Ventura 1.1 there are several ways to kern. First of all, you can kern individual letters. When you kern individual characters, you usually do so only with large characters, such as those that make up headlines or mastheads. It would be impractical to individually kern large amounts of small text such as body text.

Figure 13.15 shows an example of text before and after kerning. Notice the difference in space between the characters in the kerned text, especially between *W* and *A* and between *A* and *V*. The *W*, *A*, and *V* are kerned closer together, while *N* and *E* are kerned together for effect.

To kern an individual letter, use the Text mode and select the letter by darkening with the mouse. Then click the Set Font Properties button in the Side-bar. Specify a value for the Kern setting.

Be aware that when you kern, there may be more or less kerning in the printed version of your document than in what you see on the screen. This is due to the difference in resolution between printed

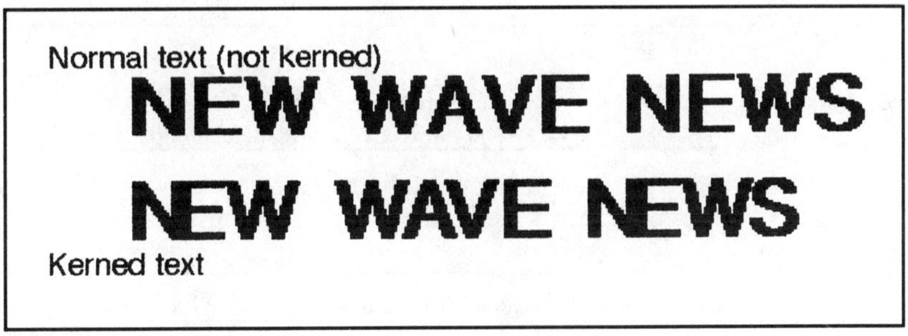

Normal text (not kerned)

NEW WAVE NEWS

NEW WAVE NEWS

Kerned text

Figure 13.15: Kerning Text

text and text on the screen. Allow yourself enough time to perform a few trial printouts of kerned material.

Figure 13.16 shows the results of kerning the masthead in the sample document. The letter *o* in *World* is kerned 1½ points and the *e* in *News* is kerned 1 point.

AUTOMATIC KERNING WITH TAGS

With Version 1.1, in addition to kerning character by character, Ventura can kern *globally* with some fonts. That is, you can kern throughout all paragraphs that are similarly tagged, moving every *V* closer to a preceding or subsequent *A*, and so on for other letter combinations. However, the program can only do this if the font already contains the kerning information: that is, information about which pairs of characters should be kerned and how much. This information is provided when you use PostScript fonts, but not when you use others, such as the fonts for the LaserJet.

To kern globally, use the Paragraph mode to select a paragraph whose tag you wish to kern with. With the paragraph selected, pull down the Paragraph menu and click Typographical Controls. You'll see the dialog box shown in Figure 13.17. Set Automatic Kerning to On and give the OK.

Two other commands can affect kerning you perform in this manner. First, you can use the Page menu's Page Layout command. By clicking the appropriate button, you can set kerning Globally On or Globally Off. When you set Automatic Kerning On for any paragraph tag, the setting will only take place as long as kerning is kept

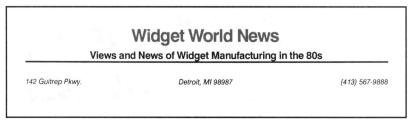

Figure 13.16: The Masthead from the Sample Document after Kerning

globally on. If you switch kerning globally off, automatic kerning is temporarily suspended. Automatic kerning can slow down processing, so you may want to turn it globally off as you work with a document. Even so, the automatic kerning status stays with a paragraph tag. When you turn kerning back on, all appropriately tagged paragraphs receive kerning treatment once again. This command does not affect kerning of individual characters, the first method of kerning we discussed.

The other command to consider is the Options menu's Set Preferences command. With this command you indicate whether you want Ventura to display automatic kerning on the screen and if so, for what size font. Displaying kerning on the screen can also slow down operations, due to the additional computations Ventura must perform. Set On-Screen Kerning to None and Ventura will only kern when you print the document. Set it to All and all appropriately tagged material will be kerned on the screen. Set it to one of the point sizes listed (between 10 to 36) and on the screen Ventura will only kern fonts of the size you indicate or larger. Again, this setting does not affect kerning you set with the Text mode's Set Font button.

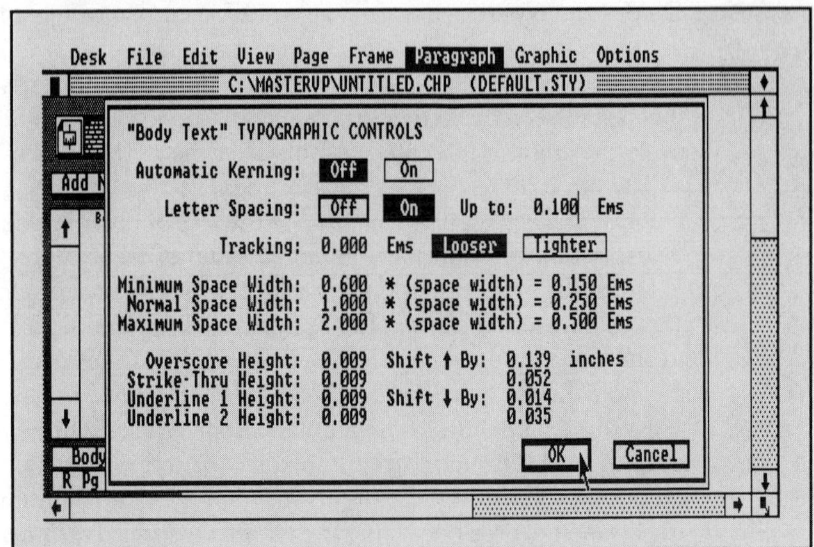

Figure 13.17: The Paragraph Menu's Typographic Controls Dialog Box

SPACING BETWEEN WORDS AND LETTERS

Let's continue to look at the dialog box for Typographic Controls and see how we can use its settings to improve the sample document. Whether you use many of the settings discussed in the next few sections depends on whether the document you are working with is justified.

Justifying a document can cause a host of problems. Inserting spacing between words and letters is an exacting chore. Many problems can therefore be avoided by simply not justifying. Use the Paragraph menu's Alignment command to accomplish this. Results can be quite acceptable, especially with vertical rules between columns, as Figure 13.18 shows. Additional improvements can be obtained by using the slower, but more thorough, algorithm for hyphenating (see Chapter 5). If you do justify the text, however, the first setting you may wish to consider is Letter Spacing.

LETTER SPACING

In the Typographic Controls dialog box, Letter Spacing can be set On or Off. When Letter Spacing is Off, Ventura will justify by adding space between words only. When Letter Spacing is On, Ventura justifies by adding space between words and within words as well—that is, between the letters that make up the word. It will add spacing up to the amount indicated in Ems after the Letter Spacing setting.

The em is an important measurement in typography. An *em* is an amount of horizontal space equal to the size of the font you're using. Thus, with a 10-point font, an em is equal to 10 points.

Consider the justified version of the sample document (Figure 13.11). The way it stands, Letter Spacing is On and set to operate up to one tenth of an em (.1 Ems). Look at the two lines at the top of the second column. The lines are loose and appear to be stretched out.

Figure 13.19 shows how adjustments to spacing affect this paragraph. In the first treatment, we've turned Letter Spacing Off. Notice how Ventura achieves justification by adding additional spacing between words only. Spacing within words is the same as it is for left-aligned text.

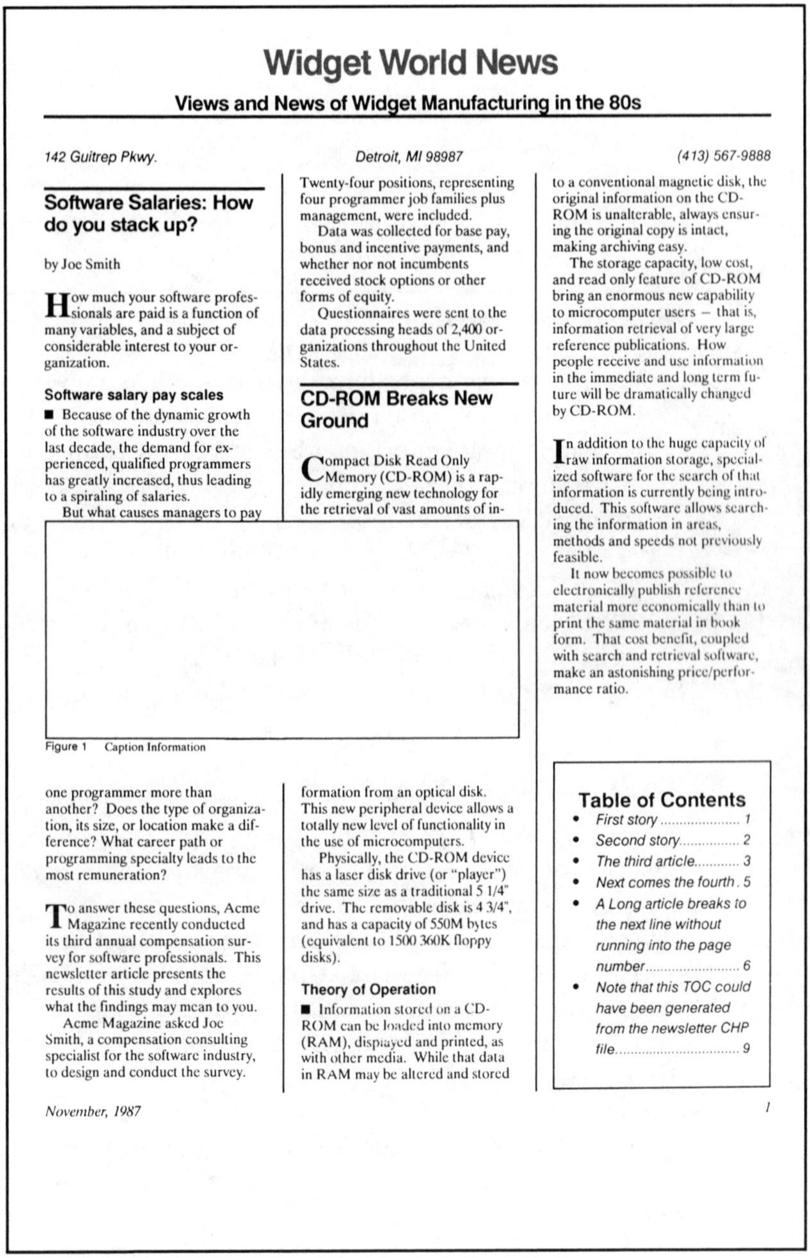

Widget World News

Views and News of Widget Manufacturing in the 80s

142 Guitrep Pkwy. *Detroit, MI 98987* *(413) 567-9888*

Software Salaries: How do you stack up?

by Joe Smith

How much your software professionals are paid is a function of many variables, and a subject of considerable interest to your organization.

Software salary pay scales

■ Because of the dynamic growth of the software industry over the last decade, the demand for experienced, qualified programmers has greatly increased, thus leading to a spiraling of salaries.

But what causes managers to pay one programmer more than another? Does the type of organization, its size, or location make a difference? What career path or programming specialty leads to the most remuneration?

To answer these questions, Acme Magazine recently conducted its third annual compensation survey for software professionals. This newsletter article presents the results of this study and explores what the findings may mean to you.

Acme Magazine asked Joe Smith, a compensation consulting specialist for the software industry, to design and conduct the survey. Twenty-four positions, representing four programmer job families plus management, were included.

Data was collected for base pay, bonus and incentive payments, and whether nor not incumbents received stock options or other forms of equity.

Questionnaires were sent to the data processing heads of 2,400 organizations throughout the United States.

CD-ROM Breaks New Ground

Compact Disk Read Only Memory (CD-ROM) is a rapidly emerging new technology for the retrieval of vast amounts of information from an optical disk. This new peripheral device allows a totally new level of functionality in the use of microcomputers.

Physically, the CD-ROM device has a laser disk drive (or "player") the same size as a traditional 5 1/4" drive. The removable disk is 4 3/4", and has a capacity of 550M bytes (equivalent to 1500 360K floppy disks).

Theory of Operation

■ Information stored on a CD-ROM can be loaded into memory (RAM), displayed and printed, as with other media. While that data in RAM may be altered and stored to a conventional magnetic disk, the original information on the CD-ROM is unalterable, always ensuring the original copy is intact, making archiving easy.

The storage capacity, low cost, and read only feature of CD-ROM bring an enormous new capability to microcomputer users — that is, information retrieval of very large reference publications. How people receive and use information in the immediate and long term future will be dramatically changed by CD-ROM.

In addition to the huge capacity of raw information storage, specialized software for the search of that information is currently being introduced. This software allows searching the information in areas, methods and speeds not previously feasible.

It now becomes possible to electronically publish reference material more economically than to print the same material in book form. That cost benefit, coupled with search and retrieval software, make an astonishing price/performance ratio.

Figure 1 Caption Information

Table of Contents

November, 1987 1

Figure 13.18: Left-Aligned Text

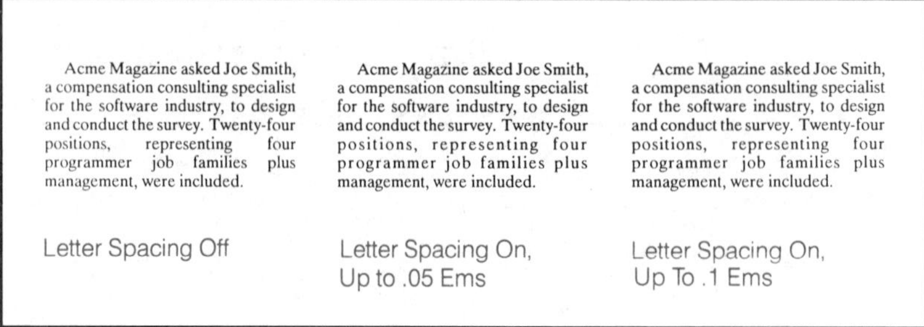

Figure 13.19: Various Letter Spacing Treatments

The second treatment shows the paragraph as it appears in Figure 13.11. Words in the loose lines are stretched out.

In the third treatment, Letter Spacing is On, but we've decreased the Up to amount by half. Although the lines are still loose, the words are stretched less and are more clearly separated. This is probably the best arrangement, although it's a matter of personal taste. In Figure 13.20 we've applied this treatment to the sample.

Whichever way you go, the lines are still loose. Better hyphenation would be in order and we'll do this later in the chapter. In fact, better hyphenation may obviate the need for letter spacing.

TRACKING

Tracking is another feature in the Typographic Controls dialog box that controls spacing. However, tracking controls *all* spacing. It decreases or increases the spacing between letters and the spacing between words. It operates whether the text is justified or not.

With tracking, you can make paragraphs looser or tighter. With a value of 0 in the Tracking field, tracking is not operational. To use tracking, enter a value and then click either Looser or Tighter as appropriate.

Tracking serves two useful purposes. First of all, you can use tracking to adjust text to fit into a fixed amount of space. Figure 13.21 shows the same sample paragraph, left-aligned in this case, with no tracking and with tracking set tighter and looser. Notice how the length of the paragraph varies with each treatment, allowing it to occupy varying amounts of space.

Widget World News

Views and News of Widget Manufacturing in the 80s

142 Guitrep Pkwy. Detroit, MI 98987 (413) 567-9888

Software Salaries: How do you stack up?

by Joe Smith

How much your software professionals are paid is a function of many variables, and a subject of considerable interest to your organization.

Software salary pay scales

■ Because of the dynamic growth of the software industry over the last decade, the demand for experienced, qualified programmers has greatly increased, thus leading to a spiraling of salaries.

But what causes managers to pay one programmer more than another? Does the type of organization, its size, or location make a difference? What career path or programming specialty leads to the most remuneration?

To answer these questions, Acme Magazine recently conducted its third annual compensation survey for software professionals. This newsletter article presents the results of this study and explores what the findings may mean to you.

Acme Magazine asked Joe Smith, a compensation consulting specialist for the software industry, to design and conduct the survey. Twenty-four positions, representing four programmer job families plus management, were included.

Data was collected for base pay, bonus and incentive payments, and whether nor not incumbents received stock options or other forms of equity.

Questionnaires were sent to the data processing heads of 2,400 organizations throughout the United States.

Figure 1 Caption Information

CD-ROM Breaks New Ground

Compact Disk Read Only Memory (CD-ROM) is a rapidly emerging new technology for the retrieval of vast amounts of information from an optical disk. This new peripheral device allows a totally new level of functionality in the use of microcomputers.

Physically, the CD-ROM device has a laser disk drive (or "player") the same size as a traditional 5 1/4" drive. The removable disk is 4 3/4", and has a capacity of 550M bytes (equivalent to 1500 360K floppy disks).

Theory of Operation

■ Information stored on a CD-ROM can be loaded into memory (RAM), displayed and printed, as with other media. While that data in RAM may be altered and stored to a conventional magnetic disk, the original information on the CD-ROM is unalterable, always ensuring the original copy is intact, making archiving easy.

The storage capacity, low cost, and read only feature of CD-ROM bring an enormous new capability to microcomputer users – that is, information retrieval of very large reference publications. How people receive and use information in the immediate and long term future will be dramatically changed by CD-ROM.

In addition to the huge capacity of raw information storage, specialized software for the search of that information is currently being introduced. This software allows searching the information in areas, methods and speeds not previously feasible.

It now becomes possible to electronically publish reference material more economically than to print the same material in book form. That cost benefit, coupled with search and retrieval software, make an astonishing price/performance ratio.

Table of Contents

November, 1987 1

Figure 13.20: The Sample with Letter Spacing Decreased

Another popular tracking application involves headlines, titles, and logos. You can use tracking to match the lengths of lines of text that would otherwise not match. For example, in Figure 13.22, tracking for the word *Universe* is tighter than normal, while tracking for the first two lines is looser, allowing all three lines of the title to match in length. (To assist in lining up the right edge on the screen, remember that you can drag the Ruler line's cross-hairs from the 0,0 mark. Use the Options command to show rulers.)

In the sample document, we could use looser tracking to fill in the page with text. However, since many lines are already too loose we won't change this setting. We'll use another technique to fill out the page.

ADJUSTING THE WIDTH OF A SPACE

Lastly, let's consider the Space Width settings. These settings allow you to control the width of a space—that is, the amount of spacing that Ventura inserts between words. Be aware, though, that it is usually unnecessary to adjust these settings.

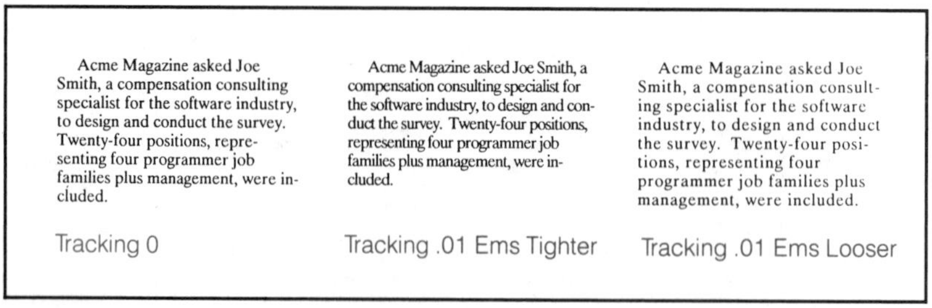

Acme Magazine asked Joe Smith, a compensation consulting specialist for the software industry, to design and conduct the survey. Twenty-four positions, representing four programmer job families plus management, were included.

Tracking 0

Acme Magazine asked Joe Smith, a compensation consulting specialist for the software industry, to design and conduct the survey. Twenty-four positions, representing four programmer job families plus management, were included.

Tracking .01 Ems Tighter

Acme Magazine asked Joe Smith, a compensation consulting specialist for the software industry, to design and conduct the survey. Twenty-four positions, representing four programmer job families plus management, were included.

Tracking .01 Ems Looser

Figure 13.21: Various Tracking Treatments

History
of the
Universe

Figure 13.22: Using Tracking to Match Line Lengths

Notice that the three settings—Minimum Space Width, Normal Space Width, and Maximum Space Width—apply only to the spacing between words. These settings operate whether letter spacing is functional or not, and they have no effect on the amount of space between letters within the same word.

As the dialog box indicates, the space widths are determined by a value that you provide, multiplied by the actual space width. The words

(space width)

represent the width of a space as contained in the width table for the font you're using.

Normally, spacing between words is the same amount as that of the standard width of a space. Thus, the value specified for Normal Space Width is usually 1. When 1 is used, the number of ems that appear is the amount given for space width in the font's width table. Ventura will use this value as the average space between words when justifying text. As necessary, Ventura will decrease the space between words, but no less than the amount you indicate for Minimum Space Width.

The Maximum Space Width setting is deceptively named. The indicated value does not limit the maximum width of a space in the way that the value for Minimum Space Width does. Regardless of what you specify as a maximum, Ventura will add as much space between words as necessary to achieve justification. However, for lines where the amount of space between words exceeds the value you've indicated for Maximum Space Width, Ventura will flag them as loose lines. These are the lines that will darken when you use the Options command to show loose lines.

Use of these settings can change the overall appearance of your document. In Figure 13.23 you can see how changing the Normal Space Width affects the distribution of space between words. The first treatment shows the text as it initially stands (although we've turned letter spacing off in order to isolate the effects of changing the space width). Although the second and third treatments are different, the impact of either is about the same. Either represents an improvement over the first treatment; spacing is more evenly distributed in the two treatments on the right.

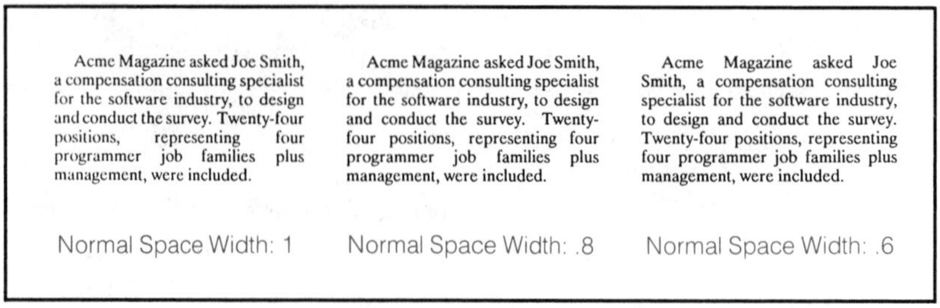

Acme Magazine asked Joe Smith, a compensation consulting specialist for the software industry, to design and conduct the survey. Twenty-four positions, representing four programmer job families plus management, were included.

Normal Space Width: 1

Acme Magazine asked Joe Smith, a compensation consulting specialist for the software industry, to design and conduct the survey. Twenty-four positions, representing four programmer job families plus management, were included.

Normal Space Width: .8

Acme Magazine asked Joe Smith, a compensation consulting specialist for the software industry, to design and conduct the survey. Twenty-four positions, representing four programmer job families plus management, were included.

Normal Space Width: .6

Figure 13.23: Changing the Space Width Setting

Using these settings, however, can sometimes cause undesirable results. Although the sample paragraph looks better with a smaller width, we won't change the setting on our sample. If we did, other paragraphs, similarly tagged, would actually become looser when this treatment was applied.

TEXT ATTRIBUTE LINES

Let's complete our examination of the Typographic Controls dialog box by looking at how to control text attribute lines. The settings grouped at the bottom of this dialog box regulate the location and size of lines created as part of the text attributes indicated. These are attributes you set by clicking them on the Text mode's Assignment list. Normally there is no need to adjust these settings.

If, however, you wish to change the thickness of your underline (from top to bottom), for instance, you could adjust the Underline 1 Height. Underline 2 Height comes into play only with double underlining. You can also change the thickness of the Overscore and Strike-thru attributes. You can also adjust the location of any of these lines by changing the corresponding Shift settings.

SETTING SOLID SPACES AND OTHER CHARACTERS

We've been examining typographic effects created with dialog boxes, but there are other means for creating some unusual characters with Ventura. For instance, you can create a variety of characters that do not appear on the keyboard. This includes such symbols as the trademark symbol, copyright symbol, registered symbol, and others. You create these using an Alt code in conjunction with the keypad, or using a word processor to enter a code into a text file. These special characters appear in Appendix E.

In addition, you can create even more nonkeyboard characters by using the Symbol font. To use it, simply assign Symbol as the face of the font (see Chapter 5). With this font, an entire set of characters, completely different from those appearing on the keyboard, appears on the screen and in print. For instance, if your using the Symbol font and you type the letter p, the Greek letter π appears. The Symbol font also makes a new set of Alt codes available as well. Appendix E lists characters in the Symbol font.

You can also enter four types of *solid spaces*. These spaces are always the same width. They will not shrink and grow in order to justify text as standard spaces do. You may find them useful with part numbers, numeric tables, and lines of computer code, for instance.

You can enter these spaces in Ventura with the keyboard, or you can type in a code with your word processor. Here is a list of the four types of solid spaces, along with the two ways to enter them:

- Em space (Ctrl-Shift-M or <_>). An em space is the same width as the point size of the font you're using. Thus, when you're using a 10-point font, an em space is 10 points wide.
- En space (Ctrl-Shift-N or < ~ >). An en space is one half the width of an em space. Thus, it's width is half that of the font size.
- Figure Space (Ctrl-Shift-F or <+>). The figure space is the same width as any one of the font's numeric digits (0 to 9). This space is useful when you need to line numbers up in columns without using tabs.
- Thin space (Ctrl-Shift-T or < | >). The thin space is the same width as a period. It is also one half the width of an en space or one quarter the width of an em space. We'll use a thin space in our sample document shortly.

SPACING BETWEEN PARAGRAPHS THAT FOLLOW ONE ANOTHER

In Chapter 5 we examined interline and interparagraph spacing. These properties, set with the Paragraph menu's Spacing dialog box, are also typographical elements (see Figure 13.24). Let's examine them more closely and consider their application with regard to our sample.

Ventura computes the spacing between paragraphs that follow each other according to the formula shown in Figure 13.25. The first value it uses is the Inter-Line setting of the first paragraph. Added to this value is either the Below setting of the first paragraph or the Above setting of the second paragraph, whichever is greater. The final value added in is the width of all ruling lines (set with the Paragraph menu) that appear between the two paragraphs.

For settings that affect spacing between paragraphs, it's generally a good idea to enter values that are multiples of the interline spacing. For that reason, use picas & points as the system of measurement. That way, lines of text in neighboring columns and on facing pages will line up. So if interline spacing is 10 points, you can create two lines of space by entering 20 points (or 1 pica, 8 points). (If you're not conversant in converting points to picas, Ventura will do it for you.

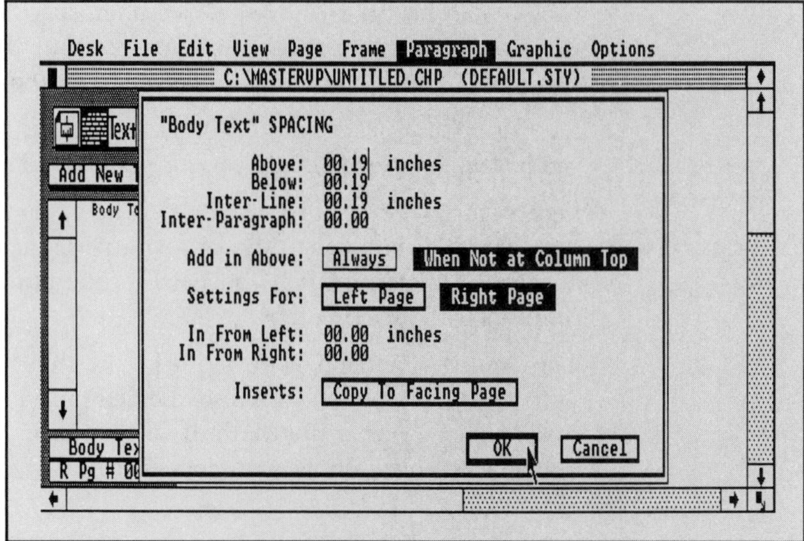

Figure 13.24: The Paragraph Menu's Spacing Dialog Box

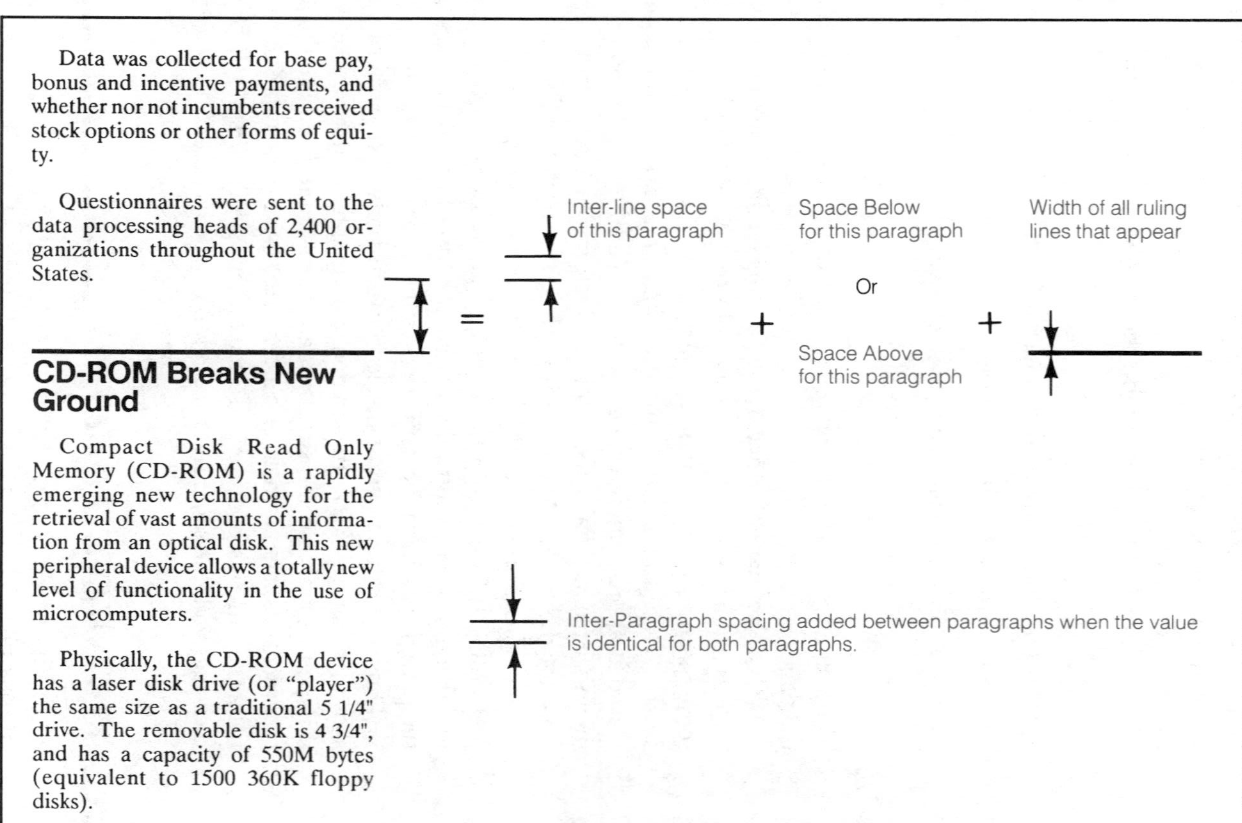

Figure 13.25: How Ventura Determines the Space between Paragraphs

You can simply enter 20 picas and when you give the OK, Ventura will convert the measurement. There may be some inconsequential rounding differences.)

In Figure 13.26, we've made the following changes to the tags indicated:

- Headline Above: 40 points (converted to 03,04)
- Headline Below: 10 points
- Subhead Above: 20 points (converted to 1,07)
- TOC Title Below: 10 points

These changes aid in setting off sections of the text and help fill out the page.

We've also made another change to the Headline tag. The way this tag was initially set up, both paragraphs that use it would always have some space above. This is desirable in the second instance (*CD-ROM Breaks*...) but it means that first use (*Software Salaries*...) would be displaced inappropriately down the first column. Use the Paragraph menu's Spacing dialog box to keep such displacement from occurring; for the Add in Above setting, click When Not at Column Top.

One other numeric setting in this dialog box is a special case. Ventura will only add in the Inter-Paragraph value when that value is identical for both paragraphs involved. Most often, this occurs when the paragraphs have the same tag, as in the case of body text.

Thus, we can add some space between body text paragraphs, as shown in Figure 13.27. In addition, paragraphs in the sample with a dropped capital and the small square block should receive the same treatment. Except for their special features, these paragraphs are essentially the same as body text. To have them similarly spaced, provide their tags with the same Inter-paragraph value as that of body text.

FINISHING TOUCHES

In Figure 13.27 you can see how 6 point spacing between paragraphs takes effect on body text and these other paragraphs. This

Widget World News

Views and News of Widget Manufacturing in the 80s

142 Guitrep Pkwy. *Detroit, MI 98987* *(413) 567-9888*

Software Salaries: How do you stack up?

by Joe Smith

How much your software professionals are paid is a function of many variables, and a subject of considerable interest to your organization.

Software salary pay scales

■ Because of the dynamic growth of the software industry over the last decade, the demand for experienced, qualified programmers has greatly increased, thus leading to a spiraling of salaries.

But what causes managers to pay one programmer more than another? Does the type of organization, its size, or location make a difference? What career path or programming specialty leads to the most remuneration?

To answer these questions, Acme Magazine recently conducted its third annual compensation survey for software professionals. This newsletter article presents the results of this study and explores what the findings may mean to you.

Acme Magazine asked Joe Smith, a compensation consulting specialist for the software industry, to design and conduct the survey. Twenty-four positions, representing four programmer job families plus management, were included.

Data was collected for base pay, bonus and incentive payments, and whether nor not incumbents received stock options or other forms of equity.

Questionnaires were sent to the data processing heads of 2,400 organizations throughout the United States.

Figure 1 Caption Information

CD-ROM Breaks New Ground

Compact Disk Read Only Memory (CD-ROM) is a rapidly emerging new technology for the retrieval of vast amounts of information from an optical disk. This new peripheral device allows a totally new level of functionality in the use of microcomputers.

Physically, the CD-ROM device has a laser disk drive (or "player") the same size as a traditional 5 1/4" drive. The removable disk is 4 3/4", and has a capacity of 550M bytes (equivalent to 1500 360K floppy disks).

Theory of Operation

■ Information stored on a CD-ROM can be loaded into memory (RAM), displayed and printed, as with other media. While that data in RAM may be altered and stored to a conventional magnetic disk, the original information on the CD-ROM is unalterable, always ensuring the original copy is intact, making archiving easy.

The storage capacity, low cost, and read only feature of CD-ROM bring an enormous new capability to microcomputer users – that is, information retrieval of very large reference publications. How people receive and use information in the immediate and long term future will be dramatically changed by CD-ROM.

In addition to the huge capacity of raw information storage, specialized software for the search of that information is currently being introduced. This software allows searching the information in areas, methods and speeds not previously feasible.

It now becomes possible to electronically publish reference material more economically than to print the same material in book form. That cost benefit, coupled with search and retrieval software, make an astonishing price/performance ratio.

Table of Contents

November, 1987 1

Figure 13.26: Improving Spacings of Headings

figure also shows other final touches, applied as follows:

- The figure and its caption have been added.
- The font for the caption has been changed. It's wise to limit the number of fonts you use. The italic font, used elsewhere on the page, serves nicely as a caption font. There is no need for it to have a separate font that's used nowhere else.
- The figure in its frame has been repositioned. Initially, the line art extended clear to the top edge of its frame. To make the spacing similar to that between column rules and text in the columns, we added a top margin of 1 pica to the frame. The amount is half that of the gutter of the underlying-page frame.
- The frame with the picture has been relocated. By moving the frame up, it doesn't interrupt the first paragraph of the second article.
- The slower, but surer, hyphenation algorithm has been implemented. It's wise to do so for text that appears within narrow columns like this.
- Line Breaks have been added to the headlines. By inserting a Line Break (Ctrl-Return) after *Software Salaries* and *CD-ROM Breaks*, we improve the readability of the headlines considerably.
- A Thin Space has been inserted between numbers and letters: specifically *550 M* and *360 K*.
- Second spaces that follow the ends of sentences have been eliminated. You can do this with Ventura in the Text mode, or you can use your word processor's search and replace capability.

Finishing touches such as these can truly enhance your documents. These capabilities show once again how sophisticated Ventura is. And despite all that the program can currently do, Xerox will undoubtedly continue to create updated versions. As they do, look for corresponding future editions of this book.

Widget World News

Views and News of Widget Manufacturing in the 80s

142 Guitrep Pkwy. *Detroit, MI 98987* *(413) 567-9888*

Software Salaries: How do you stack up?

by Joe Smith

How much your software professionals are paid is a function of many variables, and a subject of considerable interest to your organization.

Software salary pay scales

■ Because of the dynamic growth of the software industry over the last decade, the demand for experienced, qualified programmers has greatly increased, thus leading to a spiraling of salaries.

But what causes managers to pay one programmer more than another? Does the type of organization, its size, or location make a difference? What career path or programming specialty leads to the most remuneration?

To answer these questions, Acme Magazine recently conducted its third annual compensation survey for software professionals. This newsletter article presents the results of this study and explores what the findings may mean to you.

Acme Magazine asked Joe Smith, a compensation consulting specialist for the software industry, to design and conduct the survey. Twenty-four positions, representing four programmer job families plus management, were included.

Data was collected for base pay, bonus and incentive payments, and whether nor not incumbents received stock options or other forms of equity.

Questionnaires were sent to the data processing heads of 2,400 organizations throughout the United States.

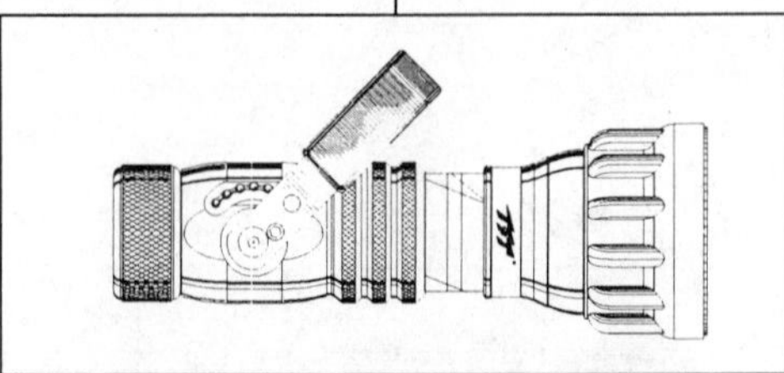

Clever CD-ROM connector that doubles as a garden hose nozzle

CD-ROM Breaks New Ground

Compact Disk Read Only Memory (CD-ROM) is a rapidly emerging new technology for the retrieval of vast amounts of information from an optical disk. This new peripheral device allows a totally new level of functionality in the use of microcomputers.

Physically, the CD-ROM device has a laser disk drive (or "player") the same size as a traditional 5 1/4" drive. The removable disk is 4 3/4", and has a capacity of 550 M bytes (equivalent to 1500 360 K floppy disks).

Theory of Operation

■ Information stored on a CD-ROM can be loaded into memory (RAM), displayed and printed, as with other media. While that data in RAM may be altered and stored to a conventional magnetic disk, the original information on the CD-ROM is unalterable, always ensuring the original copy is intact, making archiving easy.

The storage capacity, low cost, and read only feature of CD-ROM bring an enormous new capability to microcomputer users – that is, information retrieval of very large reference publications. How people receive and use information in the immediate and long term future will be dramatically changed by CD-ROM.

In addition to the huge capacity of raw information storage, specialized software for the search of that information is currently being introduced. This software allows searching the information in areas, methods and speeds not previously feasible.

It now becomes possible to electronically publish reference material more economically than to print the same material in book form. That cost benefit, coupled with search and retrieval software, make an astonishing price/performance ratio.

Table of Contents

November, 1987 1

Figure 13.27: Finishing Touches Applied

APPENDICES

APPENDIX A

Ventura's Sample Documents

FIGURES A.1 THROUGH A.20 SHOW THE SAMPLE documents that are provided with Ventura. The samples are copied into the TYPESET directory when you install Ventura.

We have made some changes in the samples as they initially appear on the disk. The samples were apparently designed to achieve their formatting effects on a PostScript printer. Printing them with a different printer, as we did with the Hewlett-Packard LaserJet Series II, can create undesirable changes. For example, dropped capitals are positioned too low and bullets are too tightly placed in the LaserJet versions of the documents. Where these changes have created poor style in the samples, they have been corrected. These corrections are discussed in Chapter 13 and noted in the examples where they were made. We have also used the Page menu's Re-Anchor Frames command to reposition the frame in &BOOK-P1, thus avoiding poor figure placement caused by the changed line length on the LaserJet.

You may wish to make additional changes as well. For example, letters touch the rules below many paragraphs (look at the *Digitizers* heading in &LSTG-P2). It would be good design to increase the spacing in order to avoid this.

Chapter files and style sheet files are paired and presented according to their common main file name: that is, that portion of the file name that precedes the period. The extensions, being the defaults, are assumed; namely, all chapter names end with the extension CHP and all style sheet names end with the extension STY. When you load chapter and style sheet files, Ventura automatically assumes the appropriate extension and filters file names accordingly. Chapter 3 contains further discussion of the system used for naming the samples and Appendix C examines file filtering.

Along with the printed versions of the samples, Tables A.1 through A.20 list the salient features for each sample. Only those features which are stored with the style sheet appear. By using the same style sheet with your document, you can have these features available.

Each table is divided into two parts. First, there are features that affect the document in general. These are accessible via the Page and Frame menus. The Frame settings apply to the underlying-page frame, which must be selected if you wish to change them.

Following these general features is a list of the paragraph tags contained within the style sheet. Body Text is always the first tag listed, followed by others alphabetically. The listings do not necessarily contain all tags for the particular style sheet; only those with features of particular interest are listed. You will probably want to explore the samples further.

Some tags occur repeatedly within the various style sheets. Two in particular are the Page Break tag (usually F8) and the Change Bar tag (usually F9). The Page Break tag causes the paragraph which follows it to begin on a new page. If you want to cause a page break, you can press an extra return between paragraphs that you want on separate pages and format the second paragraph mark with the Page Break tag. The Change Bar uses a Ruling Box Around to create a vertical bar to the left of the paragraph so tagged. The technique for creating this format is discussed in Chapter 8. Although the Change Bar tag is not initially applied to any of the sample paragraphs, we have done so in the first two samples to demonstrate this tag in action.

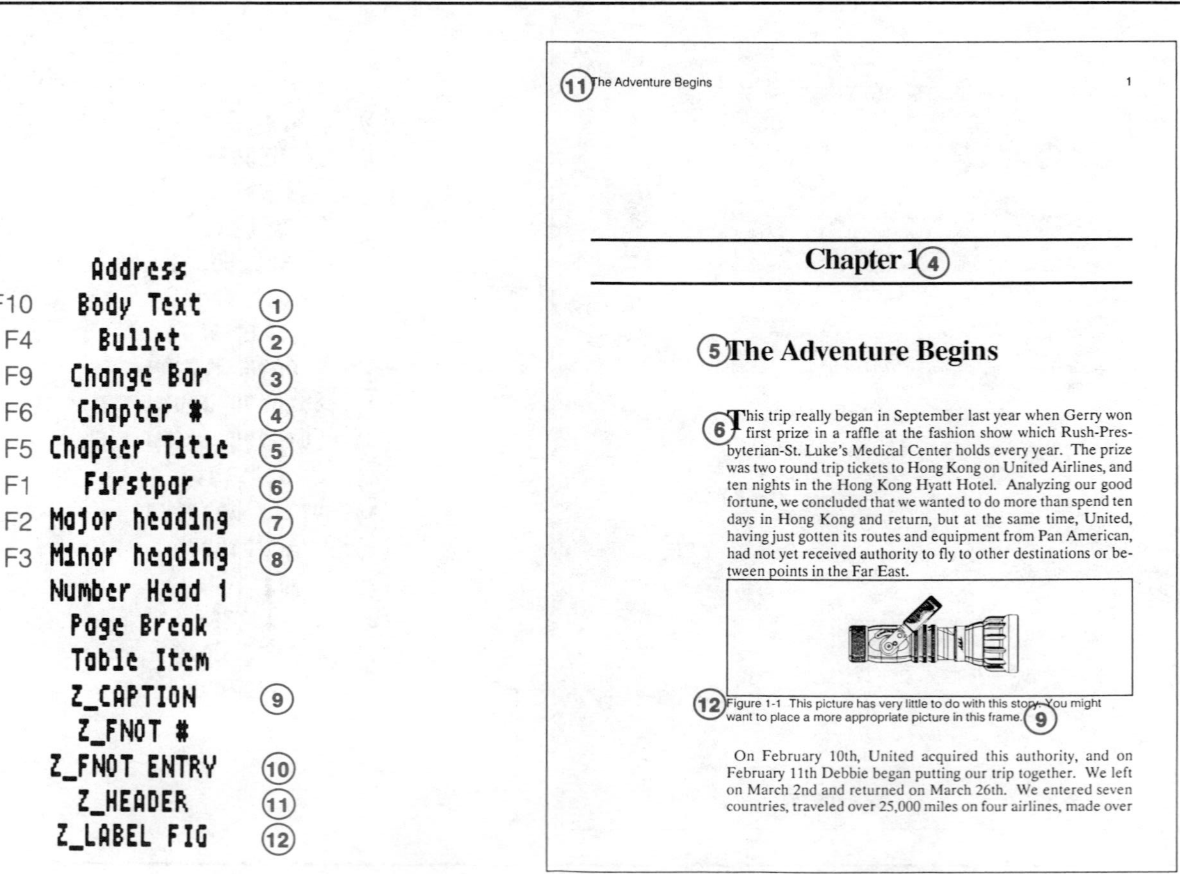

This trip really began in September last year when Gerry won first prize in a raffle at the fashion show which Rush-Presbyterian-St. Luke's Medical Center holds every year. The prize was two round trip tickets to Hong Kong on United Airlines, and ten nights in the Hong Kong Hyatt Hotel. Analyzing our good fortune, we concluded that we wanted to do more than spend ten days in Hong Kong and return, but at the same time, United, having just gotten its routes and equipment from Pan American, had not yet received authority to fly to other destinations or between points in the Far East.

Figure 1-1 This picture has very little to do with this story. You might want to place a more appropriate picture in this frame.

On February 10th, United acquired this authority, and on February 11th Debbie began putting our trip together. We left on March 2nd and returned on March 26th. We entered seven countries, traveled over 25,000 miles on four airlines, made over

Figure A.1: &BOOK-P1 Sample Pages

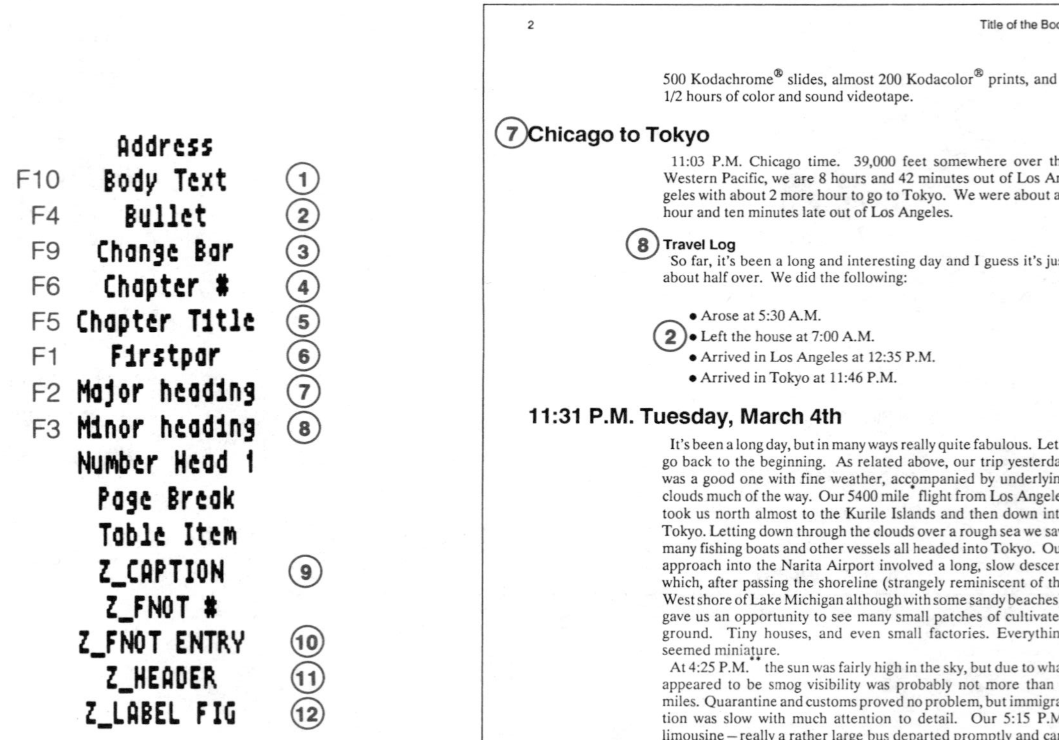

Figure A.1: &BOOK-P1 Sample Pages (continued)

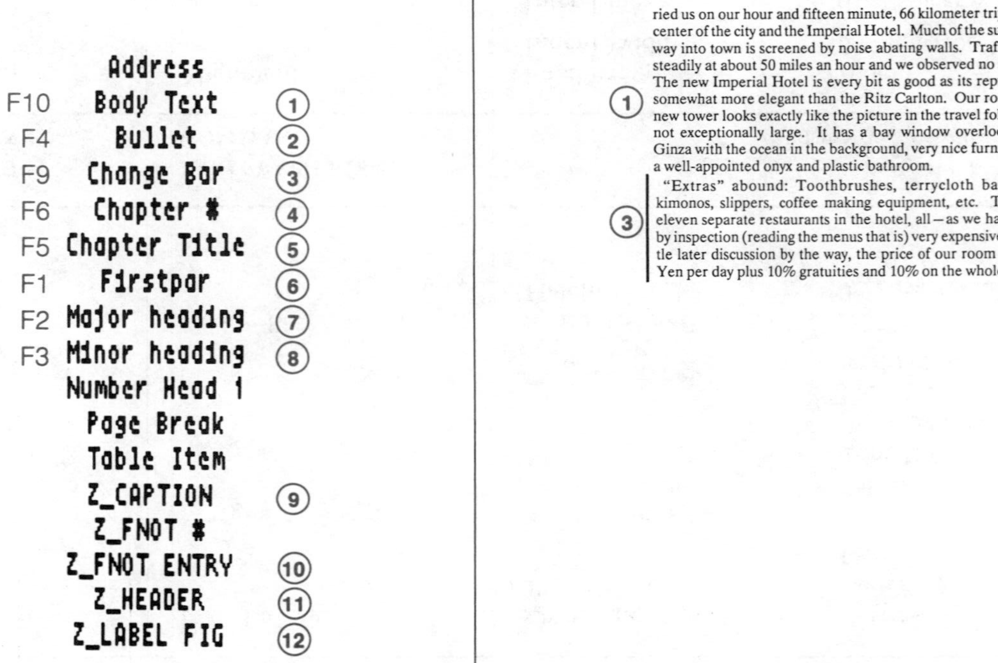

Figure A.1: &BOOK-P1 Sample Pages (continued)

MENU	COMMAND	SETTING	
Page	Page Layout	Orientation: Paper Type: Sides:	Portrait Letter Double
Frame	Margins & Columns	# of Columns: Column Width: Margins:	1 6 in. Top: 1.5'' Bottom: 1.17'' Left: 1.25'' Right: 1.25''
	Ruling Box Around	Space Above Rule 1: Height of Rule:	.75'' 0.72 fractional points (.01'')
TAG NAME AND FUNCTION KEY	**PARAGRAPH MENU COMMAND**	**SETTING**	
Body Text (F10)	Alignment	Firstline: Indent Width:	Indent 6 points (.08'')
	Spacing	Inter-Line: In From Left:	01,01 picas & points 1.5'' (09,00 picas & points)
*Bullet (F4)	Spacing	Above & Below: Inter-Line: In From Left:	3.48 fractional points 13.98 fractional points 10,00 picas & points

Tag Name and Function Key	Paragraph Menu Command	Setting	
**Change Bar (F9)	Ruling Box Around	Width:	Custom
		Height of Rule 1:	1.98 fractional points
		Custom Indent:	–6 fractional points
		Custom Width:	1.98 fractional points
Chapter # (F6)	Alignment	Alignment:	Center
	Ruling Line Above/Below	Width:	Margin
		Height of Rule 1:	1.98 fractional points
Chapter Title (F5)	Alignment	Alignment:	Center
	Above & Below:	03,00 picas & points (.5")	Spacing
†Firstpar (F1)	Special Effects	Special Effect:	Big First Char
		Space for Big First Char:	Custom, 2 lines
Major Heading (F2)	Spacing	Above:	01,01 picas & points
		Below:	00,07 picas & points
Minor Heading (F3)	Spacing	Above:	01,01 picas & points
		In From Left:	09,00 picas & points
‡Page Break (F8)	Breaks	Page Break:	After

*We increased the Indent After Bullet to 1 pica (see Chapter 13).
**Creates a vertical bar along the left edge of the paragraph (see Chapter 8). We applied this tag to the last paragraph.
†We shifted the dropped capital up 6 points (see Chapter 13).
‡Causes the next paragraph to begin on a new page.

Table A.1: &BOOK-P1 Formatting Features

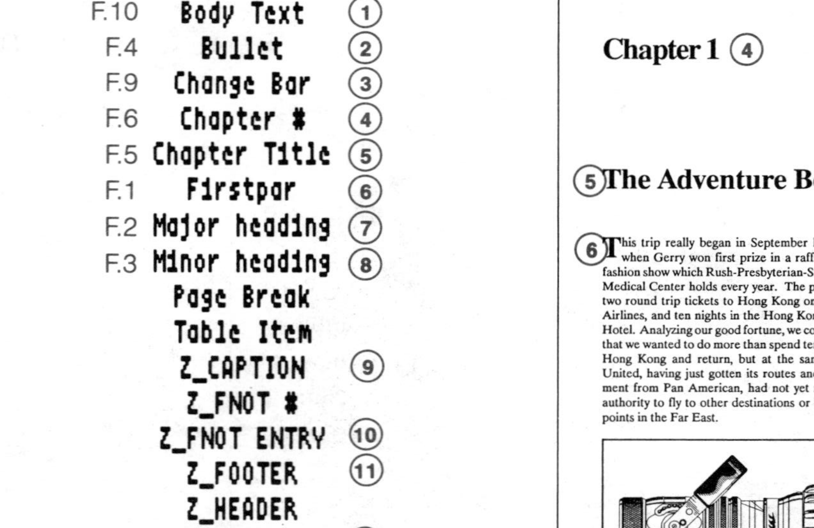

F.10	Body Text	1
F.4	Bullet	2
F.9	Change Bar	3
F.6	Chapter #	4
F.5	Chapter Title	5
F.1	Firstpar	6
F.2	Major heading	7
F.3	Minor heading	8
	Page Break	
	Table Item	
	Z_CAPTION	9
	Z_FNOT #	
	Z_FNOT ENTRY	10
	Z_FOOTER	11
	Z_HEADER	
	Z_LABEL FIG	12

Chapter 1 (4)

(5) The Adventure Begins

(6) This trip really began in September last year when Gerry won first prize in a raffle at the fashion show which Rush-Presbyterian-St. Luke's Medical Center holds every year. The prize was two round trip tickets to Hong Kong on United Airlines, and ten nights in the Hong Kong Hyatt Hotel. Analyzing our good fortune, we concluded that we wanted to do more than spend ten days in Hong Kong and return, but at the same time, United, having just gotten its routes and equipment from Pan American, had not yet received authority to fly to other destinations or between points in the Far East.

(12) Figure 1-1. Place your own picture in this (9) frame.

On February 10th, United acquired this authority, and on February 11th Debbie began putting our trip together. We left on March 2nd and returned on March 26th. We entered seven countries, traveled over 25,000 miles on four airlines, made over 500 Kodachrome® slides, almost 200 Kodacolor® prints, and 5 1/2 hours of color and sound videotape.

(7) Chicago to Tokyo

11:03 P.M. Chicago time. 39,000 feet somewhere over the Western Pacific, we are 8 hours and 42 minutes out of Los Angeles with about 2 more hour to go to Tokyo. We were about an hour and ten minutes late out of Los Angeles.

(8) Travel Log

So far, it's been a long and interesting day and I guess it's just about half over. We did the following:

(2)
- Arose at 5:30 A.M.
- Left the house at 7:00 A.M.
- Arrived in Los Angeles at 12:35 P.M.
- Arrived in Tokyo at 11:46 P.M.

(11) The Adventure Begins 1

Figure A.2: &BOOK-P2 Sample Pages

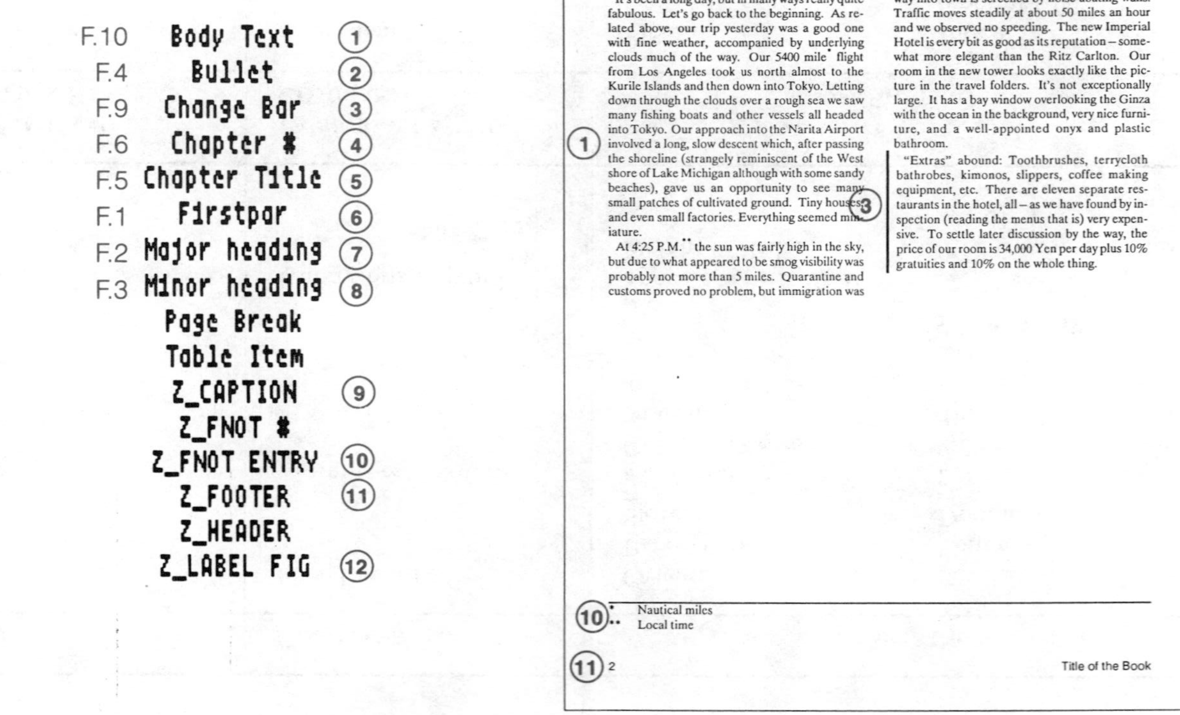

11:31 P.M. Tuesday, March 4th

It's been a long day, but in many ways really quite fabulous. Let's go back to the beginning. As related above, our trip yesterday was a good one with fine weather, accompanied by underlying clouds much of the way. Our 5400 mile* flight from Los Angeles took us north almost to the Kurile Islands and then down into Tokyo. Letting down through the clouds over a rough sea we saw many fishing boats and other vessels all headed into Tokyo. Our approach into the Narita Airport involved a long, slow descent which, after passing the shoreline (strangely reminiscent of the West shore of Lake Michigan although with some sandy beaches), gave us an opportunity to see many small patches of cultivated ground. Tiny houses and even small factories. Everything seemed miniature.

At 4:25 P.M.** the sun was fairly high in the sky, but due to what appeared to be smog visibility was probably not more than 5 miles. Quarantine and customs proved no problem, but immigration was slow with much attention to detail. Our 5:15 P.M. limousine – really a rather large bus departed promptly and carried us on our hour and fifteen minute, 66 kilometer trip into the center of the city and the Imperial Hotel. Much of the super highway into town is screened by noise abating walls. Traffic moves steadily at about 50 miles an hour and we observed no speeding. The new Imperial Hotel is every bit as good as its reputation – somewhat more elegant than the Ritz Carlton. Our room in the new tower looks exactly like the picture in the travel folders. It's not exceptionally large. It has a bay window overlooking the Ginza with the ocean in the background, very nice furniture, and a well-appointed onyx and plastic bathroom.

"Extras" abound: Toothbrushes, terrycloth bathrobes, kimonos, slippers, coffee making equipment, etc. There are eleven separate restaurants in the hotel, all – as we have found by inspection (reading the menus that is) very expensive. To settle later discussion by the way, the price of our room is 34,000 Yen per day plus 10% gratuities and 10% on the whole thing.

* Nautical miles
** Local time

2 Title of the Book

Figure A.2: &BOOK-P2 Sample Pages (continued)

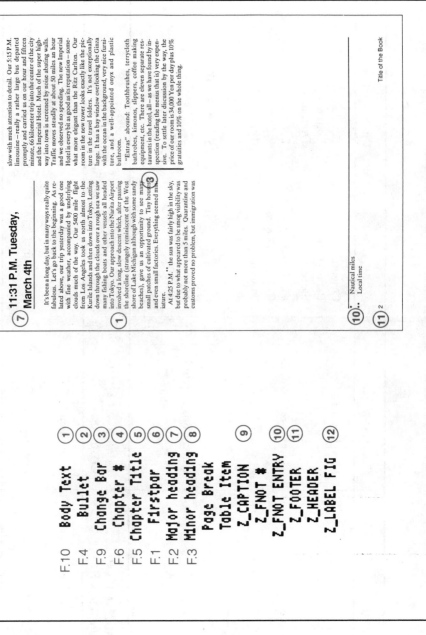

MENU	COMMAND	SETTING	
Page	Page Layout	Orientation: Paper Type: Sides:	Portrait Letter Double
Frame	Margins & Columns	# of Columns: Column Widths: Margins:	2 2.83 in. Top: 1.17" Bottom: 1.5" Left: 1.25" Right: 1.25"
	Ruling Box Around	Space Above Rule 1: Height of Rule:	.75" 0.72 fractional points (.01")
TAG NAME AND FUNCTION KEY	PARAGRAPH MENU COMMAND	SETTING	
Body Text (F10)	Alignment	Firstline: Indent Width:	Indent 6 points (.08")
	Spacing	Inter-Line:	01,00 picas & points

Tag Name and Function Key	Paragraph Menu Command	Setting	
*Bullet (F4)	Spacing	In From Left:	01,00 picas & points
**Change Bar (F9)	Ruling Box Around	Width:	Custom
		Height of Rule 1:	1.98 fractional points
		Custom Indent:	–6 fractional points
		Custom Width:	1.98 fractional points
Chapter # (F6)	Spacing	Above:	09,00 picas & points (1.5'')
		Below	06,00 picas & points (1'')
Chapter Title (F5)	Spacing	Above & Below:	03,00 picas & points (.5'')
†Firstpar (F1)	Special Effects	Special Effect:	Big First Char
		Space for Big First Char:	Custom, 2 lines
Major Heading (F2)	Spacing	Above:	01,00 picas & points
		Below:	00,10 picas & points
	Ruling Line Below	Width:	Column
		Height of Rule 1:	1.02 fractional points
Minor Heading (F3)	Spacing	Above:	01,00 picas & points
‡Page Break (F8)	Breaks	Page Break:	After

*We increased the Indent After Bullet to 1 pica (see Chapter 13).
**We applied this tag to the last paragraph.
†We shifted the dropped capital up 3 points (as Chapter 13).
‡Causes the next paragraph to begin on a new page.

Table A.2: &BOOK-P2 Formatting Features

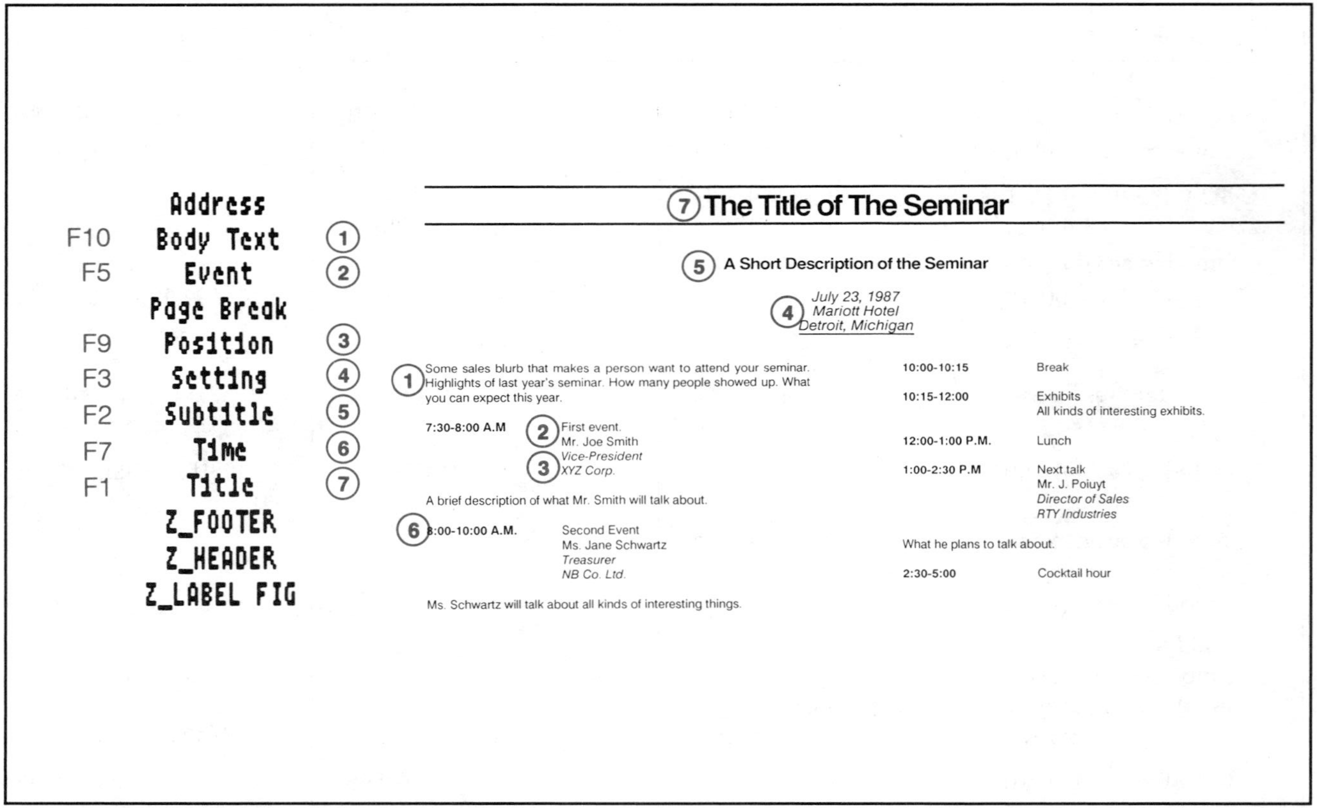

Address
F10 Body Text ①
F5 Event ②
Page Break
F9 Position ③
F3 Setting ④
F2 Subtitle ⑤
F7 Time ⑥
F1 Title ⑦
Z_FOOTER
Z_HEADER
Z_LABEL FIG

⑦ The Title of The Seminar

⑤ A Short Description of the Seminar

④ *July 23, 1987*
Mariott Hotel
Detroit, Michigan

① Some sales blurb that makes a person want to attend your seminar. Highlights of last year's seminar. How many people showed up. What you can expect this year.

7:30-8:00 A.M ② First event.
Mr. Joe Smith
③ *Vice-President*
XYZ Corp.

A brief description of what Mr. Smith will talk about.

⑥ **8:00-10:00 A.M.** Second Event
Ms. Jane Schwartz
Treasurer
NB Co. Ltd.

Ms. Schwartz will talk about all kinds of interesting things.

10:00-10:15 Break

10:15-12:00 Exhibits
All kinds of interesting exhibits.

12:00-1:00 P.M. Lunch

1:00-2:30 P.M Next talk
Mr. J. Poiuyt
Director of Sales
RTY Industries

What he plans to talk about.

2:30-5:00 Cocktail hour

Figure A.3: &BRO-L2 Sample Page

MENU	COMMAND	SETTING	
Page	Page Layout	Orientation: Paper Type: Sides:	Landscape Letter Single
Frame	Margins & Columns	# of Columns: Column Widths: Margins:	2 4.25 in. Top: 1.5'' Bottom: 1'' Left: .75'' Right: .75''
TAG NAME AND FUNCTION KEY	**PARAGRAPH MENU COMMAND**	**SETTING**	
Body Text (F10)	Spacing	Above & Below: Inter-Line:	01,00 picas & points 01,00 picas & points
*Event (F5)	Font Spacing Breaks	Style: In From Left: Line Break:	N-Italic 09,00 picas & points (1.5'') After

Table A.3: &BRO-L2 Formatting Features

Tag Name and Function Key	Paragraph Menu Command	Setting	
Page Break (F8)	Breaks	Page Break:	After
Position (F9)	Font	Style:	N-Italic
	Spacing	In From Left:	09,00 picas & points (1.5'')
	Breaks	Line Break:	Before
Setting (F3)	Font	Style:	N-Italic
	Alignment	Alignment:	Center
	Ruling Line Below	Width: Height of Rule 1:	Text 1.02 fractional points
Subtitle (F2)	Alignment	Alignment: Overall Width:	Center Frame-Wide
**Time (F7)	Breaks	Line Break:	Before
Title (F1)	Alignment	Alignment:	Center
	Overall Width:	Frame-Wide	
	Ruling Line Above/Below	Width: Height of Rule 1:	Column 1.98 fractional points

*Since Event text has no break set before it, it stays on the same line as text formatted with the Time tag.
**The Time tag has no break after it, so that text following it stays on the same line.

Table A.3: &BRO-L2 Formatting Features (continued)

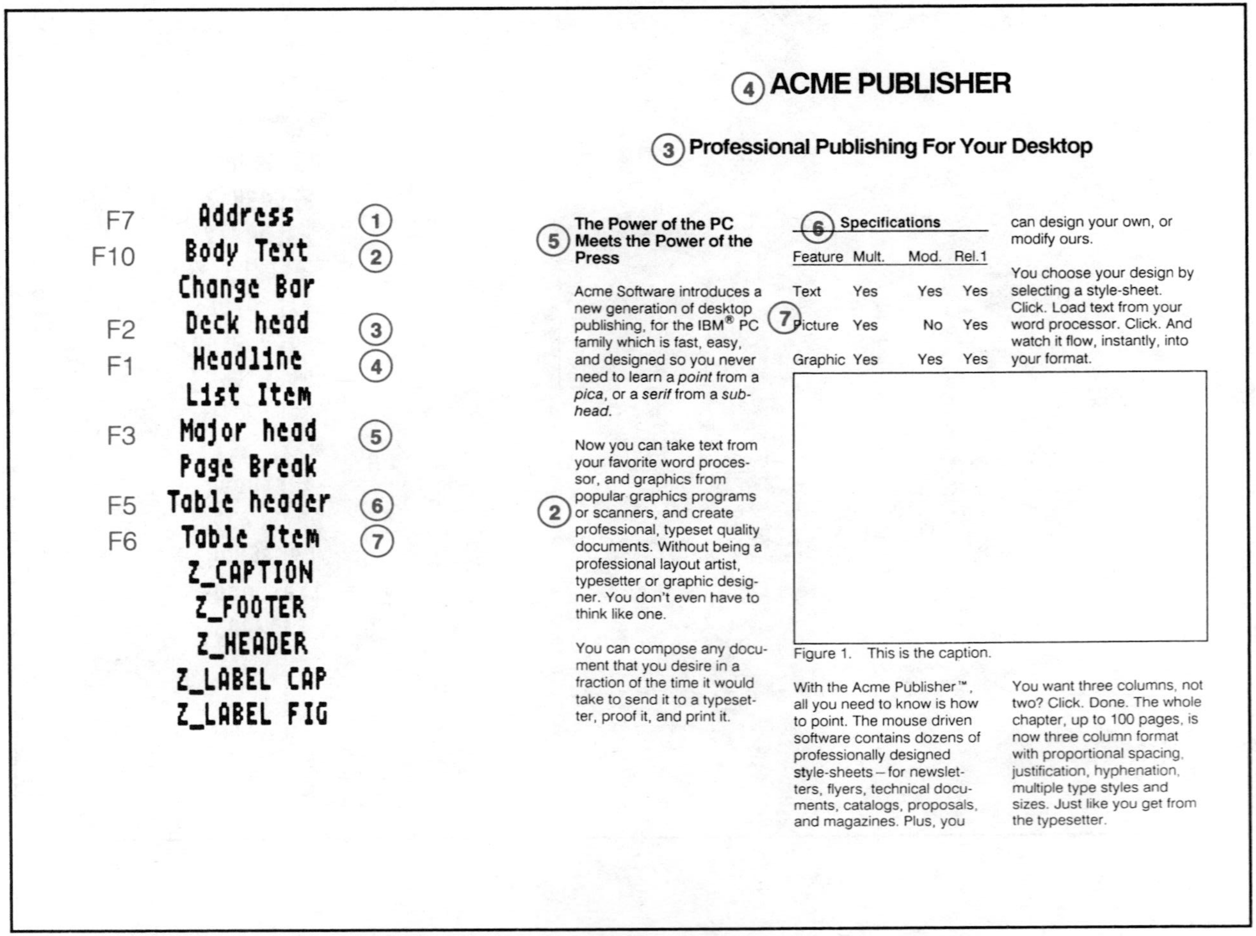

Key	Tag	
F7	Address	(1)
F10	Body Text	(2)
	Change Bar	
F2	Deck head	(3)
F1	Headline	(4)
	List Item	
F3	Major head	(5)
	Page Break	
F5	Table header	(6)
F6	Table Item	(7)
	Z_CAPTION	
	Z_FOOTER	
	Z_HEADER	
	Z_LABEL CAP	
	Z_LABEL FIG	

(4) ACME PUBLISHER

(3) Professional Publishing For Your Desktop

(5) The Power of the PC Meets the Power of the Press

Acme Software introduces a new generation of desktop publishing, for the IBM® PC family which is fast, easy, and designed so you never need to learn a *point* from a *pica*, or a *serif* from a *subhead*.

(2) Now you can take text from your favorite word processor, and graphics from popular graphics programs or scanners, and create professional, typeset quality documents. Without being a professional layout artist, typesetter or graphic designer. You don't even have to think like one.

You can compose any document that you desire in a fraction of the time it would take to send it to a typesetter, proof it, and print it.

(6) Specifications

Feature	Mult.	Mod.	Rel.1
Text	Yes	Yes	Yes
(7) Picture	Yes	No	Yes
Graphic	Yes	Yes	Yes

Figure 1. This is the caption.

With the Acme Publisher™, all you need to know is how to point. The mouse driven software contains dozens of professionally designed style-sheets – for newsletters, flyers, technical documents, catalogs, proposals, and magazines. Plus, you can design your own, or modify ours.

You choose your design by selecting a style-sheet. Click. Load text from your word processor. Click. And watch it flow, instantly, into your format.

You want three columns, not two? Click. Done. The whole chapter, up to 100 pages, is now three column format with proportional spacing, justification, hyphenation, multiple type styles and sizes. Just like you get from the typesetter.

Figure A.4: &BRO-P3 Sample Pages

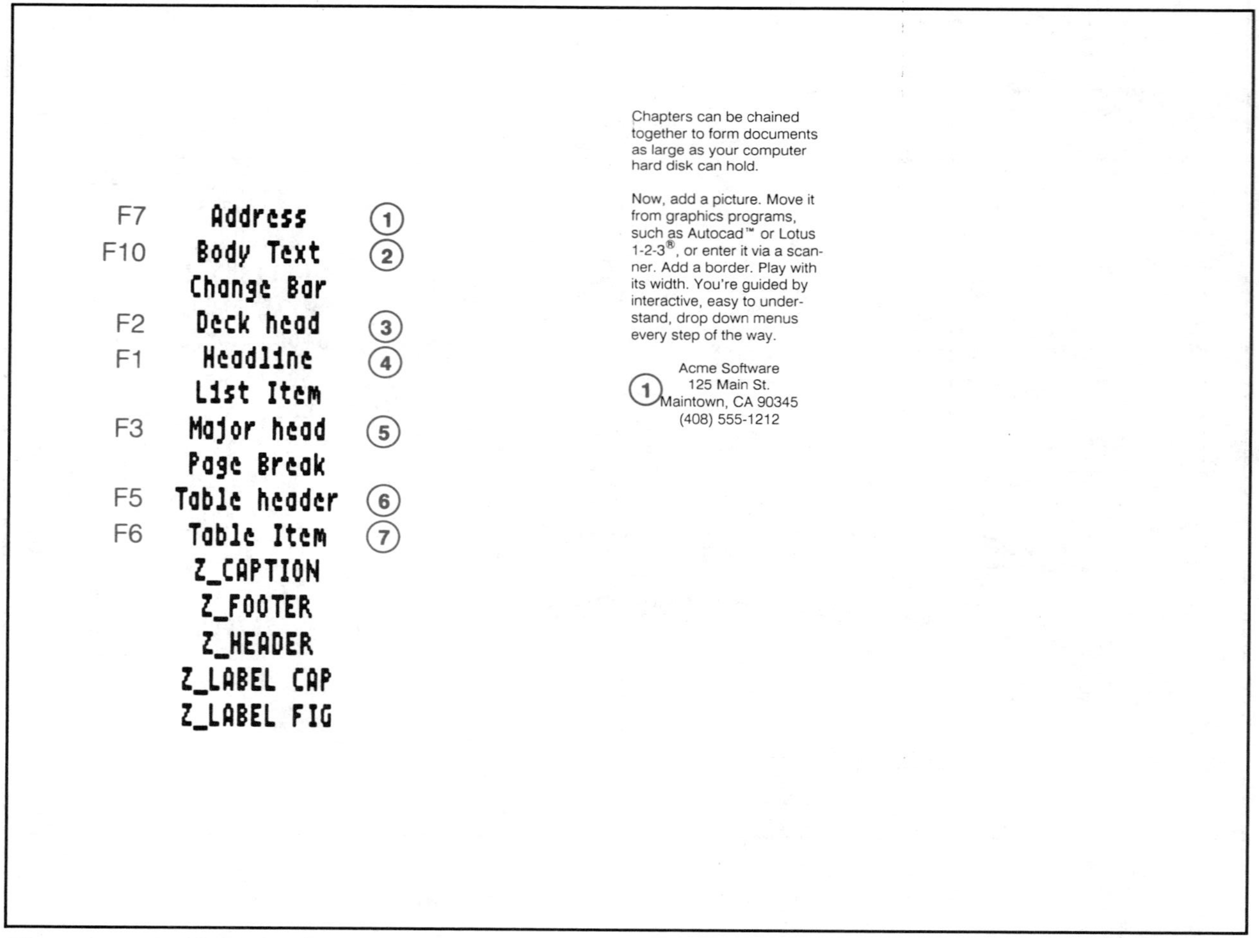

F7	Address	(1)
F10	Body Text	(2)
	Change Bar	
F2	Deck head	(3)
F1	Headline	(4)
	List Item	
F3	Major head	(5)
	Page Break	
F5	Table header	(6)
F6	Table Item	(7)
	Z_CAPTION	
	Z_FOOTER	
	Z_HEADER	
	Z_LABEL CAP	
	Z_LABEL FIG	

Chapters can be chained together to form documents as large as your computer hard disk can hold.

Now, add a picture. Move it from graphics programs, such as Autocad™ or Lotus 1-2-3®, or enter it via a scanner. Add a border. Play with its width. You're guided by interactive, easy to understand, drop down menus every step of the way.

(1) Acme Software
125 Main St.
Maintown, CA 90345
(408) 555-1212

Figure A.4: &BRO-P3 Sample Pages (continued)

MENU	COMMAND	SETTING	
Page	Page Layout	Orientation:	Portrait
		Paper Type:	Letter
		Sides:	Double
Frame	Margins & Columns	# of Columns:	3
		Column Widths:	2.17 in.
		Margins:	Top: .78"
			Bottom: .83"
			Left: .75"
			Right: .75"
TAG NAME AND FUNCTION KEY	**PARAGRAPH MENU COMMAND**	**SETTING**	
Body Text (F10)	Alignment	Alignment:	Left
	Spacing	Above & Below:	01,01 picas & points
		Inter-Line:	01,01 picas & points
Address (F7)	Alignment	Alignment:	Center
Deck head (F2)	Alignment	Alignment:	Center
		Overall Width:	Frame-Wide
	Spacing	Above:	01,01 picas & points
		Below:	03,06 picas & points

Table A.4: &BRO-P3 Formatting Features

Tag Name and Function Key	Paragraph Menu Command	Setting	
Headline (F1)	Alignment	Alignment:	Center
		Overall Width:	Frame-Wide
	Spacing	Above:	03,06 picas & points
Major head (F3)	Spacing	Above & Below:	01,01 picas & points
Page Break (F8)	Breaks	Page Break:	After
Table header (F5)	Alignment	Alignment:	Center
	Ruling Line Below	Width:	Margin
		Height of Rule 1:	1.02 fractional points
*Table Item (F6)	Tab Settings	Tab Number 1:	Left, 04,04 picas & points
		Tab Number 2:	Left, 10,00 picas & points
		Tab Number 3:	Left, 13,00 picas & points

*The tab settings are discussed in Chapter 9.

Table A.4: &BRO-P3 Formatting Features (continued)

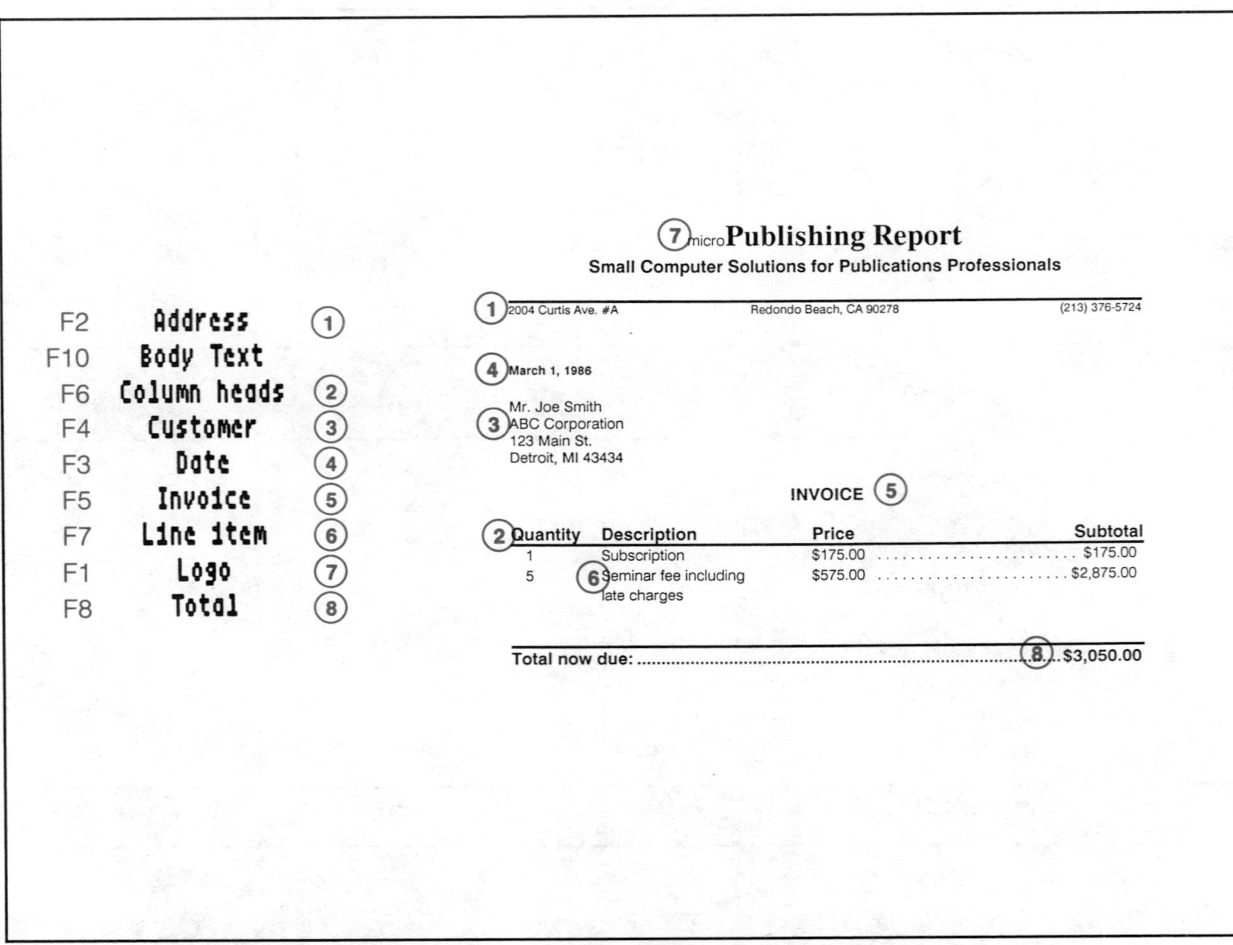

Figure A.5: &INV-P1 Sample Page

MENU	COMMAND	SETTING	
Page	Page Layout	Orientation: Paper Type: Sides:	Portrait Letter Single
Frame	Margins & Columns	# of Columns: Column Width: Margins:	1 7'' Top: 1'' Bottom: .5'' Left: .75'' Right: .75''
TAG NAME AND FUNCTION KEY	**PARAGRAPH MENU COMMAND**	**SETTING**	
Body Text (F10)	Alignment	Alignment:	Left
	Spacing	Inter-Line:	01,00 picas & points
Address (F2)	Tab Settings	Tab Number 1: Tab Number 2:	Center, 3.5'' Right, 7''
Column heads (F6)	Tab Settings	Tab Number 1: Tab Number 2: Tab Number 3: Tab Number 4:	Left, 1'' Left, 3.33'' Right, 7'' Decimal, 6.67''

TAG NAME AND FUNCTION KEY	PARAGRAPH MENU COMMAND	SETTING	
*Invoice (F5)	Ruling Line Above	Pattern: Height of Rule 1: Space Below Rule 3:	1 18 fractional points – 18 fractional points
Line item (F7)	Tab Settings	Tab Number 1: Tab Number 2: Tab Number 3:	Left, 1" Left, 3.33" Right, 6.7"
**Logo (F1)	Alignment	Alignment: Overall Width:	Center Frame-Wide
Total (F8)	Tab Settings	Tab Number 1: Tab Display: Leader Char:	Decimal, 6.7 in. Shown as Leader Char ...

*See Chapter 13 for a discussion of shaded text, like that of the word *Invoice.*
**Text attributes change the font sizes and lower the bottom line of text in the sample document.

Table A.5: &INV-P1 Formatting Features

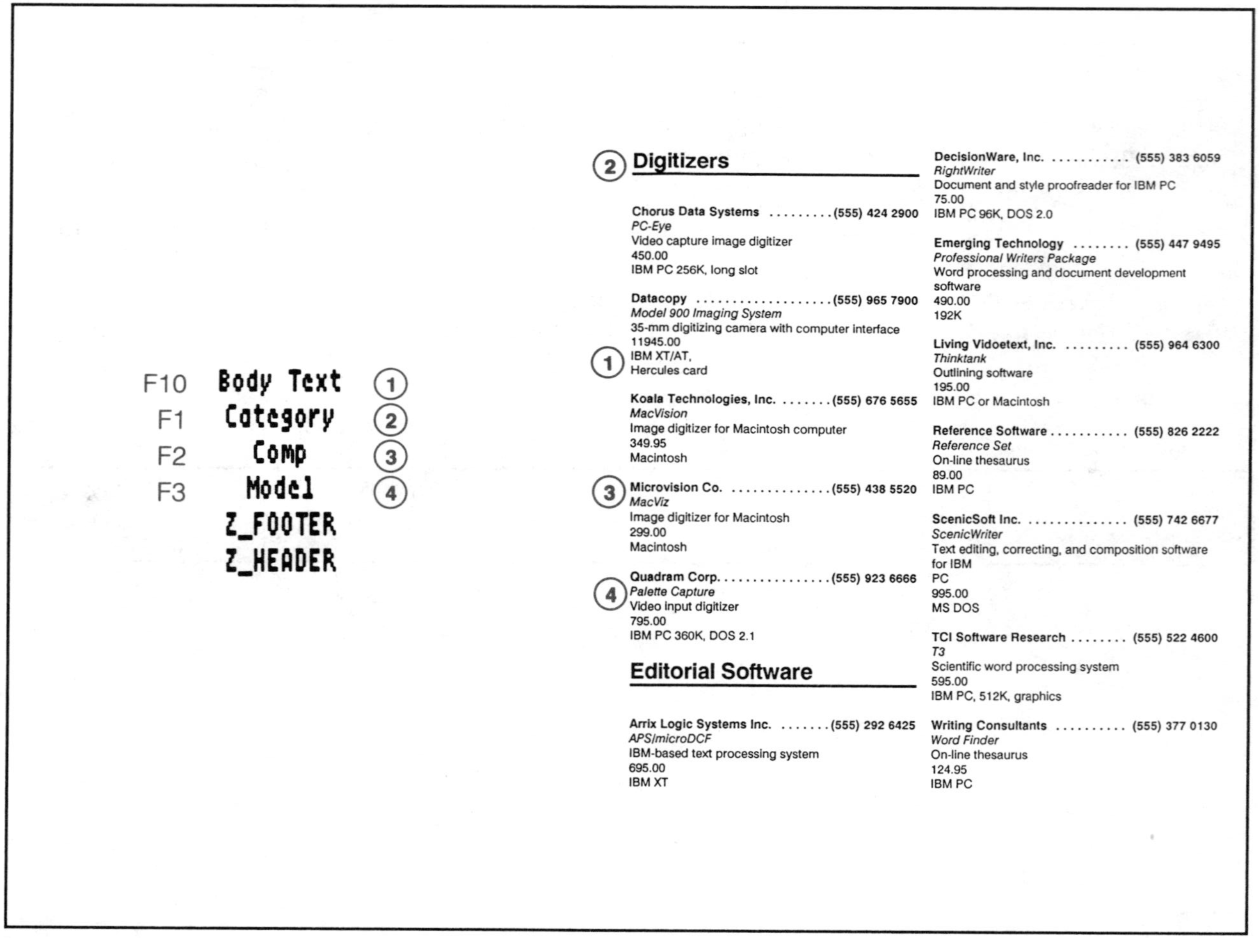

F10 Body Text (1)
F1 Category (2)
F2 Comp (3)
F3 Model (4)
Z_FOOTER
Z_HEADER

(2) **Digitizers**

Chorus Data Systems .... (555) 424 2900
PC-Eye
Video capture image digitizer
450.00
IBM PC 256K, long slot

Datacopy .... (555) 965 7900
Model 900 Imaging System
35-mm digitizing camera with computer interface
11945.00
(1) IBM XT/AT,
Hercules card

Koala Technologies, Inc. .... (555) 676 5655
MacVision
Image digitizer for Macintosh computer
349.95
Macintosh

(3) **Microvision Co.** .... (555) 438 5520
MacViz
Image digitizer for Macintosh
299.00
Macintosh

(4) **Quadram Corp.** .... (555) 923 6666
Palette Capture
Video input digitizer
795.00
IBM PC 360K, DOS 2.1

Editorial Software

Arrix Logic Systems Inc. .... (555) 292 6425
APS/microDCF
IBM-based text processing system
695.00
IBM XT

DecisionWare, Inc. .... (555) 383 6059
RightWriter
Document and style proofreader for IBM PC
75.00
IBM PC 96K, DOS 2.0

Emerging Technology .... (555) 447 9495
Professional Writers Package
Word processing and document development software
490.00
192K

Living Vidoetext, Inc. .... (555) 964 6300
Thinktank
Outlining software
195.00
IBM PC or Macintosh

Reference Software .... (555) 826 2222
Reference Set
On-line thesaurus
89.00
IBM PC

ScenicSoft Inc. .... (555) 742 6677
ScenicWriter
Text editing, correcting, and composition software for IBM
PC
995.00
MS DOS

TCI Software Research .... (555) 522 4600
T3
Scientific word processing system
595.00
IBM PC, 512K, graphics

Writing Consultants .... (555) 377 0130
Word Finder
On-line thesaurus
124.95
IBM PC

Figure A.6: &LSTG-P2 Sample Page

MENU	COMMAND	SETTING	
Page	Page Layout	Orientation:	Portrait
		Paper Type:	Letter
		Sides:	Double
Frame	Margins & Columns	# of Columns:	2
		Column Widths:	3.17"
		Margins:	Top: .83"
			Bottom: .83"
			Left: 1"
			Right: 1"
TAG NAME AND FUNCTION KEY	**PARAGRAPH MENU COMMAND**	**SETTING**	
Body Text (F10)	Alignment	Alignment:	Left
	Spacing	Inter-Line:	01,00 picas & points
Category (F1)	Spacing	Above:	01,00 picas & points
		Below:	01,10 picas & points
	Ruling Line Below	Width:	Column
		Height of Rule 1:	1.98 fractional points
Comp (F2)	Tab Settings	Tab Number 1:	Right, 3.17"
		Tab Display:	Shown as Leader Char
		Leader Char:	...
Model (F3)	Font	Style:	N-Italic

Table A.6: &LSTG-P2 Formatting Features

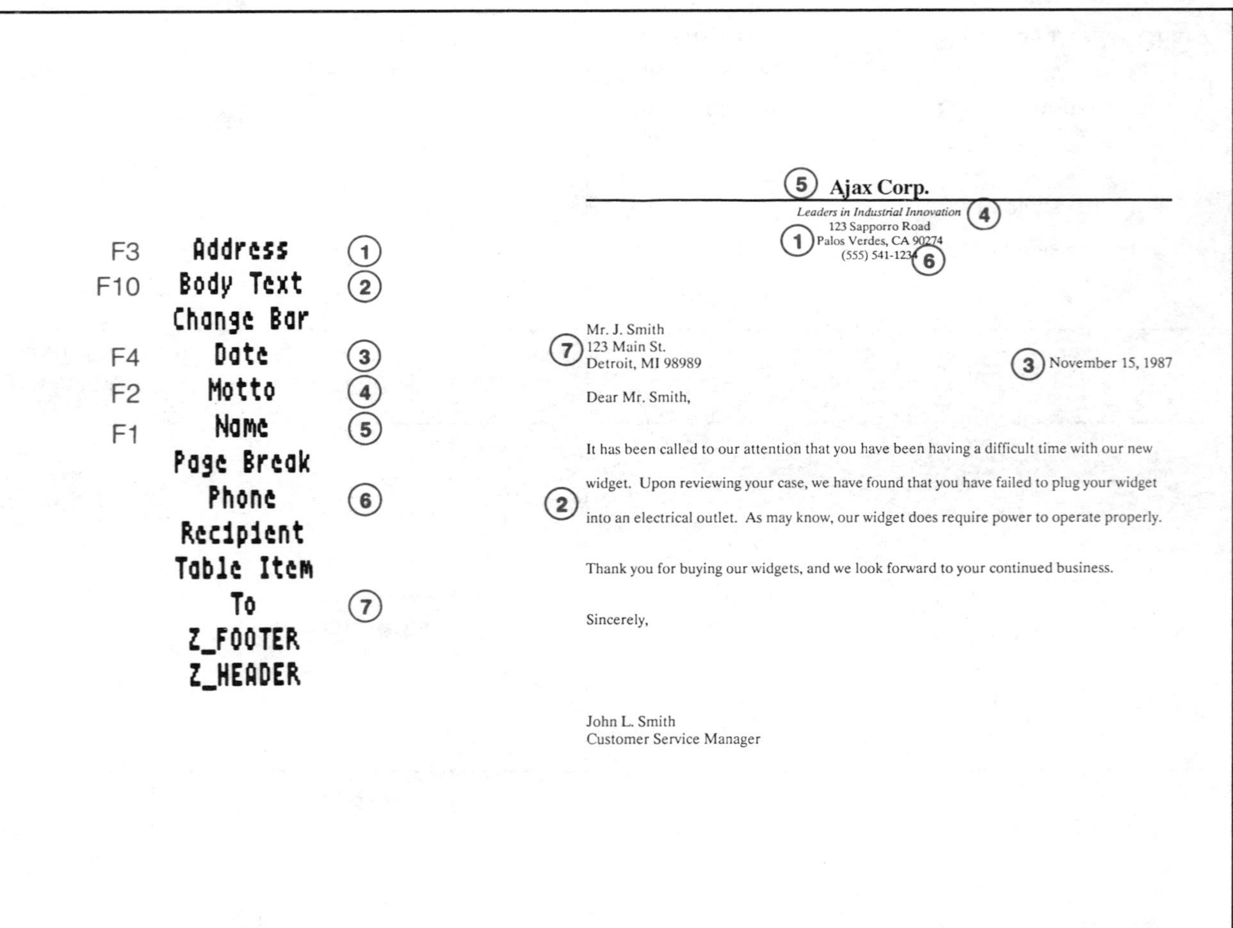

Figure A.7: <R1-P1 Sample Page

MENU	COMMAND	SETTING	
Page	Page Layout	Orientation:	Portrait
		Paper Type:	Letter
		Sides:	Single
Frame	Margins & Columns	# of Columns:	1
		Column Width:	6.5"
		Margins:	Top: .58"
			Bottom: .5"
			Left: 1"
			Right: 1"
TAG NAME AND FUNCTION KEY	**PARAGRAPH MENU COMMAND**	**SETTING**	
*Body Text (F10)	Alignment	Alignment:	Left
	Spacing	Above & Below:	01,01 picas & points
		Inter-Line:	02,04 picas & points
Address (F3)	Alignment	Alignment:	Center
Change Bar (F9)	Ruling Box Around	Width:	Custom
		Height of Rule 1:	1.02 fractional points
		Custom Indent:	–6 fractional points
		Custom Width:	1.98 fractional points

Table A.7: <R1-P1 Formatting Features

TAG NAME AND FUNCTION KEY	PARAGRAPH MENU COMMAND	SETTING	
**Date (F4)	Alignment	Alignment:	Right
	Breaks	Line Break:	After
		Next Y Position:	Beside Last Line of Prev.
Motto (F2)	Alignment	Alignment:	Center
	Font	Style:	N-Italic
Name (F1)	Alignment	Alignment:	Center
	Ruling Line Below	Width:	Frame
		Height of Rule 1:	1.98 fractional points
Page Break (F8)	Breaks	Page Break:	After
Phone	Alignment	Alignment:	Center
†To	Spacing	Interline:	01,01 picas & points

*The large value in the Spacing menu's Inter-Line setting creates double spacing.
**These settings allow the date to appear at the right on the line on which the previous paragraph ends.
†Keeps single spacing within the paragraph.

Table A.7: <R1-P1 Formatting Features (continued)

Key	Tag	No.
F10	Body Text	1
F8	Bullet	2
F7	Byline	3
F5	Creditline	4
F4	Deckhead	5
F3	Firstpar	6
F1	Headline	7
	Lift	8
F2	Subhead	9
	Z_CAPTION	10
	Z_FOOTER	
	Z_HEADER	
	Z_LABEL FIG	

(7) **Laser Printers Arrive**

(5) **Speedier, Less Costly Laser Printers Are Changing the Computer Business**

(3) *by Joseph Smith*

(4) *Joseph Smith pioneered the publishing revolution by being the first to use the phrase Professional Publishing.*

(11) Figure -I-
Japanese Sales (10)

(6) As laser printers gain more attention with lower prices, higher speeds and quality output, high-end dot-matrix printers are starting to lose some of their appeal.

Though PC users are still buying dot-matrix printers, the laser printer is giving them an alternative to think about, according to industry observers.

Laser printers, though relatively expensive, are being used more in networked environments where the distributed use of the printer justifies the expense, several analysts said. The non-impact printers also catch user interest because they are less noisy, offer sharper graphics (commonly 300-by-300 dots per inch) and can produce from eight to 10 pages per minute.

Competing Technologies (9)

- Daisy Wheel
- (2) Dot Matrix
- Laser printers
- Laser printers with write-white engines and copier options, using dry powder toner.

Laser printers still have a few areas that could be improved, according to George Jones, a key industry analyst. He noted that there are no standards

(8) **This is a liftout. It highlights a key quote or statement in the article.**

in controllers for laser printers and but the cost of using a laser is now less than a dot matrix on a cost-per-copy per minute basis.

Figure -II-
The Author

The laser printer provides sharper graphic images, Jones noted, and the laser now has the wealth of software support dot-matrix printers have always enjoyed. So, if a user moves to a laser printer from a dot-matrix printer "he can run much of his graphics software and get better graphics resolution," Jones said.

"The next step is developing generic graphics drivers which support lasers at 300-by-300 resolution. That's when you will see a huge impact on dot-matrix printers, both in price and the number of units shipping," he said, adding that it will be a year to 18 months before this happens.

Jones was quick to point out that he never sees dot-matrix printers disappearing. "Multiple-part forms are still important, and an impact printer is needed for that." He also noted that people will always want hard copies for their files or interoffice memos, and the quickest, most cost-efficient way of doing that is through a low-cost dot-matrix printer – without having to wait in line for a share laser printer. Current sales figures seem to bear Jones out. In its June 1985 Store Board Survey, market-research firm Laser Computing of Alamo, Texas, polled over 600 computer specialty stores finding that, while laser-printer sales are up, they have not eclipsed dot-matrix printers.

Figure A.8: &MAG-P3 Sample Page

Key	Tag	No.
F10	Body Text	1
F8	Bullet	2
F7	Byline	3
F5	Creditline	4
F4	Deckhead	5
F3	Firstpar	6
F1	Headline	7
	Lift	8
F2	Subhead	9
	Z_CAPTION	10
	Z_FOOTER	
	Z_HEADER	
	Z_LABEL FIG	11

Laser Computing analyst Todd Wiggins said he expects dot-matrix printers to continue competing with laser printer in the future. He also said the two technologies can work well together. "If you've got a laser shared by six to 10 people, you may still have dot-matrix printers for drafts of your own work. I think there's room for both [types] for a while," he said.

(1) As the prices of laser printers fall, more PC users may choose them over dot-matrix printer. Wiggins said the current value of the laser-printer market is about $450 million, expected to grow to about $2.2 billion by 1990.

Bill James product marketing manager with Acme Hardware which produces impact as well as non-impact printers, said both have a category in which they're most efficiently used.

He said dot-matrix printers are suited for "fast utility output, like internal documents, and for operational documents such as multi-part forms used with invoices. These are things that you don't need full-font printer for.

As for laser-printer applications, James said they are good in areas "where people don't need multiple-part forms, where they need to output data with high quality and speed – like in a group doing systems programming or an accounting department."

Figure A.8: &MAG-P3 Sample Page (continued)

MENU	COMMAND	SETTING	
Page	Page Layout	Orientation: Paper Type: Sides:	Portrait Letter Double
Frame	Margins & Columns	# of Columns: Column Widths: Margins:	3 2.17" Top: .75" Bottom: .75" Left: .75" Right: .75"
TAG NAME AND FUNCTION KEY	PARAGRAPH MENU COMMAND	SETTING	
Body Text (F10)	Alignment	Alignment: First Line: Indent Width:	Justified Indent 6.00 fractional points
	Spacing	Above & Below: Inter-Line:	01,01 picas & points 00,10 picas & points
Bullet (F8)	Alignment	First Line: Indent Width:	Indent 01,01 picas & points

Table A.8: &MAG-P3 Formatting Features

Tag Name and Function Key	Paragraph Menu Command	Setting	
	Special Effects	Special Effect: Indent After Bullet:	Bullet 01,00 picas & points
Byline (F7)	Font	Style:	N-Italic
Creditline (F5)	Font	Style:	N-Italic
Firstpar (F3)	Special Effects	Special Effect: Space for Big First Char:	Big First Char 1 line
Headline (F1)	Alignment	Alignment: Overall Width:	Center Frame-Wide
Lift	Ruling Line Above & Below	Width: Height:	Frame 1.98 fractional points

Table A.8: &MAG-P3 Formatting Features (continued)

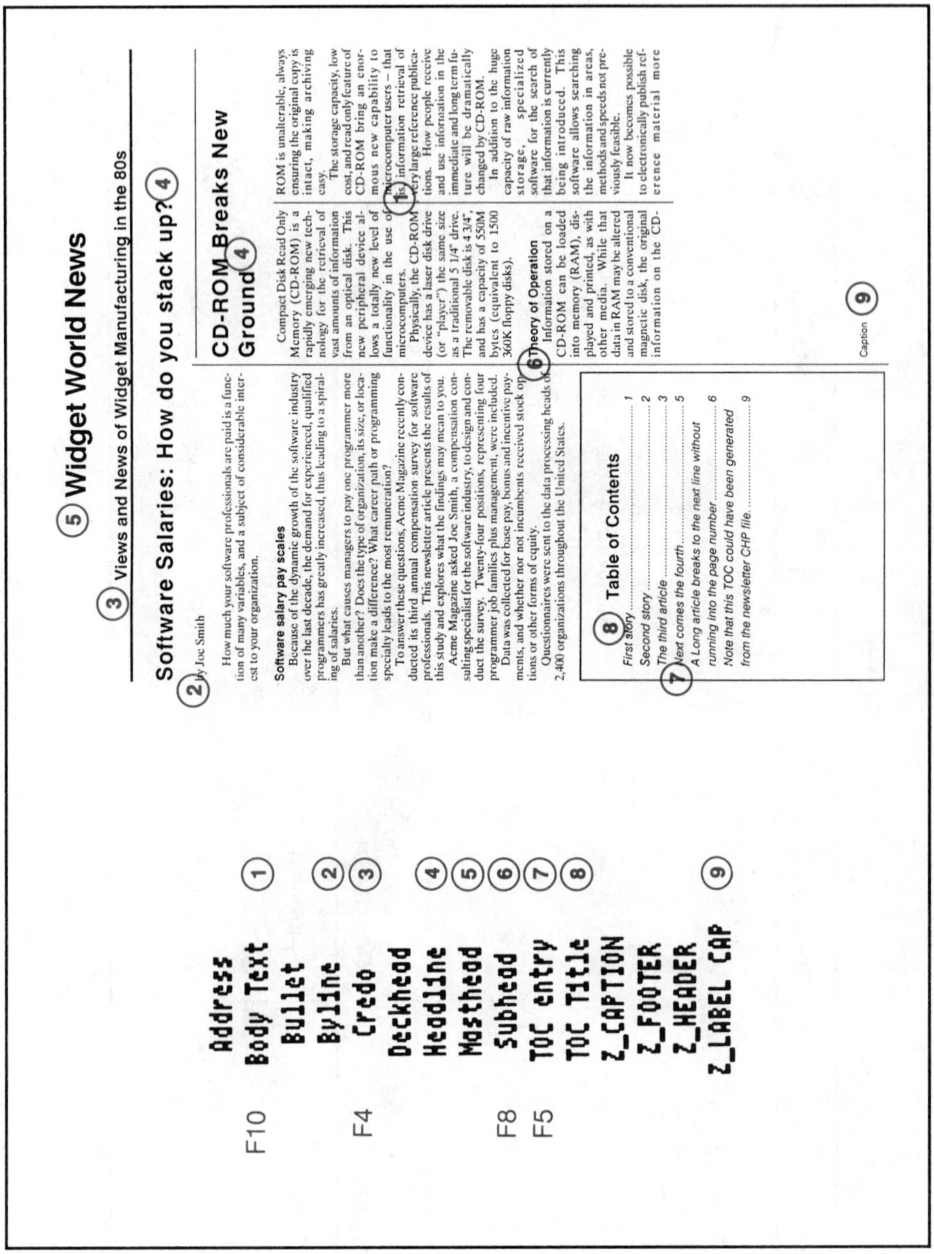

F10 Address
Body Text ①
Bullet
Byline ②
F4 Credo ③
Deckhead
Headline ④
Masthead ⑤
F8 Subhead ⑥
F5 TOC entry ⑦
TOC Title ⑧
Z_CAPTION
Z_FOOTER
Z_HEADER
Z_LABEL CAP ⑨

⑤ Widget World News

③ Views and News of Widget Manufacturing in the 80s

Software Salaries: How do you stack up? ④

② by Joe Smith

How much your software professionals are paid is a function of many variables, and a subject of considerable interest to your organization.

Software salary pay scales

Because of the dynamic growth of the software industry over the last decade, the demand for experienced, qualified programmers has greatly increased, thus leading to a spiraling of salaries.

But what causes managers to pay one programmer more than another? Does the type of organization, its size, or location make a difference? What career path or programming specialty leads to the most remuneration?

To answer these questions, Acme Magazine recently conducted its third annual compensation survey for software professionals. This newsletter article presents the results of this study and explores what the findings may mean to you.

Acme Magazine asked Joe Smith, a compensation consulting specialist for the software industry, to design and conduct the survey. Twenty-four positions, representing four programmer job families plus management, were included.

Data was collected for base pay, bonus and incentive payments, and whether nor not incumbents received stock options or other forms of equity.

Questionnaires were sent to the data processing heads of 2,400 organizations throughout the United States.

⑧ Table of Contents

CD-ROM Breaks New Ground ④

Compact Disk Read Only Memory (CD-ROM) is a rapidly emerging new technology for the retrieval of vast amounts of information from an optical disk. This new peripheral device allows a totally new level of functionality in the use of microcomputers.

Physically, the CD-ROM device has a laser disk drive (or "player") the same size as a traditional 5 1/4" drive. The removable disk is 4 3/4", and has a capacity of 550M bytes (equivalent to 1500 360K floppy disks).

⑥ Theory of Operation

Information stored on a CD-ROM can be loaded into memory (RAM), displayed and printed, as with other media. While that data in RAM may be altered and stored to a conventional magnetic disk, the original information on the CD-ROM is unalterable, always ensuring the original copy is intact, making archiving easy.

The storage capacity, low cost, and read only feature of CD-ROM bring an enormous new capability to microcomputer users – that ① is, information retrieval of very large reference publications. How people receive and use information in the immediate and long term future will be dramatically changed by CD-ROM.

In addition to the huge capacity of raw information storage, specialized software for the search of that information is currently being introduced. This software allows searching the information in areas, methods and speeds not previously feasible.

It now becomes possible to electronically publish reference material more

Caption ⑨

Figure A.9: &NEWS-P2 Sample Page

MENU	COMMAND	SETTING	
Page	Page Layout	Orientation: Paper Type: Sides:	Portrait Letter Double
Frame	Margins & Columns	# of Columns: Column Widths: Margins:	2 3.42" Top: .75" Bottom: .75" Left: .75" Right: .75"
TAG NAME AND FUNCTION KEY	**PARAGRAPH MENU COMMAND**	**SETTING**	
Body Text (F10)	Alignment	Alignment: First Line: Indent Width:	Justified Indent 01,00 picas & points
	Spacing	Above & Below: Inter-Line:	0 00,10 picas & points

TAG NAME AND FUNCTION KEY	PARAGRAPH MENU COMMAND	SETTING	
Credo (F4)	Alignment	Alignment:	Center
	Ruling Line Below	Width: Height of Rule 1:	Column 1.98 fractional points
Headline	Alignment	Overall Width:	Frame-wide
Masthead	Alignment	Alignment:	Center
TOC Title	Alignment	Alignment:	Center
TOC entry (F5)	Spacing	In From Left & Right:	01,00 picas & points
	Tab Settings	Tab Number 1: Tab Display: Tab Location: Leader Char:	Right Shown as Leader Char 3.17" …

Table A.9: &NEWS-P2 Formatting Features

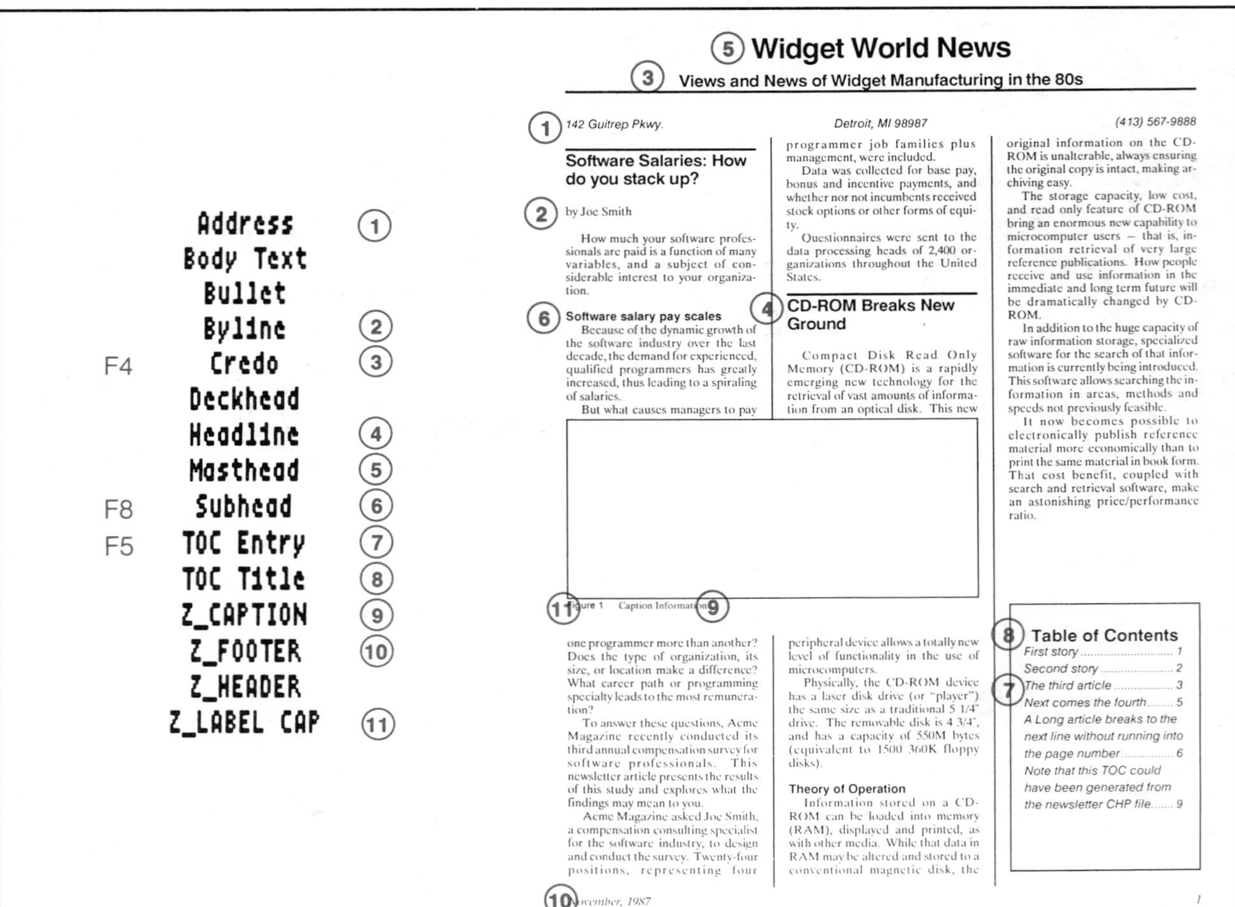

Address ①
Body Text
Bullet
Byline ②
F4 Credo ③
Deckhead
Headline ④
Masthead ⑤
F8 Subhead ⑥
F5 TOC Entry ⑦
TOC Title ⑧
Z_CAPTION ⑨
Z_FOOTER ⑩
Z_HEADER
Z_LABEL CAP ⑪

⑤ **Widget World News**

③ Views and News of Widget Manufacturing in the 80s

① *142 Guitrep Pkwy.* *Detroit, MI 98987* *(413) 567-9888*

Software Salaries: How do you stack up?

② by Joe Smith

How much your software professionals are paid is a function of many variables, and a subject of considerable interest to your organization.

⑥ **Software salary pay scales**

Because of the dynamic growth of the software industry over the last decade, the demand for experienced, qualified programmers has greatly increased, thus leading to a spiraling of salaries.

But what causes managers to pay one programmer more than another? Does the type of organization, its size, or location make a difference? What career path or programming specialty leads to the most remuneration?

To answer these questions, Acme Magazine recently conducted its third annual compensation survey for software professionals. This newsletter article presents the results of this study and explores what the findings may mean to you.

Acme Magazine asked Joe Smith, a compensation consulting specialist for the software industry, to design and conduct the survey. Twenty-four positions, representing four programmer job families plus management, were included.

Data was collected for base pay, bonus and incentive payments, and whether nor not incumbents received stock options or other forms of equity.

Questionnaires were sent to the data processing heads of 2,400 organizations throughout the United States.

⑪ Figure 1 Caption Information ⑨

④ **CD-ROM Breaks New Ground**

Compact Disk Read Only Memory (CD-ROM) is a rapidly emerging new technology for the retrieval of vast amounts of information from an optical disk. This new peripheral device allows a totally new level of functionality in the use of microcomputers.

Physically, the CD-ROM device has a laser disk drive (or "player") the same size as a traditional 5 1/4" drive. The removable disk is 4 3/4", and has a capacity of 550M bytes (equivalent to 1500 360K floppy disks).

Theory of Operation

Information stored on a CD-ROM can be loaded into memory (RAM), displayed and printed, as with other media. While that data in RAM may be altered and stored to a conventional magnetic disk, the original information on the CD-ROM is unalterable, always ensuring the original copy is intact, making archiving easy.

The storage capacity, low cost, and read only feature of CD-ROM bring an enormous new capability to microcomputer users — that is, information retrieval of very large reference publications. How people receive and use information in the immediate and long term future will be dramatically changed by CD-ROM.

In addition to the huge capacity of raw information storage, specialized software for the search of that information is currently being introduced. This software allows searching the information in areas, methods and speeds not previously feasible.

It now becomes possible to electronically publish reference material more economically than to print the same material in book form. That cost benefit, coupled with search and retrieval software, make an astonishing price/performance ratio.

⑧ **Table of Contents**

⑩ *November, 1987* *1*

Figure A.10: &NEWS-P3 Sample Page

MENU	COMMAND	SETTING	
Page	Page Layout	Orientation: Paper Type: Sides:	Portrait Letter Double
Frame	Margins & Columns	# of Columns: Column Widths: Margins:	3 2.11'' Top: .76'' Bottom: .76'' Left: 1'' Right: .5''
TAG NAME AND FUNCTION KEY	**PARAGRAPH MENU COMMAND**	**SETTING**	
Body Text (F10)	Alignment	Alignment: First Line: Indent Width:	Justified Indent 01,00 picas & points
	Spacing	Above & Below: Inter-Line:	0 00,10 picas & points
Address	Font	Style	N-Italic
	Tab Settings	Tab Number 1: Tab Number 2:	Center, 3.5'' Right, 7''

Table A.10: &NEWS-P3 Formatting Features

Tag Name and Function Key	Paragraph Menu Command	Setting	
Credo (F4)	Alignment	Alignment:	Center
	Ruling Line Below	Width:	Column
		Height of Rule 1:	1.98 fractional points
Headline	Alignment	Overall Width:	Column-wide
	Ruling Line Above	Width:	Column
		Height of Rule 1:	1.98 fractional points
Masthead	Alignment	Alignment:	Center
TOC Entry (F5)	Spacing	In From Left & Right:	01,00 picas & points
	Tab Settings	Tab Number 1:	Right
		Tab Display:	Shown as Leader Char
		Tab Location:	1.92”
		Leader Char:	...
TOC Title	Alignment	Alignment:	Center

Table A.10: &NEWS-P3 Formatting Features (continued)

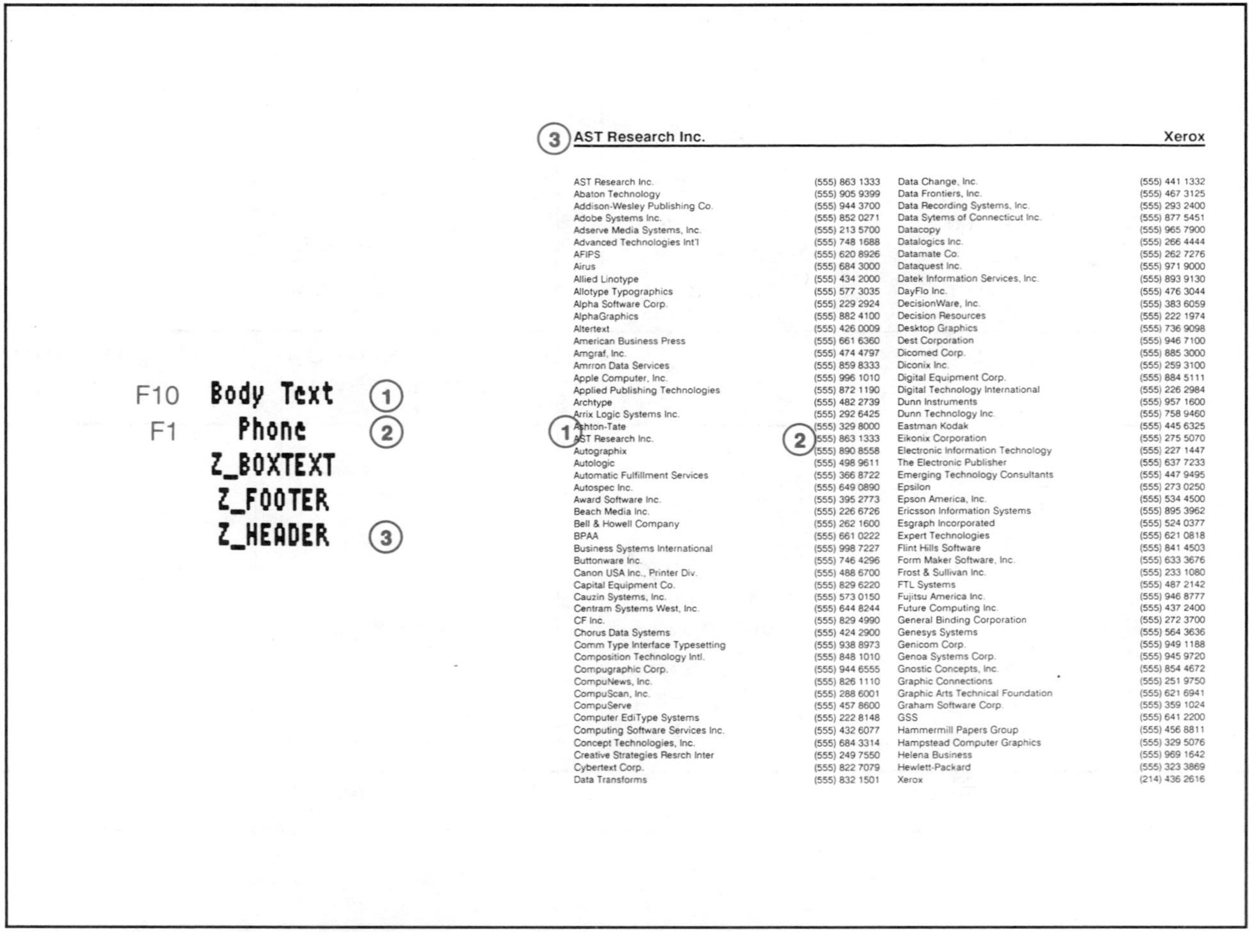

F10 Body Text (1)
F1 Phone (2)
Z_BOXTEXT
Z_FOOTER
Z_HEADER (3)

(3) AST Research Inc. Xerox

AST Research Inc. (555) 863 1333
Abaton Technology (555) 905 9399
Addison-Wesley Publishing Co. (555) 944 3700
Adobe Systems Inc. (555) 852 0271
Adserve Media Systems, Inc. (555) 213 5700
Advanced Technologies Int'l (555) 748 1688
AFIPS (555) 620 8926
Airus (555) 684 3000
Allied Linotype (555) 434 2000
Allotype Typographics (555) 577 3035
Alpha Software Corp. (555) 229 2924
AlphaGraphics (555) 882 4100
Altertext (555) 426 0009
American Business Press (555) 661 6360
Amgraf, Inc. (555) 474 4797
Amrron Data Services (555) 859 8333
Apple Computer, Inc. (555) 996 1010
Applied Publishing Technologies (555) 872 1190
Archtype (555) 482 2739
Arrix Logic Systems Inc. (555) 292 6425
(1) Ashton-Tate (555) 329 8000
AST Research Inc. (2) (555) 863 1333
Autographix (555) 890 8558
Autologic (555) 498 9611
Automatic Fulfillment Services (555) 366 8722
Autospec Inc. (555) 649 0890
Award Software Inc. (555) 395 2773
Beach Media Inc. (555) 226 6726
Bell & Howell Company (555) 262 1600
BPAA (555) 661 0222
Business Systems International (555) 998 7227
Buttonware Inc. (555) 746 4296
Canon USA Inc., Printer Div. (555) 488 6700
Capital Equipment Co. (555) 829 6220
Cauzin Systems, Inc. (555) 573 0150
Centram Systems West, Inc. (555) 644 8244
CF Inc. (555) 829 4990
Chorus Data Systems (555) 424 2900
Comm Type Interface Typesetting (555) 938 8973
Composition Technology Intl. (555) 848 1010
Compugraphic Corp. (555) 944 6555
CompuNews, Inc. (555) 826 1110
CompuScan, Inc. (555) 288 6001
CompuServe (555) 457 8600
Computer EdiType Systems (555) 222 8148
Computing Software Services Inc. (555) 432 6077
Concept Technologies, Inc. (555) 684 3314
Creative Strategies Resrch Inter (555) 249 7550
Cybertext Corp. (555) 822 7079
Data Transforms (555) 832 1501

Data Change, Inc. (555) 441 1332
Data Frontiers, Inc. (555) 467 3125
Data Recording Systems, Inc. (555) 293 2400
Data Sytems of Connecticut Inc. (555) 877 5451
Datacopy (555) 965 7900
Datalogics Inc. (555) 266 4444
Datamate Co. (555) 262 7276
Dataquest Inc. (555) 971 9000
Datek Information Services, Inc. (555) 893 9130
DayFlo Inc. (555) 476 3044
DecisionWare, Inc. (555) 383 6059
Decision Resources (555) 222 1974
Desktop Graphics (555) 736 9098
Dest Corporation (555) 946 7100
Dicomed Corp. (555) 885 3000
Diconix Inc. (555) 259 3100
Digital Equipment Corp. (555) 884 5111
Digital Technology International (555) 226 2984
Dunn Instruments (555) 957 1600
Dunn Technology Inc. (555) 758 9460
Eastman Kodak (555) 445 6325
Eikonix Corporation (555) 275 5070
Electronic Information Technology (555) 227 1447
The Electronic Publisher (555) 637 7233
Emerging Technology Consultants (555) 447 9495
Epsilon (555) 273 0250
Epson America, Inc. (555) 534 4500
Ericsson Information Systems (555) 895 3962
Esgraph Incorporated (555) 524 0377
Expert Technologies (555) 621 0818
Flint Hills Software (555) 841 4503
Form Maker Software, Inc. (555) 633 3676
Frost & Sullivan Inc. (555) 233 1080
FTL Systems (555) 487 2142
Fujitsu America Inc. (555) 946 8777
Future Computing Inc. (555) 437 2400
General Binding Corporation (555) 272 3700
Genesys Systems (555) 564 3636
Genicom Corp. (555) 949 1188
Genoa Systems Corp. (555) 945 9720
Gnostic Concepts, Inc. (555) 854 4672
Graphic Connections (555) 251 9750
Graphic Arts Technical Foundation (555) 621 6941
Graham Software Corp. (555) 359 1024
GSS (555) 641 2200
Hammermill Papers Group (555) 456 8811
Hampstead Computer Graphics (555) 329 5076
Helena Business (555) 969 1642
Hewlett-Packard (555) 323 3869
Xerox (214) 436 2616

Figure A.11: &PHON-P2 Sample Page

MENU	COMMAND	SETTING	
Page	Page Layout	Orientation:	Portrait
		Paper Type:	Letter
		Sides:	Single
Frame	Margins & Columns	# of Columns:	2
		Column Widths:	3.4''
		Margins:	Top: .75''
			Bottom: .75''
			Left: .75''
			Right: .75''
TAG NAME AND FUNCTION KEY	**PARAGRAPH MENU COMMAND**	**SETTING**	
Body Text (F10)	Alignment	Alignment:	Left
	Spacing	Above & Below:	0
		Inter-Line:	00,10 picas & points
	Breaks	Line Break:	Before
*Phone (F1)	Alignment	Alignment:	Right
	Breaks	Line Break:	After
Z_HEADER	Ruling Line Below	Width:	Frame
		Height of Rule 1:	1.98 fractional points

*Since the Phone tag does not have a line break before, phones appear on the same line as company names.

Table A.11: &PHON-P2 Formatting Features

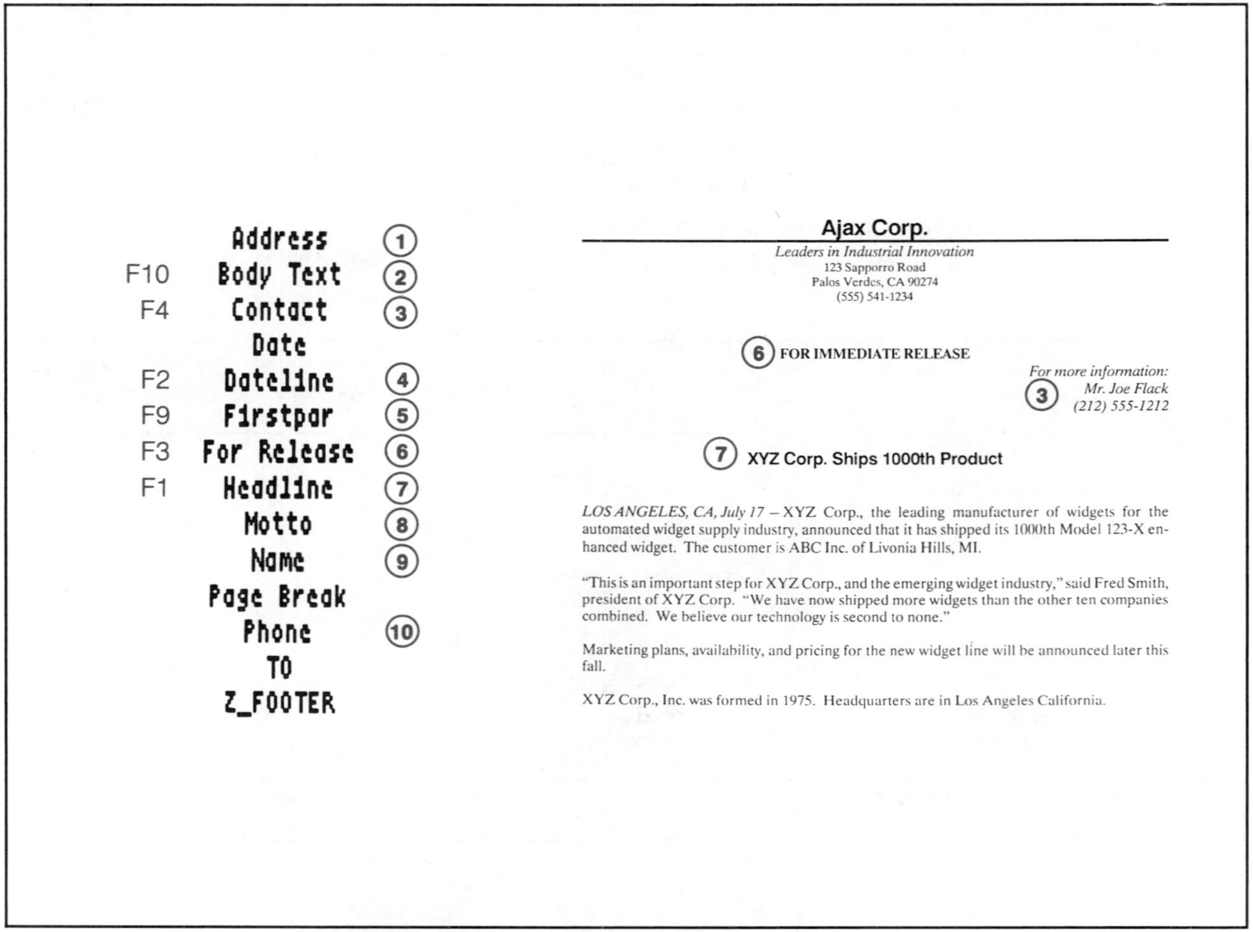

Key	Tag	No.
	Address	1
F10	Body Text	2
F4	Contact	3
	Date	
F2	Dateline	4
F9	Firstpar	5
F3	For Release	6
F1	Headline	7
	Motto	8
	Name	9
	Page Break	
	Phone	10
	TO	
	Z_FOOTER	

Ajax Corp.

Leaders in Industrial Innovation
123 Sapporro Road
Palos Verdes, CA 90274
(555) 541-1234

(6) **FOR IMMEDIATE RELEASE**

For more information:
(3) *Mr. Joe Flack*
(212) 555-1212

(7) **XYZ Corp. Ships 1000th Product**

LOS ANGELES, CA, July 17 – XYZ Corp., the leading manufacturer of widgets for the automated widget supply industry, announced that it has shipped its 1000th Model 123-X enhanced widget. The customer is ABC Inc. of Livonia Hills, MI.

"This is an important step for XYZ Corp., and the emerging widget industry," said Fred Smith, president of XYZ Corp. "We have now shipped more widgets than the other ten companies combined. We believe our technology is second to none."

Marketing plans, availability, and pricing for the new widget line will be announced later this fall.

XYZ Corp., Inc. was formed in 1975. Headquarters are in Los Angeles California.

Figure A.12: &PREL-P1 Sample Page

Menu	Command	Setting	
Page	Page Layout	Orientation: Paper Type: Sides:	Portrait Letter Single
Frame	Margins & Columns	# of Columns: Column Width: Margins:	1 6.5" Top: .58" Bottom: .5" Left: 1" Right: 1"
Tag Name and Function Key	**Paragraph Menu Command**	**Setting**	
Body Text (F10)	Alignment	Alignment:	Justified
	Spacing	Above & Below: Inter-Line:	0 01,01 picas & points
Address	Alignment	Alignment:	Center
Contact (F4)	Alignment	Alignment:	Right
*Dateline (F2)	Break	Line Break:	Before

Tag Name and Function Key	Paragraph Menu Command	Setting	
**Firstpar	Alignment	Relative Indent:	Length of Previous Line
	Breaks	Line Break:	No
For Release (F3)	Alignment	Alignment:	Center
Headline (F1)	Alignment	Alignment:	Center
Motto	Alignment	Alignment:	Center
	Font	Style:	N-Italic
Name	Alignment	Alignment:	Center
	Ruling Line Below	Width: Height of Rule 1:	Frame 1.98 fractional points
Page Break (F8)	Breaks	Page Break:	After
Phone	Alignment	Alignment:	Center

*Allows text with the Firstpar tag to follow on the same line. See Chapter 5.
**No line break and a relative indent causes the text to follow right after Dateline text.

Table A.12: &PREL-P1 Formatting Features

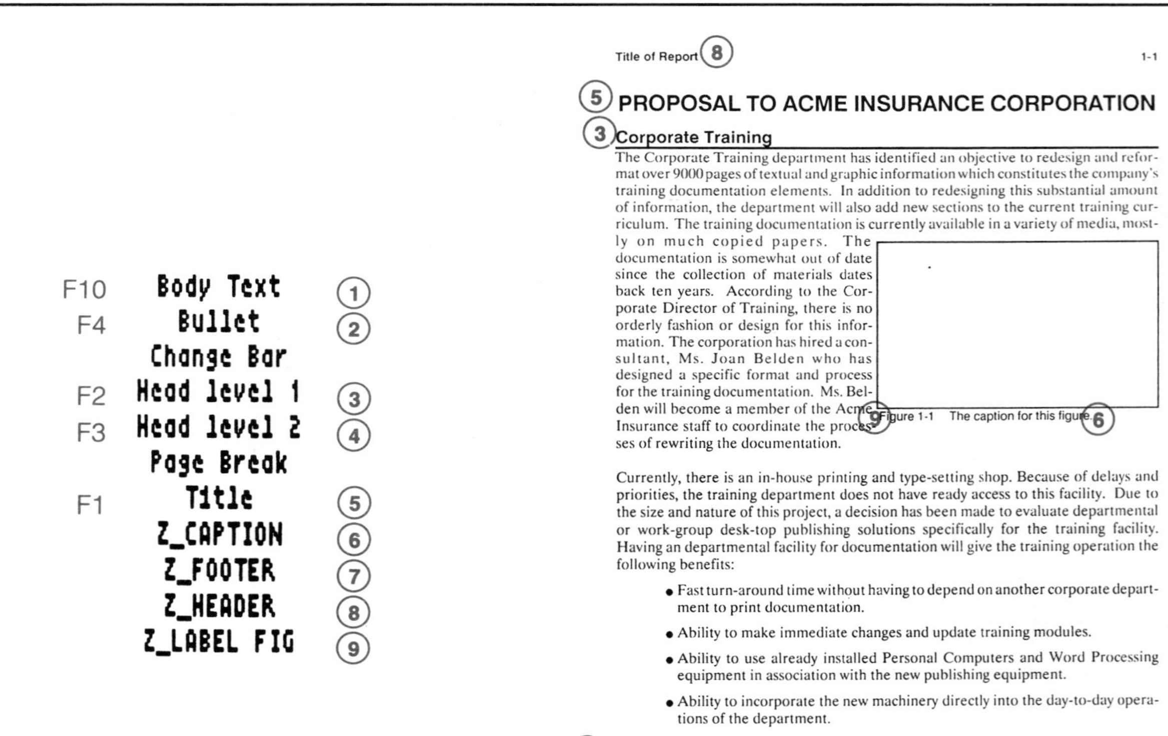

Title of Report 8 1-1

5 PROPOSAL TO ACME INSURANCE CORPORATION

3 Corporate Training

The Corporate Training department has identified an objective to redesign and reformat over 9000 pages of textual and graphic information which constitutes the company's training documentation elements. In addition to redesigning this substantial amount of information, the department will also add new sections to the current training curriculum. The training documentation is currently available in a variety of media, mostly on much copied papers. The documentation is somewhat out of date since the collection of materials dates back ten years. According to the Corporate Director of Training, there is no orderly fashion or design for this information. The corporation has hired a consultant, Ms. Joan Belden who has designed a specific format and process for the training documentation. Ms. Belden will become a member of the Acme Insurance staff to coordinate the processes of rewriting the documentation.

9 Figure 1-1 The caption for this figure. 6

Currently, there is an in-house printing and type-setting shop. Because of delays and priorities, the training department does not have ready access to this facility. Due to the size and nature of this project, a decision has been made to evaluate departmental or work-group desk-top publishing solutions specifically for the training facility. Having an departmental facility for documentation will give the training operation the following benefits:

- Fast turn-around time without having to depend on another corporate department to print documentation.
- Ability to make immediate changes and update training modules.
- Ability to use already installed Personal Computers and Word Processing equipment in association with the new publishing equipment.
- Ability to incorporate the new machinery directly into the day-to-day operations of the department.

4 The TXN Solution

It is the recommendation of TXN Corporation that Acme Insurance consider the 3544 graphic workstation as the input terminal for the redesign/reformat processes in the training facility. TXN was the first company to offer this unique type of workstation. In 1976, we introduced the 9967 professional computer which had the power of combining textual and graphic elements on the same screen. Now, ten years later, after

7 Page 1

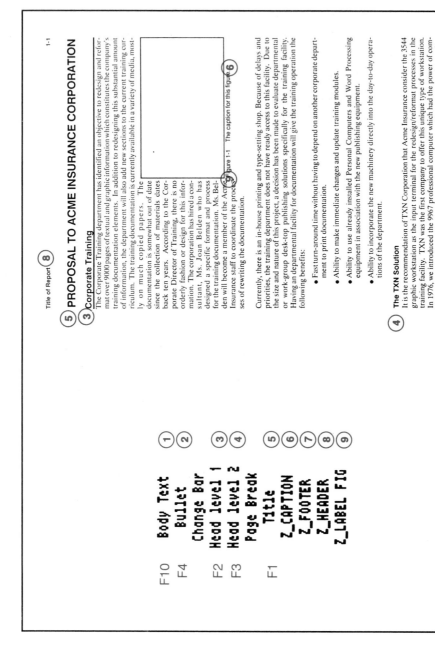

Figure A.13: &PRPT-P1 Sample Pages

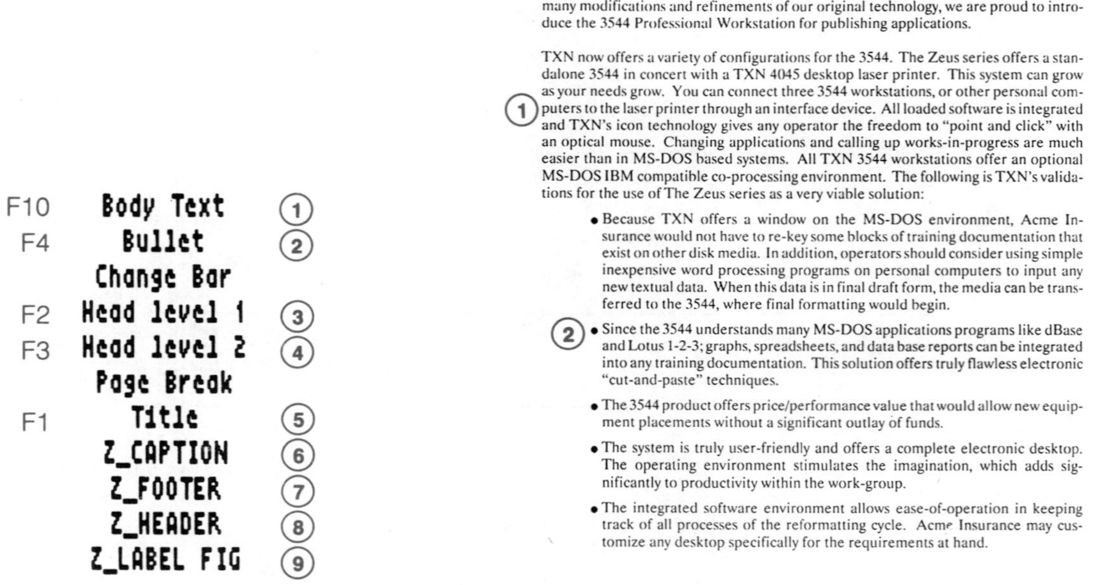

F10	Body Text	(1)
F4	Bullet	(2)
	Change Bar	
F2	Head level 1	(3)
F3	Head level 2	(4)
	Page Break	
F1	Title	(5)
	Z_CAPTION	(6)
	Z_FOOTER	(7)
	Z_HEADER	(8)
	Z_LABEL FIG	(9)

1-2 Title of Chapter

many modifications and refinements of our original technology, we are proud to introduce the 3544 Professional Workstation for publishing applications.

(1) TXN now offers a variety of configurations for the 3544. The Zeus series offers a standalone 3544 in concert with a TXN 4045 desktop laser printer. This system can grow as your needs grow. You can connect three 3544 workstations, or other personal computers to the laser printer through an interface device. All loaded software is integrated and TXN's icon technology gives any operator the freedom to "point and click" with an optical mouse. Changing applications and calling up works-in-progress are much easier than in MS-DOS based systems. All TXN 3544 workstations offer an optional MS-DOS IBM compatible co-processing environment. The following is TXN's validations for the use of The Zeus series as a very viable solution:

- Because TXN offers a window on the MS-DOS environment, Acme Insurance would not have to re-key some blocks of training documentation that exist on other disk media. In addition, operators should consider using simple inexpensive word processing programs on personal computers to input any new textual data. When this data is in final draft form, the media can be transferred to the 3544, where final formatting would begin.
- (2) Since the 3544 understands many MS-DOS applications programs like dBase and Lotus 1-2-3; graphs, spreadsheets, and data base reports can be integrated into any training documentation. This solution offers truly flawless electronic "cut-and-paste" techniques.
- The 3544 product offers price/performance value that would allow new equipment placements without a significant outlay of funds.
- The system is truly user-friendly and offers a complete electronic desktop. The operating environment stimulates the imagination, which adds significantly to productivity within the work-group.
- The integrated software environment allows ease-of-operation in keeping track of all processes of the reformatting cycle. Acme Insurance may customize any desktop specifically for the requirements at hand.

Page 2

Figure A.13: &PRPT-P1 Sample Pages (continued)

MENU	COMMAND	SETTING	
Page	Page Layout	Orientation:	Portrait
		Paper Type:	Letter
		Sides:	Double
Frame	Margins & Columns	# of Columns:	1
		Column Width:	6''
		Margins:	Top: 1''
			Bottom: 1''
			Left: 1.25''
			Right: 1.25''
TAG NAME AND FUNCTION KEY	**PARAGRAPH MENU COMMAND**	**SETTING**	
Body Text (F10)	Alignment	Alignment:	Justified
	Spacing	Above & Below:	0
		Inter-Line:	01,01 picas & points
		Inter-Paragraph:	01,01 picas & points
*Bullet (F4)	Spacing	Above & Below:	07,00 pica & points
		In From Left:	03,00 pica & points (.5'')
	Special Effects	Special Effect:	Bullet
		Indent After Bullet:	01,00 pica & points
Change Bar (F9)	Ruling Box Around	Width:	Custom
		Height of Rule 1:	1.02 fractional points
		Custom Indent:	–6 fractional points
		Custom Width:	1.98 fractional points
Head level 1 (F2)	Ruling Line Below	Width:	Margin
		Height of Rule 1:	1.98 fractional points

*Spacing Above and Below creates the space between the bulleted items.

Table A.13: &PRPT-P1 Formatting Features

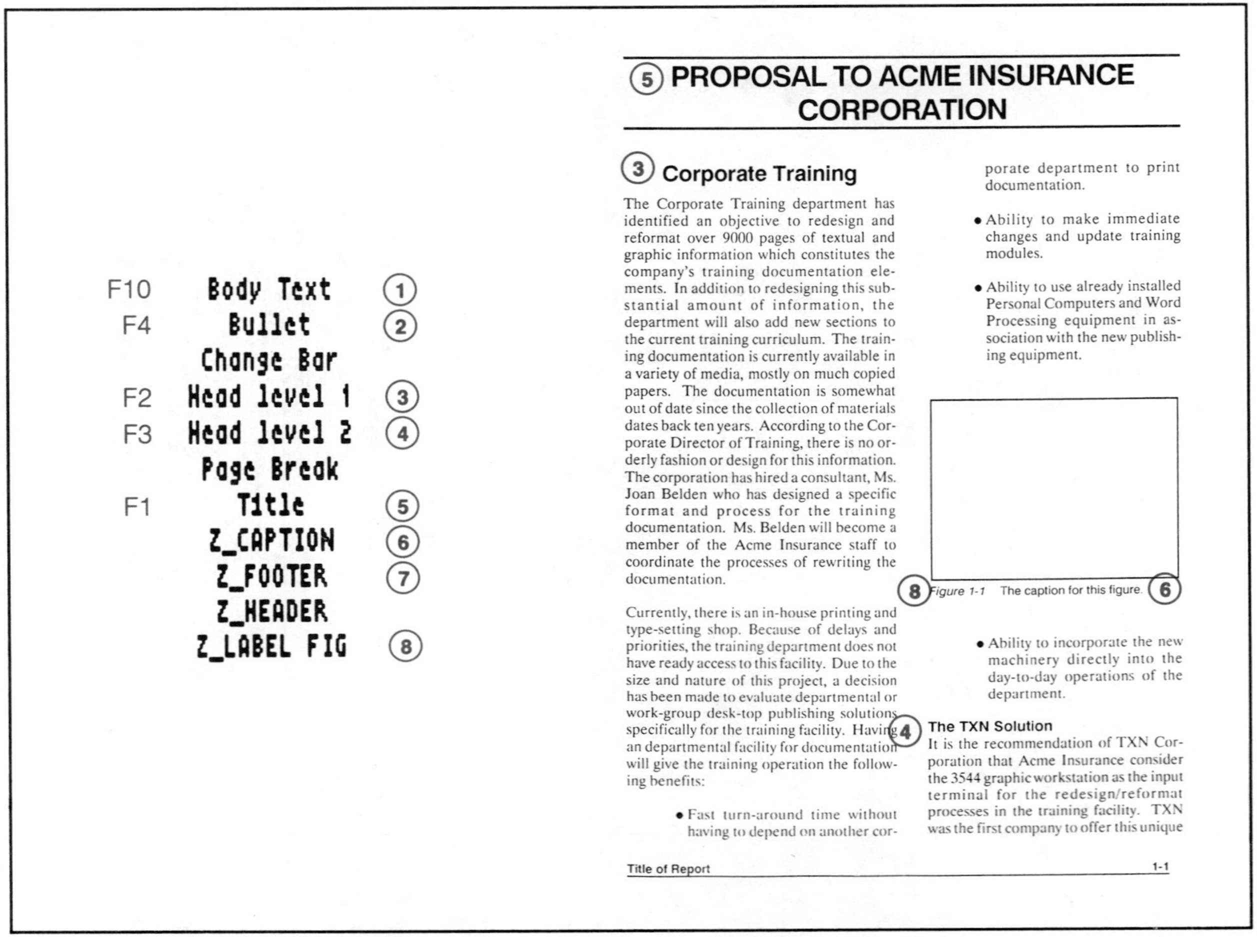

F10	Body Text	1
F4	Bullet	2
	Change Bar	
F2	Head level 1	3
F3	Head level 2	4
	Page Break	
F1	Title	5
	Z_CAPTION	6
	Z_FOOTER	7
	Z_HEADER	
	Z_LABEL FIG	8

(5) PROPOSAL TO ACME INSURANCE CORPORATION

(3) Corporate Training

The Corporate Training department has identified an objective to redesign and reformat over 9000 pages of textual and graphic information which constitutes the company's training documentation elements. In addition to redesigning this substantial amount of information, the department will also add new sections to the current training curriculum. The training documentation is currently available in a variety of media, mostly on much copied papers. The documentation is somewhat out of date since the collection of materials dates back ten years. According to the Corporate Director of Training, there is no orderly fashion or design for this information. The corporation has hired a consultant, Ms. Joan Belden who has designed a specific format and process for the training documentation. Ms. Belden will become a member of the Acme Insurance staff to coordinate the processes of rewriting the documentation.

Currently, there is an in-house printing and type-setting shop. Because of delays and priorities, the training department does not have ready access to this facility. Due to the size and nature of this project, a decision has been made to evaluate departmental or work-group desk-top publishing solutions specifically for the training facility. Having an departmental facility for documentation will give the training operation the following benefits:

- Fast turn-around time without having to depend on another corporate department to print documentation.
- Ability to make immediate changes and update training modules.
- Ability to use already installed Personal Computers and Word Processing equipment in association with the new publishing equipment.

(8) Figure 1-1 The caption for this figure. (6)

- Ability to incorporate the new machinery directly into the day-to-day operations of the department.

(4) The TXN Solution

It is the recommendation of TXN Corporation that Acme Insurance consider the 3544 graphic workstation as the input terminal for the redesign/reformat processes in the training facility. TXN was the first company to offer this unique

Title of Report 1-1

Figure A.14: &PRPT-P2 Sample Pages

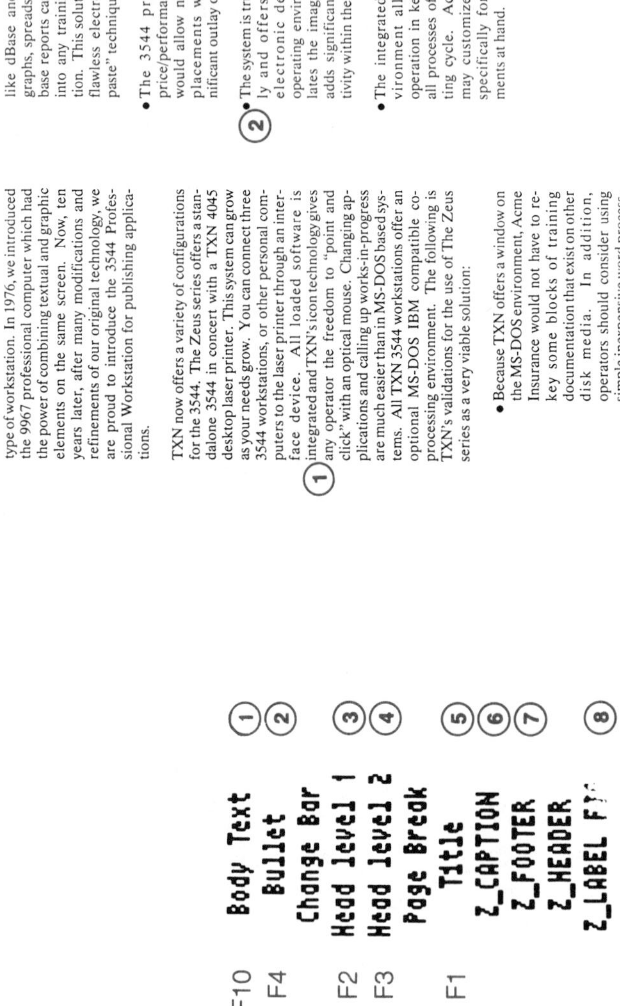

F10 Body Text (1)
F4 Bullet (2)
Change Bar
F2 Head level 1 (3)
F3 Head level 2 (4)
Page Break
F1 Title (5)
Z_CAPTION (6)
Z_FOOTER (7)
Z_HEADER
Z_LABEL F (8)

type of workstation. In 1976, we introduced the 9967 professional computer which had the power of combining textual and graphic elements on the same screen. Now, ten years later, after many modifications and refinements of our original technology, we are proud to introduce the 3544 Professional Workstation for publishing applications.

TXN now offers a variety of configurations for the 3544. The Zeus series offers a standalone 3544 in concert with a TXN 4045 desktop laser printer. This system can grow as your needs grow. You can connect three 3544 workstations, or other personal computers to the laser printer through an interface device. All loaded software is (1) integrated and TXN's icon technology gives any operator the freedom to "point and click" with an optical mouse. Changing applications and calling up works-in-progress are much easier than in MS-DOS based systems. All TXN 3544 workstations offer an optional MS-DOS IBM compatible co-processing environment. The following is TXN's validations for the use of The Zeus series as a very viable solution:

- Because TXN offers a window on the MS-DOS environment, Acme Insurance would not have to re-key some blocks of training documentation that exist on other disk media. In addition, operators should consider using simple inexpensive word processing programs on personal computers to input any new textual data. When this data is in final draft form, the media can be transferred to the 3544, where final formatting would begin.
- Since the 3544 understands many MS-DOS applications programs like dBase and Lotus 1-2-3; graphs, spreadsheets, and data base reports can be integrated into any training documentation. This solution offers truly flawless electronic "cut-and-paste" techniques.
- The 3544 product offers price/performance value that would allow new equipment placements without a significant outlay of funds.
- (2) The system is truly user-friendly and offers a complete electronic desktop. The operating environment stimulates the imagination, which adds significantly to productivity within the work-group.
- The integrated software environment allows ease-of-operation in keeping track of all processes of the reformatting cycle. Acme Insurance may customize any desktop specifically for the requirements at hand.

(7) 1-2 Title of the Chapter

Figure A.14: &PRPT-P2 Sample Pages (continued)

MENU	COMMAND	SETTING	
Page	Page Layout	Orientation: Paper Type: Sides:	Portrait Letter Double
Frame	Margins & Columns	# of Columns: Column Widths: Margins:	2 3'' and 2.83'' Top: .97'' Bottom: .97'' Left: 1.25'' Right: 1.25''
TAG NAME AND FUNCTION KEY	**PARAGRAPH MENU COMMAND**	**SETTING**	
Body Text (F10)	Alignment	Alignment:	Justified
	Spacing	Above & Below: Inter-Line: Inter-Paragraph:	0 01,01 picas & points 01,01 picas & points
*Bullet (F4)	Spacing	Above & Below: In From Left:	01,01 pica & points 03,00 pica & points (.5'')

Table A.14: &PRPT-P2 Formatting Features

TAG NAME AND FUNCTION KEY	PARAGRAPH MENU COMMAND	SETTING	
	Special Effects	Special Effect: Indent After Bullet:	Bullet 01,00 pica & points
Change Bar (F9)	Ruling Box Around	Width: Height of Rule 1: Custom Indent: Custom Width:	Custom 1.02 fractional points –6 fractional points 1.98 fractional points
Head level 1 (F2)	Alignment	Alignment:	Center
Page Break (F8)	Breaks	Page Break:	After
Title (F1)	Ruling Line Above	Width: Height of Rule 1:	Frame 1.98 fractional points
	Ruling Line Below	Width: Height of Rule 1:	Margin 1.98 fractional points
*Spacing Above and Below creates the space between the bulleted items.			

Table A.14: &PRPT-P2 Formatting Features (continued)

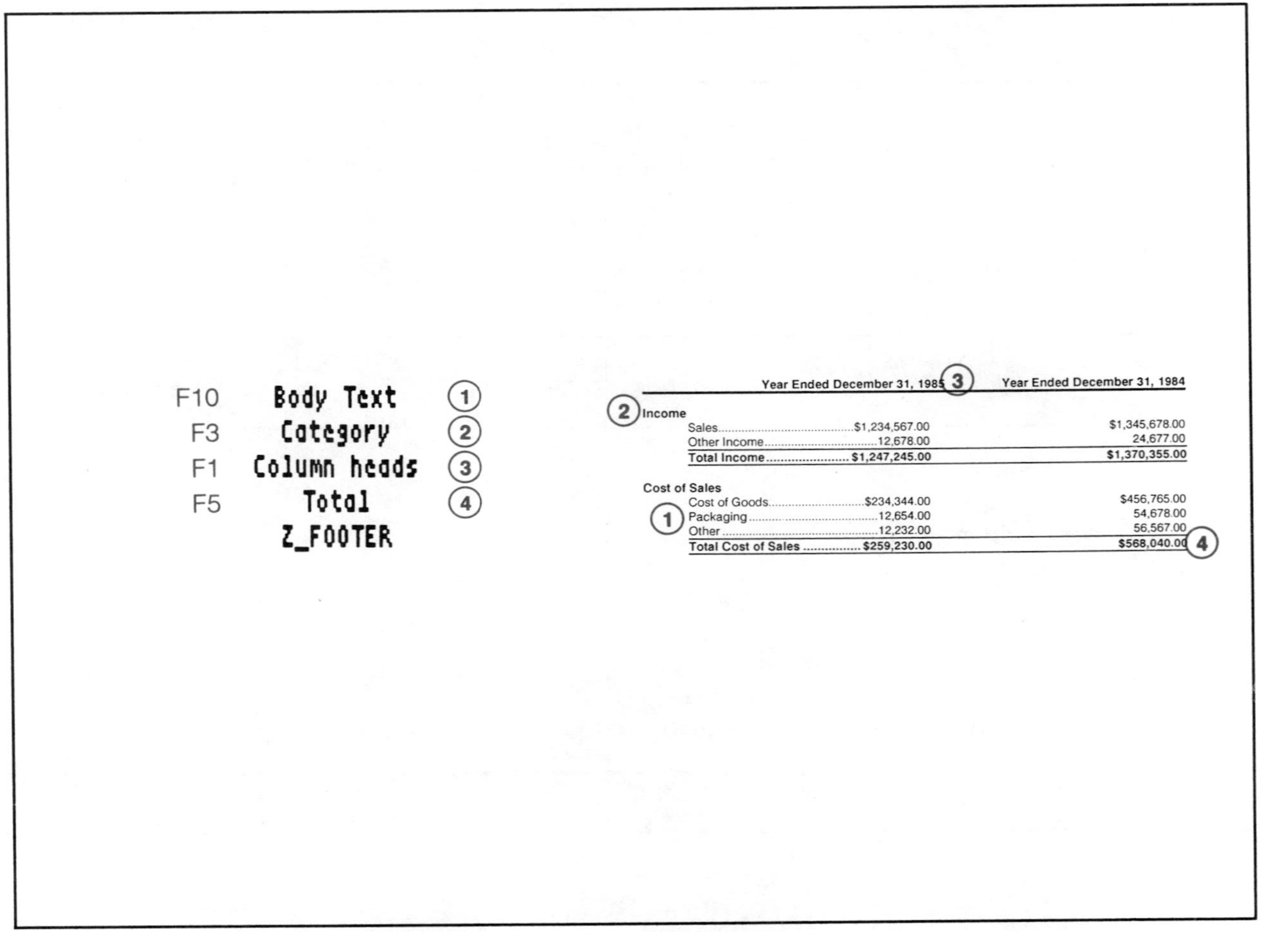

Key	Tag	
F10	Body Text	1
F3	Category	2
F1	Column heads	3
F5	Total	4
	Z_FOOTER	

	Year Ended December 31, 1985 (3)	Year Ended December 31, 1984
(2) **Income**		
Sales	$1,234,567.00	$1,345,678.00
Other Income	12,678.00	24,677.00
Total Income	**$1,247,245.00**	**$1,370,355.00**
Cost of Sales		
Cost of Goods	$234,344.00	$456,765.00
(1) Packaging	12,654.00	54,678.00
Other	12,232.00	56,567.00
Total Cost of Sales	**$259,230.00**	**$568,040.00** (4)

Figure A.15: &TBL-P1 Sample Page

MENU	COMMAND	SETTING	
Page	Page Layout	Orientation:	Portrait
		Paper Type:	Letter
		Sides:	Single
Frame	Margins & Columns	# of Columns:	1
		Column Width:	6.5''
		Margins:	Top: .75''
			Bottom: .75''
			Left: .75''
			Right: .75''
TAG NAME AND FUNCTION KEY	**PARAGRAPH MENU COMMAND**	**SETTING**	
Body Text (F10)	Alignment	Alignment:	Left
		First Line:	Indent
		Indent Width:	03,00 pica & points (.5'')
	Spacing	Above & Below:	0
		Inter-Line:	01,00 picas & points

TAG NAME AND FUNCTION KEY	PARAGRAPH MENU COMMAND	SETTING	
	Tab Settings	Tab Number 1: Tab Display: Leader Char: Tab Number 2: Tab Display:	Decimal, 3'' Shown as Leader Char ... Decimal at 5.83'' Shown as Open Space
Column heads (F1)	Tab Settings	Tab Number 1: Tab Number 2:	Center, 2.33'' Center, 5''
	Ruling Line Below	Width: Height of Rule 1:	Text 1.98 fractional points
Total (F5)	Tab Settings	*Same tab settings as Body Text*	
	Ruling Line Above & Below	Width: Height of Rule 1:	Text 1.02 fractional points

Table A.15: &TBL-P1 Formatting Features

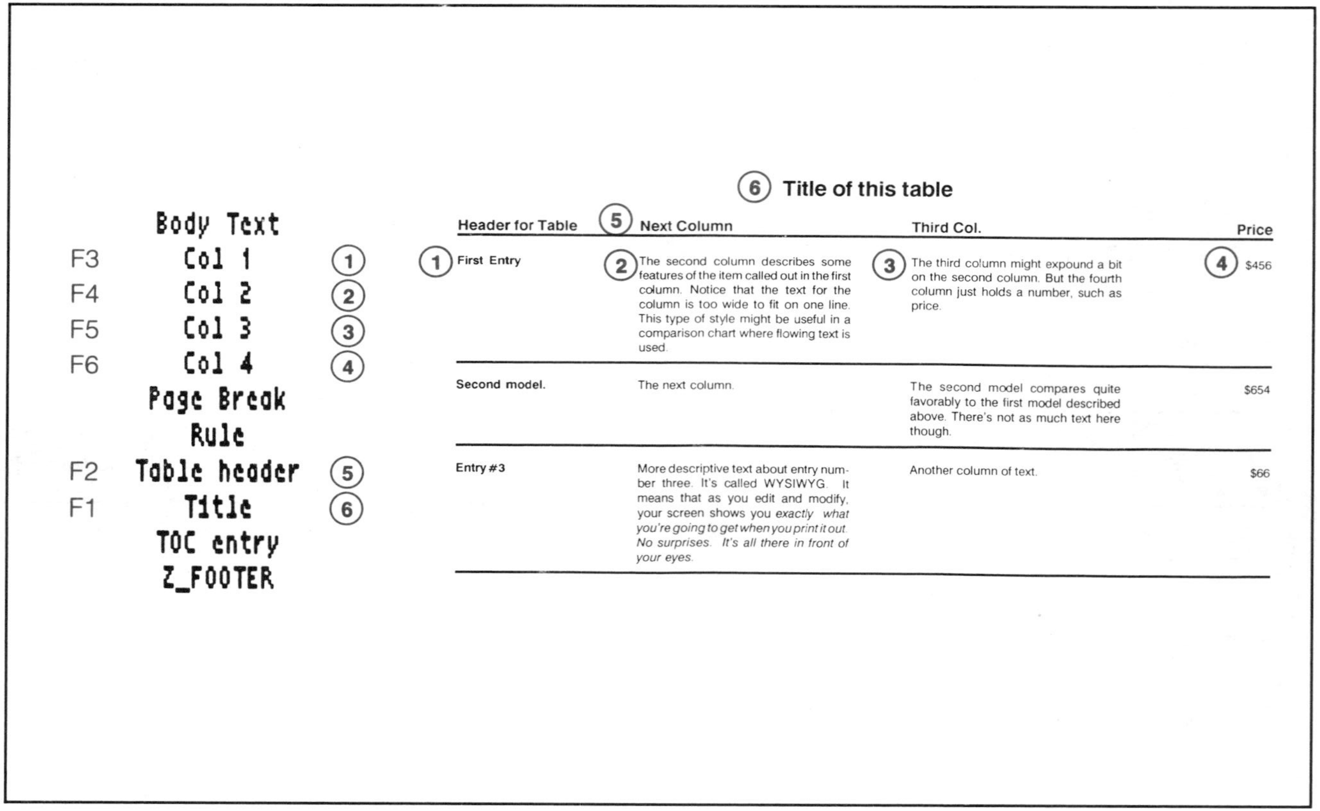

	Body Text	
F3	Col 1	(1)
F4	Col 2	(2)
F5	Col 3	(3)
F6	Col 4	(4)
	Page Break	
	Rule	
F2	Table header	(5)
F1	Title	(6)
	TOC entry	
	Z_FOOTER	

(6) **Title of this table**

Header for Table	(5) Next Column	Third Col.	Price
(1) **First Entry**	(2) The second column describes some features of the item called out in the first column. Notice that the text for the column is too wide to fit on one line. This type of style might be useful in a comparison chart where flowing text is used.	(3) The third column might expound a bit on the second column. But the fourth column just holds a number, such as price.	(4) $456
Second model.	The next column.	The second model compares quite favorably to the first model described above. There's not as much text here though.	$654
Entry #3	More descriptive text about entry number three. It's called WYSIWYG. It means that as you edit and modify, your screen shows you *exactly what you're going to get when you print it out. No surprises. It's all there in front of your eyes.*	Another column of text.	$66

Figure A.16: &TBL2-L1 Sample Page

MENU	COMMAND	SETTING	
Page	Page Layout	Orientation: Paper Type: Sides:	Landscape Letter Single
Frame	Margins & Columns	# of Columns: Column Width: Margins:	1 9'' Top: .75'' Bottom: .75'' Left: 1'' Right: 1''
TAG NAME AND FUNCTION KEY	**PARAGRAPH MENU COMMAND**	**SETTING**	
Body Text (F10)	Alignment	Alignment:	Justified
	Spacing	Above & Below: Inter-Line: Inter-Paragraph:	0 01,00 picas & points 01,00 picas & points
See Chapter 9 for a discussion of the tags in this sample.			

Table A.16: &TBL2-L1 Formatting Features

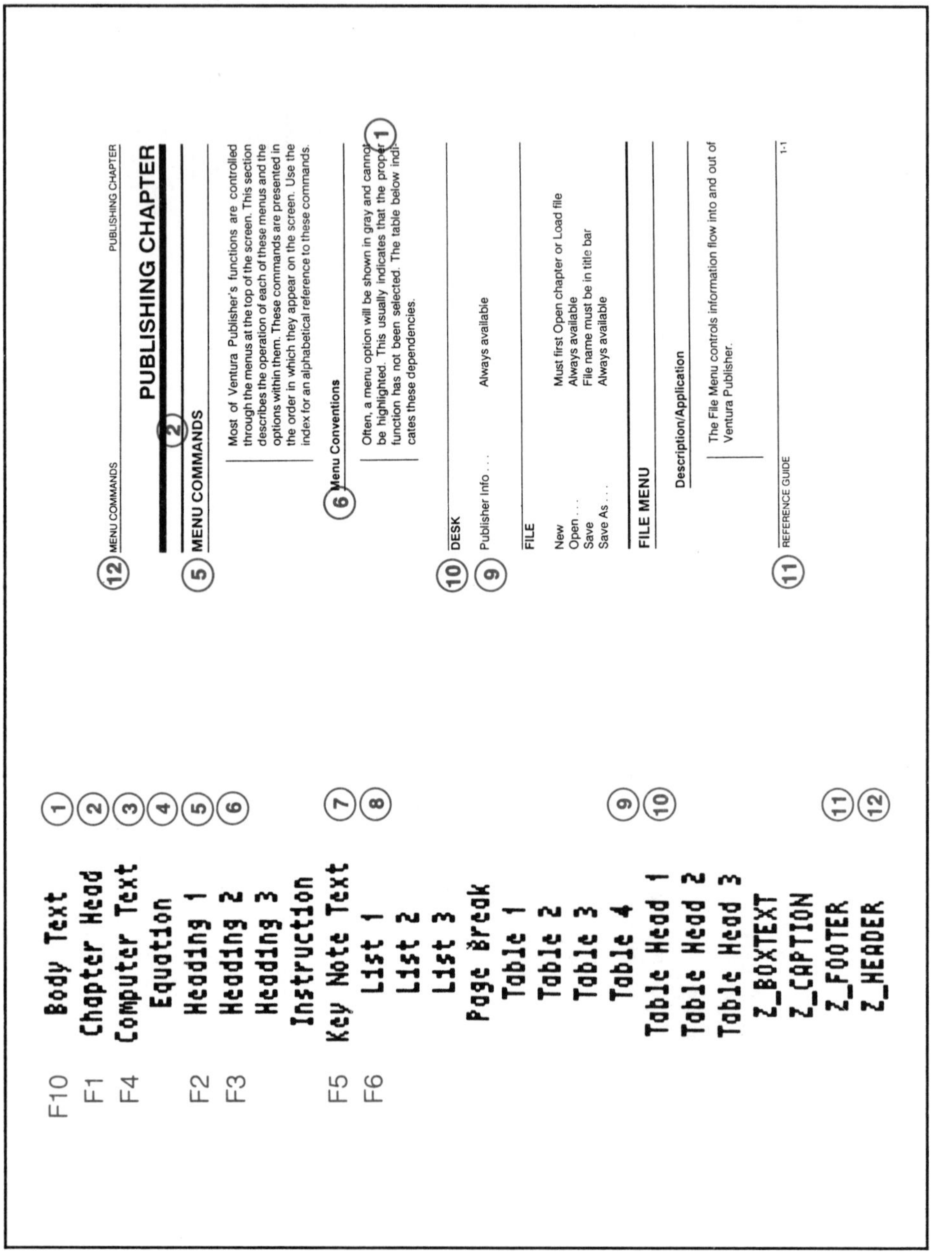

Key	Tag	#
F10	Body Text	1
F1	Chapter Head	2
F4	Computer Text	3
	Equation	4
F2	Heading 1	5
F3	Heading 2	6
	Heading 3	
	Instruction	
F5	Key Note Text	7
F6	List 1	8
	List 2	
	List 3	
	Page Break	
	Table 1	
	Table 2	
	Table 3	
	Table 4	9
	Table Head 1	10
	Table Head 2	
	Table Head 3	
	Z_BOXTEXT	
	Z_CAPTION	
	Z_FOOTER	11
	Z_HEADER	12

(12) MENU COMMANDS PUBLISHING CHAPTER

PUBLISHING CHAPTER (2)

(5) MENU COMMANDS

Most of Ventura Publisher's functions are controlled through the menus at the top of the screen. This section describes the operation of each of these menus and the options within them. These commands are presented in the order in which they appear on the screen. Use the index for an alphabetical reference to these commands.

(6) Menu Conventions

Often, a menu option will be shown in gray and cannot be highlighted. This usually indicates that the proper (1) function has not been selected. The table below indicates these dependencies.

(10) DESK

(9) Publisher Info . . .	Always available

FILE

New	Must first Open chapter or Load file
Open . . .	Always available
Save	File name must be in title bar
Save As . . .	Always available

FILE MENU

Description/Application

The File Menu controls information flow into and out of Ventura Publisher.

(11) REFERENCE GUIDE 1-1

Figure A.17: &TCHD-P1 Sample Pages

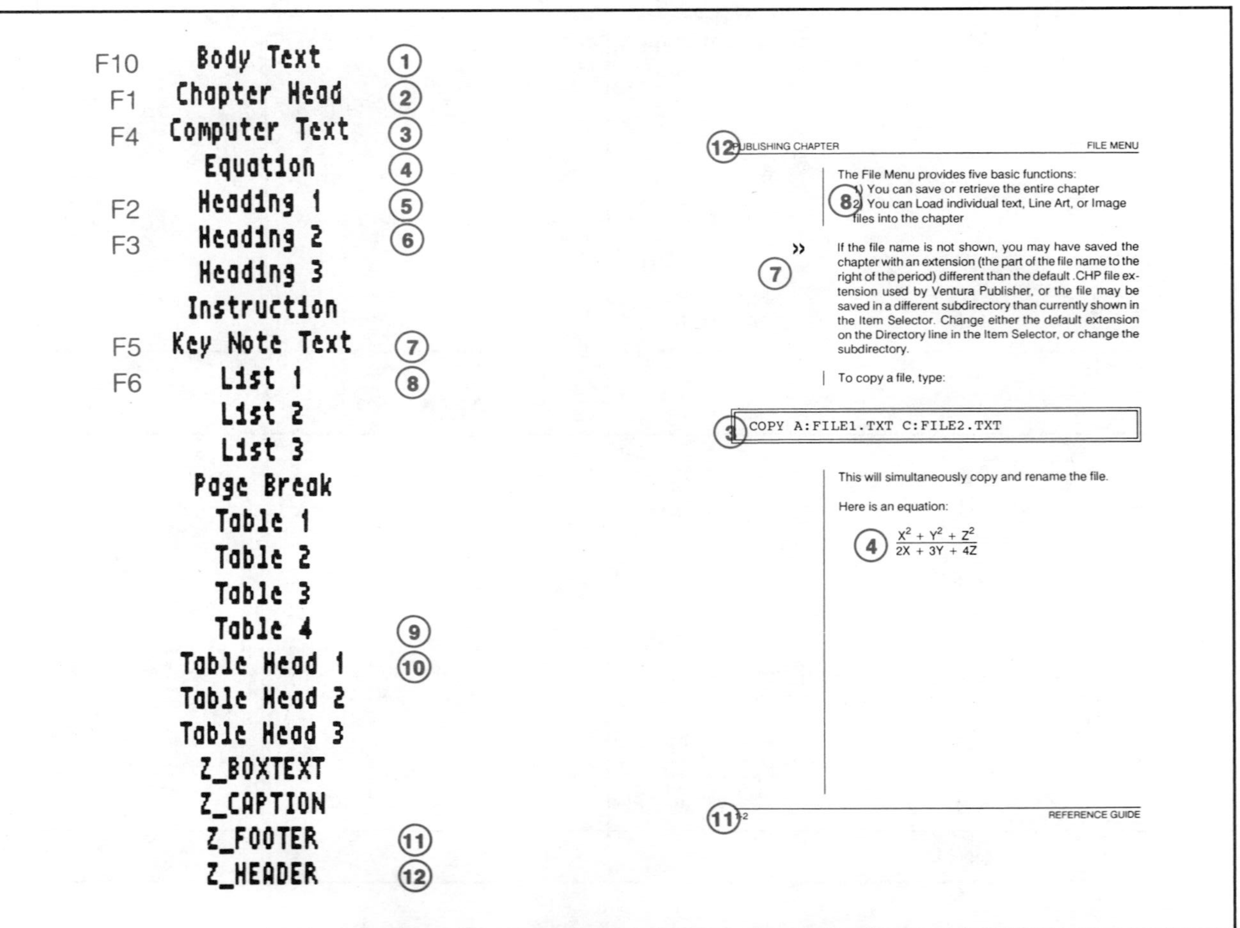

F10 Body Text 1
F1 Chapter Head 2
F4 Computer Text 3
Equation 4
F2 Heading 1 5
F3 Heading 2 6
Heading 3
Instruction
F5 Key Note Text 7
F6 List 1 8
List 2
List 3
Page Break
Table 1
Table 2
Table 3
Table 4 9
Table Head 1 10
Table Head 2
Table Head 3
Z_BOXTEXT
Z_CAPTION
Z_FOOTER 11
Z_HEADER 12
12 PUBLISHING CHAPTER
FILE MENU
The File Menu provides five basic functions:
8 1) You can save or retrieve the entire chapter
2) You can Load individual text, Line Art, or Image files into the chapter
7 »
If the file name is not shown, you may have saved the chapter with an extension (the part of the file name to the right of the period) different than the default .CHP file extension used by Ventura Publisher, or the file may be saved in a different subdirectory than currently shown in the Item Selector. Change either the default extension on the Directory line in the Item Selector, or change the subdirectory.
To copy a file, type:
3 COPY A:FILE1.TXT C:FILE2.TXT
This will simultaneously copy and rename the file.
Here is an equation:
4 $\frac{X^2 + Y^2 + Z^2}{2X + 3Y + 4Z}$
11 1-2
REFERENCE GUIDE

Figure A.17: &TCHD-P1 Sample Pages (continued)

MENU	COMMAND	SETTING	
Page	Page Layout	Orientation:	Portrait
		Paper Type:	Letter
		Sides:	Double
Frame	Margins & Columns	# of Columns:	1
		Column Width:	4.5''
		Margins:	Top: 1.92''
			Bottom: 1.92''
			Left: 2''
			Right: 2''
	Vertical Rules	Rule 1 Position:	18,00 picas & points
		Rule 1 Width:	.48 fractional points
TAG NAME AND FUNCTION KEY	**PARAGRAPH MENU COMMAND**	**SETTING**	
Body Text (F10)	Alignment	Alignment:	Justified
	Spacing	Above:	01,00 picas & points
		Inter-Line:	01,00 picas & points
Chapter Head (F1)	Alignment	Alignment:	Right
	Ruling Line Below	Width:	Frame
		Height of Rule 1:	6.00 fractional points
Computer Text (F4)	Ruling Box Around	Width:	Custom
		Space Above Rule 1:	4.74 fractional points
		Height of Rule 1:	.54 fractional points
		Space Below Rule 1:	1.98 fractional points
		Height of Rule 2:	.54 fractional points
		Space Below Rule 2:	4.74 fractional points
		Custom Indent:	6.24 fractional points
		Custom Width:	28,00 picas & points (4.67'')

TAG NAME AND FUNCTION KEY	PARAGRAPH MENU COMMAND	SETTING	
Equation	Tab Settings	Tab Number 1:	Center, 2.25"
Heading 1 (F2)	Ruling Line Above	Width:	Frame
		Height of Rule 1:	1.98 fractional points
		Space Below Rule 1:	4.02 fractional points
	Ruling Line Below	Width:	Frame
		Space Above Rule 1:	1.98 fractional points
		Height of Rule 1:	.66 fractional points
Heading 2 (F3)	Spacing	In From Left:	04,00 picas & points (.67")
	Ruling Line Below	Width:	Margin
		Space Above Rule 1:	1.98 fractional points
		Height of Rule 1:	.66 fractional points
Key Note Text (F5)	Special Effects	Special Effect:	Bullet
		Show Bullet As:	»
		Indent After Bullet:	03,00 pica & points (.5")
Table Head 1	Ruling Line Above	Width:	Column
		Height of Rule 1:	.48 fractional points
List 1 (F6)	Spacing	In From Left:	08,00 picas & points (1.33")

Table A.17: &TCHD-P1 Formatting Features

F10	Body Text	1
F9	Bullet	2
F1	Chapter Head	3
F2	Major Heading	4
F3	Minor Heading	5
	Page Break	
F7	System Prompt	6
F5	Table Head	7
F6	Table Item	8
	User Response	
F4	Warning	9
	Z_CAPTION	10
	Z_FOOTER	11
	Z_LABEL FIG	12
	Z_SEC1	13
	Z_SEC2	14
	Z_SEC3	15

(13) **1. USER INTERFACE** (3)

(14) **1.1. WYSIWYG** (4)

(12) Figure 1-1
(10) This is the caption for the figure. It is anchored below **WYSIWYG**

Ventura Publisher is designed to provide What You See (on the screen) Is What You Get printed (WYSIWYG). This means that the computer display should match as closely as possible, at all times, what you will see on the final printed page. Of course, the difference between the technology used to display a page on a CRT screen, and the technologies used to print a page on a laser printer or typesetter, do create some unavoidable differences. In particular,becausethecomputerCRTscreencannotproduceanywherenearthesameresolu tion of a printer or typesetter, and because what is displayed is shown in a different aspect ratio (height to width ratio), the space between words and between lines may appear to be bigger or smaller than the printed page under certain circumstances. Several thin ruling lines, with little space between, may show on the screen as one thick line.

(15) **1.1.1 Keyboard Keys** (5)

Various keys on the keyboard perform special functions:

- The keyboard Cursor keys control the Text Cursor (The text cursor is displayed as a thin vertical line.)
- (2) The Home key goes to the first page of the document.
- The End key goes to the last page of the document.
- The Pg Up key goes to the previous page.
- The Pg Dn key goes to the next page.

1.2. ITEM SELECTOR

1.2.1 Description

The display shown in Figure 10-2 is called an Item Selector. The Item Selector is used for saving and retrieving files.

(11) 1-A WYSIWYG

Figure A.18: &TDOC-P1 Sample Pages

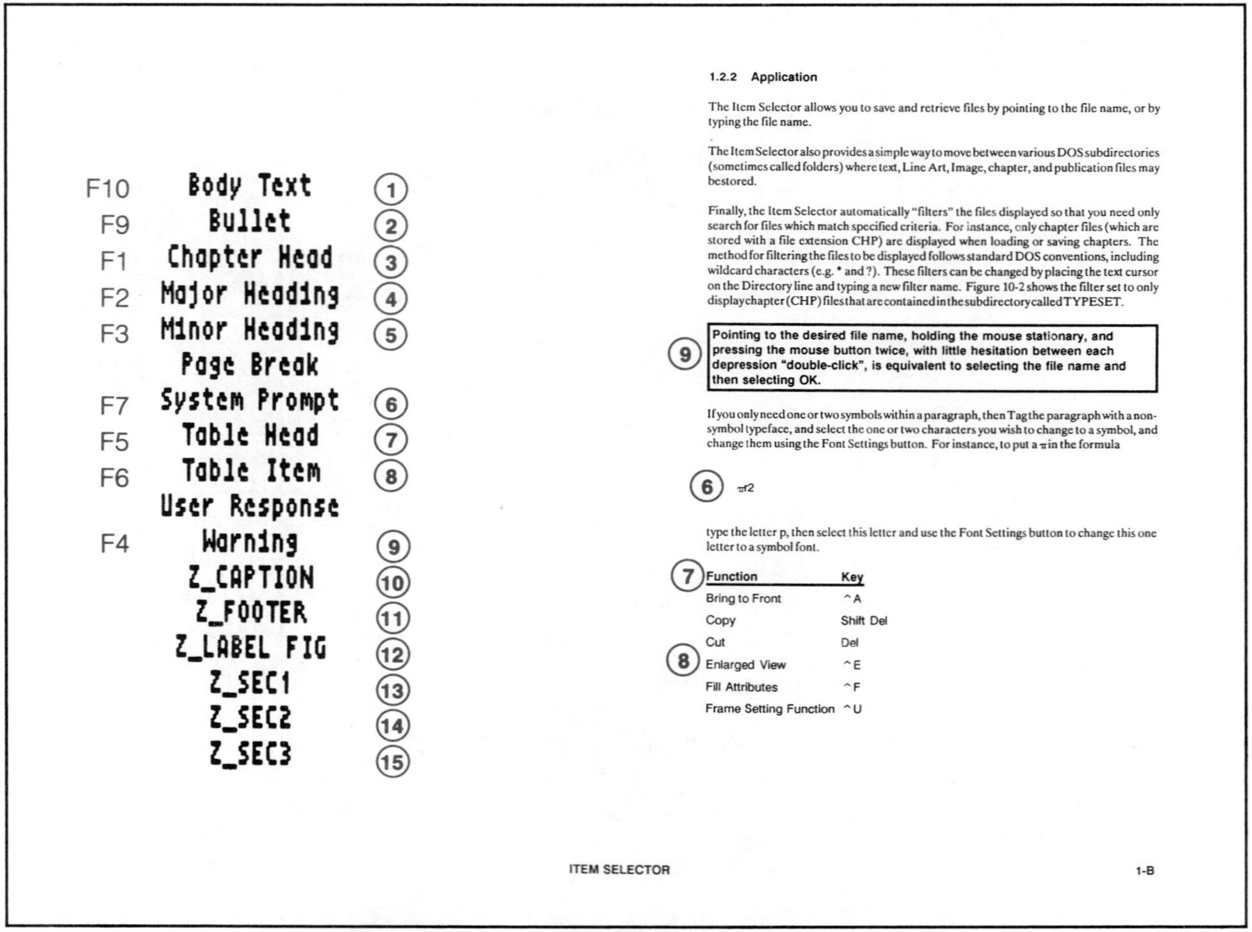

F10	Body Text	1
F9	Bullet	2
F1	Chapter Head	3
F2	Major Heading	4
F3	Minor Heading	5
	Page Break	
F7	System Prompt	6
F5	Table Head	7
F6	Table Item	8
	User Response	
F4	Warning	9
	Z_CAPTION	10
	Z_FOOTER	11
	Z_LABEL FIG	12
	Z_SEC1	13
	Z_SEC2	14
	Z_SEC3	15

1.2.2 **Application**

The Item Selector allows you to save and retrieve files by pointing to the file name, or by typing the file name.

The Item Selector also provides a simple way to move between various DOS subdirectories (sometimes called folders) where text, Line Art, Image, chapter, and publication files may bestored.

Finally, the Item Selector automatically "filters" the files displayed so that you need only search for files which match specified criteria. For instance, only chapter files (which are stored with a file extension CHP) are displayed when loading or saving chapters. The method for filtering the files to be displayed follows standard DOS conventions, including wildcard characters (e.g. * and ?). These filters can be changed by placing the text cursor on the Directory line and typing a new filter name. Figure 10-2 shows the filter set to only displaychapter (CHP) filesthat are containedinthe subdirectorycalledTYPESET.

(9) **Pointing to the desired file name, holding the mouse stationary, and pressing the mouse button twice, with little hesitation between each depression "double-click", is equivalent to selecting the file name and then selecting OK.**

If you only need one or two symbols within a paragraph, then Tag the paragraph with a non-symbol typeface, and select the one or two characters you wish to change to a symbol, and change them using the Font Settings button. For instance, to put a π in the formula

(6) πr2

type the letter p, then select this letter and use the Font Settings button to change this one letter to a symbol font.

(7) Function	Key
Bring to Front	^A
Copy	Shift Del
Cut	Del
(8) Enlarged View	^E
Fill Attributes	^F
Frame Setting Function	^U

ITEM SELECTOR 1-B

Figure A.18: &TDOC-P1 Sample Pages (continued)

MENU	COMMAND	SETTING	
Page	Page Layout	Orientation:	Portrait
		Paper Type:	Letter
		Sides:	Double
Frame	Margins & Columns	# of Columns:	1
		Column Width:	6.5"
		Margins:	Top: 1"
			Bottom: 1"
			Left: 1"
			Right: 1"
TAG NAME AND FUNCTION KEY	**PARAGRAPH MENU COMMAND**	**SETTING**	
Body Text (F10)	Alignment	Alignment:	Justified
	Spacing	Above & Below:	0
		In From Left:	9 picas & points (1.5")
Bullet (F9)	Special Effects	Special Effect:	Bullet
		Indent After Bullet:	01,00 picas & points
Chapter Head (F1)	Breaks	Line Break:	After

TAG NAME AND FUNCTION KEY	PARAGRAPH MENU COMMAND	SETTING	
	Ruling Line Below	Width: Height of Rule 1:	Margin 3.00 fractional points
Major Heading (F2)	Breaks	Line Break:	After
	Ruling Line Below	Width: Height of Rule 1:	Frame 1.98 fractional points
Minor Heading (F3)	Breaks	Line Break:	After
Warning (F4)	Ruling Box Around	Width: Height of Rule 1: Space Below Rule 1:	Margin 1.98 fractional points 1.98 fractional points
*Z_SEC1, -2, -3	Breaks	Line Break:	Before

*Break settings for section numbers and headings cause the text for these tags to stay on the same line.

Table A.18: &TDOC-P1 Formatting Features

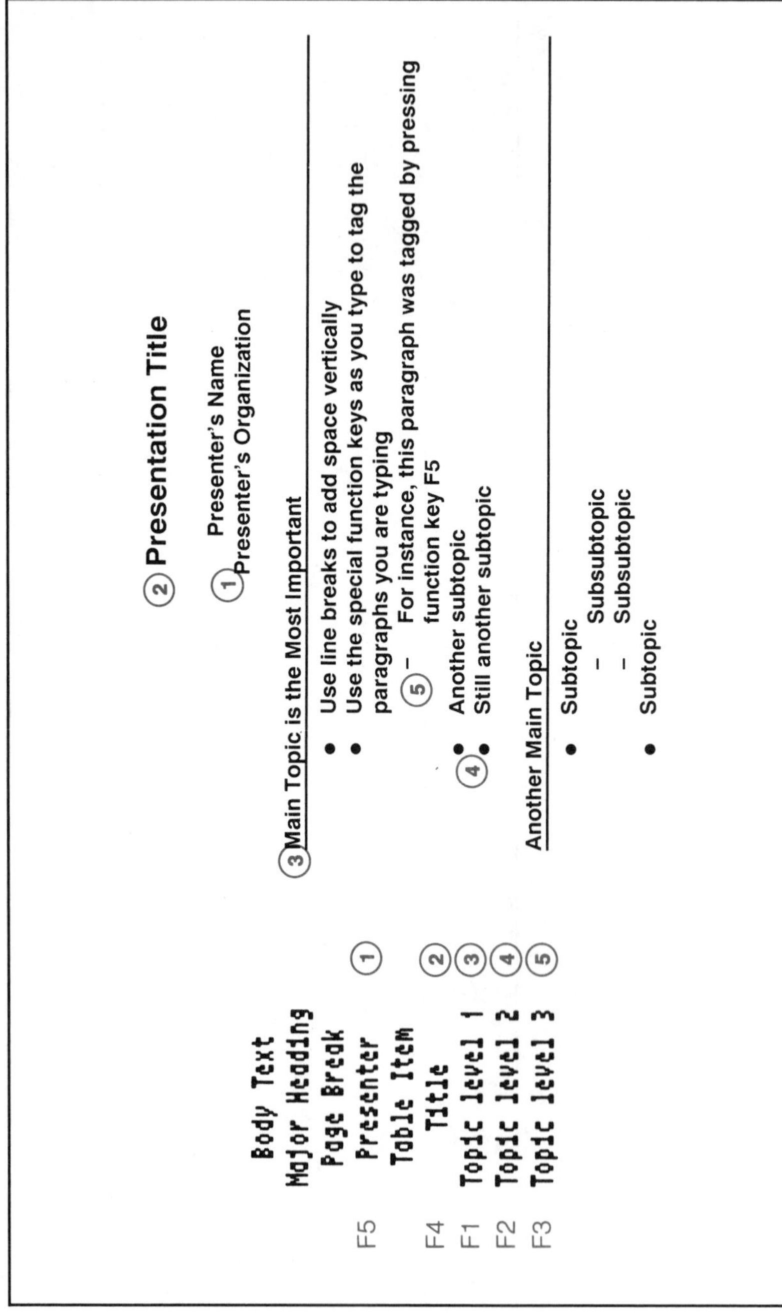

Figure A.19: &VWGF-L1 Sample Page

MENU	COMMAND	SETTING	
Page	Page Layout	Orientation: Paper Type: Sides:	Landscape Letter Single
Frame	Margins & Columns	# of Columns: Column Width: Margins:	1 9" Top: 1" Bottom: 1" Left: 1" Right: 1"
TAG NAME AND FUNCTION KEY	**PARAGRAPH MENU COMMAND**	**SETTING**	
Body Text (F10)	Alignment	Alignment:	Left
	Spacing	Above & Below: Inter-Line:	0 01,09 picas & points
Presenter	Alignment	Alignment:	Center
Title (F4)	Alignment	Alignment:	Center
Topic level 1 (F1)	Ruling Line Below	Width: Height of Rule 1:	Margin 1.98 fractional points
Topic level 2 (F2)	Spacing	In From Left:	6 picas & points (1")
	Special Effects	Special Effect: Indent After Bullet	Bullet 3 picas & points (.5")
Topic level 3 (F3)	Spacing	In From Left:	12 picas & points (2")
	Special Effects	Special Effect: Show Bullet As: Indent After Bullet	Bullet – 3 picas & points (.5")

Table A.19: &VWGF-L1 Formatting Features

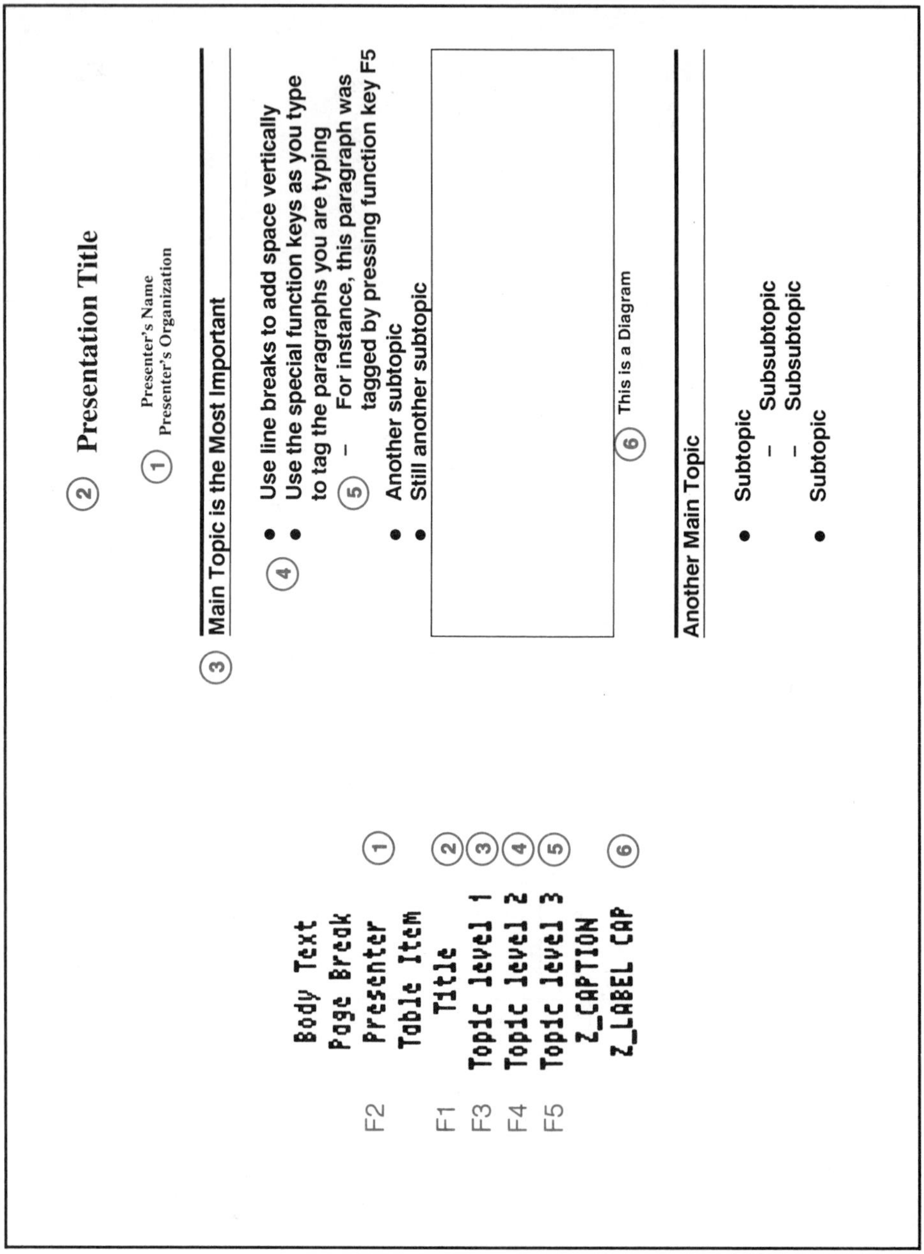

Key	Tag	
	Body Text	
	Page Break	
F2	Presenter	①
	Table Item	
F1	Title	②
F3	Topic level 1	③
F4	Topic level 2	④
F5	Topic level 3	⑤
	Z_CAPTION	
	Z_LABEL CAP	⑥

② **Presentation Title**

① Presenter's Name
Presenter's Organization

③ **Main Topic is the Most Important**

④
- Use line breaks to add space vertically
- Use the special function keys as you type to tag the paragraphs you are typing
  - ⑤ For instance, this paragraph was tagged by pressing function key F5
- Another subtopic
- Still another subtopic

⑥ This is a Diagram

Another Main Topic

- Subtopic
  - Subsubtopic
  - Subsubtopic
- Subtopic

Figure A.20: &VWGF-P1 Sample Page

MENU	COMMAND	SETTING	
Page	Page Layout	Orientation:	Portrait
		Paper Type:	Letter
		Sides:	Single
Frame	Margins & Columns	# of Columns:	1
		Column Width:	6.5"
		Margins:	Top: 1"
			Bottom: 1"
			Left: 1"
			Right: 1"
TAG NAME AND FUNCTION KEY	**PARAGRAPH MENU COMMAND**	**SETTING**	
Body Text (F10)	Alignment	Alignment:	Left
	Spacing	Above & Below:	0
		Inter-Line:	01,09 picas & points
Page Break	Breaks	Page Break:	After
Presenter (F2)	Alignment	Alignment:	Center

Table A.20: &VWGF-P1 Formatting Features

Tag Name and Function Key	Paragraph Menu Command	Setting	
Title (F4)	Alignment	Alignment:	Center
Topic level 1 (F1)	Ruling Line Above	Width: Height of Rule 1:	Frame 3.00 fractional points
	Ruling Line Below	Width: Height of Rule 1:	Margin 1.02 fractional points
Topic level 2 (F2)	Spacing	In From Left:	6 picas & points (1'')
	Special Effects	Special Effect: Indent After Bullet:	Bullet 3 picas & points (.5'')
Topic level 3 (F3)	Spacing	In From Left:	12 picas & points (2'')
	Special Effects	Special Effect: Show Bullet As: Indent After Bullet:	Bullet – 3 picas & points (.5'')
Z_LABEL CAP	Alignment	Alignment	Center

Table A.20: &VWGF-P1 Formatting Features (continued)

APPENDIX B

Alternative Setups for Ventura

MOST PEOPLE USE VENTURA WITH A MOUSE, standard RAM up to 640K, and a standard graphics monitor. However, other setups are possible. The program is designed so that you can use it, if necessary, without a mouse; you can also use Ventura with extended RAM and with large (full-page) displays. We look at these alternative setups in this appendix.

OPERATING VENTURA WITHOUT A MOUSE

Although most people use Ventura with a mouse, it is possible to operate the program without one. You may find that you need this option if you have a mouse that isn't working or if you've removed it for use on a different computer.

There are also some users who aren't aware of Ventura's hardware needs and who acquire the program without buying a mouse. Even though you can learn Ventura without using a mouse, it's not really advisable. It's easier to use the program without a mouse once you've become conversant with using Ventura with a mouse.

When installing Ventura, you have the option of specifying No Mouse. However, you are not required to use this installation option in order to use Ventura without a mouse. The techniques discussed here will work if you've installed Ventura for a particular brand of mouse as well.

Ventura's strategy for mouseless operation makes the keypad perform double duty. Normally, the directional arrows on the keypad control the keyboard (or text) cursor on the screen. When using Ventura without a mouse, you can toggle the operation of some of the keypad keys. As you do, these keys change between Normal mode, where the arrow keys control the keyboard cursor, and Mouse mode, where the arrow keys control the mouse cursor. To switch between modes, you press the Ctrl key and the Shift key on the right. When you do, you'll hear a beep tone, indicating that the change has taken place. Pressing Ctrl-right Shift again causes the operating mode to switch back.

When the keypad keys are in the Mouse mode, the Home key (which normally displays the first page in the document) duplicates clicking the mouse button. Pressing and releasing it is the same as if you click the mouse. The End key (which normally displays the last page in the document) simulates a press-and-hold or drag operation with the mouse button. Pressing the End key is the same as pressing the mouse button and holding it down. You release the theoretical mouse button by pressing the Home key. The other keys on the keypad—PgUp, PgDn, Del, and Ins—are not affected and operate the same in both keypad modes.

With the keypad in the Mouse mode, it is sometimes necessary to move the mouse cursor a smaller amount than the arrow keys allow. By pressing and holding the Shift key as you use the keypad arrows, you move the mouse cursor in smaller increments, allowing you to fine-tune its position.

Other keys pressed in combination with the Home and End keys sometimes work as they do when used with the mouse button. For example, you can use the Shift key with Home and End to select text. You can also use Shift-Home to select multiple paragraphs that you wish to tag similarly or to select multiple frames or graphics. However, you cannot use the Alt key to crop pictures or the Shift key to add multiple frames, as you can when using Alt and Shift with the mouse. You cannot use the Ctrl key to select frames in sequence that are stacked on top of one another as Ctrl-mouse does.

Moving the mouse cursor with the keypad arrows is quite a bit slower than using a mouse. Therefore, be sure to learn and use the keyboard shortcuts extensively when using Ventura without a mouse. For instance, use Ctrl-U, -I, -O, and -P to change operating modes rather than the Mode buttons. Use Ctrl-2 instead of clicking the Addition button and Ctrl-X to redisplay the last dialog box you worked with. The keyboard shortcuts are discussed and listed in Chapter 2.

Switching the operation of the keypad can be especially confusing as you work with dialog boxes. For that reason, keep the switching to a minimum. Generally, keep the keypad in the Mouse mode. Instead of using the mouse cursor or the keypad arrows to move the keyboard cursor from field to field, use the Tab key. Use Shift-Tab to move the keyboard cursor back to a previous field. Use the Return key to give the OK rather than clicking the OK button.

Canceling a dialog box is also slowed when you are in mouse mode. You must move the mouse cursor to the bottom left corner of the dialog box to reach the Cancel button before you can press Home to cancel. Therefore, take care and try to display the correct dialog box.

In the Item Selector box, you'll probably find that it's faster to type in drives, directories, and file names than to click them on the Item Selector list or use the Backup button. Again, use Tab and Shift-Tab to change fields. Use the Esc key to clear out previous names that are no longer applicable.

You can use a keyboard enhancer, such as SmartKey, to assist in using Ventura without a mouse, by creating macros that speed up the keypad arrows (see Chapter 12). For instance, you could make pressing Alt-→ the same as pressing the → key six times. This speeds moving the mouse cursor around the screen with the keypad arrows. Remember, though, that using resident programs, such as a keyboard enhancer, can limit the size of your Ventura chapters.

You can also create macros that trigger the various pull-down menus. To program the keyboard enhancer to do this, start with the mouse cursor in the bottom right corner. This will allow the macro to control the most extreme situation, and all others as well. Start recording with the keyboard enhancer and then use the arrow keys to move the mouse cursor all the way to the left, then up the left edge of the screen to the menu line, and finally across the menu line to the menu name of your choice. Then end the macro. You could use this technique, for instance, to make Alt-F trigger the Frame menu.

Don't forget that with a keyboard enhancer, the Function keys are up for grabs, if you're willing to give up their usual function of tagging paragraphs. By using the Function keys you can make various operations available with one keystroke.

USING A RAM DISK

If your computer has extended memory available (at least 1.2 MB in all), you'll probably wish to put it to use with Ventura. To do so, you can create a *RAM drive* (or *virtual disk*) and set up Ventura to use it.

In normal operations, Ventura uses your computer memory to store and manipulate text as you work on it. However, with large chapters, Ventura may run out of RAM. When that happens, Ventura will spill portions of the chapter over to the disk drive, (called *swapping to disk*), and retrieve the material as necessary. Because disk drives contain moving parts, they are slow compared to RAM. Therefore, Ventura's operations can become significantly slower when material spills over.

A RAM drive is a portion of computer memory that you configure so that it operates like a disk drive. With Ventura, you can use extended memory for this purpose. A drive letter is assigned to the memory so that, as far as the program is concerned, this memory constitutes a disk drive. Ventura will use it to hold spillover portions of the chapter as necessary.

To use a RAM drive, you must first create it. To do this, use the software that accompanies the extended memory when you purchase it. With an AT computer and DOS 3.0 and higher, you can use DOS's VDISK command. The size of the RAM drive should be at least 500K.

Next, you must inform Ventura of the RAM drive's existence. You do this by adding a code to the last line of the VP.BAT file, located in the root directory. Use ASCII mode in your word processor to do this (see Chapter 12). The code you add consists of a slash, the letter O, and an equal sign, followed by the disk-drive letter assigned to your RAM drive and a colon. Thus, if your RAM drive is drive E, you would add

```
/O=E:
```

so that the line in your VP.BAT would look like this:

```
DRVRMRGR VP %1 /S = SD_GENS5.EGA/M = 32/O = E:
```

Note that since this line also indicates the monitor, screen font, and mouse that you are using, yours may differ quite a bit from this example.

USING LARGE DISPLAYS

Monitors with large displays, such as the Genius full-page display, usually have several operating modes. Some programs cannot use the complete display and so these modes regulate the screen as required by the program in use.

When you install Ventura, you specify the monitor you will use. If the monitor operates in several modes, it's important to make sure it's configured for the full-page display whenever you use Ventura. This can be accomplished automatically by including a line in the VP.BAT file that invokes the proper mode whenever you load Ventura.

With the Genius display, this is accomplished by adding

```
vhr mds
```

to at the beginning of the VP.BAT file. Be sure you add the line before the DRVRMRGR command, as this is the command that invokes Ventura.

APPENDIX C

Dos Conventions and Ventura

VENTURA FOLLOWS DOS'S DESIGN CONVENTIONS FOR directories and wild cards. This appendix examines these conventions.

DIRECTORIES

Because a hard disk can store so much data, DOS organizes the disk so that it's easier for you to use. Just as you can divide a desk drawer into sections, so too can you divide your hard disk. That way, you can find files when you need them.

At the topmost level, storage for your computer is divided into disk drives. Clicking the Backup button in the Item Selector box repeatedly will ultimately display a list of the disk drives. Disk drives are indicated with a letter (which Ventura always capitalizes) and a colon. Thus, if your system has three disk drives, A, B, and C, they would be indicated like so:

```
A:
B:
C:
```

Disk drives, in turn, are divided into *directories*. By selecting a disk drive, you display its directories. The main directory of a disk drive is the *root directory*. This is the directory that exists before dividing the disk drive into other directories. The root directory is indicated by a backslash (\) after the disk-drive letter and colon. Thus, the root directory of drive C is indicated by

```
C:\
```

Directories that branch off the root directory are indicated by the name of that directory, following the disk-drive letter, colon, and the backslash. Thus, your drive C may have a directory for Microsoft Word, called WORD, in addition to Ventura's VENTURA and TYPESET directories. These three directories would be indicated like so:

```
C:\WORD
C:\VENTURA
C:\TYPESET
```

Directories themselves can be divided into additional directories, or *subdirectories*. These are indicated with another backslash and the name of the subdirectory. For example, your WORD directory may be divided into MEMOS, REPORTS, and FORMS. These subdirectories would be indicated like so:

```
C:\WORD\MEMOS
C:\WORD\REPORTS
C:\WORD\FORMS
```

WILD CARDS

A DOS wild card, like a wild card in a game of poker, acts as a substitute. Wild cards allow you to "filter" the files that are to be operated upon, based on some criteria you specify. You can filter when using the Item Selector box to open a chapter or load associated files. This decreases the number of files displayed, narrowing your file search. You can also use wild cards to delete matching files with the File menu's DOS File Ops command.

DOS uses two wild cards: the asterisk and the question mark. Ventura honors them both. The asterisk acts as a substitute for any number of characters. By typing an asterisk, a period, and a given extension, for instance, you can select all files that end with the extension you specify. The filter you specify in this manner follows the directory name, separated with a backslash.

For instance, documents created with Microsoft Word all end with DOC. To filter for Word documents in the MEMOS directory, you would specify

```
C:\WORD\MEMOS\*.DOC
```

You can also use the asterisk as a substitute for extensions. Thus, if you want to see all the files that begin with the name JONES, you'd use JONES.* as your search pattern. This will display JONES-.DOC, JONES.BAK, JONES.PCX, and so on, depending on what files are present in the indicated directory.

Use an asterisk after an initial letter to display all files beginning with that letter. Thus, specifying J* would display all files beginning with J, regardless of the rest of the name or the extension.

The question mark is DOS's other wild card. The question mark acts as a substitute for one character only. You can combine the question mark with the asterisk to create complex search patterns. Thus, to display all files with two letter extensions beginning with W, you'd specify *.W? for the filter. Again, this filter would be used in conjunction with a drive and directory, as in the following example:

```
C:\MASTERVP\*.W?
```

This filter would display all files ending with WP and WS. It would suppress the display of files with three-letter extensions, such as WOK, as well as files whose extensions begin with letters other than W.

APPENDIX D

Suppliers of Fonts

The following companies provide fonts for Ventura:

Adobe Systems, Inc.
1870 Embarcadero Road
Palo Alto, CA 94303
(415) 852-0271

Bitstream, Inc.
215 First Street
Cambridge, MA 02142
(617) 497-6222

CES
509 Cathedral Parkway, #10-A
New York, NY 10025
(800) 251-2223

Conographic Corporation
16802 Aston Street
Irvine, CA 92714
(714) 474-1188

Font Center
509 Marin Street, #227
Thousand Oaks, CA 91360
(805) 373-1919

Font Factory
2400 Centro Parkway, Suite J2
Houston, TX 77092
(713) 358-6954

Hewlett-Packard
PO Box 3640
Sunnyvale, CA 94088
(800) 538-8787

LaserMaster Corporation
7156 Shady Oak Road
Eden Prairie, MN 55344
(800) USA-TYPE

SoftCraft, Inc.
222 State Street, Suite 400
Madison, WI 53703
(800) 351-0500

StraightForward
3901 Via Oro Avenue
Long Beach, CA 90810
(800) 553-3332
(800) 237-9680 (in California)

SWFTE International
PO Box 5773
Wilmington, DE 19808
(800) 237-9383

Ventura Publisher User's Group
675 Jarvis Drive
Morgan Hill, CA 95037
(408) 778-1125

VS Software
VideoSoft, Inc.
PO Box 6158
Little Rock, AR 72216
(501) 376-2083

Weaver Graphics
Fox Pavilion
PO Box 1132
Jenkintown, PA 19046
(215) 884-9286

APPENDIX E

Special Characters and Codes

THIS APPENDIX CONSISTS OF TWO PARTS. THE FIRST section is a list of character sets available with Ventura. This section is drawn from the Ventura sample document CHARSET.CHP, located in the TYPESET directory. You can load and print this document yourself. We've added the keyboard shortcuts that appear toward the end of the listing.

Char Set 1 is the character set that Ventura normally uses. Char Set 2 is the set that appears when you format text with the SYMBOL font. The use of this font is discussed in Chapter 13.

The second section of the appendix is a listing of the text codes. These are codes that may appear in the word processed version of your text files in order to set an effect in place. You can also insert them yourself by typing them in. The codes are discussed in Chapter 12.

	Char Set 1	*Char Set 2*
1-31	not used	
32	space	space
33	!	!
34	"	∀
35	#	#
36	$	∃
37	%	%
38	&	&
39	'	∋
40	(	(
41	)	)
42	*	∗
43	+	+
44	,	,
45	-	−
46	.	.
47	/	/
48	0	0
49	1	1
50	2	2
51	3	3
52	4	4
53	5	5
54	6	6
55	7	7
56	8	8
57	9	9
58	:	:
59	;	;
60	<	<
61	=	=
62	>	
63	?	?
64	@	≅
65	A	Α
66	B	Β
67	C	Χ
68	D	Δ
69	E	Ε
70	F	Φ
71	G	Γ
72	H	Η
73	I	Ι
74	J	ϑ
75	K	Κ
76	L	Λ
77	M	Μ
78	N	Ν
79	O	Ο
80	P	Π
81	Q	Θ
82	R	Ρ
83	S	Σ
84	T	Τ
85	U	Υ
86	V	ς
87	W	Ω
88	X	Ξ
89	Y	Ψ
90	Z	Ζ
91	[	[
92	\	∴
93	]	]
94	^	⊥

Table E.1: The Ventura Character Sets

	CHAR SET 1	CHAR SET 2
95	_	_
96	‘	‾
97	a	α
98	b	β
99	c	χ
100	d	δ
101	e	ε
102	f	φ
103	g	γ
104	h	η
105	i	ι
106	j	ϕ
107	k	κ
108	l	λ
109	m	μ
110	n	ν
111	o	ο
112	p	π
113	q	θ
114	r	ρ
115	s	σ
116	t	τ
117	u	υ
118	v	ϖ
119	w	ω
120	x	ξ
121	y	ψ
122	z	ζ
123	{	{
124	|	|
125	}	}
126	~	~
127		
128	Ç	
129	ü	
130	é	′
131	â	≤
132	ä	⁄
133	à	∞
134	å	ƒ
135	ç	♣
136	ê	♦
137	ë	♥
138	è	♠
139	ï	↔
140	î	←
141	ì	↑
142	Ä	→
143	Å	↓
144	É	°
145	æ	±
146	Æ	″
147	ô	≥
148	ö	×
149	ò	∝
150	û	∂
151	ù	•
152	ÿ	÷
153	Ö	≠
154	Ü	≡
155	¢	≈
156	£	…
157	¥	|
158	¤	—

Table E.1: The Ventura Character Sets (continued)

	CHAR SET 1	CHAR SET 2	KEYBOARD SHORTCUT
159	ƒ	↵	
160	á	ℵ	
161	í		
162	ó		
163	ú	℘	
164	ñ	⊗	
165	Ñ	⊕	
166	ª	∅	
167	º	∩	
168	¿	∪	
169	“	⊃	Ctrl-Shift-[
170	”	⊇	Ctrl-Shift-]
171	‹	⊄	
172	›	⊂	
173	¡	⊆	
174	«	∈	
175	»	∉	
176	ã	∠	
177	õ	∇	
178	Ø	®	
179	ø	©	
180	œ	™	
181	Œ	Π	
182	À	√	
183	Ã	·	
184	Õ	¬	
185	§	∧	
186	‡	∨	
187	†	⇔	
188	¶	⇐	
189	©	⇑	Ctrl-Shift-C
190	®	⇒	Ctrl-Shift-R

	CHAR SET 1	CHAR SET 2	KEYBOARD SHORTCUT
191	™	⇓	Ctrl-Shift-2
192	„	◊	
193	…	⟨	
194	‰	®	
195	●	©	
196	–	™	Ctrl-[
197	—	Σ	Ctrl-]
198	°	⎛	
199	Á	⎜	
200	Â	⎝	
201	È	⎡	
202	Ê	⎢	
203	Ë	⎣	
204	Ì	⎧	
205	Í	⎨	
206	Î	⎩	
207	Ï	⎪	
208	Ò		
209	Ó	⟩	
210	Ô	∫	
211	Š	⌠	
212	š	⎮	
213	Ù	⌡	
214	Ú	⎞	
215	Û	⎟	
216	Ÿ	⎠	
217	ß	⎤	
218			
219			
220			
221			
222			
223			

Table E.1: The Ventura Character Sets (continued)

<table>
<tr><th>EFFECT</th><th>CODE</th></tr>
<tr><td>Color</td><td><C___></td></tr>
<tr><td>Discretionary Hyphen</td><td><-></td></tr>
<tr><td>Double underline</td><td><C = ></td></tr>
<tr><td>Inserted text:</td><td></td></tr>
<tr><td> Anchor</td><td><$&___></td></tr>
<tr><td> Footnote</td><td><$F___></td></tr>
<tr><td> Hidden text</td><td><$H___></td></tr>
<tr><td> Index</td><td><$I___></td></tr>
<tr><td>Italics</td><td><I></td></tr>
<tr><td>Jump of base line</td><td><J___></td></tr>
<tr><td>Kerning</td><td><K___></td></tr>
<tr><td>Line break</td><td><R></td></tr>
<tr><td>NoBreak Space</td><td><N></td></tr>
<tr><td>Normal</td><td><D></td></tr>
<tr><td>Overscore</td><td><O></td></tr>
<tr><td>Point size</td><td><P___></td></tr>
<tr><td>Small</td><td><S></td></tr>
<tr><td>Spaces:</td><td></td></tr>
<tr><td> Em space</td><td><_></td></tr>
<tr><td> En space</td><td>< ~ ></td></tr>
<tr><td> Thin space</td><td>< | ></td></tr>
<tr><td> Figure space</td><td>< + ></td></tr>
<tr><td>Strike-thru</td><td><X></td></tr>
<tr><td>Subscript</td><td><v></td></tr>
<tr><td>Superscript</td><td>< ^ ></td></tr>
<tr><td>Type weight:</td><td></td></tr>
<tr><td> Bold</td><td><B></td></tr>
<tr><td> Light</td><td><L></td></tr>
<tr><td> Medium</td><td><M></td></tr>
<tr><td>Typeface</td><td><F___></td></tr>
<tr><td>Underline</td><td><U></td></tr>
</table>

Table E.2: Codes for Text Effects

INDEX

MASTERING VENTURA Samples Disk

The easiest way for you to use Ventura is by applying style sheets and adapting sample documents. Now, direct from the author, you can receive a disk of professionally prepared style sheets and sample documents.

- Samples include a resume, letter, memo, book, organizational chart, form, brochure, financial report, newsletter, table, and other formats.
- Features of the formats are listed and clearly discussed.
- Function keys are listed and assigned in a consistent manner, allowing you to switch style sheets easily.
- Tags are carefully organized to allow you to apply them quickly.
- Files are ready to install on your disk, altogether or one by one.

- -

To order, simply fill out this coupon or send the information on a separate piece of paper. Mail to Matthew Holtz, 455 Hyde St. #93, San Francisco, CA 94109. Include a check for $20, payable to Matthew Holtz. (California residents please add appropriate sales tax.) Please allow 4-6 weeks for delivery.

Please send me __ copies of the *Mastering Ventura* samples disk.

____
Name

____
Address

____
City State Zip

____
Phone

SYBEX Computer Books are different.

Here is why . . .

At SYBEX, each book is designed with you in mind. Every manuscript is carefully selected and supervised by our editors, who are themselves computer experts. We publish the best authors, whose technical expertise is matched by an ability to write clearly and to communicate effectively. Programs are thoroughly tested for accuracy by our technical staff. Our computerized production department goes to great lengths to make sure that each book is well-designed.

In the pursuit of timeliness, SYBEX has achieved many publishing firsts. SYBEX was among the first to integrate personal computers used by authors and staff into the publishing process. SYBEX was the first to publish books on the CP/M operating system, microprocessor interfacing techniques, word processing, and many more topics.

Expertise in computers and dedication to the highest quality product have made SYBEX a world leader in computer book publishing. Translated into fourteen languages, SYBEX books have helped millions of people around the world to get the most from their computers. We hope we have helped you, too.

OPTION	EFFECT
FILE	
New	Clears the displayed chapter from the screen so you can create a new one.
Open Chapter	Retrieves a chapter and its related files from the disk for editing.
Save (^ S)	Saves the displayed chapter and its associated files.
Save As	Makes a copy of the displayed chapter by saving it on disk with a new name.
Abandon	Abandons the edits made to the current chapter and reloads the chapter from disk.
Load Text/Picture	Loads a word-processed text file or picture file and adds its name to the Assignment list.
Load Diff. Style	Retrieves a style sheet. Links it with the displayed chapter when the chapter is saved.
Save as New Style	Makes a copy of the style sheet in use by saving it with a new name.
To Print	Initiates the printing process.
DOS File Ops	Allows you to delete files from the disk and to make and remove DOS directories.
Quit	Brings the work session with Ventura to an end.
EDIT	
Cut (Del)	Deletes the selected text, frames, or graphics (depending on the mode) to the clipboard.
Copy (Shift-Del)	Copies the selected text, frames, or graphics (depending on the mode) to the clipboard.
Paste (Ins)	Inserts text, frames, or graphics (depending on the mode) from the clipboard.
Insert Footnote	Inserts footnote references into the text and sets up footnotes at the bottom of the page.
Insert/Edit Index	Inserts new index references into the text and allows you to edit existing entries.
Insert/Edit Anchor	Allows you to create frame anchors or relocate existing anchors.
Remove Text/File	Allows you to remove a text or picture file from a frame or from the Assignment list.
File Type/Rename	Allows you to rename a text file or change its word processor format.
VIEW	
Facing Pages View	Displays a two-page spread on the screen.
Reduced View (^ R)	Shows documents sized smaller than their printed versions.
Normal View (^ N)	Shows the document the same size as its printed version.
Enlarged View (^ E)	Shows documents twice the size of their printed versions.
Frame Setting (^ U)	Activates the Frame mode. Used to create and manipulate frames.
Paragraph Tagging (^ I)	Activates the Paragraph mode. Used to tag paragraphs and set up tag formats.
Text Editing (^ O)	Activates the Text mode. Used to edit text and assign text attributes.
Graphic Drawing (^ P)	Activates the Graphics mode. Used to operate the graphics features.
PAGE	
Page Layout	Sets portrait or landscape; letter, legal, and so on; single/double sides; and global kerning.
Widows & Orphans	Controls the number of isolated lines permitted at the top or bottom of a page or column.
Chapter Counter	Sets the style and number of chapter numbers.
Page Counter	Sets the style and number of page numbers.
Auto-Numbering	Automatically inserts section numbers and set their style.
Renumber Chapter (^ B)	Updates the numbering defined by page auto-numbering.
Re-Anchor Frames	Moves frames to the page on which their anchors appear.
Headers & Footers	Controls text that is placed repeatedly at the top and bottom of each page.
Turn Header On/Off	Removes or redisplays headers (defined with Page Headers & Footers)
Turn Footer On/Off	Removes or redisplays footers (defined with Page Headers & Footers)
Footnotes Settings	Controls the format of footnotes, created with the Insert Footnote option.
Insert/Remove Page	Inserts or removes pages of the document.
Go To Page (^ G)	Displays the specified page or a page relative to the document or selected file.